ENGLISH G

| G9 |

access 4

Cornelsen

English G Access
G9 Ausgabe 2019 · Band 4
Schülerbuch

Im Auftrag des Verlages herausgegeben von
Jörg Rademacher, Mannheim

Erarbeitet von
Laurence Harger, Wellington, Neuseeland
Cecile Niemitz-Rossant, Berlin

unter Mitarbeit von
Dr. Annette Leithner-Brauns, Dresden,
Birgit Ohmsieder, Berlin, Mervyn Whittaker, Bad Dürkheim *sowie* Peadar Curran, Berlin (Übungen, Grammar and Practice)

in Zusammenarbeit mit der Englischredaktion
Dr. Philip Devlin und Ralph Williams (koordinierende Redaktion)
Gareth Evans, Bonnie Glänzer, Stefan Höhne (Redaktionsleitung), Dr. Hie-Jung You *und beratend* Filiz Bahsi, Ulrike Berendt, Dr. Sophie Burt, Solveig Heinrich, Renata Jakovac *und* Lothar Teworte (digitales Schülerbuch)
Lizenzmanagement Sophie Dupiech

Beratende Mitwirkung
Friederike von Bremen, Hannover; Peter Brünker, Bad Kreuznach; Anette Fritsch, Dillenburg; Uli Imig, Wildeshausen; Christina Diehr, Geldern; Thomas Neidhardt, Bielefeld; Wolfgang Neudecker, Mannheim; Dr. Andreas Sedlatschek, Esslingen; Sieglinde Spranger, Chemnitz; Marcel Sprunkel, Köln; Sabine Tudan, Reichenau; Britta Weber, Aachen; Harald Weißling, Mannheim

Fotos
Nigel Wilson Photography, Bristol

Umschlaggestaltung und Layoutkonzept
hawemannundmosch, Berlin

Layout und technische Umsetzung
SPi Global, Chennai, Indien

Soweit in diesem Buch Personen fotografisch abgebildet sind und ihnen von der Redaktion fiktive Namen, Berufe, Dialoge und Ähnliches zugeordnet oder diese Personen in bestimmte Kontexte gesetzt werden, dienen diese Zuordnungen und Darstellungen ausschließlich der Veranschaulichung und dem besseren Verständnis des Buchinhaltes.

Begleitmaterial zu English G Access · G9 · Band 4

978-3-06-036394-0	Workbook mit Audios online
978-3-06-036398-8	Workbook mit Audios online und interaktiven Übungen
978-3-06-036466-4	Vokabeltaschenbuch
978-3-06-036454-1	Wordmaster Band 4
978-3-06-036450-3	Klassenarbeitstrainer
978-3-06-035880-9	Grammarmaster
978-3-06-036430-5	E-Book
978-3-06-035888-5	Englisch-Module für DAZ Lernende

www.cornelsen.de

Die Webseiten Dritter, deren Internetadressen in diesem Lehrwerk angegeben sind, wurden vor Drucklegung sorgfältig geprüft. Der Verlag übernimmt keine Gewähr für die Aktualität und den Inhalt dieser Seiten oder solcher, die mit ihnen verlinkt sind.

Dieses Werk berücksichtigt die Regeln der reformierten Rechtschreibung und Zeichensetzung.

Alle Drucke dieser Auflage sind inhaltlich unverändert und können im Unterricht nebeneinander verwendet werden.

Druck und Bindung: Firmengruppe APPL, aprinta Druck, Wemding

1. Auflage, 1. Druck 2020	1. Auflage, 1. Druck 2020
broschiert	gebunden
978-3-06-036389-6	978-3-06-036390-2

ISBN 978-3-06-036430-5 (E-Book)

PEFC zertifiziert
Dieses Produkt stammt aus nachhaltig bewirtschafteten Wäldern und kontrollierten Quellen.
www.pefc.de
PEFC/12-31-006

English G Access · G9 · Band 4 **enthält folgende Teile:**

Units	die vier Kapitel des Buches
Access to cultures	andere Kulturen kennenlernen und verstehen
Text File	eine Sammlung englischer Gedichte, Geschichten und Sachtexte
Grammar & Practice (GAP)	Grammatikerklärungen und Übungen zum Wiederholen
Skills & Media Competence (SMC)	eine Beschreibung wichtiger Lern- und Arbeitstechniken
Vocabulary	das Wörterverzeichnis zum Lernen der neuen Wörter jeder Unit
Dictionary	alphabetisches Wörterverzeichnis zum Nachschlagen

In den Units findest du diese Überschriften:

Looking at language	Beispiele sammeln und sprachliche Regeln entdecken
Language help	Hilfe in Form von sprachlichen Regeln
Practice	Aufgaben und Übungen
Access to words	Wortschatz systematisch ausbauen
Mediation course	zwischen Englisch und Deutsch besser vermitteln
Study skills	Einführung in Lern- und Arbeitstechniken
Background file	Informationen über Land und Leute
The world behind the picture	vom Bild in den Film – Videoclips mit Aufgaben
Text	Textauszug aus einem Roman oder einer Autobiographie

Du findest auch diese Symbole:

(Lautsprecher)	Audios zum Herunterladen: *www.cornelsen.de/codes (Webcode kuheqe)*
www	zusätzliche Materialien, die du unter *www.cornelsen.de/codes* finden kannst (Webcode: *rusasu*; Kaleidoscope-Videos: *niwaza*)
■■■■■	Übungssequenz: neue Grammatik intensiv üben und dann anwenden
Early finisher	zusätzliche Aktivitäten und Übungen für Schüler/innen, die früher fertig sind
More help	zusätzliche Hilfen für eine Aufgabe
You choose	zwischen zwei Aufgaben auswählen
EXTRA	zusätzliche Aktivitäten und Übungen für alle
My Book	schöne und wichtige Arbeiten sammeln
Your task	Was du gelernt hast, kannst du in der Lernaufgabe am Ende jeder Unit noch mal zeigen und dich auch selbst einschätzen.
(Ohr) (Sprechblase) (Buch) (Stift)	Hören Sprechen Lesen Schreiben
EN DE	Mediation (zwischen zwei Sprachen vermitteln)
MK	auch mit digitalen Medien lernen
(Symbole)	Partnerarbeit Partnercheck Gruppenarbeit Kooperative Lernform

	You learn about …	Texts
Arrival USA 	· Key facts USA · Differences between America and Germany	
Unit 1 New York 	· Neighbourhoods · Multicultural NYC · Immigration · Sights of NYC · Talking about likes, dislikes, interests and skills · Describing people and places	A Twenty Years 9/11 The towers and the pools B Weird moments at Washington Square Park C Take a Walk on New York's Highline **Background file** Stories of Manhattan neighborhoods (p. 22) **Text** *Putting Makeup on the Fat Boy* (excerpt from a novel, p. 32)
Kaleidoscope	**1 The first Americans** 2 Sport, National parks, Music	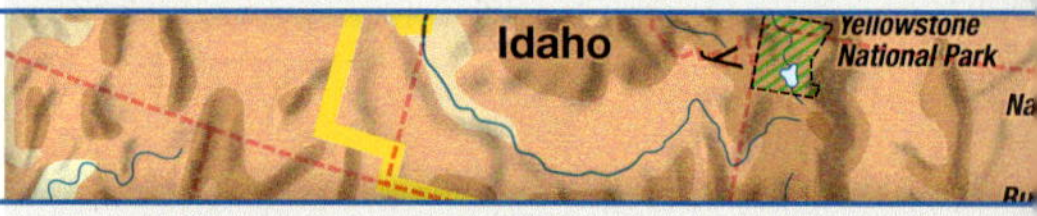
Unit 2 New Orleans 	· Music · Thanksgiving · Hurricane Katrina · Cajun food · History: Slavery and civil rights · Making suggestions **Your task (Lernaufgabe)** Give a talk about objects that are important to you and/or your family. (p. 60)	A A chat and a shock post B Grandma Betty's memory box Civil Rights C The guest **Background file** African Americans: From the age of slavery to the present (p. 50) **Text** Melba Pattillo and the Little Rock Nine (excerpt from an autobiography, p. 56)
Access to cultures 1	Meeting new people	

Skills | **Language**

8

Working with explainer videos
Collecting and processing information about the United States (p.10)

12 | Part A 14 | Part B 24 | Part C 28 | Skill in focus: Listening

Viewing
New York sights
People and places
Hanging out in Brooklyn (p. 14)

Mediation course
Key information (p. 18)

Using digital tools
Presenting information about a city (p. 23)

Study skills
Writing a summary of an article (p. 30)

MyBook
Write a dialogue or a picture story (p. 35)

Access to words
American English / British English (p. 20)

Grammar
The gerund as subject / object
The gerund after prepositions
Gerund or infintive after certain verbs
Adverbial clauses (place, comparison)

Pronunciation
British and American English (p. 21)

36

38 | Part A 40 | Part B 46 | Part C 52 | Skill in focus: Reading

Access to cultures
Gator and gumbo (p. 41),
Alligator hunting in Louisiana (p. 52)

Mediation course
Relevant information (p. 43)

Using digital tools
Making a history timeline (p. 22)

Study skills
Skimming a text (p. 53)

Viewing
A musician in New Orleans (p. 55)

MyBook
Write a letter or an interview (p. 59)

Access to words
Talking about food and cooking (p. 42)

Grammar
Conditional 1 (Revision)
Conditional 2 (Revision)
Conditional 3
Adverbs of degree

Pronunciation
Word flow (p. 48)

62

	You learn about …	Texts
Unit 3 California 	• National parks and environmental issues • Volunteering • Entertainment, film, TV • History: American expansion in California • Saying the right thing • Talking about arrangements **Your task (Lernaufgabe)** Write a report about something exciting that happened in your area. (p. 86)	A At the marine reserve B At the Starview Hotel, L.A. Mr. Miller's interview with Brandon C Celebrities and paparazzi, Wildfire **Background file** The Spanish missions and the Gold Rush A magnet for millions (pp. 76–77) **Text** A future without water? (excerpt from the novel *Dry*, p. 84)
Unit 4 South Dakota 	• School life, school system • First love • Smalltown life • Native Americans • Reporting a conversation **Your task (Lernaufgabe)** Present yourself to a class at a school in South Dakota. (p. 111)	A A date with Kaya B Tension below the surface Kaya reports C Mount Rushmore: For and against Bad news for Drew **Background file** The Lakota The Dakotas (p. 96) **Text** *The Absolutely True Diary of a Part-Time Indian* (excerpt from a novel, p. 108)
Access to cultures	Making requests	

Text File	Text 1	Text 2	Text 3
	1 WTC… Freedom Tower	*Underground New York*	*Amazing Grace*
	Non-fictional text	Excerpt from a novel	History of a song

126 More help
134 Early finisher
146 Partner pages

151 Grammar and Practice
192 Skills and media competence
214 Vocabulary

236 English sounds
237 Dictionary English–German
267 Dictionary German–English

Pro Unit können mehrere Klassenarbeiten vorgesehen werden, die Schwerpunkte sowohl im Bereich der Beherrschung der sprachlichen Mittel als auch der kommunikativen Kompetenzen bilden können. (Weitere Hinweise in *Vorschläge zur Leistungungsmessung*)

Skills	Language		
Access to cultures Being polite (p. 67) **Mediation course** Cultural differences 1 (p. 69) **Viewing** A state with many faces (p. 70) **Study skills** Make an outline for a report (p. 83) **MyBook** Write a report (p. 87) **Using digital tools** Sharing and commenting on classwork	**Access to words** Adjectives: synonyms and antonyms (p. 82) **Grammar** *will-* and *going to-*future (Revision); *will* for spontaneous decisions, *present progressive for the future* Defining and non-defining relative clauses	64 Part A 66 Part B 72 Part C 78	Skill in focus: Writing
Mediation course Cultural differences 2 (p. 92) **MyBook** Write about a local monument (p. 102) **Study skills** Using a German-English dictionary (p. 106) **Viewing** Bloodlines (p. 107) **Using digital tools** Making a slide show	**Access to words** Word building (suffixes *-ful* and *-less*) (p. 105) **Grammar** Present and past tenses: simple and progressive (Revision) State and activity verbs Indirect speech The definite article	88 Part A 90 Part B 98 Part C 102	Skill in focus: Speaking
		112	

Text 4	Text 5	Text 6	114
Hollywood Fame	Native Americans	Ghost dance	
Celebrity in songs	Non-fictional text	Song	

294 Lösungen Early finisher
297 Arbeitsanweisungen
298 Irregular verbs
300 Countries and continents
302 Quellenverzeichnis
304 Giving feedback to your classmates

Arrival USA

Imagine! You're starting a journey through the USA. What do you expect to see and do in this city?

What other images of the USA come to your mind? Describe them. Name two places you'd like to go to.

1 Reading the map

a) Look at the map. Are the two places you chose on page 8 on it? Find them if you can and describe where they are.

b) Look at the map again and the key. Say what they tell you about the USA.
→ www *List of the 50 states*

2 Overview USA

a) Watch the video. Make a list of the topics it covers.

b) Compare your lists and say what you learned about each topic. What did you find most interesting or surprising? Explain why.

3 First impressions

a) What differences between the USA and Germany do you know of? Make a list.

b) Watch a video about a German student in the USA. What differences does he see? Compare his impressions with your points from a).

4 Two different countries

a) Imagine you visit the USA for the first time. Say which aspects of life you would find most attractive/interesting/strange/…

b) An American visits Germany for the first time. What differences between the two countries do you think they would notice?

New York

1 Travelling by underground

a) In two words, say what you think about travel by underground. Here are some ideas.

clean · dirty · cheap · expensive
boring · exciting · dangerous · safe
easy · complicated · fast · slow

b) Explain your choice in a) and give examples. If you've used the underground in cities like London or New York, describe your experience.

2 On the New York subway

a) Work in groups of three. Choose one photo each. Describe what you can see and the atmosphere in your photo to your partners.

➔ *SMC 20: Describing a picture (p. 208)*

b) You will hear the thoughts of the people in photo C. Listen and match each voice to the right person in the photo.

Compare your results.

c) Listen again. Say which of these places in New York each person is thinking about.

- *Brooklyn*
- *Central Park*
- *Chinatown*
- *Coney Island*
- *Ellis Island*
- *Fifth Avenue*
- *The High Line*
- *Little Italy*
- *Lower East Side*
- *The Statue of Liberty*
- *Washingon Square Park*
- *The 9/11 Memorial*

How do they feel about the places and why?

d) In two minutes, look through the pages of this unit. How many of the places in c) can you find? Note the page number for each place.

Compare your results. Name one place you'd like to learn more about and say why.

A *Times Square, NYC*

C *New Yorkers on the subway*

B *Waiting on the platform*

1 New York sights

a) Everybody knows something about New York from films, TV, books or holidays. Look at these New York places. Say which ones you recognize and what you could do there.

A

B

C

b) Find each place on the New York map on the front inside cover. How far are they from each other?

2 Manhattan: People and places

a) You will see a film about four people. Each person is in a different neighbourhood of Manhattan. Watch the film without sound. Take notes on the different areas you see.

Use your notes to describe what you saw.
– *In the first part, there were narrow streets.*
– *Yes, and there were old buildings with metal steps too.*

b) Watch the film with sound. Take notes on each person and what they're thinking. Then say how they feel about the city.

3 Making the film: Music

Each part of the film has different music. Watch the whole film again. Then describe the music and say how well it matches the feelings of the four people.

D

E

4 Brooklyn: Hanging out with friends

a) Brooklyn is the New York borough with the highest population. Find it on the map on the front inside cover. Describe where it is in relation to Manhattan.

b) You will see a four-part film about young people in Brooklyn. In the first part, they meet on a stoop. Watch, and then describe the people, what they're doing, and the atmosphere between them.

c) Watch the next three parts of the film. Take notes on what happens. Use your notes to write three questions about each part.

d) Swap your questions with a partner and write down answers to their questions.

e) Watch again and check your answers from d).

EXTRA Say what impression of New York the people and places have given you.

Workbook 2 (p. 3)

1 A newspaper article

Describe the photos in the article. Then explain what you think the headline means.

Twenty Years 9/11

by Judd Wozencraft, September 11th, 2021

It was a warm September morning. Hundreds of New Yorkers walked towards their offices at the World Trade Center. They felt the sun on their faces, maybe stopped for a coffee before they entered the buildings. None of them knew that this was the last time. It was just another day.

Then, at 8:46 am, the North Tower of the World Trade Center burst into a ball of fire. It had been hit by American Airlines Flight 11, the first of four planes that would crash within 76 minutes. At 9:03, a second plane flew into the South Tower. At 9:37, just outside Washington DC, the Pentagon was hit. And at 10:03, the fourth plane crashed in the Pennsylvania countryside. Altogether, 2,977 people died.

The Twin Towers as Flight UA 175 hits the South Tower

The four planes had been hijacked by the al-Qaida terrorist network in a carefully planned attack on the US. 19 terrorists, who had got onto the planes as normal passengers, forced their way into the cockpits and took control. The first three planes hit the al-Qaida targets. The fourth was flying towards Washington DC, but the passengers fought back and managed to crash the plane in a field. This brave action saved many lives in the US capital.

Emergency services at the ruins of the Twin Towers

In New York, there were scenes of panic and chaos as the Twin Towers burned. Thousands ran for their lives, but for those on the top floors there was no escape. As fire and smoke took over the buildings, over 200 people jumped to their deaths. Within less than two hours, both skyscrapers collapsed. A thick cloud of dust and smoke spread out over the whole neighborhood. For the people in the streets below, it seemed as if the world was ending.

9/11 has stuck in the minds of everyone who was alive at the time. Today, even 20 years later, the images of that morning feel as fresh as ever.

2 Understanding the text

Say what event the article refers to. Describe what happened, when, where and who was involved.

3 Historic events

The author writes that "9/11 has stuck in the minds of everyone who was alive at the time." Give examples of other kinds of events that stick in people's minds. Explain why you think we remember them.

4 The towers and the pools

3:30 pm. The school bell rang. The end of another day at Stuyvesant High School.

"Hey guys," cried Jasmine when she saw Tyler and Alex at the lockers. "Do you want to hang out?"

"Sorry," said Alex. "I love hanging out with you two, but I have chess practice today. See you." Then he grabbed his backpack and walked off.

"What about you, Tyler?" Jasmine asked.

"Well," said Tyler, "I have to take some photos."

"Again?" laughed Jasmine. "You really like taking photos, don't you?"

"Sure," said Tyler. "But I enjoy being with you too. Why don't you come? I need these photos for the school newspaper. I want to join their team."

"OK," said Jasmine. "So where are we going?"

"I don't know," Tyler replied. "I just need some cool shots. Any ideas?"

"The Statue of Liberty? We could take the ferry."

"Taking the ferry is expensive," said Tyler. "And anyway, I'd prefer something nearer."

"The 9/11 Memorial? It's only four blocks away."

"You mean those huge pools?" said Tyler. "Maybe that's not such a bad idea. It's the 9/11 anniversary soon. So the school newspaper would probably be quite interested."

❖

"Hmm," said Jasmine as they reached the memorial. "Getting it in one photo will be hard."

"I don't want to photograph the whole thing," Tyler replied. "I just need some interesting details. That's what makes a good photo."

"What about that?" Jasmine suggested. She pointed to a white rose next to one of the names on the metal edge of the first pool.

Tyler shook his head. "I want something more exciting," he said and looked across the pool. "Hey," he cried. "It's cool how all the water disappears into that dark hole in the middle!" For a moment the two friends listened as the water roared below them. "What a sound!" said Tyler.

"It must be at least 30 feet deep," Jasmine added.

Tyler took out his camera and leaned a few more inches over the edge. Suddenly he heard a voice behind him: "Leaning over the memorial like that is not a good idea. I'll have to arrest you guys."

The friends turned around and saw a policeman.

"We're so sorry," said Jasmine.

The policeman's face broke into a smile. "Just joking! You kids never saw the towers, did you?"

"We weren't even born then," replied Jasmine.

"They stood right where these pools are. They were the world's highest buildings once. But now so many folks are buried here – some of my mates too. To me, being here is like being at a cemetery."

Jasmine and Tyler didn't know what to say.

"Right," said the policeman. "I'd better go now." He said goodbye and walked away.

"That was heavy ..." whispered Tyler.

"Yes," Jasmine agreed. "But I guess he felt we should think about what we were looking at."

5 The 9/11 Memorial

a) Scan the text for information about the 9/11 memorial and note it down. Then tell your partner what you learned.

b) Discuss how Tyler and the policeman see the memorial. Do you think Tyler's view changes? Give reasons for your opinion.

WWW Find out more about New York's skyscrapers.

Text file 1 (p. 114)

The 9/11 Memorial Plaza

The memorial

In a large plaza with 400 trees, two pools cover the area where the Twin Towers once stood. 30-foot high waterfalls rush down into a deep hole at the center of each pool.
The names of the victims of the 9/11 attack are cut into panels around the pools. The memorial opened ten years after the attack on the World Trade Center.

The museum

There are three main exhibitions. One explores the events before, during and after 9/11. The second looks at the lives of the people who died in the attack. In addition, you can see the last column of one of the original towers.
Visitors to the museum can also watch a program of films free of charge.
You can take as long as you like to see the museum. Visits last 2 hours on average.

Essential visitor information

The memorial is open daily from 7:30 A.M. to 9 P.M. Admission is free. Red arrows on the map show entrances to the memorial.
The museum opens daily at 9 A.M. It closes at 8 P.M. Sunday to Thursday and at 9 P.M. on Friday and Saturday. The last admission to the museum is two hours before closing time.
Standard tickets cost $24 for adults and $15 for under-18s. Children under six enter free of charge. For reductions for seniors, college students and veterans, check online.

You're spending a day in Manhattan with your parents.
You've suggested a visit to the 9/11 Memorial. Your parents ask you some questions about it:

1 Wo müssen wir genau hin?
2 Was zeigt das Museum?
3 Wie lange dauert ein Besuch im Museum?
4 Wie früh können wir ins Museum hinein?
5 Was kostet der Eintritt ins Museum?
6 Gibt es für dich eine Ermäßigung?

1 Scan the text.

a) Scan the brochure and find answers to your parents' questions.
Take notes in English. Make sure your notes only contain the information you need.

b) Compare your notes. Add important information and take out facts you don't need.

2 Put your information into your language.

a) Agree on a good way to answer your parents' questions in German in your own words.
You needn't translate the brochure word for word.

b) Join another pair. Act out the conversation. One pair plays the parents, the other the kids.

Mediation skills

This is what you need to do to find and explain important information:
Scan the text • *Take notes* • *Use your own words when you give information*

➔ *SMC 9: Mediation (p. 200)*

Language help

a) You already know that you can use the *-ing*-form after the verbs *like* or *love*.

- *I like swimming.*
- *I love hanging out with you.* (p. 17)
- *You really like taking photos.* (p. 17)

This *-ing*-form is called a *gerund*. In the examples above, the *gerund* is the object of the sentence.

b) You can also use a *gerund* as the subject of a sentence. Look at these examples:

- *Swimming is great fun.*
- *Taking the ferry is expensive.* (p. 17)
- *Getting it in one photo will be hard.* (p. 17)

Go to page 17 and find two more examples of the gerund as a subject (ll. 40–55).

➜ *GAP 9: The gerund (p. 168)*

1 Activities and hobbies (Gerunds as object/subject)

a) Talk about the activities in the box. Use these phrases with a gerund, e.g. *I hate cleaning my room.*

☺	😐	☹
I love … I like … I enjoy …	I don't mind …	I don't like … I hate …

clean my room · play computer games · shop for clothes · take out the rubbish · lie on the beach · go to the dentist · wash the dishes · stand in front of the class

b) Write five sentences about the advantages (+) and disadvantages (–) of the hobbies in the box. Use the ideas below or your own ideas., e.g. *Cooking is great fun, but it takes a lot of time.*
Then compare your sentences.

cook · do sport · draw · go to museums · learn a language · play an instrument · play chess · read · sing in a choir · swim · work in the garden · /…

+
is an awesome hobby
is a way to make friends
keeps you healthy
can help you to relax /…

–
is boring
takes a lot of time
costs a lot of money
can be difficult /…

2 A weekend in New York City (Gerunds as object/subject)

Two British teens discuss what to do in New York. Complete the text with the gerund of the right verbs.

be · do (x2) · go · queue · see · spend (x2) · stand · take · try on · visit

Zara: I like [1]… to museums. What about you?
Dom: [2]… museums is OK, but it can be boring.
Zara: What do you enjoy [3]…, then? Do you like [4]… in the fresh air? Central Park isn't far.
Dom: [5]… time in a park isn't a good idea. You can do that everywhere. What I like [6]… on a city holiday is [7]… all the main sights.
Zara: How about the big shops on Fifth Avenue?
Dom: Shops? Do you really like [8]… clothes and [9]… money on things you don't need?
Zara: Maybe the Statue of Liberty, then?
Dom: That's a cool idea. And [10]… the ferry is a good way to see the harbour too.
Zara: It says here online that you have to wait 90 minutes for a ferry. And I hate [11]….
Dom: I don't mind [12]… in a queue for that! You can go to the shops while I'm waiting, if you like.

More help *p. 126*   **Early finisher** *p. 136 (Grammar challenge)*

TIP

The UK and the US have a lot in common, including the language they speak.
However, there are several differences between British English (BE) and American English (AE), and people do not always understand each other. Here are some of the main differences:

- Different words for the same thing (e.g. flat/apartment, autumn/fall)
- Different spelling of the same words (e.g. colour/color, centre/center)
- Different pronunciation of the same words (e.g. city, stop)

1 Different words

a) In each column below, match the two words with the same meaning. Decide which word is BE and which is AE and make a list. Use a dictionary if you need help.

apartment : cookie	*elevator : yard*	*holiday(s) : queue*	*pullover : trainers*
autumn : French fries	*flashlight : match*	*jam : mum*	*restroom : store*
biscuit : fall	*football : rubbish*	*line : trousers*	*shop : underground*
candy : mobile	*game : lift*	*mom : vacation*	*sneakers : toilet*
cell phone : flat	*garbage : soccer*	*pants : sidewalk*	*subway : takeout*
chips : sweets	*garden : torch*	*pavement : jelly*	*takeaway : sweater*

flat ⟷ apartment
autumn ⟷ ...

More help p. 126

b) Complete both texts with words from a).
Partner A: Use BE in Text 1 and AE in Text 2. **Partner B:** Use AE in Text 1 and BE in Text 2.

Then compare your answers and check that you have the correct AE/BE words.

1

I got out of the subway/underground and walked along King Street. The leaves on the trees were yellow. It was [1]... Suddenly, a bike appeared from nowhere and almost hit me. "Hey!" I shouted. "You can't ride on the [2]... like that!"
When I got to Jake's, I rang the bell. Nobody answered, so I took out my [3]... and called him. "The bell isn't working," he said. "I'll come down." Some minutes later, he came to the door. He was carrying a [4]...
"Why do you need that?" I asked.
"The stairs are dark," he said. "The [5]... isn't working either, so we have to walk up to my [6]..."
Then I remembered that we wanted to watch [7]... together. It was the big [8]... between England and the USA. "So what about your TV?" I asked. "I hope that isn't broken too."

Early finisher p. 134

2

It was the summer holidays/vacation. Dad was planting flowers in the [1]... "Why don't you put on some old clothes and help him?" asked my mother. So I found an old [2]... and a pair of [3]... with holes in the knees, put them on, and went outside.
" [4]... says I should help you," I said to Dad.
"Why not pick the strawberries?" Dad said. "Then, if you like, you could make [5]... with them later."
I like cooking and baking – my cakes and [6]... are very popular – so I picked three buckets of fruit.
"Good work," said Dad. "You must be hungry. Why not get yourself a [7]...? Here's some money."
In the [8]... at the hamburger restaurant, there was just one guy in front of me. He got his food, turned and then walked straight into me. In a second, I was covered in burger, ketchup and [9]...!
It was lucky that I was still wearing my old clothes.

2 Different spelling

The same words are sometimes written differently in BE and AE.

- There are two main differences:
  BE *–our* e.g. honour, colourful   AE *–or* e.g. honor, colorful
  BE *–re* e.g. metre   AE *–er* e.g. meter
- Other differences with words you know include:
  BE *grey, practise (verb), programme, traveller* AE *gray, practice (verb), program, traveler*

a) The following sentences contain nine words in American English spelling.
Find them and say what the correct British English spelling is.

1 Manhattan is 13.4 miles (about 22 kilometers) from north to south.
2 New Yorkers are famous for their sense of humor.
3 The Statue of Liberty is just one of the famous sights in New York Harbor.
4 Chinatown is a colorful neighborhood in the south of Manhattan.
5 Times Square is a favorite tourist attraction right in the center of New York.
6 You can check the theater program to find out what shows there are on Broadway.

Some of the shows on Broadway, NYC

b) You will hear five sentences. Listen and write them down. Use AE spelling for all the words.
In each sentence, there are two words with a different spelling from BE.

Check each other's sentences.

Early finisher p. 134

3 Different pronunciation

LISTENING TIP
American English pronunciation of some words is different from what you have learned. Knowing the differences will help you to understand more easily.

a) Listen to a British and an American speaker. Say how they pronounce the orange words.
The city was so hot on Tuesday.
We went to see my aunt on her farm.

b) You will hear five short dialogues. Decide if the speakers use British or American English.
The way they say the words below will help you.

Dialogue 1: *city · dirty · pity · pretty*
Dialogue 2: *problem · project · rock · pop · topic*
Dialogue 3: *new · student · stupid · studio*
Dialogue 4: *glasses · can't · grass · danced*
Dialogue 5: *father · here · later · armchair · corner*

Workbook 7–8 (pp. 6–7)
→ GAP 20 (p. 190): AE and BE

Signs in Chinese, Chinatown, Manhattan

A street in Little Italy, Manhattan

The San Gennaro Festival, Little Italy, Manhattan

With its five boroughs, New York is the United States' largest city with 8.4 million people. It is also a city with hundreds of neighborhoods. There are 53 in the borough of Manhattan alone. Some of their names, like Upper West Side or Lower East Side are geographical descriptions. Others, like the Meatpacking District, the Garment District or the Financial District, tell us about the activities that were once done there, or still are. Many of the names also remind us that New York has been a melting pot of nations. Everyone has heard of Chinatown, which today is home to 100,000 people with a Chinese background. Other names show us how, over centuries, immigrants from Europe have shaped the city. The names Harlem and Greenwich Village (once Greenwicjk) were given by Dutch settlers in the 17th century. Chelsea, which got its name in the 18th century, was called after an area in southwest London. And later, huge waves of immigration produced names like Little Germany or Little Italy.

In the 19th and early 20th centuries, millions of Europeans crossed the Atlantic to make a new home in the United States, including 5 million Germans and over 3 million Italians. Those who settled in New York usually lived with people from their old homelands. Little Germany flourished until the end of the 1800s, with German schools, churches, libraries, markets and newspapers. Little Italy was a center of Italian life up to the 1970s, and today it still has a very Italian face with many restaurants and cultural events. The San Gennaro Festival, for example, takes place in September every year and goes on for 11 days. It goes back to 1926, when immigrants from Naples came together to celebrate the patron saint of their old home city. Events like these show how, for many Americans, the country of their ancestors still has a special place in their hearts and helps to shape their identity. Some years ago, when she was giving a concert in Italy, New York singer Lady Gaga spoke about her Italian roots. "Today I met my Italian cousins … I am thinking about how my grandparents abandoned such a beautiful place and all the sacrifices they made. Being here makes me feel I have made them proud."

A neighborhood where many of the poorest immigrants settled in the 19th century was the Lower East Side. It was the first home for many Irish people who arrived in huge numbers after the Irish famine of the 1840s and did the worst-paid jobs. As their situation improved, many Irish moved to other neighborhoods, and new immigrants took their place. Towards the end of the century, the biggest groups were Russians, Poles and Jews who had just escaped from the hard conditions in the Russian Empire. Around 1900, the Lower East Side had become the capital of Jewish America. A Jewish immigrant at that time came to a place where he found Jewish stores, banks, libraries and synagogues.
Today, with over 1.1 million Jewish inhabitants, New York is the world's largest Jewish city. Since the 1960s, many Jews have moved away from the the Lower East Side, and many of its synagogues are now used for other purposes. However, it is still a place with which American Jews identify strongly. Visitors to the area will see many Jewish businesses, including bakeries and diners like Katz's Delicatessen, which opened in the 1880s.

Until recently, Katz's was just one in a row of one-story shops on East Houston Street. Today, however, it stands next to a tall modern building. This is perhaps a symbol of how the area is changing as people with more money move in. Since the 1980s, central Manhattan has become more and more fashionable. Neighborhoods like the Meatpacking District, Soho or Greenwich Village, where once ordinary workers lived, are now top addresses for people from all over the world. Today they come, not to escape poverty, but to enjoy the way of life in one of our planet's most amazing metropolises.

Bialystoker Synagogue, Lower East Side, Manhattan

Katz's survives in a changing neighborhood

Cool lifestyle in Greenwich Village – a musician plays for the public in Washington Square Park.

a) Explain what the names of Manhattan's neighborhoods can tell us about New York and its history.

b) Read the quotation from Lady Gaga again (ll. 42–46). Then suggest reasons why the connection to the country of their ancestors is important to many Americans.

c) Find a list of Manhattan neighborhoods online. Choose one and search for a picture and key information. Then make a short neighborhood profile.

1 Weird moments at Washington Square Park

Jasmine has made a comic about an afternoon she spent in a New York park with Tyler and Alex. Describe your first impression of Jasmine's comic. Compare it with any other comics you know.

2 Understanding the text

Form a buzz group. Say all you can about the atmosphere in the park. Describe how Jasmine, Tyler and Alex feel about the place.

3 The end of the game

a) Say who you think wins the chess game. Give a reason for your opinion.

b) Listen to Tyler and Alex talk after the game. Say how each of them reacts to the result.

4 Have a go

At the beginning of the comic, Tyler says: *I can imagine getting some crazy photos here.* Say what you can (and can't) imagine doing in Washington Square Park.

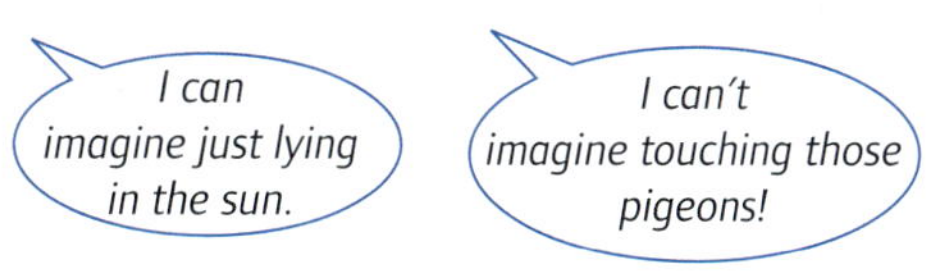

Looking at language

You often use two verbs together.
Sometimes the second verb is an infinitive: *We **decided** **to meet** at Washington Square Park.*
Sometimes it is a gerund: *I can **imagine** **getting** some crazy photos here.*

Find these verbs in the comic on pp. 24–25 and note down the form of the second verb:
decide, enjoy, expect, hate, imagine, keep, prefer, start, suggest, want
Be careful! Three of the verbs are used twice in the text.

Now complete these rules:
Verbs that always take the … include *dislike, enjoy, finish,* …, …, *mind, practise,* and …
Verbs that always take the … include *agree,* … *expect, hope, offer, plan* and …
Some verbs like *begin, hate, like, love,* … and … can take either the … or the …

➜ *GAP 10: The gerund or the to-infinitive (p. 170)*

1 On the ferry to the Statue of Liberty (Gerund or infinitive)

Two British teens on holiday in New York have just got onto the ferry to the Statue of Liberty. Complete their conversation. Choose the correct form of the verbs in brackets: gerund or infinitive.

Zara: It's exciting up here on deck. I'm glad we decided 1… (do) this. When do we leave?
Dom: You keep 2… (ask) that. It's only two minutes now.
Zara: Oh, we're starting already! I can't wait to get to the Statue of Liberty.
Dom: There are some great views up there. I hope 3… (get) lots of cool photos. And it's only 377 steps to the top!
Zara: I can't imagine 4… (climb) so many steps.
Dom: Well, people who don't like 5… (walk) can take a lift half the way up.
Zara: Phew! Maybe I'll do that. So do you have any other plans for this trip?
Dom: Well, I'm just planning 6… (hang out). Do you want 7… (meet) again tomorrow?
Zara: Oh, I've decided 8… (spend) a day in the museums tomorrow. But you probably wouldn't enjoy 9… (look) at art all day.
Dom: Well, maybe we can meet later – when you've finished 10… (see) all those pictures.
Zara: Actually, I've agreed 11… (see) my friend Todd then. He's suggested 12… (go) to the cinema. But you can come too if you don't mind 13… (hang out) with the two of us and 14… (watch) a film.
Dom: I'll think about it. Hey, look! We've arrived. I didn't expect 15… (get) here so quickly.

Early finisher ➜ *p. 136 (Grammar challenge)*

2 Free time in New York (Gerund or infinitive)

a) In a group chat, five friends are texting each other about what they want to do in New York. Find the right ending for their texts and choose the correct form of the verbs in brackets.

1 Luc: I'm keen on paintings, so I'd enjoy ...
2 Jack: I love the theatre, so I'm hoping ...
3 Ava: I want to see a lion, so I'm planning ...
4 Kim: I need a new coat, so I wouldn't mind ...
5 Nat: I'd just like to relax, so I can imagine ...

a (go) shopping on Fifth Avenue.
b (hang out) in Washington Square Park.
c (visit) the Museum of Modern Art.
d (see) a show on Broadway.
e (spend) an afternoon at the zoo.

b) Write sentences like in a) about your plans for next weekend and compare them with a partner.

More help p. 126 Workbook 11–12 (p. 8)

3 I hope you're all looking forward to ... (Gerunds after prepositions)

Language help

You can use a gerund like a noun after a preposition. Compare these sentences:

- *You're good **at** chess.*
- *You're good **at** playing chess. (p. 25)*
- *How **about** a game with this guy?*
- *How **about** having a game with this guy? (p. 25)*

GAP 11: The gerund after prepositions (p. 172)

Cindy Liu is welcoming people to a walking tour of Chinatown. Complete her announcement with the correct prepositions and gerund forms of the verbs below.

Hi, everyone. I'm Cindy. I hope you're all looking forward [1]... [2]... Chinatown today. I know *I'm* very excited [3]... [4]... you my neighborhood. Our tour is just over two miles – from East Broadway to Lafayette Street and back – but I know you're all keen [5]... [6]...! We'll see all the sights, including Columbus Park, where everyone meets up for card games. If you're good [7]... [8]..., maybe you can even join in! We'll also pass New York's oldest Chinese store, so how [9]... [10]... there to buy some souvenirs? Finally, I'm sure you'll all be interested [11]... [12]... traditional Chinese food. I know some good places for street snacks, but if you prefer the idea [13]... [14]... to a restaurant, I can suggest a few.

about (x2) · at · in · of · on · to

explore · go · play · show · stop · try · walk

More help p. 127 Early finisher p. 135 Workbook 13–14 (p. 9)

4 A day out in Manhattan

Imagine you both live in New York. Your friends Claire and Max are visiting the city. You're planning a day out with them. You want to find two activities both friends would enjoy.

a) **Partner A:** Go to p. 146 and read about Claire. **Partner B:** Go to p. 150 and read about Max.

b) Ask and write down your partner's answers:
What is Max/Claire interested in?
What does he/she like doing?
Is there anything he/she doesn't like doing?

c) Agree on two activities for the day out.
Partner A: Well, Max likes ..., so he might enjoy going to ...
Partner B: Yes, but he/Claire hates ..., so ...

Early finisher p. 135

1 A magazine article

a) Find the High Line on the map of NYC on the inside front cover.

b) Look at the three pictures. Then say what you think the article will be about.

c) Read the article and explain what the three sub-headings refer to.

d) Scan the article for these numbers and dates and explain what you find out about them.

50 · 1930s · 1980 · 1991 · 36
9,740 · 2014 · 8 million

e) Imagine you live near the High Line. Suggest ways that New York City could make the park more attractive for local New Yorkers.

Early finisher p. 135

2 Let's go to the High Line

a) Jasmine, Alex and Tyler discuss where to go on a sunny afternoon. Listen and choose the correct answer to each question (a, b, c or d).

1 Tyler is against going to the High Line because
  a he doesn't like flowers
  b he doesn't like the views from the park
  c he thinks it has nothing for young people
  d there are too many skaters.

2 Jasmine says that *A Different World* was an event where teens were able to
  a get tips from adults
  b dance and play music
  c make their own pizza
  d meet other teens from around the world.

3 Jasmine wants to work at the High Line because
  a it's only a few hours every week
  b she needs to make some money
  c she would hate working in a restaurant
  d she wants to help her local area.

b) Say if Tyler's opinion about the High Line changes. Explain your answer.

Take a Walk

Tracks from the past

There's something different about New York's High Line. First, it is one of the narrowest parks in the world. Although it is one and a half miles long, it is only 50 feet at its widest point. What also makes it special is that it lies between 18 and 30 feet above the city's busy streets.

The High Line started life in the 1930s as a railroad that carried goods to factories on Manhattan's West Side. Part of the tracks even cut through the area's blocks and went right into factory buildings. It was built where tracks had run directly at street level. These older tracks were dangerous and very unpopular. Hundreds of people, including many children, had been killed by the passing trains. At the new, higher level, it was possible to move goods faster and more safely than before.

By the 1960s, however, more goods were being moved by trucks than by trains, and the line became much less busy than it had been. It was decided to close it, and in 1980 a train full of frozen turkeys made the last journey along the tracks. Over time, plants and trees began to grow where the trains had traveled.

Workbook 16–17 (pp. 10–11)

... on New York's High Line *by Caitlin Moore*

Imagining the future

What can you do with an old structure that nobody uses any more? New York city leaders saw the High Line as just a ruin, and wanted to tear it down. For a time, it wasn't clear if the High Line would survive. In 1991, part of the line was destroyed to make space for an apartment block. But two New Yorkers, Joshua David and Robert Hammond, whose homes were nearby, protested. For them, the tracks were a wild and wonderful garden that would make a great park for local people. They believed that people should be able to hang out and relax where they lived.

In 2003, David and Hammond organized an 'Open Ideas Competition', in which 720 people from 36 countries all over the world took part. Many of them had brilliant ideas, even though they weren't always very practical. One saw the High Line as a 9,740-foot swimming pool, another as a country field with real cows, while a third imagined a long roller coaster.

Although the ideas were very different, they had one thing in common: they wanted to create an open space in which New Yorkers and their guests could experience the city in a new, exciting way.

A big success?

Between 2006 and 2014, the High Line became a park. Everywhere you go, there are wild flowers or local shrubs, and you can still see old tracks below them. Plants bloom at different times of year and the wind spreads their seeds. The park also has a lawn and a sun deck. There are cafés, an indoor market, works of art and a theater. You'll probably even see a dance or music performance. However, although the park is an awesome place, there are rules too. For example, riding a bike, skating and football aren't allowed.

The High Line offers teens just as much as it offers adults. They can join the Green Council and work with the park's gardeners to look after its many plants. Or they can join the Teen Arts and Culture Council and help to organize performances or other art events in summer.

Today, the High Line is more popular than anyone had ever expected. With over 8 million visitors a year it has become New York's biggest tourist attraction. Unfortunately, far fewer local people visit the park than the planners had originally hoped. New York City is now trying to find ways to make them use it more often.

A summary is a short version of a text which includes all the main information from the original text.

a) Read these rules for a summary. Note down whether you think they are *dos* or *don'ts*.

1 Do name the text type, topic and author in the opening sentence(s).
2 ... keep your summary much shorter than the original text (up to a third).
3 ... use the present tense to say what the writer or text describes or explains.
4 ... use the present tense to report past events.
5 ... cover all the main points.
6 ... include lots of details.
7 ... copy whole sentences from the original.
8 ... use your own words.
9 ... include your own opinion about the topic.

b) Read this summary of the article on pp. 28–29. Then check your answers from a) and change them if necessary. You can look back at the original text if you need to.

Take a walk on New York's Highline *Summary by Jasmine Wong*
Caitlin Moore's article describes the history of the High Line, a famous park in New York, and gives information about the park today.
The writer explains that the High Line was once a railroad. It was built high above the ground in the 1930s so that trains could move goods quickly and safely into factories. Before that, the tracks had run on the streets.
However, by the 1960s, very few trains used the line. It was closed in 1980 and became a ruin. Then, in 2003, two New Yorkers organized a competition to find a new way to use it. They asked people to send in ideas. Although many of the ideas weren't practical, everyone wanted to make the line into a public space.
In the end, the High Line was turned into a park, and opened in 2014. You can still see the old tracks below the plants. The park has many attractions, like a market, cafés and a theater. Millions of visitors go there every year. However, Moore points out that few local people use it, so the city is trying to find ways to make it more attractive for them and not just for tourists.

c) You are going to write a summary of another article. With your partner, first discuss what kind of information you will need to get from the text (e.g. text type). Then check your ideas.

➜ *SMC 7: Writing a summary (p. 198)*

d) Read the article about Ellis Island on page 213 and write your summary.
It can be up to a third of the length of the original text. You can use some phrases from the box.

PHRASES TO USE IN A SUMMARY

- The article is about ... / deals with ...
- The article describes ...
- The main topic is ...
- The article is written by ...
- The writer explains ... /points out ...

Ellis Island, NYC

e) Read your partner's summary and use the *dos* and *don'ts* to give him or her feedback.
Think about your partner's feedback and decide what changes you want to make.

Language help

You can join two clauses with different linking words. Look at examples from pp. 28–29:

1 *Plants and trees began to grow* ***where*** *the trains had traveled*. (p. 28)
2 *The High Line is more popular* ***than*** *anyone had ever expected*. (p. 29)
3 *The High Line offers teens just* ***as*** *much* ***as*** *it offers adults*. (p. 29)
4 *Many of them had brilliant ideas,* ***even though*** *they weren't always very practical*. (p. 29)

Translate the underlined clauses above into German. Then say how the word order is different.

➜ *GAP 16: Adverbial clauses (p. 182)*

1 This is Manhattan! (*where*)

Clauses with *where* give information about a place.
Match 1–5 with a–e and join the clauses with *where*, e.g. This is Manhattan! It's where you'll find most …
Tip: Remember to leave out *there*!

1 This is Manhattan! It's …
2 Welcome to Fifth Avenue! This is …
3 You'll find the 9/11 Memorial …
4 Don't miss the High Line, which was built …
5 Climb to the top of the Statue of Liberty! It's …

a You can get a free view across New York there.
b The WTC Twin Towers once stood there.
c You'll find most of New York's sights there.
d You can shop in really expensive stores there.
e Railroad tracks once ran through the city there.

2 A blog post from New York (*than, as … as*)

You can use *more/less … than* and *as … as* to compare things.
Complete the blog post. Use these words in the correct place: *as, less, more, than*.

Today I got to Central Park! I enjoyed it just [1]… much [2]… I had thought I would. It's much bigger [3]… it looked on the map. And it's lovely too, much [4]… beautiful [5]… I had imagined. It even has [6]… attractions [7]… you'll find in Hyde Park in London, including a castle and some forests. And there are lakes with boats. Taking one out cost [8]… money [9]… I had expected, so I spent two hours on the water. Unfortunately, there were lots of other boats too, so it wasn't [10]… relaxing [11]… I had hoped. However, I really loved the views of New York's skyline. They were actually even better [12]… they looked in the tourist brochures.

More help (p. 127)

3 Chinatown and Little Italy (*although, (even) though, even if*)

Words like *although, (even) though* and *even if* describe contrasts. A contrast clause can come in first or second position. Put the words in blue into the correct order to make contrast clauses.

1 Chinatowns five Although in New City York there are, most people only know of the one in Manhattan.
2 You really feel as if you're in China there, even in though middle of the York New in you're.
3 Try and have a walk through the neighborhood, you if even there for meal a Chinese don't stop.
4 Little Italy has kept its name, most though even Italians years ago away moved.
5 It's an expensive neighborhood today, originally poor immigrants though the home of it was.
6 Little Italy Although cheap the restaurants in aren't, huge numbers of tourists eat there.

More help (p. 127)   Early finisher p. 136 (Grammar challenge)

EXTRA Prepare a three-minute presentation for your class about a New York attraction. Use at least three sentences with a clause like those in 1–3.

Putting Makeup on the Fat Boy

(adapted and abridged from the novel by Bil Wright)

Look at the picture on page 33. Then say what you think the story will be about.

Chapter 1

When I was twelve, I convinced my mother to let me do her makeup for Parents' Night. When I was finished, my sister, Rosalia, who was fifteen, said, "Ma, aren't ya even gonna say anything?"
Ma said to me, "All right, so it looks nice, Carlos. But I don't think I should be encouraging something like this. I'm not gonna go to your school and tell your teacher, 'See my face! Isn't it pretty? My son did my makeup. Didn't he do an excellent job?'"
Rosalia asked, "Why not?"
Ma said, "You know why not! Don't make me say it."
Rosalia put her hands on her hips. "You know what, Ma? Carlos is talented, that's what he is. He's probably gonna be famous one day for being so talented, and you should be happy he can do something this good so young!"

After Ma went to Parents' Night, Rosalia and I went to McDonald's. Rosalia told me again she thought I was talented and that I was gonna be famous. I asked her to buy me an extra bag of chocolate chip cookies and an all-chocolate sundae to prove she really meant it.

By the time I got to Sojourner Truth/John F. Kennedy Freedom High School, I knew if other people could get paid as makeup artists, I could too. I already had a job after school being an assistant to all the teachers in a day care program. I didn't love my job, but I did love being able to go shopping for makeup at Little Ricky's on Thirteenth Street, where they had the wildest stuff. I'd run home, lock my bedroom door, and try it out immediately. Sitting on the side of my bed, studying my face in my two-sided makeup mirror (one for normal view, one for super-close-up) was like school after school. It was me practicing the thing that I knew would make me famous someday.
No matter what any of them said, the girls at school had to admit I was an expert. And the boys who got away with eyeliner because they were supposedly rockers even asked me for tips on how to put it on straight. I was really happy to tell them, because crooked eyeliner is so whack, it makes me nuts. My friend Angie suggested, "Carlos, now that You're sixteen, you should come to Macy's and try to get a part-time job at a makeup counter." She worked there on Saturdays and she bugged me from the beginning of school in September. "You have to go and apply for a job before the holidays. That's when they need all the help they can get. I bet you could work for any company you wanted – Chanel, Bobbi Brown, Dolce & Gabbana. Any of them." [...]

"Angie, do you think a famous store like Macy's would really hire me? I don't have any professional experience."
And good old Angie said, "Honey, all we have to do is get you an application. Then we'll come up with a fake résumé. We'll put my cell number on it. When they call, I'll answer, 'Greenberg's Department Store' and tell them, 'Carlos Duarte? You'd be lucky to get him! He's fabulous!'"

(to) **convince** [kən'vɪns] überzeugen (to) **encourage** [ɪn'kʌrɪdʒ] fördern **hip** [hɪp] Hüfte (to) **prove** [pruːv] beweisen **day care** Tagesbetreuung (to) **lock** [lɒk] abschließen **No matter what …** Egal, was … (to) **admit** [əd'mɪt] zugeben (to) **get away with sth.** mit etwas ungestraft davonkommen **supposedly** [sə'pəʊzɪdli] angeblich **straight** [streɪt] gerade **crooked** ['krʊkɪd] schief **whack** [wæk] (*AE, infml*) extrem schlecht **nuts** [nʌts] (*infml*) verrückt (to) **bug** [bʌg] (*infml*) ärgern (to) **apply** [ə'plaɪ] sich bewerben (to) **hire** ['haɪə] einstellen **application** [ˌæplɪ'keɪʃn] Bewerbung **fake** [feɪk] gefälscht **résumé** ['rezəmeɪ] (*AE*) Lebenslauf

Chapter 5

Friday morning it happened. I was in history class when my thigh vibrated.

I got up and ran out, even though it's totally against the rules. "Hello, hello!" I shouted in the hallway.

"This is Valentino, the manager of FeatureFace Cosmetics at Macy's." He said it like he was saying, *This is Meryl Streep, and I've been nominated for a zillion Oscars.* "Is Carlos Duarte there?"

"This is Carlos," I said, trying to sound like Meryl too, except in *The Devil Wears Prada*.

"We want to see you tomorrow for an interview. We have two slots available. An eleven and a one thirty."

As soon as he got out "One thirty," I said, "Eleven."

"Fine. Bring your résumé and a model for your makeup demonstration."

"Of course," I said, like it was old, old information for a pro like me.

"Don't be late. We have a very full schedule on Saturday and we don't tolerate lateness." Now *he* was definitely Meryl in *Prada*.

"I won't. I'm never late," I babbled. "Thank you."

But he didn't hear any of it, because he'd already hung up.

Chapter 6

I saw his head first, then the top part of his body, then the bottom. In sections. He was a giraffe in a black V-neck sweater, black pants, and about thirty silver bracelets, fifteen on each arm. [...]

"I'm Valentino," he announced. And he still wasn't looking at me or my sister.

"I'm Carlos Duarte," I said as though I'd said it hundreds of times in professional situations, "and this is my model, Rosalia."

He looked down somewhat, but he still never focused on me. "Where have you worked before?"

I put my red book bag on the counter and quickly unzipped it. "I have my résumé here," I said, suddenly out of breath as though I'd run ten miles to get there.

"Just tell me where the last place you worked was. As a makeup artist." His voice sounded like a stapler.

"Well, I go to school, so I haven't done it full-time. But I..." I was stalling, trying to think of a name to give him. Of course I'd practiced it, but I hadn't ever imagined the creature in front of me asking the question. "I worked on Saturdays and holidays at Bobby's, downtown."

"Bobby's downtown?" Still looking over the top of my head, he said it like it was one clearly made-up word. "And you say you're in school?"

"Yes, but I'm only applying for part-time right now. And Christmas."

"And other than this... Bobby's..." Valentino stared at my fake résumé like a bird had crapped on it.

---

thigh [θaɪ] Oberschenkel **slot** Zeitfenster **hang up** auflegen **bracelet** ['breɪslət] Armband **somewhat** ['sʌmwɒt] etwas, ein bisschen **unzip sth.** [ˌʌn'zɪp] den Reißverschluss von etwas aufmachen **stapler** ['steɪplə] Heftmaschine **stall** ['stɔ:l] Zeit gewinnen wollen **crap** [kræp] kacken

"I don't recognize any of these… places." Just then Miss Rapunzel rushed up to Valentino. "Craig Denton is here, Val. He came in the other side. He asked where you were." […]

"Our account executive is here today visiting. Couldn't have happened at a busier time," Valentino said, and sniffed. He put my résumé on the counter. "Why don't you get ready to work with your model, so I can see what you did at… Bobby's. I'll be back. Lissette will get you whatever you tell her you need." […]

As soon as he was gone, Lissette Rapunzel asked softly, as though I was trying to light a brand-new gas oven with a book of matches, "Have you ever done this before?"
"Yes," I lied breezily. "Of course."
"You should just keep talking to me, telling me everything You're doing," she whispered. "When Valentino comes back, just keep talking. And don't forget to sell the product, baby!" […]

Lissette came back and put the cleanser and Softwipes on the counter next to me. "Thank you, Lissette. By the way, I love your hair."
I was used to using my fingers for everything. But when I started to rub the concealer under Rosalia's eye, Lissette made a sound like she was choking, so I got the hint. "FeatureFace also has these wonderful brushes you can use. No one uses their fingers anymore," I said, and Lissette couldn't stop herself from laughing. A few minutes later I could hear Valentino talking to Craig Denton as I got to Rosalia's eye shadow. They were coming toward us. I was feeling so good, I got even louder.
"Now I'm going to use FeatureFace's incredible Perfect Pink as the base. You can see it's a subtle, more neutral pink – which my customers love – and we're using it to hold our color down. And we'll put a deeper, richer pink on top …" […]

Valentino and Craig Denton were now right behind Lissette! They'd stopped talking, and both of them were watching me.
"The thing that's so great about FeatureFace's shadows is how they create so much dimension with such little effort!" I had no idea what I was saying, really. It was everything I'd ever studied mixed with every ad and commercial for makeup I'd ever seen.
"You're very good for someone so young. How long have you been working for us?" I kept brushing Rosalia's eyelids, not able to speak. Was this guy really speaking to me? *How long have you been working for us?*
"He doesn't." Valentino sounded dry, but not as dry as he had when he'd been talking to me. Not at all. "This is an interview. I'm not sure he has as much experience as we'd like."
"Oh, come on," Craig Denton said, and I could tell he was smiling even though I was too nervous to look at him. "He obviously knows what he's doing. And he's definitely a good salesman."
"Yes," Valentino said in this tone that could have been agreeing to having his cavities drilled.
"I'll be curious to see what this looks like when you're finished – what is your name?"
"Carlos Duarte," I said, wishing I could have announced it in the voice I used when I was daydreaming something like this was happening.
"Well, if I'm still here, Lissette, you come get me."
"Absolutely, Craig," Lissette bubbled.
"I'm not sure you *will* still be here, Craig." Valentino sighed. "He's going very slowly. As far as I'm concerned, he should have finished the first look already –"

"You know, Val, speed is something that comes with time. When he's been doing it for as long as you have" – Craig Denton chuckled – "I'm sure he'll be as fast as you are." […]

---

rush up to sb. [rʌʃ] auf jn. zustürzen **account executive** [ə'kaʊnt‿ɪɡˌzekjətɪv] Kundenkontobetreuer/in **sniff** schniefen **match** Streichholz **lie** [laɪ] lügen **breezily** ['bri:zɪli] locker **cleanser** ['klenzə] Reinigungsmilch **concealer** [kən'si:lə] Gesichtsabdeckcreme **choke** [tʃəʊk] ersticken **hint** Hinweis **brush** [brʌʃ] Pinsel **eye shadow** ['ʃædəʊ] Lidschatten **incredible** [ɪn'kredəbl] unglaublich **base** [beɪs] Basis **effort** ['efət] Mühe **commercial** [kə'mɜ:ʃl] Werbespot **obviously** ['ɒbviəsli] offensichtlich **drill a cavity** ['kævəti] ein Zahnloch bohren **bubble** ['bʌbl] blubbern **As far as I'm concerned, …** [kən'sɜ:nd] Was mich angeht, … **chuckle** ['tʃʌkl] kichern

"Fine," Valentino snapped. "When he's finally finished the first look, Lissette, let us know." And they went around the corner to another part of the FeatureFace counter.

As soon as they'd gone, Rosalia squealed, "Ooo, Carlos!"

"Do you know how fabulous that is?" Lissette said.

"Who is he?" I asked.

"Craig Denton, the Manager of Retail Operations. And he oversees all the FeatureFace retail outlets in the city. He started on the floor, then was a counter manager like Valentino, then got promoted to MRO."

"And does it matter if he likes what I'm doing?"

"Let's put it this way: If he likes what he sees, Valentino would have to explain why he *didn't* hire you."

---

snap at sb. [snæp] jn. anblaffen **squeal** [skwiːl] kreischen, quieken **retail operations** [ˌriːteɪl‿ˌɒpəˈreɪʃnz] Einzelhandel **floor** *hier:* Verkaufsabteilung **Let's put it this way**. Wollen wir es so sagen.

1 The road to Macy's

a) Choose the correct answer for each question: a, b or c.

1 When Carlos does his mom's makeup, she
- a) likes the result.
- b) doesn't like the result.
- c) tells his teachers how talented he is.

2 While Carlos is at high school, he
- a) has an afternoon job in a makeup shop.
- b) practises doing makeup on girl students.
- c) gives advice on makeup to boy students.

3 When Angie tells Carlos to apply to Macy's, he
- a) agrees immediately.
- b) takes some time to think about it.
- c) asks her to help him with a fake résumé.

4 Valentino phones Carlos because he wants to
- a) offer him an interview.
- b) tell him that Macy's has nothing to offer.
- c) talk about Meryl Streep.

5 When Carlos arrives at Macy's, Valentino
- a) doesn't introduce himself.
- b) gives him a friendly welcome.
- c) asks him questions about his résumé.

6 Lissette advises Carlos
- a) to talk when doing someone's makeup.
- b) not to talk when doing someone's makeup.
- c) never to try and sell a makeup product.

7 At FeatureFace, Craig Denton has a
- a) higher position than Valentino.
- b) lower position than Valentino.
- c) similar position to Valentino.

8 Lissette thinks that
- a) Valentino wants to hire Carlos.
- b) Craig Denton wants to hire Carlos.
- c) Valentino and Craig want to hire Carlos.

b) Compare your results. Say what part(s) of the text helped you to choose each answer.

2 Carlos and Valentino

You choose a) or b) My Book

a) Imagine you are one of these characters: Rosalia, Lissette, Craig Denton or Valentino. You tell a friend about how you experienced Carlos' interview at Macy's. Write a short dialogue.

b) Imagine Carlos is starting his first day at Macy's. He says hi to Valentino. How will their conversation continue? Make a short picture story with speech bubbles.

Workbook 23 (p. 13)

Workbook Checkpoint 1 (pp. 14–17)

a) Look at ten screenshots from two videos about Native Americans. Then match each caption to <u>one</u> of the images.
   1 *Others were farmers.*
   2 *European settlers drove them from their land.*
   3 *Many died of disease.*
   4 *There were different cultures and traditions.*
   5 *The first settlers moved across the continent.*
   6 *Some of them built cities.*
   7 *Many were hunters.*

b) Think of captions for the three other images.

c) Watch the videos. Note down other key information about Native Americans.

d) Look again at the screenshots above. Then agree on two more screenshots to make from each of the two videos. Share your screenshots with the class and explain your choice.

a) Look at the screenshots from three videos about sport, national parks and music. Say what you think the videos might tell you about each topic.

b) Watch the videos. After each video, note down the main points you can remember.

c) Compare notes. Say which of the three topics you'd like find out more about, and why.

EXTRA An Album on the USA

Make one page on a topic that interests you: a city, Native Americans, baseball, landscapes, break dance, etc.

Collect information and pictures, and write a text for you page.

www Watch the videos again if you want to.

New Orleans

A Mardi Gras in Rue Bourbon

B A brass band in the French Quarter

1 Your first impressions

a) Describe photos A–E. Discuss what seems similar to and different from your home area. Then name one thing you would like to find out more about.

- *Photo A is of a street festival. I can see … It reminds me of … although … looks different.*
- *In photo B there is / there are …*

b) Find New Orleans on the map of the United States on pages 10–11. Say what information it gives you about the location.

2 Arriving in New Orleans

Listen to Tyler and his parents.
Note down what you learn about New Orleans.

b) Compare your notes.
Then say if you think Tyler will enjoy his stay in New Orleans. Give reasons.

EXTRA My Book Write a short text. Say

- what you know about New Orleans
- why you would/wouldn't like to go there

Read out your texts and give feedback.

Your task

At the end of this unit:
Give a talk about objects/photos/… that are important to you and/or your family.

C *A flooded street after Hurricane Katrina*

D *Ships at Baton Rouge Bridge*

E *An alligator in the swamps of the Mississippi River*

1 A chat and a shock post

Look at the pictures Tyler sent in the chat with his friends. Then say what you think he tells them.

Yesterday

Hey guys! It's so WARM in N'Awlins. 80 degrees! 9:27 pm

Jasmine
Hey, palm trees! 9:29 pm

Right in front of Grandma Betty's house. It's kinda tropical here. 9:30 pm

Jasmine
Lucky you! So is it really all sunny weather, music and Cajun food down there? 9:31 pm

Well, there's a lot of music. 9:32 pm

Jasmine
Is that a banjo? 9:32 pm

It's a gourd banjo. It's Dad's new favorite toy. He's been playing it since we got here. If he doesn't stop soon, I'll go crazy! 🙂 9:33 pm

Jasmine
Hey, Tyler. You're in the city of music. 😂 Anyway, what's it like downtown? 9:34 pm

Just one big party! 9:34 pm

Alex
That's the French Quarter, right? 9:35 pm

Jasmine
Typical. Tyler always heads straight for the fun places. I like those balconies! 9:35 pm

Yeah, that's the style here. 9:36 pm

2 Understanding the text

a) Read the chat. Note down what it tells you about different aspects of New Orleans.

Weather – very hot, tropical …

b) Write a message to Tyler. Name two things you'd like to do in New Orleans and comment on one of his photos.
Read your text to a partner.

3 A friend of yours?

a) Describe Dean Syme's post. Then say how you think Tyler feels about it, and why.

b) **Think:** Note down ideas for advice to Tyler.

Pair: Agree on the two best ideas.

Share: Discuss your best ideas. Agree on one to present to the class.

Jasmine
So you have the music and the sun. How about that famous New Orleans food? 9:38 pm

Alex
You ate alligator? Disgusting. 9:43

Jasmine
Poor alligator! I wouldn't eat any if you gave me 100 dollars. 9:44 pm

But it's real tasty – like chicken. If you give me 100 bucks, I'll eat it again. 🙂. 9:46 pm

Jasmine
Hmmm. Isn't there anything else you can recommend? 9:47 pm

This is THE place for food. 9:48 pm

I had gumbo there today. 9:48 pm

Alex
?????? 9:49 pm

Stew with sausage and shrimp. 9:50 pm

Alex
Sounds weird. Are you going to eat that kind of stuff at Thanksgiving too? 9:51 pm

No way. We're going to have turkey. Grandma Betty bought this huge bird. It's going to be a great party. 9:52 pm

Today

MeanManhattanMan
Eating alligator, Tyler? Yuck! So typical of you people. Keep your Deep South habits outta NYC!

Hey guys! Can you believe what this kid posted!? 9:05 am

Jasmine
If I were you, I'd block him. 9:48 am

Good advice, but I don't even know him. How can he know where I am? 9:49 am

Alex
That's Dean Syme. He probably saw the photos of your trip on my timeline. I feel embarrassed. 9:52 am

That guy's your friend?? 9:54 am

4 Food and you

a) Describe the different attitudes in the chat to gator and gumbo.

b) Read the box on the right. Would you try these dishes? Why (not)?
Describe an unusual dish that you have tried.

c) What is typical German food? Discuss what other cultures might think about it.

Access to cultures: Gator and gumbo

Alligator is eaten in southern states like Florida and Louisiana. Most meat comes from alligator farms and is used in lots of different dishes.

Gumbo is a stew with vegetables, herbs and spices, fish and meat (sometimes alligator!), and other ingredients. It is typical of local Cajun food, which combines Native American, African and European cooking traditions.

1 Good food

a) Make a table like this and add words from the box. Then add other food words that you know.

vegetables	meat	+dairy products	other
carrot	bacon	butter	oil

+ new words

bacon · +beans · +beef · butter · cheese · chicken · curry +powder · +flour · +garlic · +lentils · +muffin · +mushrooms · +nuts · +oil · +onions · +parsley · pepper · +peppers · +pork · +rice · +salt · +spinach · spaghetti · +tinned tomatoes

b) **Partner A:** You want to make spaghetti with tomato sauce.
Partner B: You want to make chicken curry with rice.
Choose ingredients from your table. Add others if you like. Then tell your partner your ingredients.

2 How to cook it

a) You will hear four short dialogues in which people talk about cooking food.
Listen and say how they cook in each dialogue: +*bake* · +*boil* · +*fry* · +*roast*.

b) Match each way of cooking from a) to the correct picture.

A +frying pan

B +oven

C oven

D +saucepan

c) Choose the correct word.

1 boil/fry water
2 boil/bake lentils
3 bake/roast bread
4 boil/fry a steak
5 bake/boil spaghetti
6 bake/roast a cake
7 bake/boil biscuits
8 bake/fry sausages
9 bake/roast a turkey
10 fry/roast eggs
11 bake/fry muffins
12 boil/roast rice

3 Everyday English: I'd recommend this

a) Work in groups of four. Recommend and describe a dish you like to your partners.
Say if you'd like to try your partners' dishes.

It's a vegetarian/meat dish.
It's a typical Turkish/… dish.
It's made with spinach/eggs/…
The eggs are boiled/…
The meat is fried/… with …

It tastes / It's a bit / It's very: +bitter. / +hot. / +sour. / +spicy. / sweet.

I think it's (really): amazing. / delicious. / interesting. / tasty. / yummy.

– *A: I'd recommend … It's a typical German dish. It tastes … I think it's delicious. Why don't you try it?*
– *B: I like the sound of that. / I'm not sure if I'd enjoy that. / No, I don't fancy that. / …*

b) Vote to find the most popular dish in your group.

Early finisher p. 137

 Workbook 3–4 (p. 19); Wordbank 2

You are going to explain a German menu to a visitor from the United States.
First you will practise skills to help you to do this well.

a) Read the menu. Then check in class that everyone knows what all the dishes are.

Restaurant Rote Mühle

Suppen

Linsensuppe mit Würstchen	2,90
Rindergulaschsuppe (scharf)	3,10
Knoblauchsuppe	2,70

Salate

Griechischer Bauernsalat mit Gurken, Tomaten, Feta, Oliven und Jogurt-Dressing	7,50
Blattsalat mit Putenstreifen und Curry-Dressing	7,90
Salat Rote Mühle mit Rucola, Tomaten und Ei und Honig-Senf-Dressing	8,10

Hauptgerichte

Schweineschnitzel mit Petersilienkartoffeln und Pilzen	10,50
Cordon Bleu mit Bratkartoffeln und Salatbeilage	11,90
Leberkäse mit Kartoffelsalat und Spiegelei	9,10
Riesencurrywurst mit Pommes	8,90
Schweinebraten mit Knödeln und Rotkohl	10,90
Seelachsfilet mit Salzkartoffeln und buntem Gemüse	12,50
Ofenkartoffel mit Käse überbacken und Quark	11,90
Vollkornspaghetti mit Spinat und Sahnesauce	8,90
Gemüselasagne mit Tomatensauce und Salatbeilage	10,40

Nachspeisen

Gemischtes Eis mit heißen Himbeeren	4,10
Kaiserschmarrn mit Apfelmus	7,80

b) Imagine you have to explain the menu to these four people:
1 Dom's a vegetarian 2 Zara doesn't eat pork 3 Pip hates spicy food 4 Jo's allergic to tomatoes
Decide which information is useful for each person. Say which dishes you could leave out, and why.

c) Practise paraphrasing words you can't translate into English.
– ***Gurke***, *that's a long vegetable, dark green on the outside and light green on the inside. It doesn't have a very strong taste. You often find it in salads.*
– ***Ofenkartoffel***, *that's a big potato that's baked in …*

d) Take turns to play the American visitor.
Partner A: Go to p. 146 and read your role card.
Partner B: When your partner has read the card,
- find out what kind of food they like
- find dishes on the menu you think they'd like
- describe the dishes and recommmend one.

Phrases
- Well, then I needn't tell you about the meat dishes.
- I don't know the English word, so I'll try to explain it.
- I can ask the waiter what kind of meat it is.

Now change roles. Partner B: Your role card is on p. 150.

Mediation skills

This is what you need to do when you explain a German text (e.g. a menu) to someone.
- *Decide which information is relevant.*
- *Translate or paraphrase keywords.*

→ *SMC 10: Selecting relevant information (p. 200)* → *SMC 11: Paraphrasing (p. 201)*

REMEMBER

Read these sentences from p. 41 and complete the rule about verb forms in conditional sentences.

- *If you give me 100 bucks, I'll eat it again.* (Conditional 1)
- *Poor alligator! I wouldn't eat any if you gave me 100 dollars.* (Conditional 2)

In conditional 1 sentences, we use the … in the *if*-clause and the … in the main clause.
In conditional 2 sentences, we use …

➜ *GAP 7: Conditional sentences 1 and 2 (p. 164)*

1 REVISION A note from Mom (Conditional sentences 1)

Jasmine finds a note from her mom. Complete it with the correct form of the verbs in the box.

Hi Jaz! If I [1]… work on time, I [2]… home at six. You [3]… some chocolate in the cupboard if you [4]… a snack. But remember, if you [5]… too much, you [6]… hungry at dinner time. About dinner tonight: If you [7]…, I [8]… spaghetti. But if you [9]… that again, I [10]… to the market on my way home. By the way, your dad has lost his key, so if he [11]… back early, you [12]… let him in. Mom xx

be · not be · eat · find · get · go · have to · leave · like · make · want · not want

More help p. 128

2 REVISION ... if people ate less meat (Conditional sentences 2)

Three friends are talking about food.
Complete their dialogue. Match the sentence halves and put the verbs into the correct form.

1. Dom: There … (be) more space to grow plants
2. Zara: But if I … (become) a vegetarian,
3. Dom: I'm sure you … (like) vegetarian food
4. Zara: And if I … (learn) how to cook,
5. Dom: Look, Todd, you … (feel) healthier
6. Todd: Well, I … (eat) less chocolate
7. Dom: If you … (buy) fruit instead,
8. Todd: If fresh fruit … (not cost) so much,

a. if you … (try) a few dishes.
b. you … (probably enjoy) it.
c. if you … (not eat) so much sweet food.
d. if people … (eat) less meat.
e. then maybe I … (buy) some.
f. I … (have to) give up bacon and sausages.
g. I … (be able to) make a meal for our friends!
h. if it … (not be) so delicious.

More help p. 128

3 REVISION Crazy situations (Conditional sentences 1 and 2)

Make as many conditional sentences 1 and 2 as you can to talk about the pictures below.

Conditional 1
If the girl isn't careful, that dog will bite her.

Conditional 2
If I met that dog, I'd be scared.

1

2

3

More help p. 128 Early finisher p. 139 (Grammar challenge)

 Workbook 6–7 (p. 21)

4 Help! My kids want to become vegetarians

a) The letter below has several words you haven't learned yet in this book.
Read it paragraph by paragraph.
With a partner, first discuss the meaning of each word you don't know. Then use a dictionary if you need to.

b) Say who you think the letter is written to and why the writer is worried.

TIP
When you read, you can often understand new words without looking them up.
For example, they may be similar to a German word or an English word you already know.
Or the meaning may be clear from the context.
➜ *SMC 23: Dealing with unknown words (p. 210)*

Dear Mara,

We've always been a family of meat-eaters, especially on festive occasions like Thanksgiving and Christmas. Even on normal days we enjoy a juicy steak or a meaty stew. Or at least until last week. That was when my two kids broke the news that they want to become vegetarians.

My daughter, who has just turned 12, says there are countless health reasons for giving up meat, but I disagree with that. We humans evolved because we ate meat. It's against nature to go without it completely. My daughter says your body gets all the protein it needs from things like cheese, eggs, lentils, tofu, etc. But I feel that a totally meat-free lifestyle is a big health risk, especially for adolescents.

My daughter also says she is against animal cruelty. The kind of factory farming we have in this country today disgusts her. I kind of agree with that, but it's just one of those things we have to accept. I'd offer to buy organic meat, but we aren't made of money and we couldn't afford it.

My son, who is 14, also goes on about health and animal cruelty, but his main reason for wanting to change his diet is the environment. His biggest worry is the destruction of the rainforest. Do I know, he keeps asking me, that an area equal to the state of Florida is destroyed every year, just so that we can grow food for factory-farmed animals? And what kind of future will our planet have if we go on like this? Of course I know this, and I worry about it too, so it isn't so easy for me to convince him that it's risky to do without meat at his age.

What can I say to my kids to make them see sense? I wouldn't mind cutting down a bit on meat, but cutting it out completely would be a major mistake.

Worried mom, Louisiana

5 Everyday English: If I were you ... (Giving advice)

a) Think of how Mara could to reply to the worried mom from Lousiana and make notes.
In a double circle, share your ideas. Note down any good ideas that you hear.
– *A: If I were Mara, I'd tell the worried mom …*
– *B: I'd suggest that …*
– *C: I think it would be a good idea if …*

b) Write Mara's reply to the worried mom. Try and use some of these phrases.

In my opinion, …	If I were you, I would/wouldn't …
I think you should …	If you try to …, your kids will …
Why don't you …?	If you explain why …, maybe …

Early finisher *p. 137*

1 Grandma Betty's memory box

Say what you think a memory box might be.

After dinner, Tyler's dad picked up the old banjo again and started to play. Tyler groaned.
"Ooh … that old thing needs some tuning," said Grandma Betty. "It's hurting my ears."
Aunt D'Avila reached over. "Give it to me."
She tightened its strings and started playing.
"Hey! *You* play really well Aunt D'Avila," said Tyler.
"Oh thank you, Tyler," cried D'Avila. "I found this old banjo at the back of an old closet years ago."
"Yes!" said Grandma Betty. "D'Avila ran into the room. She was screaming 'Mama! Do you know what *this* is?' I thought she had found gold!"
"Well, to me it *was* like finding gold! A gourd banjo! In my own house!"
"I wish I had found it," said Tyler's dad. "I would have screamed too."
"What's so special about it?" Tyler asked.
"This instrument has a history," D'Avila replied. "Our history. It goes back to the days of slavery."
Tyler's grandmother took the instrument in her arms. "It belonged to my daddy, your great-grandfather. It reminds me of the days when he sat out on the porch and played this song."
Grandma Betty began to sing softly: *"We give you beans for your breakfast, beans for your dinner … beans most every night!"*
"I wish I had known him, Grandma," said Tyler. "Do you have a picture of him?"
"D'Avila, honey, go to my room and bring down my box – you know which one.

❖

Tyler took something from the square box.
Grandma Betty laughed. "My alligator teeth! A boy I knew gave them to me. I was just 16 then." She held them up to her ears. "See … they're earrings. He killed the alligator himself, or so he said. He thought I'd like that. But I couldn't wear them! That kind of jewelry is *not* my style!"
"But you wouldn't have kept the earrings if you hadn't liked him," laughed Tyler.
Grandma Betty seemed not to hear him. She was looking through the other things in the box.
"Here they are!" she cried and pulled out a pile of old photos. "Tyler, this is your great-grandfather. And, look, here's your grandpa on our wedding day. He was a great man. And this is about the sit-ins." She gave Tyler an old newspaper article.
"Sit-ins?"
"The protests against segregation. Here in New Orleans. Your grandpa and I took part in them."
"Cool," said Tyler. "*I* would have been afraid."
"I would have been afraid too, Tyler – without all the others. But together we felt strong."

2 Understanding the text

a) Make groups of three. Each student chooses one of these objects from the text:
- *gourd banjo*
- *alligator teeth*
- *newspaper article*

Explain to your partners what the text says about your object and how Grandma Betty feels about it.

b) What would you put in a memory box? Share ideas with the class and give reasons.
- *I'd put … in a memory box.*
- *It's important/special to me because …*
- *It reminds me of the time when …*

WWW Find out more about the history of the gourd banjo and listen to a song.

3 Civil rights

New Orleans Sit-ins and the End of Segregation

New Orleans, September 16, 2020

Sixty years ago today, Rudy Lombard, who is black, and his friend Lanny Goldfinch, who is white, walked into a diner in downtown New Orleans. With two other black friends, they took seats at a whites-only counter. Immediately they were asked to leave. They didn't. Instead they sat quietly till the police came and arrested them. This was one of the city's first sit-ins.

In the early 1960s, segregation was the rule, not just in restaurants. Blacks could not go to the same movie theaters as whites, relax in the same parks or learn at the same schools. In streetcars, they sat at the back and had to give up their seat whenever a white wanted it. Public telephones, restrooms and waiting rooms were "White only" or "Colored only". The signs were everywhere.

Lombard was a leader of the civil rights protests in New Orleans. All over the city, there were sit-ins in restaurants, libraries and other public places which practiced discrimination against blacks. Many of those who took part were students, both white and black. Today, not everyone realizes how dangerous it was to stand up against segregation. Through their actions, the protesters took great risks. They were often arrested, some of them spent time in prison, and some lost their jobs. Many were beaten up – some were even murdered. But they never gave up and finally, after two years, segregation was ended in the city of New Orleans. "It's important to remember the courage of those who spoke out," Mayor Mitch Landrieu said today.

One of those who spoke out was Dodie Smith-Simmons. As a young girl she had played with white children in her neighborhood. But when her white friends got older, their parents no longer allowed them to play with her. "They started calling me names, they threw rocks at me," she said. "That was hard to understand. These were my friends! But it shows they weren't born with prejudices. They were taught them."

John Hubbard, who also took part in the protests, remembers traveling as a child with his mother on a streetcar. Why couldn't he sit in the front with the whites, he asked her. "They're waiting for you to change it," she told him.

And that is what Hubbard did, together with Lombard, Smith-Simmons and the thousands of others who wanted a better life for the next generation. They changed the system. Life for their children would have been completely different if they had given up the fight.

4 Protesting against segregation

Think: Make notes about these points:
- types of discrimination against black people
- how and why people protested

Pair: Compare your ideas and organize them in a table.

Share: Present your table to another pair.

Text file 3 (p. 118)

5 Have a go

Imagine you had been in New Orleans in 1960. Say what you *would* or *wouldn't have done*.

I would have / I wouldn't have

joined the protest · spoken out · said nothing
ordered a meal for the protesters
talked to the people behind the counter
gone to a different restaurant · …

Looking at language

a) Look at these sentences from page 46. Are the people talking about the past **or** about something that could happen now or in the future?

"I wish I had found it," said Tyler's dad. "I would have screamed too." (ll. 15–16)
"I wish I had known him, Grandma," said Tyler. (l. 27)
"Cool," said Tyler. "I would have been afraid." (l. 50)
"But you wouldn't have kept the earrings if you hadn't liked him." (ll. 38–39)

b) Choose the correct answers to complete the rules.

The *would have*-form is followed by the simple past / past participle form of a verb.
When you wish something about the past / the future, use the past perfect after *wish*.
In an *if*-clause about the past, you use the simple past / past perfect.

1 I would have stayed inside (*would have*-form)

Write a sentence about what you *would have done* in these situations. Use the ideas in brackets.

1 A: We went for a walk in the rain yesterday.
B: In the rain? (stay at home)
I would have stayed at home.

2 A: Eva was late again yesterday. So I waited ten minutes and then I went home.
B: Only ten minutes? (wait a bit longer)

3 A: Our host family in France gave us frogs' legs for dinner.
B: The poor frogs. (ask for something else)

4 A: I didn't really enjoy Kim's party, but I stayed till the end.
B: Really? (leave early)

5 A: I bought a pair of pink trainers yesterday.
B: Pink! (buy a different colour)

6 A: I gave my dad a pair of socks for his birthday.
B: Socks aren't so interesting! (give him a book or a DVD)

2 Would've, could've, ...

LISTENING TIP
In spoken English, native speakers usually use short forms of conditional 3 verbs.
Instead of *I would have done* ..., they say *I would've done* ... or *I'd've done* ..., etc.
Knowing these pronunciation patterns will help you to understand native speakers.

a) You will hear six sentences with short conditional 3 forms.
Listen and match each sentence (a–f) to phrases 1–6 below. You will hear each sentence twice.

1 it couldn't've been
2 I'd've helped
3 they shouldn't've told
4 I could've given
5 we wouldn't've come
6 she'd've texted

b) Write down the full form of the phrases in a): *It could not have been ...*
Listen again to the short forms and pay attention to the difference.

c) Now practise dialogues 1–6 in exercise 1. Take turns to read A and B.
Try to use short conditional forms.

3 I wish I had been more careful (*wish* + past perfect)

a) Look at pictures A–D. Think about possible reasons why each situation happened.
Now imagine you are the person in the pictures. Make sentences with *I wish* … for each situation.
– I wish I had got up earlier. / I wish I hadn't …

A

B

C

D

More help p. 129

b) Now imagine that you are speaking to the people in the pictures.
Show that you feel sorry about their situation. Make comments like this:
– That was bad luck. I bet you wish you had got up earlier.

Early finisher p. 138

4 You wouldn't have broken your leg … (Conditional sentences 3)

a) Imagine you're talking to the person in the hospital bed. Complete the *if*-clauses for this sentence:
You wouldn't have broken your leg …

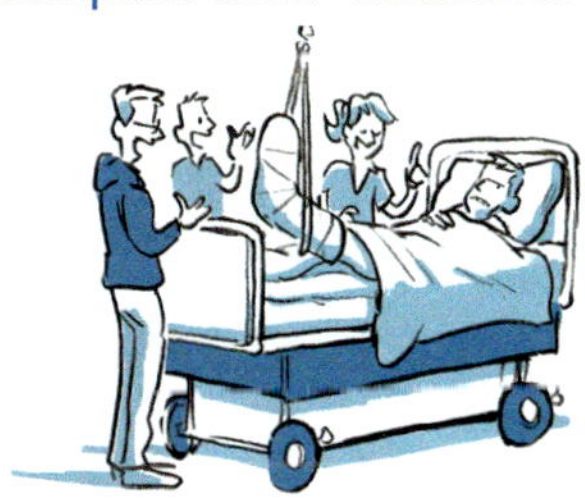

1 … if you … (look) where you were going.
if you had looked where you were going.
2 … if you … (come) down the stairs more carefully.
3 … if you … (not climb) that tall tree yesterday.
4 … if you …

b) Now make conditional 3 sentences for the people in exercise 3. Use the verbs in the box.

1 If I … home earlier, I … in time for the bus.
2 If I … my umbrella, I … so wet.
3 If I … my backpack, I … the lamp.
4 If I … so fast, I … into the tree.

be · not break · not crash · not drive · not get · leave · remember · take off

c) Write a dialogue with a person from a picture in exercise 3. Use one conditional 3 sentence.
Act out your dialogue.

More help p. 129 Early finisher p. 139 (Grammar challenge)

5 Something went wrong

a) Write a short story (75–100 words) for *one* of these endings:
1 *I wish I had listened to their advice.*
2 *We wouldn't have met if the train hadn't been late.*
3 *If I had known that, I wouldn't have gone there.*

b) Read out your stories, but not the ending. Can your partner guess the right sentence?

18th century: Black slaves work on a sugar cane plantation.

Leland, Mississipi 1939: A movie theater for black people only

Little Rock, Arkansas 1959: White protesters oppose the ending of segregation in schools.

African Americans in the age of slavery

Black people are about 13% of the population of the United States. Today, most of them call themselves African Americans. Their history goes back to the early 17th century when their ancestors were taken by Europeans from Africa, and sold in the Americas as slaves.

Until the middle of the 19th century, it was quite normal for people in North America to own slaves. George Washington, for example, the first president of the United States, owned hundreds of slaves. Slavery played an important role in the American economy, particularly in the southern states, where slaves worked on big plantations, often under very cruel conditions.

From the early 19th century, opinions about slavery began to change, especially in the North, where many political leaders were calling for all slaves to be freed. The South, however, was strongly against ending slavery. This was one of the main issues between North and South in the bloody civil war that started in 1861. After the northern states won in 1865, all slaves were freed.

The first century of "freedom"

Although black people were no longer slaves, their new "freedom" did not make them equal citizens, particularly in the South. There, new laws stopped them from buying property and forced them to keep working for white landowners. They were also unable to take part in political life. Only people who paid a special tax or had passed a reading and writing test were allowed to vote. But the tax was too high for most black people, and many couldn't read or write. These laws did not affect poorer white people: if your grandfather had voted, you could vote too. White people's grandfathers had voted. Black people's hadn't.

For most of the 20th century, the belief that white people were better than black people shaped society in the southern states. They had separate schools, separate swimming pools, separate public restrooms. The standard for white people was always higher. Their schools had better equipment. They sat at the front of a streetcar, not at the back. And if a town had only one of something, like a movie theater, it was always for white people only.

But by the 1950s, calls for change were getting louder. In 1955, the Supreme Court ordered the end of segregation in schools. Two years later, a federal law made it illegal to stop black people from voting. In the South, however, most white people were against these changes. There were many protests and black people still faced obstacles when they tried to vote.

The Civil Rights movement

In the late 1950s, civil rights leaders began to organize boycotts, sit-ins and marches against discrimination. Before long, a movement of protest had spread across the South. One of the leaders, the pastor Dr. Martin Luther King Jr., had organized a bus boycott in Alabama in 1955 and had since become a national figure and a powerful voice for black America. King is best known for his speech to over 300,000 people at the historic March on Washington in 1963. His words still move people today: "I have a dream that my four little children will one day live in a nation where they will not be judged by the color of their skin but by the content of their character." A year after the march, the President signed the Civil Rights Act, which outlawed discrimination and ended segregation in public places. In 1968, King was shot dead on the balcony of his motel in Memphis, Tenessee.

Washington, 1963: Martin Luther King makes a speech at the Lincoln Memorial.

African Americans in society today

In 2013, Washington celebrated the 50th anniversary of the civil rights march with speeches by the President and by King family members. Dr. King's daughter and sister also rang a bell that had once hung in a church where he had often spoken. The ceremony's motto was "Let Freedom Ring".

But can we really say that discrimination has ended? Certainly, the situation of African Americans is better today than in the 1960s. There are successful black people in all areas of American life, from billionaire TV personality Oprah Winfrey to Barack Obama, the first black president, who was elected in 2008, and then again in 2012.

However, although black people *can* be successful, it is far harder for them than for white people. Black people are more likely to grow up in poor neighborhoods and don't have the same chances in education. They are twice as likely to be out of work and five times more likely to be stopped by the police. Police violence against black people is a major issue.

2013 was not just a year of celebration. It also saw the birth of *Black Lives Matter,* a movement which started in response to the high number of black deaths at police hands. It quickly spread. In 2016, three black football players kneeled in support of the movement while the national anthem was played at the start of a game. Many people were offended by this gesture, but for others it has become a symbol of protest as the struggle for black equality continues.

Washington, 2013: President Barack Obama (2009–2017) at the Let Freedom Ring celebration

Santa Clara, CA, 2016: Eric Reid, Colin Kaepernick and Eli Harold kneel during the national anthem.

MK Use a digital tool to make a timeline of black history in the USA. Use information from the text and your own research. Present your timeline to another pair and give feedback.

➜ *Giving feedback (p. 304)*

1 The guest

On Thursday afternoon – Thanksgiving Day – Grandma Betty's was like a madhouse. There were four cooks in her small kitchen. Everyone was preparing a different dish. There were large oval plates with sweet potatoes, big round bowls of cranberry sauce, pumpkin pies and a huge turkey.
"I can't wait to eat this," said Tyler impatiently. "It all looks very tasty."
Just then the bell rang. "I'll go," said Tyler and ran to open the door. Before him stood a big man in a blue cotton shirt. Around his neck hung a leather cord with a long alligator tooth.
"You must be Tyler," the man said. "It's really nice to meet you. Betty has told me all about you."
"Is that you, Eugene?" called Grandma Betty. "Come over to the kitchen and spend a little time with us. Dinner will be ready in an hour."

❖

At dinner, Grandma Betty sat next to Eugene. "You look absolutely beautiful, Betty," said Eugene. "And I really like those earrings."
Tyler looked at his grandma. She seemed a little embarrassed. At that moment, her memory box flashed through his mind. He looked at Eugene. "Er ... can I ask you something?"
"Of course you can," said Eugene.
"The tooth on your chain. Where did you get it?"
Eugene looked at Tyler. "From a gator," he replied. "It was the first one I ever killed."
"*You* killed an alligator?" said Tyler.
"Sure," said Eugene. "It was me and my daddy. I was fairly young then, probably about your age."
"How do you hunt them?" Tyler asked.
"It's like fishing," said Eugene. "You move your boat through the water really quickly. Then, when you see a gator, you have to be completely silent. You throw out a line, and you hook him. But your hook is really big and sharp, right?"
"And then what?" asked Tyler.
"Well, as soon as you get the gator fairly close to your boat, you shoot him. And here's some advice – make sure he's quite dead before you pull him into your boat, or he'll pull *you* into the water."
"Man, that's awfully cruel," Tyler frowned. "I can't *believe* you can do that. It shouldn't be allowed."
"But Tyler," said his dad. "You ate alligator at the French Market and you really enjoyed it."
Tyler said nothing. Then Grandma Betty spoke. "You look a bit upset, Tyler," she said. "Here, have some more turkey. And you too, Eugene."
"Betty, it was absolutely delicious, but I couldn't eat another bite. I say it's time for some music!"
Eugene took a harmonica from his pocket and played a few notes. Then Aunt D'Avila picked up the gourd banjo.
"I haven't seen one of those for centuries," laughed Eugene. "What are we going to play?"

2 Understanding the text

a) Summarize the text in 60–80 words.
While Tyler's family are still cooking, Eugene ...

b) Say how you think Betty and Eugene feel about each other. Give reasons for your opinion.

c) Describe Tyler's attitude to hunting alligators. Say if you think it changes, and why (not).

Access to cultures: Alligator hunting

Louisiana has strict rules on alligator hunting. You need official permission, and can only hunt for a limited number of weeks. If you aren't local, you may only hunt with an official guide.

Are there similar activities with similar rules in your country? What are they?

Skimming is a reading skill that can help you to check if a text has information you need. It is different from *scanning*, which you have already learned about.

a) Scan the text below to find out when Thanksgiving became a federal holiday. Then say what you look for when you scan: general information *or* specific details.

Thanksgiving – America's favorite holiday

On the fourth Thursday in November every year, families all over the United States come together to celebrate Thanksgiving.

On the move

Over 40 million people are on the move around the holiday, the busiest traveling time of the year. So if you're in a car or waiting for a train, plane or bus on the Wednesday before Thanksgiving or the Sunday after, expect delays.

Traditional Thanksgiving turkey dinner

Not just turkey

Thanksgiving has been a federal holiday since 1863, although the tradition is much older. And on the day, roast turkey has been eaten for many years. For millions of families this traditional turkey dinner, with cranberry sauce, sweet potatoes and those delicious pumpkin pies, is the most important part of the celebration. There are also many other traditional activities which Americans look forward to, like watching a Thanksgiving Day parade, playing games, talking and, especially, watching football, as three games are shown live on TV.

One holiday ends, another begins

Another great American tradition takes center stage on the day after Thanksgiving: shopping. On "Black Friday", as it is called, many stores open early and have big sales. It is seen as the first day of the Christmas shopping season.

b) You *skim* a text to find the main ideas and decide if you want to read it in detail. You skim like this:

1 Read the **heading** (or **title**) and **sub-headings**.
2 Look at the **pictures**, **photos** or **graphics** and read their **captions**.
3 Read the **first sentence** of **every paragraph**, not the whole text.

Now skim the text on Thanksgiving and say what information you get.

c) Work in groups of three. Imagine each of you has to give a presentation on a different topic.

Partner A: Wildlife in the Louisiana swamps
Partner B: New Orleans swamp tours
Partner C: The people of the swamps

Go to pp. 147–149. Skim the three texts there and decide which one you should read. Then say which text you chose and why.

➜ *SMC 1: Skimming and scanning (p. 192)*

Early finisher p. 138

Language help

a) Adverbs of degree make the meaning of an adjective or adverb stronger or weaker:
*"You look absolutely **beautiful**."* (Strong degree)
*"You move your boat through the water really **quickly**."* (High degree)
*"I was fairly **young**, probably about your age."* (Medium degree)
*She seemed a little **embarrassed**.* (Weak degree)

b) With strong adjectives (e.g. *beautiful, delicious, terrible*), we use strong adverbs of degree. Compare *"It was absolutely **delicious**."* with *"It all looks very **tasty**."* (p. 52).
It would be unusual to say *absolutely tasty* or *very delicious*.

Find eight adverbs of degree on page 52 (1, ll. 33–46). Say how they affect the word that follows.

➜ *GAP 15: Adverbs of degree (p. 108)*

1 Very big or absolutely huge? (Adverbs of degree)

a) Make a table. Then decide how strong the adverbs in the box are. Add them to your table.
TIP: Remember that the adverb *quite* has two different meanings.

Strong (4)	High (3)	Medium (2)	Low (2)
absolutely			a bit

~~a bit~~ · ~~absolutely~~ · a little · awfully · completely · fairly · quite · really · totally · very

b) Find the adverbs of degree and match them to the most suitable adjectives.

1 absolutely · big · huge · very
very big, absolutely huge
2 difficult · fairly · impossible · totally
3 absolutely · cheap · free · very
4 very · delicious · tasty · absolutely
5 a bit · hungry · starving · absolutely
6 a bit · totally · quiet · silent
7 amazing · nice · quite · very
8 fairly · absolutely · bad · disgusting
9 completely · dead · ill · quite

More help p. 129

c) Complete this sentence. Then write five more with the pairs from b).

1 I know I asked for a very big portion of chips, but when it arrived at our table it was …

Compare your sentences with a partner.

2 After the party (Adverbs of degree)

Complete this text about the morning after Thanksgiving. Use the adverb of degree that fits best.

After the Thanksgiving party, Tyler was [1]… (a bit/really) tired and slept until 12 the next day. When he finally woke up, the sun was shining strongly through his window. "It's [2]… (awfully/fairly) bright in here," he groaned. "I wonder what time it is."
At that moment, Grandma Betty called out.
"It's [3]… (completely/quite) late," she said. "Aren't you going to have any breakfast today?"
Tyler had eaten so much the night before that he wasn't feeling [4]… (a little/very) hungry.
"No thanks, Grandma Betty," he called back.
"Are you (a bit/quite) sure?" his grandma asked.
"Grandma," Tyler said. "I'm [5]… (completely/fairly) happy to stay just where I am."
"I'm making waffles," Grandma Betty called again.
"OK, Grandma," said Tyler. "Maybe I am [6]… (a bit/totally) hungry." Then he jumped out of bed, got dressed [7]… (absolutely/very) quickly and ran to the kitchen. He could [8]… (absolutely/fairly) never say no to waffles.

Early finisher p. 139 (Grammar challenge)

1 A musician in New Orleans

a) Watch the film. Does it make you want to visit New Orleans and/or meet Ado? Explain why/why not.

b) Make a table with these headings:
- The city
- The narrator

Watch the film again and note down what you learn about the city of New Orleans and the narrator Ado.

Think of two alternative titles for the film and write them down.

c) Discuss your alternative titles. Choose the best one and tell your class.

2 Making the film: Sound and atmosphere

a) Look at these four stills from the film and describe the atmosphere. Say what kind of sound (words, music, sound effects) you would expect to hear.

1

2

3

4

b) Watch the film again and check the sound for each still. Is it as you expected? Say how the sound influences the atmosphere in a film.

3 Making the film: Picture material

Watch part of the film again and say what times in Ado's life it shows. What materials does the film-maker use for the different times?

The film shows Ado when he was a young child. The film-maker uses …

Yes, and then it shows …

Melba Pattillo and the Little Rock Nine (from the autobiography **Warriors Don't Cry**)

In 1955, the US Supreme Court ended segregation in schools. All schools now had to open their doors to black students as well as white. Some states did not want to do this. One of them was Arkansas. In September 1957, nine students in Little Rock, the Arkansas capital, tried to move from their school for blacks to the white-only Central High School. Outside the school, angry crowds of white people protested. The Governor of Arkansas sent in the National Guard to keep the black students out. In the end, the Little Rock Nine were only able to enter the school after the US president had sent soldiers to protect them.

One of the Little Rock Nine was 15-year-old Melba Pattillo. This excerpt from her autobiography, **Warriors Don't Cry**, *in which she describes her experience, contains some of the offensive words that many whites used about blacks at that time.*

US soldiers protect the Little Rock Nine as they arrive at Central High School

Melba Pattillo on her way to school

As I entered the classroom, a hush fell over the students. The guide pointed me to an empty seat, and I walked toward it. Students sitting nearby quickly gathered their books and moved away. I sat down, surrounded by empty seats, feeling unbearably selfconscious. Still, I was relieved to be off my feet. I was disoriented, as though my world were blurred and leaning to the left, like a photograph snapped from a twisted angle and out of focus. A middle-aged woman, whom I assumed to be the teacher, ignored me.

"Open your book to page twelve," she said, without allowing her eyes to acknowledge me. "Are you gonna let that nigger coon sit in our class?" a boy shouted as he glared at me. I waited for the teacher to say or do something.

"Now, class, if you've done the homework, then you know –" A loud voice cut her off, shouting, "We can kick the crap out of this nigger." The heckler continued. "Look, it's twenty of us and one of her. They ain't nothing but animals."

Again, I waited for the teacher to speak up, but she said nothing. Some of the students snickered. The boy took his seat, but he kept shouting ugly words at me throughout the rest of the class. My heart was weeping, but I squeezed back the tears. I squared my shoulders and tried to remember what Grandma had said: "God loves you, child; no matter what, he sees you as his precious idea."

Walking the gauntlet to my next class was even more harrowing. I had to go out behind the school, through the girls' dressing room, down a long concrete walkway, and onto the playing field. "You'd better watch yourself," the guide warned as

Supreme Court [suˈpriːm], [kɔːt] Oberstes Gericht **National Guard** Nationalgarde **hush** Stille **unbearably selfconscious** [ʌnˈbeərəbli] *hier:* extrem verlegen **relieved** [rɪˈliːvd] erleichtert **blurred** verschwommen **snapped from a twisted angle** von einem schrägen Winkel aufgenommen **assume** annehmen **acknowledge** [əkˈnɒlɪdʒ] würdigen **nigger coon** nigger *und* coon *sind beide herabwürdigende Begriffe, die damals von vielen Weißen verwendet wurden.* **heckler** Zwischenrufer/in **snicker** kichern **ugly** hässlich **weep** weinen **precious** kostbar **squeeze back** zurückdrücken **square your shoulders** sich stählern **walk the gauntlet** [ˈɡɔːntlət] Spießruten laufen **harrowing** erschütternd

Testament, *a sculpture by John and Kathy Deering, stands in the grounds of Arkansas State Captiol. The monument to the Little Rock Nine was completed in 2005, almost 50 years after they stood up against segregation.*

we moved at high speed through the hostile students. As we went outside to the walkway in the back of the school, I could hear the roar of the crowd in front of the school. It was even more deafening than the jeers immediately around me. On the playing field, groups of girls were tossing a volleyball. The teacher appeared to be a no-nonsense person. With a pleasant smile, she pointed me to a spot near the net and warned the other girls not to bother me.

"Let's keep the game going, girls," she said in a matter-of-fact way. The girls paused for a moment, looked at one another, looked at me, and then began tossing the ball back and forth. For just one instant, I was actually concerned about whether or not I could hit the ball and score. It took me a moment to realize it was whizzing awfully close to my head. I ducked, but they hit me real hard, shouting and cheering as they found their target. And even as I was struggling to escape their cruelty, I was at the same time more terrified by the sound of the angry crowd in the distance. It must be enormous, I thought. How would the police keep them back?

"Get inside, Melba. Now!" The face of the gym teacher showed both compassion and alarm as she quietly pointed to a group of women some distance away, jumping over the rear fence as they shouted obscenities at me. "Hurry!"

I started to run for my life.

"Nigger ... nigger ... " one woman cried, hot on my heels. "Get the nigger." Three of them had broken away from the pack and were gaining on me. I was running at top speed when someone stuck out a foot and tripped me. I fell face forward, cutting my knee and elbow. Several girls moved closer, and for an instant I hoped they were drawing near to extend a hand and ask me if I needed

---

hostile [ɔːl'ðəʊ] feindlich **deafening** ['defnɪŋ] ohrenbetäubend **jeers** *(pl)* Spott **no-nonsense** entschlossen **toss** werfen **concerned** [kən'sɜːnd] besorgt **duck** sich ducken **target** ['tɑːgɪt] Ziel **struggle** kämpfen **compassion** [kəm'pæʃn] Mitgefühl **alarm** Sorge **obscenity** Obszönität **gain on sb** jm. einholen **trip sb.** jm ein Bein stellen help. "The nigger is down," one shouted. "She's bleeding. What do you know. Niggers bleed red blood. Let's kick the nigger." I saw the foot coming my way and grabbed it before it got to my face. I twisted it at the ankle like I'd seen them do at the wrestling match. The girl fell backward. As I scrambled to my feet, I looked back to see the brigade of attacking mothers within striking distance, shouting about how they weren't going to have me in school with their kids. I ran up the stairs, hoping I could find my way back to the office. With the mothers close on my heels, shouting their threats, the twisted maze of the hallway seemed even more menacing. I felt I could have gotten lost forever as I struggled to find the door that led to the office and safety, opening first one, then another. I raced through a honeycomb of locker rooms and dead-end hallways.

After several minutes of opening the wrong doors and bumping into people who hit me or called me names, I was in tears, ready to give up, paralyzed by my fear. Suddenly Grandma's voice came into my head: "God never loses one of his flock." Shepherd, show me how to go, I said. I stood still and repeated those words over and over again until I gained some composure. I wiped my eyes, and then I saw blood running down my leg and onto my saddle shoe. It was too much! I pressed my thumb to the wounded area to try to stop the bleeding.

"I've been looking for you." The stocky guide's voice was angry, but I was so glad to see her I almost forgot myself and reached to hug her. "And just where do you think you are going? You are only supposed to travel through the school with me." She looked at my leg but said nothing, then looked away.

"Yes, ma'am, but – "

"But nothing. Let's go to shorthand class." She didn't know it, but she was the answer to my prayer. I looked over my shoulder to see the group of mothers standing still, obviously unwilling to come after me with a school official at my side. I choked back tears and speeded my steps.

"Hello, honey, welcome. We're just beginning. I'm Mrs. Pickwick." The warm voice of the tiny darkhaired woman comforted me. Although she was petite, I quickly discovered that my shorthand teacher was definitely not one to tolerate any hanky-panky. When students moved away from me, hurling insults, she gave them a stern reprimand. "If you move, you move to the office and see the principal," she said without so much as a hint of compromise in her voice.

As I headed for the last row of empty seats by the window, she called out to me, "Melba, stay away from the window." Her voice was sympathetic, as though she really cared what happened to me. As I turned back to follow her orders, I caught a glimpse of the crowd across the street from the front of the school. I was so transfixed by the sight, I couldn't move. The ocean of people stretched farther than I could see – waves of people ebbing and flowing, shoving the sawhorses and the policemen who were trying to keep them in place. There were lots of uniformed policemen, but the crowd must have outnumbered them a hundredfold. Every now and then, three or four people broke through and dashed across the street toward the front of the school. The police would run after them.

"Melba, please take your seat."

Slowly, reluctantly, I turned away and stumbled to my seat. As I sat there, trying to focus on the shorthand book before me, I could hear some of the things the crowd was shouting. "Get the niggers," and "Two, four, six, eight, we ain't gonna integrate."

Although I could not erase the images or the sounds of those people outside, somehow

---

extend austrecken **twist** verdrehen **ankle** Knöchel **within striking** in Schlagdistanz **close on my heels** dicht auf den Fersen **twisted maze** verworrener Irrgarten **menacing** ['menəsɪŋ] bedrohlich **honeycomb** ['hʌnikəʊm] Bienenwabe **gain composure** [kəm'pəʊʒə] Fassung gewinnen **wounded area** Wundstelle **stocky** stämmig **be supposed to do sth.** etwas tun sollen **shorthand** Kurzschrift **choke back tears** Tränen unterdrücken **tolerate hanky-panky** Unfug tolerieren stern reprimand strenge Rüge **catch a glimpse of sth.** etwas kurz sehen **hurl insults** Beleidigungen um sich werfen **transfixed** gefesselt **shove** [ʃʌv] schieben **sawhorse** ['sɔːhɔːs] Barriere **dash** rasen **reluctantly** [rɪ'lʌktəntli] widerwillig **stumble** stolpern **erase** [ɪ'reɪz], *AE:* [ɪ'reɪs] ausradieren **sincere** [sɪn'sɪə] aufrichtig **determined** entschlossen

Mrs. Pickwick was so sincere and determined to be as normal as possible that I actually listened to what she had to say about shorthand. I even managed to draw several shorthand characters on my tablet as the noise got louder and louder. I looked up from my notes to see my guide entering the door. She wore a frown and was redfaced and perspiring. Something was awfully wrong. It was written all over her face. "Come with me now. To the principal's office," she called out nervously. This time she collected my books and shoved them into my arms. I walked even faster than before. We were almost running. "Don't stop for anything," she shouted at me over the noise. As I followed her through an inner office past very official-looking white men, I was alarmed by the anxious expressions on their faces. I was led to an adjoining anteroom – a smaller office, where some of the eight had gathered. Two of the girls were crying. I stood near the door, which was ajar enough so that although I could not see who was speaking, I could hear much of the men's conversations. I heard their frantic tone of voice, heard them say the mob was out of control, that they would have to call for help.

"What are we gonna do about the nigger children?" asked one. "The crowd is moving fast. They've broken the barricades. These kids are trapped in here."

"Good Lord, you're right," another voice said. "We may have to let the mob have one of these kids, so's we can distract them long enough to get the others out."

"Let one of those kids hang? How's that gonna look? Niggers or not, they're children, and we got a job to do."

Hang one of us? They were talking about hanging one of my friends, or maybe even me. My knees were shaking so badly I thought I would fall over. I held my breath, trying not to make any noise. The two men discussing our fate were just on the other side of the door. I turned my back to the partially opened door, at the same time moving closer to it so I could hear more.

A man's voice said, "They're children. What'll we do, have them draw straws to see which one gets a rope around their neck?"

"It may be the only way out. There must be a thousand people out there, armed and coming this way."

"Some of these patrolmen are throwing down their badges," another breathless voice said. "We gotta get them out of here."

1 Understanding the text

Decide if these statements are true for false. Refer to the text to support your answer.

1 The students in Melba's first class are friendly to her.
2 In Melba's volleyball lesson, she hits one of her classmates with the ball.
3 During the volleyball lesson, Melba hears loud shouting outside the school.
4 Melba leaves the playing field to escape a group of angry women.
5 Melba's grandma comes to school to help her.
6 In Melba's shorthand class, her teacher tries to stop other students from being rude to her.
7 From the classroom window, Melba sees that the crowd outside is getting calmer.
8 As soon as Melba gets to the principal's office, she feels much safer.

2 Melba and her teachers

a) Make groups of three.
Each student chooses one of the three teachers from Melba's first day at school.
Go back to the text and make notes on how they behaved towards Melba.

b) Use your notes to tell your partners what you found out.

c) My Book You choose i) or ii)

i) Write a letter (150–200 words) to one of Melba's teachers. Say how you would have felt in their class if you had been Melba.

ii) Imagine you interview Melba. Think of questions and how she might answer. Then write a short dialogue (150–200 words).

---

perspire [pəˈspaɪə] schwitzen **anxious** [ˈæŋkʃəs] besorgt **gather** sich versammeln **frantic** verzweifelt **trapped** gefangen **fate** [ˈæŋkl] Schicksal **have sb. draw straws** jn. Lose ziehen lassen **armed** bewaffnet

Workbook 18 (p. 27)

Workbook Checkpoint (pp. 28–31)

Your task

Your digital memory box

In this unit, you read how Tyler's grandma keeps things that are special to her in a memory box.

Your task is to create a digital memory box. Then you'll give a short talk on it.

STEP 1

Choose two or three objects to put in your memory box and photograph them. Your objects can be

- old or new
- worth a lot of money or no money
- things for special occasions or everyday things
- things you can wear, play with, use for work, read, look at, listen to, …

Look around your room or home to get ideas.

STEP 2

In class, discuss which digital tools you can use to make your memory box.
You can make a single document for the class, or each student can make their own document.
Decide

- how to arrange your photos (e.g. in a grid, a mind map, …)
- what information to give about each object (its age, where it comes from, why it is important, …)
- how to arrange your information (e.g. with titles, captions, …)

Then prepare your memory box for your talk in class.

STEP 3

Practise your talk. The phrases below can help you:

- My objects are …
- The first thing I'd like to talk about is …
- As you can see, it's red. It's made of …
- It belongs/belonged to …
- I've had it since …
- It's been in my family since …
- It's at least 20/30/... years old.
- It comes from …
- It's worth quite a lot of money.
- It isn't worth much/anything, but …
- I/we/… use/used it to …
- It's special to me/my mum/… because …
- If I/she/… had/hadn't bought …, then …
- If we … had/hadn't gone to …, then …

STEP 4

Decide how to present your memory box: in class, in groups or in pairs.
Then give your talk and answer any questions.

How did you do?

How can you do better?

Content	
Did you give enough information about the objects you presented?	• Think about important facts you may have left out and add them to your document.
Were you able to explain words your classmates didn't understand?	• Think of two objects and practise paraphrasing them.
Could you answer your classmates' questions?	• When you prepare a talk, think of questions people might ask and how to answer them.
Structure	
Did you lead your audience through your talk?	• Make a list of the phrases that would have helped and practise them, e.g. – *The first/next/… thing I'd like to show you…*
Did you sum up your talk at the end?	• Summing up helps your audience to remember your main ideas. Think of how to put these ideas in one or two sentences, e.g. *Well, I've shown you three things altogether. They show different things about my life / how important sport is in our family / …*
Did you ask for questions?	• Answering questions helps your audience to understand your ideas better. Try to remember to ask for questions after you've summed up.
Delivery	
Was the speed of your talk OK?	• Record your talk while you're practising to check your speed and how clearly you speak.
Did you speak clearly?	• We often speak too quickly or unclearly when we're nervous. Remember, you needn't feel nervous if you have prepared well. Tell yourself that before you start. Taking a deep breath before you speak can also help you to relax.
Did you look at your classmates while you were speaking?	• Practise moving your head slowly from one side of your audience to the other. Make eye contact with different people for two seconds.
Did you show them the objects as you spoke?	• Remember that a talk is easier to understand if the speaker uses both pictures and words.

➜ *SMC 21: Giving a presentation (p. 209)*

Meeting new people

1 At a party

a) Describe what is happening in the picture below. Say what you think the atmosphere is like. How well you think the people know each other?

b) Imagine you're at a party where you don't know the other guests. Say how you would feel. Would you start a conversation or wait for someone to speak to you? What would you talk about?

2 A conversation at a party

a) Brad and Jenna meet at a party in New Orleans. Listen and note down what they talk about.

b) Compare your notes and make sure that you've understood the dialogue.

c) Read these tips about having a conversation with someone you've just met. Then listen to the dialogue again and find examples for each tip.

Starting conversations at social events

- *Find a way to break the ice, e.g. make a compliment, comment on the music, etc.*
- *In the US, introduce yourself early in the conversation.*
  (But in the UK, people often wait longer before they give their names.)
- *When you introduce yourself, give details to help the other person understand who you are.*
- *Don't assume that the other person knows a lot about where you come from.*
- *If the other person gets any facts wrong, don't make a big thing of it.*
- *To keep the conversation going, look out for topics that interest both of you.*
- *Always try to respond positively to what the other person says.*
- *Introduce people you know.*

d) Compare your results from c). Say if you agree with the tips and explain why.

3 Thinking about language

a) For each of the phrases 1–7, find as many possible endings in the box as you can.

1 It's nice to …
2 I don't think …
3 You probably haven't …
4 Oh, you mean …
5 So what are you doing …?
6 I've always wanted to …
7 I must introduce you to …

been there before • heard of Krefeld
here in New Orleans • I've seen you before
meet you • Munich • my best friend
my exchange partner • over the next few days
see the French Quarter • see you again
the French market • visit that part of Germany
we've met • Wyatt

b) Use phrases like those in a) to complete the dialogue.

A: *Hi, I don't* [1]*… My name's Anna.*
B: *Hi, Anna – it's* [2]*… I'm Ben. So where are you from?*
A: *You probably* [3]*… of Elgin. It's a city in Illinois, not far from Chicago.*
B: *Chicago! I've always* [4]*…*
A: *You should! It's a great city.*
B: *So* [5]*… here in New Orleans?*
A: *Just seeing the sights with my dad. We really love that area with all the old buildings.*
B: *Oh you* [6]*… the French Quarter? I grew up there.*
A: *You did!. Hey I* [7]*… Dad. He'd love to meet you.*

4 A guest from Germany

a) Brad introduces Max, his German exchange partner, to Jenna.
Listen to Max and Jenna. Does their conversation go well? Note examples to support your view.

b) Do you agree on how well the conversation went? Discuss your examples.

c) Listen to Max and Jenna again. What could Max do differently when he meets new people? Discuss your ideas and suggest phrases he could use.

5 Talking to other guests

a) Find a partner.
Partner A: You are an American teenager.
Partner B: You are A's exchange partner from Germany.
Discuss and agree on basic information for your roles (e.g. names, hometowns, interests, etc.).

b) All the members of your class are guests at a party in America.
Walk around and meet the other guests. Try to do all of the following:

- *break the ice with another guest*
- *introduce yourself*
- *find out about the guest*
- *keep the conversation going*
- *introduce your exchange partner to the other guest*

California

1 Images of California

a) Look at the photos.
Make notes on what you can see in them.

b) Use your notes to describe the photos.
Take turns.

- *Photo … shows a huge city/desert/…*
- *In the background, there are skyscrapers/…*
- *In the foreground, you can see shrubs/…*
- *It's similar to/completely different from …*
- *There's a big contrast between …*

Say which of the photos is closest to your idea of California and explain why.

- *Photo A/B/… is closest to my idea of California because …*
- *For me, California means … . I think you can see that in photo …*

2 Facts and figures

a) → *pp. 10–11* On the map, find all the information you can about the state of California (size, coast, cities, …).

b) Compare what you found out.
What else do you know about California, the Golden State? Tell your group.

Your task

At the end of this unit:
Write a report about an exciting event in your area.

B

E

1 At the marine reserve

Say why you think people visit marine reserves.

On Saturday morning, Hailey Miller's father drove her from their home in San Francisco to the marine reserve at Moss Beach. Hailey was a volunteer there. She had started just the week before and she couldn't stop talking about it. "Today I'm going to take a school group to the tide pools. Maybe they'll have lots of questions – about the anemones, the starfish, … I hope I'll be able to answer them all." After 30 minutes, they arrived at the reserve. "Have fun!" her dad called. "See you later."

❖

Hailey was waiting for her school group in the parking lot when a car arrived and a couple got out. They were speaking a foreign language. "German?" she thought.
"How are you doing today?" she asked them. The woman looked at Hailey and stretched.
"My back hurts," she said. "The bed at the motel just wasn't comfortable."
Hailey wasn't quite sure what to say. "Er …" she began. "I hope everything else was OK."
"Well," said the man. "The bathroom is quite dirty. We're going to complain about it later."
"Oh …," said Hailey.
The man went on: "Where are the tide pools?"
"Sorry?" said Hailey. "Oh, right, they're that way. I can give you directions, if you like."
But the couple walked off. Before long, Hailey's group arrived and she led them to the tide pools. "Look!" shouted one of the students and ran towards some seals which were relaxing in the sun. "Wait!" Hailey called out. "Don't get too near or they'll get angry. People have been bitten, you know. Come and have a look at this tide pool."
Just then she spotted the couple from before. The man had his hand in a tide pool.
"Excuse me!" Hailey shouted. "This is a reserve! Please stick to the rules and don't touch things. No shells, no stones, and especially no wildlife!"
The man shouted back crossly: "How can I know that? Why isn't there a sign?"

❖

At five, Hailey's parents arrived to pick her up.
"Had a good day?" Mr. Miller asked.
"Awesome! I can't wait for next weekend."
"Hailey, I have a surprise for you," said her dad. "We're going to spend next weekend in L.A.!"
"L.A.?" cried Hailey. "But then I won't be able to come here! Why can't I stay at home?"
"Hailey," said Mrs. Miller. "Your dad's going to interview Brandon Williams!"
"The TV star? Will I be able to meet him?"
Mr. Miller nodded. "I can probably arrange that."
"OK," said Hailey. "I *could* miss the reserve once."
"I'm sure you'll love L.A.," said Mrs. Miller. "And now, let's find that nice restaurant where we can sit outside and watch the sunset."

2 Understanding the text

a) Explain what Hailey does in her volunteer job. Then say if she likes the job. Find lines in the text to support your answer.

b) Is Hailey polite to the German visitors? Is she surprised by how they speak to her? Give reasons for your answers.

c) Say how Hailey's feelings change in her conversation with her parents (ll. 43–56). Then listen to the recording and say how the reader shows us how Hailey feels.
– The way she says "awesome" shows …
Now practise reading the lines aloud.

 Workbook 2 (p. 33)

1 At the restaurant

a) A German couple talk to the hostess and a waiter. Listen and say which statements are true.

1 The hostess offers the couple a menu.
2 The hostess asks the Germans to leave.
3 The German couple have to wait.
4 The waiter asks if they've had a good day.
5 The waiter wants to know what they did.
6 The waiter introduces himself.

b) Listen to Hailey and her parents. Say what she thinks about the German visitors, and why.

c) Listen to another scene from the restaurant. Do you think Hailey changes her opinion of the two Germans? Give reasons.

Access to cultures: Being polite

In some social situations in the USA, people often behave differently from people in Germany.

- At restaurants, people wait in line until the host or hostess shows them their table.
- Always look out for signs (like *Please wait to be seated*). This will help you to follow rules.
- In shops and at tourist attractions, people smile when you arrive. Please smile back.
- People often introduce themselves, usually with their first names. It's nice if you do the same.
- If a stranger asks you a polite question, it's best to give a short, positive answer. Try not to say anything negative (even if it is true). Don't give a lot of details.
- There is a saying: "If you can't say something nice, don't say anything at all!" But people usually find a friendly way to say things. Try to do the same.

2 Wotcha mean? (Pronunciation: Word flow)

a) Listen to a conversation. Say who is talking and what the situation is.

b) Listen again. Note the order of these phrases.

1 What do you mean?
2 How are you?
3 Have a good day.
4 Let me ask …
5 Thanks so much.
6 I don't know.
7 Glad to hear it.
8 You can't miss it.

c) Listen. Try to say the phrases like the speaker.

LISTENING TIP

When we speak, we don't pronounce words separately, pause, and then say the next word. Words flow naturally into each other. A common phrase like *What do you mean?* often sounds like *Wotcha mean?*

3 Everyday English: Saying the right thing

a) Explain why the answers to these questions are not so good. Think of a better way to reply.

1 How are you this morning? — *Well, I woke up with a headache.*
2 Is everything all right, sir? — *No, everything isn't all right.*
3 How do you like our town? — *It's OK, but it's a bit noisy.*
4 Could you wait in line, please? — *Why? That table is free.*
5 My name's Tim, by the way. — *Oh right.*
6 Can I help you? — *No, that isn't necessary.*

b) Act out short dialogues with the good answers.

Workbook 3 (p. 33)

REMEMBER

You've already learned two ways of talking about the future. Look at these examples from p. 66.

- *Today I'm going to take a school group to the tide pools.*
- *Maybe they'll have lots of questions.*

Find two more examples of the *going to*-future and of the *will*-future in the text on p. 66.
Then complete these rules:

1 We use the ...-future to make predictions. We often use it with *I think*, *I'm sure*, *I hope* or *maybe*.
2 We use the ...-future to talk about intentions or plans for the future.

➜ *GAP 5: The future (p. 160)*

1 REVISION I think Hailey will ... (*will*-future)

Hailey's mom said: *"I'm sure you'll love L.A."* Discuss what you think she will/won't do there.

I think I don't think	Hailey will she'll want to	have a nice chat with Brandon Williams take a selfie with the Hollywood sign visit a big movie studio
I hope I'm sure	she'll she won't	...

More help p. 130

2 REVISION Dom and Zara's plans (*going to*-future)

Dom and Zara and talking about their plans. Use the *going to*-future to complete their dialogues.

Zara: Dom, shall we watch a film later?
Dom: What [1]... (you/watch)? Not a love story, I hope. [2]... (I/not watch) one of those.
Zara: Actually, [3]... (I/watch) *Battle of Britain*.

Zara: Dom, [4]... (your dad/drive) us into town?
Dom: Sorry, not today. [5]... (he/take) Mum to the airport. Let's cycle instead.
Zara: [6]... (I/not cycle). It's much too far.

Dom: Zara, let's go to the beach tomorrow.
Zara: No, thanks. [7]... (I/stay) at home tomorrow.
Dom: Come on! What [8]... (you/do) at home?
Zara: Nothing much. [9]... (I/just read) my book.

Dom: Zara, [10]... (we/get) a present for George?
Zara: Why? Is it his birthday?
Dom: Yes, and he says [11]... (he/have) a big party.
Zara: But [12]... (he/invite) *us*?

3 REVISION Friends and their plans (*will*-future or *going to*-future)

Some friends are discussing plans. Complete their dialogues with the correct form of the given verbs.

Tim: I [1]... my grandma this weekend.
Flo: That's nice. I hope you [2]... a good time.
Tim: Thanks. I think it [3]... probably ... fun.
(be/have/visit)

Jon: Maybe I [4]... you on Saturday?
Sam: Sorry, but I [5]... my dad in the garden all day.
Jon: [6]... you ... in the garden on Sunday too?
(help/see/work)

Ben: I [7]... a presentation on starfish next week.
May: Cool topic! I'm sure everyone [8]... it.
Ben: Thanks. I hope you [9]... and watch me.
(come/give/love)

Liz: [10]... you ... for next week's test?
Pip: No, I [11]... anything.
Liz: Well, I am, because I don't think it [12]... easy.
(be/not do/prepare)

More help p. 130 Early finisher p. 142 (Grammar challenge)

You are going to explain to a visitor some everyday things Germany does to protect the environment.

a) First look at the pictures on this page. Say how they are connected with the topic.
Then suggest reasons why foreign visitors might not understand what these objects are used for.

b) You are in a supermarket with an American visitor who asks you some questions.
Complete the dialogue. Use information from the machine instructions below.
Then take turns to act out your dialogue.

A: Hey, look at that machine. What's it for?
B: …
A: That's cool. The machine gives me the money, right?
B: Well, not exactly, you …
A: Hey, I have a drinks can in my bag. I can put it in here, right?
B: Actually, it looks a bit squashed and it says here that …
A: Oh, that's a pity.

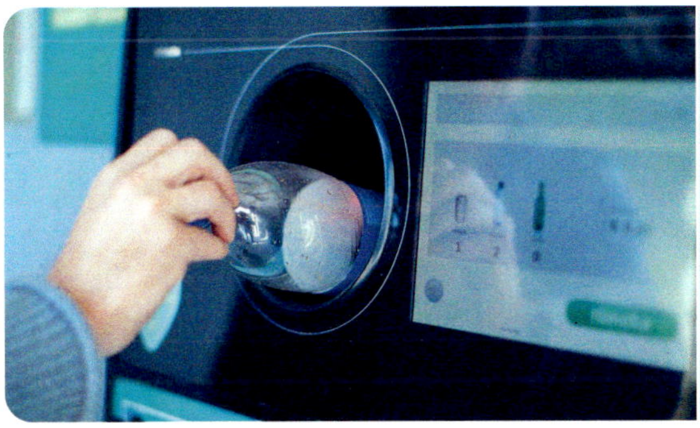

Pfandrückgabe
1 Pfandgut darf nicht verformt sein.
2 Pfandgut darf keine Restflüssigkeit enthalten.
3 Pfandgut mit Boden voraus einlegen.
4 Pfandgut langsam einlegen – nicht werfen!
5 Nach letzter Eingabe Knopf drucken
6 Pfandbon nur in dieser Filiale einreichen!

c) You read the following question on an online forum. Use the information below to write an answer.

Hi, I've just moved here from the States.
Can someone explain why we have four different color trash cans?

Gelbe Tonne
Hier hinein gehören Kunststoff, Weißblech und Aluminium, z. B. Folien, Konservendosen oder Plastiktüten.

Braune Tonne
Bioabfall kommt in diese Tonne: Gemüse, Obst, Eierschalen, Kaffeefilter, Teebeutel, Blumen, Gartenabfälle.

Blaue Tonne
Papier, Pappe, Karton, Kataloge, Zeitungen, Zeitschriften gehören in die blaue Tonne.

Graue Tonne
Für Restabfälle: die Abfälle, die übrig bleiben (alles, was nicht in die anderen Tonnen kommt).

Early finisher p. 140

Mediation skills

Remember that people from other countries may do some everyday things differently from in Germany and that it might be necessary to explain them.

➔ *SMC 12: Cultural differences (p. 201)*

3 The world behind the picture

1 A state with many faces

Choose the three places that interest you most. Then find a partner and explain your choice.

A

B

C

D

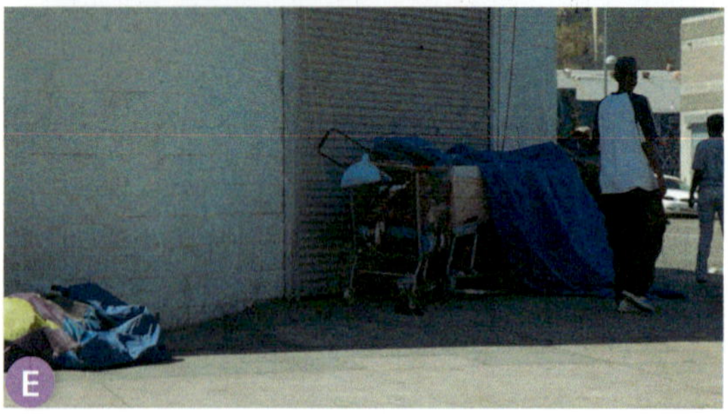
E

F

G

H

I

J

2 Discovering California

a) Watch the introduction to the film.
Then explain how the film-maker tries to interest the viewer in his subject.

b) Watch the film. Match these places to the photos in 1. Note down what you learm about them.

1 Big Sur
2 Central Valley
3 Hollywood
4 Joshua Tree National Park
5 Los Angeles
6 Mission District
7 Pier 39
8 Sequoia National Park
9 Skid Row
10 Venice Beach

c) In small groups compare the information you noted down.
Tell your partners which places you found most interesting, and why.
Have you changed your mind about your "top three" from p. 70? Explain why (not).

3 California road trip

a) **Think:** On a map of California find your "top three" places.
Would they fit well into a California road trip?
If not, choose one or two new places that would make a good road trip through the state.

b) **Pair:** Compare your results from a).
Agree on four places to visit on your road trip.
Plan your route and decide how long to stay at each place.

c) **Share:** Join another pair.
Use a map of California to present your ideas for a road trip.
– *We're starting here in San Francisco/…, where we're going to visit …*
– *Then we're going to drive … miles to …*
– *Our road trip will end in …*

4 Making the film: Atmosphere

a) The film shows two sides of Los Angeles: Hollywood and Skid Row.
Watch the sequence again. Say how you see the atmosphere in each place, and why.

boring · busy · depressing · exciting · happy · lively · lonely
negative · positive · relaxed · sad · tough · uncomfortable

b) Watch the sequence again. This time count the shots.
Which part has more shots: Hollywood or Skid Row? Which part has longer shots?

c) Discuss how the length of the shots and the speed of the music affect the atmosphere.
– *There are a lot of short shots of … with fast music.*
– *Yes, this makes it seem …*

d) Say how light and colour affect the atmosphere of the film.

Early finisher p. 140

1 At the Starview Hotel, L.A.

Think back to the text on p. 66. Why is Hailey in L.A.? How did she feel about going there?

It's almost noon. Hailey's dad is about to go to his interview with teen star Brandon Williams.

Hailey sits down at the bar. The barman continues drying glasses. Hailey sighs loudly.

Hailey waits for her drink. It doesn't come. She hears footsteps and looks around.

Hailey follows Ava. She's so excited she almost feels faint. But she doesn't get very far …

2 True or false?

Decide if these statements are true or false.

1 Hailey is allowed to take part in the interview. f
2 The barman quickly offers Hailey a drink. f
3 Hailey recognizes a famous woman in the bar. t
4 A man helps Hailey to meet Ava Aspen. f

3 Hailey's feelings

Look at each picture again.
Say how you think Hailey feels in each situation.

EXTRA Make two more frames with pictures and speech bubbles to continue the story.

4 Mr. Miller's interview with Brandon

Star *Review*

"It can be tough" Brandon reveals

by DAN MILLER

Brandon, the 16-year-old star of the popular family sitcom **Dad, I'm home***, met me at L.A.'s Starview Hotel. We had just started talking when he got an emergency call. A wildfire that had started in Corral Canyon was moving fast towards his home. Brandon's first thoughts were of Hobo, his dog. "I've got to get back to him," he told me. "Can we continue our interview in the car?" We were joined by my daughter, a huge fan of Brandon. As we raced back in his limousine, we both learned a lot about life as a child actor and about his hopes for the coming year.*

So, how did you get the role of Toby?
I saw an advertisement for an audition, so I decided to have a go. I was nervous, but it went well. And six weeks later, they offered me the role.

That all sounds quite easy …
No, it was a hard process. Then I had just a week to read my scripts. And that was during school!

Do you still go to a normal school?
Usually, I do. I'm in tenth grade. But when I'm filming, I'm tutored on set. It can take hours to set up each take … or to switch sets … so I'm busy with my geography or math book during that time.

Can you concentrate?
Yes, although it can be tough, and I get some funny reactions, like when someone pats my head and says "Cute, you're doing your homework".

We can't wait for the next season of* Dad, I'm home*. What can you tell us about it?
Well, they're sending me the scripts next week so I can't say much yet. But I know there will be changes in Toby's life – some good, some not so good. The filming will be fun. We're making two episodes here in Hollywood and then we're shooting the rest in Canada.

What are you doing this summer? Any plans?
My mom has arranged a really cool vacation. We're going to Europe for a few weeks in July.

Sounds fantastic! Where are you going exactly?
We're starting in Paris. Then we're doing a cruise on the Rhine. And we're going to London too – we're staying there till the end of the month.

What are you going to do in these exotic places?
I haven't made many plans yet, but maybe I'll climb the Eiffel Tower. And one thing for sure: I'm definitely going to visit Buckingham Palace!

5 Understanding the text

Put these points from the text in the right order.

a Brandon's education
b danger at Brandon's home
c holiday plans
d how Brandon's career as an actor started
e the next season of *Dad, I'm home*

6 Have a go

Talk about what you have arranged to do this weekend.

A: What are you doing at the weekend?
B: I'm meeting Lukas on Saturday morning and in the afternoon I'm … On Sunday, …
What are you doing?

Looking at language

You already know how to use the future with *will* and the *going to*-future:
- *Maybe I'll climb the Eiffel Tower. (p. 73, ll. 45–46)*
- *I'm definitely going to visit Buckingham palace. (p. 73, ll. 46–47)*

The texts on pp. 72 and 73 contain two new ways of talking about the future.

a new way to use *will* (p. 72)
- *No, I'll go with you.*
- *I'll call you when we're finished.*

the present progressive (p. 73)
- *They're sending me the scripts next week. (l. 31)*
- *We're making two episodes here in Hollywood. (ll. 34–35)*

Find other examples of these verb forms on p. 72 and on p. 73 (ll. 29–47).

Now decide which explanation (a, b or c) matches each new future form.

a) You use … if you're not sure that something will happen
b) You use … if you decide to do something at the moment you're speaking.
c) You use … if you're talking about something that has already been arranged.

Say what tense is usually used in German in situations like these. ➜ *GAP 5–6: The future (pp. 160–162)*

1 Hailey's busy diary (Present progressive for the future)

Hailey and her friend Maria are trying to arrange a date. Complete their dialogue. Use the present progressive and any information you need from Hailey's diary.

Maria: What [1]… (you do) Saturday? I'm free all day.
Hailey: Sorry, [2]… (I work) at … from … next Saturday.
Maria: [3]… (you work) there on Sunday too?
Hailey: No, but Mom and I [4]… (have) … . What about Thursday? [5]… (I not do) anything then.
Maria: Sorry, I can't do Thursday. Monday maybe?
Hailey: No. sorry. [6]… (I meet) … on …, and [7]… (we meet) on … too. And on Tuesday [8]… (I play) … . But wait! [9]… (I not play) on … this week. So maybe then?

Mon	After school: Bruce ♥
Tue	4.30 pm Tennis
Wed	After school: Bruce ♥
Thu	
Fri	~~4.30 pm Tennis~~
Sat	9 am–5 pm Nature reserve
Sun	Lunch at Grandma's

2 I'll help you (Spontaneous *will*)

a) Complete B's reactions to A. Use *I'll …* or *I won't …* in each sentence.

	A:	B:
1	I can't do this exercise. I don't understand it.	Just a moment. I'll help you if I can.
2	Would you like something to drink?	Yes, please. I'll …
3	Don't forget it's your grandma's birthday tomorrow.	Don't worry, …
4	The dog's barking. He wants to come back inside.	OK, …
5	I can't have lost my phone. I had it a minute ago.	What's your number? …
6	No, you can't use my bike. You always give it back dirty.	Please, I promise …

b) Check each other's sentences. Suggest improvements if necessary.

3 Text messages (Present progressive or spontaneous *will*)

Read the text messages and use the notes below to write a reply to each one. Use the present progressive or the *will*-future for the coloured verbs.

1 Hey! What's up? Can we meet this evening?

Sorry • play football • phone you • weekend

Sorry mate, but I'm playing …

2 How's it going? What are you doing in the holidays?

OK • visit uncle New York • send card when there

3 Hi. We need someone to feed the cat this weekend. Do you think Jack could do it?

not sure • ask him • but think he go • London

4 My computer isn't working – again! Can you help me, please?

OK have a look • not do anything else this evening

More help p. 130 Workbook 8 (p. 36)

4 Questions and answers (*going to*-future or spontaneous *will*)

Choose the correct future form to complete the dialogues: *going to* or *will*.

Tim: Are you going to Jan's costume party?
Flo: Yes, I 1… (dress up) as a pirate. And you? What 2… you … (dress up) as?
Tim: Good question. I 3… (have to) think about it.

Ben: Do you have any plans for the weekend?
May: Yes. I 4… (play) my new computer game. Do you want to play too?
Ben: Er – I'm not sure. I 5… (let) you know later.

Pip: It's much too hot in here.
Liz: Is it? OK, I 6… (open) a window.
Pip: But it's so loud outside.
Liz: OK, if you prefer, I 7… (not open) it.

Jon: Can I use your good camera?
Sam: Sure, I 8… (give) it to you tomorrow. What do you need it for?
Jon: I have to take photos for a project I 9… (do).

5 Summer camp (Future, mixed forms: present progressive, *will*, *going to*)

Ben and Liz are talking about summer camp. Complete their dialogue with a suitable future form.

Liz: I 1… (go) to summer camp in July.
Ben: Really? I 2… (not go) to camp again this year. Maybe I 3… (stay) at home for a change.
Liz: Oh dear, that 4… (not be) much fun.
Ben: Don't worry about me. I'm sure I 5… (think) of something interesting to do.
Liz: I don't think that 6… (be) as much fun as camp. There's a lot on this year's program.
Ben: For example?
Liz: One second, I 7… (show) you the program.
Ben: Hmm, there *are* a lot of activities. What 8… you … (choose)?
Liz: Well, first I 9… (join) the riding team.
Ben: I hope you 10… (not fall off) your horse.
Liz: Haha! Listen, why don't you take the program and read it? Maybe you 11… (find) something you like. Then you can come too.
Ben: OK, I 12… (think) about it.

More help p. 131 Early finisher p. 142 (Grammar challenge)

Workbook 9–10 (p. 36)

The Santa Clara Mission in the 18th century

The Santa Barbara Mission today

1849: San Francisco during the Gold Rush

1906: San Franciso 57 years after the Gold Rush

The Spanish missions

In the 16th century, Spain began to build an empire in south and central America, which included such countries as present-day Colombia, Peru and Mexico. Although the Spanish also claimed California – and gave it its name – for a long time they took little interest in this remote part of their empire. Then, in 1769, they began to send missionaries there to spread the Catholic religion among the Native American population. These new settlers set up missions, to which they gave names like San Francisco, Los Angeles or Santa Clara, and which later became the cities we know today.

From the beginning of the 19th century, the Spanish gradually lost control over their American empire. In 1821, Mexico became independent from Spain with California as part of the new republic. However, in 1848, after a war with United States, Mexico was forced to give up California. Then, two years later, on 9th September 1850, California officially became the 31st state of the United States.

The Gold Rush

A second important event around this time was the discovery of gold in 1848, near where the city of Sacramento stands today. The news quickly reached San Francisco – a small town with about 800 people – and from there it spread around the world. A year later, thousands of people – the Forty-Niners – were heading for California. Many of them sold all that they had to pay for the difficult journey. All of them hoped to get rich quickly. Some of them did. The gold that was found over the next few years was worth millions.

A new world replaces the old

For thousands of years, different Native American groups had lived in California. The population was small, just 300,000 when the Spanish missions came in 1769. By 1848, it had fallen to 100,000. Most Native Americans died from diseases which the settlers brought, to which they had no immunity.
By contrast, the non-native population – US citizens, Europeans, Chinese, Mexicans – grew from about 1,000 in 1848 to 380,000 by 1860. In the decades that followed, more and more settlers came. They farmed the land and built cities, roads and railroads. As this new world grew, the native peoples lost their land, livelihood and culture, and often even their lives.

A land of dreams

Since the days of the Gold Rush, millions of people have moved to California. About 40 million live there today. What makes the Golden State so inviting is its magical mix of climate, geography, opportunity and lifestyle. Like the gold diggers, people who come to California are people with dreams – of becoming rich and famous, of a better life for themselves, or of a better society. Here are just a few examples.

Oranges: A symbol of the Golden State

The film industry is a huge attraction. In the 1910s, it moved from New York to Hollywood. Good weather all year round, and different landscapes nearby, made Hollywood perfect for filming. Today, actors everywhere dream of a career in the world's movie capital. Another magnet is Silicon Valley. It was here that the microprocessors at the heart of today's digital devices were first developed. As the global center of technology and social media, California is a highly attractive destination for the world's best IT specialists.

Silicon Valley: Birthplace of the microprocessor

For many, California promises change and freedom. In the 1960s, it was a center of the hippie movement – young people who said no to money and goods, and shocked society with their political views, bright clothes, open ideas on love and sex, and revolutionary music. Big hits like Scott McKenzie's *San Francisco (Be Sure to Wear Flowers in Your Hair)* express the spirit of that time. In the 1970s, San Francisco became a center for gay people, who could live there more freely than in most other parts of America in those days. The city is now widely seen as the gay capital of the United States.

2018: At San Francisco's Pride March

Waking up from the dream?

California is a land of hope, but it also faces dangers. No society survives without water, and climate change and drought are reducing the supply. A third of the water in Southern California's cities comes from the Colorado River, which California shares with seven other states. But this great river is drying up – a major problem for the state and a worry for many. The 2018 novel *Dry* (part of which you can read on pp. 84–86) imagines a situation in which California's water runs out – just a fantasy or maybe the end of the Californian dream?

The Hoover Dam: The 140-foot-high white ring shows the drop in the Colorado River water level.

You choose Choose task a) or b). Then research your topic and write a short text.

a) You are a Native American in the 18th century. Describe the arrival of the Spanish missions.

b) You have moved to California (any time between 1849 and now). Explain your reasons.

1 Celebrities and paparazzi

Before you read the article, listen and describe the scene as Hailey arrives at Brandon's home. What questions do the reporters ask her? What do you think they will write?

Hollywood TZ #1 TEEN CELEB MAG! NEWS PHOTOS VIDEOS STYLE

Brandon's new flame!

If you thought teen celebrities only go out with other stars, think again! On Saturday afternoon, Hailey Miller of San Francisco was spotted as she got out of Brandon Williams's shiny limousine.

Brandon had just got back to his $7.5-million home in Corral Canyon after news that an unstoppable wildfire was moving towards it. Talk about unstoppable: in just a few days, Hailey's picture has gone viral. Everyone is asking: Who is *she*? And what about Brandon and Margot Peters, star of *High School Forever*? Are they finished after just two weeks? Can Brandon – sweet, responsible Toby in *Dad, I'm home* – really be so cruel?

Our reporters have been working to find all the answers. It seems that new girl Hailey and Brandon were both in the Starview Hotel when he heard about the wildfire. She was waiting for him at the hotel bar, but became impatient. Hotel workers tell us she shouted at security guards until they let her into the VIP lounge, where Brandon was giving an interview.

So who is the new girl at Brandon's side? Hailey is a volunteer environment worker. Her social media quote: "Our coast is in danger! Protecting the environment is our only hope!" You won't find Ms. Miller in Beverly Hills boutiques. She isn't into fashion. Her idea of a good time is saving starfish at Moss Beach. So what do these two have in common? The answer, it seems, is animals. Brandon, we hear, loves watching animal programs on Discovery Channel.

Our reporters are in place at Moss Beach, La Jolla and Redondo Beach. They'll bring you the latest, not just on seals and starfish, but on Brandon Williams and the environment girl. Stay posted! You won't be disappointed.

2 Understanding the text

a) Read these statements.
Are they true according to the article?
Find the lines that tell you.

1 Hailey was in the Starview Hotel at the same time as Brandon.
2 Hailey was waiting for Brandon at the bar.
3 She wanted to enter the VIP lounge to see Brandon.
4 She travelled home with Brandon in his car.
5 Hailey is Brandon's girlfriend.

b) Remember what you read on pp. 72–73.
Now say which statements really are true.

3 Hailey's reaction

Hailey's friend Maria read this article.
Listen to their phone conversation about it.

Describe the two girls' reactions to the article. Say how you would have reacted in Hailey's situation.

EXTRA Which celebrities have you read about recently? Say what you read and what you thought about it.

Early finisher p. 141
Text file 4 (pp.120–121)

4 Wildfire!

Thousands evacuated from Malibu's Corral Canyon

Sunday, December 5

Jana Maisel, Jason Goldstein and Rob Wilkins

Almost 50 homes in the Malibu canyons have been destroyed and thousands of residents evacuated in California's worst wildfire for over 20 years.

1,300 more homes are without power and will stay cut off until workers have been able to reach the burnt areas.

The fire, which started yesterday in Corral Canyon, spread quickly in the 60-mph winds. The cause of the fire is not yet known. However, there are reports of an illegal campfire, which police are investigating.

More than 800 firefighters were in action into the early hours of Sunday morning. They were supported by two planes and 18 helicopters, which fought the fire from the air.

A helicopter drops water on the Malibu wildfire.

Evacuated residents have spent the night in schools and churches, which will stay open as long as necessary. Some residents could be allowed back into their houses today.

One of the residents was Brandon Williams, who plays Toby in the TV show *Dad, I'm home*. In a message on his website he says, "I'm just so happy that my family, our house and Hobo my dog are all right. My heart goes out to the people who lost their homes."

California has a major problem with droughts, which are becoming more and more frequent. This has been the state's driest year for a century. Experts say that climate change will make droughts even longer in the future.

There is almost certainly a link between drought and the growing danger of wildfires. "Everything is just so dry," says Jeff Watkins, who works for California's forest service. "That's why the fires spread so fast. And the sad thing is: they're often caused by people that don't think."

Watkins has some important advice for California's residents and visitors. "There isn't much you can do about the weather," he says. "But there are rules everyone should stick to. For example, never throw a lit cigarette out of your car window. And remember: you can only make campfires when *we* give you a permit."

5 Find the information

a) Read the article and take notes on:
- where and when the wildfire started
- the cause of the fire
- the effects of the fire
- the work of the firefighters

b) Compare your answers.

c) Find the reasons that are given in the article for the wildfires in California.

www Find out more about climate change in the USA.

6 Comparing the two articles

a) Say which topics come up in both articles. What is the main topic of each article?

b) Discuss these questions:
- Which article is more emotional?
- Which article is more neutral?
- Which article gives more facts?

Give reasons for your opinion.

c) Imagine you saw both articles in a magazine. Which one would you read first? Write a short text to explain why.

REMEMBER

a) You have already learned how to make relative clauses. Look at these examples from p. 79.
- *My heart goes out to the people who lost their homes.*
- *The fires … are often caused by people that don't think.*

These are called *defining* relative clauses. They give key information about the word they follow. Without them, the main clause would not make complete sense.

b) In *defining* relative clauses, you can leave out the relative pronoun *(who, which, that)* if it is the object of the clause. These are called contact clauses. Look at these examples from p. 79.
- *There isn't much you can do about the weather. (or … that/which you can do …)*
- *But there are rules everyone should stick to. (or … that/which everyone should stick to.)*

Note: If a verb takes a preposition (e.g. *stick to rules*), it comes at the end of a contact clause.

➔ *GAP 13: Relative and contact clauses (p. 176)*

1 REVISION Touring celebrity homes (Defining relative clauses)

Someone has posted a question about tours in L.A. on an online forum. They have had one answer. Complete the two texts. For each gap, use a word from the box with *who* or *which*.

anyone · driver · guide · one · something · tours

Hi all, I'll be in L.A. next weekend. I'd love to go on one of those [1]… show you where the big stars live. But there are so many! Maybe someone knows a good [2]… isn't too expensive? I'd like to have a [3]… knows what they're talking about – and of course a [4]… stops often enough for photos. Can [5]… has been on one of these tours recommend [6]… would be right for me? Thanks, Amy

anything · fences · friends · website · someone · star

Amy, please don't do [7]… costs money and doesn't give you much! If you have a car, ask [8]… knows L.A. to be your guide and drive around with them. Mostly, you'll see the high [9]… guard the houses, but NOT much of the house or the [10]… lives there. Most of my [11]… did a tour like this were disappointed. Do something else, e.g. there's a good [12]… lists locations where famous films were shot. Enjoy L.A., Georgie

2 REVISION Hailey and Brandon (Defining relative clauses: contact clauses)

Use the sentences in brackets to make relative clauses for the sentence beginnings. Only use *who* or *which* to join the clauses if necessary.

1 This is the Starview. It's the hotel … (Hailey and her dad are staying at this hotel.)
   It's the hotel Hailey and her dad are staying at.
2 You don't know Hailey? She's the girl … (She works at Moss Beach Nature Reserve.)
3 If you have any questions about marine life, she's the person … (You can talk to her.)
4 And Hailey is also the girl … (Brandon Williams was photographed with her.)
5 Brandon is the teen actor … (He was interviewed by Hailey's dad.)
6 *Dad, I'm home* is the name of the TV show … (The TV show made Brandon famous.)
7 Hailey is a big fan of *Dad, I'm home*. And Brandon is the actor … (She likes him most.)
8 Right now, Hailey and Brandon are the couple … (Nearly everyone is talking about them.)

Early finisher ➔ p. 141

Language help

The text on p. 79 also has examples of a second kind of relative clause.

- *The fire, which started yesterday in Corral Canyon, spread quickly in the 60-mph winds.*
- *However, there are reports of an illegal campfire, which police are investigating.*

Relative clauses like these give us extra information about the word they refer to.
They are called *non-defining* relative clauses. The main clause makes sense without them.

Find four more examples of *non-defining* relative clauses in the text on p. 79 (ll. 17–45) and write them down. Then choose the right options to complete these rules:

- Always/Never use commas to separate non-defining relative clauses from the rest of a sentence.
- You can use the relative pronouns *who/which/that* but not *who/which/that*.
- You can/cannot leave out the relative pronoun.

→ *GAP 14: Defining and non-defining relative clauses (p. 178)*

3 The Hollywood sign (Non-defining relative clauses)

Make relative clauses from these phrases to complete the sentences about the Hollywood sign. Add the correct relative pronoun (*who* or *which*) and commas where needed.

are made of metal · had built expensive houses in the area · is over $320,000 in today's money
today is home to many celebrities · was built in 1923 · was called Harry Chandler

1 The Hollywood sign ... one of L.A.'s biggest attractions.
2 The sign was the idea of the owner of the *L.A. Times* ...
3 Chandler ... wanted to use the sign as an advertisement.
4 The famous white letters ... are 45 feet high.
5 The project cost $21,000 ...
6 There are great views of the sign from Beverly Hills ...

4 The Walk of Fame (Defining and non-defining relative clauses)

Use the sentences in brackets to make relative clauses.
Choose the right gap for each clause. Decide which clauses are non-defining and add commas.

1 Tourists (...) nearly always visit the Walk of Fame (...).
(*They come to Hollywood.*)
2 The 70-year-old Walk (...) has about 3,000 stars (...).
(*It is 1.6 miles long.*)
3 On each star (...) you'll see the name of a celebrity (...).
(*They made their name in music or film.*)
4 So you can take a selfie (...) with some of the stars (...).
(*You like them best.*)
5 Many young visitors (...) look for Daniel Radcliffe's star (...)
(*It was presented to him in 2015.*)
6 Radcliffe (...) is the only Hogwarts student (...) with a star.
(*He is famous for playing Harry Potter.*)

More help *p. 131* **Early finisher** *p. 142 (Grammar challenge)*

Adjectives help to make a text clearer and more interesting.
As you learn more adjectives, it is important to organize them well. One way to do this is to use lists of synonyms and antonyms. Using synonyms and antonyms in your writing will also improve your style.

1 Synonyms

A synonym is a word that means the same or almost the same as another. You already know quite a few.

a) Identify the four synonyms in these phrases from the text on p. 77. Then add a fifth synonym.
a huge attraction · a big hit · a great river · a major problem

b) Match the adjectives in box 1 to a synonym in box 2 and put them in a table.

1: angry · correct · crazy · famous · fantastic · loud · normal · quiet · sick · small · strange · sweet · tasty

2: awesome · calm · cross · cute · delicious · legendary · ill · legendary · little · mad · noisy · right · typical · weird

angry	cross
correct	...
...	

2 Antonyms

An antonym is a word which means the opposite of another word.

a) Think of antonyms for the adjectives in the box and make a table.

dangerous · dark · dirty · dry · easy · expensive · interesting · kind · long · loud · quick · right · sad · small · stupid · traditional

dangerous	safe
dark	...
...	

More help p. 131

b) You can also use prefixes to make antonyms. The table below contains examples you already know. Use a prefix to make antonyms of the adjectives in the box. Then add them to a table. Use a dictionary to check, if necessary.

comfortable · correct · expensive · fair · friendly · important · interesting · lucky · necessary · perfect · polite · popular · possible · practical · probable · regular · responsible · usual

un-	il-	im-	in-	ir-
unhappy	illegal	...	...	...

3 Beverly Hills (Writing a description)

a) Read the text. Find synonyms for the green words and rewrite the red phrases with antonyms.

It's easy to like Beverly Hills, the city with good views of the L.A. skyline and of the famous Hollywood sign. And it's not just the big houses of celebrities you can see there. On a normal day, it's possible that you will spot some of the stars in person. And even if you're unlucky, you can still visit the awesome museums or enjoy the calm atmosphere in the nice green parks. And there's lots of tasty food you can try at one of the city's many restaurants. Of course, Beverly Hills is an expensive place, so it's not unimportant to plan your visit so you know exactly what you can expect.

b) Write a short description of a place or person. Then find alternative ways to phrase some ideas.
Compare and discuss your text with a partner.

Early finisher p. 141

Workbook 15 (p. 39)

Before you write a report, you can make an outline to help you to structure your facts.
On this page you will make an outline for a report about how Hailey helped to rescue a baby whale.

STEP 1 – How to make an outline

Look carefully at the model outline on the left. Then add one word to each gap to complete the tips.

Report outline

1 Title
ideas
2 Introduction
keywords
(Who? What? Where? When?)
3 Main body
- Sub-heading
keywords
(What happened? / Why? / How?)
- Sub-heading
keywords
(What happened? / Why? / How?)
4 Conclusion
ideas for one or two sentences

TIPS

A report has ... main parts:
a title, ..., ... and a conclusion. You can use this structure to make an outline.

First, make **headings** for each part.
Note down some ... for a catchy title.
Add ... under headings 2 and 3.

If you have a lot of information for the **main body**, you can make ... and arrange your keywords under them.

Keywords should answer questions like *who?* ..., ..., and ... in the introduction. In the main body, they answer questions like ..., ..., and ... .

Finally, think of ideas for one or two good ... to sum up or round off your report.

STEP 2 – Make an outline

a) Listen to the start of the radio report. In your outline, note down ideas for a title.

b) Listen again. This time, add keywords for the introduction to your outline.

c) Look at these sub-headings and keywords. Then listen to what happens.
Note down keywords for the main events. Decide which sub-heading they go under.

3 Main body
- Baby whale in trouble
...
Preparing the rescue
ropes and knives, ...

TIP

In a report, you usually mention events in the order in which they happened. In your outline, try to arrange your facts in that order.

d) Listen to the rest of Hailey's adventure and note down the details.
Think of two or three more sub-headings to arrange these details under.

e) Compare parts 1–3 of your outlines. Make changes if you wish.
Then discuss ideas for the conclusion. Add the two ideas you like best to complete your outline.

EXTRA Use your outline to write a report about Hailey's adventure.

Workbook 16–18 (pp. 39–41)

A future without water?

Dry, *a novel by Neal and Jarrod Shusterman, is set in California and tells the story of how the lives of different teenagers are affected when the state's water supply is suddenly cut off during a long period of drought. In this excerpt from the novel, Alyssa and her brother Garrett are at home in Los Angeles with their parents when the news breaks.*

The dry bed of the Los Angeles River

Before you read, think about the different ways you use water every day and share your ideas in class.

"Shush!" Mom says. She rarely shushes Dad. She'll shush me and Garrett all day, but my parents never shush each other. It's an unspoken rule. She's watching the TV, where a news anchor is blathering about the "flow crisis." That's what the media's been calling the drought, ever since people got tired of hearing the word "drought." Kind of like the way "global warming" became "climate change," and "war" became "conflict." But now they've got a new catchphrase. A new stage in our water woes. They're calling this the "Tap-Out."

Uncle Basil emerges from his vapor cloud long enough to ask, "What's going on?"

"Arizona and Nevada just backed out of the reservoir relief deal," Mom tells him. "They've shut the floodgates on all the dams, saying they need the water themselves."

Which means that the Colorado River won't even reach California anymore.

Uncle Basil tries to wrap his mind around it. "Turning off the entire river like it's a spigot! Can they do that?"

My father raises an eyebrow. "They just did." [...]

As we pull into the Costco parking lot we can see the crowd. It seems like our entire neighborhood had the same idea. We do nothing but slowly circle in search of an empty space. Finally Uncle Basil pulls out his Costco card and hands it to me. "You two go in. I'll meet you inside when I find a place to park."

I wonder how he'll get in without his card, but then, Uncle Basil finds ways around any situation. Garrett and I hop out and join the hordes of people flooding the entrance. Inside it's like Black Friday at its worst – but today it's not televisions and video games people are after. The carts in the checkout line are stocked with canned goods, toiletries, but mostly water. The essentials of life. [...]

"This cart sucks," Garrett says. He's right. One wheel is bent, and the only way to push it is to lean it on the other three wheels. I look back toward the entrance. There were only a couple of carts left when I grabbed this one. They'll all be gone now.

"It'll do," I tell him.

Garrett and I forge our way through the crowds toward the back left corner, where the water pallets are. As we do, we overhear bits and pieces of conversations.

"FEMA's already slammed with Hurricane Noah," one woman tells another. "How are they going to help us, too?"

"It's not our fault! Agriculture uses eighty percent of the water!"

"If the state spent more time finding new sources of water, instead of fining us for filling our

---

Shush! Ruhe! **rarely** selten **news anchor** Nachrichtensprecher(in) **blather** ['blæðə] faseln **catchphrase** Schlagwort **emerge** [ɪ'mɜːdʒ] erscheinen **vapor cloud** Rauchwolke **wrap your mind around something** [ræp] etwas verstehen **spigot** ['spɪgət] Wasserhahn **Costco** US-Großhandelsmarkt **cart** Einkaufswagen **checkout line** Kassenschlange **canned good** Dosenware **suck** ätzend sein **bent** verbogen **overhear** zufällig hören **FEMA's already slammed** die Krisenbehörde ist schon voll beschäftigt **fine** Geldstrafe auferlegen swimming pools," one woman says, "we wouldn't be in this position."

Garrett turns to me. "My friend Jason has a giant aquarium in his living room, and he didn't get fined."

"That's different," I explain to him. "Fish are considered pets."

"But it's still water."

"Then go drink it," I say, shutting him up. I don't have time to think about other people's problems. We have our own to worry about. But it looks like I'm the only one who cares, because Garrett has already gone off to hunt for free samples.

As I push the cart, it keeps veering to the left and I have to lean heavily on the right side to prevent the bent wheel from acting like a rudder.

As I approach the rear of the warehouse, I can see that it's the most crowded spot, and as I reach the last aisle to see the water pallets, I realize I'm too late. The pallets are already empty. [...]

Behind me, people who can't see that the water pallets are empty keep pushing forward.

Eventually some employee will have the good sense to put a sign out front that says NO WATER, but until they do, customers will keep piling in, pushing toward the back, creating a suffocating crowd, like the mosh pit of a concert.

On a hunch, I maneuver my way to the side aisle, and to the racks of canned soda, which are also beginning to disappear. But I'm not here for soda.

As I look around the stacks of drinks, I find a single case of water that someone abandoned there maybe yesterday, when it wasn't such a precious commodity. I reach for it, only to find it pulled away at the last second by a thin woman with a beak of a nose. She stacks it on top of her cart like a crown on top of her canned goods. "I'm sorry, but we were here first," she says. And then her daughter steps forward – a girl I recognize from soccer – Hali Hartling. She's annoyingly popular and thinks she's much better at soccer than she really is. Half the girls in school want to be like her, and the other half hate her because they know they'll never come close. Me, I just put up with her. She's not worth the energy for me to be anything but indifferent.

Although she always seems to bleed confidence, right now she can't even look me in the eye – because she knows, just as her mother knows, that I had that water first. As her mother pulls their cart away, Hali leans closer to me. "I'm sorry about that, Morrow," she says earnestly, calling me by my last name like we do in soccer.

"Didn't I share my water with you at practice last week?" I point out to her. "Maybe you could return the favor and share a few bottles with me."

She looks back to her mother, who's already moving down the aisle, then back to me with a shrug.

"Sorry, they don't sell them by the bottle here. Just by the case." And then she gets a little bit red in the face, and turns to leave before it becomes a full-fledged flush.

I take in my surroundings. Crowds are still getting thicker, and things are vanishing from the shelves at an alarming rate. Even the sodas are gone now. Stupid! I should have grabbed some.

I hurry back to my empty cart before someone else can take it. There's no sign of Uncle Basil yet, and Garrett is probably off stuffing his face with something greasy. The Gatorade he requested is all gone, too. Finally I spot Garrett

He's down one of the frozen aisles, pizza sauce all over his face. He wipes his mouth with his shirt, knowing I'll comment. But I don't bother – because I see something. Just past the frozen vegetables and ice cream, there's a chest packed with ice. Enormous bags of it. I can't believe people are such limited thinkers that they haven't thought of this themselves! Or maybe they have, but denied that they could possibly be so desperate. I open the door and reach for a bag.

"What are you doing? We need water, not ice."

"Ice is water, Einstein," I tell him. I go for a bag, and realize they're a lot heavier than I had anticipated.

---

hunt suchen **prevent** verhindern **rudder** Ruder **eventually** [ɪ'ventʃuəli] irgendwann **suffocating** ['sʌfəkeɪtɪŋ] erstickend **on a hunch** einer Intuition folgend **aisle** [aɪl] Gang **soda** Limonade **abandoned** verlassen **precious commodity** kostbare Ressource **put up with** ertragen **indifferent** gleichgültig **bleed confidence** Selbstvertrauen ausstrahlen **return the favor** sich revanchieren **before it becomes a full-fledged flush** bevor sie ganz rot im Gesicht wird **take in the surroundings** die Umgebung wahrnehmen **vanish** verschwinden **at an alarming rate** mit erschreckendem Tempo **stuff** vollstopfen **bother** sich die Mühe machen **chest** Truhe **deny** [dɪ'naɪ] nicht zugeben **desperate** verzweifelt **anticipate** erwarten

"Help me!" Together Garrett and I heave one bag of ice after another into our cart, until it's piled as high as it can get. By now other people have taken notice, and have crowded the ice case, beginning to empty it.

The cart is ridiculously heavy now, and almost impossible to push – especially with a bad wheel. Then, as we struggle with the cart, the jammed wheel scraping across the concrete floor, a man in a business suit comes up behind us. He smiles.

"That's quite a load there," he says. "Looks like you could use some help."

He doesn't wait for us to answer before grabbing the cart's handle, and wrestling it forward far more effectively than we did.

"Crazy here today," he says jovially. "Crazy everywhere, I'll bet."

"Thank you for helping us," I tell him.

"Not a problem. We all need to help one another."

He smiles again, and I return the grin. It's good to know that difficult times can bring out the best in people.

Bit by bit, with short but steady lurches, we get the cart to the front of the store, and into one of the snaking checkout lines.

"I suppose that's my workout for the day," he chuckles.

I look at our cart, and decide that one good turn deserves another. "Why don't you take a bag of ice for yourself," I suggest.

His smile doesn't fade. "I have an even better idea," he says. "Why don't you take a bag of ice for yourselves, and I'll keep the rest."

For a moment I think he's joking, but then realize he's dead serious. "Excuse me?"

He manufactures a heavy sigh. "You're right, that really wouldn't be fair to you. Tell you what, why don't we split it down the middle? I'll take half, you take half."

He says it like he's being generous. As if the ice is his to give. He's still smiling, but his eyes scare me. "I think my offer is more than fair," he says.

I begin to wonder what business he's in, and if it's all about cheating people but making them think they're not being cheated. It's not going to fly with me but his hands are firmly locked on the handle of our cart, and there's nothing to prove that it's ours and not his.

"Is there a problem here?"

It's Uncle Basil. He's arrived just in time. He glares at the man coldly for a moment, then the man takes his hands off the cart.

"Not at all," he says.

"Good." Uncle Basil says. "I'd hate to think you were harassing my niece and nephew. People get arrested for that."

The man holds eye contact with our uncle for a moment more before folding. He looks at the ice, his expression bitter, then leaves, not taking as much as a single bag.

1 Understanding the text

a) Complete these sentences to sum up the text.
1 On a TV news show, Alyssa's family learn that ...
2 Alyssa arrives at Costco and realizes that ...
3 The only cart they can find is one that ...
4 At the water pallets, Alyssa can see that ...
5 Finally, she finds one case of water, but ...
6 Alyssa sees an ice chest and realizes that ...
7 A man helps Alyssa push her cart, but then ...
8 When Uncle Basil finally arrives, ...

b) Compare Mrs. Hartling's behaviour with that of the man in the business suit.

2 Surviving without water

a) Work in groups of four. Make a placemat on an A3 piece of paper. Think of problems which could be caused if you suddenly had no water supply.

b) Turn the placemat and read the other ideas. Discuss and agree on the four most serious problems. Write them in the middle.

c) Think of possible solutions to your group's four problems. Then present your ideas in class.

Workbook 19 (p. 41)

ridiculously [rɪˈdɪkjələsli] *hier:* extrem **scrape** scharren **concrete** [ˈkɒŋkriːt] Beton **jovial** [ˈdʒəʊviəl] freundlich **chuckle** laugh **good turn** gute Tat **deserve** verdienen **fade** verblassen **generous** [ˈdʒenərəs] großzügig **cheat** betrügen **fly** *hier:* funktionieren **prove** [pruːv] beweisen **glare** zornig anstarren **harass** [ˈhærəs] belästigen **get arrested** verhaftet werden

Workbook Checkpoint pp. 42–45

Write a report

A USA-German student partnership programme has asked for articles for its online magazine. The idea is to give readers a picture of life in their partner country.

Write a report about an exciting or interesting event in your home area. Here are some ideas:

- an environment protest
- a sports event
- a local festival

You can also look online, in local newspapers or ask your parents or teacher for ideas.

STEP 1

Get information

You choose a), b) or c).

a) Go to the event yourself. Take a notebook and write down as much as you can.
Remember: Your notes should answer important *wh*-questions.
Take photographs.

b) Interview someone who was at the event.
Prepare questions for your interview partner. Include as many *wh*-questions as possible.

c) Get your information through the media.
Take notes. Make sure they answer important *wh*-questions.

STEP 2

Make an outline

Use your notes from Step 1.

Swap outlines. Comment on your partner's.

➔ *p. 83: Making an outline for a report*

STEP 3

Write a first draft

Look back at the two articles on pp. 78–79. How were their styles different?
Choose the better model for your report.
Now use your outline to write your report. Make sure each paragraph has a topic sentence.

STEP 4

Give feedback and revise

Swap your outlines and your first drafts. Read each other's work carefully.
Use the feedback sheet at the back of the book to assess each other's report.

➔ *Giving feedback (p. 304)*

My Book Decide what changes you should make. Then revise your first draft. If you can, add photos.

STEP 5 MK

Share your reports

Make a private website for your class and upload all the reports.
Then read and comment on some of the other reports.

South Dakota

1 Faces of South Dakota

a) For each picture note down three adjectives to describe what you see in it.
Use ideas from the box or a dictionary.

beautiful · boring · calm · cool · cute
dangerous · depressing · dramatic · empty
exciting · exotic · funny · impressive · pretty
rocky · scary · silent · small · vast

b) Work in groups of three. Each student describes two of the pictures to the group. Say what your two photos tell you about South Dakota.

c) → *pp. 10–11* Say what the map tells you about South Dakota (size, landscapes, etc.). Say how it fits with the photos.

2 If photos could talk

You choose a) or b).

a) Imagine the places, people and animals in the photos could tell stories. Choose one photo. Write down what they would say.

b) Imagine you visited one of the places in the photos. Write down what you experienced.

Your task

At the end of this unit:
Present yourself to a class from a South Dakota school.

A sculpture of Sitting Bull by the Missouri on the Standing Rock Reservation

Wild horses on a prairie in the Black Hills region

The faces of four presidents have been carved into the rocks at Mount Rushmore.

Fields on a South Dakota farm

A cowboy with bison in Custer State Park

The historic small town of Deadwood was built during the Black Hills Gold Rush (1870s).

1 A date with Kaya?

Describe the picture. Say what the people in the foreground might be talking about.

It was breakfast time. Drew Schmidt was looking at his texts when his dad entered the kitchen. "The car's all yours, son," he said and slapped the keys on the counter. "Drive carefully!"
"Thanks, Dad. I appreciate it."
Only minutes later Drew was behind the wheel on the way to school.
He was turning into the Mobridge-Pollock High School parking lot when the car behind his honked. It was Rob, Drew's best friend. As always, he was in his old Ford – the one with the words "Go Tigers" in big orange letters on the back window.
"Hey!" Rob called. "You don't usually drive."
"But I am driving this week," Drew shouted. "Dad's working from home, so he doesn't need the car."
Rob nodded his head. "Not bad! Not bad at all."
"Yeah … and, it looks like I'm going to the high school rodeo finals this June."
"Hey! How do you know?"
"Coach thinks I'm doing well. He said my times were almost perfect. So I just need to keep it up."
"No wonder you look so happy."
The two boys got out of their cars and headed for the school door. As they were walking towards their classroom, Drew suddenly stopped. There she was at the water fountain. She bent down for a drink and tucked her long black hair behind her ear. Drew's eyes lit up. He leaned towards Rob. "The other reason I'm in such a good mood is standing right there … I'm going to talk to her."
"Play it cool, man," Rob advised.
But Drew was already walking towards Kaya Red Hawk.
"Kaya! I was watching you during practice. You looked really great. Your technique is excellent."
"Really? I wish Coach agreed with that. He thinks I'm too slow. I need to speed up if I want to qualify for the finals."
"It just takes practice," said Drew. "Uh, maybe we could practice together, I mean, if we could find some horses somewhere."
"Well, my uncle owns a ranch on the Standing Rock Rez. He always says I can ride his horses whenever I want. Problem is, I don't have a car."
"Well … I can drive you. What do you say? This Saturday?"
Kaya smiled. At that moment the bell rang and Drew didn't hear her answer. Before he could ask again, one of her friends had pulled her away.
Drew looked at Rob and smiled.
"Hey, man – what's up?" Rob asked.
"I just got a date with Kaya Red Hawk."
"You're joking," laughed Rob. "I don't believe it!"
"No," said Drew. "It's true … er … I think."

2 Understanding the text

Complete these sentences about the text.

1 Drew can drive to school because …
2 He's happy about the rodeo finals because …
3 Kaya suggests going to … because …
4 Rob finds it hard to believe that …

3 What happens next?

Form a buzz group. In two minutes, say

- if you think Drew and Kaya will go on a date
- why or why not
- if you think they would enjoy being together.

Access to cultures: Two typical American high schools

Top: The pledge of allegiance at Hingham
Bottom: Hingham school cafeteria

Top: Supporting the Mobridge school team
Bottom: Baseball at Hingham

Mobridge-Pollock High School (MPHS), South Dakota and Hingham High School, Massachusetts, are 1,800 miles apart. MPHS is small, with only 200 students, but the two schools are similar in most ways. However, a German exchange student will notice differences to school at home.

High school is for ages 14–18 (grades 9–12). There is no other kind of public school, so whether you're the next Einstein or a slower learner, you work together. School starts early (8 at Hingham, 8:10 at MPHS), with lessons till the middle of the afternoon. The day is divided into periods of 50–60 minutes. During the first period, there is usually a roll-call, when teachers read out the names from the register to check that all the students are there. There is a lunch break in the cafeteria, with different times for different grades.

Many students drive to school. This is legal in South Dakota from age 14 – in Massachusetts you have to wait till you're 16 to get your driver's licence. Both MPHS and Hingham offer their students driving lessons.

Like most schools, MPHS and Hingham start the day with the pledge of allegiance to the US and its flag. Then lessons follow. All students do basic courses like math, science, language, writing, literature and social studies. They can also choose other subjects, or learn practical skills. Students are given regular assignments which they have to pass (grades A, B, C or D). If they fail (grade F), they have to do extra work to improve their level.

When lessons end, students often stay for some of the school clubs (e.g. drama, music, chess) or for sport. Playing for your school against other schools is a big honour, but even if you don't make the team, it's important to come along and cheer. In smaller places like Mobridge, the whole town comes out to support the school teams. There, on big game days you can see the words "Go Tigers!" everywhere.

a) Read the text and note down how American high schools are different from or similar to yours.
Compare notes. Add to them if necessary.

b) Watch a film about Hingham High School and add to your notes from a).
In class, discuss what you prefer about US schools and what you prefer about yours.

You are going to explain your school rules to an exchange student at your school.
Remember: Rules in other countries may be different from yours (e.g. stricter or less strict).
If you know about the other country, it will be easier to explain what your guest needs to know.

a) Work in groups of four. Each student writes down key information on one topic from the MPHS rules.

MPHS School Rules

Lateness

A student who misses the first five minutes of a class will not be allowed to attend that class without a pass from a teacher or the central office. A student who misses the first fifteen minutes of a class will be marked as "late". A student who is marked "late" ten times must attend two sessions at the end of the school day from 3:30 – 5:00. A letter will be sent to the parents.

Classroom rules

1 No food or drinks are allowed.
2 No book bags are allowed.
3 Cell phones should be turned off when you enter the classroom.
4 Tablets and other electronic equipment can only be used in class with a teacher's permission.

Lockers and locker searches

Although each student will be given a school locker, the lockers are the property of the school. The school wishes to make sure that all lockers are taken care of. For this reason, teachers may check that lockers are clean and that nothing has been stolen. These checks can take place at any time without the student's permission.

Leaving the school grounds

Students who need to leave the school building or grounds during the school day for any reason must have written permission from their parents.
Before they leave, they must also go to the principal's office and get permission to leave.

b) Use your notes to tell your group what you found out about rules at MPHS. Then compare the MPHS rules with your school's. Do they deal with similar points? Are they stricter or less strict?

www Read these rules if you aren't sure what your school rules are.

c) **Partner A:** Tell an American guest about your school rules.
– *Lessons start at … in the morning.*
– *You have to … / You needn't … / You aren't allowed to …*
Partner B: You are the American guest. Listen to A and ask questions.
– *Where can I get a pass if I'm late?*
– *Do I have to …? / Am I allowed to …?*

Mediation skills

When you explain something to foreign visitors, their questions might seem strange to you.
Think of what you know about the visitor's country and point out what's different in Germany.

→ *SMC 12: Cultural differences (p. 201)*

REMEMBER
The simple present is used for regular actions or to make a general statement.
The present progressive is used for activities that are in progress (now, today, this week, etc.).
- *"Hey!" Rob called. "You **don't** usually **drive**."*
- *"But I **am driving** this week," Drew shouted.*

➔ GAP 1: The present tenses (p. 152)

1 REVISION Rob's clubs (Simple present or present progressive?)

a) Rob's Uncle Zeb asks about his school clubs. Put the verbs in the simple present.

Zeb: What clubs [1]… (you be) in, Rob?
Rob: [2]… (I play) on the school soccer team.
Zeb: Soccer? What position [3]… (you play) in?
Rob: [4]… (I be) one of the goalkeepers.
Zeb: So [5]… (you not shoot) many goals then? Ha!
Rob: [6]… (I not score) many, but [7]… (I save) a lot.
Zeb: So, how often [8]… (you have to) train?
Rob: [9]… (We usually train) on Mondays and Fridays. But [10]… (I not always manage) to go on Fridays. My [11]… (choir meet) twice a month on Friday afternoons and [12]… (Mom not let) me miss that!

b) Rob has just arrived at choir practice. Put the verbs in the present progressive.

Rob: Hey, guys? What [1]… (you do)? Why [2]… (you hang out) outside? Let's go in.
Tara: [3]… (We not stand) here for fun. [4]… (We wait) for Mr Graber. He hasn't arrived yet.
Liz: He's usually early. [5]… (I start) to get worried.
Hal: [6]… (I just get) bored. [7]… (Bel and I think) about going home.
Liz: Come on, Hal! [8]… (You not be) fair.
Tara: Hey, what's that noise? [9]… (somebody's phone ring)?
Rob: It's mine. [10]… (Mr Graber call) me. Mr Graber! Are you OK? [11]… (We just talk about) you.

2 REVISION At break in Mobridge (Simple present or present progressive?)

a) Use the simple present or the present progressive to complete the text.

The sun [1]… (shine) in Mobridge today, so lots of students at MPHS [2]… (relax) outside during break.
On the right of the picture, Jane Lenz [3]… (sit) next to her best friend, Sally Koch. Jane [4]… (check) facts in a book and Sally [5]… (take) notes. They often [6]… (help) each other with their school work. Jane [7]… (be) from Mobridge, but Sally [8]… (not live) quite as near to MPHS. Every day she [9]… (travel) 37 miles from Pollock in the school bus. At the moment she [10]… (learn) to drive. When she [11]… (get) her driver's license, she [12]… (want) to drive to school every day.

b) Write a text about the boys in the picture. Say what you think they're doing with the phone.
Ryan Abbott is sitting next to Jared Adamu.

Early finisher p. 143

REMEMBER

The simple past is used to say that an action took place in the past.
The past progressive is when an action was in progress in the past.

- *Drew's eyes **lit up**. He **leaned** towards Rob. (The actions were completed.)*
- *Drew **was** already **walking** towards Kaya Red Hawk. (The action was still going on.)*

You can use the two forms together when a shorter action interupts a longer one.

- *Then, as they **were walking** towards their classroom, Drew suddenly **stopped**.*

➜ *GAP 2: The past tenses (p. 154)*

3 REVISION Yesterday in Mobridge (Simple past or past progressive?)

Use the simple past or the past progressive to complete texts A–D.

Rob [1]... (see) Kaya while he [2]... (walk) down Main Street in Mobridge yesterday afternoon. He [3]... (smile) and [4]... (shout) her name a few times, but Kaya [5]... (not hear) him. She [6]... (listen) to music and she [7]... (not look) around when he [8]... (call) her.

Drew's mom [1]... (walk) down Main Street when a young exchange student from Europe [2]... (come) up to her. He [3]... (look) for the post office and [4]... (ask) Drew's mom for directions. She [5]... (go) towards the post office anyway, so she [6]... (offer) to take him there.

More help *p. 132*

While Kaya's mom [1]... (shop) in Mobridge she [2]... (decide) to stop for a coffee. She [3]... (go) into a diner where she [4]... (spot) her friend Angela. Angela [5]... (sit) on her own, so Kaya's mom [6]... (sit down) at the same table and the two women [7]... (talk) and [8]... (laugh) about old times.

Sally [1]... (cycle) down Main Street yesterday when she [2]... (notice) a dog on the sidewalk. Suddenly the dog [3]... (see) a cat and [4]... (run) out in front of Sally's bike. Fortunately, Sally [5]... (not go) very fast and she [6]... (ride) very carefully. She [7]... (stop) in time and [8]... (not hit) the dog.

Early finisher *p. 143*

 Workbook *7 (p. 49)*

Language help

a) You already know that the progressive form of verbs is used for activities in progress.
- *Drew Schmidt **was looking** at his texts when his dad entered the kitchen.*

However, verbs that describe states (not activities) cannot be used in the progressive.
Typical state verbs include: *hate, know, like, mean, need, own, seem, think, understand, want.*
Look at these examples from the text on p. 90.
- *He's working from home this week so he **doesn't need** it.*
- *Coach **thinks** I'm doing well.*
- *"You're joking," laughed Rob. "I **don't believe** it!"*

b) Some verbs have different meanings and can be both activity and state verbs, for example: ***have, look, see, smell, taste, think***.
- *Drew Schmidt **was looking** at his texts when his dad entered the kitchen. (**anschauen**)*
- *No wonder you **look** so happy. (**aussehen**)*
- *You **looked** really great. (**aussehen**)*

➜ *GAP 3: State and activity verbs (p. 156)*

4 What does this word mean? (State verbs and activity verbs)

a) Match the verbs from the box to the gaps in the sentences and put them into the simple present.

1 What ... this strange word on this line ...? I ... it.
2 Dom ... football, so he ... to watch tomorrow's match.
3 Who ... this blue bike? Can I use it if you ... it at the moment?
4 Brrr! I ... I'll wear a coat when I go out later. It ... to be a bit cold today.
5 Can you suggest something from the menu? I really ... what I ... to eat.

hate · not know
mean · not need · own
seem · think
not understand
want · not want

More help p. 132

b) Choose the right verb for each pair of sentences. Then put them into the correct present form.

1 a) Mom ... those big red roses. b) Those big red roses ... beautiful.
2 a) This soup ... delicious! b) Don't burn your tongue while you ... it.
3 a) What ... you ... at over there? b) At your drawings – they ... really cool!
4 a) I ... about my birthday party. b) ... you ... everyone will come?
5 a) I ... such a bad headache. b) Sorry it's so loud, but we ... a party.

have · look
smell
taste · think

5 The choir's summer party (State verbs and activity verbs)

Rob and Tara are talking about their choir's summer party. Complete their dialogue.
Choose the right verb for each gap and put it into the simple present or present progressive.

Rob: Hey, Tara! [1]Do you know who [2]... with the choir's summer party this year? (help, know)

Tara: Well, I [3]... Hal and Liz [4]... a list of volunteers. Why? [5]... *you* ... to help? (make, think, want)

Rob: I [6]... about it. I [7]... to play a bigger role in the choir this year. And anyway, I [8]... parties. (like, think, try)

Tara: Well, Liz [9]... a big lunch. I'm sure she [10]... some help with the cooking. [11]... you ... time for that? (have, need, plan)

Rob: [12]... you ...? You [13]... that there's nothing I [14]... more than cooking. (hate, joke, know)

Tara: I [15]... you, Rob! You [16]... it up. I'm sure you're an awesome cook. (not believe, make)

More help p. 132 Early finisher p. 145

1853: Teepees in a Lakota community

A Lakota hide painting

The Crazy Horse Memorial in the Black Hills remembers the great Lakota leader.

1890: Hundreds of children, women and men were killed in the Massacre of Wounded Knee.

Traditional life and culture

The Lakota are one of the native nations of North America's Great Plains. For centuries, they have lived in present-day North and South Dakota. Traditionally, they were hunters. Thanks to the šúŋkawakáŋ – "horse" in English – which was introduced to America by European settlers, they were able to follow bison across the endless plains. As nomads, they lived in teepees (made of bison hide), which were easy to take with them as they moved about.

Like all Native Americans, the Lakota have a close relationship with nature. They see Earth as a mother, a giver of life. Humans, animals, rivers, mountains and forests are all connected and – as part of the natural world – they are sacred. Like Earth, the sun is also important in Lakota beliefs. The Sun Dance, which celebrates the renewal of Earth and its people, was once a major annual ceremony. Symbols like the horse, the bear, bison or the sun are often used in Lakotan hide paintings, which record important events.

From the 1850s to the present

Until the 1850s, the Lakota had good relations with the USA, at that time just 30 states in the east. In the Treaty of Fort Laramie in 1851, the United States recognized Lakota land rights. However, the next decades saw bloody conflict. As white settlers moved west, the US government supported them, and broke the promises they had made to the native population. In the fight to defend their land, the Lakota won some victories. Under the legendary leaders Crazy Horse and Sitting Bull, they defeated the US army in the Battle of Bighorn in 1876. But, in the end, the USA was stronger. After a terrible massacre by the US army in 1890, the Lakota gave up their fight for freedom.

After the wars, the Lakota were forced onto reservations much smaller than the land they had owned. Their living standard was low. They could not use their language or practise their religion. The Sun Dance was forbidden.
It was only in the 1960s that life began to improve. Today, the Lakota govern themselves on reservations. Their language is taught in schools, although the number of speakers is falling. And in education, jobs and health, they are still at a disadvantage. Altogether 170,000 people identify as Lakota.

US westward expansion and the Dakotas

When the United States became independent in 1776, there were 13 states on the Atlantic coast. During the 1800s, as millions of European immigrants arrived, the country expanded fast towards the Pacific. In those days, many white people believed that God had chosen them to settle the continent. By 1900, the number of states had grown to 45. North and South Dakota joined the Union as the 39th and 40th states in 1889.

Until the 1850s, there were less than 5,000 white settlers in the Dakotas. But soon their numbers began to grow and, in 1861, the United States set up the Dakota Territory with a government to keep the peace there. A year later, the US Homestead Act promised 65 hectares of land to every new settler, and the numbers increased again. Another wave followed in 1875 when gold was found in the Black Hills. By 1889, when the Dakotas joined the United States, the white population had grown to about 500,000. The largest group of settlers was German, which is why the capital of North Dakota is called Bismarck, after the German chancellor.

The Dakotas today

Although the population of the Dakotas continued to grow for some decades, they never became big states and today they are among the most thinly populated in the US. Together, their land area is bigger than Germany's but their population is just a little higher than that of the city of Düsseldorf.
For many people, North and South Dakota are typical examples of small-town and rural America. Farming has always been one of the main economic activities there. However, fewer people can live from the land today, and many are moving to the larger towns of Fargo, Bismarck (ND), Sioux Falls and Rapid City (SD). Tourism is becoming more and more important in the regional economy with over 30 million visitors a year. Visitors come to see the dramatic landscape, the bison and monuments like Mount Rushmore. Hunting and fishing are popular tourist activities.

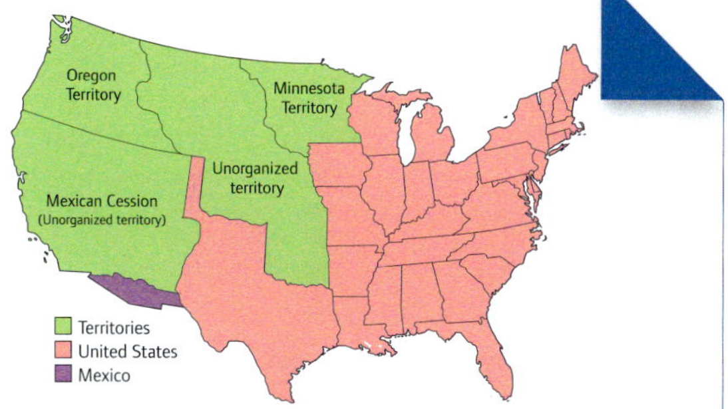

Map of the United States in 1848

1877: Gold miners in the city of Deadwood

	Area (sq. km)	Population
ND	183,272	755,393
SD	199,905	865,454
D'dorf	217	645,923
GER	357,386	83,020,000

Pierre, South Dakota's capital, has a population of only 14,000.

MK Imagine you had lived in the Dakotas in the years between 1860 and 1890. Choose a perspective. You are either a Lakota <u>or</u> a white settler.

a) Tell your story. In a short slide show, describe some of the key events you experienced. Make five slides. For each slide, find an image, write a heading and a short text (about 30 words).

b) Join up with a pair who chose the other perspective and present your slide show.

1 Tension below the surface

Say what you think the title of this text means.

On Saturday, Drew and Kaya drove through the flat fields of wheat to Standing Rock Reservation. When they got to Kaya's uncle's ranch, they borrowed two horses and spent the whole morning practicing for the school rodeo team.

Drew: Hey, Kaya! You're getting much better. There's no way you won't make the team.
Kaya: Thanks, Drew. You've been so helpful. How about a burger before we drive back home?
Drew: I'd love to, but I don't have time. I have to get home. My brother Austin gets back from college in a couple of hours.
Kaya: Oh, OK. That's cool.
Drew: Yeah, he's bringing his girlfriend. We're driving to Rapid City next weekend. Austin wants to show her Mount Rushmore.
Kaya: Oh, right.
Drew: It's a great place, isn't it?
Kaya: Actually, I've never seen it.
Drew: So what are you doing on the weekend? You can join us if you're interested. Why don't we spend the day together?
Kaya: Thanks Drew, but I don't want to go there.
Drew: Why not? Mount Rushmore is a great national monument.
Kaya: Not now, Drew. I'll explain later.
Drew: Oh, look, someone's coming.
Kaya: Hey, Rhett, Cody! How are you doing?
Rhett: Hi Kaya. I didn't expect to see you here.
Kaya: Right, we're practicing for the high school rodeo. We've borrowed horses from Uncle Chayton. Oh, by the way, this is Drew.
Rhett: Hi Drew. I'm Rhett. Cody and I are Kaya's cousins.
Drew: Hi guys! Nice to meet you.
Cody: Practicing? With a šúŋkawakáŋ like that. You can't be serious.
Kaya: Hey, Cody. You know my Lakota isn't good. What's a shunk… whatever you said?
Cody: Šúŋkawakáŋ? It means horse. It's the one good thing the white man brought here to America.
Kaya: Cody, this isn't the time. Sorry, Drew.
Drew: No stress, Kaya. It's not a problem.
Cody: You know, Kaya, the problem is that you live in Mobridge. You should move to the rez and live here like us. Then you might understand a bit more Lakota.
Rhett: Let's go, Cody. We have work to do.

2 Kaya's feelings

Look at these lines from the text.
Say how you think Kaya feels when she says them. Explain your view.

- How about a burger before we drive back home (ll. 9–10)
- Oh, OK. That's cool. (l. 14)
- Thanks Drew, but I don't want to go there. (l. 24)
- Cody, this isn't the time. Sorry, Drew. (l. 44)

3 The atmosphere in the text

a) Find and describe as many moments of tension in the text as you can.
b) Describe how Kaya, Drew and Cody behave. Then discuss your views on it.
- *I think Kaya was right/wrong when she …*
- *In my opinion, Drew/Cody/… should/shouldn't have …*
- *It was weird/… when …*

4 Kaya reports

Kaya and Drew didn't talk much on the drive back to Mobridge. When they got to Kaya's house, she smiled and waved as he drove off. Then, as she walked slowly through the garden, a woman's voice called out from the porch.

Jodi: Kaya! You're back. Come and sit with me.

Kaya: Aunt Jodi! What are you doing here?

Jodi: I came to see you. Where have you been?

Kaya: I was practicing for the rodeo out on the rez – and guess what?

Jodi: Tell me.

Kaya: I met Rhett and Cody. Cody spoke Lakota. He used a funny word. He said it meant horse.

Jodi: Šúŋkawakáŋ?

Kaya: That's it. You know, he advised me to move to the rez. To learn Lakota.

Jodi: Well, Cody has some very strong opinions.

Kaya: Yes. And actually, he's a bit rude too.

Jodi: What do you mean?

Kaya: He said the horse was the one good thing the white man had brought here to America.

Jodi: Is that rude, honey?

Kaya: But Drew was there with me.

Jodi: Drew? Who's that?

Kaya: Just a guy from school. He's a great rider and he was helping me to practice.

Jodi: He sounds nice. Are you seeing him again?

Kaya: Well, Drew told me that he and his brother Austin were driving to Rapid City next weekend and he said I could join them if I was interested. He suggested spending the day together.

Jodi: In Rapid City? What do they want to do there?

Kaya: Austin's girlfriend is here. Drew said he wanted to show her Mount Rushmore.

Jodi: Mount Rushmore! You didn't say you'd go, did you?

Kaya: Noooo! I told him I'd never seen it. And I said that I didn't want to go there.

Jodi: Well that was fairly clear. How did he react?

Kaya: He said Mount Rushmore was a great national monument.

Jodi: But didn't you explain …?

Kaya: I said I'd explain, Jodi, but then Rhett and Cody arrived.

Jodi: Didn't you tell him on the drive back?

Kaya: I just couldn't. Cody was so rude to Drew, and Drew was really nice about it. It wasn't the right moment for a lesson on Mount Rushmore.

Jodi: I see what you mean, Kaya. But you'll have to say something sooner or later.

5 Understanding the text

Who says these lines from the text? About who, and why?

1 He used a funny word.
2 He has some very strong opinions.
3 And actually, he's a bit rude too.
4 He sounds nice.
5 I told him that I'd never seen it.
6 How did he react?
7 Didn't you tell him on the drive back?

6 Have a go

Drew said to Kaya: "Mount Rushmore ***is*** a great national monument."
Kaya reported to Jodi: He said that Mount Rushmore ***was*** a great national monument.

Imagine Drew said these things. Report them.

South Dakota is one of the smallest US states.
The population is almost 900,000.
The capital city is Pierre.

Looking at language

In the text on p. 98, Cody says: *It means horse. (l. 41)*
On p. 99, Kaya tells her aunt what Cody said: *He said it meant horse. (ll. 11–12)*

Look at these statements from p. 98. Then find out how Kaya reports them in the text on p. 99. Write down the verbs and say how they change.

- *Thanks Drew, but I don't want to go there.*
- *We're driving to Rapid City next weekend.*
- *Actually, I've never seen it.*
- *You can join us if you're interested.*
- *I'll explain later.*
- *It's the one good thing the white man brought here.*

Say what other changes you can find in the reported sentences.

➔ *GAP 17: Indirect speech (p. 184)*

1 Kaya said ... (Indirect speech)

Report Kaya's statement like this: *Kaya said that she lived ...*

1 "I live with my mom in Mobridge."
2 "I want to make the rodeo team in summer."
3 "Drew Schmidt offered to help me."
4 "We practised at my uncle's ranch."
5 "Drew is visiting Mount Rushmore soon."
6 "I don't want to go with him."
7 "I haven't told him the reason."
8 "I'll have to explain it to him soon."

2 Planning the choir party (Indirect speech)

Liz and Hal are organizing the MPHS choir party. Liz has spoken to some choir members about it. Imagine you're Liz. Report to Hal what everyone said.

1 Tara: I'm vegetarian. I can make a cheese dish.
Tara said she was vegetarian and she could ...
2 Tara: I'll ask my mom to make some apple juice.
And she told me ...
3 Ben: I really love apple juice. I can bring some paper cups.
4 Ben: I've never cooked before, but I'll try to make a salad.
5 Sue: My dad isn't working next week. I'll ask him to make some pizzas.
6 Brad: I don't know how to bake a cake, but I can buy one.
7 Rob: I'm not very good at cooking, but I can make great sandwiches.
8 Rob: I wasn't able to go to last year's party, so I can't wait for this year's.

More help ➔ *p. 133*   Early finisher ➔ *p. 144*

3 Jana said she could speak a little Chinese (Indirect speech)

In groups of three, take turns to play A, B and C. Use ideas from the table or think of your own.

Partner A	Partner B	Partner C
I can speak a little Chinese.	*What did Jana say?*	*She said she could speak a little Chinese.*

I can speak a little Chinese.	*I don't know how to ride a horse.*
It will be quite warm tomorrow.	*It isn't raining at the moment.*
I've been a Dortmund fan all my life.	*I won't have time to do my homework today.*
I'll be 16 on my next birthday.	*My friend is having a party at the weekend.*
I didn't have any breakfast this morning.	*Most Germans learn English at school.*

4 Drew's dad told him to hurry up (Indirect speech: *ask, tell, advise, remind, suggest*)

REMEMBER
You already know different ways to report commands, requests, suggestions, etc.
a) *ask, tell, advise, remind* + *me/you/him/…* + *to* + infinitive.
Cody: *You should move to the rez and live here like us. (p. 98, ll. 47–48)*
Kaya: *He advised me to move to the rez. (p. 99, ll. 14–15)*

b) *suggest* + gerund
Drew: *Why don't we spend the day together? (p. 98, l. 23)*
Kaya: *He suggested spending the day together. (p. 99, ll. 30–31)*
➔ *GAP 18: Indirect commands (p. 186)*

a) Report some things Drew's parents said to him last week. Decide which reporting verb to use: *ask, tell, advise, remind* or *suggest*. Sometimes more than one of these verbs is possible.

Mr Schmidt:
1 "Hurry up, Drew. You'll be late for school."
Drew's dad told him to hurry up.
2 "Why don't you invite Kaya for dinner?"
He suggested inviting Kaya for dinner.
3 "Clean out the car, please."
4 "Can you help me in the garden this evening?"

Mrs Schmidt:
5 "Go to bed a bit earlier if you feel tired."
6 "Can you help me to carry this box?"
7 "Don't forget to call your grandma."
8 "Why don't you phone her after dinner?"
9 "Get a weekend job if you need more money."
10 "Don't leave your dirty socks on the floor."

b) Make similar sentences about yourself.
My mum/sister/… asked me not to play my music so loudly.

Early finisher ➔ *p. 145 (Grammar challenge)*

5 An interview about the internet and social media

a) Ask your partner these questions and write down their answers.

1 Can you use the internet when you want to?
2 Do you use social media
- on your home computer?
- on your phone?
- at school?

3 Are you following any interesting people at the moment? What do they do?
4 Do you have a blog?
What kind of posts do you write?
5 Which websites and apps do you use most?
What do you use them for?
6 Do you have any internet tips for
- other teens?
- your parents or teachers?

b) Work with students from other pairs. Say what you learned about your partner in a).
– *Jana told me that she had a music blog. She said that she wrote …*
– *Lukas advised me to download an app for …*

1 Mount Rushmore: For and against

Work on the 60-foot-high heads of the four presidents (George Washington, Thomas Jefferson, Abraham Lincoln and Theodore Roosevelt) at Mount Rushmore began in 1927 and was finished in 1941. The sculptures were made to attract tourists to South Dakota, and today nearly three million come every year – more than to any other place in the state.
As the two comments below show, people can react very differently to this national memorial.

Sarah Kelada

We went on a class trip to South Dakota to see the giant faces in the Black Hills. As I walked along Mount Rushmore's Avenue of Flags and saw the presidents' faces in the mountain before me, it was clear what this place is: a symbol of power, a monument to patriotism.
The memorial was paid for with taxpayers' money and it is looked after by the National Park Service. It is one of the places where America shows the world how great it is.
However, it is on Native American land in Paha Sapa, the Black Hills, which are sacred to the Lakota people. The same Black Hills that were promised to the Lakota forever in 1868, but were taken away from them a few years later when white people discovered gold there.
Those presidents didn't care about the role of nature in Lakota beliefs. Instead, they helped to kill the people who had lived there for centuries and steal their land. Many Native Americans find the memorial extremely offensive. How would people feel if they sprayed graffiti on the cathedral in Rapid City?

Darren Wright

As I walked along Mount Rushmore's Avenue of Flags, I was blown away by one of our country's most wonderful sights. This huge, awesome work of art made me proud to be an American! It is hardly surprising that it is found on lists of the "Wonders of the Modern World".
The monument is dedicated to four presidents who played a major role in building the United States. That's why they were chosen for this memorial to our nation. Their 60-foot granite faces will gaze for ever over the Black Hills as a symbol of the power of our nation. History will always remember them.
I stayed around for the evening ceremony in the amphitheater. It began with a 20-minute movie about the history of the monument. Then, as the national anthem played in the background, huge floodlights lit up the presidents' faces against the cloudless night sky. As I watched, like many other Americans in the crowd, I felt tears of pride run down my face.

2 Different opinions

a) List reasons why the writers are for or against Mount Rushmore. Compare your lists in class.

b) Explain why you would or would not visit Mount Rushmore.

www Read about the Crazy Horse Memorial. Does it change your view of Mount Rushmore?

3 Monuments and memorials

a) Think of the monuments in your region. Decide which one you would take an American visitor to see. Explain your choice to the class.

b) My Book Write a text (100 words) to recommend the monument you chose to your visitor.

4 Kaya's decision

Say what you think Kaya's decision might be.

Friday afternoon. School was over. Even though it was already June, Drew felt a chill in the air as he walked through the high school's double doors. After dinner the night before, his dad had asked for the car keys back. Now, whenever he wanted to go somewhere, Drew would have to ask someone for a ride.
Rob came up and suggested going for a pizza. "Let's go to Joe's! Then I'll give you a ride home."
"OK," said Drew glumly.
Next to the school, a group of students was talking and laughing. Drew could hear Kaya's voice.
"Just a minute, Rob," he said. "I have to ask Kaya something." He walked over to Kaya's group and led her away from her friends.
"So have you decided yet? Will you come with us to Mount Rushmore?" he asked.
"I can't do it, Drew."
"Why not?"
"Because Mount Rushmore is an insult to the Lakota people. I don't want to go there. Ever. The Black Hills are sacred to us, Drew."
"But there are lots of other things we could do in Rapid City as well," Drew said.
Kaya sighed as she looked into Drew's disappointed face. "I know, Drew. But I still can't go to Mount Rushmore."
"OK, then. I only asked you to come because I thought it would be fun. I don't want to cause any problems."
"Drew, I'd like to do something with you. But I just can't go to the Black Hills. Uh … why don't you stay here on the weekend?"
"You mean not go with my family?"
Rob came up from behind. "Hey man, I can't wait any longer! I need that pizza now!"
"I've changed my mind," said Drew and looked away. "I'm going home."
Rob shook his head in surprise. "What? Are you sure?"
"Yeah, I'm sure."
"OK then. I'll give you a ride."
"No thanks. I'll walk. I don't want to go by car."
"But it's over five miles, Drew!"
"Yeah, so what? I need to think."
"Think about what?"
"About life … you know, that kind of thing."

5 Understanding the text

a) Explain Kaya's reasons for her decision. What does she suggest to Drew? How does Drew react?

b) Imagine you're Drew. Write down your thoughts as you walk home.
Text file 5–6 *(pp. 122–125)*

6 Where's Drew?

Listen and find out where Drew is, and why. Say how Kaya finds out and how she reacts.

EXTRA Imagine Kaya and Drew meet at school the next week. What will they say? Write their conversation and act it out.

We often make one word from another by adding a suffix like *-ful*, *-less* or *-ness*, e.g.:
noun: cloud > **adjective:** *cloudless* **adjective:** dark > **noun:** *darkness*
Knowing about suffixes will help you to understand words you haven't learned yet.
Using suffixes is also a good way to increase your vocabulary.

1 Adjectives from nouns (Suffixes: *-ful* and *-less*)

The suffixes *-ful* and *-less* are opposites: *-ful* means "with a lot of …"; *-less* means "without …"

a) Complete the sentences with adjectives. Find the best word in one of the boxes and add a suffix.

1 Kaya had a … night. She lay awake in bed for hours.
2 Exam week at school can be a … time, even for the best students.
3 I opened the window and let the breeze into the hot, … room.
4 Our school football team has been so … this year. We've won all our matches!
5 Cody and Rhett took part in a … demonstration where no one got hurt.
6 That play was so long – it seemed …! I thought it would never finish.

-ful: colour · event · peace · stress · success · truth

-less: air · end · home · moon · rain · sleep

b) Make adjectives from the words you didn't need in a) and use them to write your own sentences.

More help p. 133

2 Nouns from adjectives (Abstract nouns with the suffix *-ness*)

Nouns can be concrete or abstract. Concrete nouns describe material objects, e.g. *dog, house, tree*.
An abstract noun does not describe a material object: e.g. *courage, danger, fame, pride*.
You can make abstract nouns from adjectives with the suffix *-ness*:, e.g. *happiness, sadness*.
If an adjective ends in *-y*, it is usually changed to an *i* when you add the suffix, e.g. *happiness, silliness*.

Drew talks about South Dakota. Rewrite his sentences. Use nouns with *-ness* where you need them.

1 The people in South Dakota are so friendly.	I love the *friendliness* of the people *in South Dakota*.
2 They're kind and helpful too.	They're also known for their … and … .
3 I never feel lonely in Mobridge.	… just isn't a problem for … .
4 I love the empty roads and fields.	The … of the … is something I love.
5 The dark nights make it easy to see the stars.	The … at night makes it … .
6 It's amazing how bright they are.	Their … is simply … .

More help p. 133

3 Your sentences (Suffixes: *-ful*, *-less* and *-ness*)

a) Choose five words from the box.
Use a dictionary to find out which of the suffixes *-ful*, *-less* or *-ness* can be used with them. Sometimes more than one suffix is possible.

b) Write a sentence with each of the words you found in the dictionary:
bitter: There was a lot of bitterness when our team lost the match.

c) Compare your sentences. Early finisher p. 144

d) In class, share sentences for each of the words in the box.

bitter · child · clever · cloud · fair · friend · great · heart · help · ill · job · life · mad · nervous · power · shy · skill tear · tired · rest

Language help

In English the definite article (*the*) isn't used before a noun in some cases.
Look at some examples from the texts on pp. 102–103.

abstract nouns	e.g. *history, life, nature, patriotism, power, pride, …* ***History** will always remember them. / … a monument to **patriotism***
plural nouns	e.g. *Native Americans, people, taxpayers, …* *How would **people** feel if …? / The memorial was paid for with **taxpayers'** money.*
some places and meals	e.g. *church, hospital, school, prison, … / breakfast, lunch, dinner* *School was over. / After dinner the night before, …*

However, we use the definite article when we give these nouns a more specific meaning.

*… a movie about **the history** of the monument.*
*They helped to kill **the people** who had lived there for centuries.*
*Next to **the school**, a group of students was talking and laughing.*

➔ *GAP 19: The definite article (p. 188)*

1 Life on the rez (Abstract nouns without the definite article)

a) Decide if these nouns are abstract or concrete and make two lists. Add more nouns to each list.

education · flag · love · skates · friendliness · time · moon · sailor · energy · ball · art · history · machine · sport · power · boyfriend · change · chaos · fashion · meal · friend · picture · pride · nature · jeans · statue · school · environment

b) Cody speaks about life on the rez. Add the definite article (*the*) if necessary to complete his speech.

Many people say that [1]… life on [2]… reservation is quite tough. But it is here that we can really enjoy [3]… freedom. For me, [4]… best thing about living here is being so close to [5]… nature. As a Lakota, I want to do as much as possible to help [6]… environment. So I'm very excited about [7]… new wind farm we're building right here on [8]… rez. We need to do something about [9]… climate change and [10]… wind energy will help [11]… planet to survive. Another thing I like here is that we can learn [12]… Lakota language and speak it every day. In my opinion, [13]… education is [14]… key to keeping our culture alive.

2 Everyday life in Mobridge (The definite article: Plurals, places, meals)

Choose the right word from the box to complete each pair of sentences. Add *the* if necessary.

> breakfast · farmers · hospital · lunch · people · school

1 a) MPHS is the name of … that Drew goes to.
  b) At what age do kids in S. Dakota start …?
2 a) … for Grade 9 student at MPHS starts at 12.
  b) … you get there is cheap and healthy.
3 a) … don't think Mobridge is very exciting.
  b) Drew knows … who own that diner.
4 a) Drew eats jelly on toast for … before school.
  b) … I had at the Mobridge diner was really tasty.
5 a) How many doctors work at … in Mobridge?
  b) Drew was ill once and spent a week in …
6 a) … don't grow much fruit in South Dakota.
  b) … that Drew knows all grow wheat.

Early finisher *p. 145*

A bilingual (German-English) dictionary helps you to find the English words you need. You can find good dictionaries online. You can also use a print dictionary.

Aufsatz | German-English

Aufsatz der
1 *(Schule) BE* essay ['eseɪ], *AE* paper ['peɪpə]
einen Aufsatz über Goethe schreiben
write an essay on Goethe
2 *(Abhandlung)* paper
3 *(Möbel)* top section ['tɒp ˌsekʃn]

behandeln | German-English

behandeln transitives Verb
1 treat [triːt]
jn. mit Antibiotika behandeln
treat sb. with antibiotics
2 *(Thema, Fall)* deal with [diːl]
Das Buch behandelt die Geschichte der Kelten.
The book deals with the history of the Celts.

Note | German-English

Note die
1 *(Musik)* note; *(gedruckte Noten)* sheet music
Kannst du Noten lesen? Can you read music?
2 *(Schule) BE* mark [mɑːk], *AE* grade [greɪd]
3 **eine persönliche Note** a personal touch [tʌtʃ]

Prüfung | German-English

Prüfung die
1 exam [ɪg'zæm], examination [ɪgˌzæmɪ'neɪʃn]; test
eine Prüfung machen do/sit/take an exam;
eine Prüfung bestehen/nicht bestehen
pass/fail an exam
2 *(technische Überprüfung)* inspection [ɪn'spekʃn]
3 *(von Dokumenten)* check [tʃek]

nützlich | German-English

nützlich Adjektiv
1 *(hilfreich)* useful, handy, helpful
2 *(vorteilhaft)* beneficial [benə'fiʃl]
Antonym: nutzlos

vorbereiten | German-English

vorbereiten transitives Verb
1 *(Mahlzeit; Reise)* prepare [prɪ'peə]
Wir sind dabei, unseren Urlaub vorzubereiten.
We're making preparations for our holiday.
2 **sich auf etwas vorbereiten** prepare for sth.
Ich bereite mich auf die mündliche Prüfung vor.
I'm preparing for my oral exam.

a) Read the following tips. Then use the dictionary search results above to do the tasks.

TIP 1 Remember that words often have more than one meaning.
- Find the English word for *Note* that you can use to say how you did in your class test.
- Find another example of a "school word" which also has other meanings.

TIP 2 British and American English may use different words for the same thing.
- Find two examples.

TIP 3 Nouns can take a different verb in English than in German.
- Find the three verbs you can use to say *eine Prüfung machen* in English.

TIP 4 You may need different prepositions in English and German, e.g. **im** Internet = **on** the internet.
- Find the English for *sich vorbereiten* and *einen Aufsatz schreiben*.
- What are the prepositions in the German examples? What are they in the English ones?
- Find a verb which takes a preposition in English, but not in German.

TIP 5 In online dictionaries, antonyms and/or synonyms are often given.
- Where would you click to find the opposite of *nützlich* in English?

b) Look at the dictionary entries again. What kind of information do they give you? Make a list.
- different meanings of a word ...

➔ *SMC 24: Using a dictionary (p. 210)*

1 Bloodlines

(by Christopher Nataanii Cegielski)

Bloodlines is a short film which tells a story about relationships in a Native American family.

a) Look at this still from the film and describe the mood between the characters.
Then watch the beginning of the film.
What else can you say about the family?

b) Now watch the rest of the film and take notes about what happens.
Compare your ideas.

c) During the whole film, the characters never talk about their feelings.
Discuss how you think they feel towards each other as the story continues.

Now imagine what they are thinking in the stills on the right.
Write a short dialogue in which the father and the older boy say how they feel.

2 Making the film: Shots

a) Look at these stills from the film.
Describe what you can see in each shot.

b) Match the shots to the follow definitions.
- This shot tells you more about the situation the characters are in.
- This shot helps you to understand where the action takes place.
- This shot shows the feelings of one of the characters.

Now watch some scenes from the film again and find examples of each kind of shot.

1 *long shot*

2 *medium shot*

3 *close-up*

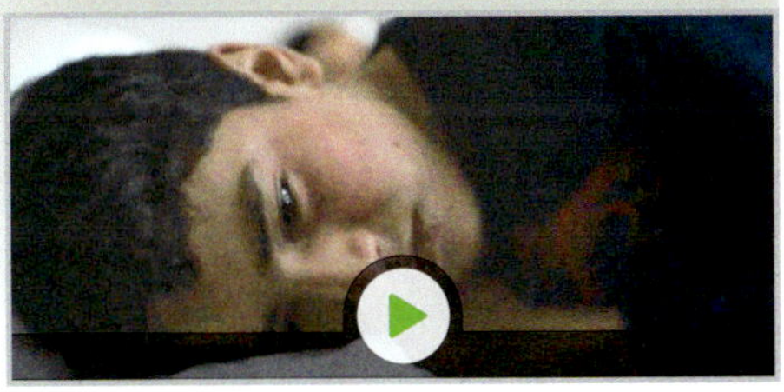

The Absolutely True Diary of a Part-Time Indian (an excerpt from the novel)

Sherman Alexie's novel is about a Native American teenager called Junior who is a member of the Spokane tribe and lives on a reservation in the north-west of the USA. The novel focuses on the differences between the completely different worlds of the reservation and the nearby town where mostly white Americans live. This excerpt takes place after the death of Junior's grandmother.

Sherman Alexie

We held Grandmother's wake three days later. We knew that people would be coming in large numbers. But we were stunned because almost two thousand Indians showed up that day to say goodbye.

[...]

Yep, about two thousand Indians (and a few white folks) sat and stood on the football field as we all said goodbye to the greatest Spokane Indian in history.

I knew that my grandmother would have loved that send-off.

It was crazy and fun and sad.

My sister wasn't able to come to the funeral. That was the worst part about it. She didn't have enough money to get back, I guess. That was sad. But she promised me she'd sing one hundred mourning songs that day.

We all have to find our own ways to say good-bye.

Tons of people told stories about my grandmother.

But there was one story that mattered most of all.

About ten hours into the wake, a white guy stood. He was a stranger. He looked vaguely familiar. I knew I'd seen him before, but I couldn't think of where. We all wondered exactly who he was. But nobody knew. That wasn't surprising. My grandmother had met thousands of people. The white guy was holding this big suitcase. He held that thing tight to his chest as he talked.

"Hello," he said. "My name is Ted."

And then I remembered who he was. He was a rich and famous billionaire white dude. He was famous for being filthy rich and really weird.

My grandmother knew Billionaire Ted!

Wow.

We all were excited to hear this guy's story. And so what did he have to say?

We all groaned.

We'd expected this white guy to be original. But he was yet another white guy who showed up on the rez because he loved Indian people SOOOOOOOO much.

Do you know how many white strangers show up on Indian reservations every year and start telling Indians how much they love them?

Thousands.

It's sickening.

And boring.

"Listen," Ted said. "I know you've heard that before. I know white people say that all the time. But I still need to say it. I love Indians. I love your songs, your dances, and your souls. And I love your art. I collect Indian art."

Oh, God, he was a collector. Those guys made Indians feel like insects pinned to a display board. I looked around the football field. Yep, all of my

---

wake Totenwache **stun** verblüffen **send-off** Verabschiedung **mourning** ['mɔːnɪŋ] trauernd **tons of sth.** (*infml*) eine Menge etwas **familiar** bekannt **filthy rich** (*infml*) stinkreich cousins were squirming like beetles and butterflies with pins stuck in their hearts.

"I've collected Indian art for decades," Ted said. "I have old spears. Old arrowheads. I have old armor. I have blankets. And paintings. And sculptures. And baskets. And jewelry."

Blah, blah, blah, blah.

"And I have old powwow dance outfits," he said. Now that made everybody sit up and pay attention.

"About ten years ago, this Indian guy knocked on the door of my cabin in Montana."

Cabin, my butt. Ted lived in a forty-room log mansion just outside of Bozeman.

"Well, I didn't know this stranger," Ted said. "But I always open my door to Indians."

Oh, please.

"And this particular Indian stranger was holding a very beautiful powwow dance outfit, a woman's powwow dance outfit. It was the most beautiful thing I'd ever seen. It was all beaded blue and red and yellow with a thunderbird design. It must have weighed fifty pounds. And I couldn't imagine the strength of the woman who could dance beneath that magical burden."

Every woman in the world could dance that way.

"Well, this Indian stranger said he was in a desperate situation. His wife was dying of cancer and he needed money to pay for her medicine. I knew he was lying. I knew he'd stolen the outfit. I could always smell a thief."

Smell yourself, Ted.

"And I knew I should call the police on this thief. I knew I should take that outfit away and find the real owner. But it was so beautiful, so perfect, that I gave the Indian stranger a thousand dollars and sent him on his way. And I kept the outfit."

Whoa, was Ted coming here to make a confession? And why had he chosen my grandmother's funeral for his confession?

"For years, I felt terrible. I'd look at that outfit hanging on the wall of my Montana cabin." Mansion, Ted, it's a mansion. Go ahead; you can say it: MANSION!

"And then I decided to do some research. I hired an anthropologist, an expert, and he quickly pointed out that the outfit was obviously of Interior Salish origin. And after doing a little research, he discovered that the outfit was Spokane Indian, to be specific. And then, a few years ago, he visited your reservation undercover and learned that this stolen outfit once belonged to a woman named Grandmother Spirit."

We all gasped. This was a huge shock. I wondered if we were all part of some crazy reality show called *When Billionaires Pretend to be Human*. I looked around for the cameras.

"Well, ever since I learned who really owned this outfit, I've been torn. I always wanted to give it back. But I wanted to keep it, too. I couldn't sleep some nights because I was so torn up by it."

Yep, even billionaires have DARK NIGHTS OF THE SOUL

"And, well, I finally couldn't take it anymore. I packed up the outfit and headed for your reservation, here, to hand-deliver the outfit back to Grandmother Spirit. And I get here only to discover that she's passed on to the next world. It's just devastating."

We were all completely silent. This was the weirdest thing any of us had ever witnessed. And we're Indians, so trust me, we've seen some really weird stuff.

"But I have the outfit here," Ted said. He opened up his suitcase and pulled out the outfit and held it up. It was fifty pounds, so he struggled with it. Anybody would have struggled with it.

"So if any of Grandmother Spirit's children are here, I'd love to return her outfit to them." My mother stood and walked up to Ted.

"I'm Grandmother Spirit's only daughter," she said. My mother's voice had gotten all formal. Indians are good at that. We'll be talking and laughing and carrying on like normal, and then,

---

collector Sammler/in **pin sth.** etwas aufspießen **squirm** [skwɜːm] sich winden **powwow** ['paʊwaʊ] *eine Form von Kulturveranstaltung von nordamerikanischen Ureinwohnern* **mansion** ['mænʃn] Villa **beaded** aufgereiht **thunderbird** Donnervogel **burden** Last **desperate** verzweifelt **cancer** Krebs **Whoa** [wəʊ] Brr! **confession** Geständnis **cancer** Krebs (*Krankheit*) **hire sb.** jn. anstellen **Interior Salish** ['seɪlɪʃ] *Gruppe von nordamerikanischen Ureinwohnern* **undercover** verdeckt **gasp** keuchen **human** menschlich **be torn** hin- und hergerissen sein **take it** (*infml*) etwas verkraften **hand-deliver sth.** etwas persönlich überreichen **struggle** kämpfen

BOOM, we get all serious and sacred and start talking like some English royalty.

"Dearest daughter," Ted said. "I hereby return your stolen goods. I hope you forgive me for returning it too late."

"Well, there's nothing to forgive, Ted," my mother said. "Grandmother Spirit wasn't a powwow dancer."

Ted's mouth dropped open.

"Excuse me," he said.

"My mother loved going to powwows. But she never danced. She never owned a dance outfit. This couldn't be hers."

Ted didn't say anything. He couldn't say anything.

"In fact, looking at the beads and design, this doesn't look Spokane at all. I don't recognize the work. Does anybody here recognize the beadwork?"

"No," everybody said.

"It looks more Sioux to me," my mother said. "Maybe Oglala. Maybe. I'm not an expert. Your anthropologist wasn't much of an expert, either. He got this way wrong."

We all just sat there in silence and mulled that over.

Then he packed his outfit back into the suitcase, hurried over to his waiting car, and sped away.

For about two minutes, we all sat quiet. Who knew what to say?

And then my mother started laughing. And that set us all off.

Two thousand Indians laughed at the same time.

We kept laughing.

It was the most glorious noise I'd ever heard.

And I realized that, sure, Indians were drunk and sad and displaced and crazy and mean, but, dang, we knew how to laugh.

When it comes to death, we know that laughter and tears are pretty much the same thing.

And so, laughing and crying, we said good-bye to my grandmother.

And when we said goodbye to one grandmother, we said goodbye to all of them.

Each funeral was a funeral for all of us. We lived and died together.

All of us laughed when they lowered my grandmother into the ground.

And all of us laughed when they covered her with dirt.

And all of us laughed as we walked and drove and rode our way back to our lonely, lonely houses.

1 Understanding the text

Decide which statements about Ted are true. Refer to the text. Correct the false statements.

1 Ted is a rich Native American.
2 He has no interest in Native American culture.
3 He explains how he got a powwow outfit.
4 He is keen on keeping the outfit as a souvenir.
5 He doesn't find the outfit's owner.
6 Everyone is angry when Ted drives away.

2 Ted's character

a) Read these lines 40–43, 74 and 89 again. Discuss what they tell you about Junior's attitude towards Ted and other white people like him.

b) Do you think Junior's view of Ted is fair? Give reasons.

EXTRA Imagine Ted writes a blog post about his experience on the reservation. How does he feel? What has he learned? Write his post.

Workbook 19 (p. 55)

carry on weitermachen **hereby** hiermit **goods** Gegenstände **forgive sb.** jm. verzeihen **Sioux** [suː]; **Oglala** *Gruppen von nordamerikanischen Ureinwohnern* **way wrong** (*infml*) sehr falsch **mull sth. over** etwas überdenken **glorious** herrlich **displaced** vertrieben

Workbook Checkpoint (pp. 56–59)

Your task

A presentation: Introduce yourself to your American class

You are on a school exchange in Mobridge, South Dakota.
In a short presentation, introduce yourself to your class and tell them something about yourself.

STEP 1
Collect ideas
- your name, age, etc.
- information about your home area and your school
- your impressions of school in Mobridge
- your impressions of South Dakota, places you've seen
- experiences you've had there
- people you've met and conversations you've had

➔ *SMC 25: Ordering and structuring vocabulary (p. 211)*

STEP 2
Find vocabulary you need
- Make a list of words you need to look up.
- Find the words in an online or print dictionary. ➔ *p. 106*

STEP 3
Structure your content
- Decide what to say in your introduction, in the main body of your presentation and in the conclusion.
- Use cards with keywords and number them or use digital note cards on your phone.

➔ *SMC 4: Structuring texts (p. 195)*

STEP 4
Find visuals to go with your content
- a picture of your family, friends, hometown
- photos you have taken in South Dakota

Prinzipalmarkt – a famous street

STEP 5
Think of language you can use to
- introduce yourself and your topics
  - *Good morning everyone. My name is … and this morning I'd like tell you about …*
- lead your audience through your presentation
  - *First I'm going to talk about … · Now I'd like to move on to …*
- talk about your experiences, people you've met, things they've told you.
  - *One day when I was walking down Main Street, …* ➔ *pp. 94–95*
  - *I met an old man who told me that …* ➔ *pp. 100–101*

STEP 6
The presentation
- Practise your presentation. ➔ *SMC 21: Giving a presentation (p. 209)*
- Take turns to give your presentations. Give feedback after each one. ➔ *Giving feedback (p. 304)*

Making requests

1 Everyday requests

a) **Think:** What kind of things do you ask other people to do – at home, at school, at a club, etc.? Make a list.

b) **Pair:** Compare your lists. Do you ask other people to do the same kind of things? Describe how you feel if someone says no to a request. How do you feel when they say yes?

– I often have to ask my little brother to be quiet.
– I sometimes ask my mum to …
– I feel hurt/sad/happy if someone says yes/no.
– I don't mind if …

c) **Share:** Join up with another pair. Sum up your discussion from b). Then think of different ways to complete this sentence and agree on the best two:
If you want someone to say yes to your request, it is important to …

2 At a school environment project

a) Chad and Darius are taking part in a recycling project at a high school in South Dakota. Darius asks Chad to do two things. Listen and say what they are.

b) Listen again and complete the phrases he uses to make his requests:

1 … go and find another one.
2 … fill it up.

c) Sabina, an exchange student from Germany, is also taking part in the project. Listen. Then say what she asks Chad and Darius to do and write down the phrases she uses.

Sabina, Chad and Darius at work on their project

d) Listen again to the dialogue between Sabina, Chad and Darius. Say which description of Sabina you agree with most and explain why.

1 She sounds polite.
2 She sounds rude and doesn't care.
3 She sounds rude, but doesn't mean to be.
4 She sounds neither rude nor polite.

3 Thinking about language

a) Using the right phrases can help you to avoid sounding rude in a foreign language.
Read the tip below. Then think of other ways that Sabina could make her requests from 2.
Would you advise her to use these phrases? Why (not)?

TIP

When you make a request in the United States or in Great Britain, it is important to say please. However, just saying please doesn't always make you sound polite.

If your request is too direct, you can easily sound like you're giving orders. This is why polite requests in English are very often indirect, especially when you aren't talking to family members or close friends.

Phrases for making polite requests

1 It would be great if you could ...
2 I wonder if you could ...?
3 I don't suppose you could ...?
4 Do you think you could ...?
5 Do you have time to ...?
6 Would you mind (doing, helping, etc.) ...?
7 What do you think about (doing, etc.) ...?

b) Comment on the American/British way of making requests.
Explain how it is different or similar in your language.

4 At the end of an afternoon's work

a) Darius, Chad and Sabina are finishing their afternoon's work. Listen to their dialogue.
Note the three phrases from the box Darius uses to show appreciation. Put them into a table.

Don't mention it. · It was nothing. · My pleasure.
No problem. · Thanks a million.
Thanks so much. · That's so kind of you.
We really appreciate it. · You shouldn't have.
You're the best. · You're welcome.

Showing appreciation	Reacting
...	...

b) Listen again. How does Chad react to Darius? Note two phrases and add them to the table.

c) Complete the table with all the other phrases from the box.

d) Discuss which phrases sound best to you and practise them together.

5 Your dialogue

a) You are a group of American and German students at work on a project. Decide what your project is (e.g. a film evening, a sports event, cleaning a beach) and what tasks need to be done.
Prepare a dialogue which includes several requests. Use phrases from 3 and 4.

b) Practise your dialogue. Then act it out for another group.

Text 1

1 WTC... Freedom Tower

1 *1 World Trade Center* opened in 2014. New Yorkers often call it "Freedom Tower". To get an idea why, look at the building's dimensions. It is 196 by 196 feet, the same area as each of the twin towers which collapsed on September 11, 2001, after two hijacked airplanes flew into them. While we're still at ground level: The base[1] of the building is like a box with concrete[2] walls, 186 feet high. These walls are covered in glass panels[3] which light up at night. They have no windows.

Can you guess why not?

To protect the building from truck bombs and other attacks at ground level.

2 54 high-speed elevators travel up to the top of the building. Let's take one of the express elevators that go non-stop to the restaurant and observation deck and reach a speed of 2,000 feet a minute.
The observation deck is 1,362 feet above ground – exactly the height of the old World Trade Center 2 building. To the top of the glass parapet[4] it is 1,368 feet – the height of the old World Trade Center 1 tower.

How long do you think it takes to go the top?

It takes about 45 seconds to reach the top. That's really fast!

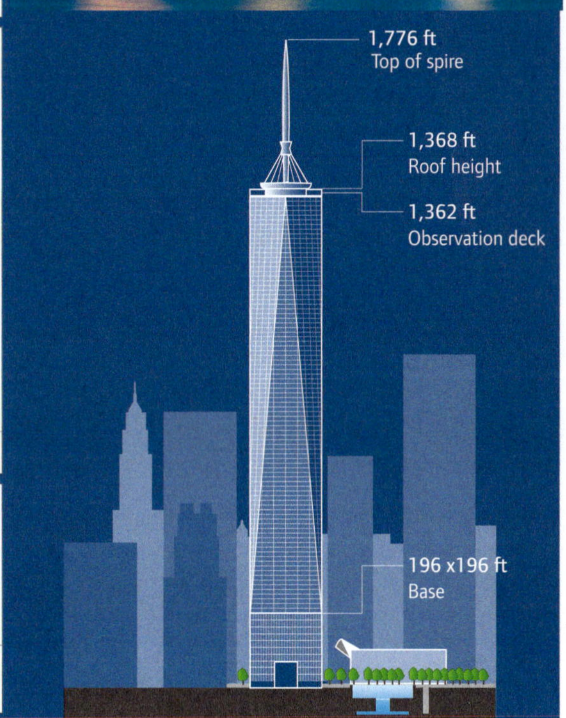

3 Although you can't climb to the top of the antenna (unless you're King Kong!), its height of 1,776 feet above ground is important too.

What is important about that number?

1776 is the year that the United States declared[5] its independence[6] from Britain.

4 Now, after you have enjoyed all the incredible[7] views of Manhattan and all five boroughs of New York City, you can take the elevator back down ... and in less than a minute you are back on the street, not far from from the 9/11 Memorial – those two deep fountains where the old twin towers once stood. One more thing: when you are walking around Manhattan at night, don't forget to watch out for the Freedom Tower antenna which lights up the night sky like a gigantic lighthouse.[8]

a) Say what connections you see between the dimensions of *1 World Trade Center* and the and the name *Freedom Tower*.

b) Explain why *1 WTC* is a popular tourist attraction.
Would you visit it too? Give reasons.

[1] **base** [beɪs] Sockel [2] **concrete** ['kɒnkriːt] Beton [3] **panel** ['pænəl] Platte [4] **parapet** ['pærəpet] Brüstung [5] (to) **declare** [dɪ'kleə] **erklären** [6] **independence** Unabhängigkeit [7] **incredible** [ɪn'kredəbl] unglaublich [8] **lighthouse** Leuchtturm

Text 2

Underground New York from the novel by Cecile Rossant

Describe graffiti you know in your town and the places you find it. Say if you think it is art. Is it OK to spray graffiti anywhere? Discuss.

Sister and brother Zoe and Basti from Darmstadt are visiting their cousins Rick and Debby, who live in NYC. Rick is 16 and along with his friends Moog and Raul wants to show Zoe and Basti the Freedom Tunnel – a sight you won't find in any travel guide. But is the adventure worth the risk?

"Next stop: 125th Street – Martin Luther King Boulevard,"said the voice over the speakers. It had been a long slow ride on the Uptown local train and they were all standing in front of the doors, ready to get off when the train pulled into the station.
"Moog, Raul! Hey, man!" yelled Rick to the two boys who walked towards them. Rick came up to a chubby[1] but tall boy and they gave each other a soul shake: they touched forearms[2] then slid down to their hands, ending in a hook action with three of their fingers. Rick's friend was wearing a big white T-shirt and long, baggy[3] cargo shorts. He was smiling as if he was ready to tell a joke. The other boy was wearing a black woolen hat and was even taller and skinnier than Basti. He walked up to Rick and performed the same greeting, adding a shoulder bump to the mix.
"These are my cousins, Basti and Zoe," said Rick.
"Hi, I'm Moog and this is Raul," he said and put out his hand. "You guys live in Germany, right?"
"Yes, we live in Darmstadt – it's close to Frankfurt. You know Frankfurt?" asked Basti.
"I know frankfurters – you know the kind you can eat – hot dogs," said Moog and laughed.
"Well, we are Frankfurters … but not that kind. We call hot dogs *Wiener Würstchen* – have you ever heard of them?" asked Basti.
"Yeah, yeah – we sometimes call hot dogs wieners, but I've never heard that other word, what was it … worstchain?"
"Yes, something like that," said Basti laughing.
"OK, we can continue with the language lesson later. I think we should head out now while the sun is still high," said Raul and started to walk towards the stairs. […]

"That's the tunnel entrance," said Moog pointing to a dark, square opening with grass and even small trees growing on top. They walked along a gravel[4] path next to the tracks until they reached the tunnel opening.
"I think we should wait here for a train to go by," said Rick.
"Really, man?" said Raul, shaking his head.
"Yeah, come on, Rick. If one just passed by, we might have to wait here another half an hour," added Moog, kicking a few bits of gravel towards the metal tracks.
"Well, I don't think one just went by. We would have heard it. We weren't that far away. And besides, this is Basti and Zoe's first time down here and their second day in New York! If anything happens, man, it will be my fault. I want to make it as safe as possible," said Rick, kicking a few more pebbles[5] at the tracks.
"Rick – you, Zoe and I could also wait here. Moog and Raul should go ahead if they want," suggested Basti.

---

[1] **chubby** ['tʃʌbi] mollig [2] **forearm** ['fɔːrɑːm] Unterarm [3] **baggy** ['bægi] weit (geschnitten) [4] **gravel** ['grævəl] Schotter
[5] **pebble** ['pebl] Kieselstein

"I don't …" – whatever Rick was going to say, the thundering[1] sound of an approaching[2] train was cutting him off. The five kids jumped back into the green area just as the train raced by, kicking gravel and dust into the air. It blew its horn as if to say: I know you kids are there. As soon as the train passed, Moog started running into the tunnel screaming like a madman.

"Stop! Wait!" shouted Rick, but Moog didn't turn back.

"We should all check our watches. It's 11:05 now. That means the next train will be at 11:45. OK?"

"OK, OK … now, let's get going!" said Raul impatiently[3], shifting[4] his backpack on his back and taking a few wide strides[5] into the tunnel.

"Wow!" he screamed, "look at that light!" The tunnel was about 6 meters high and 18 meters wide. Although it was bright and sunny outside, the tunnel was very dark. About every 20 meters, sunlight from openings above cut into the tunnel's thick darkness. You could almost touch the light with your fingers.

"Oooh eeee!" That was Moog and the tunnel echoed[6] back and made funny changes to his voice.

Raul tried out his voice with a loud "Hellooooo, hellooo …," then Zoe echoed him, "Haaaaallo, haaaallo …" […]

Crunch, crunch, crunch was the sound of the stones under their feet as they went deeper into the tunnel. Gravel and dirt[7] mixed with all kinds of garbage that covered the ground next to the tracks. There were empty cans[8] of spray paint, old clothes, shoes, blankets[9], and plastic dolls[10] with dirty faces. The air became cooler and had a strange smell of rusty[11] metal, machine oil, old garbage and earth. The colors that had filled their eyes that morning were gone: the green of the trees, the blue sky, and the bright sunlight. Now there were the grays, browns and blacks of this underworld. Color appeared only in the explosion of graffiti on the tunnel walls. […]

When Raul and Moog found an empty section[12] of wall, they set down their bags, took out their paints and started shaking the cans. Rick, Basti and Zoe stopped to watch. Soon the two boys were doing a kind of hip hop dance in front of the wall while spraying on their names. Moog wasn't Moog's real name. He shared it with the rabbit robot character that Zoe had seen on some of Rick's stickers. As the rabbit's ears and face began to appear on the tunnel wall, Rick, Zoe and Basti walked on into the darkness of the tunnel. To the left and to the right colorful graffiti burst[13] out from the walls. "Man, this is great stuff!" said Rick. "There should also be real paintings down here. Here! Look at this!" Rick jumped in front of a long wall painting that was over three meters high and about 30 meters long. […]

"This is a painting by a guy who called himself 'Freedom'," explained Rick. "The tunnel is named after him. I've read about him on the Internet. His real name is Chris Pape and he even lived down here for a while. There are a lot more of his paintings further down in the tunnel," said Rick. He realized that he sounded like a museum guide who explains the artwork to a small group of tourists. So he quickly said, "Now I need to find a good place to do my own work." The best places directly under the light from above were all taken.

"How about here?" suggested Basti and stopped. He pointed to an area where somebody had started a graffiti but not finished it. The wall was white in some places, but there was still a large area that was untouched.

"That's great, Basti," said Rick excitedly. He dropped his bag and took out all of his spray cans. "Can you start shaking some of these? You can also use them if you want. You could even just write 'Basti the Frankfurter, 2009'!"

"I'll just start with the shaking," said Basti.

"I'm going to walk on and take some more pictures," said Zoe.

"Do you want me to come with you?" asked Basti vigorously[14] shaking one of the cans.

---

[1] **thundering** ['θʌndərɪŋ] donnernd [2] **approaching** [ə'prəʊtʃɪŋ] sich nähernd [3] **impatiently** [ɪm'peɪʃntli] ungeduldig [4] (to) **shift** [ʃɪft] verschieben [5] **stride** [straɪd] Schritt [6] (to) **echo** ['ekəʊ] widerhallen [7] **dirt** [dɜːt] Schmutz [8] **can** [kæn] Dose [9] **blanket** ['blæŋkɪt] Decke [10] **doll** [dɒl] Puppe [11] **rusty** ['rʊsti] rostig [12] **section** ['sekʃn] Abschnitt [13] (to) **burst** [bɜːst] explodieren [14] **vigorously** ['vɪgərəsli] energisch

"No, that's all right. I'll be back very soon, don't worry."
Zoe took a sip of water from her bottle and headed out. [...]

At each spot where light entered, the wall below was washed in light.[1] It was just like an art gallery or a museum, where strong spot lights light up the paintings on the walls. And there were paintings here, too – real paintings. [...]

Copies of Leonardo da Vinci, or was it Michelangelo? One had the face of an angel.

Another was just the body of a woman and a man like those old Greek statues with no arms and no heads. She reached 107th Street – she knew because the sign on the wall told her. Below the little sign was the strangest painting she had seen yet. It was a picture of a figure in a black sweat jacket with a spray paint can for a head.
"Wow, komisch ..." she heard herself say outloud. [...]

Zoe checked her watch. 11:35! She had been wandering alone for over 20 minutes so there must be another train soon. The others were blocks away. What did Rick say? Get as far away from the tracks as possible. Get out of sight of the train driver. Find a niche[2] in the wall. Press yourself against the wall before the train comes. That means NOW! Zoe was scared – her hands were shaking. "I've got about eight minutes." She ran over the tracks to the wall. She tried to get around a pile[3] of garbage, but by mistake[4] she stepped on a soft and very dirty teddy bear that lay in her path. She saw an opening or door on the other side. Zoe ran over. There was a door. There were even a few steps leading up to it. Painted on the wall next to the door were the words 'Home Sweet Home'. No train can come up here, she thought and hopped[5] up the steps. She pushed open the door and stepped in.[6] It was totally dark inside the room. My flashlight![7] she thought happily and reached inside her backpack. Flick went the switch. She heard a sound. Movement. A little snort.[8] With the light illuminating[9] the little room, Zoe met eye to eye with an old man. He was sitting at a large metal desk and looked at her with a surprised look.
"Entschuldigung! Ich ... I ... I'm sorry ..."
"German! You're German?!" said the man in a gruff[10] voice. "Who are you?"
"My name is Zoe. I was just ..."
"And you're German, right?"

1 The Freedom Tunnel

a) Describe the Freedom Tunnel.
Name the risks of walking through it.

b) Explain why the Freedom Tunnel attracts graffiti artists.

c) Say if you would walk through this tunnel.
Give reasons why or why not.

2 The man in the tunnel

Who is the man Zoe meets?
Give him a name and create a short biography.
Explain why he is down there and why is he so interested in the fact that Zoe is German.

---

[1] **washed in light** mit Licht ausgeleuchtet [2] **niche** [niːʃ] Nische [3] **pile** [paɪl] Haufen [4] **by mistake** aus Versehen
[5] (to) **hop** springen [6] (to) **step in** hineingehen [7] **flashlight** ['flæʃlaɪt] (AE) Taschenlampe [8] **snort** [snɔːt] Schnauben
[9] (to) **illuminate** [ɪ'luːmɪneɪt] aufleuchten [10] **gruff** [grʌf] rau

… Amazing grace, how sweet the sound,

Text 3

Amazing Grace: History of a song

Name the most popular songs that both you and your family know and sing.

Imagine: A hymn which was written in the 1770s by a British slave trader is sung 240 years later by the first African American president of the United States, Barack Obama, in front of 5,500 people. The hymn, *Amazing Grace*[1], is one of the most popular songs ever. It has been recorded thousands of times and there are countless[2] performances every year. Where does it come from? Why is it so popular? And why did President Obama sing it?

The story of *Amazing Grace* begins with Englishman John Newton, a seaman in the Atlantic slave trade. Newton liked to curse[3], drink and make fun of his captain. There is a story that he angered[4] his captain so often that he was once forced to work on a plantation as a slave as punishment.

John Newton (1725–1807)

Then, in 1748, Newton's ship was caught in a storm off the coast of Ireland. He called out to God to save him, and survived. From then on, he promised, he would lead a Christian[5] life. It is sometimes said that he wrote the first verse of *Amazing Grace* while his boat was being repaired[6]. However, Newton continued his work in the slave trade for over six years before becoming a priest in the Church of England.

During his time as a priest, Newton wrote many hymns. He published[7] *Amazing Grace* in a 1770s collection, but without a melody. It was probably chanted[8] in Newton's church services, not sung. Some years later, in 1789, the hymn travelled across the Atlantic and quickly became popular in the United States. At first it was sung to many different tunes[9], but in 1835 the composer William Walker linked the words to the melody "New Britain". That version, the one we know today, became a standard hymn in different American churches, and was especially popular as a gospel song among African Americans.

Mahalia Jackson, who performed in concert halls around the world, singing at a Civil Rights rally[10] in 1957

In the 20th century, *Amazing Grace* was also adopted[11] by movements of protest. African Americans, who knew it as a hymn, sang it at anti-discrimination marches in the 1950s and 60s. Later, it was sung by the protesters against the Vietnam War (1955–1975). Some of them didn't realize that it was originally a hymn.

Although written in Britain, by the 20th century *Amazing Grace* had been forgotten there. Then, in 1970, American folk singer Judy Collins recorded a version which reached #5 in the UK music charts.

---

[1] **amazing grace** [ə'meɪzɪŋ], [greɪs] erstaunliche Gnade [2] **countless** ['kaʊntləs] zahllos [3] (to) **curse** [kɜːs] fluchen [4] (to) **anger** ['æŋgə] ärgern [5] **Christian** ['krɪstʃən] christlich [6] (to) **repair** [rɪ'peə] reparieren [7] (to) **publish** ['pʌblɪʃ] veröffentlichen [8] (to) **chant** [tʃɑːnt] im Chor sprechen [9] **tune** [tjuːn] Melodie [10] **rally** ['ræli] Kundgebung [11] (to) **adopt** [ə'dɒpt] übernehmen

I once was lost but now am found,

That saved a wretch[1] like me.

Was blind, but now I see.

The song travelled back across the Atlantic to Britain, and to other countries around the world. It has since been recorded by singers like Aretha Franklin, Rod Stewart, Celine Dion and Beyoncé. In 1972, a new version, played for the first time with bagpipes, was recorded by a Scottish regiment in the British Army. It reached #1 in the UK charts and #11 in the US. Today, around the world, the bagpipe version is often played at the funerals of police officers and soldiers killed in service.

What is unusual about *Amazing Grace* is the way it appeals[2] to people whatever their age, race[3], region, religion or political beliefs[4]. Is it the words or the music that move the listener? Or a combination of both? Or the different styles of the many recordings, which offer something to many tastes?

Whatever the reason, the song seems to give people hope and strength at difficult times, whether they're campaigning[5] for a better world or at times of sadness[6] and loss[7].

It was at such a moment that President Obama sang *Amazing Grace* in public[8] in 2015. Some days earlier, a 21-year-old white man had murdered the Reverend Clementa Pinckney and eight other African Americans at a church in Charleston, South Carolina. Obama had come to honour[9] the victims[10]. In his speech, he spoke of how he understood the Christian idea of grace. It was the power of grace, he said, which helped the families of the victims to forgive[11] the killer of their loved ones. It was grace which showed up the mistakes that America had made. And it was grace, he believed, that would help people to change America for the better and build goodwill[12] between all races. At the end of his speech the President slowly started singing the first verse of *Amazing Grace*. The church leaders behind him and the audience joined him in song.

President Barack Obama singing Amazing Grace in 2015.

1 English hymn to world hit

a) Say what you think the first four lines of *Amazing Grace* meant to John Newton.

b) Describe the "journey" of *Amazing Grace* from English hymn to world hit.
Then say what you think of the song.

2 The President's speech

Watch part of President Obama's speech. Describe how the audience reacts to his words and his singing.

Say why you think he sang.

[1] **wretch** [retʃ] Sünder/in [2] (to) **appeal to sb.** [ə'pi:l] jn. ansprechen [3] **race** [reɪs] ethnische Gruppe [4] **belief** [bɪ'li:f] Glaube, Meinung [5] (to) **campaign** [kæm'peɪn] sich einsetzen [6] **sadness** ['sædnəs] Traurigkeit [7] **loss** [lɒs] Verlust [8] **in public** ['pʌblɪk] in der Öffentlichkeit [9] (to) **honour** ['ɒnə] ehren [10] **victim** ['vɪktɪm] Opfer [11] (to) **forgive sb.** [fə'gɪv] jn. vergeben [12] **goodwill** [ˌgʊd'wɪl] Wohlwollen

Text 4

Who wants to be a celebrity?

Hollywood *by Madonna*

Everybody comes to Hollywood
They wanna make it in the neighbourhood
They like the smell of it in Hollywood
How could it hurt you when it looks so good?
Shine your light now
This time it's got to be good
You get it right now
Cause you're in Hollywood

There's something in the air in Hollywood
The sun is shining like you knew it would
You're riding in your car in Hollywood
You got the top down and it feels so good

Everybody comes to Hollywood
They wanna make it in the neighbourhood
They like the smell of it in Hollywood
How could it hurt you when it looks so good?

I lost my memory in Hollywood
I've had a million visions bad and good
There's something in the air in Hollywood
I tried to leave it but I never could

Shine your light now
This time it's got to be good
You get it right now yeah
Cause you're in Hollywood
There's something in the air in Hollywood
I've lost my reputation bad and good
You're riding in your car in Hollywood
You got the top down and it feels so good

Music stations always play the same songs
I'm bored with the concept of right and wrong

Everybody comes to Hollywood
They wanna make it in the neighbourhood
They like the smell of it in Hollywood
How could it hurt you when it looks so good?

Shine your light now
This time it's got to be good
You get it right now yeah
Cause you're in Hollywood
Cause you're in Hollywood
Cause you're in Hollywood
In Hollywood
In Hollywood
In Hollywood

Check it out
This bird has flown

Shine your light now
This time it's got to be good
You get it right now yeah
Cause you're in Hollywood
Cause you're in Hollywood
Cause you're in Hollywood
In Hollywood
In Hollywood
In Hollywood

Push the button
Don't push the button
Trip the station
Change the channel
...

(to) **make it** [meɪk] es schaffen, Erfolg haben (to) **shine your light** [ʃaɪn] ein leuchtendes Beispiel sein **top** [tɒp] (Auto)Dach **memory** ['meməri] Gedächtnis **vision** ['vɪʒn] Vision **reputation** [ˌrepju'teɪʃn] Ruf **station** ['steɪʃn] (Radio)Sender **concept** ['kɒnsept] Konzept **button** ['bʌtn] Knopf (to) **trip the station** [trɪp] den Sender ausschalten

Fame *by David Bowie*

Fame makes a man take things over
Fame lets him loose, hard to swallow
Fame puts you there where things are hollow (fame)
Fame, it's not your brain, it's just the flame
That burns your change to keep you insane (fame)

Fame, (fame) what you like is in the limo
Fame, (fame) what you get is no tomorrow
Fame, (fame) what you need you have to borrow
Fame, (fame) it's mine, it's mine, it's just his line
To bind your time, it drives you to crime (fame)

Is it any wonder I reject you first?
Fame, fame, fame, fame
Is it any wonder you are too cool to fool? (fame)
Fame, bully for you, chilly for me
Got to get a rain check on pain (fame)

Fame
Fame, fame, fame
Fame, fame, fame
Fame, fame, fame, fame
Fame, fame, fame, fame
Fame, fame, fame
Fame, what's your name?
Fame

Madonna, the American singer, songwriter and actor who was born in 1958, has sold over 300 million records. Her song *Hollywood* came out in 2003.

David Bowie, the British singer and songwriter, was born in 1947 and died in 2016. His song *Fame*, which came out in 1975, was his first #1 hit in the United States.

a) Read the text of *Hollywood*. Then say
- what picture of Hollywood it gives you
- what Hollywood promises the people who go there.

b) Read the text of *Fame*. What is the song's message about being famous? Which lines of the song tell you this?

c) Say what link you see between the two songs.

d) Give examples of how people can become famous.

e) Listen to the two songs. Say which one you prefer, and why (the words, the music …?).

fame [feɪm] Berühmtheit (to) **let sb. loose** [luːs] jn. loslassen, befreien (to) **swallow** ['swɒləʊ] schlucken **hollow** ['hɒləʊ] hohl **brain** [breɪn] Gehirn **flame** [fleɪm] Flamme **insane** [ɪn'seɪn] verrückt (to) **bind** [baɪnd] binden (to) **drive** [draɪv] treiben **crime** [kraɪm] Verbrechen, Kriminalität (to) **reject** [rɪ'dʒekt] ablehnen (to) **fool** [fuːl] betrügen **bully for you** ['bʊli] Gratuliere! (ironisch) **chilly** ['tʃɪli] frostig **rain check** ['reɪntʃek] Gutschein **pain** [peɪn] Schmerz

Text 5

Native Americans

Before reading, say what the images on p. 123 tell you about the Native American peoples.

1 Ancient civilizations

When, in the 15th century, Europeans started arriving in North America and claiming[1] the lands for their kings and queens back home, the continent was not empty. People already lived there, and had done so for about 16,000 years. Civilizations had grown and declined.[2] The Ancestral Pueblo culture, for example, had existed for over 1,000 years before starting to die out around 1300. Climate change in the Southwest led to drought and famine, and the people were forced to leave their settlements,[3] like the cliff dwellings[4] at Mesa Verde, Colorado, and move away to find food.

2 Over 500 Nations

When the Europeans arrived, millions of people already lived all over the continent in more than 500 different tribes, from the east to the west coasts, from the ice-covered Arctic North to the hot Southwest. These nations spoke hundreds of different languages, far more than in Europe at that time, and there was great cultural variety.[5] The map below shows the ten different "culture areas" of the native population.
Each area is a different landscape and climate zone and was home to tribes with similar lifestyles.

Native American Culture Areas

3 Lifestyes and livelihoods.[6]

Native American lifestyles differed greatly. Some tribes were nomadic. Others were sedentary,[7] and built permanent settlements, where they lived from hunting and gathering (getting food from wild animals and plants) or from crops like corn, squash[8] and beans, which they grew on farms. These lifestyles were influenced[9] by landscape and climate. In the cold Subarctic, people had to move around to find food. But where land was fertile,[10] or nature provided[11] enough food, tribes were usually sedentary. In the Northwest, for example, where there were a lot of fish, whales, seals, etc., people lived in villages in solid wood houses.

Lifestyles were influenced by other factors too. For example, before European contact, Plains Indians lived in villages from hunting and farming. But after the Spanish introduced horses around 1750, they became nomadic, followed herds of buffalo, and lived in tepees made of buffalo skins. As the tepee shows, the dwellings of Native Americans were influenced by their lifestyles, as well as by the climate and the available building materials. Dwellings differed greatly, from the tepee, to the stone and adobe houses of the Southwest, to the longhouses of the Eastern Woodlands. You can see some examples on the next page.

[1] (to) **claim** beanspruchen [2] (to) **decline** [dɪˈklaɪn] untergehen [3] **settlement** [ˈsetlmənt] Siedlung [4] **dwelling** Unterkunft
[5] **variety** [vəˈraɪəti] Vielfalt [6] **livelihood** [ˈlaɪvlihʊd] Lebensunterhalt [7] **sedentary** [ˈsedntri] sesshaft [8] **squash** [skwɒʃ] Kürbis
[9] (to) **influence** [ˈɪnfluəns] beeinflussen [10] **fertile** [ˈfɜːtaɪl] fruchtbar [11] (to) **provide** [prəˈvaɪd] bereitstellen

Area Northwest Coast
Tribe Tlingit
Dwelling Wooden cabin
Lifestyle Sedentary
Livelihood Hunting and fishing

Only in this area did tribes traditionally make totem poles.

Area Southwest
Tribe Pueblo
Dwelling Adobe house
Lifestyle Sedentary
Livelihood Mainly farming

Some adobe houses are up to 800 years old. The ladder, a traditional feature, reaches up to heaven.

Area Southwest
Tribe Apache
Dwelling Wickiup
Lifestyle Nomadic
Livelihood Hunting/Gathering

Wickiups could be built quickly with simple materials.

Area Great Plains
Tribe Oglala Lakota
Dwelling Tepee
Lifestyle Nomadic from c. 1750
Livelihood Buffalo

This historical photo shows a girl on a reservation in South Dakota in 1891. By this time, white settlers had killed most of the buffalo, which had given the Lakota their food, clothes and housing. The Lakota had lost their livelihood and their land.

Area Southwest
Tribe Ancestral Pueblo
Dwelling Cliff dwelling
Lifestyle Sedentary
Livelihood Mainly farming

'Apartment blocks' like these at Mesa Verde were built against cliffs to make them easier to defend or maybe be closer to seep springs[12] (water). They could house many families.

Area Eastern Woodlands
Tribe Iroquois
Dwelling Longhouse
Lifestyle Sedentary
Livelihood Mainly farming

Longhouses housed clans of up to 60 people. Inside, mats were used to divide them into rooms.

Area Southeast
Tribe Cherokee
Dwelling Asi
Lifestyle Sedentary
Livelihood Mainly farming

Asis were permanent structures which took a long time to build. Cherokee villages were made up of large numbers of them.

[12] **seep spring** ['siːp sprɪŋ] Sickerquelle

4 How many?

It is difficult to say how many people lived in North America before European contact, but many historians suggest a figure of around 10 million. The first time Native Americans were counted across the United States was in the 1890 census.[1] By then the figure had fallen to under half a million. What had happened?

Native American population in the present-day area of the USA

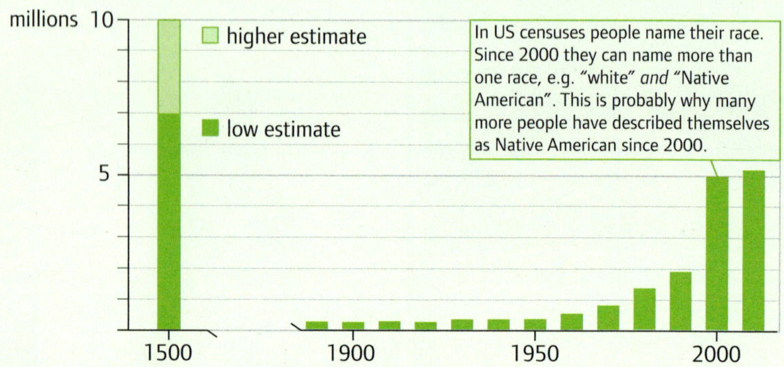

5 Disease

When Europeans started sailing to the Americas after Christopher Columbus's famous voyage to the New World in 1492, they had more than people, animals, weapons and other goods on board.

Their ships were full of invisible[2] guests too – the viruses that caused diseases like smallpox[3] or chicken pox.[4]

These diseases were common in Europe and Asia, so people there had some immunity to them. But the diseases did not exist in the Americas, so native people had no immunity.

The diseases moved from community to community much faster than Europeans themselves and huge numbers died from them. For that reason, European settlers and explorers often arrived in villages and country that seemed almost empty – most of the people who once lived there had died from European diseases and their communities had collapsed.

6 Loss[5] of land and livelihood

Between 1600 and 1900 tens of millions of Europeans came to make a new life in North America. These settlers, with the help of the US government, pushed the native people off their traditional lands. Although the US government made treaties[6] with Native American tribes which gave them land rights, it often broke these treaties and took the land away again. The tribes were forced to live on reservations, very often on poor land that settlers did not want. If they tried to resist[7] losing their lands, the US government often made war on them.

7 Recovery[8]

By the late 19th century, there were only about 350,000 Native Americans left in North America. Since then, their numbers have recovered as they have won more rights. They can govern themselves in their reservations (though most Native Americans live in cities like any other Americans) and are working hard to keep their cultures and languages alive.

a) **Find these numbers or dates in the text and say what they refer to:**

16,000 · 1300 · 500 · 1750 · 10 million · 1492 · 1600–1900 · 350,000

b) **Explain what the graph above tells us about Native Americans in North America. Say why you think there is no information about the period 1500–1890.**

c) You choose **Find out more about one of these topics and report to the class.**

two of the dwellings on p. 125 | a war between Native Americans and whites | Native-American life today

[1] **census** ['sensəs] Volkszählung [2] **invisible** [ɪn'vɪzəbl] unsichtbar [3] **smallpox** Pocken [4] **chicken pox** Windpocken [5] **loss** Verlust
[6] **treaty** ['triːti] Vertrag [7] (to) **resist** [rɪ'zɪst] Widerstand leisten [8] **recovery** [rɪ'kʌvəri] Erholung, Aufschwung

Text 6

Ghost dance by Robbie Robertson - from the album *Music for the Native Americans*

Crow[1] has brought the message
to the children of the sun
for the return of the buffalo
and for a better day to come

You can kill my body
You can damn[2] my soul[3]
for not believing in your god
and some world down below

Chorus:
You don't stand a chance[4]
against my prayers
You don't stand a chance
against my love
They outlawed[5] the Ghost Dance
but we shall live again,
we shall live again

My sister above
She has red paint
She died at Wounded Knee
like a latter day saint[6]

You got the big drum in the distance[7]
blackbird in the sky
That's the sound that you hear
when the buffalo cry

Chorus:
You don't stand a chance …

Crazy Horse was a mystic
He knew the secret of the trance
And Sitting Bull the great apostle
of the Ghost Dance

Come on Comanche
Come on Blackfoot
Come on Shoshone
Come on Cheyenne

We shall live again

Come on Arapaho
Come on Cherokee
Come on Paiute
Come on Sioux

We shall live again

Canadian **Robbie Robertson**, born 1943, became famous as the lead guitarist of *The Band*, Bob Dylan's backing group and a cult rock group in their own right.[8] The son of a Mohawk Native American mother and a Jewish father, Robertson spent part of his childhood[9] on the Six Nations Reservation. He returned to his native roots[10] with his 1994 album *Music for the Native Americans*.

The Ghost Dance by the Oglala Lakota at Pine Ridge, 1890

The **Ghost Dance** movement began amongst the Paiute tribe in the 1870s and then spread all over the West. It was a reaction to the poverty,[11] hunger and disease of life on the reservations. Those who did the Ghost Dance believed it would make the white settlers disappear and return the land, buffalo and a good life to the Natives. Although the Ghost Dance movement was peaceful, it alarmed many white Americans and the government outlawed it. The conflict this caused ended in December 1890 with the shooting of Lakota leader Sitting Bull and the massacre of 153 Lakota, mainly women and children, at Wounded Knee on the Pine Ridge Reservation, SD.

a) Read about the ghost dance movement. Then listen to the song and say what sort of music it is and what makes it sound Native American.

b) Use what you have found out to explain the meaning behind the following lines of the song: *ll.3–4, ll.9–19, l.14, l.16, l.19, ll.27–28*

---

[1] **crow** [krəʊ] Krähe [2] (to) **damn** [dæm] verdammen [3] **soul** [səʊl] Seele [4] (to) **stand a chance** eine Chance haben [5] (to) **outlaw** ['aʊtlɔː] gesetzlich verbieten [6] **latter day saint** [lætə], [seɪnt] Heilige(r) der Letzten Tage [7] **distance** ['dɪstəns] Ferne [8] **in their own right** selbst [9] **childhood** ['tʃaɪldhʊd] Kindheit [10] **root** [ruːt] Wurzel [11] **poverty** ['pɒvəti] Armut

2 A weekend in New York City (Gerunds as object or subect)

p. 19 **Part A Practice**

**Two British teens discuss what to do in New York.
Complete the text with the gerund of the correct verb in brackets.**

Zara: I like (go/visit) [1]going to museums. What about you?
Dom: (Go/Visit) [2]... museums is OK, but it can be boring.
Zara: What do you enjoy (be/do) [3]..., then? Do you like (be/spend) [4]... in the fresh air? Central Park isn't far.
Dom: (Be/Spend) [5]... time in a park isn't a good idea. You can do that anywhere. What I like (do/go) [6]... on a city holiday is (queue/see) [7]... all the main sights.
Zara: How about the big shops on Fifth Avenue?
Dom: Shops? Do you really like (take/try) [8]... on clothes and (spend/stand) [9]... money on things you don't need?
Zara: Maybe the Statue of Liberty, then?
Dom: That's a cool idea. And (go/take) [10]... the ferry is a good way to see the harbour too.
Zara: It says here online that you have to wait 90 minutes for a ferry. And I hate (queue/visit) [11]... .
Dom: I don't mind (spend/stand) [12]... in a queue for that! You can go to the shops while I'm waiting, if you like.

1 Different words

p. 20 **Access to words**

a) In each pair of words you can find the BE and AE for the same thing. Decide which is which. Then make two lists. Use a dictionary if you need help.

apartment : flat	*elevator : lift*	*holiday(s) : vacation*	*pullover : sweater*
autumn : fall	*flashlight : torch*	*jam : jelly*	*restroom : toilet*
biscuit : cookie	*football : soccer*	*line : queue*	*shop : store*
candy : sweets	*game : match*	*mom : mum*	*sneakers : trainers*
cell phone : mobile	*garbage : rubbish*	*pants : trousers*	*subway : underground*
chips : French fries	*garden : yard*	*pavement : sidewalk*	*takeaway : takeout*

flat ⟷ apartment
autumn ⟷ ...

2 Free time in New York (Gerund or infinitive)

p. 27 **Part B Practice**

b) Write sentences like in a) about your plans for next weekend and compare them with a partner. You can use the table below for ideas and help with your sentences.

I'm keen on / **I like**	art / computer games / Italian food / football / music / nature / sport / ...	so	I can imagine / I'd enjoy / I wouldn't mind	going ... / spending ... / staying ... / visiting ... / ...
I need	a light for my bike / new football boots / a new phone / some toys for my cat / a present for my mum / ...		I'm planning / I'm hoping / I'm expect	to go / to spend / to stay / to visit / ...
I want to / **I'd like to**	be outside/ do something different / go into town / see something new / spend some time with my dad / ...			

3 I hope you're all looking forward to … (Gerunds after prepositions)

p. 27 Part B Practice

Cindy Liu is welcoming people to a walking tour of Chinatown. Complete her announcement. Choose the correct preposition and verb for each gap and put the verb into the gerund.

Hi, everyone, I'm Cindy. I hope you're all looking forward [1] to [2] exploring Chinatown today. I know *I'm* very excited [3]… [4]… you my neighborhood. Our tour is just over two miles – from East Broadway to Lafayette Street and back– but I know you're all keen [5]… [6]…! We'll see all the sights, including Columbus Park, where everyone meets up for card games. If you're good [7]… [8]…, maybe you can even join in! We'll also pass New York's oldest Chinese store, so how [9]… [10]… there to buy some souvenirs? Finally, I'm sure you'll all be interested [11]… [12]… traditional Chinese food. I know some good places for street snacks, but if you prefer the idea [13]… [14]… to a restaurant, I can sugest a few.

- about – stop
- about – show
- at – play
- in –try
- of – go
- on – walk
- ~~to – explore~~

2 A blog post from New York (*that, than, as … as*)

p. 31 Part C Practice

You can use clauses with *that, than, as … as* to compare things.
Complete the blog post by a tourist in New York. Use the words from the box.

Today I got to Central Park! I enjoyed it just [1]… much [2]… I had thought I would. It's the biggest city park [3]… I've ever seen. And it's lovely too, much [4]… beautiful [5]… I had imagined. It even has [6]… attractions [7]… you'll find in Hyde Park in London, including a castle and some forests. And there are lakes with boats. Taking one out cost [8]… money [9]… I had expected, so I spent two hours on the water. Unfortunately, there were lots of other boats too, so it wasn't [10]… relaxing [11]… I had hoped. However, I really loved the views of New York's skyline. They were actually even better [12]… they looked in the tourist brochures.

- as … as (2x)
- less … than (1x)
- more … than (2x)
- than (1x)
- that (1x)

3 Chinatown and Little Italy (*although, (even) though, even if*)

p. 31 Part C Practice

You can use *although, (even) though* or *even if* to make contrasts.
Contrast clauses can come in first or second position in a sentence.
Put the words in the boxes into the correct order to make contrast clauses.

1. [in New York City] [Although] [five Chinatowns] [there are] [,] **most people only know of the one in Manhattan.**
2. You really feel as if you're in China there, [New York] [in the middle of] [you're] [even though] [.]
3. Try and have walk through the neighborhood, [a Chinese meal there] [even if] [stop for] [you don't] [.]
4. Little Italy has kept its name, [most Italians] [even though] [years ago] [moved away] [.]
5. It's an expensive neighborhood today, [poor immigrants] [though] [the home of] [it was originally] [.]
6. the restaurants [Although] [in Little Italy] [cheap] [aren't] [,] huge numbers of tourists eat there.

1 REVISION A note from Mom (Conditional sentences 1)

← p. 44 Part A Practice

Jasmine finds a note from her mom. Complete it with the correct form of the verbs in brackets.

Hi Jaz, If I [1]... (leave) work on time, I [2]... (be) home at six. You [3]... (find) some chocolate in the cupboard if you [4]... (want) a snack. But remember, if you [5]... (eat) too much, you [6]... (not be) hungry at dinner time. About dinner tonight: If you [7]... (like), I [8]... (make) spaghetti. But if you [9]... (not want) that again, I [10]... (go) to the market on my way home. By the way, your dad has lost his key, so if he [11]... (get) back early, you [12]... (have to) let him in. Mom xx

2 REVISION ... if people ate less meat (Conditional sentences 2)

← p. 44 Part A Practice

Three friends are talking about food. Put the verbs into the correct form to complete their dialogue.

1 Dom: There ... (be) more space to grow plants if people ... (eat) less meat.
2 Zara: But if I ... (become) a vegetarian, I ... (have to) give up bacon and sausages.
3 Dom: I'm sure you ... (like) vegetarian food if you ... (try) a few dishes.
4 Zara: And if I ... (learn) how to cook, I ... (be able to) make a meal for our friends.
5 Dom: Look, Todd, you ... (feel) healthier if you ... (not eat) so much sweet food.
6 Todd: Well, I ... (eat) less chocolate if it ... (not be) so delicious.
7 Dom: If you ... (buy) fruit instead, you ... (probably enjoy) it.
8 Todd: If fresh fruit ... (not cost) so much, then maybe I ... (buy) some.

3 REVISION Crazy situations (Conditional sentences 1 and 2)

← p. 44 Part A Practice

Make as many conditional sentences 1 and 2 as you can to talk about these pictures

Conditional 1: If the girl isn't careful, that dog will bite her.
Conditional 2: If I met that dog, I'd be scared.

1

2

3

These sentence beginnings can help you.

If the small dog stops barking, ...
If the big dog gets angry, ...
If the girl takes her dog away, ...

If I were the big dog, ...
If I owned the small dog, ...
If I had a dangerous dog, ...

If the alligator is hungry, ...
If the alligator eats the fish, ...
If the boy isn't careful,...

If I were the fish, ...
If I went fishing, ...
If the boy fell into the water, ...

If the boy says sorry, ...
If the monkey likes ice cream, ...
If the woman's jacket is new, ...

If it was my jacket, ...
If the ice cream was mine, ...
If I were the monkey, ...

3 I wish I had been more careful (*wish* + past perfect)

p. 49 Part B Practice

a) Look at pictures A–D. Think about possible reasons why each situation happened.
Now imagine you are the person in the pictures. Make sentences with *I wish …* for each situation.
– I wish I had got up earlier. / I wish I hadn't …
The ideas below the pictures can help you.

A

B

C

D

A
- *wake up earlier*
- *run faster*
- *not go to bed so late*
- *do more sport*

B
- *not go outside*
- *check my weather app*
- *take an umbrella*
- *wear a raincoat*

C
- *not go into the shop*
- *take off my my rucksack*
- *see the lamp on the table*

D
- *see the tree*
- *ask Mum to drive*
- *take a taxi*
- *not drive so fast*

4 You woudn't have broken your leg … (Conditional sentences 3)

p. 49 Part B Practice

c) Write a short dialogue with a person from one of the pictures in 3. Use one conditional 3 sentence.
You can use the ideas below.
Act out your dialogue.

A
A: I missed the bus this morning.
B: I guess you wish you (run) faster.
A: Or if I (wake up) earlier, I (not be) late.

B
A: I got very wet yesterday.
B: Do you wish you (not go) outside?
A: Well, if I (wear) a coat, I (not get) wet.

C
A: I have to pay for that lamp I broke.
B: I bet you wish you (be) more careful.
A: Yes, if I (be) more careful, I (not break) it.

D
A: I had an accident in my car yesterday.
B: I bet you wish you (take) a taxi.
A: Right, if I (take) a taxi, I (not hit) that tree.

1 Very big or absolutely huge? (Adverbs of degree)

p. 54 Part C Practice

b) Match each adverb of degree to the most suitable adjective.

Adverbs of degree	Adjectives	
1 absolutely · very	big · huge	*very big, absolutely huge*
2 fairly · totally	difficult · impossible	
3 absolutely · very	cheap · free	
4 absolutely · fairly	delicious · tasty	
5 a bit · totally	hungry · starving	
6 a bit · completely	quiet · silent	
7 quite · very	nice · amazing	
8 a bit · absolutely	bad · disgusting	
9 completely quite	dead · ill	

1 I think Hailey will ... (*will*-future)

p. 68 Part A Practice

Hailey's mom said: *"I'm sure you'll love L.A."* Discuss what you think she will/won't do there.

I think I don't think Maybe I hope I'm sure	Hailey will she'll want to she'll she won't	have a nice chat with Brandon Williams spend time in the L.A. Natural History Musuem do a bus tour of famous people's homes meet lots of movie stars go and see the Walk of Fame visit a big movie studio go to Disneyland take a selfie with the Hollywood sign go to Venice beach buy some cool clothes in expensive shops

3 Friends and their plans (*will*-future or *going to*-future)

p. 68 Part A Practice

Some friends are discussing plans. Complete their dialogues with the correct form of the gven verbs.

Tim: I [1]... (visit) my grandma this weekend.
Flo: That's nice. I hope you [2]... (have) a good time.
Tim: Thanks. I think it [3]... probably ... (be) fun.

Jon: Maybe I [4]... (see) you on Saturday?
Sam: Sorry, but I [5]... (help) my dad in the garden all day.
Jon: [6]... you ... (work) in the garden on Sunday too?

Ben: I [7]... (give) a presentation on starfish next week.
May: Cool topic! I'm sure everyone [8]... (love) it.
Ben: Thanks. I hope you [9]... (come) and watch me

Liz: [10]... you ... (prepare) for next week's test?
Pip: No, I [11]... (not do) anything.
Liz: Well, I am, because I don't think it [12]... (be) easy.

3 Text messages (Present progressive or spontaneous *will*)

p. 75 Part B Practice

Read the text messages and complete the replies with the correct forms of the verbs.

1
Hey! What's up? Can we meet this evening?
Sorry mate, but (I · play) football tonight. (I · phone) you at the weekend, OK?

2
How's it going? What are you doing in the holidays?
I'm OK, thanks. (I · visit) my uncle in New York. (I · send) you a card when I'm there.

3
Hi. We need someone to feed the cat this weekend. Do you think Jack could do it?
I'm not sure.(I · ask) him, but I think (he · go) to London.

4
My computer isn't working – again! Can you help me, please?
OK (I · have) a look. (I · not do) anything else this evening.

5 Summer camp (Future, mixed forms: present progressive, *will*, *going to*)

p. 75 **Part B Practice**

Ben and Liz are talking about summer camp. Choose the correct future form to complete their dialogue.

Liz: [1]… (I'll go/I'm going) to summer camp in July. I can't wait.
Ben: Really? [2]… (I'm not going/I won't go) to camp again this year. Maybe [3]… (I'm staying/I'll stay) at home for a change.
Liz: Oh dear, that [4]… (isn't being/won't be) much fun.
Ben: Don't worry about me. I'm sure [5]… (I'll think/I'm thinking) of something interesting to do.
Liz: I don't think that [6]… (is being/will be) as much fun as camp. There's so much on this year's program.
Ben: For example?
Liz: One second, [7]… (I'll show/I'm showing) you the program.
Ben: Hmm, there *are* a lot of activities. What [8]… (are you choosing/are you going to choose)?
Liz: Well, first [9]… (I'm going to join/I'll join) the riding team.
Ben: I hope [10]… (you won't fall off/you aren't falling off) off your horse.
Liz: Haha, very funny. Listen, why don't you take the program and read it? Maybe [11]… (you'll find/you're going to find) something you like. Then you can come too.
Ben: OK, [12]… (I'll think/I'm going to think) about it.

4 The Walk of Fame (Defining and non-defining relative clauses)

p. 81 **Part C Practice**

Decide if the relative clauses below are defining or non-defining. Add commas where needed.

1 Tourists *who come to Hollywood* always visit the Walk of Fame.
2 The 70-year old Walk *which is 1.6 miles long* has about 3,000 stars.
3 On each star you'll see the name of a celebrity *who made their name in music or film.*
4 So you can take a selfie with some of the stars *you like best.*
5 Many young visitors look for Daniel Radcliffe's star *which was presented to him in 2015.*
6 Radcliffe *who is famous for playing Harry Potter* is the only Hogwarts student with a star.

2 Antonyms

p. 82 **Access to words**

An antonym is a word which means the opposite of another word.

a) Match the adjectives in box 1 to an antonym in box 2 and put them in a table.

1: dangerous · dark · dirty · dry · easy · expensive · interesting · kind · long · loud · quick · right · sad · small · stupid · traditional

2: boring · bright · cheap · clean · clever · cruel · difficult · happy · large · modern · quiet · safe · short · slow · wet · wrong

dangerous	safe
dark	…
…	

4 Yesterday in Mobridge (Simple past or past progressive?)

p. 94 Part A Practice

Look at the pictures and complete the text.
Use the correct form of the verb: simple past or past progressive.

Rob [1]saw • was seeing Kaya while he [2]walked • was walking down Main Street in Mobridge yesterday. He [3]smiled • was smiling and [4]shouted • was shouting her name a few times, but Kaya [5]didn't hear • wasn't hearing him. She [6]listened • was listening to music and she [7]didn't look • wasn't looking around when he [8]called • was calling her.

Drew's mom [1]walked • was walking down Main Street when a young exchange student [2]came • was coming up to her. He [3]looked • was looking for the post office and [4]asked • was asking Drew's mom for directions. She [5]went • was going towards the post office anyway, so she [6]offered • was offering to take him there.

4 What does this word mean? (State verbs and activity verbs)

p. 95 Part A Practice

Match the verbs in brackets to the gaps in the sentences and put them into the simple present.

1 What ... this strange word on this line ...? I ... it. (mean, not understand)
2 Dom ... football, so he ... to watch tomorrow's match. (hate, not want)
3 Who ... this blue bike? Can I use it if you ... it at the moment. (not need, own)
4 Brrr! I ... I'll wear a coat when I go out later. It ... to be a bit cold today. (seem, think)
5 Can you suggest something from the menu? I really ... what I ... to eat. (not know, want)

5 The choir's summer party (State verbs and activity verbs)

p. 95 Part A Practice

Rob and Tara are talking about their choir's summer party. Complete their dialogue.
Put the verbs in brackets into the correct form.

Rob: Hey, Tara! [1]Do you know who [2]... (help) with the choir's summer party this year?
Tara: Well, I [3]... (think) Hal and Liz [4]... (make) a list of volunteers. Why? [5]... *you* ... (want) to help?
Rob: I [6]... (think) about it. I [7]... (try) to play a bigger role in the choir this year. And anyway, I [8]... (like) parties.
Tara: Well, Liz [9]... (plan) a big lunch. I'm sure she [10]... (need) some help with the cooking. [11]... (have) you ... time for that?
Rob: [10]... you ... (joke)?! You [11]... (know) that there's nothing I [12] ... (hate) more than cooking.
Tara: I [13]... (not believe) you, Rob! You [14]... (make) it up. I'm sure you're an awesome cook.

1 Planning the choir party (Indirect speech)

p. 100 Part B Practice

Liz and Hal are organizing the MPHS choir party. Liz has spoken to some choir members about it. Imagine you're Liz. Report to Hal what everyone said.

1 Tara: I'**m** vegetarian. I **can** make a cheese dish.
*Tara said she **was** vegetarian and she **could** make a cheese dish.*
2 Tara: I'**ll ask** my mom to make some apple juice.
And she said she ... her mom to make some apple juice.
3 Ben: I really **love** apple juice. I **can bring** some paper cups.
Ben said he really ... apple juice and that he ... some paper cups.
4 Ben: I'**ve never cooked** before, but I'**ll try** to make a salad.
And he said he ... before, but he ... to make a salad.
5 Sue: My dad **isn't working** next week. I'**ll ask him** to make pizzas.
Sue said her dad ... next week, and she ... him to make pizzas.
6 Brad: I **don't know** how to bake a cake, but I **can buy** one.
Brad said he ... how to bake a cake, but he ... one.
7 Rob: I'**m not** very good at cooking, but I **can make** great sandwiches.
Rob said he ... very good at cooking, but he ... great sandwiches.
8 Rob: I ***wasn't able*** to go to last year's party, so I **can't wait** for this year's.
And he said he ... to go to last years's party, so he ... for this year's.

1 Adjectives from nouns (Suffixes: *-ful* and *-less*)

p. 104 Access to words

b) Make adjectives from the words you didn't need in a) and use them to write your own sentences. You can use some of the ideas below.

-ful: colour · event · truth

a colouful room/painting/garden
an eventful afternoon/day/life
a truthful answer/statement/person

-less: home · moon · rain

a homeless child/dog/person
a moonless night/evening/sky
a rainless month/summer/region

2 Nouns from adjectives (Abstract nouns with the suffix *-ness*)

p. 104 Access to words

Drew talks about South Dakota. Make nouns with *-ness* from the green adjectives. Then choose the correct place for each noun in the sentences on the right.

1 The people in South Dakota are so friendly.	I love the ... of the people ... in South Dakota.
2 They're kind and helpful too.	They're also known ... for their and ... .
3 I never feel lonely in Mobridge.	... just isn't a problem for ... me in Mobridge.
4 I love the empty roads and fields.	The ... of the ... roads and fields is something I love.
5 The dark nights make it easy to see the stars.	The ... at night makes it ... easy to see the stars.
6 It's amazing how bright they are.	Their ... is simply ... amazing.

One day, two stories

p. 20, exercise 1 Access to words

Fatima is a British girl on holiday in New York. She meets her American friend Paul. They both write down what they did that day. First read Paul's version. Then put Fatima's version in the right order.

Paul		Fatima
First thing in the morning, my cell phone rang.	a	I had only eaten a few biscuits. I was starving!
It was Fatima. She asked to meet me in front of my apartment.	b	Paul's place isn't far from from the underground station, so I was there quite quickly.
I live close to the subway, so it didn't take her long to get there.	c	When we finally went shopping, there were no nice trainers. So I looked for new trousers instead.
Fatima wanted a new pair of sneakers and she asked me to help her choose some. I said yes.	d	Paul had had enough, so I let him choose what to do next. And that meant watching hours of football on the TV in his room!
On the way to the store, we walked past some kids who were eating French fries on the sidewalk.	e	"That was a long queue for pizza," I said. We took our pullovers off and sat on them on the grass.
"That makes me hungry," she said. She'd only had a couple of cookies for breakfast.	f	We decided to get a takeaway. It was autumn, but the sun was out, so we wanted to eat it in the park.
"We should get takeout and eat in the park. " I said. It was a warm fall day. Too warm for sweaters.	g	I woke up, got dressed and called Paul on his mobile.
Lots of people had the same idea: we stood in line for ten minutes before we got our pizza.	h	On on our way, we walked past some people who were eating chips on the pavement.
When we finally got to the store, Fatima couldn't find any sneakers. Instead she tried on seventeen pairs of pants!	i	"Nice trainers," I said when I got there. "I need a new pair. Can we go into town and get some?" "Good idea," he said.
"Now it's my turn to decide what to do," I said. We went back to my place and watched some soccer.	j	"We should hang out," I said. "Let's meet on the street by your flat."

Missing letters

p. 21, exercise 2 Access to words

Complete the sentences with the letters from the box. Then decide if the sentences are BE or AE.

1 I think gray is a really boring … …. I never wear it. Blue, red and green are what I like.
2 I don't really have a fav…ite TV pro… …. I like everything!
3 I want to go to Paris to pr… … my French. And have a good time, of course! I love the fashion, too: their clothes are so col… ….
4 The … … of town was crowded. There were thousands of people everywhere. It took me ten minutes to walk a hundred … ….
5 Airports are really exciting places. They are full of tra… … from all over the world.
6 Ladies and gentlemen, thanks for coming. It is an … … for me to speak to you today.

gra · met · ~~ray~~ · vel
col · ise · or · act
hon · ful · ers · our
ter · ers · our · mme
our · cen

Ping-pong prepositions

p. 26, exercise 1 Part B

Choose the right prepositions from the box to replace *ping* and the best other words to replace *pong*.

1 I like eating, but I'm not very good *ping pong*: I can only make sandwiches!
2 Greenwich Village is full *ping* interesting *pong*. Look, I bought this T-shirt here!
3 Broadway is famous *ping* its many *pong*: there are so many great shows you can see in them.
4 I can't eat most pizzas: I'm allergic *ping* milk products, so I can't eat any *pong*.
5 I'm not worried *ping* flying in storms. I know *pong* are actually safer than cars.
6 My English is much better now. My teacher is very proud *ping* the *pong* I've made this year.
7 I love New York It's very different *ping pong* like San Francisco and Dallas: bigger, more exciting, and with more to see and do.

about · at
cheese
cities · cooking
for · from
of (x2) · planes
progress · stores
theaters · to

Two British tourists in Manhattan

p. 27, exercise 3 Part B

a) First complete the story with the missing words. Some letters have been given to help you.

It's impossible to [1] _ _ e all the sights in every [2] _ _ _ _ _ _ _ _ h _ _ d in Manhattan in one day, but we managed to do a lot, and we certainly took a lot of [3] _ h _ _ _ _: our cameras were busy!
We started the day with a great [4] _ r _ _ _ _ _ _ t in Katz Delicatessen, the world-famous restaurant: a great place for our first meal of the day. We had to [5] _ u _ _ _ for 20 minutes, but when we got in, the food was [6] _ _ l _ _ _ _ u _. We loved it.
We thought about going to the Museum of Modern Art, but decided not to. Not because we think museums are [7] _ o _ _ _ _ – I find them really interesting – but we didn't have all day and thought we would [8] _ p _ _ d too long there. So we walked to the 9/11 [9] _ e _ _ _ _ _ _ and read the names of all the many [10] v _ _ _ _ _ _. I didn't know that there were two [11] _ o _ _ _ of water where the Twin Towers once [12] _ _ o _ _. We saw an exhibition in one of the three [13] _ u _ _ _ m _ there, and learned more about the events before, during and after the attack.
We stopped for lunch in Little Italy, where we shared a [14] _ _ z _ _. It was so big we couldn't finish it!
We both wanted to see the Statue of Liberty, but we couldn't buy any [15] _ _ c _ _ _ _ to go inside and climb to the top – they sell out very quickly. Instead, we did a [16] _ o _ _ tour on the river, and got some great [17] v _ _ _ _ of the city from the [18] h _ _ _ _ u _ – and took even more photos!

b) To find out where the writer had dinner, put the letters in the orange boxes in the right order.

What am I ?

p. 28, exercise 1 Part C

You'll find me in NYC. Millions of people visit me every day. What am I? Here are some clues:

1 My first is in *coffee*. It isn't in *tea*, but it rhymes with it.
2 My second is in *Queens* but not in *Manhattan*.
3 My third is in *now* and in *then*, but not in *today*.
4 My fourth sounds like something you drink with a biscuit.
5 My fifth sounds like you …, not like like I *am*.
6 My sixth is the first of 26, and it's also in *last*.
7 You'll find the last of my first word four times in this line.
8 My next word rhymes with dark, and has the same number of letters.
9 You don't have to wait in line to see me. The first letter of my second word comes before queue!

Answers (p. 294)

Sentence building (Gerunds as object/subject)

p. 19, exercise 2 Part A Practice

Write sentences. Match A, B and C and decide if you need a gerund or another form of the verb.

	A	B	C
1	Swimming (swim) in the sea	the dentist, but it's	... (write) really boring.
2	He's so impatient that	... (play) video games, and	people in other countries ... (live).
3	I enjoy ... (play) sport more	is much nicer than	something we all ... (have to) do.
4	Nobody likes ... (go) to	... (learn) about how	in a pool, in my opinion.
5	... (travel) helps you	he hates ... (wait)	... (talk) to my mates is another.
6	One of my favourite hobbies is	stories, but I ... (find)	and it ... (keep) me healthy too.
7	I don't mind ... (read)	than ... (watch) it,	for longer than 5 minutes.

Remember, remember (Gerund or infinitive)

p. 26, exercise 1 Part B Practice

First check how the meaning of remember can change. GAP 10.2, (p. 170)

a) Choose the correct form of the verb in brackets.

1 Do you remember ... (meet) Jane before? I don't, but she says we met last year.
2 It's lucky I remembered ... (take) my umbrella. It rained for hours!
3 I remembered ... (buy) everything except the cheese. Is butter OK instead?
4 My grandpa remembers ... (go) to one of the first Beatles concerts in Liverpool in the 1960s.
5 I remember ... (see) Dorothy on her skateboard and ... (think) "I want one of those".

b) Complete the dialogue with the correct form of a verb from the box.

bring · buy · invite · put · see · tell

Max: Right, so we're nearly ready for the party. Where are the paper plates? I can't see them. You did remember [1]... some with you, didn't you?
Kim: Yes. And I remember [2]... them on the table in the kitchen.
Max: Really? I don't remember [3]... them there. Ah, they're on the chair. Good, you remembered [4]... small and large plates. I hope they were cheap. I'm surprised nobody is here yet. Did you remember [5]... everyone?
Kim: Yes. I remember [6]... them the party would be at your house.

Two out of three (Adverbial clauses)

p. 31, exercise 3 Part C Practice

To complete these sentences, you need to fill two of the three gaps.
Choose the correct words from the box. You will need some of them more than once.

as · less · more · than · though · where

1 New York is a great city, but it's even ... expensive ... we had ... thought it would be.
2 There weren't ... many ... people at the 9/11 Memorial ... I had expected.
3 Central Park is ... lots of people go to relax, ... it's not the biggest ... park in New York.
4 Even ... we stayed ... many of the famous sights are, we didn't see ... everything in Manhattan.
5 Lots of ... young people like the Bronx, but it doesn't attract ... many tourists ... Manhattan does.
6 Even ... New York is an expensive place, a tasty meal ... in Chinatown may cost less ... you think.

Food words

p. 42, exercise 3 Access to words

Daisy, Helen, Mark, Paul, and Richard are five friends. They're talking about food.
First read the facts and complete the sentences with the right options. Then decide who says what.

Facts
- There is one vegetarian. It's not one of the boys.
- Mark has to be really careful about what he eats He has an allergy.
- Paul doesn't like green vegetables.
- Richard can eat everything.
- Daisy doesn't eat spicy food.

Options
spaghetti/tinned/onions
~~lentil~~/~~garlic~~/~~mushrooms~~/~~spicy~~
dairy/cheese/butter/oil
baked/fried/boiled/bacon
pork/rice/mushrooms/spinach

1	Helen:	I don't eat meat. My favourite meal is lentil curry with garlic and mushrooms. I love spicy food.
2	...:	I don't understand why people don't like some food. I love it all. My favourite vegetables are potatoes. They can be ..., ... or .... I love them particularly with ... and cheese.
3	...:	I can't eat ... products like ... or ..., so I normally use ... when I cook.
4	...:	My mum loves Italian food, so we eat a lot of ..., which she makes with fresh or ... tomatoes, ... and salt.
5	...:	My favourite dish is ... with ... and ..., but I don't like ....

Advice for teens

p. 45, exercise 5 Part A Practice

a) Dr Bell gives advice to teens. Complete her statements with the right words from the box.

agreed · dentist · enjoys · exercise · hear · instrument · serious · sports · tired

1 This could be a [a]... problem, so in my opinion you should definitely make an appointment to see a [b].... You need professional help.

2 If you went jogging or swimming, or did some other [a]..., you'd probably feel [b]... at the end of the day. And [c]... is good for you, anyway.

3 It would be a good idea if you [a]... to do something you like one day, and something she [b]... next time. You'll both do something you like.

4 These days you can learn to play almost any [a]... online, and you can wear headphones so nobody can [b]... you. Your parents won't even notice!

b) Now match Dr Bell's statements from a) to the teens' problems below.

Jay:	My tooth really hurts. Every time I eat something it is very painful. It's been like this for several days now and I'm really worried. What should I do?
Harriet:	I really want to learn the piano and join a band, but my parents say it'll be too noisy and there isn't enough room for a piano at home.
Aanan:	My best friend and I argue a lot these days because we can never agree what to do. We liked the same things a few years ago, but now our tastes in music and films are different. Going to the cinema or a concert just isn't as easy as it once was. What should I do?
Tilly:	I find it hard to sleep at night. I go to bed at the normal time, but then I stay awake for hours.

Answers (p. 294)

I wish ...

p. 49, exercise 3 **Part B Practice**

Complete the sentences with the words in brackets and add any other words you need.
Careful! In each pair of sentences, one sentence is negative.

1 **We didn't see the beginning of the film. We were late.**
a) I wish *we had left earlier* (leave earlier) b) I wish *we hadn't missed the first scene* (miss/first scene)

2 **I couldn't see the screen very clearly. I left my glasses at home.**
a) I wish ... (forget/glasses) b) I wish ... (remember/take/glasses)

3 **It was a horror film. It gave my friend Jack bad dreams.**
a) My friend Jack wishes ... (chose/different film) b) He wishes ... (be so frightening)

4 **We were sitting right at the back. There were no seats in the middle. I couldn't see the screen clearly.**
a) I wish ... (seats/be closer/screen) b) I wish ... (sit/so far back)

5 **In fact, the whole evening was pretty bad. It wasn't a good idea to go out.**
a) I wish ... (stay/home) b) I wish ... (go out)

Thanksgiving wordsearch

p. 53 **Study skills**

Complete the text with words from the wordsearch. The numbers in brackets tell you how many letters each word has.
They can be horizontal or vertical, and from right to left or left to right!

It was President Lincoln who introduced the [1]... (7) of Thanksgiving, which is [2]... (10) on the [3]... (6) Thursday of November each year.

As everyone knows, the [4]... (11) dinner is turkey. However, not so many people know that in 1947 President Truman added a new tradition when he decided to officially [5]... (4) one lucky turkey from being [6]... (5). This has been repeated by every [7]... (9) since.

On such an important day, it is natural that [8]... (8) like to be together. In fact, the average family will travel at least 240 [9]... (5) to share the day with loved ones. People make over 24 [10]... (7) plane journeys for the event, although most journeys are made by [11]... (3).

Another fact some people forget: The USA is not the only country that has Thanksgiving. It is also an important [12]... (3) in Canada.

a	n	n	a	d	r	u	q	h	o	k	t
z	g	o	s	a	v	e	w	t	r	u	h
u	k	h	y	y	q	x	k	r	a	c	o
x	w	o	g	e	o	r	g	u	t	b	m
e	r	l	m	i	l	e	s	o	i	e	a
a	m	i	w	y	k	x	o	f	m	n	s
t	i	d	p	r	e	s	i	d	e	n	t
e	l	a	n	o	i	t	i	d	a	r	t
n	l	y	q	w	k	z	g	o	r	l	a
z	i	x	y	f	a	m	i	l	i	e	s
u	o	d	e	t	a	r	b	e	l	e	c
z	n	c	a	r	o	l	g	q	y	o	z

The right pair (Conditionals 1 and 2)

p. 44. exercise 3 Part A Practice

Choose the right pair of verbs (green or blue) to complete the dialogue. Then put them in the correct form: conditional 1 or conditional 2.

1 A: Have you ever been to New Orleans?
B: No, actually, but if I ... lucky, I ... there next year.
have · go
be · be

2 A: I just can't work out how to find the answer.
B: If I ... you, I ... a different way of solving the problem
be · find
want · be

3 A: Hurry, the film starts at seven!
B: Yes, if we ... soon, we ... the beginning.
not leave · miss
leave · see

4 A: What are your plans for this afternoon?
B: I don't know. If the weather ... so bad right now, I ... to the beach.
not be · go
not have · swim

5 A: Did Jamie live in the USA for a few years?
B: I don't know. I ... him tomorrow if I ... him in college.
see · tell
ask · see

6 A: This is delicious! You're such a good cook.
B: If you really ... it, I ... you some to take home with you.
eat · promise
like · give

Sentence halves (Conditionals 2 and 3)

p. 49, exercise 4 Part B Practice

Match the sentence halves. Put the verbs in brackets into the correct conditional form.

1 If I ... (go) to bed earlier
2 If you ... (go) to bed earlier
3 Your mum would have been upset
4 Your mum would be really happy
5 Fred would go to the concert
6 Freya would have hated the concert
7 If I ... (see) the accident,
8 If someone ... (be) hurt in an accident

a if you ... (give) her some flowers.
b I wouldn't have felt so tired when I got up.
c if you ... (make) her go with you.
d I would have called 911 for help.
e would you know how to help them?
f if the tickets ... (not be) so expensive.
g you would find it easier to get up in the mornings.
h if you ... (forget) her birthday.

Rephrasing sentences (Adverbs of degree)

p. 54, exercise 2 Part C Practice

Rephrase the sentences. In each sentence, use one of adverbs and one of the adjectives on the right.

1 There weren't very many people on the beach.
The beach was ...
awfully · fairly · totally
crowded · empty · full

2 Wow! That was such a tasty meal!
The meal was ...
absolutely · a bit · fairly
awful · delicious · nice

3 It's not very warm in this room.
This room is ...
a bit · awfully · totally
cold · low · hot

4 It's really loud in this street, isn't it?
This street is ...
a little · very · completely
calm · noisy · quiet

5 Alex was a bit rude to me yesterday.
Alex wasn't ...
absolutely · a little · very
impolite · polite · unfriendly

Answers (p. 295)

Mixed up rubbish

p. 69, exercise 2 **Mediation**

a) Read the texts. Make words with the letters in the boxes to fill the gaps.

Jutta	Every morning I clear up the breakfast things and do the recycling. Luckily, everything goes in the same bin so it's nice and easy. What did I recycle today? Let me think: we had some fruit, an omelette and toast, so I threw away the half the [1]apple I didn't eat, the [2]... ... and a [3]... that had gone all black so nobody wanted it. Oh yes, and Mum asked me to throw out the [4]... she had got for her birthday last week.	anabna · refsowl geg leslhs · ~~palpe~~
Markus	I had quite a lot of paper to recycle this week, actually. I got a [1]... from a clothes shop I like, but I don't need it so put it in the recycling bin, together with two [2]... from the weekend, and some old sports [3]... I read ages ago. I also threw away a pair of old [4]... that have holes in them.	zagimenas · ckoss spansrewep rehorbcu
Stefan	We love coffee so we always have a lot of [1]... ... to recycle. Also, I prefer home-made fruit drinks to ones you buy at supermarkets. Yesterday I needed fifteen [2]... for the juice I made. They are in the bin now. I also had a few [3]... to recycle, and the [4]... my two new pairs of shoes came in. And I found a couple of plastic [5]...	clapist gasb egroans · slotbet ceffeo liftres oxebs
Simone	We had a takeaway last night. I threw away a piece of [1]... that nobody wanted and the [2]... it came in. When he was younger, my brother collected film [3]... and also [4]... ... of the films he went to – don't ask me why. He asked me to throw them away too.	nameic scetkit xbo · stopers zapiz

b) Decide if these statements are true or false. Correct the false sentences.

1 Jutta put everything in the blue bin.
2 Markus put things in the blue and grey bins.
3 Simone put things in three bins.
4 Stefan didn't put anything in the yellow bin.

Who's the celebrity?

p. 71, exercise 4 **The world behind the picture**

First find the missing words to complete the sentences.
The coloured boxes make the name of a celebrity who got a star on the Walk of Fame in 1975.

1 The Walk of Fame is over two m _ _ _ _ long.
2 It runs for 15 _ _ _ _ k _ on Hollywood Boulevard and into Vine Street.
3 The stars are all about six _ e _ _ apart.
4 Stars are not free: each one _ _ _ t _ around $40,000.
5 In 2020, Batman, who started as a _ a _ _ _ o _ character in a comic, got his star.
6 Each year about 25 new people _ _ _ n the club of famous people with stars.
7 Living stars must attend the _ e _ _ _ _ y where their star is presented to the public.
8 A group of five people decides who gets the _ _ _ o _ r of getting a star in their name.
9 One embarrassing fact is that there are spelling mistakes in nine of the stars' _ _ m _ _.

Join the words

p. 78, exercise 3 **Part C**

Read the sentences. To complete them, make words with the letters in the table.

pable	com	dis	ity
ry	cel	~~shi~~	sec
vir	cove	nel	uns
~~ny~~	ur	chan	mon
top	ebr	ity	al

1 My car is not new, but I've just cleaned it so it's all nice and shiny .
2 People think the life of a ... is easy, but it's not. It's hard to have a private life, for example.
3 Last season our baseball team won every game in three different competitions. We were absolutely ... .
4 Every blogger hopes that one of their posts will go ... and be read by millions.
5 The President is always surrounded by at least ten ... guards.
6 Sandy and I have a lot in ... : we both love sports, play the guitar and enjoy action movies.
7 Life in California changed after the ... of gold there. Millions came and the cities grew.
8 What ... is the film on? I think it's starting now and I'd like to watch it.

Unusual definitions

p. 80, exercise 2 **Part C Practice**

Match the three sentence parts to make definitions.
Add the missing relative pronouns (*who* or *which*) if necessary. Leave them out wherever possible.

Part 1	Part 2	Part 3
1 A cell phone is a device	7 to do the things	13 you wouldn't have without them.
2 A secret is something	8 becomes more comfortable	14 finally agrees with you.
3 A teacher is a person	9 lots of teens	15 when your alarm goes off.
4 An argument is a discussion	10 goes on till the other person	16 can't live without.
5 A bed is a piece of furniture	11 you tell everyone	17 to tell nobody.
6 Tomorrow is the best time	12 helps you solve problems	18 people told you to do today.

Find the words

p. 82, exercise 3 **Access to words**

Read the clues and find the words.

1 It's the opposite of *correct*, and it rhymes with the opposite of *short*.
2 It means the same as *cross*, and looks and sounds a little like how you feel when you need to eat.
3 It's the opposite of *quiet*, and rhymes with the word for a large group of people.
4 It means the same as cute and it rhymes with something vegetarians don't eat.
5 This word describes people, is a synonym of *big* and rhymes with the opposite.
6 It has five letters, means the same as *strange*, and rhymes with the hair on a person's face.

Answers (p. 295)

Vacation questions (*going to*-future)

p. 68, exercise 3 **Part A Practice**

Read the dialogue and complete the questions with the verbs in brackets.
Use the going to-future. Sometimes you need to use question words (e.g. *What …? / How …?*, etc.)

Fred: [1]… (spend) the summer in Malibu again?
Lyn: Yeah, Mom has booked the same vacation home there as last summer.
Fred: Lucky you! [2]… (stay) there for?
Lyn: Only for two weeks this year.
Fred: Two whole weeks! [3]… (do) down there?
Lyn: Lie on the beach, of course.
Fred: [4]… (not do) anything else?
Lyn: Of course not, silly. You go to Malibu for the sun. Anyway, what about you? [5]… (stay) at home here in San Francisco or [6]… (travel) somewhere else?
Fred: Yes, I'm going to take part in a great volunteering project
Lyn: [7]… (volunteer)?
Fred: On Ocean Beach. We're going to help keep the beach clean.
Lyn: [8]… (volunteer) with?
Fred: With Kylie and Samir. They worked there last year. They said it was awesome.
Lyn: It sounds interesting. [9]… (write) about it on your blog? I want to read all about it.
Fred: Of course! And you can send me photos from Malibu.

Making a dialogue (*will*-future or *going to*-future)

p. 75, exercise 5 **Part B Practice**

First put the dialogue in the right order.
Then put the verbs in the right tense: *will*-future or *going to*-future.

1 Ben: Hmm. Maybe after school.
2 Ben: It's Mack's birthday on Friday. Do you know what you … (give) him as a present?
3 Liz: OK, let's take the bus. I … (meet) you at the bus stop after the last lesson.
4 Liz: Oh, I want to go into town too. Can I come with you?
5 Ben: I don't know yet, but I'm sure I … (find) something. I think I … (go) into town later and look around.
6 Ben: Yes, that … (be) fun.
7 Liz: When … you (go) … ?
8 Liz: Well, Kim told me he loves tennis, so I … (buy) him a lesson with a coach. What about you?

Mixed up sentences (Relative clauses)

p. 81, exercise 4 **Part C Practice**

Put the phrases in the right order to make sentences. Then add punctuation to each sentence.

1 of cinema TV and theatre /celebrates stars / which is a major tourist attraction / The Walk of Fame /

2 that many towns and / The Walk of Fame / cities have copied / began in L.A. / which is an idea

3 The Walk of Fame / in Los Angeles which / is a famous attraction / we visited last year

4 series of books and films / made J.K. Rowling famous / Harry Potter which is a / and also a play

5 Potter films / much as the books / which he saw / Ian didn't enjoy the Harry / last year as

6 was the star / of celebrities on / of the Harry Potter films / the Walk of Fame / Daniel Radcliffe who / is one of thousands

School words

p. 93, exercise 2 **Part A Practice**

Use the letters in the grid on the right to make words that complete the sentences. Each word must use the central letter E. You can use a letter more than once in each word.

1 I'll meet you in the _ _ _ _ _ _ _ _ _ after history class. We can have lunch there together.
2 At the start of the day the teacher takes the _ _ _ _ _ _ _ _ to make sure everyone is there.
3 We're doing a cool project in our social _ _ _ _ _ _ _ class this month.
4 We've got to hand in our English _ _ _ _ _ _ _ _ _ _ tomorrow, so I'm going to finish it at home tonight.
5 The teachers always say that the best way to get good _ _ _ _ _ _ is to study hard and pay attention in class.
6 I'm nervous because the history _ _ _ _ is tomorrow. It lasts two hours and has fifty questions.
7 My brother isn't so good at languages, but he's very good at _ _ _ _ _ _ _. He loves experiments.
8 Our school day is divided into several _ _ _ _ _ _ _ of about 60 minutes.

C	A	T	I
P	G	D	O
R	E		F
M	U	S	N
L	X	B	Y

The fire alarm puzzle

p. 94, exercise 3 **Part A Practice**

a) Jack, Bryan and Sally were at school yesterday when the fire alarm went off. Complete the clues for the puzzle with the right verbs. Use the past progressive or simple past.

1 The student who [a]... in the library [b]... to music when they [c]... the fire alarm and [d]... at the meeting point first because the library is next to the main door. (arrive / hear / not listen / study)

2 The student who [a]... in the cafeteria [b]... the alarm for several seconds because they [c]... to loud music on their phone (listen / not hear / sit)

3 Bryan, who [a]... an assignment when the alarm [b]... to ring, calmly [c]... his books in his bag, but [d]... the last of the three friends to get to the meeting point. (not be / not do / put / start)

4 The student who [a]... the last to join their two friends outside [b]... a coffee in the cafeteria, which is a long way from the school entrance (be / have)

5 Jack [a]... an assignment, and Sally [b]... on her own when the alarm [c].... (not do / go off / work)

b) Now solve the puzzle: Decide where the students were, what they were doing, and in which order they got to the school meeting point outside.

	Jack	Bryan	Sally
Room: Cafeteria / Library / Classroom	...	...	...
Activity: Doing an assignment / Helping a classmate / Listening to music	...	...	...
Got to school meeting point: First / Second / Third	...	...	...

Answers (pp. 295–296)

An invitation to a party

p. 100, exercise 2 **Part B Practice**

a) Two friends are talking on the phone. Their sentences are in the wrong order. Put them in the correct order. Allan's first statement has been done for you.

Allan	Bea
1 "I'm having a party next week."	…
2 "It's on Saturday. That's a better day for parties."	A "A club! What a brilliant idea!"
3 "Just one more thing. Bring your dancing shoes. You'll need them."	B "Great. I'll definitely be there by 9."
4 "Actually, Dad has arranged a room at a club."	C "Saturday! Then I can come to your house and help you get ready."
5 "I'm having a PARTY. Next week."	D "Sorry. I didn't hear you."
6 "The club opens at 8.30 pm. You can come any time from then."	E "I hope it isn't on Friday. I have plans that day."

b) Bea told another friend about her phone call. Use indirect speech to complete what she said.

Bea: Allan told me he [1]… a party. I said I [2]… it [3]… on Friday and explained that I [4]… plans that day. But it was OK. He told me the party [5]… on Saturday. I said I [6]… help him to get ready but he told me that his dad [7]… a room at a club. What a brilliant idea! Anyway, Allan said that the club [8]… at 8.30 and that I [9]… come any time after that. And do you know what he said next? He told me I [10]… my dancing shoes!

Find the suffixes

p. 104, exercise 3 **Access to words**

Add the correct suffix (*-ful*, *-less* or *-ness*) to the words given and use them to complete each text.

A colour / dark / sleep	D heart / power / sad
I had a fantastic time last weekend. I stayed over at a friend's house. They gave me a very [1]…room – with green, red, and blue walls, although of course in the [2]… you can't tell. Unfortunately, I had a [3]… night because it was so hot.	I can't understand people who are cruel to animals. I think it's absolutely [1]…. Many animals are [2]… to defend themselves. You can see a look of great [3]… in the animals' eyes. It's just not fair.
B power / stress / shy	E cloud / happy / peace
When I was younger I found being with other people quite [1]…. What helped me with my [2]… was when I joined the football team. They accepted me, and we got good results. Being a part of a winning team is a [3]… feeling!	I love camping in the wild, far away from everything. On [1]… nights I can sit and look at the stars for hours. It's so [2]… and quiet – it fills me with [3]….
C bitter / event / home	F end / help / lonely
I saw a film about a woman who had a very [1]… life. She started two companies, but then lost all her money. She was even [2]… for a while and slept on the streets. People were really bad to her. The amazing thing was she never felt any [3]… towards the people who were so cruel.	I have a big family, so [1]… is not a problem for me: I always have someone to do things with and, here in the city, there is an almost [2]… choice of activities. If I have problems I try to solve them myself, but my parents are very [3]… and often give me advice.

Sentence halves (State and activity verbs)

p. 95, exercise 5 Part A Practice

Match the sentence halves.
Then decide if the verb in brackets is a state verb or an activity verb and write down the correct form.

	A		B
1	Kim is in the kitchen, where she	a	(have) a picnic this afternoon.
2	The cake Kim made yesterday	b	(think) about having a costume party.
3	Let's hope it doesn't rain because we	c	(look) much younger than that.
4	It doesn't matter if it rains because I	d	(taste) the food for tonight's dinner.
5	I'm not sure what to do on my birthday, but I	e	(look) for one online.
6	I'm not sure when Grandma's birthday is, but I	f	(have) a very good umbrella.
7	My mum is almost 50, but she	g	(taste) OK, but it's a bit dry.
8	My mum wants a new computer and she	h	(think) it's in late September.

What did they say? (Indirect speech)

p. 101, exercise 4 Part B Practice

a) Read what speakers 1–6 said. Then decide which sentence (a–f) they said next.

1 **Jack:** The restaurant will be full.
2 **Clara**: I haven't eaten yet.
3 **Tom**: There's nothing to do at home.
4 **Lily**: It's Grandpa's birthday.
5 **Harry**: I'm sorry I can't join you at the beach.
6 **Vera**: It's going to rain later.

a You should take an umbrella.
b Remember to give him a call.
c Have a nice time there!
d You should reserve a table.
e Can you make me a sandwich, please?
f Let's go to the cinema.

b) Write sentences to report what the people said.
For a–f, use the reporting verb that fits best: *advise*, *ask*, *remind*, *suggest*, *tell*.

Jack said that the restaurant would be full and advised us to reserve a table.

The or no *the*? (The definite article)

p. 105, exercise 2 Part C Practice

Read the sentences and decide how many of the underlined definite articles are correct.

1 Do you know [a] the people who live in [b] the house next to [c] the church? I think they're [d] the teachers.

2 I enjoy most lessons at [a] the school, but [b] the history is my favourite. Knowing about [c] the past helps you understand [d] the life in general.

3 I love watching [a] the television documentaries about [b] the nature. I believe we must do more to fight [c] the problems such as [d] the climate change.

4 In my opinion, one of [a] the best things about learning [b] the languages is that it can help you to understand how [c] the other people in different parts of [d] the world think.

Answers (p. 296)

4 A day out in Manhattan

p. 27

Partner A:

Claire

Claire is in the Big Apple to have fun.
She wants to meet people of her own age.
Please don't expect her to be quiet and listen to a guide!
She likes travelling and loves having people around her.
Doing any kind of sport is what she likes best.
Claire's favourite food is Asian, and she has heard that finding that in New York is easy.
You wouldn't think so, but she is really good at playing chess too.

Mediation course: Explaining a menu

p. 43

d) Partner A:

When your partner has read their role card,

- find out what kind of food they like
- find dishes on the menu you think they'd like
- explain what they are and suggest some dishes.

Then read your role card and answer your partner's questions.

What you eat
You are a vegetarian who sometimes eats fish.
You love all kinds of cheeses and potato dishes.
You don't like to eat a lot at each meal.
You love soups and vegetable dishes and salads.

4 Study skills: Skimming a text

p. 53

c) Work in groups of three. Imagine you have to do a presentation.
Each of you has a different topic:

Partner A: New Orleans swamp tours
Partner B: The people of the swamps
Partner C: Wildlife in the Louisiana swamps

Skim texts 1–3 on pages 147–149 and decide which one you should read in detail.
Then say which text you chose and why.

1 Animals of the wetlands

The Honey Island Swamp is home to snowy white egrets.

Mammals
There are many wild mammals in the Louisiana wetlands. Examples are the coyote, muskrat, Norway rat and red fox. Armadillos also live in the wetlands as well as large mammals like the black bear.

Reptiles
Maybe the most famous of swamp animals, the American alligator is quite common. But it is still in danger. Several kinds of snakes make their home in the Louisiana wetlands. America's largest freshwater turtle, the alligator snapping turtle, shares the habitat with its cousin, the common snapping turtle.

Birds
Some of America's tallest birds love the fish in the Louisiana wetlands. Brown pelicans, which are endangered, also take advantage of the plentiful fish. Raptors live in the marshes of southern Louisiana.

4 Study skills: Skimming a text

p. 53

2

What should you expect from kayaking in a swamp?

A perfect day
Imagine this: it's a perfect day, 79 degrees and sunny. The cypress trees rise like monuments to nature from the Pearl River where we start. Two guides start you on an easy tour, down river, so that you can learn how to paddle. Yes, the river isn't slow everywhere. And watch out for the bushes because there are poisonous snakes … But isn't that why you're out here? For nature – beautiful and dangerous?

Meet the locals
As you paddle down river you see some of Louisiana's culture – swamp houses and boats are hidden in the trees or are on the river itself. If you run into other paddlers, they're wonderfully friendly.

Almost religious
As the trip goes on, you begin to paddle in and out of trees and go where other tours wouldn't take you. You find yourself in the middle of a swamp forest of cypresses and old oaks. The beauty of this view is almost religious: the sun streams through trees, and vines and Spanish moss hang from branches high and low. Nature is quietly buzzing around you, and if you can take a moment to be quiet and just watch, you might see alligators or other animals around the river.

4 Study skills: Skimming a text

p. 53

3 What is Cajun?

In America's largest swamp, the bayous and wetlands of Louisiana, lives a people like no other

Where their name comes from

After Britain beat France in the Seven Years' War in the late 18th century, French settlers from a part of Canada they called Acadia moved to Louisana's swamp country. The French called them "les Acadiens" or "les 'Cadiens". Later came the Americans, who could not pronounce "Acadien" or "Cadien". Instead they said "Cajun" and in this way gave the people of the swamps their name.

Way of life

The Cajuns today still continue many of the traditions of the first Acadiens who came to live in the swamps, like hunting alligators. They are a thrifty, hard-working and religious folk. But they are also known for their "joie de vivre" and this expresses itself in the community festivals, dancing and food of bayou life. With their herbs, spices and other ingredients they make some of the most tasty dishes in North America.

Cajun music

Cajun music is known as Zydeco. Its traditions go back to the music of the French settlers of Canada. It is sometimes sad, sometimes happy, and sometimes both at the same time. In the past, the fiddle was the main instrument, but the accordion has become important too. Cajun music became more famous in 2007, when the Grammy Award for Best Zydeco Album was created.

4 A day out in Manhattan

p. 27

Partner B:

Max

Max is a quiet boy who likes watching events and people in everyday situations.
He doesn't mind being in the city, but likes being in the countryside more.
He is a talented musician and loves listening to live music.
Max is interested in the history of places and enjoys meeting people from all kinds of backgrounds.
One thing he can't stand is travelling by subway.
He also hates it when people make fun of him or laugh at him.

Mediation course: Explaining a menu

p. 43

d) Partner B:
Read your role card then answer your partner's questions.

What you eat
You like all kinds of meat, but hate fish.
You like some kinds of cheese but not strong ones like blue cheese or Limburger.
You want to try very traditional German food.
You tend to eat a lot.

When your partner has read their role card,
- find out what kind of food they like
- find dishes on the menu you think they'd like
- explain what they are and suggest some dishes.

Dieser Teil dieses Buches fasst zusammen, was du in den fünf Units deines Englischbuches über englische Grammatik lernst. Auf den linken Seiten stehen Erklärungen und Beispielsätze, auf den rechten Seiten Übungen.

→ Unter cornelsen.de/webcodes (Webcode: *hiwapi*) kannst du nachsehen, ob du die Übungen richtig bearbeitet hast. Dort findest du auch eine Übersicht grammatischer Fachbegriffe.

Inhalt

Inhalt		Seite
1	REVISION **Present tenses** Zeitformen der Gegenwart 1.1 **Simple present** Die einfache Form der Gegenwart 1.2 **Present progressive** Die Verlaufsform der Gegenwart 1.3 **Simple present and present progressive contrasted** *Simple present* und *present progressive* im Vergleich	152
2	REVISION **Past tenses** Zeitformen der Vergangenheit 2.1 **Simple past** Die einfache Form der Vergangenheit 2.2 **Past progressive** Die Verlaufsform der Vergangenheit 2.3 **Simple past and past progressive contrasted** *Simple past* und *past progressive* im Vergleich	154
3	**State verbs and activity verbs** Zustands- und Tätigkeitsverben 3.1 REVISION **State verbs** Zustandsverben 3.2 **Activity verbs** Tätigkeitsverben	156
4	REVISION **Simple past and present/past perfect contrasted** *Simple past* und *present/past perfect* im Vergleich 4.1 **Present perfect or simple past?** *Present perfect* oder *simple past?* 4.2 **Simple past or past perfect?** *Simple past* oder *past perfect?*	158
5	**Future tenses** Zeitformen der Zukunft 5.1 REVISION ***Going to*-future** Das Futur mit *going to* 5.2 REVISION ***Will*-future** Das Futur mit *will* 5.3 **More information on *will*** Weitere Informationen zu *will*	160
6	**Present tenses with a future meaning** Zeiten der Gegenwart mit Zukunftsbezug 6.1 **Present progressive with a future meaning** *Present progressive* mit Zukunftsbezug 6.2 **Simple present with a future meaning** *Simple present* mit Zukunftsbezug	162
7	REVISION **Conditional sentences 1 and 2** Bedingungssätze 1 und 2	164
8	**Conditional sentence 3** Bedingungssatz 3	166
9	**The gerund** Das Gerundium	168
10	**The gerund or the *to*-infinitive** Das Gerundium oder der *to*-infinitive	170
11	**The gerund after prepositions and in certain phrases** Das Gerundium nach Präpositionen und in bestimmten Wendungen	172
12	REVISION **The passive** Das Passiv	174
13	REVISION **Relative and contact clauses** Relativsätze mit und ohne Relativpronomen	176
14	**Defining and non-defining relative clauses** Bestimmende und nicht bestimmende Relativsätze 14.1 **Defining relative clauses** Bestimmende Relativsätze 14.2 **Non-defining relative clauses** Nicht bestimmende Relativsätze	178
15	**Adverbs** Adverbien 15.1 REVISION **Adverbs of manner** Adverbien der Art und Weise 15.2 **Adverbs of degree** Gradadverbien	180
16	**Adverbial clauses** Adverbiale Nebensätze 16.1 REVISION **Adverbial clauses** Adverbiale Nebensätze 16.2 **Adverbial clauses of place** Adverbiale Nebensätze des Ortes 16.3 **Adverbial clauses of comparison** Adverbiale Nebensätze des Vergleichs 16.4 **Adverbial clauses of contrast** Adverbiale Nebensätze des Gegensatzes	182
17	**Indirect speech** Indirekte Rede	184
18	**Indirect requests, commands, advice and suggestions** Bitten, Aufforderungen, Ratschläge und Vorschläge in indirekter Rede	186
19	**The definite article** Der bestimmte Artikel 19.1 **Abstract and concrete nouns** Abstrakte und konkrete Nomen 19.2 **Some buildings and meals** Einige Gebäude und Mahlzeiten	188
20	**British and American English** Britisches und amerikanisches Englisch	190

1 REVISION Present tenses Zeitformen der Gegenwart

1.1 Simple present Die einfache Form der Gegenwart

Positive statements	Bejahte Aussagesätze
*Dave **plays** football on Mondays and tennis on Thursdays.* *It never **snows** in August.*	◀ Wenn du darüber redest, was **regelmäßig** (jeden Tag, immer, oft, meistens) oder **nie** geschieht, dann verwendest du das *simple present*.
*Water **boils** at 100° Celsius.*	◀ Du verwendest das *simple present* auch, um allgemeine Aussagen zu machen.
Questions	Fragen
Do** you **like** your new friends? – **Yes, I do. ***Does** John **drink** his tea with milk? – **No, he doesn't**.*	◀ Fragen im *simple present* bildest du mit ***Do*** … bzw. (bei *he/she/it*) mit ***Does*** …
***Where do** you **go** after school today? – To the library.* ***Why do** you **eat** so many sweets? It's not healthy.*	◀ Fragen mit Fragewörtern *(When, Where, What, Why, How)* bildest du wie Entscheidungsfragen.
Negative statements *I **don't want** to watch this video. It's boring.* *Sam **doesn't know** anything about his girlfriend.* ➔ *p.93, exercise 1*	Verneinte Aussagesätze Eine Aussage im *simple present* verneinst du mit ***don't* + Infinitiv** bzw. (bei *he/she/it*) mit ***doesn't* + Infinitiv**.

1.2 Present progressive Die Verlaufsform der Gegenwart

*What **are** you **doing**?* ***I'm writing** text messages to my friends.* *Look – the dog **is eating** your scone!* *Dad **is working** a lot from home these days.*	◀ Du verwendest das *present progressive*, wenn du sagen willst, – was jemand **gerade** macht oder – was **gerade** passiert. Das *present progressive* bildest du mit ***am/are/is* + *-ing*-Form** des Verbs.
1 *I can't believe this. My brother **is making** me a sandwich.* 2 *Oh no, **I'm getting** sick.* ➔ *p.93, exercise 1*	**!** Vorsicht: 1 Ein stummes ***e*** fällt weg: *make* → making 2 Du verdoppelst den Konsonanten nach einem einzelnen, betonten Vokal: *get* → *ge**tt**ing*, *swim* → *swi**mm**ing*

1.3 Simple present and present progressive contrasted *Simple present* und *present progressive* im Vergleich

*I **do** yoga <u>every morning</u>.* *I'**m talking** to you <u>right now</u>. **Are** you **listening**?*	◀ Während das *simple present* Gewohnheiten und allgemeine Aussagen ausdrückt, beschreibt das *present progressive* Handlungen, die gerade stattfinden. Signalwörter für das – *simple present: always, usually, often, sometimes, never, every morning, on Saturdays, in summer, …* – *present progressive: (right) now, just, today, …*
*I **love** this pair of shoes. Can you buy them for me, Mum?* *Henry's grandparents **own** this beautiful cottage.* ➔ *p.93, exercise 2*	**!** Zustandsverben (*love, believe, own* usw.) bildest du in der Regel immer mit dem *simple present*.

IN ENGLISH:
- You use the **simple present** when you talk about routines and facts.
- You use the **present progressive** to say what somebody is doing now.

1 Exercises

1 Present tenses

a) Complete the facts about New York City with the correct verbs from the box. Use the simple present.

~~be~~ · cost · flow · happen · have · live · shine · speak · stand · take

1. New York City is the largest city in the United States.
2. Nearly 8.5 million people ... in the city.
3. New York ... a lot of names: the Big Apple, the city that never sleeps, for example.
4. A lot of New Yorkers ... more than one language every day.
5. The Hudson river ... through New York.
6. The Statue of Liberty ... on Ellis Island.
7. A child's ticket to visit the top of the statue ... $12.
8. At sunset on May 28 and July 13 every year, the sun ... along some New York streets.
9. The same thing ... at sunrise on Dec 5 and Jan 8.
10. A lot of New Yorkers and tourists ... beautiful photos on these days.

b) Complete the sentences about Mary and Brad. Use the simple present.

1. Mary and Brad are cousins, but they ... in different countries. (be, live)
2. Where ... Mary ...? In Manchester, in the UK. Her family ... a house. Mary ... a room with her little sister. (live, own, share)
3. What about Brad? Brad and his family ... an apartment in New York in the US. Brad ... any brothers or sisters. (have, not have)
4. Brad and Mary ... each other very often in person, but they ... *SnapTalk* to stay in contact. (not see, use)
5. The cousins ... the same age – 14. Mary ... in Year 9, but in New York they ... it eighth grade – Brad's grade. (be, be, call)
6. Mary ... to school. And Brad? Brad ... the school bus. Brad's mum ... the city streets ... too dangerous for bikes. (think, be, cycle, take)
7. Mary and Brad's fathers ... brothers. They ... twins, but they ... very similar. (be, not be, look)
8. What ... the brothers ...? Mary's dad ... for a bank. He ... a lot. Mary ... him when he ... away. (be, do, miss, travel, work)
9. Brad's dad ... a police officer. He sometimes ... at night and at the weekends. Brad often ... about his dad. (be, worry, work)

c) Complete the statements and questions. Use the present progressive.

1. What's that noise? Is someone screaming (scream)? — That's my dad. He ... in the shower again. (sing)
2. Look! The little boy ... (cry). He must be lost. — It's OK. Look. His mother ... (go) over to him.
3. Dad, what ... you ... (do) with my favourite T-shirt? — This old thing? I ... (throw) it away. It's full of holes.
4. Why ... Brian ... (stand) there? — He ... (wait) for Miss Murphy. I think he's in trouble again.
5. I need the computer, Mum. ... you ... it (use)? — That's OK. I ... (not use) it at the moment.
6. ... Dad ... (come) with us? — Yes. He ... (get) ready upstairs.
7. ... you ... (take) more selfies? — No! I ... (try) to make a video call at the moment.
8. Look. Across the road. Someone ... (wave) at us. — That's my crazy friend Luke. Oh God! What ... he ... (wear)?
9. Hi Paul. Where are you? I ... (phone) from the beach. — Tom, hi. We're here too. We ... (lie) on the beach right now – beside the ice cream van.

d) Mary and Brad want to meet on SnapTalk. Complete the text and put the verbs into the correct form. Use the simple present or the present progressive.

It[1]'s (be) eight o'clock on Wednesday evening in Mary's house. Mary [2]... (get) ready to call her cousin Brad in New York on *SnapTalk*. The cousins [3]... (not call) each other *every* Wednesday, but they [4]... (try) to do it as often as they [5]... (can). At the same time in New York, Brad [6]... (just come) in the door of his family's apartment. It [7]... (be) three o'clock in the afternoon right now in New York. Brad [8]... (finish) school at 2 o'clock on Wednesdays, so Wednesday [9]... (be) the best day for both of the cousins to call. Now Brad [10]... (make) a sandwich. He often [11]... (have) a snack when he [12]... (arrive) home from school. His parents[13] ... (not be) home at the moment because they [14]... (work). Brad's dad sometimes [15]... (have) a day off on Wednesdays, but not this week. Back in Manchester, Mary [16]... (look for) her headset. OK, now she [17]... (have) it and she[18] ... (be) ready. Two clicks on her mouse. *SnapTalk* [19]... (ring) now. Over in New York right now, Brad [20]... (sit) on the sofa and [21]... (eat) his sandwich. ***Buzz, buzz*** Brad: "Mary, hi!" Mary: "Hey cousin, what [22]... you ... (do)?" Brad: "Nothing. I [23]... (just have) a snack. You?" Mary: "I [24]... (try) to finish my history homework. Maybe you[25] ... (can) help. What [26]... you ... (know) about World War II?" Brad: "Well, a lot about the American side. What exactly [27]... you ... (want) to know?"

2 REVISION Past tenses Zeitformen der Vergangenheit

2.1 Simple past Die einfache Form der Vergangenheit

*It **was** late when Jane **arrived** home. She **took** off her coat, **drank** a cup of hot milk and then **went** to bed, but she **couldn't fall** asleep. She **turned** on the radio and **listened** to her favourite music show.*

◀ Wenn du über **Vergangenes berichtest** – z.B., wenn du eine Geschichte erzählst –, benutzt du überwiegend das *simple past*.

*The two boys **got** out of their cars and **headed** for the school door.*

meet → ***met***	***bring*** → ***brought***
become → ***became***	***sell*** → ***sold***

◀ Das *simple past* beschreibt auch eine **Abfolge von Handlungen** in der Vergangenheit.

◀ **Unregelmäßige** Verben haben eine eigene Form für das *simple past*, die du einzeln lernen musst.

→ *Liste der unregelmäßigen Verben, S. 298–299*

*The accident **happened** two years ago.*

Signalwörter für das *simple past: last Saturday, yesterday, two years ago, in 2010, …*

2.2 Past progressive Die Verlaufsform der Vergangenheit

Use and form

*When I got up, the cat **was sleeping** next to me.*
Die Katze schlief (gerade) neben mir, als ich aufwachte.

Gebrauch und Form

◀ Mit dem *past progressive* drückst du aus, dass zu einem **Zeitpunkt in der Vergangenheit**
– etwas **gerade** passierte
– jemand **gerade** dabei war, etwas zu tun.

*He **was turning** into the Mobridge-Pollock High School parking lot when the car behind his honked.*

Das *past progressive* bildest du mit ***was/were + -ing*-Form** des Verbs: *I was playing … / You were playing … / …*

Negative statements

*Jo **wasn't sleeping** in his bed, he **was playing** with his new app.*
*You **weren't studying** for the test, you **were talking** on the phone the entire time.*

Verneinte Aussagesätze

*Eine Aussage im past progressive verneinst du mit **was/were + not + -ing*-Form** des Verbs. Kurzformen: wasn't, weren't*

Questions

__Were you__ cleaning your room at 2 o'clock?
__Was Drew__ watching Kaya during practice?

Fragen

In Fragen vertauschst du Subjekt und *was/were*.

2.3 Simple past and past progressive contrasted *Simple past* und *past progressive* im Vergleich

*We **travelled** to Vancouver last fall.*
*Dad **left** early this morning. He **had** an important meeting.*

◀ Das *simple past* drückt eine abgeschlossene Handlung in der Vergangenheit aus.

*Drew Schmidt **was looking** at his texts when his dad **entered** the kitchen.*

➜ *p.94, exercise 3*

◀ Das *past progressive* verwendest du oft, um zu beschreiben, was gerade vor sich ging, als eine neue Handlung (im *simple past*) einsetzte.

IN ENGLISH:

- You use the **simple past**
  – when you talk about things in the past (e.g. when you tell a story)
  – when you want to say or ask when something happened
  – when you talk about a new action in the past.
- You use the **past progressive** when you talk about an action that was going on at a point in the past.

2 Exercises

2 Past tenses

a) Complete the historical facts about New York with the correct form of the simple past.

1. The Dutch built the first European village that later … the city of New York. (build, become)
2. These first Dutch settlers … their region New York, they … it New Amsterdam. (call, not call)
3. When the British … control of the area in 1664, they … the name so they … it to New York. (change, not like, take)
4. New York … one of the 13 colonies that … against the British during the War of Independence. (be, fight)
5. The first U.S. flag … 13 stripes, but it … 50 white stars like today – there … only 13. (be, have, not have)
6. Washington D.C. … the U.S. capital until 1790 – before that it … New York City. (be, not become)
7. Americans … the Statue of Liberty – France … it as a gift to the U.S. in 1885. (not build, give)
8. New York City … quickly in the 20th century – the population … from 3.5 to 8 million. (grow, rise)

b) Use the verb in brackets to complete each pair of sentences.
You will need the simple past in one sentence and the past progressive in the other.

1. a) Tom read all Harry Popper books, one after the other.
   b) Mary was reading in bed when suddenly all the lights went out. (read)
2. a) Brad … the answer to the last question when the teacher said to stop.
   b) I … an email to my Grandma and then turned off the computer. (write)
3. a) An old lady … heavy bags out of the store as John arrived.
   b) John … the old lady's bags to the car for her. (carry)
4. a) When Linda broke her ankle, she … in the park.
   b) Brian … four miles in the park yesterday. (run)
5. a) The boys … loudly in the library when the lady asked them to be quiet.
   b) Ben … to Linda on the phone but forgot to ask her about the homework. (talk)
6. a) Lucy: You took my sweets when I … !
   b) Anne: Miriam and Jennie … at each other once at the party. (not look)
7. a) I saw you and Jane during the break. What … you … about?
   b) I … once or twice during the movie – It wasn't very funny. (laugh)
8. a) Belinda … out all her birthday candles in one go.
   b) During our walk on the hill, the wind … so hard that we couldn't hear each other. (blow)

c) Complete the sentences with one verb in the simple past and one in the past progressive.

1. I was crossing (cross) the road when the accident happened (happen).
2. Paul … (listen) to music so he … (not hear) the phone.
3. I … (jump) onto the bus just as the doors … (close).
4. The strange man in the park … (shout) so crazily that somebody … (call) the police.
5. The teacher … (not notice) that Ralph … (make) funny faces behind her back.
6. The prisoner … (escape) as the police … (take) him to jail.
7. When my dad … (grow up), he … (not get) a lot of pocket money.
8. When Miss Murphy … (walk) into the classroom, Kevin … (pretend) to be her.
9. July … (give) Mike a note when Luke … (grab) it out of her hand.

d) Complete the sentences with the right verbs from the box. Use the simple past or the past progressive.

leave · look · lose · play · ~~sing~~ · teach · wait

1. Jennie was singing along to her favourite song when the CD player broke.
2. I didn't know what the word meant so I … it up in the dictionary.
3. Our team … 0-1 until we scored two goals in the last five minutes and won the game.
4. Mike and Toby … one game of cards and then they watched some TV.
5. When Anne arrived home late, her parents … for her in the living room.
6. My friends … the park as I arrived, but they decided to stay a bit longer.
7. My dad … me how to swim when I was five years old.

3 State and activity verbs Zustands- und Tätigkeitsverben

3.1 REVISION State verbs Zustandsverben

*The book **doesn't sound** interesting to me.*
*Emily **seems** happy at her new school.*
*Kaya's uncle **owns** a ranch on the Standing Rock Rez.*

*I **don't believe** their story.*
*How **do** you **know**?*
*Anna **didn't understand** what Julie **meant**.*

*Lucy **doesn't like** people who talk a lot.*
*I **don't mind** waiting for you here.*
*We **prefer** brown bread to white bread. It's healthier.*

➜ *p.95, exercises 4–5*

Zustandsverben *(state verbs)* beschreiben Zustände.
Zu den Zustandsverben gehören

- Verben, die **Eigenschaften, Besitz oder Zugehörigkeit** ausdrücken, z.B. *be, seem, sound, mean* („bedeuten"), *cost, need, own, belong, …*
- Verben des **Meinens und des Wissens**, z.B. *believe, know, mean* („meinen"), *remember, imagine, recognize, understand, …*
- Verben des **Mögens und Wollens**, z.B. *like, love, dislike, hate, mind, prefer, want, …*

Sie werden in der Regel nur in der *simple form* verwendet.

3.2 Activity verbs Tätigkeitsverben

(in a shop window) *We **make** the best pizza in town!*
(on the phone) *Carol **is making** pancakes. Can she call you back?*

*It **gets** dark very early here in winter.*
*At 5 o'clock it **was** already **getting** dark.*

➜ *p.95, exercises 4–5*

Tätigkeitsverben bezeichnen Tätigkeiten *(do, go, make, read, …)* oder Vorgänge *(become, get, rain, …)*.

Sie können sowohl in der *simple form* als auch in der *progressive form* verwendet werden.

		State	Activity
(to) have	*Julie has dark hair.*	haben	
	Julie is having a shower.		duschen
	We were having fun/a great time.		Spaß/eine tolle Zeit haben
(to) look	*Do I look silly with my hair like this?*	aussehen	
	I didn't see him. I wasn't looking.		(hin)schauen, gucken
(to) smell	*The flowers smell wonderful.*	riechen	
	Sophie is smelling the roses.		an etwas riechen
(to) taste	*The pizza tastes good.*	schmecken	
	I'm tasting the soup now.		kosten, probieren
(to) think	*Coach thinks I'm doing well.*	denken, meinen	
	He was thinking of moving to Paris.		überlegen, nachdenken

Einige wenige englische Verben können als Zustands- oder als Tätigkeitssverben verwendet werden (mit jeweils **unterschiedlichen Bedeutungen** im Deutschen).

IN ENGLISH

- **State verbs** describe
  - states or what someone owns (e.g. *be, own*),
  - what someone knows or thinks (e.g. *believe, know, imagine*) and
  - wishes or likes/dislikes (e.g. *love, hate, want*).

  You use state verbs with the simple form of the verb.
- **Activity verbs** refer to activities or processes. You can use them with the simple and the progressive form.
- A few verbs are used as state verbs (in the simple form) and as activity verbs (in the progressive form). The meanings of the verbs then change.

3 Exercises

3 State and activity verbs

a) Complete the facts with the correct verbs. Use the simple present.

belong · believe · cost · ~~imagine~~ · not mind · prefer · not remember · not understand

1. **Ben:** Do you think Jamie is enjoying his holiday? **Alice:** I imagine he's having great fun.
2. **Ken:** Wow. Look at this. 33% of Americans … that UFOs are real.
3. **Teacher:** Who … this jacket … to? It shouldn't be on the classroom floor.
4. **Vicky:** What about this skirt? **Elaine:** No. I … the other one. The colours are nicer.
5. **David:** Dad says I can't have a new phone because it … too much. He's going to give me his old one.
6. **Tourist:** Onde fica o metro? **Brad:** I'm sorry. I … . Can you speak English?
7. **Jennie:** Brian, have you seen my phone? **Brian:** Yes, somewhere, but I … where.
8. **Dad:** Julie, what would you like for dinner – pizza or burgers? **Julie:** I … , Dad. I'm so hungry, I'll eat anything.

b) Complete the short dialogues with the verbs in brackets.
Put one verb into the simple present and the other into the present progressive.

1. **Ben:** Look at Dad. He doesn't usually like (not like) parties. **Mum:** But he … (enjoy) himself now!
2. **Jason:** What's the name of that player on the other team? **Keith:** Which one? **Jason:** Him over there. He … (look) at us now. **Keith:** Oh yeah. He told me his name before the game, but I … (not remember) it now.
3. **Brad:** Psst! Tracy! … you … (understand) question number four? **Tracy:** Shh! I … (do) question number three now.
4. **German student:** Mr. Becker, what … peace … (mean)? **English teacher:** … you … (talk) about world *peace* or a *piece* of bread?
5. **Justin:** No, you can't have the computer. I … (use) it. **Jenny:** But you've had it for ages. I … (need) it now.
6. **Lisa:** You … (seem) a bit tired, Orla. **Orla:** I am. I … (get up) early this week to take Rex for his walk. Dad usually does it, but he's away.

c) Complete the sentences with the correct verbs from the orange box.

1. At the Chocolate Museum, the kids	having	the different kinds of chocolate.
2. David	have	so good in his new suit.
3. Brian, your trainers	is looking	awful.
4. Gary	looks	about his test tomorrow.
5. My teacher	smell	people shouldn't eat meat.
6. Are you	is smelling	fun?
7. Mum	tastes	for her car keys right now.
8. Rex	are tasting	you – he does that with every visitor.
9. Do you	thinks	any sisters or brothers?
10. This ice cream	is thinking	like strawberry.

d) Three friends start a band together and are talking about a name for it.
Complete their talk with the verbs in the simple or progressive form of the present.

Oliver: Hi Luke! Where's Kim?
Luke: She 1's coming (come). She 2… (put) her bike at the back of the house.
Kim: Hi Oliver! I 3… (look forward) to our first band practice today.
Oliver: Yeah, me too. But first, we 4… (need) a name for the band. 5… you … (have) any ideas?
Luke: Yeah - *The Fantastic Three*. What 6… you … (think)?
Oliver: It 7… (sound) like we're superheroes, not a rock band. How about *Three will rock you?*
Kim: Sorry, I 8… (not like) it. I 9… (prefer) something short. I 10… (know)! What about the first letters of our names? K– L–O.
Luke: Kim, *klo* 11… (mean) *toilet* in German. I 12… (not think) we 13… (want) a name like that.
Oliver: No, that's no good. Um.
Kim: What's the matter, Oliver? You 14… (look) angry.
Oliver: I'm not. I 15… (think). Got it! Let's take the first *two* letters of your name, Kim – K-I. *Kilo*!
Luke: *Kilo*! I 16… (love) it. *Kilo* play *heavy* rock, man!

4 REVISION Simple past and present/past perfect contrasted

Simple past und *present/past perfect* im Vergleich

4.1 Present perfect or simple past? *Present perfect* oder *simple past?*

*We've **bought** tickets for the football game tonight! Now we can all go together.*

*Ron **has given** me his mobile. Now I can call my brother.*

◄ Du kannst auch das *present perfect* verwenden, um über etwas Vergangenes zu sprechen, das noch Auswirkungen auf die Gegenwart oder die Zukunft hat. Der genaue Zeitpunkt in der Vergangenheit ist dabei unwichtig.

cook → cooked	***live → lived***
be → been	***keep → kept***
fall → fallen	***spend → spent***

◄ Das *present perfect* bildest du mit ***have/has* + 3. Form des Verbs** (Partizip Perfekt; englisch: *past participle*).
→ *Liste der unregelmäßigen Verben, S. 298–299*

__Have__ you __been__ to the new shopping mall yet?
We__'ve invited__ Dean to our Halloween party.

• *Present perfect:*
– wenn du fragen willst, **ob** etwas geschehen ist
– wenn du sagen willst, **dass** etwas (irgendwann) geschehen ist.

I __went__ to the new shopping mall last weekend.
Helen __asked__ me for help an hour ago.
What time __did__ you __visit__ your grandpa yesterday?

• *Simple past:*
wenn du sagen oder fragen willst, ***wann*** etwas geschehen ist, wie z.B. *yesterday, last year, an hour ago, in 2012*.

4.2 Simple past or past perfect? *Simple past* oder *past perfect?*

*It **hadn't rained** for days.*

◄ Das *past perfect* bildest du mit ***had*** (Kurzform: ***'d***) und der **3. Form des Verbs** (Partizip Perfekt; englisch: *past participle*).

The first lesson __had__ already __started__ when I __arrived__.
Die erste Unterrichtstunde hatte schon begonnen, als ich ankam.

• *Past perfect:* wenn du sagen willst, dass etwas **noch vor etwas anderem in der Vergangenheit** stattgefunden hat.

Handlung 1 *(past perfect)* geschah vor **Handlung 2**:
The first lesson had started ***I arrived***

When I __got__ on the bus, I __had lost__ my purse.
Als ich in den Bus stieg, hatte ich (schon) mein Portemonnaie verloren.

When I __got__ on the bus, I __lost__ my purse.
Ich habe mein Portemonnaie verloren, als ich in den Bus gestiegen bin. (= Ich habe beim Einsteigen oder im Bus mein Portemonnaie verloren.)

◄ Beachte die Bedeutungsunterschiede je nachdem, ob du das *past perfect* oder das *simple past* verwendest.

After Ellen __finished__ / __had finished__ her piano lesson, she __met__ some friends.
Nachdem Ellen mit ihrer Klavierstunde fertig war, traf sie sich mit ein paar Freunden.

◄ Mit *after* und *before* brauchst du das *past perfect* nicht, um die Reihenfolge der Handlungen hervorzuheben. Du kannst das *past perfect* aber benutzen. Die Bedeutung ändert sich dabei nicht.

*I had **already** eaten dinner when the pizza arrived.*
*Grandpa had **never** been to another country before.*

! Im *past perfect* stehen Adverbien (wie *already, ever, never, just, usually, often, always*) in der Regel zwischen *had* und der *past participle* Form.

IN ENGLISH:

- You use the **present perfect** to say that something has happened.
- You use the **simple past** to say when something happened.
- You use the **past perfect** to say that something had happened before something else happened later in the past.

4 Exercises

4 Simple past and present/past perfect contrasted

a) Complete the dialogues with the correct form of the present perfect. Use the verbs in brackets.

1. **Ben:** I've written most of my story for English class, but I ... of a good ending yet. (not think, write)
2. **Keith:** ... your parents ... about buying you a smartphone? **Tim:** They ... me yet. (decide, not tell)
3. **Brian's mum:** Brian, you ... again! You ... this shirt once and it's already too small. (grow, only wear)
4. **Neil:** I don't believe it. *Wolf359* ... again! No one ... him in *Fourth Knight*. (ever beat, win)
5. **Orla:** ... anyone ... my black jeans? **Mum:** ... you ... under your bed? (look, see)
6. **Linda:** ... you ... a chance to talk to the new girl yet? **Julie:** Maria? Sure. She ... me to her house. (have, even invite)
7. **Tracy:** I wonder what's wrong with Anne. I ... her a lot of texts, but she still ... me. (not answer, send)
8. **James:** This tent smells bad! **Luke:** I know. We ... it a long time, but we ... it for ages. (have, not use)
9. **Jen:** ... you ... the pizza yet, Dad? Because I ... again. I'd like salami instead of ham. (think, order)
10. **Maria:** I ... a lot of new friends at school. **Mum:** That's great. You ... there a few days. (only be, already make)
11. **Anne:** Hey Tracy. Sorry I ... to your texts until now. I ... my phone. (just find, not reply)
12. **Grandma:** What ... you ... to your lovely blond hair?! It's pink! **Lucy:** I ... a colour in it. Don't worry. It'll wash out. (do, put)

b) Complete the sentences with the verbs in the correct tense. Use the simple past or present perfect.

1. Dad: Have you thought (think) about what you want for your birthday?
   Tom: Actually Dad, on my way home from school I ... (see) a new Samson phone in the shop.
2. Mum: Ben, there you are. Come and watch the movie with us. You ... (not miss) much – it only ... (begin) a few minutes ago.
3. Marie: Hi Alice. What ... your parents ... (say) about your results in last week's French test? My mum and dad ... (not be) very pleased about mine.
   Alice: I still ... (not show) them yet.
4. Linda: Yesterday's German homework ... (be) difficult. I ... (have to) ask my dad to help.
   Julian: My dad can't help. He ... (learn) German at school, but he ... (forget) most of it.
5. Mike: Oh no! Look. Barry ... (bring) his little brother with him.
   Luke: Oh man. The last time he ... (come), we ... (can not) have any fun.
6. Orla: You should see the new Adventurers movie. We ... (go) to see it at the weekend and it ... (be) great.
   Matilda: Maybe I will. I ... (not be) to the cinema for ages.
7. Peter: ... you ... (see) Adrian's latest Snaptalk post?
   Thomas: No. Show me. The last time he ... (post), it ... (be) very funny.
8. Lucy: Wow! Look! They ... (make) the water park even better. That pool ... (not be) there last summer.

c) Complete the sentences with the verbs. Put <u>one</u> verb in the past perfect and the other(s) in the past simple.

1. Mary couldn't (can not) follow the movie because she had missed (miss) the beginning.
2. The exercise was difficult because I ... (not read) the grammar information on the other page before I ... (start) it.
3. Tom's mum: I ... (want) to say goodnight to you, but you ... (fall) asleep already.
4. After the third lesson I ... (feel) very hungry because I ... (not have) any breakfast.
5. Peter ... (want) Ben to delete the video but Ben ... (already send) it to lots of people.
6. No one ... (tell) Jill about the secret birthday party, so she ... (get) a real surprise when she ... (open) the door.
7. Peter ... (get) bad results in the history test because he ... (not listen) to the teacher's study tips.
8. When the band ... (practise) many times, they finally ... (record) their NewTube video.
9. After they ... (listen) to their father's story, the kids ... (be) all quite scared.
10. Rob ... (hurry) as fast as he ... (can) but the bus ... (go) already.
11. Jane's father ... (not believe) that she ... (finish) all her homework so quickly.
12. I ... (suggest) *Jurassic Wars*, but Tommy ... (see) it twice, so we ... (watch) *Spider Boy* instead.
13. James: I ... (can not) answer question four because I ... (not revise) the chapter on Bismarck.
14. The kids in 8D really ... (miss) Miss Fisher when she ... (retire) because she ... (be) their class teacher for years.
15. When Hal and Bob ... (check) their *NewTube* page they ... (saw) that two thousand people ... (watch) their video.

5 Future tenses Zeitformen der Zukunft

5.1 REVISION The *going to*-future Das Futur mit *going to*

*Today **I'm going to take** a school group to the tide pools.*
*We**'re going to spend** next weekend in L.A.!*
➜ *p.68, exercises 2–3 • p.75, exercises 4–5*

◄ Wenn du **Vorhaben, Pläne, Absichten** für die Zukunft beschreiben willst, verwendest du *am/are/is going to* + Infinitiv.

5.2 REVISION The *will*-future Das Futur mit *will*

*Grandpa **will be** 75 in March.*

◄ Mit *will/won't* + Infinitiv sagst du, was in der Zukunft geschehen wird.

*He probably **won't invite** many guests to his birthday party.*
*Ann hopes it**'ll snow** on Christmas this year.*

Wenn **Vermutungen** geäußert werden, steht häufig *I (don't) think, I'm (not) sure, maybe* oder *probably*. Oft sind es Dinge, die wir nicht beeinflussen können, z.B. Vorhersagen über das Wetter.

*I'm sure you**'ll love** L.A..*
Ich bin mir sicher, dass du L.A. liebst.

! Im **Deutschen** benutzen wir oft das Präsens, wenn wir Vermutungen äußern oder Vorhersagen machen.
Im **Englischen** steht das *will-future*.

*Someone **will** definitely **find** a solution.*
Irgendjemand wird bestimmt eine Lösung finden.
*He probably **won't find** a solution to this problem.*
Er wird wahrscheinlich keine Lösung für das Problem finden.
*Maybe they**'ll have** lots of questions - about the anemones, the starfish, ...*
Vielleicht haben sie viele Fragen - ...
➜ *p.68, exercises 1,3*

Vergleiche auch die **Stellung der Adverbien** wie *probably, maybe* oder *definitely* im Deutschen und Englischen.
Im Englischen ändert sich die Position des Adverbs in verneinten Sätzen. Das Adverb steht vor *won't*.

5.3 More information on *will* Weitere Informationen zu *will*

1 *You've left your keys at home? Don't worry. I**'ll give** you mine.*
Du hast deine Schlüssel zu Hause gelassen. Keine Sorge! Ich gebe dir meine Schlüssel.

2 *Wait, I**'ll open** the door for you.*
Warte, ich mach dir die Tür auf.

3 *I**'ll call** you when we're finished.*
Ich werde dich anrufen, wenn wir fertig sind.

➜ *pp.74–75, exercises 2–5*

Du verwendest das *will*-future auch, wenn du dich spontan (beim Sprechen) zu etwas entschließt.

Oft geht es dabei um **Angebote** (Sätze 1 und 2) oder **Versprechen** (Satz 3).

IN ENGLISH:
- You use the ***going to*-future** to describe intentions and talk about plans.
- You use the ***will*-future** to say what we know or think will happen.
- You also use the ***will*-future** to make a spontaneous offer or promise to someone.

5 Exercises

5 Future tenses

a) Use the correct form of the *going to*-future to complete the statements and questions.

1. **Jen**: Why are your old toys in the car? **Tim**: We're going to take (take) them to the children's hospital tomorrow.
2. **Mum**: Why didn't you finish the rest of the pizza, Brian? **Brian**: Because I ... (eat) it later.
3. **Lisa**: Miss Bond forgot to give us our test results. **Mary**: No, she ... (tell) us the results after the break.
4. **Pete**: Hey Philip! I thought you didn't have time to come with us. **Philip**: I don't. But I ... (not stay) very long.
5. **Dad**: Look at the kitchen! It's so dirty. Who ... (clean) it? **Barry**: Not me. It's not my fault. It was Susie.
6. **Mum**: I hope you ... (not post) that awful photo of me on your *Friendbook* page. **Fran**: Don't worry, Mum.
7. **Tina**: Where ... you and your family ... (go) on holiday this summer? **Julian**: My parents haven't decided yet.
8. **Tony**: Joe ... (not play) on the team next year. He says he doesn't enjoy it any more.
9. **Teacher**: Children, be quiet. I ... (give) the next boy or girl who speaks without permission extra homework.
10. **Mike**: Is *Fourth Knight* finished? **Terry**: No, it isn't. They ... (make) a new version in a few weeks.

**b) Complete the dialogues with the correct verbs and adverbs from the box.
Use the *will*-future. Pay attention to the position of the adverb.**

~~be~~ · probably come · cost · get · probably go · help · say · definitely win · send · phone

1. **Brian:** I'm going to Tom's house, Mum. **Mum:** When will you be home, Brian?
2. **Lucy:** The weather app on my phone says that the weather ... warmer later in the week.
3. **James:** Who do think will win the game tomorrow? **Ben:** Manchester ... – I'm sure of it.
4. **Linda:** Have a great holiday, Jennie! **Jennie:** Thanks. I ... you a postcard.
5. **Kevin:** Don't go yet. The bus ... in a minute. It's usually late.
6. **Dad:** ... you ... us when you arrive? **Tracy:** Of course, Dad.
7. **Jamie:** I can't find my phone anywhere!! **Mum:** Don't worry, Jamie. I ... you to look.
8. **Computer store man:** I looked at your broken laptop. I think it ... less to buy a new one.
9. **Tina:** Well, have your mum and dad decided about your holiday yet? **Julian:** Not yet. I guess we ... to Scotland, again.
10. **Tracy:** I think you should ask your parents if you can go to the concert, Elaine. Who knows? Maybe they ... yes.

c) Complete the dialogues with the *going to* future or the *will*-future.

Orla: (Phone rings) Hi Matilda. Can I call you back later? We [1] 're going to have (have) our dinner in a minute.
Matilda: Oh sorry. Don't worry. I [2] ... (write) you a message instead.

Mum: Tell me, Jane. Who [3] ... you ... (invite) to your birthday party?
Jane: Here's the list. Have a look.
Mum: You forgot Lisa. [4] ... you ... (add) her name to the list, please?

Ben: Hi Luke. Nice flowers. Are they for me?
Luke: No. I [5] ... (give) them to my mother. It's Mother's Day today.
Ben: Really? Oh. I think I [6] ... (get) some for my mum, too. Where did you get them?
Luke: Follow me and I [7] ... (show) you.

Gemma: (At the cinema) Oh no. Look at all the people in the ticket queues. We [8] ... (miss) the beginning of the movie.
Mary: Maybe we [9] ... (miss) the trailers. That's not so bad. Where are you going? You're not leaving, are you?
Gemma: No. I [10] ... (stand) in the other queue – it's shorter. We [11] ... (see) who gets to the counter first.
Mary: OK. I [12] ... (stay) here and whoever is first buys the tickets.

Jack: Why are you taking a photo of your old *Gamestation*?
Bobbie: I [13] ... (sell) it on *TBay*.
Jack: Don't do that. You [14] ... (not get) very much money for it. What about the video game store? Sometimes they take old *Gamestations* and you can buy a new one cheaper.
Bobbie: It's a good idea, but Mum and Dad [15] ... (buy) me a new one for my birthday anyway. I still need games for the new one. Let's go to the store now. Maybe they [16] ... (give) us a game at a lower price. [17] ... you ... (put) the *Gamestation* in its box while I tell Mum what we [18] ... (do)?
Jack: Sure.

6 Present tenses with a future meaning Zeiten der Gegenwart mit Zukunftsbezug

6.1 Present progressive with a future meaning *Present progressive* mit Zukunftsbezug

*We'**re making** two episodes here in Hollywood and then we'**re shooting** the rest in Canada.*

*What **are** you **doing** on Sunday? **Are** you **going** skiing again?*

◄ Wenn etwas für die Zukunft fest verabredet ist, kannst du auch das *present progressive* benutzen. Es muss aber deutlich sein, dass es sich um etwas Zukünftiges handelt, z.B. durch eine **Zeitangabe** *(on Sunday, tomorrow)* **oder aus dem Zusammenhang**.

*We'**re going** to Europe for a few weeks in July.*
*Where **are** you **going** exactly? – We'**re starting** in Paris.*
*Josh **is visiting** his cousin tomorrow.*

Man nennt diese Verwendung des *present progressive* manchmal ***diary future***, weil es dabei oft um Verabredungen geht, die schon im Terminkalender eingetragen sind.

➜ *pp.74–75, exercises 1,3,5*

6.2 Simple present with a future meaning *Simple present* mit Zukunftsbezug

*The next train to Cardiff **leaves** at 8:25.*
*Our French classes **start** on Monday.*

◄ Auch das *simple present* kann futurische Bedeutung haben. Du verwendest es, wenn du über ein zukünftiges Geschehen sprichst, das durch einen **Fahrplan, ein Programm oder Ähnliches** genau festgelegt ist.

*The café **opens** at 10 am on Sundays.*
*The sun **goes** down at 5:54pm today.*
*What time **does** your plane **arrive** in New York?*

◄ Häufig verwendete Verben sind u.a. *arrive, leave, go, open, close, start, stop.*

Diese Verwendung des *simple present* bezeichnet man auch ***timetable future***.

IN ENGLISH:

You can also use the present tenses of a verb to talk about the future:

- You can use the **present progressive** to talk about what you have planned to do in the future (= diary future).
- You can use the **simple present** for future events that are listed in a timetable or programme (= timetable future).

6 Exercises

6 Present tenses with a future meaning

a) Look at the Smith family's calendar for next week. Then write sentences about their plans with the correct form of the present progressive.
1. On Monday afternoon, Mr Smith is going to the hairdresser.
2. On Tuesday, Lucy and Jane ... in the park at three o'clock.
3. On Wednesday, Mrs Smith ... at the gym at 5pm.
4. Lucy's friend Jane ... at 4.30pm on Thursday.
5. On Thursday afternoon, Jake ... Jamal. He ... for his Maths test instead.
6. On Friday evening, Mr and Mrs Smith ... at Luigi's restaurant.
7. Everyone ... the house on Saturday morning.

Monday
Afternoon - Dad – go hairdresser
Tuesday
Lucy – meet Jane in the park @3pm
Jake – go to baseball training
Wednesday
Jake – have video call with Joe
Mom – do yoga at the gym @5pm
Thursday
Lucy – Jane come to tea @4.30pm
Jake – ~~meet Jamal~~ revise
Friday
Jake – Maths exam!
Lucy – swimming pool
Mom & Dad – dinner at Luigi's Italian restaurant @8pm
Saturday
Everyone – clean the house
Jake – play baseball game
Sunday
have lunch @ Grandma & Grandpa's @1pm
Evening? – movie/game night?

b) Look again at the Smith family's calendar. Then make questions about their family's plans. Add a verb in the progressive form to each question.
1. What time / Jake / baseball training / on Tuesday?
   What time is Jake going to baseball training on Tuesday?
2. When / Jake and his friend Joe / video call?
3. Where / Lucy / on Friday?
4. Mr Smith: Where / you / your baseball game on Saturday, Jake?
5. Lucy: When / we / lunch / at Grandma and Grandpa's?
6. What / the Smiths / on Sunday evening?

c) Complete the sentences with the verbs from the box. Use the simple present.

be · ~~begin~~ · not finish · land · leave · open
start · take place · finish

1. The baseball game begins at 3pm and ... around 6pm.
2. Dad: Brian, can you go to the bakery and get some bread rolls? It ... in ten minutes.
3. Mum: My appointment at the hairdresser ... at three o'clock next Monday.
4. Paul: When should we go to the airport tomorrow, Mum? When ... Dad's plane ... ?
5. The school exams ... in the school gym next month.
6. The earliest train to Liverpool next Saturday ... London at 5.30am.
7. Luke: Mum. The concert tomorrow ... until 11.45pm. Can you pick us up then?
8. Kevin: Hi Tom. I can't wait for your party next week. What time ... it ... ?

d) The sentences need the right verb. Put the verbs into the correct form. Use the simple present or the present progressive.

1. Football training	not come	at 5pm tomorrow on pitch number three.
2. The last bus	finish	the town centre at 11pm.
3. Brian and his family	go	back from their holidays until Friday.
4. Don't forget that school	leave	early tomorrow – it's Wednesday.
5. The new Pk Maxx store	meet	its doors next Monday, 2nd June.
6. Next Thursday, Kevin	open	me in front of the library.
7. Grandma	starts	us next weekend.
8. Jane and I	take place	to the mall after school today.
9. The next Fourth Knight tournament	visit	online next Saturday.

7 REVISION Conditional sentences 1 and 2 Bedingungssätze 1 und 2

7.1 Conditional sentence 1 Bedingungssatz 1

If he ***doesn't stop*** *soon, I'****ll go*** *crazy!*
Wenn er nicht sofort aufhört, werde ich verrückt!

*We'****ll play basketball*** *in the schoolyard if it* ***doesn't rain****.*
Watch out! If you ***fall****, I* ***won't hold*** *you.*

1 *If Amy doesn't have to go now, she* ***can*** *have lunch with us.*
Wenn Amy jetzt nicht gehen muss, dann kann sie mit uns Mittag essen.
2 *If you miss me, just* ***visit*** *me.*
Wenn du mich vermisst, komm mich einfach besuchen.

➜ *p.44, exercises 1,3*

◂ Bedingungssätze vom Typ 1 sind „Was ist, wenn … "-Sätze: Sie beschreiben, was unter bestimmten Bedingungen geschieht oder nicht geschieht.

Im ***if-Satz*** steht das *simple present*. Im **Hauptsatz** steht meist das *will-future*.

◂ Im Hauptsatz können auch *can, must, could, should* + Infinitiv (Satz 1) oder ein Imperativ (Satz 2) stehen.

7.2 Conditional sentence 2 Bedingungssatz 2

If Alan ***spent*** *more time with his friends, he* ***would be*** *very happy.*
Wenn Alan mehr Zeit mit seinen Freunden verbringen würde, dann wäre er überglücklich.

If I ***were*** *you, I'****d block him****.*
I ***wouldn't eat*** *any, if you* ***gave*** *me 100 dollars.*

If Mark ***read*** *this email, he* ***might get*** *angry.*
… könnte er sauer werden.

If I ***were*** *in Africa, I* ***could*** */* ***might see*** *many wild animals.*
… könnte ich / würde ich vielleicht viele Tiere in der Wildnis sehen.

➜ *p.44, exercises 2–3*

◂ Bedingungssätze vom Typ 2 sind „Was wäre, wenn…"-Sätze: Du verwendest sie, wenn du dir eine Handlung oder Situation vorstellst, die eher unwahrscheinlich ist.

Im ***if-Satz*** steht das *simple past*. Im **Hauptsatz** steht meist *would* + Infinitiv (Kurzform: *'d*).

◂ Im Hauptsatz können auch *might* + Infinitiv oder *could* + Infinitiv stehen.

! Beachte, dass im *if*-Satz oft ***were*** statt *was* steht. *Was* ist aber auch möglich.
If I were/was a bird/in Africa …

ZUSAMMENFASSUNG:

Bedingungssatz 1	*If*-Satz	Hauptsatz
If they score another goal, they will win. Das Spiel hat erst begonnen bzw. ist noch nicht vorbei. Der Sprecher denkt, es ist wahrscheinlich, dass sie noch ein Tor machen.	*simple present*	*will*-future, *can/must/could/should* + infinitive oder ein Imperativ
Bedingungssatz 2		
If they scored another goal, they would win. Das Spiel ist fast vorbei. Der Sprecher denkt, es ist unwahrscheinlich, dass sie noch ein Tor machen.	*simple past*	*would/could/might* + infinitive

IN ENGLISH:

- In **conditional 1 sentences** you describe a condition in the *if*-clause and its consequence in the main clause.
- You use **conditional 2 sentences** when you imagine an action or situation which is probably not going to happen.

7 Exercises

7 Conditional sentences 1 and 2

a) Match the sentence parts and put the verbs in the correct form to make conditional 1 statements and questions.

1. If you see (see) Mike,
2. Your sister ... (not give) you her dress again
3. If you ... (want) to get that part of the song right,
4. We ... (miss) the beginning of the film
5. If I tell you something,
6. I ... (let) you borrow my Wintendo
7. Someone ... (steal) your bike
8. Billy, if your homework ... (be) late again,

a) will you ask him to call me?
b) if you ... (lend) me your Gamestation.
c) you ... (have to practise) more often.
d) if we ... (not leave) now.
e) if you ... (make) it dirty.
f) ... you ... (promise) not to tell anyone?
g) I ... (have to write) a letter to your parents.
h) if you ... (leave) it there.

b) Here are some tips about learning English. Use one modal verb and one main verb from each box to complete the conditional 1 sentences. Several modal verb combinations are possible. One sentence needs the imperative form.

~~can~~ can could mustn't should shouldn't

sing not panic ~~speak~~ try not worry write

1. If you know English, you can speak with people all over the world.
2. If you can't remember an English word, you ... to explain it with other English words.
3. If you don't understand everything an English speaker says, you ... – just ask them to speak more slowly.
4. If you want a fun way to practise English, you ... along with English songs.
5. You ... your own sentences if you need more practice with conditional 1.
6. If you make mistakes when you speak English, ... too much – nobody's perfect.

c) Complete the conditional 2 statements and questions.

1. Sorry, Barry, if I didn't have (not have) so much homework to do, I would come (come) with you.
2. What's the first thing you ... (change) if you ... (be) head teacher of the school, Jennie?
3. My dad ... (not have to) be away as often as he does if he ... (not work) as a lorry driver.
4. If you ... (see) someone drop a lot of money, ... you ... (keep) it or tell the person?
5. I ... (have) a bedroom all to myself if we ... (live) in a house and not this small apartment.
6. We ... (visit) our grandparents more often if they ... (not live) so far away.
7. If my legs ... (be) longer, I ... (be) a better basketball player.
8. What ... you ... (do) if you ... (be) me?
9. If my uniform ... (not be) so grey, I ... (not hate) it so much.

d) Look at the conditional 1 and 2 sentences. Then match the first parts of the conditional sentences with the correct ending. Put the verbs in a-h into the right form.

1. If Miriam could have any pet in the world,
2. I'll miss our science teacher Mr Brophy
3. My parents wouldn't like it
4. If my mum calls your mum,
5. You should practise a language – if you don't use it,
6. If it were my birthday party,
7. The world will get hotter
8. If you tell Henry the truth,

a) I ... (not invite) Jane.
b) if we ... (not use) cleaner energy instead of oil and coal.
c) if we ... (change) teachers next year.
d) she would choose (choose) a black panther.
e) I'm sure he... (not be) angry.
f) if I ... (post) photos of them as babies on the internet.
g) you ... (lose) it.
h) ... she ... (let) you sleep over at my house?

e) Complete the conditional statements and questions with the verbs from the box.
Put the verbs into the correct form. Use conditional 1 or conditional 2.

be (2x) · ~~not be~~ · not come (2x) · drive · fly · have to · call · ~~fall~~ · not get · have · not revise · not speak · not think · tell

1. Watch out! If you aren't careful, you'll fall!
2. If nobody ... cars in the city, the air ... cleaner and life less noisy.
3. I ... English as well as I do if my father ... from Ireland.
4. Where ... you ... to if you ... wings?
5. If you ... for tomorrow's test, you ... good results.
6. You ... my brother was so cool if you ... grow up with him.
7. Dad, if Jennie ..., ... you ... her that I'm in Alice's house?
8. If the bus ... soon, we ... late for school.

8 Conditional sentence 3 Bedingungssatz 3

Use and form Gebrauch und Form

1 *If Ellen had asked her dad, he would have given her some money.*
Wenn Ellen ihren Vater gefragt hätte, dann hätte er ihr ein wenig Geld gegeben.
2 *If the shops hadn't been closed, we would have gone shopping.*
Wenn die Geschäfte nicht geschlossen hätten, wären wir einkaufen gegangen.

◂ Bedingungssätze vom Typ 3 sind „Was wäre gewesen, wenn …"-Sätze. Du verwendest sie, wenn du dir eine Handlung oder Situation in der Vergangenheit vorstellst, die nicht passiert ist.
Der *if*-Satz nennt eine Bedingung, die nicht erfüllt wurde: Ellen hat ihren Vater nicht gefragt (Satz 1). In Satz 2 haben die Geschäfte nicht geöffnet.
Der Hauptsatz drückt aus, was geschehen wäre, wenn die Bedingung im *if*-Satz erfüllt worden wäre: Dann hätte er ihr ein wenig Geld gegeben (Satz 1). Dann wären wir einkaufen gegangen (Satz 2).

*But you **wouldn't have kept** the earrings if you **hadn't liked** them.*
Aber du hättest die Ohrringe nicht behalten, wenn du sie nicht gemocht hättest.

◂ Bedingungssätze vom Typ 3 drücken aus, was unter bestimmten Bedingungen geschehen oder nicht geschehen wäre.

Bedingung	**Folge für die Zukunft**
*If you **hadn't liked***	*you **wouldn't have kept***
past perfect	*would (not) have + past participle*

Im ***if*-Satz** steht das *past perfect*. Im **Hauptsatz** steht meist *would (not) have + past participle*.

*If it hadn't rained, we **could / might** have gone swimming.*
…, hätten wir schwimmen gehen können / wären wir vielleicht schwimmen gegangen.

◂ Im Hauptsatz können auch *could have* + past participle oder *might have* + past participle stehen.

*If she'**d** (=had) called me, I'**d** (=would) have answered the phone.*

! Die Kurzform *'d* steht im *if*-Satz für ***had***, im Hauptsatz aber für ***would***.

➜ *p.49, exercise 4*

More information

Weitere Informationen

***I wish I had found** it. I would have screamed too.*
Ich wünschte, ich hätte es gefunden. Ich hätte auch geschrien.
***I wish I had known** him, Grandma.*
Ich wünschte, ich hätte ihn gekannt, Oma.

◂ Wenn du dir wünschst, dass etwas anders gelaufen wäre oder du anders gehandelt hättest, verwendest du Phrasen wie *I wish I had/I hadn't done …*

***I would have been** afraid.*
I hätte Angst gehabt.

◂ Wenn du etwas Vergangenes kommentierst, benutzt du oft Phrasen wie *I wouldn't have done that / I would have …*

➜ *pp.48–49, exercises 1–3*

ZUSAMMENFASSUNG:

Bedingungssatz 3	***If*-Satz**	**Hauptsatz**
If they had scored another goal, they would have won.	*past perfect*	*would/could/might + have + past participle*
Das Spiel ist vorbei. Sie haben kein weiteres Tor gemacht und haben deshalb nicht gewonnen.		

IN ENGLISH:

You use **conditional 3 sentences** when you talk about an action or situation which did not happen in the past.

8 Exercises

8 Conditional sentence 3

a) Complete the sentences with "would (not) have" and the verbs from the box. Put the verbs in the correct form.

not be · buy · choose · know · ~~tell~~ · use

1. Pete: The teacher gave me extra work because I threw paper in class, but it was Danny who threw it.
   Julie: I would have told the teacher that Danny did it.
2. Tracy: It was my birthday yesterday.
   Jen: What?! I didn't know that. Why didn't you tell me? I ... you a present.
3. John: I'm glad you asked me to go with you to the party.
   Linda: Me too. It ... as much fun without you.
4. Jane: I can't believe the boys' team didn't know the answer to that last quiz question.
   Lucy: I can't either. Even my little sister ... the answer to that question.
5. Tim: What did you think of my presentation?
   James: I thought it was good except for the last part. I ... a picture to make it more interesting.
6. Orla: I decided to have my birthday party in the park. What do you think?
   Matilda: I ... somewhere inside. What if the weather is bad?

b) Complete the conditional 3 sentences.

1. If we had taken (take) a taxi, we wouldn't have been (not be) late for the concert.
2. If I ... (be) more careful, the accident ... (not happen).
3. We ... (not get) lost if Dad ... (look) at the map.
4. I ... (not believe) it if I ... (not see) it with my own eyes.
5. If you ... (not study) so hard, you ... (not get) such good results.
6. If Paul ... (have) more money, he ... (buy) a better phone.
7. Elaine ... (not lose) her money if she ... (put) it somewhere safe.
8. Mum ... (not be) so angry with me if I ... (tell) her the truth from the start.

c) Match the sentence parts and put the verbs in the correct form to make conditional 3 sentences.

1. The kids would have been (be) in a lot of trouble
2. I ... (buy) a ticket for you too
3. We ... (have to) walk
4. If we ... (look) at a weather app before our walk,
5. If Tracy ... (tell) me it was a secret,
6. Joe ... (go) to the party
7. If it ... (not rain) so much,
8. I'm sure your sister ... (not mind) so much

a) if you ... (ask) her for her bike instead of just taking it.
b) the holiday ... (be) great.
c) I ... (not tell) Susan.
d) if he ... (not be) ill.
e) if I ... (know) you wanted to go to the concert.
f) if the teacher had caught (catch) them.
g) if your dad ... (not pick) us up after the movie.
h) we ... (know) it would be so cold.

d) Use the information from the sentences to write conditional 3 sentences.

1. You didn't give me your email address. I didn't write to you.
   If you had given me your email address, I would have written to you.
2. Linda didn't finish her presentation because her dad's computer was broken.
3. You went to bed late. You felt so tired in school today.
4. Tim's mum fell over his books because he left them on the floor.
5. Brian was ill because he ate so much chocolate.
6. I didn't go to the park with my friends because I had so much homework to do.
7. Paul didn't tell the truth before. His parents didn't believe what he said.
8. Daniel spent all his money on a magazine. He didn't have enough money for sweets.
9. I didn't write down the homework. I forgot what it was.

9 The gerund Das Gerundium

9.1 Use and form Gebrauch und Form

*I love **drawing**.*
*Dan hates **dancing**.*

Wenn die *-ing*-Form eines Verbs die **Funktion eines Nomens** hat, nennst du sie Gerundium (englisch: *gerund*).
Vergleiche: *I love pop music*. (*love* + Nomen)
I love drawing. (*love* + *-ing*-Form)

*My hobbies are **singing, swimming** and **reading**.*

◀ Die *-ing*-Form bildest du durch Anhängen von *-ing* an den Infinitiv: *(to) sing -> sing**ing***.

The gerund as object

Das Gerundium als Objekt

*Pam doesn't like **cleaning**.*
*Bill's brother enjoys **surfing**.*

Das Gerundium (und seine Erweiterung) kann wie ein Nomen **Objekt** eines Satzes sein.

*Alex likes **playing** tennis after school.*
Alex spielt gern nach der Schule Tennis.

◀ Wie ein Verb kannst du das Gerundium erweitern, z. B. durch ein Objekt *(tennis)* oder eine Orts- oder Zeitangabe *(after school)*.

The gerund as subject

Das Gerundium als Subjekt

***Drawing** isn't easy.*
***Travelling** can be expensive.*

Das Gerundium (und seine Erweiterung) kann wie ein Nomen auch **Subjekt** eines Satzes sein.

***Getting** it in one photo will be hard.*
***Chilling** in Washington Square Park is fun.*
Chillen im Washington Square Park macht Spaß. / Es macht Spaß, im Washington Square Park zu chillen.

◀ Auch hier kannst du das Gerundium erweitern, z. B. durch ein Objekt *(it)* oder eine Orts- oder Zeitangabe *(in one photo, in Washington Square Park)*.

! Im Deutschen gibst du das Gerundium oft durch einen Infinitiv mit „zu" oder durch ein Nomen wieder.

➜ *p.19, exercises 1–2*

9.2 The gerund after verbs Das Gerundium nach Verben

*But I **enjoy being** with you too.*
Aber ich bin auch gern mit dir zusammen.

*I can't **imagine living** anywhere else.*
Ich kann mir nicht vorstellen, irgendwo anders zu wohnen.

*Tyler **suggested visiting** Birdman.*
Tyler schlug vor, den Vogelmann zu besuchen.

➜ *p.19, exercises 1–2*

Nach einigen Verben – z.B. *enjoy, finish, imagine, mind, miss, practise, suggest* – steht (anders als im Deutschen) immer ein Gerundium.

IN ENGLISH:

- A **gerund** is an *-ing* form which is used like a noun.
- Gerunds can be the object or the subject of a sentence, e.g. *I love playing tennis.* or *Playing tennis is fun.*
- Some verbs only take the gerund, e.g. *enjoy, finish, imagine, mind, miss, practise, suggest*.

9 Exercises

9 The gerund

a) Complete the sentences with a verb in its gerund form.

know · meet · ~~play~~ · read · share · take · walk · win

1. Mary practises playing the piano every day.
2. I don't like … my room with my little brother.
3. John: My sister is so curious. She likes … everything about everybody.
4. Orla: I love … in bed before I go asleep.
5. Tim: Could you imagine … a million pounds? What would you do with all that money?
6. Jane: My sister is away on a school exchange. I miss … to school with her in the mornings.
7. Sophia: Hi Matilda! Would you mind … me outside the library tomorrow?
8. Brian: My favourite hobby is … photos, especially nature photos.

b) Put the responses in the short dialogues in the correct order. You will need to put one verb in the gerund form.

1. Miriam: What was your favourite part of your holiday?
   Tracy: the Grand Canyon / see Seeing the Grand Canyon.
2. Paula: We lost another game. We must be the worst team ever.
   Fran: is / everything / not / win
3. Elaine: Jamie! Why are you covered in mud?
   Jamie: work / the garden / you / in / dirty / makes
4. Mum: Why are you wearing earphones when it's homework time?
   Jane: me / to music / listen / helps / think
5. Dad: Why aren't you with Mum and your sister?
   Tara: the Ice Queen / because / boring / for the sixth time / is / watch
6. Tim: Miss Yourell, I'm not sure what kind of story I should write.
   Teacher: some ideas / write / is / a good start / down
7. Anne: Do you want to come to the library to study for the test?
   Lucy: idea / brilliant / is / revise / a
8. Joe: It's not fair! You're allowed out until 10 o'clock, but I must be home before eight.
   Ben: advantages / older / be / has

c) Complete the kids' conversation with two of the verbs in brackets. Put one of the verbs in the gerund form.

1. Zara: I like doing yoga. What about you, Mia? (do, like, make)
2. Mia: Yoga's OK, but I … … team sports. They're more fun. (dislike, prefer, play)
3. Pete: I'm a nature man. I … … outdoor activities. In the countryside. (be, do, love)
4. Zara: Pete the nature man – that's funny! What do you … … in the wild? (be, enjoy, do)
5. Pete: Zara the city girl – that's funnier! … … outside under the stars - that's what I love. (expect, imagine, sleep)
6. Zara: I'm not a city girl. I don't … … camping, but I wouldn't sleep outside, only inside the tent. (go, mind, love)
7. Mia: I'm surprised, Pete. Don't you … … able to play your *Gamestation* when you're in the countryside? (be, mind, miss)
8. Pete: I have a *Wintendo Twitch*, not a *Gamestation*. It's like a tablet – I can take it with me and … … ! (go, keep, play)

d) Join the sentence parts to make one sentence. Complete the sentences using the gerund of the verbs in the boxes.

For the subjects:

be · eat · play · spell

1. My sister wants to give up
2. … chess helps Tim
3. The boys don't like
4. … English words isn't
5. Linda hates
6. … a Hollywood actor
7. Jane finds
8. … fruit and vegetables
9. Our English teacher suggested

For the objects:

go · keep · sing · clean · wait

a. always easy.
b. is Mark's dream.
c. … in front of people difficult.
d. is good for you.
e. … for someone, but she always arrives late herself.
f. going to violin lessons.
g. … a special notebook for our vocabulary.
h. … their rooms.
i. to relax in the evening.

10 The gerund or the *to*-infinitive Das Gerundium oder der *to-infinitive*

10.1 Verbs with no differences in meaning Verben ohne Bedeutungsunterschiede

She ***began learning / to learn*** *judo when she was eight.*
Sie fing an Judo zu lernen, als sie acht war.
Tyler ***hates missing / to miss*** *a good shot.*
Tyler hasst es, eine gute Aufnahme zu verpassen.
But Birdman's pigeons were insulted. And they ***started showing / to show*** *Alex their feelings.*
… und sie begannen Alex ihre Gefühle zu zeigen.

◂ Nach ***begin/start, hate, like, love, prefer*** kann – bei gleicher Bedeutung – ein Gerundium oder ein *to*-Infinitiv stehen.

Mum ***would prefer to move*** *to a small village, but Dad* ***would hate to live*** *in the country.*
Meine Mutter würde es bevorzugen in ein kleines Dorf zu ziehen, aber mein Vater würden es hassen, auf dem Land zu leben.

! Nach *would like, would love, would hate, would prefer* kann nur der *to*-Infinitiv stehen.

➔ *pp.26–27, exercises 1–2*

10.2 Verbs with differences in meaning Verben mit Bedeutungsunterschieden

I mustn't ***forget to call*** *Brad – it's his birthday.*
Ich darf nicht vergessen Brad anzurufen – es ist sein Geburtstag.
I'll never ***forget meeting*** *Brad for the first time.*
Ich werde nie (den Moment) vergessen, als ich Brad das erste Mal getroffen habe.

Remember to bring *your umbrella.*
Denk dran, deinen Schirm mitzubringen.
Jude ***remembers running*** *the marathon last year.*
Jude erinnert sich daran, dass er letztes Jahr den Marathon gelaufen ist.

Nancy ***stopped to buy*** *some bread.*
Nancy hielt an, um ein wenig Brot zu kaufen.
"Mr. Keller told me everything. ***Stop lying****, Pete."*
"… Hör auf zu lügen, Pete."

I'll ***try to spend*** *less money for clothes.*
Ich werde versuchen, weniger Geld für Anziehsachen auszugeben.
He couldn't open the door, so he ***tried kicking*** *it.*
… Deshalb probierte er, sie einzutreten.

➔ *pp.26–27, exercises 1–2*

Bei ***forget, remember, stop*** und ***try*** hängt es von der Bedeutung ab, ob sie mit *to*-Infinitiv <u>oder</u> mit Gerundium stehen:

- *forget to do sth.* = vergessen, (später) etwas zu tun
  forget doing sth. = vergessen, dass man (in der Vergangenheit) etwas getan hat
- *remember to do sth.* = daran denken, (später) etwas zu tun
  remember doing sth. = sich daran erinnern, dass man etwas getan hat
- *stop to do sth.* = anhalten, um etwas zu tun
  stop doing sth. = aufhören, etwas zu tun
- *try to do sth.* = versuchen, etwas zu tun
  try doing sth. = etwas ausprobieren

IN ENGLISH:

- Some verbs like *begin/start, hate, like, love* and *prefer* can take **the gerund or the *to*-infinitive**. The meanings of the verbs do not change.
- Verbs like *forget, remember, stop* and *try* have different meanings when they are followed by a gerund <u>or</u> a *to*-infinitive.

10 Exercises

10 The gerund or the *to*- infinitive

a) The Jones family are in the kitchen and are talking about their weekend plans.
Complete the sentences with the two verbs in brackets. Put one verb in the gerund or the *to*-infinitive form. Put the other verb in its correct form, too.

1. Dad: What would you like to do this weekend, kids? (do, like)
2. Susan: I … … to the zoo. We haven't been there for ages. (go, suggest)
3. Mark: I don't understand why Susan … … at animals so much. (enjoy, look)
4. Mum: OK, Mark. Where would you … … ? (go, prefer)
5. Mark: The Science Museum. Susan, stop it! She … … me under the table. (keep, kick)
6. Dad: Susan, stop that, please. OK, kids. If you can't agree on what you … … , Mum and I will decide. (do, want)
7. Mum: The Science Museum website says they have … … the new space travel part. That sounds interesting. (build, finish)
8. Dad: It does. OK, we'll go to the Museum this weekend and, Susan, the weekend after, we … … to the zoo. (go, promise)

b) Put the first verb into the correct form and use the gerund/the *to*-infinitive with the second form.
You can use the gerund <u>and</u> the *to*-infinitive forms here. The meanings of the verbs do not change.

~~begin~~ · not like · love · paint · play · prefer · ~~rain~~ · run · start · wear

1. The children ran inside when it began raining / began to rain.
2. Thursday is Gemma's favourite school day because she has double Art and she … … .
3. The P.E. teacher blew the whistle and the kids … … as fast as they could.
4. Mary … … glasses, but she needs them.
5. I … … team sports – that's why I picked volleyball and not tennis at the sports summer camp.

c) Complete the pair of sentences using the verb in the box. Put one of the verbs in brackets into the gerund form and the other into the *to*-infinitive form. Here the meanings of the verbs change.

1. **forget**
   a) Brian: Although I was very young, I'll never forget flying (fly) on a plane the first time.
   b) Mum: Oh no, Julie forgot to pack (pack) her lunch for school. She's going to be hungry.
2. **stop**
   a) On our way home from Liverpool, we … (eat) at a *McBurger* restaurant.
   b) Dana believes that everyone should … (eat) animals.
3. **try**
   a) Pete … (reach) the geography book on the top shelf, but he was too short.
   b) Then he … (stand) on a chair and he was able to get it.
4. **remember**
   a) Teacher: OK, children. Please … … (give) your parents the letter about the school trip.
   b) Jamie: Mum, have you seen my phone? I … … (leave) it on the kitchen table, but it's not there now.

11 The gerund after prepositions and in certain phrases
Das Gerundium nach Präpositionen und in bestimmten Wendungen

11.1 The gerund after prepositions Das Gerundium nach Präpositionen

1 *Never cross a street* ***without looking***.
Überquere nie eine Straße, ohne zu schauen.
2 *You can improve your English* ***by watching*** *British TV.*
…, indem du britisches Fernsehen schaust.
3 *I suggested visiting Birdman. Alex wasn't* ***keen on doing*** *that either.*
Ich schlug vor, den Vogelmann zu besuchen. Alex war auch nicht begeistert, dies zu tun.
4 *She was* ***looking forward to meeting*** *Jim in the park.*
Sie freute sich darauf, Jim im Park zu treffen.

➜ *p.27, exercises 3–4*

Wenn auf eine Präposition *(about, at, for, in, instead of, of, without, …)* ein Verb folgt, dann steht dieses Verb als Gerundium.

Die Präposition kann
– alleine stehen (Sätze 1 und 2) oder
– mit einem anderen Wort fest verbunden sein (Sätze 3 und 4).

Im Folgenden findest du eine Reihe von nützlichen **Wendungen mit Präposition + Gerundium**.

Adjektiv + Präposition + Gerundium:

(to) be	***afraid/tired of***	***doing*** *sth.*	Angst haben vor / genug haben von; etwas satt haben
	excited about		gespannt sein auf; aufgeregt sein wegen
	good/bad at		gut/schlecht sein in; etwas gut/schlecht können
	interested in		interessiert sein an; sich interessieren für
	keen on		begeistert sein von; interessiert sein an

Nomen + Präposition + Gerundium:

the	***chance of***	***doing*** *sth.*	Chance, (günstige) Gelegenheit (zu)
	danger of		Gefahr (zu)
	hope of		Hoffnung (zu/auf)
	idea of		Idee, Gedanke (zu)
	reason for		Grund für
	way of		Art und Weise, Weg (zu)

Verb + Präposition + Gerundium:

(to)	***believe in***	***doing*** *sth.*	glauben an
	decide against		sich entscheiden gegen
	dream of/about		träumen von
	look forward to		sich freuen auf
	talk about/of		reden von
	think of		denken an; in Betracht ziehen
	worry about		sich Sorgen machen wegen/um

11.2 The gerund in certain phrases Das Gerundium in bestimmten Wendungen

John is busy ***preparing*** *dinner.*
John ist damit beschäftigt, das Abendessen vorzubereiten.
The band had a great time ***performing*** *at the festival.*
Die Band genoss es sehr, auf dem Festival aufzutreten.
I had a hard time ***finding*** *my way in London.*
Ich fand es schwierig, mich in London zurechtzufinden.
It wasn't much fun ***waiting*** *for the bus in the rain.*
Es war nicht gerade ein Vergnügen, … zu warten.
It's not worth ***watching*** *the film. It's boring.*
Es lohnt sich nicht, den Film anzuschauen. …

Es gibt eine Reihe von Wendungen, in denen du das Gerundium verwendest. Dazu gehören:
- ***be busy doing sth.*** (beschäftigt sein mit …)
- ***have a great time doing sth.*** (eine großartige Zeit haben …; es genießen …)
- ***have a hard time / have a problem doing sth.*** (Schwierigkeiten / ein Problem haben …)
- ***it is (no) fun doing sth.*** (es ist (k)ein Vergnügen …)
- ***it is (not) worth doing sth.*** (es lohnt sich (nicht) …)

IN ENGLISH:
- Verbs which follow a **preposition** take the form of a gerund.
- There are **certain phrases** that are used with the gerund.

11 Exercises

11 The gerund after prepositions and in certain phrases

a) Complete the sentences with a preposition from the box and the verb in brackets. Use the gerund form.

about · at · at · in · ~~of~~ · of · on

1. Mary is leaving for school early this morning because she is afraid of being (be) late again.
2. Brad's dad: Why do you want to come with me to work tomorrow?
   Brad: Because I'm interested … … (learn) about what you do.
3. Keith is good … … (juggle), so he is really happy about the school circus project.
4. Ben: What is brown and sticky?
   Lucy: We're tired … … (hear) your old jokes, Ben.
   Ben: A stick!
5. Jason is excited … … (go) on his class trip.
6. Dave did badly in the test again. So he isn't very keen … … (tell). his parents his results.
7. Kevin: Shopping with Dad always takes a long time – he's bad … … (decide) what he wants to buy.

b) Complete the sentences with the verbs, nouns, and prepositions in brackets. Put the verbs in their gerund form.
1. A good reason for learning English is that people speak it all over the world. (for, learn, reason)
2. The fans waited in the … … … their favourite star outside the concert hall. (hope, of, see)
3. Even the … … … in front of people makes Jane shake. It's a pity because she has a lovely voice. (idea, of, sing)
4. Think about it. I'm sure you'll find a … … … the problem. (of, solve, way)
5. There's very little … … … lost when you have a smartphone. (chance, get, of)
6. In wet weather, the … … … is too high so the old tower is closed. (danger, slip, of)

c) Complete the underlined verbs and use the gerund form for the other.
1. Linda and Miriam <u>have</u> been talking about going to the Taylor Swish concert for weeks. (about, go, talk)
2. They <u>have</u> even … … … their hair colour to blond, like Taylor's. (change, of, think)
3. But after talking to their mothers, they <u>have</u> … … … it. (against, decide, do)
4. They <u>don't</u> really … … … everything Taylor does. (believe, copy, in)
5. They <u>have</u> … … … their favourite singer in real life for years. (about, dream, see)
6. They <u>are</u> … … … along with Taylor. (look forward, sing, to)
7. We left home early because we <u>were</u> … … … late for the concert. (about, be, worry)

d) Jody, a New York teenager, is asked to give some tips to people visiting New York.
Use a word and a verb in its gerund form to complete his tips.

Words: busy · ~~no fun~~ · worth · time · time · problem

Verbs: climb · see · shop · spend · go · ~~wait~~

1. It's no fun waiting in line for tickets, so tell your parents to buy tickets online for attractions.
2. You'll have a hard … … everything in one visit to the Natural History Museum, so go there twice.
3. While your parents are … … in Macy's department store, you can eat ice cream on the 7th floor.
4. A visit to the crown of the Statue of Liberty is a bad idea if someone has a … … steps – there are 393!
5. It's definitely … … a day at Coney Island fun park.
6. You'll have a great … … on the Coney Island Cyclone ride – it's amazing!

12 REVISION The passive Das Passiv

Use Gebrauch

*Two women **were caught** last night when they tried to break into a shop.*
***Was** anyone **killed** in the storm?*

◄ Du findest das Passiv oft in **Nachrichten, Zeitungsberichten** (z.B. über Unfälle oder Verbrechen), **technischen Beschreibungen** und auf **Schildern**.

*Parking is **allowed** from 6 am to 6 pm.*
Man darf (hier) von 6 bis 18 Uhr parken.

! Im **Deutschen** verwenden wir oft einen Aktivsatz mit „man".
Im **Englischen** steht ein Passivsatz.

*Dad's car **was stolen** yesterday.*
*This ring **was made** in Italy.*
*Our living room **hasn't been painted** yet.*

◄ Passivsätze drücken aus, was mit etwas oder jemandem geschieht.
Du verwendest sie oft, wenn nicht wichtig (oder bekannt) ist, wer die Handlung ausführt. Passivsätze wirken auch oft **höflicher** auf den Zuhörer.

*Lord of the Rings was written **by** J. R. R. Tolkien.*
Herr der Ringe wurde von J. R. R. Tolkien geschrieben.

◄ Wenn du in einem Passivsatz den „Täter" oder „Verursacher" nennen willst, benutzt du die Präposition ***by*** („von", „durch") + Nomen.

ZUSAMMENFASSUNG:

Simple present	*Free food **is offered** …*	… wird angeboten …
Simple past	*Free food **was offered** …*	… wurde angeboten …
Present perfect	*Free food **has been offered** …*	… ist angeboten worden …
Past perfect	*Free food **had been offered** …*	… war angeboten worden …
***will*-future**	*Free food **will be offered** …*	… wird angeboten werden …
***going to*-future**	*Free food **is going to be offered** …*	… wird angeboten werden …
Modal auxiliaries	*Free food **can/could be offered** …*	… kann/könnte angeboten werden …

Das Passiv wird mit einer Form von ***be*** und der **3. Form des Verbs** (Partizip Perfekt; *past participle*) gebildet.
Liste der unregelmäßigen Verben, S. 298–299

IN ENGLISH:

- **Passive sentences** are often used in newspaper articles, technical descriptions and on signs.
- They describe what happens to people or things.
- You can use *by* + noun in a passive sentence to say who does the action.
- You use a passive sentence to be more polite and less direct.
- You form passive sentences with a form of *be* + past participle.

12 Exercises

12 The passive

a) Complete the sentences about Central Park with the correct passive forms.
Use simple present or simple past.

1. On July 21, 1853, a law was made to keep the land on Manhattan Island as a park.
2. The designers named it "Greensward", but it ... (call) Central Park by New Yorkers.
3. The park ... (plan) to seem bigger than it really was.
4. Twenty-eight miles of footpaths ... (build) through the park.
5. They designed seven lakes and forests ... (plant), too.
6. The Ramble is an area of Central Park that ... (allow) to grow naturally wild.
7. The Ramble ... (use) today by many people as a place to watch birds.
8. Central Park is the most popular park in the US – it ... (visit) by twenty-five million people every year.

b) Rewrite the underlined sentences. Use the passive with *by* … .

1. Do you like my bracelet? My best friend made it.
   It was made by my best friend.
2. Have you heard this song? Sam Smith sings it.
3. I love this picture. Leonardo da Vinci painted it.
4. I want to visit that castle. King Ludwig built it.
5. Try the biscuits. Students in my class made them.
6. Let's buy this fruit. Local farmers grew it.
7. I love this tea. The Royal Family drink it.
8. Do you know this book? J. K. Rowling wrote it.
9. This tree is old. My great grandpa planted it.
10. There's our new library. The Queen opened it.
11. I got a postcard yesterday. My uncle sent it.

c) Write these active sentences about Brad's school in the passive form.
Use *by* + noun if it is important to say who does the action.

1. They are closing Brad's school on Friday because the building is too old.
   Brad's school is being closed on Friday because...
2. They will teach the last lessons in the building tomorrow.
3. They are building a new school at the moment.
4. Buses will take the students to a different school.
5. They will finish the new school in six months.
6. They are already making plans for the opening celebration.
7. The Mayor of New York is going to open the new school.
8. They have chosen Brad from his class to stand beside the Mayor.
9. Local TV are going to do a report.
10. Thousands of New Yorkers will see Brad on television.

d) Here are some rules and information from the New York subway. Write them in the passive form.

1. Travellers may bring bags onto subway trains.
   Bags may be brought onto subway trains.
2. The police may check your bags for dangerous things.
3. You can take pets onto the subway.
4. You must keep pets in an animal travel box or bag.
5. You must buy a *Metrocard* before entering the subway platform.
6. We sell *Metrocards* at subway station stores and ticket machines.
7. You can use the *Metrocard* on buses in New York, too.
8. You may eat food on the subway.
9. Travellers cannot open the subway train doors – except in emergencies.

13 REVISION Relative and contact clauses Relativsätze mit und ohne Relativpronomen

13.1 Relative clauses Relativsätze mit Relativpronomen

Relative pronouns *who, which* and *that*

1 *Ann hates people **who** don't tell the truth.*
Ann hasst Leute, die nicht die Wahrheit sagen.

2 *I forget most of the books **which** I read.*
Ich vergesse die meisten Bücher, die ich lese.

3 *What's the name of the film **that** we watched yesterday?*
… der Name des Films, den wir gestern gesehen haben?

Relativpronomen *who, which* and *that*

1 Mit Relativsätzen beschreibst du genauer, über wen oder was du sprichst. Das Relativpronomen ***who*** steht nur in Relativsätzen, die Personen beschreiben: *people/friends who …*

2 Das Relativpronomen ***which*** steht nur in Relativsätzen, die Dinge und Tiere beschreiben: *the door/thing/dog which …*

3 Das Relativpronomen ***that*** kannst du für Dinge, Tiere und Personen verwenden.

13.2 Contact clauses Relativsätze ohne Relativpronomen

1 *Ann hates people **who** don't tell the truth.*
… Menschen, **die** nicht die Wahrheit sagen.

Das Relativpronomen kann Objekt oder Subjekt des Relativsatzes sein.

In **1** ist das Relativpronomen ***who*** das **Subjekt** des Relativsatzes. Es steht direkt vor dem Verb und darf nicht weggelassen werden.

*Who was the man **who** was talking to Jeremy at the bus stop?*
… der Mann, **der** mit Jeremy gesprochen hat
*Who was the man [who] **Jeremy** was talking to at the bus stop?*
… der Mann, mit dem **Jeremy** gesprochen hat

! Vergleiche die Bedeutungsunterschiede, die durch die unterschiedliche Satzstellung im Relativsatz entstehen.

2 *I forget most of the books **which I** read.*
… die meisten Bücher, ***die* ich** lese.

In **2** ist das Relativpronomen ***which*** das **Objekt** des Relativsatzes. Auf das Relativpronomen folgt das Subjekt des Relativsatzes, und dann das Verb.

This is the best joke [that] you've ever made.
This is the best joke you've ever made.

◄ Wenn das Relativpronomen Objekt ist, fällt es oft weg. Relativsätze **ohne Relativpronomen** nennt man ***contact clauses***.

John went to that school.
*That's the school John went **to**.*
Das ist die Schule, **auf** der John war.

➜ *p.80, exercise 2*

! Im **Deutschen** steht die Präposition in einem Relativsatz vor dem Relativpronomen.
Im **Englischen** folgt die Präposition nach dem Verb (wie im Originalsatz, z.B. *John went to that school*) und steht oft am Ende eines Satzes.

IN ENGLISH:

- You use **relative clauses** with *who, which* and *that* to give more detail about people, animals or things.
- The relative pronoun can be the subject or the object of the relative clause.
  - When it is the subject, you mustn't leave it out.
  - When it is the object, you can leave it out.
- A relative clause without a relative pronoun is called a **contact clause**.

13 Exercises

13 Relative and contact clauses

a) Match the sentence halves and join them with *who* or *which*.

1. A dime is a coin	who	a) is not one of the 50 US states.
2. *Birdman* is a man	which	b) links Manhattan and Brooklyn.
3. Washington DC is a district in the US		c) is very important to the Native American culture.
4. The Brooklyn Bridge is a bridge		d) feeds the birds in Washington Square Park.
5. A streetcar is a kind of tram		e) makes sure players follow the rules.
6. Storytelling is a tradition		f) takes place on 19th June.
7. Juneteenth is an African American celebration		g) is worth ten American cents.
8. A referee is the person		h) can be found in some American cities.

b) The teacher asked the class to name amazing things they would like to have or invent. Read the students' answers and choose the correct noun from the list to complete the sentences. Use a relative pronoun – *which* or *that*.

an exercise book   a clock   ~~clothes~~   a machine   a phone   a robot
a skateboard   a social media site   vegetables

1. Billy: I'd invent clothes that/which never get dirty.
2. Jamie: I'd like to have … … corrects my spelling.
3. Julie: I'd invent … … wakes you up and makes you a smoothie in the morning.
4. Ben: I think … … can fly would be a great thing to invent.
5. Maria: I would invent … … gets its energy from the sun.
6. Robbie: I'd like … … cleans my bedroom for me.
7. Anne: I wish I had … … taste like sweets.
8. Miriam: I'd start … … doesn't let parents join.
9. Jacob: I'd invent … … can make meat without hurting animals.

c) Finish each sentence with a contact clause. Pay attention to the position of the preposition.

1. Listen! That's the song… (I was telling you about it.)
   Listen! That's the song I was telling you about.
2. Here's the book… (You were looking for it.)
3. Is that the bus…? (We need to take it.)
4. She's the girl… (I go to school with her.)
5. Are those the steps…? (Paul fell down them.)
6. I can't find the box… (I put the DVD into.)
7. Who were those kids… ? (Mae was talking to them.)
8. Is this the book … ? (Dad was interested in it.)

d) Jan is on exchange in America. He doesn't know what some American words mean and asks his host brother. Match the words with the descriptions. Add a relative pronoun only where needed.

a stoop   bae   a borough   a cell   a trailer   Thanksgiving

1. Bae is an informal word which/that means 'boyfriend' or 'girlfriend'.
2. … is an American holiday … we celebrate on the fourth Thursday of November.
3. … is a phone … you can fit in your pocket.
4. … is the name of the steps … lead up to the door of a house or building.
5. … is a word … describes a district or area of an American city.
6. … is a thing on wheels … you can stay or live in – in Britain it's called a caravan.

14 Defining and non-defining relative clauses Bestimmende und nicht bestimmende Relativsätze

14.1 Defining relative clauses Bestimmende Relativsätze

1 *My heart goes out to the people* ***who/that*** *lost their homes.*

2 *That's the shop* ***which/that*** *sells second-hand clothes and books and stuff.*

Bestimmende Relativsätze werden mit Relativpronomen eingeleitet:
- Bei Personen verwendet man die Relativpronomen *who* oder *that* (Satz 1).
- Bei Dingen und Tieren verwendet man die Relativpronomen *which* oder *that* (Satz 2).

Ein bestimmender Relativsatz gibt **wichtige Informationen**, die zum Verständnis des Satzes notwendig sind: Ohne die Relativsätze in Satz 1 und 2 wüsste man gar nicht, von welchen Menschen bzw. von welchem Geschäft die Rede ist.

3 *The dog* ***whose*** *owner left him in his car was barking.*
The guy ***whose*** *bike I borrowed wants it back.*

Mit dem Relativbegleiter *whose* kannst du auch bestimmende Relativsätze einleiten. *Whose* ("dessen, deren") drückt Besitz oder Zugehörigkeit aus. Hinter *whose* steht immer ein Nomen.

➜ *pp.80–81, exercises 1–2, 4*

! Im Englischen stehen vor und nach dem Relativsatz **keine Kommas**.

14.2 Non-defining relative clauses Nicht bestimmende Relativsätze

1 *California has a major problem with droughts,* ***which are becoming more and more frequent****.*

2 *One of the evacuated residents was Brandon Williams,* ***who plays Toby in the popular TV show "Dad, I'm home"****.*

Nicht bestimmende Relativsätze kommen hauptsächlich in geschriebenem Englisch vor. Sie geben **Zusatzinformationen**, die zum Verständnis des Satzes nicht unbedingt notwendig sind:
Du verstehst die Beispielsätze auch ohne die Relativsätze.

New Mexico, ***which became part of the United States in 1912,*** *has a population of about two million people.*

New Mexico, das 1912 Teil der USA wurde, hat eine Bevölkerung von ca. 2 Millionen Einwohnern.

◀ In nicht bestimmenden Relativsätzen verwendest du immer ***who, which*** oder ***whose*** – nicht aber das Relativpronomen *that*.

! Nicht bestimmende Relativsätze werden durch **Kommas** abgetrennt.

➜ *p.81, exercises 3–4*

IN ENGLISH:

- A **defining relative clause** gives necessary information about the noun that it refers to. You don't use commas with defining relative clauses.
- A **non-defining relative clause** gives extra information about the noun that it refers to. That means you can understand the main clause without the information from the relative clause. You always use commas with non-defining relative clauses.

14 Exercises

14 Defining and non-defining relative clauses

a) Make one sentence from the two sentences. Use a defining relative clause.

1. I lost a book. My grandfather had given it to me.
   I lost the book which/that my grandfather had given to me.
2. My dad told us a scary story. It wasn't true.
3. I know that player. She just scored a goal.
4. Where's the money? I left it on the table.
5. What was the name of that family? They moved last year.
6. Billy showed us some pictures. His mother had painted them.
7. Here's a photo of my grandfather. It shows him when he was my age.

b) Make one sentence from the two sentences. Use a defining relative clause.

1. An actor visited our school today. He plays *Harry Danger* on TV.
   The actor who/that plays Harry Danger on TV visited our school today.
2. A young girl was brought to hospital. She fell off her bicycle.
3. A boy sent me an sms. I met him on holidays.
4. The teacher was very nice. He taught us History last year.
5. John thought the girl was pretty. She was talking to Kate.
6. A dog was running around the park. It didn't belong to anyone.
7. The movie was boring. We saw it in the cinema last weekend.

c) Complete the sentences. Choose the best ending from the box and change it into a relative clause.

they are red, white, and blue	she is standing beside you in the photo
~~it has a big garden at the back~~	it doesn't cost a lot
it needs a lot of thought	it has milk in it
he came before Donald Trump	they stole a car

1. Peter lives in a house ... Peter lives in a house which/that has a big garden at the back.
2. The police are still looking for the thieves ...
3. Chess is a game ...
4. Brian can't eat anything ...
5. America, the UK, Russia, the Netherlands, and France all have flags ...
6. What's the name of the girl ...?
7. John wants to buy a tablet ...
8. Do you know the name of the president ...?

d) Complete the sentences. Use *that* where possible. If *that* is not possible, use *who* or *which*.

1. The person that told me the news said I shouldn't tell anyone else.
2. The game, ... was very boring, finished with no goals.
3. New York, ... has a population of over 8 million, is the biggest city in the US.
4. The pink dress was too expensive, so Julie bought the yellow one, ... was cheaper.
5. Where's the nearest shop ... sells flowers?
6. The blue tent, ... my Uncle gave us, had a big hole in it.
7. Jake, ... is in the same class as my brother, broke his leg in the accident.
8. Julie needs special earphones ... can work with her new phone.

e) Find the relative clauses in these sentences and decide if they are defining or non-defining. Add commas where you need them.

1. Robbie who has a bad temper shouted at his sister.
   Robbie, who has a bad temper, shouted at his sister. (non-defining)
2. The student who had a bad cold had to go home from school early.
3. All of the students went to the top of the tower except Anne who is scared of high places.
4. The swimmers who swam the fastest were chosen for the school team.
5. The phone that Mary found on the floor belongs to Kevin.
6. The Grand Canyon which is over 300 kilometres long is a wonder of nature.
7. The shop that sells the new Gamestation isn't far away.
8. Mr Webster who is the best teacher in the school is leaving at the end of term.

15 Adverbs Adverbien

15.1 REVISION Adverbs of manner Adverbien der Art und Weise

*"I can't wait to eat this," said Tyler **impatiently**.*
*Kevin came home after midnight. He opened the door **carefully**.*

*He speaks **quietly**.*
Er spricht leise.
*Pat is never **quiet**.*
Pat ist nie leise.

Adverbien der Art und Weise *(adverbs of manner)* verwendest du, um zu beschreiben, wie jemand etwas tut oder wie etwas geschieht.

! Im **Deutschen** haben Adverbien der Art und Weise und Adjektive dieselbe Form. **Englische** Adverbien der Art und Weise haben in der Regel eine eigene Form.

Adjective	Adverb
sad	*sad**ly***
happy	*happi**ly***
terrible	*terrib**ly***

◄ Die meisten Adverbien der Art und Weise werden gebildet, indem *-ly* an das Adjektiv angehängt wird.

*Josh is a very **fast** runner. He can run very **fast**.*
*School life can be **hard** sometimes.*
*I have to study very **hard** to get good test results.*
*My Spanish is **good**. I speak Spanish **well**.*
Mein Spanisch ist gut. Ich spreche gut Spanisch.

◄ Bei *fast, hard* und *high* haben Adjektiv und Adverb dieselbe Form. Das Adverb zu *good* heißt *well*.

! Adverbien der Art und Weise können im **Deutschen** zwischen Verb und Objekt stehen. Im **Englischen** dürfen sie nicht zwischen Verb und Objekt stehen.

15.2 Adverbs of degree Gradadverbien

*You move your boat through the water **really fast**.*
*It all looks **very tasty**.*
*Our teachers are **awfully strict**.*
*Musical instruments can be **quite / fairly expensive**.*

◄ Gradadverbien verstärken andere Wörter (z.B. *really, very, completely*) oder schwächen sie ab (z.B. *a little, quite, fairly, a bit*).
Sie stehen direkt vor dem Wort, auf das sie sich beziehen.

Strong	High	Medium	Weak
totally	*really*	*fairly*	*a bit*
absolutely	*very*	*quite*	*a little*
completely	*awfully*		
quite			

Du unterscheidest zwischen Gradadverbien, die stark, hoch, mittel oder schwach (***strong, high, medium** oder **weak***) sind. Je nachdem welches Gradadverb du wählst, kannst du ein Wort stärker oder schwächer machen.
Das Adverb *quite* hat zwei Bedeutungen: 1. völlig, ganz (*strong*) und 2. ziemlich (*medium*).

*The film we saw last night was **a bit / quite / really / totally funny**.*

Gradadverbien stehen für gewöhnlich mit Adjektiven oder Adverbien, die auch steigerbar sind.

*It's **absolutely impossible** to finish this task in one hour.*
*Then, when you see a gator, you have to be **completely silent**.*
*Betty, it was **absolutely delicious**, but I couldn't eat another bite.*

! Adjektive wie *impossible* oder *perfect*, die du nicht steigern kannst, nennt man ***strong adjectives***. Du kannst z.B. nicht sagen, dass etwas *a bit impossible* oder *very impossible* ist. Stattdessen verwendest du sie mit ***strong adverbs of degree*** wie *absolutely, totally* und *completely*.

➜ *p.54, exercises 1–2*

IN ENGLISH:
- You use **adverbs of manner** to describe how someone does something or how something is done.
- You use **adverbs of degree** to add a stronger or weaker meaning to a word. There are strong, high, medium and weak adverbs of degree that you can choose from.
- Strong adjectives (e.g. *impossible* or *perfect*) are only used with **strong adverbs of degree** like *absolutely* or *totally*.

15 Exercises

15 Adverbs

a) Complete the sentences. Use one adjective and change the other adjective into its adverb form.

1. Mum: How was your test? Brian: Good, I think. I'm sure I wrote the wrong answer for the first question, but I think I answered the rest correctly. (correct, wrong)
2. If you work in a shop, you have to behave ... even when customers are ... . (polite, rude)
3. At Helena's birthday party, her dad sang so ... that everyone was ... when he finally stopped. (happy, terrible)
4. Brian and I wanted to have a ... talk with Joe, but Joe reacted ... , and we don't know why. (angry, quiet)
5. Our team had a ... start in the game, but then we played ... and won in the end. (bad, good)
6. Although the planes fly ... over our house, they are still ... . (high, loud)
7. My teacher said it is always ... to read my homework because I write so ... . (beautiful, easy)
8. We tried ... to climb to the top, but the wind was so ... we had to come back down. (hard, strong)
9. Ben and Tom prepared their presentation much too ... - that's why it wasn't very ... . (fast, good)
10. Harold walked onto the stage to receive his ... trophy and ... showed it to everyone. (large, proud)

b) Choose the correct adverb of degree to complete the sentences.

1. **John:** Are you ready to go to Tony's place? **Ben:** Yes, but I won't stay long. I'm feeling a bit tired. (a bit, absolutely, totally)
2. **Lucy:** I hate the circus and will never go to one. It's ... cruel to make animals perform for humans! (a little, awfully, fairly)
3. **Mae:** What do you think of our new teacher? **Ann:** I ... like her. She makes learning interesting. (fairly, really, very)
4. **Linda:** Mary speaks German ... well - even Germans don't know she comes from New York. (a bit, completely, very)
5. **Ben:** I'm ... sorry about your cat. **Jill:** Thanks. He had a good, long life. (fairly, really, quite)
6. **Sarah:** Was there a fire in your area last night? **Jamie:** Yes. Our neighbour's house was ... destroyed by the fire. (a bit, awfully, completely)
7. **Rob:** Mum, this shirt is ... big for me. **Mum:** You grow so fast. In a month, it'll fit perfectly. (absolutely, a little, totally)
8. **Julie:** It's ... impossible to solve these exercises. I can't do them. **Dad:** Let's read the grammar page again. (fairly, a bit, absolutely)
9. **Bobby:** Yes! I've ... killed the last boss on the final level! **Jamie:** Wow! With a high score record, too! (a little, very, totally)

c) The adverbs of degree in these sentences sound wrong. Find them.
Then choose the alternative that best matches the meaning of the sentence.

1. Mrs Jones, this cake is a little delicious! (absolutely, fairly)
   Mrs Jones, this cake is absolutely delicious!
2. The lake was absolutely shallow – we couldn't swim in it, only walk. (really, completely)
3. Brian's party was fairly fantastic. (absolutely, very)
4. With a player like Frank Stapleton, we can't lose – he's a little brilliant. (a bit, totally)
5. Everyone got 100%! That test was a bit easy. (totally, fairly)
6. Ugh!! That tastes a little awful. I'm going to be sick! (absolutely, fairly)
7. The computer is fairly broken. It doesn't even turn on anymore. (completely, awfully)
8. A: How is your foot today?
   B: It's still totally sore, but I can walk on it without a problem. (a bit, awfully)
9. That movie was very terrible. I'm never going to watch a Steven Spielen movie again! (quite, a little)
10. A: Dad, how large is a blue whale?
    B: A blue whale? It's a little large!!! (quite, fairly)
11. A: Was your mum angry that you were home late?
    B: She was absolutely angry at first and shouted at me, but she calmed down. (a bit, really)
12. A: Did you enjoy the concert?
    B: Enjoy it? It was very amazing! (fairly, absolutely)

16 Adverbial clauses Adverbiale Nebensätze

16.1 REVISION Adverbial clauses Adverbiale Nebensätze

*Everybody cheered **at half-time**.*
*Everybody cheered **when the first half ended**.*

Adverbiale Nebensätze kannst du anstelle von Adverbialbestimmungen verwenden. Du leitest sie durch Konjunktionen wie *when, because* und *while* ein.

Es gibt unterschiedliche Arten von adverbialen Nebensätzen. In den Beispielsätzen links unterscheidest du zwischen Nebensätze der **Zeit** und des **Grundes**.

*I was happy **because I was invited to John's party.***
***Because I was invited to John's party,** I was happy.*

◂ Sie stehen oft nach dem Hauptsatz. Du setzt ein Komma, wenn der Nebensatz vor dem Hauptsatz steht.

16.2 Adverbial clauses of place Adverbiale Nebensätze des Ortes

*It was built **where tracks had run directly at street level.***
*They believed that people should be able to hang out and relax **where they lived.***
*There were a lot of kids **wherever we went.***
***Everywhere you go,** there are wild flowers.*

➜ *p.31, exercise 1*

Du leitest Nebensätze des Ortes durch folgende Konjunktionen ein:

- *where* (wo, wohin)
- *wherever* (wo, wohin auch immer)
- *everywhere* (überall wo/wohin)

16.3 Adverbial clauses of comparison Adverbiale Nebensätze des Vergleichs

*Nobody likes you **as I do.***
*The High Line offers teens just **as** much **as it offers adults.***

Nebensätze des Vergleichs kannst du einleiten mit:

- *as* (wie), *as … as* (so … wie)
- *as if / as though* (als ob)
- *than* (als)

*His dad is playing tennis **as if he is playing it for the first time.***
*Henry behaved **as though I had broken the cup.***
*Today, the High line is more popular **than anyone had ever expected.***

◂ Nach *as if / as though* und *than* kann auch das *past tense* oder *past perfect* stehen, um eine irreale Handlung zu beschreiben. Im Deutschen steht dafür der Konjunktiv.

*Nobody likes you **like I do.***

➜ *p.31, exercise 2*

! Im gesprochenen English benutzt du häufig *like* statt *as* oder *as if*.

16.4 Adverbial clauses of contrast Adverbiale Nebensätze des Gegensatzes

***Although it is one and a half miles long,** it is only 50 feet at its widest point.*
*Many of them had brilliant ideas, **even though they weren't always very practical.***
*John likes vegetables **while/whereas his sister likes meat for dinner.***

➜ *p.31, exercise 3*

Du führst Nebensätze des Gegensatzes mit diesen Konjunktionen ein:

- *although/though* (obwohl, obgleich)
- *even if / even though* (auch wenn; selbst wenn)
- *while/whereas* (während, wohingegen)

IN ENGLISH:

- **Adverbial clauses** can be used instead of adverbials.
- There are different types of adverbial clauses such as **time, reason, place, comparison** and **contrast**.
- You introduce adverbial clauses with conjunctions. They can come before or after the main clause.

16 Exercises

16. Adverbial clauses

a) Join these sentences with *when*. Remember that *when* can begin a sentence or come after the main clause. Use a comma when it introduces a sentence.

1. the kids stopped talking | the teacher asked them. The kids stopped talking <u>when</u> the teacher asked them.
2. Jody wasn't at home | I went to his house.
3. Mary arrives home | she will call me.
4. Paul doesn't turn off his lamp | he sleeps.
5. we wear our good clothes | we go to church.
6. Dad is angry | his ears go red.
7. we get a lot of sweets | we visit Grandma and Grandpa.

b) Join the sentences together to make one sentence with *because*. You use *because* at the beginning or in the middle of the sentence after the main clause.

1. Brian didn't go to the party. He didn't feel well. Brian didn't go to the party <u>because</u> he didn't feel well.
2. Matilda didn't go to see the movie. She wanted to read the book first.
3. Julie hadn't studied enough. She was nervous about the test.
4. I'm going on a school trip. I don't need to bring my schoolbooks tomorrow.
5. The kids were playing video games. They didn't notice how late it was.
6. We should get something nice for our neighbours. They looked after our cat.
7. I feel bad. I forgot Kevin's birthday.

c) Match 1-7 with a-g and join the sentences with *where*. Remember to leave out *there*.

1 + f) New York Zoo is <u>where</u> kids can go to learn all about animals.

1. New York Zoo is	a) You'll find rides and fun things to do for everyone there.
2. Central Park is	b) People arrived there to start a new life in America.
3. Coney Island is	c) A lot of theatres can be found there.
4. Ellis Island was	d) You can go there to relax and take a break from the city.
5. One World Observatory is	e) Thousands of New Yorkers celebrate the New Year there.
6. Broadway is	f) Kids can go there to learn all about animals.
7. On December 31st, Times Square is	g) You can get the best photos of New York there.

d) Complete the adverbial clauses of comparison with *as, as … as, as if* and *than*.

1. Joe's phone costs as much as my phone, but mine has a better camera.
2. In class, these exercises looked simple but they are harder … I thought.
3. I got a concert ticket for Jane, too, because she is a big fan of Lady Gaga … I am.
4. I'm sure Kevin will win the race – nobody can run … fast … he can.
5. When he heard the news, Dad looked … … he had seen a ghost.
6. Wait until you see the new Fourth Knight III game. You'll love it. It is even better … FK II!
7. Lucy wasn't happy because Linda chose the same presentation topic … she did.
8. The Gamestation was less expensive … I expected so I was able to buy an extra game for it.
9. I didn't enjoy the movie. It wasn't … funny … you said.

e) Join the sentence halves. Use the adverbials. Be careful with the order of the sentence parts.

1. **although**
   a) the kids jumped in / the water was very cold
   Although the water was cold, the kids jumped in.
   b) the sun was shining / the water was very cold
2. **even though**
   a) I was hungry / I didn't eat a lot
   b) I was hungry / I ate a lot
3. **even if**
   a) I ask nicely / Mum will say no
   b) I won't get angry / Mum says no

17 Indirect speech Indirekte Rede

17.1 Direct and indirect speech Direkte und indirekte Rede

Skye says, "It's too noisy."
Skye sagt: „Es ist zu laut."

◄ In der **direkten Rede** *(direct speech)* gibst du wörtlich wieder, was jemand sagt oder schreibt (oder gesagt oder geschrieben hat). Direkte Rede steht gewöhnlich in Anführungszeichen.

Skye says (that) it's too noisy.
Skye sagt, dass es zu laut ist.

◄ In der **indirekten Rede** *(indirect* oder *reported speech)* berichtest du, was jemand sagt oder schreibt (oder gesagt oder geschrieben hat). Die indirekte Rede wird mit Verben wie *say, tell sb., add, answer, explain, write* eingeleitet.

Cody says Šũŋkawakáŋ means horse.

! Im **Englischen** steht vor der indirekten Rede kein Komma, und das Wort *that* („dass") wird oft weggelassen.

17.2 Indirect speech: Tense changes Indirekte Rede: Veränderungen der Zeitform

I'm tired of it.
I don't want to be in the play any more!

Wenn das einleitende Verb im *simple past* steht (*she said, she told me* usw.), verwendest du in der indirekten Rede meist andere Zeitformen als in der direkten Rede: Die Zeitformen der direkten Rede werden **um eine Zeitstufe in die Vergangenheit „zurückverschoben"** (*backshift of tenses*).

*Skye told Lewis that she **was** tired of it.*
*She said she **didn't** want to be in the play any more.*

➜ *p.100, exercises 1–3*

◄ So wird z.B. das *simple present* der direkten Rede in der indirekten Rede „zurückverschoben" zum *simple past*.

Tense changes	Direct speech	Indirect speech
present ➜ past	"We **need** you."	Lewis told Skye that they **needed** her.
	"We**'re driving** to Rapid City next weekend."	Drew said they **were driving** to Rapid City next weekend.
will-future ➜ *would* + infinitive	"We**'ll** never **get** it right."	Sandra said they **would** never **get** it right.
can ➜ *could*	"You **can't be** serious."	Cody said they **couldn't be** serious.
past ➜ past (oder past perfect[1])	"Skye **started** to cry."	Lewis said that Skye **(had) started** to cry.

[1]*Past tense*-Formen der direkten Rede werden in der indirekten Rede oft beibehalten, also nicht ins *past perfect* verändert.

17.3 Indirect speech: Pronoun changes Indirekte Rede: Veränderungen der Pronomen

Ella (zu Lucy): *"**I**'ll call **you** when **we**'re back."*
Lucy berichtet ihrer Schwester:
*Ella told me that **she** would call **me** when **they** were back.*
Ella berichtet ihrem Vater:
*I told Lucy that **I** would call **her** when **we** were back.*

➜ *p.100, exercises 1–3*

◄ Wie im Deutschen werden in der indirekten Rede die Pronomen verändert, je nachdem, wer wem berichtet.

IN ENGLISH:

- In **direct speech**, we repeat word for word what someone has said or written. We usually use quotation marks: *"I'm tired," she said.*
- In **indirect speech**, we report what someone has said or written: *She said/told me (that) she was tired.*
- If the reporting verb is in the past (*said, told,* etc.), there is usually a change or "backshift" of tenses: present ➜ past; past ➜ past (or past perfect); *will* ➜ *would; can* ➜ *could.*

17 Exercises

17 Indirect speech

a) Write in your exercise book what the kids say. Use direct speech.

1.	2.	3.	4.	5.
I'm tired.	I can't go to Mae's party.	We're going on holidays next week.	I have to go straight home after school.	It's four o'clock.
Paul	Mary	Julie	Miriam	Patrick

1. Paul says, "I'm tired."

b) Now write what the kids say in a) but use indirect speech.

1. Paul says he's tired.

c) Write the direct speech as indirect speech. Use the verb *say* in the simple past.

1. Ron: I have a great idea for the history presentation.
   Ron said (that) he had a great idea for the history presentation.
2. Mary: I don't know the answer to question three.
3. James: I put my name on the list for the soccer club.
4. Music teacher: Next week's concert practice is cancelled.
5. Frieda: I have never been to Ireland.
6. Anne: I think the yellow dress is nicer than the pink one.
7. Philip: I need more money for a new guitar.
8. Joe: I prefer ice cream for dessert.
9. Lucy: I don't want to be late for school.
10. Miriam: I'm not able to swim.

d) Write the direct speech as indirect speech. Use the verbs *say* or *tell* in the simple past.

1. Paul → James "I won't be at Gemma's party tomorrow"
   Paul told/said to James (that) he wouldn't be at Gemma's party tomorrow.
2. Anne: I'm going to the Lady Gaga concert next weekend.
3. Kevin: I can't go to the cinema on Friday.
4. Jane → Alice "I have to babysit this evening."
5. James: I think the test will be hard.
6. Larry: I'm not looking forward to the test either.
7. Anna → Mike "I'll be back in a minute."
8. Linda: I'm meeting Julie tomorrow.
9. Julie: I'm going shopping with Linda after school tomorrow.
10. Miriam: I'll put the computer away when I finish the game.

e) Write the direct speech as indirect speech. Use the verbs *say* or *tell* in the simple past.

1. Keith → you: "You can have the party in my house."
   Keith said (to me) / told me (that) I could have the party in his house.
2. Jamie → Mary "I need your help with the German project."
3. Teacher → class "You can use your dictionaries in the next exercise."
4. Miriam and Helen → you "We'll help you to prepare for your party."
5. Julie → Mark "I don't know where your bag is."
6. John → Ben and Tim "I will tell you my secret later."
7. Alice → Joe "You can sit beside me if you want."
8. Tom's mum → Tom "You have to clean your room."
9. Coach → Marie "With more practice, you can be a great player."
10. Kevin → Ron "I forgot to bring your book with me."

18 Indirect requests, commands, advice and suggestions
Bitten, Aufforderungen, Ratschläge und Vorschläge in indirekter Rede

1 *"Can you take us to the hospital?"*
*I **asked** the taxi driver to take us to the hospital.*
Ich bat den Taxifahrer, uns ins Krankenhaus zu fahren.

2 *"Don't go too close to the water because it's dangerous."*
*Mum **told** me not to go too close to the water because it's dangerous.*
Mum sagte mir, ich soll nicht so nah ans Wasser gehen / forderte mich auf, nicht zu nah ans Wasser zu gehen, weil es gefährlich ist.

3 *"You should move to the rez."*
*Cody **advised** Kaya to move to the rez.*
Cody riet Kaya ins Reservat zu ziehen.

4 *"Let's go for a pizza."*
*Bobby **suggested** going for a pizza.*
Bobby schlug vor, eine Pizza essen zu gehen.
Drew: Why don't we spend the day together?
*Drew **suggested** spending the day together.*
Drew schlug vor, den Tag zusammen zu verbringen.

➜ *p.101, exercise 4*

Bitten, Aufforderungen und Ratschläge gibst du meist durch eine Infinitivkonstruktion wieder:

1 für **Bitten** verwendest du meist *ask sb. to do sth.* (bzw. *ask sb. not to do sth.*)

2 für **Aufforderungen** verwendest du meist *tell sb. to do sth.* (bzw. *tell sb. not to do sth.*)

3 für **Ratschläge** verwendest du meist *advise sb. to do sth.* (bzw. *advise sb. not to do sth.*)

4 **Vorschläge** leitest du in der indirekten Rede meist mit *suggest* ein

! Nach *suggest* darf kein *to*-Infinitiv stehen.
Also nie: ~~*He suggested to go for a pizza.*~~
Sondern: *He suggested going for a pizza./*
He suggested that we go for a pizza./
He suggested we should go for a pizza.

! **Im Englischen** steht vor *that* nie ein Komma.

IN ENGLISH:

- You can use **indirect speech** to report requests, commands, advice and suggestions.
- The ***to*-infinitive** is used with requests, commands and advice: *ask/tell/advise sb. to do sth.*
  Miss Jones told/asked me to open the window. The doctor advised me to eat more fruit.
- The *to*-infinitive cannot be used to report suggestions. You can use *suggest + -ing* or *suggest that …*:
  Miss Bell suggested talking to our parents first / suggested that we (should) talk to our parents first.

18 Exercises

18 Indirect requests, commands, advice and suggestions

a) Class 8BE are having a maths test. Report what their teacher says to them using the prompts. Put the reporting verbs into the simple past. Put the second verb into the *to*-infinitive or the-*ing* form.

1. *"You should all study unit three for the test."*
   The teacher/ suggest / study / unit three / for the test
   The teacher suggested studying unit three for the test.
2. *"Do not turn the worksheet over until I say so."*
   He / tell / the students / not / turn over / the worksheet / until / he / said / so
3. *"Read all the questions first before you start writing."*
   He / advise / them / read / all the questions first / before / they / started / writing
4. *"You can use the empty worksheet for your ideas."*
   He / suggest / use / the empty worksheet/ for the students' ideas
5. *"Robert, can you close the window beside your desk, please?"*
   He / ask / Robert / close / the window
6. *"Don't spend too much time on one question."*
   He / tell / the class / not / spend / too much time on one question
7. *"You can begin the test."*
   He / tell / the students / begin / the test
8. *"Please stop writing now."*
   He / ask / the class / stop / writing
9. *"Make sure your name is on your worksheets before you give them to me."*
   He / advise / the students / make sure / their names / were / on the worksheets

b) Tom is going to the US on a school exchange. Report what he and his family and friends say. Use the reporting verbs in brackets. Remember to change the tenses and pronouns.

1. Tom's younger sister: Can you bring me back some American sweets?" (ask)
   Tom's younger sister asked him to bring her back some American sweets.
2. Tom's mum: "Don't eat too much fast food. (tell)
3. Tom's dad: Keep your room in the host family's house clean! (tell)
4. His friend, Sally: Why don't you keep a blog during your time over in the States? (suggest)
5. His friend, Mike: You should say *bathroom* in America and not *toilet*. (advise)
6. Mike and Sally: Let's pick a day and time to do a video call every week. (suggest)
7. Tom → his parents: "Don't worry about me." (tell)
8. Tom's parents: Please call us as soon as you can. (ask)
9. Sally → Tom: "Can we take one last selfie together?" (ask)
10. Sally → Tom: "Oh no! Delete that photo and take another. It is terrible." (tell)

c) Some of the sentences are wrong. Write those sentences and correct the mistakes.

1. Joe suggested to have a picnic in the park on Saturday.
   Joe suggested having a picnic in the park on Saturday.
2. I asked you not to tell anyone about my new boyfriend.
3. Our teacher told to bring a newspaper with us to our English lesson on Thursday.
4. Mum suggested, that we go to the cinema tomorrow.
5. Lucy told me, that she didn't know where Linda was.
6. The doctor told Keith not to play sport for two weeks.
7. The teacher advised the students bringing their raincoats for the trip tomorrow.
8. The old lady asked Gary to help her to open the door.

19 The definite article Der bestimmte Artikel

19.1 Abstract and concrete nouns Abstrakte und konkrete Nomen

1 *These presidents didn't care about the role of* ***nature*** *in Lakota beliefs.*
History *will always remember them.*

2 *How would* ***people*** *feel if they sprayed graffiti on the cathedral in Rapid City?*
Many Native ***Americans*** *find the memorial extremely offensive.*

3 *What will happen if we run out of* ***oil / water****?*

4 *It began with a 20-minute movie about* ***the history*** *of the monument.*

5 ***The oil*** *that was found on his land made him very rich.*
Das Öl, das auf seinem Land gefunden wurde …

6 ***The people*** *who live here all help each other.*
Die Menschen, die hier leben, …
The prices *you have to pay for houses in this area are shocking.*
Die Preise, die man für Häuser in dieser Gegend bezahlt …

➜ p.105, exercises 1–2

Wenn du ein Nomen ganz allgemein gebrauchst, steht es ohne bestimmten Artikel (auch, wenn ein Adjektiv davorsteht).

Das gilt insbesondere für:
- **abstrakte Begriffe** (wie *nature, history, death, life, noise, peace, research, security, sport)*
- **Nomen im Plural** (wie *people, Americans, prices)*
- **Stoffbezeichnungen** (wie *air, oil, gold, tea, glass, water).*

! Solche Nomen stehen jedoch **mit bestimmtem Artikel**, wenn sie näher bestimmt sind, z.B. durch eine *of*-Fügung (4) oder einen Relativsatz (5, 6).

Anders als in den Sätzen 1 – 3, geht es in den Sätzen 4 – 6 konkret um die Geschichte des Denkmals, das Öl, das auf einem ganz bestimmten Land gefunden wurde usw.

19.2 Some buildings and meals Einige Gebäude und Mahlzeiten

1 *We go* ***to church*** *every Sunday.*
… in die Kirche (zum Gottesdienst)
He spent two years ***in prison****.*
… im Gefängnis (um eine Strafe zu verbüßen)
I know her ***from school****.*
… aus der Schule (vom gemeinsamen Unterricht)
Dad's ill. He's ***in hospital****. (AmE: in the hospital)*
… im Krankenhaus (zur Behandlung)

2 *There's a concert in* ***the church*** *on Friday.*
He works in one of the shops behind ***the prison****.*
Go straight on till you get to ***the school****, then turn left.*

I eat toast and eggs ***for breakfast****.*
Lucy will call me ***after dinner****.*

➜ p.105, exercise 3

Die Gebäudebezeichnungen *church, hospital, prison, school, college, university*

1 stehen ohne den bestimmten Artikel, wenn die **Funktion / der Zweck des Gebäudes** im Vordergrund steht
2 stehen mit dem bestimmten Artikel, wenn es um den **Ort / das Bauwerk** geht.

◀ Mahlzeiten stehen nach einer Präposition in der Regel ohne den bestimmten Artikel.

IN ENGLISH:
- We do not use the definite article when nouns are used in a general sense, e.g. abstract, material and plural nouns.
- We put **the definite article** before these nouns when they become concrete nouns. For example, when they are followed by an *of*-phrase or a relative clause.
- Some buildings are used with the definite article when we refer to the place or the building.

19 Exercises

19 The definite article

a) Some of these sentences need the definite article and some don't. Put the definite article in where it is needed.

1. Dad: Mike, can you go to the shop? We need … oil to fry our sausages.
2. My dad thinks … young people use … social media too much.
3. Since they closed … airport, it's been much quieter where I live. I actually miss … noise.
4. They closed … playground because … glass was found in … sand.
5. Many … people hope … science can help make … life better for everyone.
6. … Chinese is a difficult language for … English speakers to learn.
7. At 0°C, … water becomes ice.
8. Patrick gave an interesting presentation on … history of Ireland.
9. I really liked … pictures by Rembrandt we saw in … museum.
10. Can you imagine … life without … computers?
11. Can you close … door when you go out?
12. We didn't go swimming because … water was too cold.
13. Philip is very interested in … nature.
14. Who are … people in this photograph?
15. We lost our last three games, but we shouldn't lose … hope.

b) Complete the sentences with the given word. Use the definite article if necessary.

1. **school:** a) In Germany, school begins before 8am, but in Ireland classes begin at 9am.
   b) A lot of parents were waiting outside … to meet their children after the class trip.
2. **hospital:** a) I've never been very sick – I've never had to go to … .
   b) The mayor wants to close … in our town.
3. **prison:** a) Sometimes I hear someone playing the piano in … near where I live.
   b) In some countries people are sent to … because they don't agree with their government.
4. **university:** a) My older sister starts … next month in another city. I'm going to miss her when she's away.
   b) After school, I want to study at … where my father studied.

c) Yvonne is an American exchange student in Duisburg. She emails her friends. Complete her email with the definite article where needed.

Hi everyone,
I can't believe that I've been here in [1] the city of Duisburg for three weeks already. Time flies when you're having [2] … fun! My host family – [3] … Brauns - are wonderful and my host sister, Andrea, is really cool. Duisburgers are rather friendly – well, all [4] … people I've met so far have all been friendly. My host parents actually come from Munich and [5] … German they speak sounds quite different to their children's and to [6] … accents in [7] … books we study at [8] … school in [9] … US. One thing that's a bit hard is that [10] … family eat [11] … meat. You know that I don't. But my host-mom has been super, and we go shopping for a lot of rice, pasta, and vegetables. Doing [12] … family things together is really important to my host-family. Sunday is [13] … day everyone does things together. Back home, we go to [14] … mall on Sundays, but here, if [15] … weather is nice, we go on an *Ausflug* (a trip) to [16] … countryside, which is great because you know I love [17] … nature. I'm enjoying [18] … school a lot but studying all of [19] … school subjects in German is much harder than I expected. What's [20] … latest news from back home? Write and tell me.
Love, Yvonne.

d) Ralph, a U.S. exchange student, emails his friends about Cologne. Add ***the*** to the text if needed.

Hi guys,
Only one week left! I've nearly reached [1] the end of my exchange in Cologne. It hasn't been [2] … best experience in [3] … world, but I guess [4] … life isn't a *Ponyhof* – that's what they say here. After two months, I just miss [5] … home. I don't know if my German is any better than it was. All [6] … kids here just kept speaking English with me. I suppose I could have tried harder. I won't miss [7] … food here – they eat [8] … dark bread with everything. And I won't miss [9] … rules with my host family. [10] … Schmidt family are nice and very friendly, but [11] … parents are very strict. I miss you guys and my mom's cooking and [12] … American TV! I'm looking forward to next weekend. We're doing one last trip to see some of [13] … sights that I haven't visited yet. We're going to go on a boat trip on [14] … river Rhine and visit [15] … Imhoff Chocolate museum. Don't worry - I'll buy some candy for you guys, too. I can't wait to see you. I hope you can come to [16] … airport to meet me! Ralph

20 British and American English Britisches und Amerikanisches Englisch

20.1 Spelling Rechtschreibung

BrE	AmE
colour, neighbour	*color, neighbor*
theatre	*theater*
practise	*practice*
travelling, travelled	*traveling, traveled*
programme	*program*

Britisches (BrE) und **amerikanisches Englisch** (AmE) unterscheiden sich in unterschiedlichen Aspekten, wie z. B. Rechtschreibung, Vokabeln und Grammatik.

◀ Beide Schreibweisen sind korrekt. Allerdings ist es wichtig, nur eine Schreibweise zu benutzen. Im Englischunterricht wird die britische Schreibweise bevorzugt, da in deutschen Schulen überwiegend *British English* gelernt wird.

20.2 Vocabulary Vokabeln

flat	***apartment***
holiday	***vacation***
biscuit	***cookie***
chips	***fries***
boot	***trunk***

Einige Wörter im BrE und AmE ähneln sich gar nicht in ihrer Form. Das trifft nicht nur auf BrE und AmE zu, sondern auch auf viele andere Varietäten des Englischen. Diese Unterschiede sind oft regional und historisch bedingt.

20.3 Grammar Grammatik

Present perfect and simple past

*The bus **has just left**.*	*The bus **just left**. (The bus **has just left**.)*
***Have** you **cleaned** your room **yet**?*	***Did** you **clean** your room yet?*
*I**'ve already called** the police.*	*I **already called** the police.*

Present perfect und *simple past*

Adverbien wie *already, ever, just, never* und *(not) yet* stehen im BrE mit dem ***present perfect***.

Im AmE stehen sie oft mit dem ***simple past***. Sie können aber auch mit dem *present perfect* stehen.

Irregular verbs

burned/burnt	***burned***
learned/learnt	***learned***
*The weather **has got** nicer.*	*The weather **has gotten** nicer.*
*I **have (got)** a cold.*	*I **have** a cold.*

Unregelmäßige Verben

Es gibt Verben im BrE, die neben der regelmäßigen Form auch eine unregelmäßige Form haben. Im AmE verwendest du die regelmäßigen Form.

◀ Das *past participle* von *get* ist *gotten* im AmE.

◀ Im BrE gibt es neben *have* auch *have got*. Im AmE benutzt du einfach nur *have*.

The adverb *really*

*John is a **really** funny guy.*	*John is a **real** funny guy.*

Das Adverb *really*

Im informellen AmE benutzt du oft *real* statt *really* („sehr").

The definite article

*Dad's ill. He's **in hospital**.* (zur Behandlung)	*Dad's ill. He's **in the hospital**.*

Der bestimmte Artikel

Im AmE steht auch der bestimmte Artikel vor Gebäudebezeichnungen, die die Funktion des Gebäudes beschreiben (hier: zur Behandlung im Krankenhaus).

IN ENGLISH:

- **British English** and **American English** show differences in spelling, vocabulary and grammar.
- It is important to choose between British or American English (and not to mix the two varieties of English).

20 Exercises

20 British and American English

a) Read the short dialogues between a British and an American English speaker.
First find the right response to each British English sentence. Then write down the two words that are different in British and American English.
Example: 1 + d biscuit - cookie

British English speaker	American English speaker
1. Do you want a biscuit?	a) We're not having a vacation because my little sister is only a few weeks old.
2. Are you going on holidays this summer?	b) I had to wear my sneakers because I couldn't find my shoes.
3. Aren't the trees beautiful in the autumn?	c) I don't have a favorite. I like all kinds of music.
4. Let's get some fish and chips.	d) No, thanks. I'm not eating cookies at the moment. I'm on a diet.
5. Your mum does a lot of travelling.	e) Really? I can't remember the last time I was at the theater.
6. You mustn't wear trainers at school.	f) I don't like fish. I'll have a hamburger with my fries.
7. We're going to the theatre on Friday.	g) They sure are. I love the fall.
8. Who's your favourite singer?	h) She's a train driver! Traveling is part of the job.

b) Look at the sentences below. An American listener might not understand what the British English speaker means. Rewrite the British English sentences to make the meaning clear.
1. We're going to have chips for dinner. We're going to have French fries for dinner.
2. The lift in the underground is broken.
3. I'll wait in the queue for the tickets while you go to the toilet.
4. We're going to play football and you can be the goalkeeper.
5. Your pullover looks nice with those trousers.
6. Our school only allows trainers with white bottoms in the school gym.
7. It's very dark in the garden. Can you take that torch?
8. Can you help me take the bags out of the boot?

c) Barbara has written about her first days in England. She wants to make her English more British.
Can you find 18 more things? Pay attention to spelling, vocabulary and grammar.
1. I would like to tell you about one of my first days in London. I needed to buy some stamps at a store (shop), so I said goodbye to my host family and went for a walk.
2. I left the apartment and took the elevator.
3. When I left our building, I stopped on the sidewalk and asked someone where I could buy some stamps.
4. A friendly lady said a store was across the road and 30 feet down the street to the left.
5. I asked, "How many meters is that?" and she said "I don't know. Ten maybe?" She was right.
6. There were two people standing in the line in the store, so I had to wait a short time.
7. When it was my turn, I asked for three international stamps and I bought some candy with the change.
8. As I came out, I walked right into the center of a large group of people.
9. They were all walking to the subway station, and I was pushed that way too.
10. Most of the people were wearing sweaters with the same design.
11. I think they were all going to a soccer match.
12. I pushed my way out of the group. Back on the sidewalk, I didn't know where I was.
13. I called my host mom on my cell and told her I had gotten lost.
14. I was real happy to see her when she came to take me home.

Skills and Media Competence – Inhalt

			Seite
READING SKILLS	SMC 1	Skimming and scanning	192
	SMC 2	Marking up a text	193
WRITING SKILLS	SMC 3	The stages of writing	194
	SMC 4	Structuring texts	195
	SMC 5	Writing good sentences	196
	SMC 6	Making an outline	197
	SMC 7	Writing a summary	198
	SMC 8	Revising texts	199
MEDIATION SKILLS	SMC 9	Mediating written or spoken information	200
	SMC 10	Selecting relevant information	200
	SMC 11	Paraphrasing	201
	SMC 12	Cultural differences	201
LISTENING AND SPEAKING SKILLS	SMC 13	Listening	202
	SMC 14	Communicating in everyday situations	203
VIEWING SKILLS	SMC 15	Viewing	204
PROJECT AND PRESENTATION SKILLS	SMC 16	Teamwork	205
	SMC 17	Internet research	205
	SMC 18	Creating a good layout for a page or poster	207
	SMC 19	Making good slides for an electronic presentation	207
	SMC 20	Describing and presenting pictures	208
	SMC 21	Giving a presentation	209
	SMC 22	Peer feedback	209
STUDY SKILLS	SMC 23	Dealing with unknown words	210
	SMC 24	Using a dictionary	210
	SMC 25	Ordering and structuring vocabulary	211
	SMC 26	Making and taking notes	212

MK Die mit diesem Symbol gekennzeichneten Abschnitte enthalten Hinweise und Tipps, die dir dabei helfen, elektronische Medien beim Englischlernen einzusetzen.

READING SKILLS

1 Skimming and scanning MK

→ p. 53

Skimming *(reading for gist)* und Scanning *(reading for specific information)* sind Lesetechniken, die viel Zeit sparen, v. a. beim Lesen von langen Texten.

SKIMMING

Angenommen, du suchst Informationen zu einem bestimmten Thema, z. B. für ein Referat oder als Antwort für eine Hausaufgabe. Deine Suche im Internet liefert eine Vielzahl an Ergebnissen, die für dein Thema relevant sein könnten. Die alle gründlich zu lesen, würde zu viel Zeit kostet. Hier hilft das Skimming.

Step 1: Sieh dir die folgenden Textteile an, um zu sehen, worum es im Text geht:

- Überschrift und Unterüberschriften
- Bilder und Bildunterschriften
- den ersten Satz jedes Absatzes – dieser Satz ist meist der *topic sentence*, der die Hauptidee des Absatzes nennt
- den letzten Absatz des Textes, der oft eine Zusammenfassung des Textes enthält

Step 2: Fasse für dich selbst den Text in ein paar Worten zusammen. Wenn dir das ohne Probleme gelingt, dann weißt du, um was es in dem Text geht – und dass dein Skimming erfolgreich war.

TIPP
Mache dir um unbekannten Wortschatz erstmal keine Gedanken – dafür ist Zeit, wenn du feststellst, dass der Text für dich geeignet ist.

SCANNING

Wenn du in einem Text nach Informationen oder Antworten auf eine Frage suchst, aber nicht den ganzen Text lesen willst, reicht es oft, wenn du den Text nach Schlüsselwörtern *(keywords)* absuchst und nur dort genauer liest, wo du sie findest.

Step 1: Überlege dir *keywords*, die für dein Thema oder deine Frage relevant sind. Wenn du z. B. nach den Öffnungszeiten eines Museums usw. suchst, dann könnten das Wörter (oder Symbole) sein wie *open, (opening) hours, days,* oder Zahlen wie *8am–5pm*.

Step 2: Geh mit deinen Augen sehr schnell durch den Text und suche nach deinen *keywords*. Du kannst auch mit dem Finger in breiten Bewegungen wie bei einem „S" von oben bis unten durch den Text gehen, bis du eines oder mehrere deiner *keywords* gefunden hast.

Step 3: Lies die Textstelle, die dein *keyword* enthält, um zu sehen, ob sie die gewünschten Informationen enthält. Wenn nicht, scanne weiter.

TIPP
Wenn du mit Texten im Internet arbeitest, kann dein Browser dir viel Arbeit abnehmen.
Mit Strg+F (Cmd+F am Mac) kannst du nach deinen *keywords* suchen und nur die Textstellen lesen, in denen ein *keyword* markiert ist.

2 Marking up a text

Wenn du mit Kopien von Texten arbeitest, kannst du wichtige Informationen darin markieren, um sie einfacher wiederzufinden oder als Grundlage für die Weiterarbeit zu verwenden, z. B. wenn du eine Zusammenfassung schreiben oder mit Hilfe des Textes eine inhaltliche Frage beantworten sollst.

Step 1: Lies dir die Aufgabe genau durch und überlege, welche Informationen du zur Beantwortung brauchst. Behalte dies im Kopf, während du den Text liest.

Step 2: Lies den Text und markiere nur Informationen, die wichtig sind. Nicht jeder Satz enthält Wichtiges, und oft reicht es aus, nur ein oder zwei Wörter in einem Satz zu markieren. Hebe wichtige Informationen hervor, z. B. durch Unterstreichen, Einkreisen oder Markieren mit einem Textmarker.

Step 3: Mach dir kurze Notizen am Rand – z. B. kurze Überschriften oder Stichwörter –, die den Inhalt kurz zusammenfassen. (➜ *SMC 26*)

TIPP
1. Verwende unterschiedliche Farben für unterschiedliche Aufgaben/Fragestellungen.
2. Markiere wirklich nur Stichwörter, sonst wird es unübersichtlich.

Fifty years ago today, Rudy Lombard, who is black, and his friend Lanny Goldfinch, who is white, walked into a diner in downtown New Orleans. With two other black friends, they took

Many of those who took part were students, both white and black. Today, not everyone realizes how dangerous it was to stand up against segregation. Through their actions, the protesters

WRITING SKILLS

3 The stages of writing

Wenn deine Texte präzise und gut lesbar sind, machst du es deinen Lesern leichter, deinen Gedanken zu folgen, egal ob du eine Geschichte, einen Bericht oder eine Zusammenfassung schreibst.

Du solltest deine Texte stets gut planen und zuerst einen Entwurf erstellen, den du dann überarbeitest, bis das Ergebnis so ist, wie du es haben willst – gut lesbar, leicht zu verstehen und ohne Fehler. Dieses Vorgehen braucht Zeit, aber es macht deine Texte besser.

PLANUNGSPHASE

Step 1: Plane für diese Phase ausreichend Zeit ein und denke über folgende Fragen nach:

- über welches Thema willst du schreiben?
- was genau sollst du tun (beschreiben, erläutern, zusammenfassen …)?
- welche Dinge musst du für den geforderten Text beachten?

Step 2: Dann solltest du

- alle nötigen Informationen für dein Thema recherchieren (➡ *SMC 17*),
- Ideen/Argumente sammeln und sortieren
- und eine Outline für deinen Text (z. B. einen Bericht) schreiben. (➡ *SMC 6*)

ENTWURFSPHASE

Jetzt schreibe deinen ersten Entwurf:

- Füge deiner Outline linking words (➡ *SMC 5*) und topic sentences hinzu (➡ *SMC 4*).
- Beginne für jede neue Idee einen neuen Absatz.
- Führe deine Ideen aus und gib Beispiele (wenn das die Textsorte erfordert).
- Denk über das Ende deines Textes nach. Wenn du weißt, wie dein Text endet, ist es leichter, eine gute Einleitung zu schreiben, die darauf hinführt. (➡ *SMC 4*)

TIPP
Wenn du mehr Informationen zum Verfassen guter Texte haben möchtest, sieh dir auch die folgenden Skills files an:
- SMC 17: Internet research
- SMC 4: Structuring texts
- SMC 5: Good sentences
- SMC 6: Making an outline
- SMC 7: Writing a summary
- SMC 8: Revising texts

ÜBERARBEITUNGSPHASE

Wenn dein Entwurf fertig ist, heißt das leider noch nicht, dass dein Text auch fertig ist. Jetzt ist es an der Zeit, dass du oder jemand anderes deinen Text noch einmal kritisch durchliest. Am besten ist es, wenn du den Text mehrmals liest, jedes Mal mit einem anderen Schwerpunkt:

- Liest sich der Text gut? Ist er logisch aufgebaut und hat eine gute Struktur? (➡ *SMC 4*)
- Sieh dir die verschiedenen sprachlichen Aspekte deines Textes an: Grammatik, Rechtschreibung, Zeichensetzung, Ausdruck, *linking words, time markers* etc. (➡ *SMC 5, SMC 8*)
- Schreibe deinen Text noch einmal. Verbessere alles, was im ersten Entwurf noch nicht ganz gepasst hat. Wenn du Feedback von jemand anderem bekommen hast, sieh es dir genau an und entscheide dann, was davon du für deinen Text übernehmen möchtest.

4 Structuring texts

STRUCTURE

Ein guter Text besteht in der Regel aus den folgenden drei Teilen:

- Einleitung *(introduction)*:
  Hier steht, worum es in dem gesamten Text geht. An dieser Stelle kann auch ein Problem genannt werden, das in dem Text erörtert werden soll.
- Hauptteil *(main body)*:
  Dieser Teil ist in mehrere Absätze gegliedert und präsentiert die Details (Fakten, Beispiele etc.) zu deinem Thema.
- Schluss *(conclusion)*:
  Hier gibst du deinem Text ein passendes, interessantes Ende.

PARAGRAPHS

Längere Texte sind einfacher zu lesen und schneller zu verstehen, wenn sie in Absätze eingeteilt sind. Dabei solltest du folgende Dinge beachten:

- Fange für jeden neuen Aspekt einen neuen Absatz an.
- Beginne mit einem interessanten *topic sentence*.
- Beende deinen Text im letzten Absatz mit einer Zusammenfassung oder etwas Persönlichem.

TOPIC SENTENCES

Jeder Absatz sollte mit einem Einleitungssatz beginnen.

Dieser topic sentence beschreibt, worum es in dem Absatz geht. Wichtige Dinge, die du in einem *topic sentence* ansprechen kannst, sind z. B.

- **Orte:** *My trip to Berlin was exciting.*
- **Personen:** *The Beatles are one of the most famous bands in the world.*
- **Aktivitäten:** *Lots of people ride their bike every day.*

My Trip to New Orleans

Last summer I wanted to go to New Orleans because I like big cities.

First I had to find some information on New Orleans. So I went online and looked for websites about things to do in New Orleans. I found a website with some interesting information on the sights and I also found a list of hostels for New Orleans. I saved about five cool websites in my favourites list.

At home I started to plan for my trip. I read all the websites and took notes on museums, the sights and the best cheap cafes in the city. After a few days I knew where I wanted to go and what I wanted to do there.

I did not want to go to New Orleans alone, so I had to find someone to go with me. I called most of my friends and told them about my plan. Some of them did not want to spend their holidays in a big city and others had no money for the trip. But my friend Judith agreed to go with me. We decided to go in late August.

Judith and I spent two lovely weeks in New Orleans. We went to the French Market and enjoyed the fantastic food there. We stayed in a lovely hostel and met lots of really nice people. Before we went home we spent a whole afternoon in the French Quarter where we listened to music while we walked around.

This was one of the best summer holidays I ever had. Go to New Orleans – it's fantastic!

5 Writing good sentences

Gute Texte bestehen aus gut formulierten, abwechslungsreichen Sätzen. Die folgenden Techniken helfen dir, dich gut auszudrücken und damit den Stil deiner Texte zu verbessern.

ADJEKTIVE

Verwende Adjektive, wenn du Dinge, Orte und Menschen näher beschreiben möchtest:

- a bright face
- a fantastic trip

Stell aber sicher, dass du die Adjektive good, bad and nice nicht zu häufig einsetzt.
Ersetze sie durch andere Adjektive mit einer ähnlichen bzw. genaueren Bedeutung:

- a nice teacher: a friendly teacher, a helpful teacher, ...
- a good book: an interesting book, a funny book, ...

ADVERBIEN

Verwende Adverbien, um Handlungen näher zu beschreiben:

- They walked home slowly.
- She talked quietly.

Verwende Ausdrücke wie really, very, a bit etc., um Aussagen zu verdeutlichen oder zu verstärken:

- It was a really sad story.
- The houses are very high.

KONJUNKTIONEN

Konjunktionen wie and, but oder because geben deinen Sätzen eine klare, gut nachvollziehbare Struktur:

- We went to the London Eye, but it was very expensive.

RELATIVSÄTZE

Relativsätze verbinden Sätze oder geben mehr Informationen zu einer Sache oder einer Person:

- This is the shop which sells the best ice cream in Berlin.

ZEITANGABEN

Time markers / adverbiale Bestimmungen der Zeit helfen dem Leser, sich in einem Text oder einer Geschichte zeitlich zurechtzufinden. Verwende *time markers*, um ...

- die Reihenfolge von Ereignissen zu verdeutlichen:
  at first, next, finally, ...
- zu zeigen, wie viel Zeit zwischen einzelnen Ereignissen vergeht:
  for half an hour, just two minutes later, ...
- zu verdeutlichen, wie langsam oder schnell etwas passiert:
  immediately, it took hours, faster than I could look, ...
- zu sagen, wenn etwas zeitgleich passiert:
  while I was waiting, during the lesson, as we came round the corner, ...
- die Ereignisse eines Textes/einer Geschichte zeitlich einzuordnen:
  two summers ago, last Halloween, on my way home from school yesterday, ...

6 Making an outline

→ p. 83

In einem Bericht geht es darum, dem Leser übersichtlich und gut verständlich Fakten darzustellen, z. B. zu einem Ereignis oder einem Vorfall.

Wenn du einen Bericht schreiben sollst, kann es helfen, schon in der Planungsphase (→ *SMC 3*) eine Gliederung zu erstellen, die die zwei wichtigsten Punkte bei einem Bericht schon berücksichtigt: eine gute Struktur und die Beantwortung der *wh*-Fragen. Damit leistest du schon eine Menge Vorarbeit und erleichterst dir das Schreiben.

STRUKTUR DER GLIEDERUNG

Wie jeder Text sollte ein Bericht aus einer Überschrift, einer Einleitung, einem Hauptteil und einem Schluss bestehen. (→ *SMC 4*)

In einer Gliederung kannst du diese Struktur schon anlegen und für jeden Textteil eine Überschrift notieren sowie Stichwörter dazu ergänzen. Wenn du viele Informationen im Hauptteil unterbringen möchtest, verwende auch Unterüberschriften.

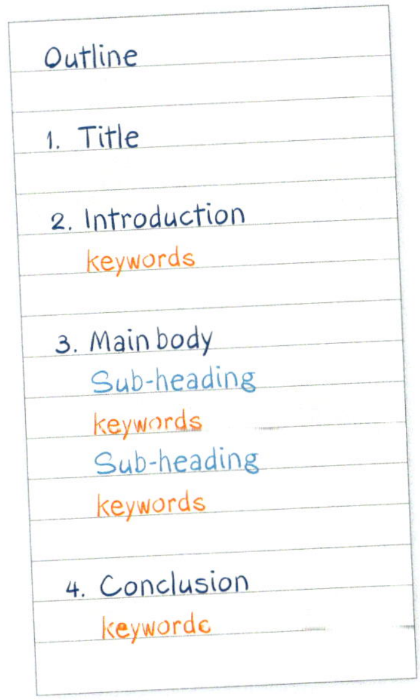

KEYWORDS

In der Einleitung eines Berichtes sagst du kurz, was passiert ist. Dabei kannst du schon knapp die wichtigsten *wh*-Fragen beantworten, bevor du im Hauptteil näher darauf eingehst.

In deiner Gliederung solltest du deswegen unter dem Abschnitt *Introduction* deine Stichworte auf die Fragen Who?, What?, When?, Where? und Why? konzentrieren.

Im Hauptteil eines Berichtes stehen dann die Details des Ereignisses, meist in chronologischer Reihenfolge. Hier werden also die *wh*-Fragen genauer beantwortet, deswegen solltest du in der Gliederung unter dem Abschnitt *Main body* weitere Stichworte zu den einzelnen Fragen sammeln.

Im Schlussabsatz bringst du deinen Bericht zu einem guten, runden Abschluss. In der Gliederung solltest du dir dafür nicht mehr als ein oder zwei Stichworte notieren.

TIPP

Ein Bericht soll objektiv sein und Fakten darstellen. Konzentriere dich bei deinen *keywords* in der Gliederung darauf, die 5 *wh*-Fragen zu beantworten:

- What happened?
- Who did what?
- When did it happen?
- Where did it happen?
- Why did it happen?

Denk daran, dass ein Bericht im *simple past* geschrieben wird. Du solltest also deine Stichworte auch gleich so notieren.

7 Writing a summary

➜ p. 30

Wenn du eine Zusammenfassung schreiben sollst, ist es wichtig, den Text gut zu kennen. Erst dann kannst du entscheiden, welche Aspekte so wichtig sind, dass sie in deiner Zusammenfassung erwähnt werden sollten – und welche nicht.
Die folgenden Schritte können dabei helfen:

PLANUNGSPHASE

Step 1: Lies den Text genau. Mach dir Notizen (➜ *SMC 26*) oder markiere wichtige Stellen im Text (➜ *SMC 2*).

Step 2: Beantworte die *wh*-Fragen Who? What? Where? When? Why? zum Text.
Du kannst dir dazu Stichworte am Rand machen.

- Who? Who does something? Who is the text about?
- What? What happens? What does person X do?
- Where? Where does it take place?
- When? When does it take place?
- Why? Why does person X act this way? Why does something happen?

Step 3: Entscheide, welche Textteile wichtige Informationen enthalten.
Beispiele,
Vergleiche, direkte Rede oder Zahlen und Ähnliches gehören nicht in eine Zusammenfassung.

TIPP
Du kannst Teile, die für deine Zusammenfassung überflüssig sind, im Text einklammern.

SCHREIBPHASE

Step 1: Schreib einen ersten Entwurf deiner Zusammenfassung:

- Beginne mit einer Einleitung, in der wichtige Informationen wie z. B. Titel, Autor/in, Thema und Hauptaussage des Textes stehen. Wenn du einen Zeitungsartikel zusammenfasst, solltest du hier auch die Quelle nennen.
- Verwende immer das simple present.
  Ausnahme hiervon: Wenn der Autor etwas beschreibt, das in der Vergangenheit oder der Zukunft liegt, z.B. in einem Zeitungsartikel, kannst du das auch so wiedergeben. Beispiel:
  The writer describes the festival in New York, which started on Saturday, 4th April. She gives details about the opening event, where the mayor gave a speech to the large crowd. She also writes about New Orleans, where next year's festival will take place.
- Kopiere nicht den Text, sondern benutze deine eigenen Worte.

LANGUAGE HELP
Folgende *phrases* können dir bei der Einleitung helfen:
- The story/text is about …
- The text deals with …
- The topic of the text is …
- The article/text shows …

Step 2: Überarbeite deine Zusammenfassung:

- Hast du alle wichtigen Aspekte genannt?
- Hast du unwichtige Details weggelassen?
- Ist dein Text durchgängig im *simple present*? (außer in den oben genannten Ausnahmen)
- Hast du deine Textteile gut verbunden? Ist dein Text logisch aufgebaut und gut zu verstehen?
- Vergiss auch nicht, den Text auf Rechtschreibung und Zeichensetzung zu checken. (➜ *SMC 8*)

8 Revising texts

Egal, ob du eine Rückmeldung von einem Partner/einer Partnerin bekommen hast oder nicht – einen Text solltest du auf jeden Fall noch einmal gut prüfen, bevor du ihn deinem Lehrer/deiner Lehrerin übergibst.

TEXTÜBERARBEITUNG

1. Stimmt die Struktur?

Jeder Text braucht
- eine Einleitung, die in das Thema einführt,
- einen Hauptteil, der das Thema ausführt,
- einen Schluss, der alles auf den Punkt bringt.

(➡ *SMC 4)*

2. Stimmt der Aufbau der Absätze?

Jeder Absatz
- befasst sich mit einem zusammenhängenden Gedanken,
- beginnt mit einem ***topic sentence***, der diesen Gedanken einführt.

(➡ *SMC 4)*

3. Stimmen die Verknüpfungen?

Gute *linking words*
- schaffen Verbindungen zwischen Sätzen oder Satzteilen,
- helfen, Zusammenhänge besser darzustellen und verständlich zu machen.

(➡ *SMC 5)*

4. Sind die Zeitangaben richtig gesetzt?

Time markers
- helfen, sich z. B. in einer Geschichte zurechtzufinden,
- machen das Geschehen anschaulicher.

(➡ *SMC 5)*

5. Enthält der Text Adjektive und Adverbien?

Adjektive und Adverbien
- erlauben nähere Beschreibungen von Personen und Dingen,
- machen Texte anschaulicher.

(➡ *SMC 5)*

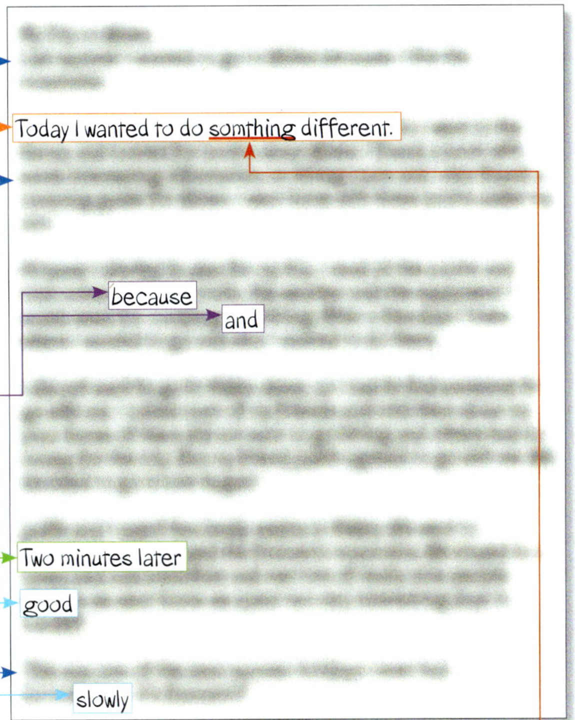

6. Hat der Text sprachliche/grammatikalische Fehler?

Überprüfe deinen Text
- auf Rechtschreibung,
- auf grammatische Formen, z. B. Verbformen, Satzbau *(word order)* usw.

Überprüfen elektronischer Texte

Textverarbeitungsprogramme haben eine Überprüfungsfunktion. Dabei werden falsch geschriebene Wörter unterstrichen. Wenn du einen Text auf dem Computer schreibst, hilft dir diese Funktion. Achte dabei auf Folgendes:

- Die Spracheinstellungen deines Programms müssen stimmen. Sonst meldet das Programm Fehler, die keine sind. Wenn z.B. die Überprüfungsfunktion auf US-Englisch eingestellt ist, werden manche Wörter als fehlerhaft unterstrichen, obwohl sie im britischen Englisch richtig geschrieben sind.
- Fehler mit Apostrophen oder bei gleichlautenden Wörtern (z.B. their, they're, there) werden nicht immer entdeckt.
- Auch andere Fehler werden nicht erkannt. Wenn du z.B. statt *bedroom* (ein Wort) *bed room* (zwei Wörter) schreibst, wird dieser Fehler nicht angezeigt, weil beide einzelnen Wörter für sich genommen richtig sind. Daher bleibt es wichtig, einen Text selbst zu prüfen und sich nicht nur auf die Überprüfung durch das Programm zu verlassen.

MEDIATION SKILLS

9 Mediating written or spoken information

➔ p. 18

Nicht jeder spricht und versteht sowohl Deutsch als auch Englisch; daher kann es vorkommen, dass du in bestimmten Situationen für Andere zwischen den Sprachen vermitteln musst – das nennt man dann Mediation.

Wie und was genau du vermitteln musst, hängt von der Situation ab und auch davon, ob du den Inhalt eines geschriebenen Textes wiedergeben oder zwischen zwei Sprechern vermitteln sollst.

Sprachmittlung bedeutet nicht Übersetzen (von Texten) oder Dolmetschen (bei Unterhaltungen), sondern das sinngemäße Übertragen von Inhalten in die andere Sprache.

MEDIATION VON SCHRIFTLICHEN ODER MÜNDLICHEN INFORMATIONEN

Wenn du Informationen in einer anderen Sprache wiedergeben sollst, geht es nicht darum, alles zu übersetzen, sondern es kommt darauf an, die wichtigsten Informationen herauszusuchen. Oft stellt dir die Person, für die du die Informationen wiedergibst, gezielte Fragen – so weißt du, worauf du achten musst.

Schriftliche Informationen

- Scanne den Text gezielt nach den geforderten Informationen. (➔ *SMC 1*)
- Mach dir keine Sorgen, wenn du nicht jedes Wort verstehst. Das ist oft nicht nötig, um die wichtigen Punkte zu verstehen und wiederzugeben.
- Wenn der Text länger ist und du viele Informationen im Blick behalten musst, markiere die wichtigsten Textstellen. (➔ *SMC 2*)
- Mach dir Notizen in deinen eigenen Worten. (➔ *SMC 26*)

Mündliche Informationen

- Achte beim Hören gezielt auf die gesuchten Informationen. (➔ *SMC 13*)
- Mach dir Notizen. (➔ *SMC 26*)
- Überlege, wie du deine Notizen am besten in der anderen Sprache wiedergeben kannst.

TIPP
Bei Mediation im Unterricht hast du in der Regel eine Aufgabenstellung, die dir sagt, worauf du beim Lesen oder Hören achten musst bzw. welche Stellen du wiedergeben sollst.
Konzentriere dich beim Lesen des Textes auf diese Stellen *(scanning)* bzw. mache dir gezielt zu diesen Stellen Notizen.

TIPP
Wenn du den Inhalt eines Texts schriftlich in einer anderen Sprache wiedergeben sollst, achte darauf, dass deine Mediation nicht länger ist als ca. 35-40% des Originaltextes, ähnlich wie bei einer *summary*. (➔ *SMC 7*)

10 Selecting relevant information

➔ p. 43

Manchmal gibt es keine gezielten Fragen oder Aufgabenstellungen, die dir sagen, welche Informationen du aus einem Text heraussuchen und wiedergeben sollst. In der Regel hast du aber trotzdem Anhaltspunkte, die sich aus der Situation ergeben oder aus dem, was dir dein Gegenüber erzählt hat.

Wenn du in einer solchen Situation bist, helfen folgende Hinweise:

- Analysiere die Situation, um abzuschätzen, um welche Informationen es gehen könnte (Restaurant, Bahnhof, Flughafen usw.).
- Wenn du unsicher bist, frage nach.
- Übersetze wichtige Stichworte direkt, wenn du die Wörter kennst.
- Umschreibe Begriffe, die du nicht kennst.

TIPP
Wenn du Informationen wiedergibst, kannst du oft Details zu einem Begriff zusammenfassen. Wenn z. B. in einem Text *twitter, Facebook, tumblr* und *Pinterest* vorkommen, kannst du *social media* sagen anstatt alle aufzuzählen.

11 Paraphrasing

➜ p. 43

Es fällt dir eventuell manchmal schwer, mündliche Aussagen oder Texte in Englisch wiederzugeben, z. B. weil

- dein Wortschatz nicht ausreicht
- dir bekannte Wörter „im Stress“ der Situation nicht einfallen
- oder spezielle Fachbegriffe auftauchen.

Wenn dir das passiert, dann solltest du versuchen, diese Wörter zu umschreiben, z. B. mithilfe von Relativsätzen wie:

It's somebody/a person who ...
It's something that you use to ...
It's an animal that ...
It's a place that/where ...

TIPP
Oft helfen beim Umschreiben auch Synonyme (gleiche Bedeutung) oder Antonyme (gegenteilige Bedeutung). Wenn du die weißt, kannst du z. B. sagen:
- It's the same as ...
- It's the opposite of ...

12 Cultural differences

➜ p. 69

Wenn du anderen Menschen hilfst, Texte oder Gehörtes zu verstehen, kann es neben Wortschatzproblemen auch noch andere Schwierigkeiten geben. Diese sind häufig in kulturellen Unterschieden begründet. Um hier helfen zu können, musst du dir beim Sprachmitteln bewusst machen, dass dein Gegenüber evtl. bestimmte Dinge nicht weiß, die für dich selbstverständlich sind, oder dass er/sie dich nicht sofort versteht, obwohl du den Inhalt korrekt übertragen hast.

Dinge, die häufig zu Missverständnissen führen, sind z. B.
- Temperaturen: 30 Grad bei uns sind heiß, in den USA eher kalt, weil in den USA Temperaturen in Fahrenheit angegeben werden, nicht in Celsius.
- Längenangaben/Geschwindigkeit: Bei uns wird das metrische System verwendet (Meter, Kilometer usw.), in den USA das *imperial system* mit *inch*, *yard* und *mile*. Das kann auch bei Geschwindigkeitsangaben zu Verwirrung führen, denn 75 *mph* (Meilen pro Stunde) sind z. B. ca. 120 km/h.

Am besten ist es, wenn du immer noch mal höflich nachfragst, ob dein Gegenüber alles verstanden hat. Wenn du dann feststellst, dass es zu einem Missverständnis gekommen ist, dann kannst du folgende Dinge probieren:
- Frage höflich nach, wo das Missverständnis ist.
- Versuche, das Missverständnis durch eine neue Erklärung zu beseitigen.
- Ergänze deine Erläuterung evtl. mit Hintergrundinformationen: Es kann sein, dass du bestimmte Dinge, die für dich völlig normal sind, erklären musst (wie z. B. Mülltrennung oder das Benutzen des Nahverkehrs).
- Sei auch offen für die Erklärungen, die du evtl. im Gegenzug bekommst – hier kannst du Dinge über das Land deines Gegenübers lernen.

LANGUAGE SKILLS

13 Listening

Im Unterricht kann es schwer sein, einem Hörtext zu folgen, weil du die Sprecher nicht sehen kannst und du dich auch noch auf die Aufgaben zum Hörtext konzentrieren musst.

Die folgenden Tipps können dir helfen.

Was mache ich vor dem Hören?

- Schau dir die Aufgabenstellung genau an. Was sollst du heraushören?
- Oft findest du zum Hörtext Überschriften und Bilder, die schon einige Fragen beantworten: Wer spricht mit wem, wo sind sie, worüber reden sie?
- Überlege, was du selbst zum Thema schon weißt und welche englischen Begriffe im Gespräch fallen könnten.

Worauf sollte ich während des Hörens achten?

- Lass dich nicht verwirren, wenn es mehrere Sprecher gibt. Versuche dann, die jeweiligen Stimmen einer Person zuzuordnen.
- Wie reden die Menschen miteinander? Gibt es einen, der den Ton angibt, oder einen, der besonders ärgerlich oder traurig klingt?
- Einiges wirst du nicht verstehen – keine Sorge, das ist nicht schlimm. Wichtiger ist, was du alles verstanden hast. Oft ergibt sich dann der Rest.

Was, wenn ich Details heraushören soll?

- Gerate nicht in Panik, wenn du denkst, du hättest etwas Wichtiges verpasst. Konzentriere dich auf die nächste wichtige Information.
- Ignoriere Hintergrundgeräusche. Wenn du bestimmte Details heraushören sollst, sind sie unwichtig und lenken nur ab.
- Mach nur kurze Notizen, z.B. Anfangsbuchstaben, Symbole und Stichworte (➔ *SMC 26*)
- Je nachdem, welche Details du heraushören sollst, können Signalwörter helfen, dem Hörtext zu folgen und dich auf die Details zu konzentrieren:
  - Aufzählungen: *and, another, too, …*
  - Gegensätze: *although, but, …*
  - Gründe, Folgen: *because, so, so that, …*
  - Vergleiche: *larger/older/… than, as … as, more, most, …*
  - Reihenfolge: *before, after, then, next, later, …*

Und nach dem Hören?

- Wenn möglich, vergleiche mit einem Partner/einer Partnerin, was ihr verstanden habt.
- Wenn du einen Text ein zweites Mal hören darfst, notiere dir nach dem ersten Hören kurz, worauf du beim zweiten Hören besonders achten willst.
- Wenn dir die eine oder andere Frage bei der Beantwortung noch Schwierigkeiten macht, dann hilft oft schlaues Raten und Kombinieren.

14 Communicating in everyday situations

Es ist nicht immer einfach, sich mit Menschen aus anderen Ländern zu unterhalten. Neben der Sprachbarriere gibt es oft auch kulturelle Unterschiede, wie das folgende Beispiel zeigt.

Lies dieses Gespräch zwischen Paul, einem deutschen Schüler, und seinem Austauschpartner Jack in den USA:

Jack: How's your school at home?
Paul: It's okay.
Jack: Oh … good. What are your favorite subjects?
Paul: Er, I don't know.
Jack: Oh, well. Maybe you'll enjoy our school too.
Paul: Maybe.
Jack: Er … want to play a game?

Das Gespräch kommt nicht so richtig in Gang, und Jack gibt irgendwann auf. Wenn man aber einige Regeln beachtet, werden Unterhaltungen einfacher und für beide Parteien erfreulicher. Vergleiche das folgende Gespräch mit dem obigen:

Jack: How's your school at home?
Paul: I like it … but of course I don't like all my teachers.
Jack: Yeah, I think that's normal. What are your favorite subjects?
Paul: I'm not sure. I like history and maths, but art and German are okay too.
Jack: Ah, my favorite subject is English. Anyway, I'm sure you'll enjoy our school too. Our history teacher is pretty cool. Have you met any of the teachers yet?
Paul: No, not yet, but I think …

Die folgenden Schritte helfen dir, wenn du dich freundlich und flüssig unterhalten willst:

Step 1: Beginne freundlich, z. B. mit etwas, was beide Gesprächspartner verbindet (der Ort, die Situation usw.).

Step 2: Halte die Unterhaltung am Laufen:
- zeige dein Interesse, indem du Fragen stellst
- vermeide einsilbige Antworten, um nicht desinteressiert oder unfreundlich zu wirken
- wenn du etwas nicht verstehst, frage nach
- wenn du etwas nicht sagen kannst, versuche es zu umschreiben oder bitte deinen Gesprächspartner um Hilfe

Step 3: Beende das Gespräch so freundlich, wie du es angefangen hast:
- bedanke dich, wenn du um Hilfe gebeten hast
- verabschiede dich freundlich

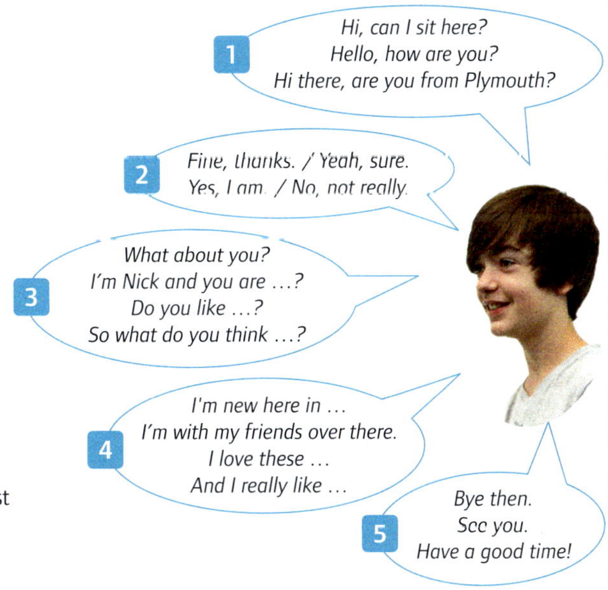

TIPP

Aussprache und Satzmelodie (z.B. bei *question tags*) sind wichtig im Englischen. Da es aber mitten in einem Gespräch nicht immer einfach ist, darauf zu achten, solltest du das Sprechen regelmäßig üben, indem du dich aufnimmst (etwa mit der Diktierfunktion deines Handys) und dich dann anhörst, um deine Aussprache zu überprüfen. Das funktioniert am besten, wenn du einen Text liest, den du auch als Audio vorliegen hast, also etwa ein Text aus dem Schülerbuch oder dem Workbook oder ein Audiobook, denn dann kannst du deine Aussprache gut mit der korrekten vergleichen.

VIEWING SKILLS

15 Viewing

Wenn du verstehst, wie Filmtechniken eingesetzt werden, um beim Zuschauer z.B. Angst, Freude, Spannung oder Lachen auszulösen, bekommst du ein besseres Verständnis dafür, wie Filme funktionieren.

Es gibt viele verschiedene Elemente, die die Atmosphäre und die Wirkung eines Filmes beeinflussen:

- Genre: Handelt es sich um einen Dokumentarfilm (documentary), einen Spielfilm (feature film) wie z. B. thriller, science-fiction/sci-fi movie, comedy oder ein drama? Oder ist es ein Videoclip oder ein Werbefilm?
- Story: Wo und wann spielt der Film (setting)? Besetzung der Rollen (cast), Schauplatz (location), Handlung (plot).
- Camera: Erst durch die Bilder der **Kamera** ist der Zuschauer in der Lage, einen Film wahrzunehmen. Die Kamera stellt das Blickfeld her und begrenzt es gleichzeitig, z. B. hinsichtlich der Beziehung der Charaktere zueinander. Auch die Stimmung oder Spannung in einer Szene wird von der Kameraführung beeinflusst. Dafür gibt es z. B. folgende Mittel:
  - Shots: Die **Kameraeinstellung** beeinflusst, wie man Szenen wahrnimmt, ob z. B. Personen oder Objekte als Nahaufnahme (close-up), aus der mittleren Distanz (medium shot) oder als Totale (long shot) gefilmt sind.
  - Editing: Filme werden in der Regel nicht chronologisch gedreht und auch nicht nur mit einer einzigen Kamera, d. h. am Ende der Dreharbeiten müssen viele einzelne Shots zu einem Film zusammengefügt werden. Dieser **Filmschnitt** bestimmt, wie eine Szene wirkt. Er bestimmt den Rhythmus – lange Einstellungen mit wenigen Schnitten wirken eher ruhig, können aber auch große Spannung erzeugen, während schnelle, harte Schnitte eher actiongeladen wirken. Wie genau eine Szene wirkt, hängt oft auch vom Zusammenspiel von Schnitt und Musik ab.
- Soundtrack: Die **Musik**, die für eine Szene gewählt wird, hat großen Einfluss darauf, wie man die Szene wahrnimmt. Eine Actionszene wird meist mit schneller, lauter Musik unterlegt, eine romantische Szene eher mit ruhiger, leiser Musik. Dies geschieht, um die Wirkung des Gesehenen zu verstärken.

long shot

medium shot

close-up

VIEWING LOG

Wenn du eine Szene oder einen ganzen Film sehr intensiv analysieren möchtest, hilft es, ein Filmtagebuch (viewing log) anzulegen, in dem du die Handlung oder einzelne wichtige Szenen sowie deine Reaktion darauf festhältst.

Das Filmtagebuch kann z. B. eine simple, zweispaltige Tabelle sein:
Spalte 1: What you noticed – images, sounds, dialogue, lighting, costumes, mood, characterization, plot, etc.
Spalte 2: Your reaction – What did you think? How did the scene make you feel?

TIPP

Wenn du über Filme sprechen möchtest, können dir folgende Redewendungen helfen:

- The film is about … / shows … / tells the story of …
- The music creates/builds/supports tension/suspense/joy …
- The actor's body language helps to create a feeling of happiness/joy/anger/suspense …
- In this scene the music/effects/camera angle … supports the plot /mood of the scene / …
- The camera movement creates a feeling of …
- The camera work/soundtrack helps to …
- The close-ups show his/her feelings.

PROJECT AND PRESENTATION SKILLS

16 Teamwork

Bei Projekten arbeitet ihr oft im Team. Dabei solltet ihr eure unterschiedlichen Fähigkeiten und Talente einbringen und bestimmte Regeln beachten. Folgende Schritte können helfen, die Arbeit zu organisieren:

Step 1: Legt Regeln für die Arbeit in der Gruppe fest, z. B. gegenseitige Unterstützung, pünktliches und zügiges Arbeiten, einander zuhören oder verschiedene Lösungen diskutieren usw.

Step 2: Sammelt Ideen für die Bearbeitung eures Themas (z. B. in einer Mindmap). Wählt gemeinsam Unterthemen aus und legt die Arbeitsschritte fest, die für die Bearbeitung nötig sind.

Step 3: Verteilt Rollen und Aufgaben nach euren Interessen und Fähigkeiten. Wenn ihr euch nicht einigen könnt, hilft Auslosen oder Würfeln. Folgende Rollen solltet ihr auf jeden Fall verteilen:
- coordinator
- writer
- researcher

Step 4: Macht einen Zeitplan für eure Arbeiten, an den sich alle halten.

Step 5: Am Ende der Arbeit sollte ein Rückblick stehen: Besprecht, was gut war und wo ihr Verbesserungsmöglichkeiten seht.

17 Internet research

Das Internet ist voller Informationen und es ist nicht einfach, genau die Informationen zu finden, die du benötigst.

Wie finde ich die Informationen, die ich brauche?

- Überlege, was die wichtigsten ***Stichwörter*** für dein Thema sind. Für das Thema "The Beatles in Hamburg" wären *Beatles* und *Hamburg* ein guter Start.
- Gib deine Stichwörter in eine ***Suchmaschine*** ein. Je mehr gute Stichwörter du eingibst, desto genauer sind die Ergebnisse. In der Infografik rechts kannst du sehen, wie du an ganz spezielle Informationen kommen kannst.
- Sieh dir mehrere ***Suchergebnisse*** an, um zu sehen, ob sie passen. Wenn du schnell ein bestimmtes Wort wie z.B. *Hamburg* finden willst, dann kannst du mit der Tastenkombination ***Strg + F*** danach suchen. Das Wort wird dann auf der Seite markiert und du kannst schnell sehen, ob die Information relevant ist.
- Achte darauf, wer die Webseite erstellt hat, um die ***Qualität*** der Suchergebnisse einzuschätzen. Sind sie eher zuverlässig (Online-Lexikon, bekannte Medien, ...) oder eher persönliche Meinungen (Forum, Fan-Seite, ...)?
- Kopiere nicht einfach ganze Artikel aus dem Internet. Mach dir Notizen und verwende deine eigenen Worte, um die Inhalte wiederzugeben.

Internet research
Tipps und Tricks

Wenn du ganz spezifische Informationen suchst, helfen diese Tricks:

Was du suchst: Artikel aus der *Wikipedia*, in denen du Informationen über die Zeit der Beatles in Hamburg findest.

Wie du danach suchst:

site:wikipedia.com "the beatles" "hamburg"

site:	" "
sucht nur auf der genannten Seite	sucht die exakten Begriffe und erzwingt das Vorkommen im Suchergebnis

Was du suchst: Einen englischsprachigen Bericht, am liebsten als PDF, über den Lebensraum von Füchsen.

Wie du danach suchst:

filetype:pdf intitle:habitat of *fox

filetype:	intitle:	*
sucht nur diesen Dateityp (pdf, doc, jpg usw.)	zeigt nur Ergebnisse, in denen dieses Wort im Titel auftaucht	sucht auch Worte wie Red Fox, Black Fox, Desert Fox usw.

- Setz dir ein Zeitlimit für deine Recherche und ordne dann dein Material. Prüfe, ob dir etwas fehlt und suche ggf. gezielt nach nur noch diesen Informationen.
- Leg alle interessanten Materialien zu deinem Thema in einem eigenen Ordner ab. Dann kannst du sie dir später genauer ansehen und auswählen, was du nutzen möchtest.

TIPP
Du kannst bei einfachen Suchanfragen auch direkt die Frage ins Suchfeld eingeben, z.B. *What is 20 oz in grams?* Die Suchmaschine sucht sich dann selbst die relevanten Stichworte heraus – hier *20 oz* und *grams* – und liefert die Antwort. Bei komplexeren Suchanfragen sind die Antworten oft besser, je genauer du dir Suchbegriffe überlegst.

Bildsuche im Internet

Die folgenden Hinweise helfen dir, wenn du für eine Aufgabe online Bilder suchen sollst, denn dabei gibt es einiges zu beachten. Zum Glück haben fast alle Suchmaschinen eine Bildsuche, die du in der Regel entweder schon vor der Suche oder bei den Ergebnissen durch das Klicken auf den "Bilder"-Knopf erreichen kannst.

Wie finde ich die richtigen Bilder?

Auch hier kommt es vor allem auf die richtigen **Suchbegriffe** an. Je genauer du suchst, d.h. je enger deine Suche ist, desto besser werden deine Ergebnisse sein und desto weniger Zeit brauchst du.

Nehmen wir an, du suchst etwas zum Eton College:

- *eton college* findet alle Bilder zu *eton* und *college*, wird aber in der Regel schon gute Ergebnisse liefern, weil die Schule berühmt ist; suchst du nach *"eton college"* bekommst du nur Ergebnisse, bei denen diese Wörter genau so in den Bildinformationen hinterlegt sind
- suchst du z.B. Bilder zu Sport und speziell Rugby am Eton College, kannst du die Suche weiter einschränken:
  eton college sports findet Bilder zu allen Sportarten und -teams an der Schule
  eton college rugby findet bevorzugt Bilder zu Rugby an der Schule
  eton college "rugby team" findet Bilder zur Rugbymannschaft der Schule
  eton college sports -rugby hingegen zeigt dir alle Sportarten *außer* Rugby an

Bedenke bei der Suche zu Orten wie Städten, Parks, Flüssen usw., dass es die mehrfach geben kann, d.h. hier musst du ggf. deine Suche um ein *UK*, *USA* oder *Canada* ergänzen, je nachdem, wonach du suchst. Städte namens Plymouth z.B. gibt es in GB, USA und Kanada.

Wie speichere ich die Bilder und wie darf ich sie nutzen?

Bilder, die du im Internet findest, haben einen **Urheber**, d.h. du darfst sie nicht so ohne Weiteres einfach speichern und verwenden.

- **Was du darfst**: Bilder speichern (rechte Maustaste -> Bild speichern unter ...) und in Präsentationen oder Postern für den Unterricht verwenden, **aber:** du musst die Quelle angeben, am besten direkt am Bild und auf diese Weise: *Quelle: Adresse der Webseite (URL)* oder im Idealfall *Name des Fotografen (+ URL)*
- **Was du nicht darfst**: Präsentationen mit fremden Fotos auf die Schulwebseite laden oder sie anderweitig veröffentlichen. Dazu brauchst du immer die Erlaubnis des Urhebers.

! Wenn du ein Bild gespeichert hast, aber nicht mehr weißt, wo es herkommt, ist das noch kein Grund zur Sorge: Du kannst bei vielen Suchmaschinen eine Suche anhand des Bildes starten.

Dazu klickst du auf das kleine Kamerasymbol in der Suchleiste und lädst dann das Bild hoch. Als Ergebnis kommt dann eine Liste mit Webseiten, auf denen das Bild verwendet wurde und du kannst gucken, wo du es gefunden hast und dir dann die Quelle kopieren/notieren.

18 Creating a good layout for a page or poster

Wenn du einen Text gestalten möchtest, z. B. für einen Vortrag, einen Blog oder als Poster für eine Präsentation, können dir folgende Hinweise helfen:

- Sortiere die Informationen, die du vermitteln willst: Was ist wichtig? Was ist ein Unterpunkt? Hast du Beispiele für Thesen/ Argumente?
- Gib deinem Produkt eine klare Struktur: Texte haben meist drei Teile (Einleitung, Hauptteil, Schluss), während Poster häufig aus Aufzählungen wichtiger Punkte bestehen. Beginne für jeden neuen Gedanken einen neuen Absatz bzw. einen neuen Stichpunkt.
- Eine Überschrift verdeutlicht, worum es in deinem Text geht. Sie soll Leser auch neugierig machen auf das, was kommt. Wenn es in deinem Produkt um mehrere Themen/Aspekte eines Themas geht, dann kannst du für einzelne Abschnitte auch Zwischenüberschriften verwenden. Das gibt dem Ganzen eine klare Struktur und hilft dem Leser, sich schnell zu orientieren.
- Ergänze dein Produkt mit passenden Fotos, Videos, Audios, Statistiken etc. Vergiss nicht anzugeben, woher die Medien stammen (➔ *SMC 17, 19*).

- Wenn nicht auf den ersten Blick erkennbar ist, was z.B. ein Bild zeigt, füge Bildunterschriften ein.
- Formatiere dein Produkt so, dass es gut lesbar ist. Dabei ist das Medium wichtig – für einen ausgedruckten Handzettel kannst du andere Schriftarten wählen als für einen Text, der am Bildschirm gelesen wird. (➔ *SMC 19*) Für ein Poster (z.B. für einen *gallery walk)* muss die Schriftgröße größer sein als für einen Ausdruck. Eine große Schriftgröße hilft dir auch, nicht zu viele Punkte auf dem Poster unterzubringen – hier ist weniger mehr.

19 Making good slides for an electronic presentation

Vieles, was für das Layout von Texten/Postern gilt, kannst du auch auf Folien für Präsentation anwenden. Es gibt aber einige Besonderheiten zu beachten. Generell gilt: gut ist, was deine Folien übersichtlich und leicht zu lesen macht.

TEXT

- Verwende möglichst wenige Folien.
- Nutze Aufzählungen mit *keywords*, keine ganzen Sätze und schreibe nicht mehr als sechs Zeilen auf eine Folie.
- Wähle eine ausreichende Schriftgröße (mindestens 30pt, gerne mehr) und eine gut lesbare Schrift und gehe sparsam mit Texthervorhebungen wie fett, kursiv, Unterstreichung um; lass einen ausreichend großen Abstand zwischen den Zeilen.
- Richte den Text linksbündig aus, außer du verfolgst ein ganz besonderes Ziel damit (z.B. zentriert zum Herausheben eines Zitats), aber mische die Ausrichtung nicht auf einer Folie. Zitate z.B. wirken oft am besten, wenn sie zentriert alleine auf einer Folie stehen.

TIPP

- Eine gute Faustregel lautet **6 x 6**: pro Folie maximal 6 Zeilen mit je maximal 6 Wörtern
- Bedenke: Folien sind eine **visuelle Unterstützung** für eine Präsentation, keine Zusammenfassung. Die Zuhörer sollen hören, nicht lesen – die Texte sollten daher auf das Wichtigste reduziert sein.
- **Vermeide Spezialeffekte** wie verspielte Übergänge, tanzende Buchstaben etc. Sie kosten viel Zeit und helfen den Zuhörern nicht.

ABBILDUNGEN

- Ein Bild sagt mehr als tausend Worte – das gilt auch für Folien: manche Inhalte kannst du ebenso mit einem passenden Bild oder einer Grafik ausdrücken.
- Suche ein Bild, dass die Aussage deines Vortrages unterstreicht: z.B. ein Foto, das eine Fragestellung gut illustriert oder eines, das das Problem gut darstellt. Es muss auch kein Foto sein – manchmal ist eine passende Grafik genauso gut, um z.B. statistische Aussagen auf den Punkt zu bringen.
- Wichtig: bei allen Bildern, die du verwendest, musst du die Quelle angeben, d.h. der Fotograf/die Fotografin, Illustrator/Illustratorin etc. sowie der Ort, wo du das Bild gefunden hast (eine Suchmaschine im Internet ist keine Quellenangabe!).

TIPP

Wenn du deine Folien/Poster nur vor der Klasse zeigst, darfst du Bilder verwenden, ohne die **Urheber** um Erlaubnis zu fragen, weil es sich um eine begrenzte Öffentlichkeit handelt. Wenn die Folien aber öffentlich zugänglich sind (z.B. auf einer Webseite oder der Schulzeitung), musst du die Urheber unbedingt um **Erlaubnis** fragen.
Als Faustregel gilt: veröffentliche kein Bild ohne Erlaubnis, das du nicht selbst gemacht hast.

20 Describing and presenting pictures

Manchmal sollst du ein Foto vor der Klasse vorstellen und es dabei beschreiben. Hier sind ein paar Hilfen.

Wie stelle ich ein Foto vor?

1 Stelle das Foto vor und sage, woher es kommt.

2 Beschreibe das Foto:

- Sage, was wo zu sehen ist: *at the top/bottom* · *in the foreground/background* · *in the middle* · *on the left/right*
- Diese Präpositionen sind auch hilfreich: *behind* · *between* · *in front of* · *next to* · *under* · *over*
- Geh bei der Beschreibung in einer bestimmten Reihenfolge vor, z.B. von links nach rechts oder von oben nach unten.

3 Sage, was dir an dem Foto gefällt oder nicht.

4 Wenn du mit der Vorstellung des Fotos fertig bist, bedanke dich fürs Zuhören und frage, ob noch jemand Fragen hat.

1 *I'd like to talk about this photo of … I found it on the internet/in a magazine/…*

2 *In the foreground you can see … I think the people in the photo are talking about …/having fun/ celebrating/…*

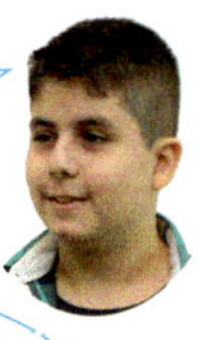

3 *I really like/don't like the photo because … It's interesting/boring/exciting/ … because …*

4 *Thank you for listening. Do you have any questions?*

21 Giving a presentation

Wie halte ich eine gute Präsentation?

Vorbereitung
- Sammle Informationen zu deinem Thema.
- Wähle eine Form der Präsentation aus, die das Thema gut veranschaulicht (Poster, Folie, Tafel, ...).
- Mach dir Notizen, z.B. auf nummerierten Karteikarten oder in einer App.
- Bereite deine Medien vor (Poster, Folie, Tafelanschrieb, ...). Schreibe groß und für alle gut lesbar.
- Übe deine Präsentation zu Hause vor einem Spiegel oder vor einem kleinen Publikum (Eltern, Großeltern, Freunde).
- Sprich laut, deutlich und langsam.

Durchführung
- Warte, bis es ruhig ist. Schaue die Zuhörer/innen an.
- Erkläre, worüber du sprechen wirst und wie deine Präsentation aufgebaut ist.
- Lies nicht von deinen Karten ab, sondern sprich möglichst frei.

Schluss
- Sage, dass du zum Ende kommst und bedanke dich fürs Zuhören.
- Frag die Zuhörer/innen, ob sie Fragen haben.

22 Peer feedback

Manchmal sollst du im Unterricht Partnern/Partnerinnen eine Rückmeldung zu einer Aufgabe geben. Das nennt man *peer feedback*.

Wozu ist *peer feedback* gut?

Gegenseitige Rückmeldungen sind für dich und deine Partner *(peers)* wichtig, denn du kannst
- jemanden loben für etwas, das er/sie gut gemacht hat,
- Hinweise geben, wo deine Partner noch Probleme haben,
- durch die Rückmeldungen selbst lernen, was du schon gut kannst und was du anders machen solltest.

Was muss ich beachten?

Bei deiner Rückmeldung solltest du drei Dinge beachten:

- Halte dich an die Punkte, zu denen du Rückmeldung geben sollst, z.B. die Aussprache, Betonung und Verständlichkeit bei einem Dialog, die Rechtschreibfehler in einem Text, das Einhalten eines roten Fadens in einer Geschichte usw. Begründe deine Einschätzungen.
- Gib deine Rückmeldung mit Respekt – niemand soll sich angegriffen fühlen. Nenne zuerst Gelungenes und mache dann Verbesserungsvorschläge zu Punkten, die noch nicht so gelungen sind.
- Wenn du eine Rückmeldung bekommst, überdenke die Vorschläge gut. Korrigiere die Fehler, die andere gefunden haben, und arbeite an den Stellen nach, wo du eventuell Probleme hattest.

What I liked	What you could do better
You chose a great photo. ☺ You spoke clearly and looked at us. ...	Next time, say what is happening in the photo. Sometimes you stood in front of the photo. ...

STUDY SKILLS

23 Understanding new words

Das Nachschlagen unbekannter Wörter kostet Zeit und ist auch nicht immer nötig. Oft geht es auch ohne den Einsatz eines Wörterbuches.

Immer gleich im Wörterbuch nachschlagen?

- Viele englische Wörter werden ähnlich wie im Deutschen geschrieben oder klingen ähnlich (z.B. *brochure, statue, insect*). Manche sehen auch einem Wort aus anderen Sprachen ähnlich, z.B. *voice (French: voix; Latin: vox)*.
- In manchen Wörtern stecken bekannte Teile, z.B. *bottle opener, snowshoe.*
- Präfixe und Suffixe wie *un-*, *re-* und *-er* helfen beim Erschließen: *listen**er** (sb. who listens), **un**happy <> happy, **re**pay (pay sb. back).*
- Bilder zum Text zeigen oft Dinge, die du im Text vielleicht nicht verstehst.
- Der Kontext, also die Wörter und Sätze um das Wort herum, kann beim Verstehen helfen, z.B. *Let's hurry. The train **departs** in ten minutes.*

TIPP
Nicht alle Wörter, die im Deutschen und Englischen ähnlich sind, haben auch dieselbe Bedeutung.
Achte daher auf false friends:
handy = praktisch, *nicht* Handy

24 Using a dictionary

Es gibt unterschiedliche Wörterbücher, in denen du nachschlagen kannst. Wenn du die Bedeutung eines unbekannten Wortes nachschlagen willst, dann benutzt du am besten ein zweisprachiges Wörterbuch (Englisch-Deutsch bzw. Deutsch-Englisch). Wenn du mehr Informationen zu englischen Wörtern haben möchtest, etwa Beispielsätze, Definitionen oder Alternativen, dann bietet sich ein einsprachiges Wörterbuch an.

ZWEISPRACHIGE WÖRTERBÜCHER

Die Leitwörter *(running heads)* oben auf der Seite helfen dir, schnell zu finden, was du suchst. Auf der linken Seite steht das erste Stichwort, auf der rechten Seite das letzte Stichwort der Doppelseite.

- *resign* ist das Stichwort *(headword)*. Stichwörter sind alphabetisch geordnet: *r* vor *s*, *ra* vor *re*, *rhe* vor *rhi* usw.
- Die kursiv gedruckten Hinweise helfen dir, die für deinen Text passende Bedeutung zu finden.
- Die Ziffern 1, 2 usw. zeigen, dass ein Stichwort unterschiedliche Bedeutungen haben oder unterschiedlichen Wortarten angehören kann (z. B. Adjektiv, Nomen, Verb).
- Beispielsätze und Redewendungen sind dem Stichwort zugeordnet.
- Unregelmäßige Verbformen, besondere Pluralformen, die Steigerungsformen der Adjektive und ähnliche Hinweise stehen oft in Klammern oder sind kursiv gedruckt.
- Die Lautschrift gibt Auskunft darüber, wie das Wort ausgesprochen und betont wird.

resort

resign /rɪˈzaɪn/
1 BERUF • *als Vorsitzender usw* zurücktreten: ***He resigned from the company.*** Er verließ das Unternehmen.
2 (*job, post*) aufgeben (*Stelle, Posten*)
3 **resign oneself to something** sich mit etwas abfinden
resignation /ˌrezɪgˈneɪʃn/
1 BERUF • *bei Unternehmen* Kündigung; *von Minister usw* Rücktritt
2 **hand in one's resignation** *von Angestelltem* kündigen; *von Minister usw* sein Amt niederlegen
3 *Gemütszustand* Resignation
resigned /rɪˈzaɪnd/ (*look, sigh*) resigniert

resit[1] /ˌriːˈsɪt/ *Verb* (→ *sit*) *BE* (*exam*) wiederholen (*Prüfung*)
resit[2] /ˈriːsɪt/ *Substantiv* • *BE* Wiederholungsprüfung
resolution /ˌrezəˈluːʃn/
1 POLITIK Beschluss, Resolution
2 *bei Problem, Streit* Lösung
3 ≈ *Entschiedenheit* Entschlossenheit

TIPP MK
Wenn du ein Online-Wörterbuch oder eine App verwenden möchtest, weil das schneller geht oder du dein Handy gerade zur Hand hast, erkundige dich vorher bei deiner Lehrerin/deinem Lehrer, welche zu empfehlen sind, denn nicht alle sind gleich gut. Fast alle funktionieren aber nach den gleichen Prinzipien wie gedruckte Wörterbücher. Am besten probierst du beides aus und siehst, was für dich das Beste ist. Bevor du allerdings ein Online-Wörterbuch im Unterricht verwendest, klärt am besten in der Klasse ab, wann und wie du das einsetzen darfst. Bei den Hausaufgaben sieht das evtl. anders aus als bei einer Klassenarbeit oder im Unterricht.

EINSPRACHIGE WÖRTERBÜCHER

Wenn du selbst einen englischen Text schreibst, kannst du ein einsprachiges englisches Wörterbuch zu Hilfe nehmen. Hier findest du mehr über ein englisches Wort heraus als in einem zweisprachigen Wörterbuch:

- Ein einsprachiges Wörterbuch erklärt die Bedeutung eines englischen Wortes auf Englisch. Da manche Wörter mehrere Bedeutungen haben, ist es wichtig, alle Einträge und Beispielsätze zu einem Wort zu lesen und mit deinem englischen Text zu vergleichen, um die korrekte Bedeutung herauszufinden.
- Das Wörterbuch hilft dir, die passende Verbindung mit anderen Wörtern zu finden, z. B. zu Verben, Präpositionen oder in bestimmten feststehenden Wendungen. Das ist nützlich, wenn du selbst einen englischen Text schreiben willst und nach den richtigen Wörtern suchst.

deadly ['dedli] *adj*
1 *able or likely to kill people* {= lethal}: This is no longer a deadly disease.
deadly to The HSN virus is deadly to chickens.
a deadly weapon The new generation of biological weapons is more deadly than ever.
2 *(only before noun)* {= complete}:
deadly silence There was deadly silence after his speech.
a deadly secret Don't tell anyone – this is a deadly secret.
deadly serious *completely serious:* Don't laugh – I am deadly serious!
3 *(informal) very boring*: Many TV programmes are pretty deadly!

25 Ordering and structuring vocabulary

→ p. 82

Warum Wortschatz sammeln und strukturieren?

Wenn du einen Text zu einem bestimmten Thema schreiben sollst, kann es helfen, vorab Vokabeln dazu zu sammeln, damit dein Text einen abwechslungsreichen Wortschatz hat und sich gut liest. Oft wird auch schon beim Sammeln eine Gliederung des Themas erkennbar. Dadurch merkst du auch schnell, welche Wörter du ggf. noch nachschlagen musst.

Diese Art, Wortschatz zu ordnen, hilft dir auch neue Vokabeln zu lernen und sie zu vernetzen, so dass sie besser in deinem Gedächtnis bleiben.

Welche Methoden gibt es?

Für das Ordnen der Wörter gibt es verschiedene Möglichkeiten. Du solltest unterschiedliche Formen ausprobieren und dann diejenige verwenden, die am besten zu dir oder der Aufgabe passt.

Einige der Formen, die du nutzen kannst, sind:

- Tabellen (***tables***)
- Diagramme (z.B. ***tree diagrams***)
- Mindmaps

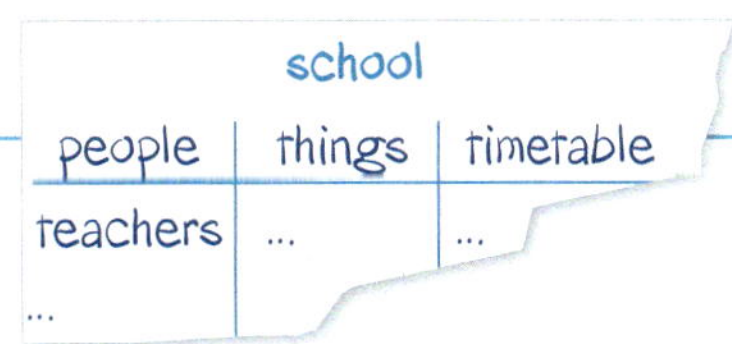

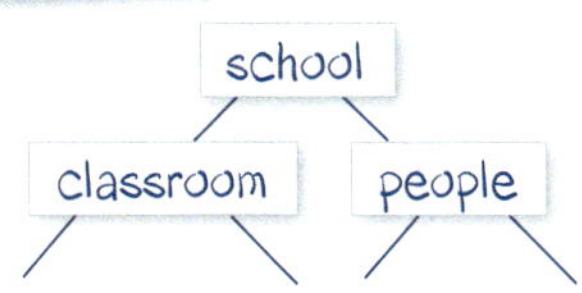

TIPP

Wenn du Wortschatz für einen Text zusammenstellst, solltest du daran denken, dass du nicht nur Nomen, sondern auch Verben, Adverbien, Adjektive etc. brauchst, sowie Varianten für Ausdrücke, die häufig vorkommen.

Synonyms and antonyms

Eine andere gute Möglichkeit zur Organisation sind Synonyme und Antonyme, die du in einer Tabelle zusammenstellst, evtl. mithilfe eines Wörterbuches oder eines Thesaurus. Mit dieser Methode kannst du nicht nur deinen bestehenden Wortschatz organisieren, sondern ihn auch erweitern. Siehe dir aber immer die Beispielsätze im Wörterbuch an, bevor du die Wörter selbst vernwendest.

word	synonym	antonym	example sentence
difficult	hard	easy	The test was very difficult.
safe	...	dangerous	Don't be afraid, this area is quite safe.
scenic	beautiful	...	We took the scenic tour along the coast.

TIPP
Wenn du ein neues Adjektiv lernst, schlag es nach, entweder online oder in einem Wörterbuch, um zu sehen, ob es Antonyme oder Synonyme mit Präfixen oder Suffixen gibt, so dass du nicht nur z.B. das Adjektiv "legal" lernst, sondern auch gleich "illegal".

26 Making and taking notes

Wenn du Informationen oder eigene Gedanken kurz für dich notierst – z.B. als Vorbereitung auf einen eigenen Vortrag oder eine Präsentation –, heißt das im Englischen making notes. Wenn du dir Notizen beim Lesen oder Zuhören machst, heißt das taking notes. Für beide Varianten gelten aber die gleichen Grundsätze.

Step 1: Achte auf keywords, die die wichtigsten Informationen enthalten, um deine Frage/Aufgabe zu beantworten oder den Inhalt eines Textes grob zu verstehen.

Step 2: Notiere nur die wichtigsten Informationen. Verwende Abkürzungen und Symbole, aber achte darauf, dass du ein System hast und immer dieselben verwendest, damit du deine Notizen auch später noch verstehst.
Markiere offene Fragen.

Step 3: Geh im Anschluss an das Lesen oder Hören nochmal durch deine Notizen und ergänze evtl. noch fehlende Informationen.

TIPP
Wenn du kein eigenes System von Abkürzungen hast, kannst du z. B. auch diese verwenden:

- the same as =
- not the same as ≠
- about the same as ≈
- and +
- becomes/will be ->
- between b/w
- for example e.g.
- important !
- not x
- with w/
- without w/o
- open question ??

The story of Ellis Island *by Jan Thompson*

The early history

Ellis Island is a mile southwest of Manhattan, and although it's small (just 200 by 600 meters) it has an important place in American history. For over 12 million immigrants who arrived in the United States between 1892 and 1954, Ellis Island was the first stop – the door to a new life in America.
In 1774, a New Yorker called Samuel Ellis bought the island and gave it his name. At that time, it was a popular place for rich people to have picnics and go fishing in their free time. However, Samuel Ellis couldn't build there because, when the sea rose up, most of the island was under water. After he died, Ellis's grandchildren sold it to the US army. This was around 1808, when the US was at war with France and the United Kingdom. The army put soldiers on Ellis Island to protect New York from enemy ships. They dropped mountains of earth into the water around the island and made it much bigger. This made it possible build there.

An immigration station

By the mid-19th century, more and more people were moving from Europe to the US. The government chose Ellis Island as the place where immigrants could stay while officials checked their papers and decided if they could enter the country. The old army buildings were pulled down and the island was made even bigger. A hospital, buildings for the immigrants to sleep in, and rooms for the government officials were built. The station opened in January 1882. Its first immigrant was Annie Moore, a 17-year-old girl from Cork in Ireland, who arrived with her brothers to meet their parents in the US. On that one day in January, almost 700 immigrants passed through the island.
Typically, only immigrants who had travelled third class on ships from Europe had to go to Ellis Island. The richer first- and second-class travelers could go straight on to New York. Immigrants who were healthy and had all the right papers usually spent about three to five hours on the island. Only two per cent of them were not allowed to enter the United States. Those unlucky people had to get back on a ship and return home.

A new life for the island

By the mid-20th century, the US government didn't need Ellis Island any more. Immigration rules had changed, and fewer immigrants from southern and eastern Europe could now move there. In November 1954, the last immigrant, Arne Peterssen, a Norwegian sailor, was sent on to New York. The immigration station on Ellis Island closed for ever.
Years went by and the buildings on Ellis Island became ruins. You could take a ferry to visit them, but there wasn't much to see. Lot of people and businesses had plans to give the island a new life – as a luxury hotel, a swimming pool and a world trade center – but they were all unsuccessful.
Finally, in 1982, President Ronald Reagan put together a group to raise money and make the island into a museum. Eight years and 160 million dollars later, the Ellis Island National Museum of Immigration opened for visitors.
Today, two million people get on the ferry every year to see the place where so many immigrants spent their first hours in America. The museum tells their stories. There is a library, a reading room and three theaters for films and live performances. Outside the main building, you can find the Wall of Honor with a list of 775,000 names: people who arrived at the immigration station, but also slaves, Native Americans, and immigrants that were never on the island. Their names tell the whole story of America and its people.

Das **Vocabulary** (S. 214–236) enthält alle Wörter und Wendungen deines Englischbuches, die du lernen musst. Sie stehen in der Reihenfolge, in der sie im Buch zum ersten Mal vorkommen.

Hier siehst du, wie das **Vocabulary** aufgebaut ist:

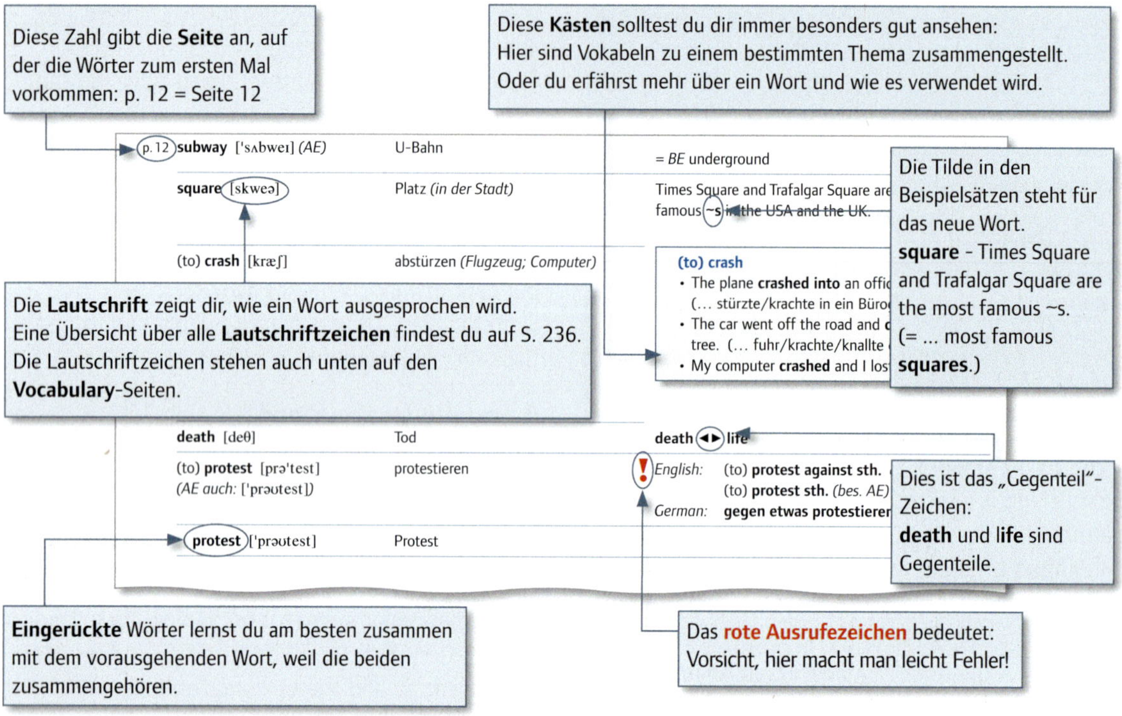

Im **Vocabulary** werden folgende **Abkürzungen** verwendet:

p. = page (Seite) pp. = pages (Seiten)

sth. = something (etwas) sb. = somebody (jemand)

jn. = jemanden jm. = jemandem

pl = *plural* (Mehrzahl)

infml = *informal* (umgangssprachlich)

AE = *American English* *BE* = *British English*

Ⓕ = *verwandtes Wort im Französischen* Ⓛ = *verwandtes Wort im Lateinischen*

Wenn du **nachschlagen** möchtest, was ein englisches Wort bedeutet oder wie man es ausspricht, dann verwende das **English – German Dictionary** auf den Seiten 237–266.

[iː] green · [i] happy · [ɪ] big · [e] red · [æ] cat · [ɑː] class · [ɒ] song · [ɔː] door · [uː] blue · [ʊ] book · [ʌ] mum · [ɜː] girl · [ə] a partner

Unit 1 New York

p. 12	**subway** ['sʌbweɪ] *(AE)*	U-Bahn	= *BE* underground — (L) sub *(unter)*
	central ['sentrəl]	zentral, Zentral-, Mittel-	! stress: **central** ['sentrəl]
	avenue ['ævənjuː]	Allee, Boulevard	(F) l'avenue *(f)*
	statue ['stætʃuː]	Statue	! pronunciation: **statue** ['stætʃuː] — (L) statua
	liberty ['lɪbəti]	Freiheit	(F) la liberté (L) libertas *f*
	square [skweə]	Platz *(in der Stadt)*	Times Square and Trafalgar Square are the most famous **~s** in the USA and the UK.
p. 14	**metal** ['metl]	Metall; Metall-	! stress: **metal** ['metl] — (F) le métal

Part A

p. 16	**newspaper** ['njuːspeɪpə] (*kurz auch:* **paper**)	Zeitung	
	(to) **crash** [kræʃ]	abstürzen *(Flugzeug; Computer)*	**(to) crash** • The plane **crashed into** an office block. (… stürzte/krachte in ein Bürogebäude.) • The car went off the road and **crashed into** a tree. (… fuhr/krachte/knallte gegen …) • My computer **crashed** and I lost lots of work.
	within [wɪ'ðɪn]	innerhalb (von)	Can you finish your project ~ a week?
	terrorist ['terərɪst]	terroristische(r, s); Terrorist/in	! stress: **terrorist** ['terərɪst] — (F) le/la terroriste (L) terrere *(erschrecken)*
	network ['netwɜːk]	Netz, Netzwerk	
	attack [ə'tæk]	Angriff	verb: (to) **attack** ~ noun: **attack**
	(to) **force your way into** sth. [fɔːs]	sich in etwas eindrängen	The door was closed and we had to ~ our **way into** the room.
	control [kən'trəʊl]	Kontrolle	Never let anyone **take ~ of** your computer. *(Kontrolle übernehmen)*
	target ['tɑːgɪt]	Ziel, Zielscheibe	The terrorists didn't hit their ~.  a **target**
	brave [breɪv]	mutig, tapfer	She was very ~: she jumped into the river and saved the little dog's life. ! • ein **mutiges** Kind = a **brave** child • ein **braves** Kind = a **well-behaved** child / a **good** child
	thousand ['θaʊznd]	tausend; Tausend	
	floor [flɔː]	Geschoss, Etage, Stockwerk	Our flat is on the third ~.
	death [deθ]	Tod	**death** ◄► **life**

[eɪ] name · [aɪ] time · [ɔɪ] **boy** · [əʊ] **old** ·
[aʊ] town · [ɪə] **here** · [eə] **where** · [ʊə] **tour**

	skyscraper ['skaɪskreɪpə]	Wolkenkratzer	**skyscrapers**  the Manhattan skyline
	(to) **collapse** [kə'læps]	einstürzen; zusammenbrechen	
	thick [θɪk]	dick	! *German* **dick** = **1. fat** *(person, animal)* **2. thick** *(book, pullover, sauce, cloud, wall, …)*
	dust [dʌst]	Staub	
	emergency [ɪ'mɜːdʒənsi]	Notfall, Not-	There's been an accident. Can you call the ~ **services** *(Not-, Rettungsdienste)*, please?
	service ['sɜːvɪs]	Dienst, Service	There's a good bus ~ in New York. I was disappointed with the bad ~ in the restaurant. (F) le service (L) servus *(Sklave)*
	neighborhood *(AE)* / **neighbourhood** *(BE)* ['neɪbəhʊd]	Viertel, Gegend, Umgebung; Nachbarschaft	We live in a great ~ with lots of shops and parks.
	as if [æz_'ɪf]	als ob	He looks **as if** he's crying. ! *German* **als ob** = **1. like** **2. as if** *(a bit more formal than* **like***)*
	(to) **stick** [stɪk], **stuck, stuck** [stʌk]	bleiben; kleben	Why do bad songs always ~ in my head? **Stick** the picture onto the poster.
	mind [maɪnd]	Verstand, Sinn, Geist	Grandpa is very old, but his ~ is still very active.
	(to) **be alive** [ə'laɪv]	leben, am Leben sein	(to) **be alive** ◄► (to) **be dead**
	image ['ɪmɪdʒ]	Bild, Abbild; Vorstellung	When I hear 'NYC', I have an ~ of skyscrapers in my head. (F) l'image *(f)* (L) *imago f*
	historic [hɪ'stɒrɪk]	historisch *(geschichtlich bedeutsam)*	The first landing on the moon was a ~ event.
p. 17	**high school** ['haɪ skuːl]	*(USA) Schule für 14- bis 18-Jährige*	
	locker ['lɒkə]	Schließfach, Spind	**lockers** 
	backpack ['bækpæk] (*BE auch:* **rucksack** ['rʌksæk])	Rucksack	 **backpacks** (*BE auch:* **rucksacks**)
	shot [ʃɒt]	Aufnahme, Foto; *(Film)* Einstellung, Szene	
	block [blɒk]	(Häuser-, Wohn-)Block	
	anniversary [ˌænɪ'vɜːsəri]	Jahrestag	May 8th is the ~ of John's death. (… Johns Todestag) (F) l' anniversaire *(m)* (L) *anniversarium*

[b] **boat** · [p] **pool** · [d] **dad** · [t] **ten** · [g] **good** · [k] **cat** ·
[m] **mum** · [n] **no** · [ŋ] **song** · [l] **hello** · [r] **red** · [w] **we** · [j] **you**

	rose [rəʊz]	Rose	Ⓕ la rose
	(to) **roar** [rɔː]	tosen, dröhnen	The waves **~ed** as the storm got stronger.
	foot [fʊt], *pl* **feet** [fiːt]	Fuß *(Längenmaß; ca. 30 cm)*	**!** **foot** = **1.** Fuß *(Körperteil)*; **2.** Fuß *(Längenmaß)* She's over six **feet** tall. (= over 1.83 metres)
	(to) **lean** [liːn]	sich lehnen; sich beugen	 He's **~ing** forward to talk to the driver.
	inch [ɪntʃ]	Zoll *(Längenmaß; 2,54 cm)*	12 **inches** = 1 foot (about 30 centimetres)
	(to) **arrest** [əˈrest]	verhaften, festnehmen	After the body was found, the police quickly **~ed** a 32-year-old man. Ⓕ arrêter qn.
	(to) **bury** [ˈberi]	begraben, beerdigen	He died on holiday in Spain and was **buried** there.
	cemetery [*BE:* ˈsemətri, *AE:* ˈseməteri]	Friedhof	an area of land where people are buried Ⓕ le cimetière
	I'd better … (= **I had better …**)	Ich sollte lieber …	It's getting late. **I'd** ~ call Mum. (= I should call …) It's cold. **You'd** ~ put on a pullover. (= You should put on …)
	I guess …	Ich nehme an, … / Ich denke, …	If he hasn't had lunch **I** ~ he'll be hungry.
p. 19	**way** [weɪ]	Art und Weise	

way ("Art und Weise")

Try to introduce your topic **in an interesting way**.	auf eine interessante Art und Weise
In this way, you will make sure that everyone enjoys your talk.	auf diese Weise
I like **the way** Oliver ended his talk.	die Art und Weise, wie …
John is like his father **in some/many ways**.	in mancher/vielerlei Hinsicht

p. 20	(to) **have** sth. **in common** [ˈkɒmən]	etwas miteinander gemein haben	We're the same age, but we don't **have** much **in** ~. Ⓛ communis, -e *(gemeinsam)*
	fall [fɔːl] *(AE)*	Herbst	= *BE* autumn
	leaf [liːf], *pl* **leaves**	Blatt	In the fall, the **leaves** fall to the ground.
p. 21	**colourful** [ˈkʌləfl]	bunt, farbenfreudig	

Part B

p. 24	**mood** [muːd]	Laune, Stimmung	*English:* (to) **be in a good/bad mood** *German:* **gute/schlechte Laune haben**
	crazy [ˈkreɪzi]	verrückt	You want to go out in this weather? You must be ~.
	weirdo [ˈwɪədəʊ] *(infml)*	Spinner/in	Don't walk through the park. It's full of **~s** at night.
	(to) **be keen on** sth. [kiːn]	wild auf etwas sein	**I'm** really ~ **on** sports. I go running every day.
	(to) **be keen on doing** sth.	wild darauf sein, etwas zu tun	**I'm not** very ~ **on** going to that party on Friday. Do we have to go?
	pigeon [ˈpɪdʒɪn]	(Stadt-)Taube	a **pigeon** Ⓕ le pigeon 

	insulted [ɪn'sʌltɪd]	beleidigt	When he said I was fat, I felt really ~.
p. 25	**suggestion** [sə'dʒestʃən]	Vorschlag	My ~ is that we stop work and go home. verb: (to) **suggest** ~ noun: **suggestion** (F) la suggestion
	move [mu:v]	Zug *(bei Brettspielen)*	(L) movere *(bewegen, sich bewegen)*
	legendary ['ledʒəndri]	legendär, berühmt	! stress: **<u>leg</u>endary** ['ledʒəndri] (F) légendaire
	Ladies and gentlemen [ˌleɪdiz‿ən 'dʒentlmən]	Meine Damen und Herren / Sehr geehrte Damen und Herren	
	timer ['taɪmə]	Zeitmesser	
	(to) **click** [klɪk]	klicken	Open the page and ~ on the link.
p. 26	**glad** [glæd]	froh, dankbar	

Part C

p. 28	(to) **take a walk** *(bes. AE)*	spazieren gehen, einen Spaziergang machen	(to) go for a walk
	track [træk]	(Bahn-)Gleis	
	railroad ['reɪlrəʊd] *(AE)*, **railway** ['reɪlweɪ] *(BE)*	Eisenbahn	**railway tracks** *(BE)*, **railroad tracks** *(AE)*
	truck [trʌk] *(BE auch:* **lorry** ['lɒri])	Lastwagen, LKW	 **trucks**

	frozen ['frəʊzn]	tiefgekühlt	
	turkey ['tɜ:ki]	Pute, Truthahn	**a turkey** **a frozen turkey**
p. 29	**(to) tear** sth. **down** [ˌteə 'daʊn], **tore** [tɔ:], **torn** [tɔ:n]	etwas abreißen	They started **~ing** the Berlin Wall **down** in 1989.
	if [ɪf]	ob	! **if** = 1. <u>ob</u> ~ I don't know **if** I can come to your party. 2. <u>wenn, falls</u> ~ I'll come to your party **if** I can.
	space [speɪs]	Platz, Raum	I need new shelves. There's no ~ for my books! (F) l'espace *(m)*
	the men **whose** homes … [hu:z]	die Männer, deren Wohnungen …	! **whose** = 1. wessen ~ **Whose** car is this? 2. dessen, deren ~ The woman **whose** car was stolen …
	(to) protest [prə'test] *(AE auch:* ['prəʊtest])	protestieren	*English:* (to) **protest against sth.** *or* (to) **protest sth.** *(bes. AE)* *German:* **gegen etwas protestieren** (F) protester
	protest ['prəʊtest]	Protest	
	even though [ˌi:vn 'ðəʊ]	auch wenn; obwohl	**Even** ~ it was already 9 am, it was still dark outside.
	practical ['præktɪkl]	praktisch	Your ideas are good, but can you give me some ~ help, too? (F) pratique

[i:] green · [i] happy · [ɪ] big · [e] red · [æ] cat · [ɑ:] class · [ɒ] song ·
[ɔ:] door · [u:] blue · [ʊ] book · [ʌ] mum · [ɜ:] girl · [ə] a partner

a **9,740-foot** swimming pool — ein 9.740 Fuß langes Schwimmbad

a 9,740-foot swimming pool, a three-pound ball

- a three-pound ball — ein drei Pfund schwerer Ball
- a 150-kilogram bear — ein 150 Kilogramm schwerer Bär
- a ten-kilometre walk — eine Zehn-Kilometer-Wanderung
- a two-hour lesson — eine zweistündige Unterrichtsstunde
- a 24-hour supermarket — ein Supermarkt, der 24 Stunden geöffnet ist
- a three-week holiday — ein dreiwöchiger Urlaub
- a 30-minute ride — eine 30-minütige Fahrt
- a 70-year-old teacher — ein 70-jähriger Lehrer

! Im Englischen steht das Nomen im Singular:
a **three-week** holiday
(nicht: a three-~~weeks~~ holiday)

a **roller coaster**

shrubs **lawn** **seeds**

	roller coaster ['rəʊlə kəʊstə]	Achterbahn	
	(to) **create** [kri'eɪt]	schaffen, erschaffen, kreieren	
	shrub [ʃrʌb]	Strauch, Busch	
	(to) **bloom** [bluːm]	blühen	
	seed [siːd]	Samen	
	lawn [lɔːn]	Rasen	
	work of art [ˌwɜːk‿əv‿'ɑːt]	Kunstwerk	(L) ars *f (Kunst)*
	performance [pə'fɔːməns]	Aufführung, Vorstellung, Auftritt	verb: (to) **perform** noun: **performance**
	awesome ['ɔːsəm] *(bes. AE, infml)*	klasse, großartig	= *BE* great, super, fantastic, cool
	council ['kaʊnsl]	Ausschuss; Rat *(Stadtrat, Gemeinderat u.Ä.)*	
	unfortunately [ʌn'fɔːtʃənətli]	leider, unglücklicherweise	We were planning a barbecue, but ~ it rained. **fortunately** (glücklicherweise) ◄► **unfortunately** (I) fortuna
p. 30	**type (of)** [taɪp]	Art, Sorte, Typ	= kind (of)
	(to) **report** [rɪ'pɔːt]	berichten	
	(to) **cover** ['kʌvə]	behandeln, abdecken	In history last term, we **~ed** the 18th century. Any more questions? – No, you've **~ed** them all. ! (to) **cover** = **1.** bedecken, zudecken; **2.** behandeln, abdecken (F) couvrir
	(to) **include** [ɪn'kluːd]	einschließen; beinhalten	Does the trip ~ a tour of the Tower of London? Our group also **~d** three children. (= Zu unserer Gruppe gehörten auch drei Kinder.)
	(to) **deal with** sth. [diːl], **dealt, dealt** [delt]	sich mit etwas beschäftigen; von etwas handeln	The film **~s with** the life of John Lennon.
p. 31	**immigrant** ['ɪmɪgrənt]	Einwanderer/Einwanderin	! stress: **immigrant** ['ɪmɪgrənt] (F) l'immigrant, e / l'immigré, e (L) immigrare

Unit 2 New Orleans

p. 38	(to) **remind** sb. [rɪ'maɪnd]	jn. erinnern	Please **remind** me that it's Grandma's birthday on Friday. I want to call her. Grandpa always says I **remind** him of his sister. ! • **remember sth.** = sich an etwas erinnern Do you **remember** her name? • **remind sb.** = jn. erinnern I mustn't forget. Please **remind** me.
	Mardi Gras [ˌmɑːdi 'grɑː]	Faschingsdienstag (*auch:* die Karnevalsfeiern in New Orleans)	
	brass band [ˌbrɑːs 'bænd]	Blaskapelle	a **brass band** 
p. 39	(to) **flood** [flʌd]	überfluten, überschwemmen	
	flood	Flut, Überschwemmung	
	hurricane ['hʌrɪkən]	Hurrikan, Orkan	
	alligator ['ælɪgeɪtə]	Alligator	! stress: <u>al</u>ligator ['ælɪgeɪtə]
	swamp [swɒmp]	Sumpf	

Part A

p. 40	**degree** [dɪ'griː]	Grad	**Temperatures** *You say:* **25 degrees Celsius / 77 degrees Fahrenheit** *You write:* **25° C / 77° F**
	Celsius (C) ['selsiəs]	Celsius	
	Fahrenheit (F) ['færənhaɪt]	Fahrenheit	
	palm tree ['pɑːm triː]	Palme	! silent "l": **palm tree** ['pɑːm triː]
	kinda ['kaɪndə] **(= kind of)** *(infml)*	irgendwie	This place looks **kind of** scary to me. ! kind of + **<u>noun</u>**: What **kind of <u>music</u>** …? Welche **Art von Musik** …? **kind of + <u>adjective</u>:** He looked **kind of <u>crazy</u>**. … **irgendwie verrückt** …
	tropical ['trɒpɪkl]	tropisch, Tropen-	
	downtown ['daʊntaʊn] *(AE)*	im Zentrum	He lives **downtown**. *(AE)* = He lives in the city centre. *(BE)*
	head for sth. [hed]	auf etwas zusteuern/zugehen/zufahren	As soon as we arrived at the coast, we **~ed for** the beach.
	balcony ['bælkəni]	Balkon	We had a super view from our ~.
	style [staɪl]	Stil	
p. 41	**disgusting** [dɪs'gʌstɪŋ]	ekelhaft, widerlich	I find the way some people eat ~. It makes me feel sick.
	chicken ['tʃɪkɪn]	Huhn; (Brat-)Hähnchen	
	buck [bʌk] *(infml)* **(= dollar ($)** ['dɒlə]**)**	Dollar	

[b] **boat** · [p] **pool** · [d] **dad** · [t] **ten** · [g] **good** · [k] **cat** · [m] **mum** · [n] **no** · [ŋ] **song** · [l] **hello** · [r] **red** · [w] **we** · [j] **you**

(to) **recommend** sth. **(to** sb.**)** [ˌrekə'mend]	(jm.) etwas empfehlen	I can ~ the music store on Baker Street. It's really cheap. (F) recommander
stew [stjuː]	Eintopf	 stew sausages shrimps
sausage ['sɒsɪdʒ]	Wurst, Würstchen	
shrimp [ʃrɪmp], *pl* **shrimp** *or* **shrimps**	Garnele	
Thanksgiving [θæŋks'gɪvɪŋ]	Erntedankfest *(amerikanischer Feiertag am vierten Donnerstag im November)*	
habit ['hæbɪt]	(An-)Gewohnheit	something people do regularly: Doing sport is a good **habit**. (L) habere *(eine Gewohnheit haben)*
(to) **block** [blɒk]	blockieren, sperren	(to) **block** emails; (to) **block** a phone number; (to) **block** sb.
advice *(no pl)* [əd'vaɪs]	Rat, Ratschlag, Ratschläge	Take my ~: Go and see a doctor. (Hör auf meinen Rat: …) ! She gave me <u>**some**</u> / <u>**a piece of**</u> **advice**. *Never:* She gave me some ~~advices~~ / ~~an advice~~.
timeline ['taɪmlaɪn]	Zeitstrahl, Zeitleiste	
embarrassed [ɪm'bærəst]	verlegen; peinlich berührt	
(to) **embarrass** sb. [ɪm'bærəs]	jn. in Verlegenheit bringen	
dish [dɪʃ]	Gericht *(Speise)*	What's your favourite ~? ~ Lasagne. ! **dish** = Gericht *(Speise)* **dishes** *(pl)* = (benutztes) Geschirr: (to) **clear/wash the dishes** das Geschirr abräumen/abwaschen
herb [hɜːb]	(Gewürz-)Kraut	Steak tastes better if you add ~**s** to it.
spice [spaɪs]	Gewürz	In winter, Grandma likes tea with ~**s** in it.
ingredient [ɪn'griːdiənt]	Zutat	What ~**s** do you need to make scones? (F) l'ingrédient *(m)*
(to) **combine** [kəm'baɪn]	kombinieren, verbinden	First, ~ the eggs with cream and add some yoghurt. (F) combiner
Native American [ˌneɪtɪv‿ə'merɪkən]	amerikanischer Ureinwohner/ amerikanische Ureinwohnerin	(L) nasci *(geboren werden)*
p. 42 **dairy products** *(pl)* ['deəri prɒdʌkts]	Milchprodukte, Molkereiprodukte	
beef [biːf]	Rindfleisch	!
pork [pɔːk]	Schweinefleisch	see table below
tinned [tɪnd]	Dosen-; in Dosen	We had ~ spaghetti for lunch today. I didn't like it.
powder ['paʊdə]	Pulver	We haven't got any fresh milk, but we've got some milk ~. (F) la poudre

	<u>**The animal**</u>	<u>**The meat**</u>	
• *English:*	**cow**	**beef**	(F) le bœuf
German:	**Kuh**	**Rindfleisch**	
• *English:*	**pig**	**pork**	(F) le porc
German:	**Schwein**	**Schweinefleisch**	

[f] **f**ather • [v] **r**iver • [s] **s**ister • [z] plea**s**e • [ʃ] **sh**op • [ʒ] televi**s**ion • [tʃ] **t**eacher • [dʒ] **G**ermany • [θ] **th**anks • [ð] **th**is • [h] **h**ere

Food words

rice [raɪs]

beans [bi:nz]
Bohnen

lentils ['lentlz]
Linsen

onions ! ['ʌnjənz]

peppers

mushrooms
['mʌʃrʊmz, 'mʌʃru:mz]

spinach (frozen)
['spɪnɪtʃ]

garlic ['gɑ:lɪk]

parsley ['pɑ:sli]
Petersilie

lemons
['lemənz]

nuts [nʌts]

butter ['bʌtə]

salt [sɔ:lt] + **pepper**

sugar ['ʃʊgə]

flour ['flaʊə]

(to) **bake** [beɪk]	backen
(to) **boil** [bɔɪl]	kochen; zum Kochen bringen

German "kochen"

- (to) **cook a meal** — (ein) Essen kochen, eine Mahlzeit zubereiten
- (to) **boil water/eggs/potatoes** — Wasser/Eier/Kartoffeln kochen
- (to) **make tea/coffee/soup** — Tee/Kaffee/Suppe kochen

! Who is going to **cook / do the cooking** this evening? — Wer kocht heute Abend?

(to) **fry** [fraɪ]	braten *(in der Pfanne)*	
(to) **roast** [rəʊst]	braten *(im Backofen)*	
frying pan ['fraɪɪŋ pæn]	Bratpfanne	
saucepan ['sɔ:spən]	Kochtopf, Stieltopf	
oven ['ʌvn]	Backofen	! pronunciation: **oven** ['ʌvn]
vegetarian [ˌvedʒə'teəriən]	Vegetarier/in; vegetarisch	
bitter ['bɪtə]	bitter	
hot [hɒt]	scharf (gewürzt)	
sour ['saʊə]	sauer, säuerlich	
spicy ['spaɪsi]	würzig, pikant	
(to) **fancy** sth. ['fænsi] *(infml)*	Lust auf etwas/zu etwas haben	I'm so hungry. I really ~ a hamburger.
p. 43 **relevant (to** sth.**)** ['reləvənt]	relevant, wichtig (für etwas)	! stress: <u>re</u>levant ['reləvənt]
allergic (to sth.**)** [ə'lɜ:dʒɪk]	allergisch (gegen etwas)	I mustn't eat that cake. I'm ~ **to** nuts. (F) allergique

frying pan

saucepan

oven

[i:] green · [i] happy · [ɪ] big · [e] red · [æ] cat · [ɑ:] class · [ɒ] song · [ɔ:] door · [u:] blue · [ʊ] book · [ʌ] mum · [ɜ:] girl · [ə] a partner

light green/blue/…	hellgrün/-blau/…	**light green/blue/… ◄► dark green/blue/…**
taste [teɪst]	Geschmack	I'm a vegetarian because I don't like the ~ of meat.
waiter ['weɪtə] **/** **waitress** ['weɪtrəs]	Kellner/Kellnerin	
menu ['menjuː]	Speisekarte	! stress: **me**nu ['menjuː]
(to) **paraphrase** ['pærəfreɪz]	umschreiben, anders ausdrücken	If you can't think of the right word, try to ~ it. (F) paraphraser
p. 44 **healthy** ['helθi]	gesund	

Part B

p. 46 (to) **tune** [tjuːn]	stimmen *(Instrument)*	Bass guitars are usually **~d** to E, A, D and G.
(to) **tighten** ['taɪtn]	spannen, festziehen, nachziehen	If you ~ the string, the note becomes higher.
string [strɪŋ]	Saite	 **strings**
closet ['klɒzɪt] *(bes. AE)*	Wandschrank *(oft begehbar)*	 a **closet**
I would have screamed too.	Ich hätte auch geschrien.	I **would have been** too scared (Ich wäre zu ängstlich gewesen.) You **could have asked** me. (Du hättest mich fragen können.) They **must have been** asleep. (Sie müssen geschlafen haben.)
slavery ['sleɪvəri]	Sklaverei	
slave [sleɪv]	Sklave, Sklavin	(F) l'esclave *(m/f)*
(to) **belong to** sb. [bɪ'lɒŋ]	jm. gehören; zu jm. gehören	I think this bag **~s to** Jill. (= I think this is Jill's bag.)
great-grandfather/ great-grandmother	Urgroßvater/ Urgroßmutter	
porch [pɔːtʃ]	Veranda *(AE)*; Vorbau, Vordach *(BE)*	 **porch** *(AE)*  **porch** *(BE)*
honey ['hʌni]	Honig; *(infml, als Anrede:)* Schatz, Schätzchen	

one/ones

If you don't want to repeat a noun, you use **one** (singular) or **ones** (plural):

Go upstairs and bring down my box, please. You know **which one**.	… Du weißt, welche.
The shops here are a lot cheaper than **the ones** in Bourbon Street.	… als die in Bourbon Street.
Which T-shirt would you like? ~ **The blue one**.	… Das blaue.

he killed the alligator **himself**	er hat den Alligator selbst getötet

[eɪ] name · [aɪ] time · [ɔɪ] boy · [əʊ] old · [aʊ] town · [ɪə] here · [eə] where · [ʊə] tour

German "selbst"

Die Reflexivpronomen **myself, yourself, themselves** usw. kennst du bereits.
Diese Pronomen werden auch verwendet, um ein Nomen (oder Pronomen) hervorzuheben (Sätze 1 und 2) oder um zu betonen, dass jemand etwas allein, ohne Hilfe getan hat (Sätze 3 und 4). Im Deutschen steht meist **selbst**.

1) The director **himself** welcomed us.	Der Regisseur selbst hieß uns willkommen.
2) The room **itself** was OK, but the view was terrible.	Das Zimmer selbst war in Ordnung, ...
3) This is good. Did you cook it **yourself**?	... Hast du es selbst gekocht?
4) It'll be cheaper if we paint the room **ourselves**.	..., wenn wir das Zimmer selbst streichen.

	jewellery *(BE)* **/ jewelry** *(AE)* *(no pl)* ['dʒuːəlri]	Schmuck	rings, earrings, etc.
	pile [paɪl]	Stapel, Haufen	I can't come, I have a ~ of work to do.
	segregation [ˌsegrɪ'geɪʃn]	Trennung *(nach Hautfarbe, Religion oder Geschlecht)*	There is ~ in some swimming pools. Men and women are not allowed to swim at the same time.
	(to) **be afraid (of** sth./sb.**)** [ə'freɪd]	Angst haben (vor etwas/jm.)	My mother **is** ~ **of** snakes.
p. 47	**civil rights** *(pl)* [ˌsɪvl 'raɪts]	Bürgerrechte	Ⓛ civis *m, f (Bürger/in)*
	diner ['daɪnə] *(AE)*	*(kleines, preiswertes)* Restaurant	
	counter ['kaʊntə] *(AE)* (*kurz für:* **countertop)**	Arbeitsplatte; Küchentheke	**counter(top)** *(AE)* **worktop** *(BE)* Ⓕ le comptoir 
	in the 1960s [ˌnaɪntiːn'sɪkstiz]	in den 60er-Jahren (des 20. Jahrhunderts)	
	movie theater ['muːvi θɪətə] *(AE)*	Kino	= *BE* cinema
	movie ['muːvi]	Film	
	streetcar ['striːtkɑː] *(AE)* **/ tram** [træm] *(BE)*	Straßenbahn	a New Orleans **streetcar** 
	all over the city / the world	in der ganzen Stadt/ auf der ganzen Welt	The singer Adele is famous ~ ~ **the world**.
	discrimination (against) [dɪˌskrɪmɪ'neɪʃn]	Diskriminierung (von)	*English:* **discrimination against** women/foreigners *German:* **Diskriminierung von** Frauen/Ausländern Ⓕ la discrimination
	both ... and ... [bəʊθ]	sowohl ... als auch ...	English is spoken ~ in Britain **and** in the USA.
	(to) **stand up (for/against** sth./sb.**)** [ˌstænd‿'ʌp]	eintreten/sich einsetzen (für/ gegen etwas/jn.)	It's important to ~ **up for** your rights. Nelson Mandela **stood up against** discrimination.
	(to) **beat** sb. **up**	jn. zusammenschlagen	
	(to) **murder** ['mɜːdə]	morden, ermorden	
	courage ['kʌrɪdʒ]	Mut, Courage	I didn't have the ~ to help them. (= I was too scared to help them.) Ⓕ le courage

[b] boat · [p] pool · [d] dad · [t] ten · [g] good · [k] cat · [m] mum · [n] no · [ŋ] song · [l] hello · [r] red · [w] we · [j] you

	(to) **speak out**	den Mund aufmachen; sich (kritisch) äußern	You can't change things if you don't ~ **out**.
	(to) **call** sb. **names**	jn. beschimpfen, jm. Schimpfwörter nachrufen	The kids **~ed him names** because of his big nose.
	prejudice (against) ['predʒudɪs]	Vorurteil (gegen), Voreingenommenheit (gegenüber)	Some people still have a ~ **against** girls and think that girls aren't good at maths. (F) le préjugé (L) prae (vor), iudicium *n (Urteil)*
	generation [ˌdʒenəˈreɪʃn]	Generation	! stress: gene**ra**tion [ˌdʒenəˈreɪʃn] (F) la génération
	system ['sɪstəm]	System	! stress: **sy**stem ['sɪstəm] (F) le système
	complete [kəm'pli:t]	vollständig, komplett	adjective: **complete** adverb: **completely** völlig, vollkommen (L) complere *(füllen)*
	(to) **complete** [kəm'pli:t]	abschließen, vollenden; vervollständigen	
p. 48	**native speaker** [ˌneɪtɪv 'spi:kə]	Muttersprachler/in	(L) nasci *(geboren werden)*
	pattern ['pætn]	Muster	I like the ~ of your pullover, but not the colour.

Part C

p. 52	**cook** [kʊk]	Koch, Köchin	
	oval ['əʊvl]	oval	! stress: **o**val ['əʊvl]
	cranberry ['krænbəri]	Preiselbeere	
	sauce [sɔ:s]	Soße	
	pumpkin ['pʌmpkɪn]	Kürbis	
	pie ['paɪ]	Obstkuchen; Pastete	**cranberries** **sauce** **pumpkin** **pumpkin pie**
	impatient [ɪm'peɪʃnt]	ungeduldig	I get ~ when I have to wait for a long time. **patient** (geduldig) ◄► **impatient** (F) impatient, e
	leather ['leðə]	Leder	
	a little	ein bisschen, ein wenig, etwas	
	(to) **flash through** sb.'s **mind** [flæʃ], [maɪnd]	jm. durch den Kopf schießen	I thought for a long time, then suddenly an idea **~ed through my ~**.
	fairly ['feəli]	ziemlich	! **fair** = „fair, gerecht“ Come on, kids, play **fair**! **fairly** = „ziemlich“ He plays chess **fairly** well. (= … **quite** well.)
	(to) **hunt** [hʌnt]	jagen	
	line [laɪn]	Leine, (Angel-)Schnur	
	hook [hʊk]	Haken	noun: **hook** ~ verb: (to) **hook** (an den Haken/an die Angel bekommen)
	sharp [ʃɑ:p]	scharf	Be careful. That knife is very ~.
	(to) **shoot** [ʃu:t], **shot, shot** [ʃɒt]	schießen; erschießen	She **shot** the thief in the leg. John Lennon was **shot** in 1980.

	awfully ['ɔːfli]	furchtbar, außerordentlich	I'm **awfully** sorry that I can't come to your party.
	cruel ['kruːl]	grausam	I don't like zoos. I think it's **cruel** to put animals in cages. (F) cruel, le (L) crudelis, -e
	harmonica [hɑː'mɒnɪkə]	Mundharmonika	
	strict [strɪkt]	streng	Emily isn't allowed to watch TV after 9 o'clock. Her parents are very ~ about that.
	limited ['lɪmɪtɪd]	beschränkt, begrenzt	The price is ~ for one month only. (F) limité, e (L) limes *m (Grenze)*
p. 53	(to) **skim a text** [skɪm]	einen Text überfliegen *(um den Inhalt grob zu erfassen)*	
	sub-heading ['sʌbˌhedɪŋ]	Zwischenüberschrift; Kapitelüberschrift	Long articles in newspapers are often broken up with ~-**headings**.
	graphics *(pl)* ['ɡræfɪks]	Grafiken	
p. 54	**totally** ['təʊtəli]	völlig, total	• adv: **totally** (völlig, total) – I **totally** disagree. (F) totalement • adj: **total** (Gesamt-) – the **total** number of students at this school (F) total, e
p. 55	**narrator** [nə'reɪtə]	Erzähler/in; Sprecher/in	

Unit 3 California

p. 64	**desert** ['dezət]	Wüste	 (F) le désert (L) deserere *(verlassen)*
	contrast ['kɒntrɑːst]	Kontrast, Gegensatz	! stress: <u>con</u>trast ['kɒntrɑːst] (F) le contraste

Part A

p. 66	**marine** [mə'riːn]	Meeres-	**marine** life, **marine** animals, **marine** scientists (L) mare *n (Meer)*
	reserve [rɪ'zɜːv]	Schutzgebiet, Reservat	
	the week before	die Woche zuvor; in der Woche davor	Last week was sunny. **The week** ~ was rainy.
	parking lot ['pɑːkɪŋ lɒt] *(AE)*, **car park** ['kɑː pɑːk] *(BE)*	Parkplatz	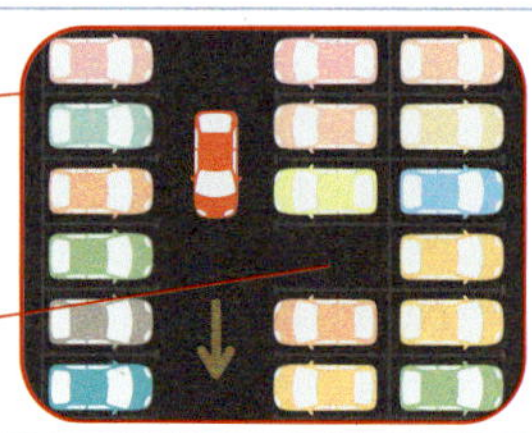
	a couple ['kʌpl]	ein Paar; ein paar	 a young couple  a couple of sandwiches

[iː] green · [i] happy · [ɪ] big · [e] red · [æ] cat · [ɑː] class · [ɒ] song · [ɔː] door · [uː] blue · [ʊ] book · [ʌ] mum · [ɜː] girl · [ə] a partner

foreign ['fɒrən]	fremd, ausländisch	a **foreign** language; **foreign** countries
(to) **stretch** [stretʃ]	sich dehnen, sich strecken	The cat **~ed** then washed himself.
motel [məʊ'tel]	Motel *(Hotel mit Zimmern und Garagen an einer Autostraße)*	
(to) **complain** [kəm'pleɪn]	sich beschweren, sich beklagen	There is a disco right next to the hotel, and a lot of guests ~ about the noise. Ⓕ se plaindre
Sorry? ['sɒri]	Wie bitte?	

sorry

Mit **sorry** kannst du ...

• **dich entschuldigen:**	**Sorry** I'm late.	**Entschuldigung**, dass ich zu späte komme.
• **sagen, dass dir etwas leid tut:**	My grandfather died last month. – Oh, **I'm sorry**.	Mein Großvater ist letzten Monat gestorben. – Oh, **das tut mir leid**.
• **nachfragen, wenn du etwas nicht richtig verstanden hast:**	We'll pick you up at the airport. – **Sorry?** It's a bit loud in here. Could you say that again?	Wir holen Sie am Flughafen ab. – **Wie bitte?** Es ist ein bisschen laut hier. Könnten Sie das wiederholen?

(to) **give** sb. **directions (to)** [də'rekʃnz]	jm. den Weg beschreiben (zu/nach)	(to) **ask for directions** ◄► (to) **give directions** (nach dem Weg fragen)
(to) **spot** sb./sth. [spɒt]	jn./etwas entdecken, erblicken	We had a picnic on the coast, and suddenly Dad **~ted** some seals.
shell [ʃel]	Muschel(schale)	
wildlife ['waɪldlaɪf]	Tierwelt, frei lebende Tiere	The ~ of Africa is very different from the ~ in Europe. You can find all kinds of ~ in our national parks.
Mr. Miller / **Mrs.** Miller *(AE)*	Herr Miller / Frau Miller	**!** In American English, **Mr** and **Mrs** are usually written with a full stop.
(to) **arrange** [ə'reɪndʒ]	organisieren, vereinbaren	Let's ~ a time to meet again next week.
p. 67 **hostess** ['həʊstəs]	Gastgeberin *(in USA auch: Frau, die in einem Restaurant die Gäste in Empfang nimmt)*	
social ['səʊʃl]	sozial, Sozial-, gesellschaftlich	**!** stress: <u>so</u>cial ['səʊʃl] Ⓕ social, e Ⓛ socius *m* (*Kamerad*)
(to) **look out for** sb./sth.	nach jm./etwas Ausschau halten	We need some bread. Can you ~ **out for** a bakery?
stranger ['streɪndʒə]	Fremde(r), Unbekannte(r)	Young children shouldn't speak to **~s**. Ⓕ l'étranger *(m)*, l'étrangère *(f)*
saying ['seɪɪŋ]	Sprichwort, Redensart	
separately ['seprətli]	einzeln, separat	adjective: **separate** – The library has a **separate** room for children's books. adverb: **separately** – All the volunteers were interviewed **separately**.
common ['kɒmən]	häufig; weit verbreitet	One of the most ~ names for girls in Britain today is Olivia. Ⓛ communis, -e *(allgemein)*

[eɪ] name · [aɪ] time · [ɔɪ] boy · [əʊ] old ·
[aʊ] town · [ɪə] here · [eə] where · [ʊə] tour

p. 68	**prediction** [prɪˈdɪkʃn]	Vorhersage, Voraussage	What is your ~ for the *Bundesliga* this year? Who will win? (L) praedicere *(vorhersagen)*
	(to) **cycle** [ˈsaɪkl]	Rad fahren, mit dem Rad fahren	= (to) **ride a bike**
p. 69	**machine** [məˈʃiːn]	Maschine, Gerät	
	can [kæn]	Dose	! *German* **Dose** = **1. tin** *(BE; for food)* **2. can** *(BE; for drink)* *In AE,* **can** *is used for food and drink.*
	(to) **squash** sth. [skwɒʃ]	etwas zerdrücken, zerquetschen	
	trash can [ˈtræʃ kæn] *(AE)*, **rubbish bin** [ˈrʌbɪʃ bɪn] *(BE)*	Mülltonne, Abfalleimer	a **rubbish bin** *(BE)* a **trash can** *(AE)*
	necessary [ˈnesəsəri]	notwendig, nötig	You can phone me on my mobile if ~. (F) nécessaire (L) necesse est *(es ist notwendig)*
	depressing [dɪˈpresɪŋ]	deprimierend	I'm sad because the news is so ~.
	lively [ˈlaɪvli]	lebendig, lebhaft	At 75, my grandma is still very ~. She goes dancing twice a week.
	relaxed [rɪˈlækst]	entspannt	verb: (to) **relax** ~ adjective: **relaxed**
	tough [tʌf]	(knall)hart, schwierig	

Part B

p. 72	**noon** [nuːn]	Mittag	
	(to) **be about to do** sth.	im Begriff sein, etwas zu tun; kurz davor sein, etwas zu tun	I was ~ **to go** to bed when the doorbell rang.
	afterwards [ˈɑːftəwədz]	nachher, danach	
	footstep [ˈfʊtstep]	Schritt	
	autograph [ˈɔːtəgrɑːf]	Autogramm	
	she **feels faint** [feɪnt]	ihr ist schwindelig	When I saw the injured dog, I **felt** ~.
	VIP [ˌviː‿aɪ ˈpiː] **(very important person)**	Prominente(r)	! pronunciation: **VIP** [ˌviː‿aɪ ˈpiː] – *not:* ~~[vɪp]~~
p. 73	(to) **reveal** [rɪˈviːl]	offenbaren, preisgeben, verraten	Please don't ~ this news to anyone.
	wildfire [ˈwaɪldfaɪə]	Waldbrand, Buschbrand	
	canyon [ˈkænjən]	Cañon	
	limousine [ˌlɪməˈziːn], [ˈlɪməziːn]	Luxuslimousine, Straßenkreuzer	
	advertisement [ədˈvɜːtɪsmənt]	Werbespot, Werbung; Anzeige, Inserat	
	process [ˈprəʊses]	Prozess, Vorgang	! stress: <u>**pro**</u>cess [ˈprəʊses] (F) le processus (L) procedere *(vorrücken, fortschreiten)*
	script [skrɪpt]	Drehbuch; Manuskript	(L) scribere *(schreiben)*
	grade [greɪd] *(AE)*	Jahrgangsstufe, Klasse	= *BE* year (L) gradus *m (Stufe)*

limousines

[b] **boat** · [p] **pool** · [d] **dad** · [t] **ten** · [g] **good** · [k] **cat** · [m] **mum** · [n] **no** · [ŋ] **song** · [l] **hello** · [r] **red** · [w] **we** · [j] **you**

(to) **tutor** sb. ['tju:tə]	jn. unterrichten, jm. Stunden geben	My big brother **~s** kids to earn money. (L) tutus, -a, -um *(sicher)*
(to) **set** sth. **up, set, set** [set]	etwas errichten, aufbauen; etwas arrangieren	It took three hours to ~ **up** the equipment. The head teacher wants to ~ **up** a meeting with our parents.
take [teɪk]	Einstellung, Take *(beim Film)*	
(to) **switch** [swɪtʃ]	wechseln	Press OPT and TAB to ~ between programs.
(to) **pat** [pæt]	tätscheln	*English:* She **patted him on the head**. *German:* Sie **tätschelte ihm den Kopf**.
cute [kju:t]	niedlich, süß	Oh, look at the baby seals! Aren't they ~?
season ['si:zn] *(bes. AE)*	Staffel *(einer Fernsehserie)*	
episode ['epɪsəʊd]	Episode	Each season has 13 ~s.
exotic [ɪg'zɒtɪk]	exotisch	We saw lots of ~ animals at the zoo. (F) exotique
for sure	klar; ganz bestimmt	'Are you coming to the game?' ~ '**For** ~.'
definitely ['defɪnətli]	sicher, bestimmt	
p. 74 (to) **be free**	frei haben	Can we meet tomorrow? **Are** you **free**?
How's it going?	Wie geht's? / Wie läuft's?	
for a change	zur Abwechslung	Can we listen to *my* music **for a** ~?

Part C

p. 78 **celebrity** [sə'lebrəti]	Berühmtheit *(berühmte Person)*	(L) celeber, celebris, celebre *(berühmt)*
flame [fleɪm]	Flamme	(L) flamma *f*
shiny ['ʃaɪni]	glänzend	What has she put on her hair? It's so nice and ~.
unstoppable [ʌn'stɒpəbl]	unaufhaltsam, unaufhaltbar	For years, Bayern Munich has been ~.
(to) **go viral** ['vaɪrəl]	sich wie ein Virus ausbreiten / sich wie ein Lauffeuer verbreiten	In just a few hours, the story of their divorce **has gone** ~.
security [sɪ'kjʊərəti]	Sicherheit, Sicherheits-	 **a security check at the airport** (F) la sécurité
guard [gɑ:d]	Wachposten, Wache	
environment [ɪn'vaɪrənmənt]	Umwelt	(F) l'environnement *(m)*
quote [kwəʊt] *(infml für* **quotation** [kwəʊ'teɪʃn])	Zitat	
Ms Miller *(BE)*, **Ms.** Miller *(AE)* [mɪz], [məz]	Frau Miller	**!** Viele Frauen möchten lieber mit **Ms** … angesprochen werden, weil am Wort **Ms** nicht zu erkennen ist, ob sie verheiratet sind oder nicht.
discovery [dɪ'skʌvəri]	Entdeckung	(F) la découverte
(to) **discover** [dɪ'skʌvə]	entdecken; herausfinden	I **~ed** some old photos of my grandparents in the attic.

[f] **f**ather · [v] **r**iver · [s] **s**ister · [z] plea**s**e · [ʃ] **sh**op · [ʒ] televi**s**ion · [tʃ] tea**ch**er · [dʒ] **G**ermany · [θ] **th**anks · [ð] **th**is · [h] **h**ere

channel ['tʃænl]	Kanal, Sender	The English **Channel** is between France and the UK. What ~ is the film on?
the latest ['leɪtɪst] *(infml)*	das Neueste	Have you heard **the** ~? Sam and Jo aren't together any more.
Stay posted. ['pəʊstɪd]	Bleib(t) auf dem Laufenden!	
disappointed (with) [ˌdɪsə'pɔɪntɪd]	enttäuscht (von)	She was ~ **with** the result of the game. She knew her team could do better.
reaction (to) [ri'ækʃn]	Reaktion (auf)	verb: (to) **react (to)** – noun: **reaction (to)**
p. 79 (to) **evacuate** [ɪ'vækjueɪt]	evakuieren	There was a fire at school today and they had to ~ the building. (F) évacuer (L) vacuus, -a, *-um (leer)*
resident ['rezɪdənt]	Bewohner/in, Anwohner/in	
power ['paʊə]	Energie, Strom; Kraft, Stärke; Macht	How much ~ does a TV use? Eating the right food can help you to build up your ~. In the old days, kings and queens had more ~ than they do today.
(to) **be cut off from** sth.	von etwas abgeschnitten/ abgetrennt sein	During the cold winter of 1999, the village **was ~ off from** the rest of the world for three months.
burnt [bɜːnt]	verbrannt	verb: (to) **burn (burned, burned)** - adjective: **burnt**
mph [ˌem piː_'eɪtʃ] **(***kurz für:* **miles per hour** [pə, pɜː]**)**	Meilen pro Stunde	55 **mph** = about 89 km/h
cause [kɔːz]	Ursache	I still don't understand the ~ of the problem. (F) la cause (L) causa *f*
(to) **cause** [kɔːz]	verursachen	I still don't understand what ~**d** the problem. verb: (to) **cause** – noun: **cause**
illegal [ɪ'liːgl]	illegal, ungesetzlich	**legal ◄► illegal** ! stress: **le**gal ['liːgl], il**le**gal [ɪ'liːgl] (F) légal, e ~ illégal, e (L) lex *f (Gesetz)*

campfire ['kæmpfaɪə]	Lagerfeuer	a **campfire**
(to) **investigate** [ɪn'vestɪgeɪt]	*(polizeilich)* untersuchen; ermitteln	The police are **investigating** the cause …
firefighter ['faɪəfaɪtə]	Feuerwehrmann/-frau	
helicopter ['helɪkɒptə]	Hubschrauber, Helikopter	(F) l'hélicoptère *(m)*
My heart goes out to …	Ich fühle mit … / Mein Mitgefühl gilt …	When I hear about all the poor people in Africa, **my ~ goes out to** them and I want to offer my help.
drought [draʊt]	Dürre, Trockenheit	
frequent ['friːkwənt]	häufig	
more and more frequent / beautiful	immer häufiger / schöner	"You get ~ **and** ~ beautiful every day, honey." My English is getting **better and better** *(immer besser)* as I get older.
expert ['ekspɜːt]	Experte/Expertin	! stress: **ex**pert ['ekspɜːt] (F) l'expert *(m)*, l'experte *(f)*
climate ['klaɪmət]	Klima	! pronunciation: **climate** ['klaɪmət] (F) le climat
link [lɪŋk]	Link, Verknüpfung, Verbindung	

[iː] green · [i] happy · [ɪ] big · [e] red · [æ] cat · [ɑː] class · [ɒ] song · [ɔː] door · [uː] blue · [ʊ] book · [ʌ] mum · [ɜː] girl · [ə] a partner

	cigarette [ˌsɪgə'ret]	Zigarette	
	permit ['pɜːmɪt]	Genehmigung, Erlaubnis(schein)	You need a ~ to go fishing here. (L) permittere *(erlauben*
	effect (on) [ɪ'fekt]	(Aus-)Wirkung (auf)	**cause ◄► effect** (F) l'effet *(m)* (L) efficere *(bewirken)*
	(to) **compare** [kəm'peə]	vergleichen	Now ~ your ideas with a partner's. (F) comparer (L) comparare
	emotional [ɪ'məʊʃənl]	emotional; gefühlsbetont	! stress: e**mo**tional [ɪ'məʊʃənl] (F) émotionnel, le
	neutral ['njuːtrəl]	neutral	! stress: **neu**tral ['njuːtrəl] (F) neutre (L) neuter, neutra, neutrum
p. 80	**location** [ləʊ'keɪʃn]	Ort, Standort; Drehort	
p. 81	**fame** [feɪm]	Ruhm	adjective: **famous** ~ noun: **fame**
p. 82	**synonym** ['sɪnənɪm]	Synonym *(bedeutungsgleiches Wort)*	Words or phrases that have the same (or almost the same) meaning are called "**~s**". (F) le synonyme
	antonym ['æntənɪm]	Antonym *(Gegensatzwort)*	
	opposite ['ɒpəzɪt]	Gegenteil	What's the ~ of "dirty"? – "Clean."
	prefix ['priːfɪks]	Präfix, Vorsilbe	Many adjectives can be made negative with the ~ "un-".
p. 83	**dramatic** [drə'mætɪk]	dramatisch	I saw a ~ film about a man who escaped from prison. (F) dramatique
	outline ['aʊtlaɪn]	Gliederung	An ~ helps you to structure your ideas before you start writing.
	possible ['pɒsəbl]	möglich	**possible ◄► impossible** (F) possible ~ impossible (L) posse *(können)*
	(to) **experience** [ɪk'spɪəriəns]	erfahren, erleben	Where's a good place to ~ a white Christmas? verb: (to) **experience** - noun: **experience**
	catchy ['kætʃi] *(infml)*	eingängig *(Melodie, Slogan)*	This song is so ~ I can't stop singing it.
	(to) **round** sth. **off (with** sth.**)**	etwas (mit etwas) abschließen, vervollständigen	They **~ed off** the meal with coffee.
	(to) **mention** ['menʃn]	erwähnen	Now that you ~ it: yes, I'm hungry too.
p. 84	**supply** [sə'plaɪ]	Vorrat; Versorgung, Lieferung	No milk in the shops! They're having ~ problems.
	excerpt (from) ['eksɜːpt]	Auszug (aus)	We're not reading the whole book, just an ~.

Unit 4 South Dakota

p. 88	**impressive** [ɪm'presɪv]	beeindruckend	This ~ church was built in 1799.
	vast [vɑːst]	riesig	Africa is a ~ continent. It's over 5,000 miles from north to south.
	sculpture ['skʌlptʃə]	Skulptur	! stress: **sculp**ture ['skʌlptʃə] (F) la sculpture
	reservation [ˌrezə'veɪʃn] (*kurz auch:* **rez**)	Reservat, Reservation	(L) *servare (retten, bewahren)*
	prairie ['preəri]	Prärie, Grasland	! stress: **prai**rie ['preəri] (F) la prairie
	region ['riːdʒən]	Region	! stress: **re**gion ['riːdʒən] (F) la région (L) regio *f*

[eɪ] name · [aɪ] time · [ɔɪ] boy · [əʊ] old ·
[aʊ] town · [ɪə] here · [eə] where · [ʊə] tour

	(to) **carve** [kɑːv]	meißeln; schnitzen	
p. 89	**bison** ['baɪsn], *pl* **bison**	Amerikanischer Bison	**a bison** 

Part A

p. 90	(to) **slap** [slæp]	knallen, klatschen	She ~**ped** the letters on his desk.
	(to) **appreciate** sb./sth. [ə'priːʃieɪt]	etwas schätzen, etwas zu schätzen wissen	Thank you. We really ~ your help.
	wheel [wiːl] (*kurz für:* **steering wheel** ['stɪərɪŋ wi ːl])	Lenkrad	! **wheel** = 1. Rad  2. *(steering wheel)* Lenkrad 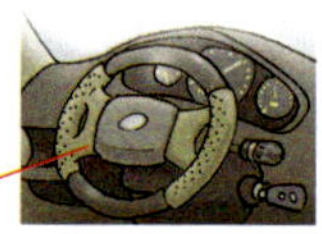 3. **wheels** *(pl; infml)* fahrbarer Untersatz 
	(to) **honk** [hɒŋk]	hupen	
	coach [kəʊtʃ]	Trainer/in	
	rodeo ['rəʊdiəʊ]	Rodeo	! stress: <u>ro</u>deo ['rəʊdiəʊ]
	final ['faɪnl]	Finale, Endspiel	! stress: <u>fi</u>nal ['faɪnl]

(to) keep, kept, kept

1) (to) **keep**	behalten aufbewahren aufheben, aufsparen	Can I **keep** your pen or do you want it back? Butter should be **kept** in a cool place. Don't eat all your biscuits now. **Keep** some for later.
2) (to) **keep** sth. **alive/fresh/warm/...**	halten, erhalten	I think we should try to **keep** our traditions **alive**. She put on some boots to **keep** her feet **warm**.
3) (to) **keep** sth. **up**	etwas aufrechterhalten, etwas fortsetzen	Dad goes to evening classes to **keep up** his English. You're doing good work. **Keep it up!**
4) (to) **keep to** sth.	sich an etwas halten	We should **keep to** our plan and go by bike.
5) (to) **keep (on) doing** sth.	etwas immer wieder/ immer weiter/ständig tun	They **kept (on) walking** till they got to a village. I tried to speak, but he **kept interrupting** me.

No wonder ... ['wʌndə]	Kein Wunder ...	His grandma has just died. ~ **No** – he looks so sad. The Grand Canyon is one of the natural ~**s** of the world. ! Dem Wort **Wunder** in der Bedeutung „übernatürliches Ereignis" entspricht das englische **miracle**: It's a **miracle** she didn't die in the car crash.
water fountain *(bes. AE)* / **drinking fountain** *(bes. BE)* ['faʊntən]	Trinkbrunnen	 (F) la fontaine
(to) tuck [tʌk]	stecken, klemmen	He ~**ed** his books under his arm and left. She ~**ed** her hair behind her ear and started writing.

(to) **advise** sb. **to do** sth. [əd'vaɪz]	jm. raten, etwas zu tun	The doctor **~d** him **to** eat more fruit. The doctor **~d** him not **to** eat so much meat.
technique [tek'ni:k]	Technik, Methode	! stress: tech**nique** [tek'ni:k]
excellent ['eksələnt]	ausgezeichnet, hervorragend	(F) excellent, e
(to) **speed up** [ˌspi:d_'ʌp]	beschleunigen, schneller werden	You're so slow! Can't you ~ **up** a bit?
(to) **qualify** ['kwɒlɪfaɪ]	sich qualifizieren	If we win this match, we'll ~ for the finals. (F) se qualifier
it takes practice ['præktɪs]	es erfordert Übung	You can't do this immediately. **It** will **take** ~.
somewhere ['sʌmweə]	irgendwo, irgendwohin	This summer I'd like to go ~ where it's nice and warm.
p. 91 **apart** [ə'pɑ:t]	auseinander, voneinander entfernt	The two houses are only 10 m ~. We took the cupboard ~ to get it out of the room.
(to) **notice** ['nəʊtɪs]	merken, bemerken	I didn't ~ Jeremy because he was so quiet. When I arrived, I **~d** that I had forgotten my money.
whether ['weðə]	ob	**Whether** you go or not, that is your decision. ! **whether** is a little more formal than **if**.
(to) **divide (into)** [dɪ'vaɪd]	(sich) teilen (in), (sich) aufteilen (in)	Now ~ **into** groups and talk about the questions. We **~d** the cake **into** eight parts. (F) diviser (L) dividere
period ['pɪəriəd] *(bes. AE)*	Unterrichtsstunde, Schulstunde	
register ['redʒɪstə]	Klassenbuch; Register, Verzeichnis	
driver's license ['draɪvəz ˌlaɪsəns] *(AE)*, **driving licence** *(BE)*	Führerschein, Fahrerlaubnis	(L) licet *(es ist erlaubt)*
basic ['beɪsɪk]	elementar, Grund-	The ~ idea is quite simple really.
literature ['lɪtrətʃə]	Literatur	! stress: **li**terature ['lɪtrətʃə] (F) la littérature (L) litterae *f*
social studies [ˌsəʊʃl 'stʌdiz]	Sozialkunde	
assignment [ə'saɪnmənt] *(AE)*	Aufgabe, Arbeitsauftrag *(in der Schule oder daheim zu erledigen)*	
(to) **pass** [pɑ:s]	bestehen *(Test, Prüfung)*	(F) passer
grade [greɪd] *(bes. AE)* *(BE auch:* **mark** [mɑ:k])	(Schul-)Note, Zensur	! **grade** = **1.** *(AE)* Klasse, Jahrgangsstufe (= *BE* ***year***) **2.** *(bes. AE)* Note, Zensur (*BE auch:* **mark**) (L) gradus *m (Stufe)*
(to) **fail** [feɪl]	nicht bestehen *(Test, Prüfung)*; durchfallen	(to) **pass a test** ◄► (to) **fail a test**
extra ['ekstrə]	zusätzlich	(L) extra *(außerhalb)*
p. 92 (to) **attend a** course [ə'tend]	einen Kurs besuchen, an einem Kurs teilnehmen	My son was ill and couldn't ~ classes today. He **~ed** the same school as his older sister.
session ['seʃn]	Sitzung, Einheit	(L) sedere *(sitzen)*
property ['prɒpəti]	Eigentum	(F) la propriété
(to) **take care of** sth. [keə]	sich (gut) um etwas kümmern; sorgfältig mit etwas umgehen	You can have my bike, but promise to **take** ~ **of** it.

[f] **f**ather · [v] **r**i**v**er · [s] **s**i**s**ter · [z] plea**s**e · [ʃ] **sh**op · [ʒ] televi**s**ion · [tʃ] **t**ea**ch**er · [dʒ] **G**ermany · [θ] **th**anks · [ð] **th**is · [h] **h**ere

	for this reason ['ri:zn]	aus diesem Grund	Year 4 will visit the museum on Friday afternoon. **For this** ~, lessons will end at 12 o'clock.
	(to) **steal** [sti:l], **stole** [stəʊl], **stolen** ['stəʊlən]	stehlen	Where is your bike? – Somebody has **stolen** it.
	at any time	jederzeit, zu jeder Zeit	**at any time** ◄► **at no time**
	grounds *(pl)* [graʊndz]	Gelände	Students need a permit to leave the school ~.
	principal ['prɪnsəpl] *(bes. AE)*	Schulleiter/ in	(L) princeps, principis *m (erster Mann)*
p. 93	**position** [pə'zɪʃn]	Platz, Position	! stress: **po<u>si</u>tion** [pə'zɪʃn] (F) la position (L) ponere *(stellen)*
p. 94	(to) **come up to** sb.	auf jn. zukommen	He **came** ~ **to** me and asked me how to get to York.
p. 95	**state** [steɪ]	Zustand	Your bedroom is in a terrible ~. Please clean it now!

Part B

p. 98	**flat** [flæt]	flach, eben	Cycling is easier in a ~ area like the Münsterland than in a hilly area like the Weserbergland. **hilly** ◄► **flat**
	wheat [wi:t]	Weizen	Is this bread made from ~?
	(to) **borrow** sth. **(from** sb.**)** ['bɒrəʊ]	sich etwas (aus)leihen (vom jm.), etwas entleihen	! • You **borrow** something from somebody: "Can I **borrow** your MP3 player?" • You **lend** somebody something: "OK, I'll **lend** you my MP3 player. But I want it back by tomorrow."
	(to) **lend** sb. sth. [lend], **lent, lent** [lent]	jm. etwas leihen	
	helpful ['helpfl]	hilfreich	
	college ['kɒlɪdʒ]	Hochschule	

Part C

p. 102	(to) **attract** [ə'trækt]	anziehen, anlocken	New York ~**s** millions of tourists every year. verb: (to) **attract** ~ noun: **attraction** (F) a tirer ~ l'attraction *(f)* (L) ad *(an, zu)* + trahere *(ziehen)*
	more than in any other place	mehr als an jedem anderen Ort	
	giant ['dʒaɪənt]	riesig, Riesen-	(F) gêant, e
	patriotism ['peɪtriətɪzəm]	Patriotismus	! stress: **<u>pa</u>triotism** ['peɪtriətɪzəm] (F) le patriotisme (L) patria *f (Heimat)*
	taxpayer ['tækspeɪə]	Steuerzahler/in	
	tax [tæks]	*(die)* Steuer	The ~ on cars in Germany is higher than the ~ on books.
	however [haʊ'evə]	aber; allerdings; jedoch	She was born in France. She isn't French, ~. (= But she isn't French.)
	sacred ['seɪkrɪd]	heilig	Cows are ~ in India. (L) sacer, sacra, sacrum
	extremely [ɪk'stri:mli]	äußerst, höchst	The Beatles were ~ popular in the 1960s. adjective: **extreme** (extrem) – adverb: **extremely** (L) extra *(außerhalb)*
	offensive [ə'fensɪv]	beleidigend, Anstoß erregend	My grandma finds some words very ~. (L) *offendere (beleidigen)*

[i:] green · [i] happy · [ɪ] big · [e] red · [æ] cat · [ɑ:] class · [ɒ] song · [ɔ:] door · [u:] blue · [ʊ] book · [ʌ] mum · [ɜ:] girl · [ə] a partner

(to) **spray** [spreɪ]	(be)sprühen, sprayen	**Spraying graffiti** is illegal. The walls were **sprayed** with **graffiti**.
graffiti [grəˈfiːti]	Graffiti	

wonderful [ˈwʌndəfəl]	wunderbar	
hardly [ˈhɑːdli]	kaum	There was ~ anyone in the streets. It was very quiet. **!** They work **hard**. Sie arbeiten **hart**. | They **hardly** work. Sie arbeiten **kaum**.
surprising [səˈpraɪzɪŋ]	überraschend	
surprise [səˈpraɪz]	Überraschung	A present? For me? That's a nice! Ⓕ la surprise adjective: **surprising** (überraschend) **surprised** (überrascht) noun: **surprise** I smiled in ~. (voller Überraschung)
(to) **be dedicated to** [ˈdedɪkeɪtɪd]	gewidmet sein *(einer Sache/Person)*	There is a monument that **is** ~ **to** the people who died in the fire.
granite [ˈgrænɪt]	Granit	
(to) **gaze** [geɪz]	blicken, starren	He **~d** for hours at the sea.
ceremony [ˈserəməni]	Zeremonie	**!** stress: __ce__remony [ˈserəməni] Ⓕ la cérémonie
national anthem [ˌnæʃnəl_ˈænnθəm]	Nationalhymne	
floodlight [ˈflʌdlaɪt]	Flutlicht(lampe)	**floodlights**
cloudless [ˈklaʊdləs]	wolkenlos	
pride (**in** sth.) [praɪd]	Stolz (auf etwas)	adjective: **proud (of** sth.**)** ~ noun: **pride (in** sth.**)**
p. 103 **whenever** [ˌwenˈevə]	wann (auch) immer; egal, wann	

whenever, wherever, whatever, whoever

At my school, we're allowed to use dictionaries **whenever** we want.	… **wann immer wir wollen**
I'll find you, **wherever** you are.	… **wo immer du (auch) bist / egal, wo du bist**
We will help you, **whatever** happens.	… **was immer auch geschieht / egal, was geschieht**
Whoever told you that was wrong.	**Wer immer dir das auch erzählt hat,** …

glum(ly) [glʌm, ˈglʌmli]	niedergeschlagen	adjective: **glum** – Don't be **glum**. Try to be more optimistic. adverb: **glumly** – "We lost again," he said **glumly**.
insult (to) [ˈɪnsʌlt]	Beleidigung (für)	I take your comment as a personal ~ **to** me. Ⓕ insulter
not (...) any longer [ˈlɒŋgə]	nicht länger; nicht mehr	I'll leave now. I **don't** want to wait for you **any** ~.
(to) **change your mind** [maɪnd]	es sich anders überlegen; seine Meinung ändern	I've **changed my** ~. I *will* wait for you.
p. 104 **suffix** [ˈsʌfɪks]	Suffix, Nachsilbe	**prefix** (Vorsilbe) ◄► **suffix** (Nachsilbe) Ⓕ le préfixe ◄► le suffixe
exam [ɪgˈzæm]	Prüfung	*English:* (to) **take an exam** *German:* **eine Prüfung ablegen**
abstract [ˈæbstrækt]	**abstrakt**	**!** stress: __ab__stract [ˈæbstrækt] Ⓛ abstractus *(weggezogen)*
concrete [ˈkɒŋkriːt]	**konkret**	**!** stress: __con__crete [ˈkɒŋkriːt] Ⓛ concretus *(zusammengewachsen)*

[eɪ] name · [aɪ] time · [ɔɪ] boy · [əʊ] old · [aʊ] town · [ɪə] here · [eə] where · [ʊə] tour

p. 105	**certain** ['sɜːtn]	bestimmte(r, s), gewisse(r, s)	Try to save a ~ amount of money each month. A ~ Mr Davidson called this morning. (L) certus
p. 106	**bilingual** [baɪ'lɪŋgwəl]	zweisprachig	(F) bilingue (L) bis *(zweimal)*, lingua *f (Sprache)*
p. 107	**relationship** [rɪ'leɪʃnʃɪp]	Beziehung, Verhältnis	(F) la relation
	long shot ['lɒŋ ʃɒt]	Totale, Totalaufnahme	
	medium shot ['miːdiəm ʃɒt]	Halbtotale	(L) medius, -a, -um *(der mittlere)*
	close-up ['kləʊs‿ʌp]	Nahaufnahme	

English sounds

English sounds

[iː] green, he, sea
[i] happy, monkey
[ɪ] big, in, expensive
[e] red, yes, again, breakfast
[æ] cat, animal, apple, black
[ɑː] class, ask, car, park
[ɒ] song, on, dog, what
[ɔː] door, or, ball, four, morning
[uː] blue, ruler, too, two, you
[ʊ] book, good, pullover
[ʌ] mum, bus, colour
[ɜː] girl, early, her, work, T-shirt
[ə] a partner, again, today

[eɪ] name, eight, play, great
[aɪ] time, right, my, I
[ɔɪ] boy, toilet, noise
[əʊ] old, no, road, yellow
[aʊ] town, now, house
[ɪə] here, year, idea
[eə] where, pair, share, their
[ʊə] tour

[b] boat, table, verb
[p] pool, paper, shop
[d] dad, window, good
[t] ten, letter, at
[g] good, again, bag
[k] cat, kitchen, back
[m] mum, man, remember
[n] no, one, ten
[ŋ] song, young, uncle, thanks
[l] hello, like, old, small
[r] red, ruler, friend, sorry
[w] we, where, one
[j] you, yes, uniform
[f] family, after, laugh
[v] river, very, seven, have
[s] sister, poster, yes
[z] please, zoo, quiz, his, music
[ʃ] shop, station, English
[ʒ] television, usually
[tʃ] teacher, child, watch
[dʒ] Germany, job, project, orange
[θ] thanks, three, bathroom
[ð] the, this, father, with
[h] here, who, behind
[x] loch

Am besten kannst du dir die Aussprache der einzelnen Lautzeichen einprägen, wenn du dir zu jedem Zeichen ein einfaches Wort merkst – das [iː] ist der **green**-Laut, das [eɪ] ist der **name**-Laut usw.

Das **Dictionary** besteht aus **zwei alphabetischen Wörterlisten**:
English – German (S. 237 – 266) und **German – English** (S. 267 – 293)

Im **English – German Dictionary** kannst du nachschlagen, wenn du wissen möchtest, was ein englisches Wort bedeutet, wie man es ausspricht oder wie es geschrieben wird.

Im **Dictionary** werden folgende **Abkürzungen und Symbole** verwendet:

sth. = something (etwas) sb. = somebody (jemand) jn. = jemanden jm. = jemandem
pl = *plural* (Mehrzahl) *infml* = *informal* (umgangssprachlich)
° Mit diesem Kringel sind Wörter markiert, die nicht zum Lernwortschatz gehören.

▸ Der Pfeil weist auf Kästen im **Vocabulary** (S. 214 – 236) hin, in denen du weitere Informationen zu diesem Wort findest.

Die **Fundstellenangaben** zeigen, wo ein Wort zum ersten Mal vorkommt.
I = Band 1 • II = Band 2 • III = Band 3 • IV 1 (18) = Band 4, Unit 1, Seite 18

1

1960s [ˌnaɪntiːn'sɪkstiz]: **in the 1960s** in den 60er-Jahren *(des 20. Jahrhunderts)* IV 2 (47)

A

a [ə] ein, eine I **once/twice a week** einmal/zweimal pro Woche II
°**abandon sb.** [ə'bændən] jn. verlassen, im Stich lassen; aussetzen
abbreviation [əˌbriːvi'eɪʃn] Abkürzung II
able ['eɪbl]: **be able to do sth.** etwas tun können; fähig sein / in der Lage sein, etwas zu tun III
about [ə'baʊt]:
1. über; von I **about me/you/...** über mich/dich/... I **about yourself** über dich selbst I **It's about a seagull.** Es geht um eine Möwe. / Es handelt von einer Möwe. I **What about ...?** Wie wäre es mit ...? II **What about you?** Und du? / Und was ist mit dir?; Und ihr? / Und was ist mit euch? I **What's your poster about?** Wovon handelt dein Poster? / Worum geht es bei deinem Poster? I
2. ungefähr II
3. be about to do sth. im Begriff sein, etwas zu tun; kurz davor sein, etwas zu tun IV 3 (72)
above [ə'bʌv] oben, darüber; über, oberhalb (von) III
absolutely ['æbsəluːtli] völlig, absolut III
abstract ['æbstrækt] abstrakt IV 4 (104)
accent ['æksənt] Akzent III
access ['ækses] Zugang, Zutritt I
accident [æksɪdənt] Unfall III
across the moor/the street [ə'krɒs] (quer) über das Moor/die Straße II
act [ækt]:
1. schauspielern II **act sth. out** etwas vorspielen I
°**2.** Gesetz
action ['ækʃn] Action; Handlung, Tat I
activity [æk'tɪvəti] Aktivität I **free-time activities** Freizeitaktivitäten I
actor ['æktə] Schauspieler/in III
actually ['æktʃuəli] eigentlich; übrigens; tatsächlich III
add (to) [æd] hinzufügen, ergänzen, addieren (zu) III
adder ['ædə] Kreuzotter II
address [ə'dres] Adresse, Anschrift I
adjective ['ædʒɪktɪv] Adjektiv II
adult ['ædʌlt] Erwachsene(r) III
advantage [əd'vɑːntɪdʒ] Vorteil III
adventure [əd'ventʃə] Abenteuer II
adverb ['ædvɜːb] Adverb II
advertisement [əd'vɜːtɪsmənt] Werbespot, Werbung; Anzeige, Inserat IV 3 (73)
advice *(no pl)* [əd'vaɪs] Rat, Ratschlag, Ratschläge IV 2 (41)
advise sb. to do sth. [əd'vaɪz] jm. raten, etwas zu tun IV 4 (90)
°**affect** [ə'fekt] beeinflussen
afraid [ə'freɪd]: be afraid (of sth./sb.) Angst haben (vor etwas/jm.) IV 2 (46)
°**African American** [ˌæfrɪkən‿ə'merɪkən] Afroamerikaner/in, afroamerikanisch
after ['ɑːftə]:
1. nachdem II
2. after breakfast nach dem Frühstück I **after that** danach III
3. run after sb. hinter jm. herrennen I
afternoon [ˌɑːftə'nuːn] Nachmittag I **in the afternoon** nachmittags, am Nachmittag I **on Saturday afternoon** am Samstagnachmittag I
afterwards ['ɑːftəwədz] nachher, danach IV 3 (72)
again [ə'gen] wieder; noch einmal I **again and again** immer wieder II
against [ə'genst] gegen II
age [eɪdʒ] Alter I **... is your age** ... ist in deinem Alter; ... ist so alt wie du II **ages ago** vor einer Ewigkeit III **a boy of your age** ein Junge in deinem Alter III **for ages** seit einer Ewigkeit, ewig lange III
ago [ə'gəʊ]: **a week ago** vor einer Woche II
agree [ə'griː]: **agree with sb.** jm. zustimmen I **agree on sth.** sich auf etwas einigen I
air [eə] Luft II
airport ['eəpɔːt] Flughafen III
alive [ə'laɪv]: **be alive** leben, am Leben sein IV 1 (16)
all [ɔːl] alles; alle I **all alone** ganz allein II **all of Plymouth** ganz Plymouth, das ganze Plymouth I **all right** okay; in Ordnung I **all the time** die ganze Zeit II **all over the city / the world** in der ganzen Stadt / auf der ganzen Welt IV 2 (47)
allergic (to sth.) [ə'lɜːdʒɪk] allergisch (gegen etwas) IV 2 (43)
alligator ['ælɪgeɪtə] Alligator IV 2 (39)
allow [ə'laʊ] erlauben, zulassen III
be allowed to do sth. etwas tun dürfen II
almost ['ɔːlməʊst] fast, beinahe I
alone [ə'ləʊn] allein I

along [ə'lɒŋ]: **along the street / the river / ...** die Straße / den Fluss / ... entlang I **sing along** (with sb.) (mit jm.) mitsingen III
aloud [ə'laʊd]: **read aloud** laut (vor) lesen II
already [ɔːl'redi] schon, bereits II
also ['ɔːlsəʊ] auch I
although [ɔːl'ðəʊ] obwohl III
altogether [ˌɔːltə'geðə] insgesamt, alles in allem III
always ['ɔːlweɪz] immer I
am: 4 am [ˌeɪ‿'em] 4 Uhr morgens I
amazing [ə'meɪzɪŋ] erstaunlich, unglaublich III
°**Americas** [ə'merɪkəz]: **the Americas** Amerika *(Doppelkontinent)*
°**amphitheatre** ['æmfɪθɪətə] Amphitheater
an [æn, ən] ein, eine I
°**ancestor** ['ænsestə] Vorfahr/in
and [ænd, ənd] und I
angry (with sb.) ['æŋgri] wütend (auf jn.) II
animal ['ænɪml] Tier I
anniversary [ˌænɪ'vɜːsəri] Jahrestag IV 1 (17)
announcement [ə'naʊnsmənt] Durchsage, Ansage III
°**annual** ['ænjuəl] jährlich
another [ə'nʌðə] ein(e) andere(r, s); noch ein(e) II
answer ['ɑːnsə]:
1. antworten; beantworten I **answer the phone** ans Telefon gehen II
2. Antwort I
ant [ænt] Ameise I
anthem ['ænθəm]: **national anthem** Nationalhymne IV 4 (102)
antonym ['æntənɪm] Antonym *(Gegensatzwort)* IV 3 (82)
any ['eni]: **Are there any ...?** Gibt es (irgendwelche) ...? I **There aren't any ...** Es gibt keine / Es sind keine ... I **not ... any more** nicht mehr II **not (...) any longer** ['lɒŋgə] nicht länger; nicht mehr IV 4 (103) **more than in any other place** mehr als an jedem anderen Ort IV 4 (102)
anybody? ['enibɒdi] (irgend)jemand? II **not ... anybody** niemand II
anyone? ['eniwʌn] (irgend)jemand? II **not ... anyone** niemand II **anyone else** sonst jemand III
anything? ['eniθɪŋ] (irgend)etwas? II **anything else?** sonst noch etwas? III **not ... anything** nichts II
Anyway, ... ['eniweɪ] Jedenfalls, ... / Wie dem auch sei, ... / Aber egal, ... II **And anyway, ...** Und überhaupt, ... III
apart [ə'pɑːt] auseinander, voneinander entfernt IV 4 (91)
apartment [ə'pɑːtmənt] Wohnung II
app [æp] App III
appear [ə'pɪə] erscheinen, auftauchen II
apple ['æpl] Apfel II
appointment [ə'pɔɪntmənt] Verabredung, Termin I
appreciate sb./sth. [ə'priːʃieɪt] etwas schätzen, etwas zu schätzen wissen IV 4 (90)
April ['eɪprəl] April I
aquarium [ə'kweəriəm] Aquarium; Aquarienhaus I
architect ['ɑːkɪtekt] Architekt/in III
are ['ɑː] bist; sind; seid I **Are you ...?** Bist du ...? I **The DVDs are ...** Die DVDs kosten ... I
area ['eəriə] Bereich; Gebiet, Gegend I
aren't [ɑːnt]: **you aren't** du bist nicht ...; du bist kein/e ...; ihr seid nicht ...; ihr seid kein/e ... I
argue ['ɑːgjuː] streiten; sich streiten III
argument ['ɑːgjumənt]:
1. Argument III
2. Streit, Auseinandersetzung III
arm [ɑːm] Arm II
armchair ['ɑːmtʃeə] Sessel I
army ['ɑːmi] Armee III
around ... [ə'raʊnd] um ... (herum) II **all around her** überall um sie herum III **around the library / the beach** in der Bücherei / auf dem Strand umher II **walk around** herumlaufen, umherspazieren II
arrange [ə'reɪndʒ]:
1. anordnen II
2. organisieren, vereinbaren IV 3 (66)
arrest [ə'rest] verhaften, festnehmen IV 1 (17)
arrive [ə'raɪv] ankommen, eintreffen I
art [ɑːt] Kunst I **work of art** Kunstwerk IV 1 (29)
article ['ɑːtɪkl] Artikel II
artist ['ɑːtɪst] Künstler/in II
as [æz], [əz]:
1. als, während II **as if** als ob IV 1 (16)
2. as a child als Kind II **as kung fu master** als Kung Fu-Master II
3. as big as so groß wie II
4. **as he said** wie er (einmal) sagte III
ashes *(pl)* ['æʃɪz] Asche *(sterbliche Überreste)* III
ask [ɑːsk] fragen I **ask a question** eine Frage stellen I **ask for sth.** um etwas bitten II **ask sb. to do sth.** jemanden bitten, etwas zu tun I **ask sb. the way** jn. nach dem Weg fragen II
asleep [ə'sliːp]: **be asleep** schlafen II
°**assess** [ə'ses] einschätzen, beurteilen
assignment [ə'saɪnmənt] Aufgabe, Arbeitsauftrag *(in der Schule oder daheim zu erledigen)* IV 4 (91)
astronaut ['æstrənɔːt] Astronaut/in III
at [æt, ət] an, bei, in I **at 88 School Street** in der Schulstraße 88 I **at Dad's** bei Papa/Vati II **at first** zuerst, anfangs, am Anfang II **at home** daheim, zu Hause I **at last** endlich, schließlich I **at least** zumindest, wenigstens II **at lunchtime** mittags I **at the moment** gerade, im Moment I **at night** nachts, in der Nacht I **at school** in der Schule I **at the weekend** am Wochenende I **not ... at all** überhaupt nicht(s), gar nicht(s); überhaupt kein/e, gar kein/e II
ate [et, eɪt] *siehe* **eat**
Atlantic [ət'læntɪk]: **the Atlantic (Ocean)** der Atlantik, der Atlantische Ozean III
atmosphere ['ætməsfɪə] Atmosphäre; Stimmung III
attack [ə'tæk]:
1. angreifen II
2. Angriff IV 1 (16)
attend [ə'tend]: **attend a course** einen Kurs besuchen, an einem Kurs teilnehmen IV 4 (92)
attic ['ætɪk] Dachboden I **in the attic** auf dem Dachboden I
°**attitude** ['ætɪtjuːd] Haltung
attract [ə'trækt] anziehen, anlocken IV 4 (102)
attraction [ə'trækʃn] Attraktion; Anziehungspunkt III
°**attractive** [ə'træktɪv] attraktiv, verlockend
audience ['ɔːdiəns] Publikum, Zuschauer/innen, Zuhörer/innen II
audition [ɔː'dɪʃn] Vorsprechen, Vorsingen, Vorspielen II
August ['ɔːgəst] August I
aunt [ɑːnt] Tante I
author ['ɔːθə] Autor/in I
autograph ['ɔːtəgrɑːf] Autogramm IV 3 (72)
autumn ['ɔːtəm] Herbst II
available [ə'veɪləbl] erhältlich, verfügbar; erreichbar *(am Telefon)* III

avenue ['ævənju:] Allee, Boulevard IV 1 (12)
awake [ə'weɪk] wach III
away [ə'weɪ] weg, fort I
awesome ['ɔ:səm] *(bes. AE, infml)* klasse, großartig IV 1 (29)
awful ['ɔ:fl] schrecklich, fürchterlich II
awfully ['ɔ:fli] furchtbar, außerordentlich IV 2 (52)

B

back [bæk]:
1. zurück I
2. Rücken II
3. Rückseite, hintere Seite II **at the back** hinten II **to the back** nach hinten II

background ['bækgraʊnd] Hintergrund II
background file ['bækgraʊnd ˌfaɪl] Hintergrundinformation(en) I
backpack ['bækpæk] Rucksack IV 1 (17)
bacon ['beɪkən] Schinkenspeck II
bad [bæd] schlecht, schlimm II
bag [bæg] Tasche, Beutel, Tüte I; Sack I **school bag** Schultasche I
bagpiper ['bægpaɪpə] Dudelsackpfeifer/in, Dudelsackspieler/in, Sackpfeifer/in III
bagpipes *(pl)* ['bægpaɪps] Dudelsack, Sackpfeife III
bake [beɪk] backen IV 2 (42)
°**bakery** ['beɪkəri] Bäckerei
balcony ['bælkəni] Balkon IV 2 (40)
ball [bɔ:l] Ball I
banana [bə'nɑ:nə] Banane III
band [bænd] Band, (Musik-)Gruppe II
°**banjo** ['bændʒəʊ] Banjo
°**bank** [bæŋk] Bank
bar [bɑ:]:
1. Riegel *(Schokolade, Müsli)*, Tafel *(Schokolade)* III
2. Bar III

bark [bɑ:k] bellen I
barman *pl* **barmen** ['bɑ:mən], ['bɑ:mən] Barkeeper III
barn [bɑ:n] Scheune II
basic ['beɪsɪk] elementar, Grund- IV 4 (91)
basket ['bɑ:skɪt] Korb I
basketball ['bɑ:skɪtbɔ:l] Basketball I
bath [bɑ:θ] Bad II **have/take a bath** baden, ein Bad nehmen II
bathroom ['bɑ:θru:m] Badezimmer I
be [bi], **was/were, been** sein I
beach [bi:tʃ] Strand I
bean [bi:n] Bohne IV 2 (42)
► S. 222 Food words
bear [beə] Bär I
beard [bɪəd] Bart II
beat, beat, beaten [bi:t] schlagen; besiegen III **beat sb. up** jn. zusammenschlagen IV 2 (47)
beautiful ['bju:tɪfl] schön II
became [bɪ'keɪm] *siehe* **become**
because [bɪ'kɒz] weil I
become [bɪ'kʌm], **became, become** werden II
bed [bed] Bett I **bed and breakfast (B&B)** Frühstückspension *(wörtlich: Bett und Frühstück)* III
bedroom ['bedru:m] Schlafzimmer I
beef [bi:f] Rindfleisch IV 2 (42) **roast beef** Rinderbraten I
been [bi:n] *siehe* **be** **Have you ever been to ...?** Bist du jemals in ... gewesen? II
beep [bi:p] piepen II
before [bɪ'fɔ:]:
1. bevor I
2. vor I **before school/lessons** vor der Schule *(vor Schulbeginn)* / vorm Unterricht I
3. (vorher) schon mal II **never/not before** (vorher) noch nie II **the week before** die Woche zuvor; in der Woche davor IV 3 (66)
4. **before long** schon bald III

began [bɪ'gæn] *siehe* **begin**
begin [bɪ'gɪn], **began, begun** beginnen, anfangen II
beginning [bɪ'gɪnɪŋ] Anfang, Beginn III
begun [bɪ'gʌn] *siehe*
behave [bɪ'heɪv] sich verhalten, sich benehmen III **well-behaved** brav IV 1 (16)
behind [bɪ'haɪnd] hinter I
°**belief** [bɪ'li:f] Glaube; Überzeugung
believe [bɪ'li:v] glauben II
bell [bel] Klingel, Glocke II
belong to sb. [bɪ'lɒŋ] jm. gehören; zu jm. gehören IV 2 (46)
below [bɪ'ləʊ] unten, darunter; unter, unterhalb (von) III
bend down [bend], **bent, bent** III
best [best]: **the best ...** der/die/das beste ...; die besten ... I **the best thing about ...** das Beste an ... III
bet, bet, bet [bet] wetten III
better ['betə] besser I **I'd better ... (= I had better ...)** Ich sollte lieber ... IV 1 (17)
between [bɪ'twi:n] zwischen I
beyond [bɪ'jɒnd] jenseits (von), über ... hinaus/hinweg III
big [bɪg] groß I **big wheel** Riesenrad I **the biggest ...** ['bɪgɪst] der/die/das größte ... I
bike [baɪk] Fahrrad I **ride a bike** Fahrrad fahren I
bilingual [baɪ'lɪŋgwəl] zweisprachig IV 4 (106)
°**billionaire** [ˌbɪljə'neə] Milliardär/in
bird [bɜ:d] Vogel I
°**birth** [bɜ:θ] Geburt
birthday ['bɜ:θdeɪ] Geburtstag I **My birthday is in May.** Ich habe im Mai Geburtstag. I **My birthday is on 5th August.** Ich habe am 5. August Geburtstag. I **When's your birthday?** Wann hast du Geburtstag? I
°**birthplace** ['bɜ:θpleɪs] Geburtsort
biscuit ['bɪskɪt] Keks, Plätzchen I
bison ['baɪsn], *pl* **bison** Amerikanischer Bison IV 4 (89)
bit [ə 'bɪt]:
1. **a bit** ein bisschen, etwas II
2. *siehe* **bite**

bite [baɪt]:
1. **(bit, bitten)** beißen II
2. Biss, Bissen III

bitten ['bɪtn] *siehe* **bite**
bitter ['bɪtə] bitter IV 2 (42)
bitterness ['bɪtənəs] Bitterkeit IV 4 (104)
black [blæk] schwarz I
blew [blu:] *siehe* **blow**
block [blɒk]:
1. (Häuser-, Wohn-)Block IV 1 (17)
2. block [blɒk] blockieren, sperren IV 2 (41)

blog [blɒg] Blog *(Weblog, digitales Tagebuch)* II
blogger ['blɒgə] Blogschreiber/in III
blond *(bei Frauen oft:* **blonde***)* [blɒnd] blond I
blood [blʌd] Blut III
°**bloody** ['blʌdi] blutig
bloom [blu:m] blühen IV 1 (29)
blow [bləʊ], **blew, blown:**
1. **blow sth. out** etwas auspusten, ausblasen II
2. **blow a whistle** pfeifen *(auf der Trillerpfeife)* III
°3. **blow sb. away** *(infml)* jn. (völlig) umhauen *(stark beeindrucken)*

blown [bləʊn] *siehe* **blow**
blue [blu:] blau I
board [bɔ:d]:
1. (Wand-)Tafel I
2. **on board (the ship)** an Bord (des Schiffes) III

boarding school ['bɔːdɪŋ skuːl] Internat II
boat [bəʊt] Boot, Schiff I
body ['bɒdi]:
1. Körper II
2. Leiche III
3. Hauptteil *(eines Textes)* III
boil [bɔɪl] kochen; zum Kochen bringen IV 2 (42)
► S. 222 Food words
book [bʊk] Buch I
boot [buːt] Stiefel II
border ['bɔːdə] Grenze III
bored [bɔːd]: **be/feel bored** gelangweilt sein, sich langweilen II
boring ['bɔːrɪŋ] langweilig I
born [bɔːn]: **be born** geboren sein/werden III
°**borough** [*AE:* 'bɜːrəʊ, *BE:* 'bʌrə] (Stadt-)Bezirk
borrow sth. (from sb.) ['bɒrəʊ] sich etwas (aus)leihen (vom jm.), etwas entleihen IV 4 (98)
boss [bɒs] Chef/in, Boss III
both [bəʊθ] beide II **both ... and ...** sowohl ... als auch ... IV 2 (47)
bottle ['bɒtl] Flasche I
bottom ['bɒtəm]: **at the bottom (of)** unten, am unteren Ende (von) II
bought [bɔːt] *siehe* **buy**
bow [baʊ] sich verbeugen, sich verneigen II
bowl [bəʊl] Schüssel II
box [bɒks] Kasten, Kiste, Kästchen I
boy [bɔɪ] Junge I
°**boycott** ['bɔɪkɒt] Boykott
boyfriend ['bɔɪfrend] Freund III
°**bracket** ['brækɪt] Klammer *(in Texten)*
brass band [ˌbrɑːs 'bænd] Blaskapelle IV 2 (38)
brave [breɪv] mutig, tapfer IV 1 (16)
bread [bred] Brot I
break [breɪk]:
1. Pause I
2. **(broke, broken)** zerbrechen, kaputt machen; brechen, kaputt gehen II
breakfast ['brekfəst] Frühstück I **have breakfast** frühstücken I
breath [breθ] Atem, Atemzug II **..., he said under his breath.** ..., sagte er flüsternd / murmelte er. III
breeze [briːz] Brise III
bridge [brɪdʒ] Brücke II
bright [braɪt] strahlend, leuchtend, hell I
brilliant ['brɪliənt] großartig, genial, glänzend II
bring [brɪŋ], **brought, brought** (mit-, her)bringen II **bring in** *(hay)* einbringen *(Heu)* II
British ['brɪtɪʃ] britisch I
brochure ['brəʊʃə] Broschüre, Prospekt II
broke [brəʊk] *siehe* **break**
broken ['brəʊkən]:
1. *siehe* **break**
2. zerbrochen, kaputt; gebrochen II
brother ['brʌðə] Bruder I
brought [brɔːt] *siehe* **bring**
brown [braʊn] braun I
°**bubble** ['bʌbl]: **speech bubble** Sprechblase
buck [bʌk] *(infml)* Dollar IV 2 (41)
bucket ['bʌkɪt] Eimer II
build [bɪld], **built, built** bauen III
building ['bɪldɪŋ] Gebäude II
built [bɪlt] *siehe* **build**
bully ['bʊli] (Schul-)Tyrann III
burger ['bɜːgə] Hamburger II
burn [bɜːn] brennen; verbrennen III
burnt [bɜːnt] verbrannt IV 3 (79)
burst into tears, burst, burst [bɜːst] in Tränen ausbrechen III
bury ['beri] begraben, beerdigen IV 1 (17)
bus [bʌs] Bus I **go by bus** mit dem Bus fahren I **bus stop** Bushaltestelle III
°**business** ['bɪznəs] Geschäft, Geschäfts-; Unternehmen, Betrieb
busy ['bɪzi] belebt, geschäftig, hektisch III **be busy** beschäftigt sein; viel zu tun haben II
but [bʌt, bət] aber I
butter ['bʌtə] Butter III
► S. 222 Food words
butterfly ['bʌtəflaɪ] Schmetterling I
buy [baɪ], **bought, bought** kaufen I
by [baɪ]:
1. von ... II
2. **by the sea** am Meer I **take sb. by the arm** jn. am Arm nehmen II
3. **go by car/bus/...** mit dem Auto/Bus/... fahren I
4. **one by one** einer nach dem anderen II °**paragraph by paragraph** Absatz für Absatz
5. **by 8 pm** bis (spätestens) 20 Uhr III
Bye. [baɪ] Tschüs. I

C

café ['kæfeɪ] Café I
cafeteria [ˌkæfə'tɪəriə] Cafeteria IV 4 (91)
°**Cajun** ['keɪdʒən] Cajun
cake [keɪk] Kuchen I
call [kɔːl]:
1. rufen; anrufen; nennen I **call out the names** die Namen aufrufen II **call sb. names** jn. beschimpfen, jm. Schimpfwörter nachrufen IV 2 (47) °**call for sth.** etwas fordern
2. *(kurz für:* **phone call**) Anruf; Telefongespräch II
called [kɔːld]: **be called** heißen, genannt werden I
calm [kɑːm] ruhig III
came [keɪm] *siehe* **come**
camera ['kæmərə] Kamera, Fotoapparat I
campfire ['kæmpfaɪə] Lagerfeuer IV 3 (79)
campsite ['kæmpsaɪt] Zeltplatz II
can [kæn]:
1. Dose IV 3 (69)
2. [kæn, kən] können I **we cannot** ['kænɒt], **we can't** [kɑːnt] ... wir können nicht ... I
canal [kə'næl] Kanal III
candle ['kændl] Kerze II
candy ['kændi] *(AE)* Süßigkeiten IV 1 (20)
canteen [kæn'tiːn] Kantine, (Schul-)Mensa I
canyon ['kænjən] Cañon IV 3 (73)
cap [kæp] Mütze, Kappe II
capital ['kæpɪtl] Hauptstadt III
captain ['kæptɪn] Kapitän/in I
caption ['kæpʃn] Bildunterschrift I
car [kɑː] Auto I **go by car** mit dem Auto fahren I **car park** ['kɑː pɑːk] *(BE)* Parkplatz IV 3 (66)
caravan ['kærəvæn] Wohnwagen II
card (to) [kɑːd] Karte (an) I
care [keə]: **take care of sth.** sich (gut) um etwas kümmern; sorgfältig mit etwas umgehen IV 4 (92)
career [kə'rɪə] Karriere III
careful ['keəfl] vorsichtig II
carnival ['kɑːnɪvl] Karneval, Fasching III
carpenter ['kɑːpəntə] Tischler/in, Zimmerer/Zimmerin III
carrot ['kærət] Möhre, Karotte III
carry ['kæri] tragen I
cart [kɑːt] Karren I
carve [kɑːv] meißeln; schnitzen IV 4 (88)
cash desk ['kæʃ desk] Kasse *(in Geschäften)* II
castle ['kɑːsl] Burg, Schloss I
cat [kæt] Katze I

catch [kætʃ], **caught, caught** fangen I
catchy ['kætʃi] eingängig *(Melodie, Slogan)* IV 3 (83)
cathedral [kə'θi:drəl] Kathedrale, Dom III
caught [kɔ:t] *siehe* **catch**
cause [kɔ:z]:
1. Ursache IV 3 (79)
2. verursachen IV 3 (79)
celebrate ['selɪbreɪt] feiern II
celebration [ˌselɪ'breɪʃn] Feier II
celebrity [sə'lebrəti] Berühmtheit (berühmte Person) IV 3 (78)
cell (phone) [sel] *(bes. AE)* Mobiltelefon, Handy IV 1 (20)
Celsius (C) ['selsiəs] Celsius IV 2 (40)
► S. 220 Temperatures
cemetery ['semətri] *(BE)*, ['seməteri] *(AE)* Friedhof IV 1 (17)
cent [sent] Cent III
center ['sentə] *(AE)* Zentrum IV 1 (20)
central ['sentrəl] zentral, Zentral-, Mittel- IV 1 (12)
centre ['sentə] Zentrum; Mitte I
century ['sentʃəri] Jahrhundert II
ceremony ['serəməni] Zeremonie IV 4 (102)
certain ['sɜ:tn] bestimmte(r, s), gewisse(r, s) IV 4 (105)
°**certainly** ['sɜ:tnli] sicher(lich), auf jeden Fall
chair [tʃeə] Stuhl I
challenge ['tʃælɪndʒ]:
1. Herausforderung III
2. challenge sb. (to sth.) jn. herausfordern (zu etwas) III
champion ['tʃæmpiən] Champion, Meister/in II
chance [tʃɑ:ns] Gelegenheit, Möglichkeit, Chance III
°**chancellor** ['tʃɑ:nsələ] Kanzler/in
change [tʃeɪndʒ]:
1. (ver)ändern; sich (ver)ändern II
change your mind es sich anders überlegen; seine Meinung ändern IV 4 (103)
2. Änderung, Veränderung II **for a change** zur Abwechslung IV 3 (74)
3. Wechselgeld II
4. umsteigen III
5. wechseln, umtauschen *(Geld)* III
channel ['tʃænl] Kanal, Sender IV 3 (78)
chaos ['keɪɒs] Chaos I
character ['kærəktə]:
1. Figur, Person *(in Roman, Film, Theaterstück)* I
°**2. character** Charakter, Wesen

charity ['tʃærəti] Wohlfahrtsorganisation; Wohltätigkeit, wohltätige Zwecke II
chat [tʃæt]:
1. chatten III
2. Chat III
cheap [tʃi:p] billig, preiswert II
check [tʃek]:
1. Überprüfung, Kontrolle I
2. (über)prüfen, kontrollieren I
cheer [tʃɪə] jubeln II
cheese [tʃi:z] Käse I
chess [tʃes] Schach I
chest [tʃest] Brust, Brustkorb II
chicken ['tʃɪkɪn] Huhn; (Brat-)Hähnchen IV 2 (41)
child [tʃaɪld], *pl* **children** ['tʃɪldrən] Kind I
°**chill** [tʃɪl] Kühle, Kälte
chips *(pl)* [tʃɪps] Pommes frites II
chocolate ['tʃɒklət]:
1. Schokolade I
2. Praline II
choice [tʃɔɪs] Wahl; Auswahl III
choir ['kwaɪə] Chor II
choose [tʃu:z], **chose, chosen** aussuchen, (aus)wählen; sich aussuchen I
chorus ['kɔ:rəs] Refrain II
chose [tʃəʊz] *siehe* **choose**
chosen ['tʃəʊzn] *siehe* **choose**
Christmas ['krɪsməs] Weihnachten III
church [tʃɜ:tʃ] Kirche II
cigarette [ˌsɪgə'ret] Zigarette IV 3 (79)
cinema ['sɪnəmə] Kino II
circle ['sɜ:kl] Kreis II
°**citizen** ['sɪtɪzn] Bürger/in
city ['sɪti] Stadt, Großstadt I
civil rights *(pl)* [ˌsɪvl 'raɪts] Bürgerrechte IV 2 (47)
°**civilization** [ˌsɪvəlaɪ'zeɪʃn] Zivilisation
°**claim sth.** [kleɪm] etwas beanspruchen
clap [klæp] *(Beifall)* klatschen II **Clap your hands.** Klatscht in die Hände. II
class [klɑ:s] (Schul-)Klasse I °**in class** im Unterricht
classical ['klæsɪkl] klassisch III
classmate ['klɑ:smeɪt] Mitschüler/in, Klassenkamerad/in I
classroom ['klɑ:sru:m] Klassenzimmer I
clean [kli:n]:
1. sauber II
2. sauber machen, putzen I
clear [klɪə]:
1. klar, deutlich II
2. räumen; abräumen III

clever ['klevə] klug, schlau I
click [klɪk] klicken IV 1 (25)
cliff [klɪf] Klippe III
climate ['klaɪmət] Klima IV 3 (79)
climate change Klimawandel IV 4 (105)
climb [klaɪm]:
1. klettern; hinaufklettern (auf) II
climb a tree auf einen Baum klettern II
2. Aufstieg, Anstieg III
climber [klaɪmə] Bergsteiger(in), Kletterer, Kletterin III
clock [klɒk] (Wand-, Stand-, Turm-) Uhr I
close [kləʊz] schließen, zumachen II
close (to) [kləʊs] nah, dicht (bei, an) II **look closely** genau hinschauen II
closet ['klɒzɪt] Wandschrank *(oft begehbar)* IV 2 (46)
close-up ['kləʊs‿ʌp] Nahaufnahme IV 4 (107)
clothes *(pl)* [kləʊðz] Kleidung, Kleidungsstücke I
cloud [klaʊd] Wolke II
cloudless ['klaʊdləs] wolkenlos IV 4 (102)
cloudy ['klaʊdi] bewölkt II
clown [klaʊn] Clown/in II
club [klʌb] Klub I **join a club** in einen Klub eintreten; sich einem Klub anschließen I
clue [klu:] (Lösungs-)Hinweis; Anhaltspunkt III
coach [kəʊtʃ] Trainer/in IV 4 (90)
coal [kəʊl] Kohle III
coast [kəʊst] Küste I
coat [kəʊt] Mantel II
cocoa ['kəʊkəʊ] Kakao II
coffee ['kɒfi] Kaffee III
make coffee Kaffee kochen IV 2 (42)
► S. 222 Food words
coin [kɔɪn] Münze I
cold [kəʊld]:
1. kalt I **be cold** frieren II
2. have a cold eine Erkältung/einen Schnupfen haben, erkältet sein II
collapse [kə'læps] einstürzen; zusammenbrechen IV 1 (16)
collect [kə'lekt] sammeln I
college ['kɒlɪdʒ] Hochschule IV 4 (98)
colon ['kəʊlən] Doppelpunkt II
colour *(AE:* **color***)* ['kʌlə] Farbe I
colourful ['kʌləfl] bunt, farbenfreudig IV 1 (21)
column ['kɒləm] Säule III

combine [kəm'baɪn] kombinieren, verbinden IV 2 (41)
come [kʌm], **came, come** kommen I **come across sb./sth.** stoßen auf, *(zufällig)* treffen III **come down with** sth. bekommen *(Krankheit)*, erkranken an III **come in** hereinkommen I **Come on, Dad.** Na los, Dad! / Komm, Dad! I **come over** herüberkommen, vorbeikommen III **come over (to)** herüberkommen (zu/nach), vorbeikommen (bei) III **come up to sb.** auf jn. zukommen IV 4 (94) **come up with sth.** haben, kommen auf *(Idee, Vorschlag)* III
comedy ['kɒmədi] Comedyshow; Komödie II
comfortable ['kʌmftəbl] bequem; angenehm III
comma ['kɒmə] Komma II
comment ['kɒment]:
1. Bemerkung, Kommentar III
°**make a comment** einen Kommentar abgeben
°2. **comment on sth.** etwas kommentieren; sich zu etwas äußern
common ['kɒmən] häufig; weit verbreitet IV 3 (68) **have sth. in common** etwas miteinander gemein haben IV 1 (20)
compare [kəm'peə] vergleichen IV 3 (79)
competition [ˌkɒmpə'tɪʃn] Wettbewerb II
complain [kəm'pleɪn] sich beschweren, sich beklagen IV 3 (66)
complete [kəm'pliːt]:
1. abschließen, vollenden; vervollständigen IV 2 (47)
2. komplett, vollständig IV 2 (47)
complicated ['kɒmplɪkeɪtɪd] kompliziert III
computer [kəm'pjuːtə] Computer I
concert ['kɒnsət] Konzert II
conclusion [kən'kluːʒn] Schluss(folgerung) III
concrete ['kɒŋkriːt] konkret IV 4 (104)
°**conditions (pl)** [kən'dɪʃnz] Verhältnisse, Bedingungen
°**conflict** ['kɒnflɪkt] Konflikt, Auseinandersetzung
°**connect** [kə'nekt] verbinden
conservation [ˌkɒnsə'veɪʃn] Umweltschutz III
consonant ['kɒnsənənt] Konsonant, Mitlaut II
content ['kɒntent] Inhalt III
context ['kɒntekst] (Text-, Satz-)Zusammenhang, Kontext II
°**continent** ['kɒntɪnənt] Kontinent
continue sth. [kən'tɪnjuː] etwas fortsetzen III
contrast ['kɒntrɑːst] Kontrast, Gegensatz IV 3 (64) °**by contrast** im Vergleich; im Gegenteil
control [kən'trəʊl]:
1. kontrollieren, beherrschen; unter Kontrolle halten/bekommen III
2. Kontrolle IV 1 (16) **take control** Kontrolle übernehmen IV 1 (16)
conversation [ˌkɒnvə'seɪʃn] Gespräch, Unterhaltung II
cook [kʊk]:
1. kochen, zubereiten III **cook a meal** (ein) Essen kochen, eine Mahlzeit zubereiten IV 2 (42) **Who is going to cook / do the cooking this evening?** IV 2 (42) Wer kocht heute Abend?
2. Koch, Köchin IV 2 (52)
► S. 222 Food words
cookie ['kʊki] *(AE)* Keks IV 1 (20)
cool [kuːl]:
1. kühl II
2. cool I
coordinator [kəʊ'ɔːdɪneɪtə] Koordinator/in III
copy ['kɒpi] kopieren, abschreiben I
°**cord** [kɔːd] Schnur
corner ['kɔːnə] Ecke I **on the corner of Church Road and London Road** Church Road, Ecke London Road II **corner shop** Laden an der Ecke; Tante-Emma-Laden I
cornflakes ['kɔːnfleɪks] Cornflakes I
correct [kə'rekt]:
1. richtig, korrekt II
2. korrigieren, berichtigen II
°**correction** [kə'rekʃn] Korrektur, Berichtigung
corridor ['kɒrɪdɔː] Gang, Korridor III
cost [kɒst], **cost, cost** kosten II
costume ['kɒstjuːm] Kostüm, Verkleidung II
cottage ['kɒtɪdʒ] Häuschen, Cottage II
cough [kɒf]: **have a cough** Husten haben II
could [kʊd, kəd]:
1. **She could feel the tears.** Sie konnte die Tränen spüren. II
2. **What could be better?** Was könnte besser sein? II
council ['kaʊnsl] Ausschuss; Rat *(Stadtrat, Gemeinderat u.Ä.)* IV 1 (29)
count [kaʊnt] zählen I **count to 100** bis 100 zählen I
counter(top) ['kaʊntə], ['kaʊntətɒp] (Küchen)Theke; Arbeitsplatte IV 2 (47)
country ['kʌntri] Land *(Staat; Gegensatz zur Stadt)* II
countryside ['kʌntrisaɪd] Landschaft, ländliche Gegend II
county ['kaʊnti] Grafschaft *(in Großbritannien)* I
couple ['kʌpl]: **a couple** ein Paar; ein paar IV 3 (66)
courage ['kʌrɪdʒ] Mut, Courage IV 2 (47)
course [kɔːs] Kurs, Lehrgang I **attend a course** einen Kurs besuchen, an einem Kurs teilnehmen IV 4 (92)
cousin ['kʌzn] Cousin, Cousine I
cover ['kʌvə] behandeln, abdecken IV 1 (30)
cow [kaʊ] Kuh II
cowboy ['kaʊbɔɪ] Cowboy IV 4 (88)
crab [kræb] Krebs I
cranberry ['krænbəri] Preiselbeere IV 2 (52)
crash [kræʃ] abstürzen *(Flugzeug; Computer)* IV 1 (16) **crash into sth.** in/gegen etwas stürzen/krachen/fahren/knallen IV 1 (16)
► S. 215 (to) crash
crazy ['kreɪzi] verrückt IV 1 (24)
cream [kriːm] Sahne I
create [kri'eɪt] schaffen, erschaffen, kreieren IV 1 (29)
crib sheet ['krɪb ʃiːt] *(infml)* Spickzettel, Merkzettel II
cricket ['krɪkɪt] Cricket I
cross [krɒs] überqueren, kreuzen; sich kreuzen II
crossword ['krɒswɜːd] Kreuzworträtsel III
crowd [kraʊd] (Menschen-)Menge II
crowded ['kraʊdɪd] voller Menschen; überfüllt III
crown [kraʊn] Krone III
cruel ['kruːl] grausam IV 2 (52)
cruise [kruːz] Kreuzfahrt, Schiffsreise, Bootsfahrt III
cry [kraɪ] schreien; weinen II
°**cultural** ['kʌltʃərəl] kulturell
culture ['kʌltʃə] Kultur III
cup [kʌp] Tasse I **a cup of tea** eine Tasse Tee I
cupboard ['kʌbəd] Schrank I
curious ['kjʊəriəs] wissbegierig, neugierig III
currency ['kʌrənsi] Währung III
curry ['kʌri] Curry(gericht) III
cut [kʌt], **cut, cut** schneiden II **Cut!** Schnitt! *(beim Filmen)* II **be cut off from sth.** von etwas abgeschnitten/abgetrennt sein IV 3 (79)

cute [kjuːt] niedlich, süß IV 3 (73)
cycle ['saɪkl] Rad fahren, mit dem Rad fahren IV 3 (68)

D

dad [dæd] Papa, Vati I
dairy products *(pl)* ['deəri prɒdʌkts] Milchprodukte, Molkereiprodukte IV 2 (42)
°**dam** [dæm] Damm, Staudamm
dance [dɑːns]:
1. tanzen I
2. Tanz II **dance floor** Tanzfläche II
danger ['deɪndʒə] Gefahr III
dangerous ['deɪndʒərəs] gefährlich I
dark [dɑːk] dunkel I
darkness ['dɑːknəs] Dunkelheit, Finsternis III
date [deɪt]:
1. Datum I
2. Verabredung, Date IV 4 (90)
daughter ['dɔːtə] Tochter II
day [deɪ] Tag I **day of the week** Wochentag I °**in those days** damals
dead [ded] tot I
deal with sth. [diːl], **dealt, dealt** sich mit etwas beschäftigen; von etwas handeln IV 1 (30)
dealt [delt] *siehe* **deal**
death [deθ] Tod IV 1 (16)
°**decade** ['dekeɪd] Jahrzehnt
December [dɪ'sembə] Dezember I
decide [dɪ'saɪd] beschließen, sich entscheiden II
decision [dɪ'sɪʒn] Entscheidung III
deck [dek] Deck *(eines Schiffes)* I
dedicated ['dedɪkeɪtɪd] **be dedicated to** gewidmet sein (einer Sache/Person) IV 4 (102)
deep [diːp] tief II
deer, *pl* **deer** [dɪə] Reh, Hirsch II
°**defeat** [dɪ'fiːt] besiegen
defend sb./sth. (against sb./sth.) [dɪ'fend] jn./etwas verteidigen (gegen jn./etwas) II
definitely ['defɪnətli] sicher, bestimmt IV 3 (73)
degree [dɪ'griː] Grad IV 2 (40)
► S. 220 Temperatures
delete [dɪ'liːt] löschen; streichen III
°**delicatessen** [ˌdelɪkə'tesn] Delikatessen, Feinkostgeschäft
delicious [dɪ'lɪʃəs] köstlich, lecker II
demonstration [ˌdemən'streɪʃn] Demonstration, Vorführung II
dentist ['dentɪst] Zahnarzt/-ärztin II
depressing [dɪ'presɪŋ] deprimierend IV 3 (69)
describe sth. (to sb.) [dɪ'skraɪb] (jm.) etwas beschreiben II
desert ['dezət] Wüste IV 3 (64)
design and technology [dɪˌzaɪn‿ənd tek'nɒlədʒi] Design und Technik I
designer [dɪ'zaɪnə] Designer/in II
desk [desk] Schreibtisch I
dessert [dɪ'zɜːt] Nachtisch, Nachspeise I
°**destination** [ˌdestɪ'neɪʃn] Reiseziel
destroy [dɪ'strɔɪ] zerstören II
detail ['diːteɪl] Detail, Einzelheit III **go into detail** ins Detail gehen, auf Einzelheiten eingehen III
°**develop** [dɪ'veləp] entwickeln
°**device** [dɪ'vaɪs] Mittel; Gerät, Apparat
dial ['daɪəl] wählen *(Telefonnummer)* III
dialogue ['daɪəlɒg] Dialog II
diary ['daɪəri] Tagebuch; Kalender I
dictionary ['dɪkʃənri] alphabetisches Wörterverzeichnis, Wörterbuch I
did [dɪd] *siehe* **do**
die [daɪ] sterben II
difference (to) ['dɪfrəns] Unterschied (zu) III
different ['dɪfrənt] verschieden; anders I °**different from** anders als
difficult ['dɪfɪkəlt] schwierig, schwer II
°**digger** ['dɪgə] Gräber/in
digital ['dɪdʒɪtl] digital III
diner ['daɪnə] *(kleines, preiswertes)* Restaurant IV 2 (47)
dining room ['daɪnɪŋ ruːm] Esszimmer I
dinner ['dɪnə] Abendessen, Abendbrot I **have dinner** zu Abend essen I
direction [də'rekʃn] Richtung III **ask for directions** nach dem Weg fragen IV 3 (66) **give sb. directions (to)** jm. den Weg beschreiben (zu/nach) IV 3 (66)
director [də'rektə] Leiter/in; Dirigent/in; Regisseur/in II
dirty ['dɜːti] schmutzig II
disadvantage [ˌdɪsəd'vɑːntɪdʒ] Nachteil III °**at a disadvantage** im Nachteil
disappear [ˌdɪsə'pɪə] verschwinden II
disappointed (with) [ˌdɪsə'pɔɪntɪd] enttäuscht (von) IV 3 (78)
disco ['dɪskəʊ] Disko II
discover [dɪ'skʌvə] entdecken; herausfinden IV 3 (78)
discovery [dɪ'skʌvəri] Entdeckung IV 3 (78)
discrimination (against) [dɪˌskrɪmɪ'neɪʃn] Diskriminierung (von) IV 2 (47)
discussion [dɪ'skʌʃn] Diskussion III
°**disease** [dɪ'ziːz] (ansteckende) Krankheit
disgusting [dɪs'gʌstɪŋ] ekelhaft, widerlich IV 2 (41)
dish [dɪʃ] Gericht (Speise) IV 2 (41)
dishes *(pl)* ['dɪʃɪz]: **wash the dishes** das Geschirr abwaschen, spülen II
dishwasher ['dɪʃwɒʃə] Geschirrspüler III
dislikes [dɪs'laɪks]: **likes and dislikes** *(pl)* Vorlieben und Abneigungen I
distance ['dɪstəns] Ferne; Entfernung III
ditch [dɪtʃ] Graben III
dive in [daɪv‿'ɪn] hineinspringen III
divide (into) [dɪ'vaɪd] (sich) teilen (in), (sich) aufteilen (in) IV 4 (91)
divorced [dɪ'vɔːst] geschieden I
dizzy ['dɪzi] schwindlig III
do [duː], **did, done** machen, tun I **do sport** Sport treiben I **Don't go.** [dəʊnt] Geh nicht. I **he doesn't have time** er hat keine Zeit I
dock [dɒk] Hafen III
doctor ['dɒktə] Arzt/Ärztin II
dog [dɒg] Hund I
dollar ($) ['dɒlə] Dollar IV 2 (41)
done [dʌn] *siehe* do
door [dɔː] Tür I
doorbell ['dɔːbel] Türklingel, Türglocke II
double ['dʌbl] Doppel- I
down [daʊn] hinunter, herunter; nach unten I **down there** dort unten; nach dort unten II
downhill [ˌdaʊn'hɪl] bergab III
downstairs [ˌdaʊn'steəz] unten; nach unten *(im Haus)* I
downstream [ˌdaʊn'striːm] flussabwärts III
downtown ['daʊntaʊn]: **in downtown New Orleans** *(AE)* im Zentrum von New Orleans IV 2 (41)
draft [drɑːft] Entwurf II
drama ['drɑːmə] Schauspiel; darstellende Kunst II
dramatic [drə'mætɪk] dramatisch IV 3 (83)
drank [dræŋk] *siehe* **drink**
draw [drɔː], **drew, drawn** zeichnen II
drawing ['drɔːɪŋ] Zeichnung II
drawn [drɔːn] *siehe* **draw**

dream [dri:m] Traum I
dress [dres] Kleid I
dress up [ˌdres_'ʌp] sich verkleiden; sich schick anziehen II
drew [dru:] *siehe* **draw**
drink [drɪŋk]:
1. **(drank, drunk)** trinken I
2. Getränk I
drinking fountain ['faʊntən] *(bes. BE)* Trinkbrunnen IV 4 (90)
drive [draɪv]:
1. **drove, driven** *(mit dem Auto)* fahren II
2. Fahrt IV 4 (99)
driven ['drɪvn] *siehe* **drive**
driver ['draɪvə] Fahrer/in III **driver's license** *(AE)*; **driving licence** *(BE)* Führerschein, Fahrerlaubnis IV 4 (91)
drop sth. [drɒp]:
1. etwas fallen lassen II
°2. Fall, Rückgang
drought [draʊt] Dürre, Trockenheit IV 3 (79)
drove [drəʊv] *siehe* **drive**
drown [draʊn] ertrinken III
drum [drʌm] Trommel I **drums** *(pl)* Schlagzeug I **play the drums** Schlagzeug spielen I
drunk [drʌŋk] *siehe* **drink**
dry [draɪ] trocken III
°**dry up** [ˌdraɪ_'ʌp] vertrocknen
during ['djʊərɪŋ] während III
dust [dʌst] Staub IV 1 (16)
DVD [ˌdi:vi:'di:] DVD I

E

each [i:tʃ] jeder, jede, jedes (einzelne) II **each other** sich (gegenseitig), einander III
ear [ɪə] Ohr II
early ['ɜ:li] früh I
earn [ɜ:n] verdienen (Geld) III
earphones *(pl)* ['ɪəfəʊnz] Ohrhörer, Kopfhörer II
earring ['ɪərɪŋ] Ohrring IV 2 (46)
earth [ɜ:θ]: **(the) earth** *(oft auch:* **Earth**) (die) Erde *(der Planet)* II **on earth** auf der Erde II
east [i:st] Osten; nach Osten; östlich III
eastbound ['i:stbaʊnd] Richtung Osten III
easy ['i:zi] einfach, leicht II
eat [i:t], **ate, eaten** essen I
eaten ['i:tn] *siehe* **eat**
°**economic** [ˌi:kə'nɒmɪk] ökonomisch
°**economy** [ɪ'kɒnəmi] (Volks-)Wirtschaft
edge [edʒ] Rand, Kante III
edit ['edɪt] bearbeiten; schneiden *(Film, Video)* I
editor ['edɪtə] Redakteur/in; Herausgeber/in III
education [ˌedʒu'keɪʃn] (Schul-, Aus-)Bildung; Erziehung III
effect (on) [ɪ'fekt] (Aus-)Wirkung (auf) IV 3 (79)
e.g. [ˌi: 'dʒi:] z.B. (zum Beispiel) II
egg [eg] Ei II
eight [eɪt] acht I
either ['aɪðə], ['i:ðə]: **not ... either** auch nicht II
°**elect sb.** [ɪ'lekt] jn. wählen
elephant ['elɪfənt] Elefant I
elevator ['elɪveɪtə] *(bes. AE)* Fahrstuhl, Aufzug, Lift IV 1 (20)
eleven [ɪ'levn] elf I
else [els] sonst III **anything else?** sonst noch etwas? III **everybody else** alle anderen; sonst jeder III **someone else** jemand anders III **what else?** was (sonst) noch? III **who else?** wer (sonst) noch? III
email ['i:meɪl] E-Mail I
embarrass sb. [ɪm'bærəs] jn. in Verlegenheit bringen IV 2 (41)
embarrassed [ɪm'bærəst] verlegen; peinlich berührt IV 2 (41)
emergency [ɪ'mɜ:dʒənsi] Notfall, Not- IV 1 (16)
emotion [ɪ'məʊʃn] Gefühl, Emotion III
emotional [ɪ'məʊʃənl] emotional; gefühlsbetont IV 3 (79)
°**empire** ['empaɪə] Reich, Imperium
empty ['empti] leer III
encore ['ɒŋkɔ:] Zugabe II
end [end]:
1. Ende, Schluss I °**in the end** schließlich, am Ende, zum Schluss
2. enden; beenden II
ending ['endɪŋ] Ende, (Ab-)Schluss II
°**endless** ['endləs] endlos
enemy ['enəmi] Feind/in II
energy ['enədʒi] Energie, Kraft III
engineer [ˌendʒɪ'nɪə] Ingenieur/in III
English ['ɪŋglɪʃ] Englisch; englisch I **in English** auf Englisch I
enjoy [ɪn'dʒɔɪ] genießen III **I enjoyed myself.** Ich habe mich amüsiert. / Ich hatte Spaß. III
enough [ɪ'nʌf] genug I
enter ['entə] betreten, hineingehen in; eintreten III
entry ['entri]:
1. Eintrag, Eintragung *(im Tagebuch, Wörterbuch)* II
2. Eintritt, Zutritt III
environment [ɪn'vaɪrənmənt] Umwelt IV 3 (78)
episode ['epɪsəʊd] Episode IV 3 (73)
°**equal** ['i:kwəl] gleich(gestellt)
°**equality** [i'kwɒləti] Gleichheit
equipment [ɪ'kwɪpmənt] *(no pl)* Ausrüstung III
escape [ɪ'skeɪp]:
1. fliehen III
2. Flucht III
°**especially** [ɪ'speʃəli] besonders
etc. (et cetera) [et'setərə] usw. (und so weiter) II
EU [ˌi: 'ju:]: **the EU** die EU III
euro (€) ['jʊərəʊ] Euro III
Europe ['jʊərəp] Europa III
European Union [ˌjʊərəpi:ən 'ju:niən] Europäische Union III
evacuate [ɪ'vækjueɪt] evakuieren IV 3 (79)
even ['i:vn] sogar II **even if** selbst wenn II **not even** (noch) nicht einmal II **even though** auch wenn; obwohl IV 1 (29)
evening ['i:vnɪŋ] Abend I **in the evening** abends, am Abend I
event [ɪ'vent] Ereignis II
ever ['evə] jemals II **Have you ever been to ...?** Bist du jemals in ... gewesen? II **better than ever** besser als je zuvor II **for ever** (für) immer; ewig II
every day/colour/boat ['evri] jeder Tag / jede Farbe / jedes Boot I
everybody ['evribɒdi] jeder; alle I **everybody else** alle anderen; sonst jeder III
everyday ['evrideɪ] Alltags- I
everyone ['evriwʌn] jeder; alle I **everyone else** alle anderen; sonst jeder III
everything ['evriθɪŋ] alles II
everywhere ['evriweə] überall II
exact [ɪg'zækt] genau III
exam [ɪg'zæm] Prüfung IV 4 (104)
example [ɪg'zɑ:mpl] Beispiel II **for example** zum Beispiel II
excellent ['eksələnt] ausgezeichnet, hervorragend IV 4 (90)
except [ɪk'sept] außer, bis auf II
excerpt (from) ['eksɜ:pt] Auszug (aus) IV 3 (84)
exchange [ɪks'tʃeɪndʒ] Austausch III
excited [ɪk'saɪtɪd] aufgeregt, gespannt I

exciting [ɪk'saɪtɪŋ] aufregend, spannend I
exclamation mark [ˌeksklə'meɪʃn mɑːk] Ausrufezeichen II
Excuse me, … [ɪk'skjuːz miː] Entschuldigung, … / Entschuldigen Sie, … II
exercise ['eksəsaɪz] Aufgabe, Übung I
exercise book ['eksəsaɪz bʊk] Schulheft, Übungsheft I
exotic [ɪg'zɒtɪk] exotisch IV 3 (73)
°**expand** [ɪk'spænd] sich ausdehnen
°**expansion** [ɪk'spænʃn] Ausdehnung
expect sth. [ɪk'spekt] etwas erwarten III
expensive [ɪk'spensɪv] teuer II
experience [ɪk'spɪəriəns]:
1. *(no pl)* Erfahrung(en) III
2. erfahren, erleben IV 3 (83)
expert ['ekspɜːt] Experte/Expertin IV 3 (79)
explain sth. to sb. [ɪk'spleɪn] jm. etwas erklären, erläutern I
explore [ɪk'splɔː] erkunden, erforschen III
°**express sth.** [ɪk'spres] etwas ausdrücken
expression [ɪk'spreʃn]: **facial expression** Gesichtsausdruck, Mimik III
extra ['ekstrə] zusätzlich IV 4 (91)
extremely [ɪk'striːmli] äußerst, höchst IV 4 (102)
eye [aɪ] Auge I

F

face [feɪs] Gesicht I
facial expression [ˌfeɪʃl‿ɪk'spreʃn] Gesichtsausdruck, Mimik III
fact [fækt] Tatsache, Fakt III **in fact** eigentlich, in Wirklichkeit III
factory ['fæktri] Fabrik III
factual ['fæktʃʊəl] sachlich, Sach-; faktisch; den Tatsachen entsprechend III
Fahrenheit (F) ['færənhaɪt] Fahrenheit IV 2 (40)
► S. 220 Temperatures
fail [feɪl] nicht bestehen *(Test, Prüfung)*; durchfallen IV 4 (91)
faint [feɪnt]: **she feels faint** ihr ist schwindelig IV 3 (72)
fair [feə] fair, gerecht IV 2 (52)
fairly ['feəli] ziemlich IV 2 (52)
fall [fɔːl]:
1. **fell, fallen** fallen, stürzen; hinfallen I **fall asleep** einschlafen I
2. *(AE)* Herbst IV 1 (20)
fallen ['fɔːlən] *siehe* **fall 1.**
false [fɔːls] falsch III
fame [feɪm] Ruhm IV 3 (81)
family ['fæməli] Familie I **the Smith family** (die) Familie Smith I **family tree** (Familien-)Stammbaum I **a family of four** eine vierköpfige Familie III
°**famine** ['fæmɪn] Hungersnot
famous (for) ['feɪməs] berühmt (für, wegen) II
fan [fæn] Fan, Anhänger/in I
fancy sth. ['fænsi] Lust auf etwas/zu etwas haben IV 2 (42)
fantastic [fæn'tæstɪk] fantastisch II
°**fantasy** ['fæntəsi] Fantasie
far [fɑː] weit (entfernt) I
farm [fɑːm]:
1. Bauernhof, Farm I;
°2. bebauen
farmer ['fɑːmə] Bauer/Bäuerin, Landwirt/in I
farmhouse ['fɑːmhaʊs] Bauernhaus III
°**farming** ['fɑːmɪŋ] Landwirtschaft
fashion ['fæʃn] Mode II
°**fashionable** ['fæʃnəbl] modisch
fast [fɑːst] schnell I
fat [fæt] dick, fett II
father ['fɑːðə] Vater I
favourite *(AE:* **favorite***)* ['feɪvərɪt]: **my favourite photo** mein Lieblingsfoto I
February ['februəri] Februar I
fed [fed] *siehe* **feed**
°**federal** ['fedərəl] Bundes-
feed [fiːd], **fed, fed** füttern I **feeding time** Fütterungszeit I
feedback ['fiːdbæk] Rückmeldung, Feedback III
feel [fiːl], **felt, felt** fühlen; sich fühlen I **I don't feel well.** Mir geht's nicht gut. / Ich fühle mich nicht gut. II **I feel sick.** Mir ist schlecht. II
feeling ['fiːlɪŋ] Gefühl I
feet [fiːt] *plural of* **foot** II
fell [fel] *siehe* **fall**
felt [felt] *siehe* **feel**
felt pen [ˌfelt 'pen] Filzstift II
fence [fens] Zaun II
ferry ['feri] Fähre I
festival ['festɪvl] Fest, Festival II
few [fjuː]: **a few** ein paar, einige II **quite a few** ziemlich viele IV 3 (82)
field [fiːld] Feld, Acker, Weide II
fight [faɪt]:
1. **(fought, fought)** kämpfen I **fight sb.** jn. bekämpfen; gegen jn. kämpfen II
2. Kampf, Schlägerei III
figure ['fɪgə]:
1. Zahl, Ziffer III
2. Figur, Gestalt III
file [faɪl]: **background file** Hintergrundinformation(en) I
fill [fɪl] füllen III
film [fɪlm]:
1. filmen I
2. Film I
final ['faɪnl]:
1. letzte(r, s), End- III
2. Finale, Endspiel IV 4 (90)
finally ['faɪnəli] endlich, schließlich III
°**financial** [faɪ'nænʃl] finanziell
find [faɪnd], **found, found** finden I **Find someone who …** Finde jemanden, der … I **find sth. out** etwas herausfinden II
fine [faɪn] fein II **Fine, thanks.** Gut, danke. I
finger ['fɪŋgə] Finger II
finish ['fɪnɪʃ]:
1. enden I
2. **finish sth**. etwas beenden; mit etwas fertig werden/sein I
°3. vervollständigen; abschließen
finished ['fɪnɪʃt]: **We're finished.** Wir sind fertig. I
fire ['faɪə] Feuer II
firefighter ['faɪəfaɪtə] Feuerwehrmann/-frau IV 3 (79)
fireplace ['faɪəpleɪs] Kamin II
firework ['faɪəwɜːk] Feuerwerkskörper II **fireworks** *(pl)* Feuerwerk II
first [fɜːst] zuerst, als Erstes I **the first day** der erste Tag I **at first** zuerst, anfangs, am Anfang II
fish [fɪʃ], *pl* **fish** Fisch I
°**fishing** ['fɪʃɪŋ] Angeln, Fischen
fit sth. into/into sth. [fɪt] etwas in etwas einpassen III
five [faɪv] fünf I
flag [flæg] Fahne, Flagge II
flame [fleɪm] Flamme IV 3 (78)
flash [flæʃ]:
1. Lichtblitz II **a flash of lightning** ein Blitz II
2. **flash through sb.'s mind** jm. durch den Kopf schießen IV 2 (52)
flashlight ['flæʃlaɪt] *(AE)* Taschenlampe IV 1 (20)
flat [flæt]:
1. Wohnung I
2. **flach, eben** IV 4 (98)
flew [fluː] *siehe* **fly**
flock [flɒk]: **flock of sheep/goats** Schaf-/Ziegenherde III **flock of birds** Vogelschar III

flood [flʌd]:
1. überfluten, überschwemmen IV 2 (39)
2. Flut, Überschwemmung IV 2 (39)

floodlight ['flʌdlaɪt] Flutlicht(lampe) IV 4 (102)

floor [flɔː]:
1. Fußboden I
2. Geschoss, Etage, Stockwerk IV 1 (16)

flour ['flaʊə] Mehl IV 2 (42)
► S. 222 Food words

°**flourish** ['flʌrɪʃ] blühen

flow [fləʊ] fließen III

flower ['flaʊə] Blume; Blüte II

flown [fləʊn] *siehe* **fly**

flute [fluːt] Querflöte III

fly [flaɪ], **flew, flown** fliegen II

focus ['fəʊkəs] Mittelpunkt, Schwerpunkt III

folk music ['fəʊk ˌmjuːzɪk] Volksmusik III

follow ['fɒləʊ] folgen I **Follow me.** Folg(t) mir. I

food [fuːd] Essen; Lebensmittel; Futter I

foot [fʊt], *pl* **feet** [fiːt] Fuß II *(auch Längenmaß; ca. 30 cm)* IV 1 (17) **a 9,740-foot swimming pool** ein 9.740 Fuß langes Schwimmbad IV 1 (29)
► S. 219 a 9,740-foot swimming pool

football ['fʊtbɔːl] Fußball I

footprint ['fʊtprɪnt] Fußabdruck II

footstep ['fʊtstep] Schritt IV 3 (72)

for [fɔː, fə]:
1. für I **What's for lunch?** Was gibt es zum Mittagessen? I **What's for homework?** Was haben wir als Hausaufgabe auf? I **for ever** (für) immer, ewig II **for example** zum Beispiel II **for miles** meilenweit II
2. for hours/weeks/... seit Stunden/Wochen/... III

°**forbidden** [fə'bɪdn] verboten

force [fɔːs]: **force your way into sth.** sich in etwas eindrängen IV 1 (16) °**force sb. to do sth.** jn. zwingen, etwas zu tun; jn. dazu bringen, etwas zu tun

foreground ['fɔːgraʊnd] Vordergrund II

foreign ['fɒrən] fremd, ausländisch IV 3 (66)

forest ['fɒrɪst] Wald II

forget [fə'get], **forgot, forgotten** vergessen I

forgot [fə'gɒt] *siehe* **forget**

forgotten [fə'gɒtn] *siehe* **forget**

fork [fɔːk] Gabel II

form (of) [fɔːm]:
1. form (of) Form (von) I
2. bilden, formen III

fortunately ['fɔːtʃənətli] glücklicherweise IV 1 (31)

forward ['fɔːwəd]: **look forward to sth.** sich auf etwas freuen II

fought [fɔːt] *siehe* **fight**

found [faʊnd] *siehe* **find**

fountain ['faʊntən]: **water fountain** *(bes. AE)* Trinkbrunnen IV 4 (90)

four [fɔː] vier I

free [friː]:
1. frei I **free time** Freizeit, freie Zeit I **free-time activities** Freizeitaktivitäten I **be free** frei haben IV 3 (74)
2. kostenlos II
°**3. free sb.** jn. befreien

°**freedom** ['friːdəm] Freiheit

°**freeze frame** ['friːz freɪm] Standbild

French [frentʃ] Französisch I

frequent ['friːkwənt] häufig IV 3 (79)

fresh [freʃ] frisch II

Friday ['fraɪdeɪ, 'fraɪdi] Freitag I

friend ['frend] Freund/in I

friendly ['frendli] freundlich I

fries *(pl)* [fraɪz] *(American English)* Pommes frites II

frog [frɒg] Frosch I

from [frɒm, frəm] aus, von I **from ... to ...** von ... bis ... I

front [frʌnt] Vorderseite, vordere Seite II **at the front** vorn II **in front of** vor *(räumlich)* I **to the front** nach vorn II

frown [fraʊn] die Stirn runzeln II

frozen ['frəʊzn] tiefgekühlt IV 1 (28)
► S. 222 Food words

fruit [fruːt] Obst, Früchte; Frucht I **fruit salad** Obstsalat I

fry [fraɪ] braten *(in der Pfanne)* IV 2 (42)

frying pan ['fraɪɪŋ pæn] Bratpfanne IV 2 (42)

full (of) [fʊl] voll II **full moon** Vollmond II **full sentence** ganzer Satz II **full stop** Punkt *(Satzzeichen)* II

fun [fʌn] Spaß I **have fun** Spaß haben, sich amüsieren I **That sounds fun.** Das klingt nach Spaß. I **fun park** Vergnügungspark II **make fun of sb./sth.** sich über jn./etwas lustig machen III

funeral ['fjuːnərəl] Trauerfeier III

funny ['fʌni] witzig, komisch I

furniture *(no pl)* ['fɜːnɪtʃə] Möbel III

further ['fɜːðə] weiter II **furthest** am weitesten II

fuss [fʌs]: **make a fuss about sth.** großen Wirbel um etwas machen III

future ['fjuːtʃə] Zukunft; zukünftige(r, s) II

G

gallery ['gæləri] Galerie III

gallop ['gæləp] galoppieren III

game [geɪm] Spiel I

°**gap** [gæp] Lücke

garbage ['gɑːbɪdʒ] *(AE)* Müll, Abfall IV 1 (20)

garden ['gɑːdn] Garten I

gardening ['gɑːdnɪŋ] Gärtnern, Gartenarbeit I

garlic ['gɑːlɪk] Knoblauch IV 2 (42)
► S. 222 Food words

°**garment** ['gɑːmənt] Kleidungsstück

gate [geɪt] Tor, Pforte, Gatter II

gave [geɪv] *siehe* **give**

°**gay** [geɪ] schwul, lesbisch

gaze [geɪz] blicken, starren IV 4 (102)

gel [dʒel] Gel II

generation [ˌdʒenə'reɪʃn] Generation IV 2 (47)

gently ['dʒentli] behutsam, sanft III

geography [dʒi'ɒgrəfi] Geografie I

German ['dʒɜːmən] Deutsch; deutsch I **in German** auf Deutsch I

°**gesture** ['dʒestʃə] Geste, Handbewegung

get [get], **got, got:**
1. bekommen II **Did you get it?** *(infml)* Hast du es verstanden/kapiert/mitbekommen? II
2. get sth. (sich) etwas besorgen, (sich) etwas holen II
3. gelangen, (hin)kommen I **get in(to) a car/taxi** in ein Auto/Taxi einsteigen II **get on a bus/train/plane** in einen Bus/Zug/ein Flugzeug einsteigen II **get off a bus/plane/train** aus einem Bus/Flugzeug/Zug aussteigen II **get out of a car/taxi** aus einem Auto/Taxi aussteigen II
4. get angry/cold/... wütend/kalt/... werden I **get ready (for)** sich fertig machen (für), sich vorbereiten (auf) II
5. get on vorankommen, zurechtkommen II
6. get up aufstehen I

ghost [gəʊst] Geist, Gespenst I

giant ['dʒaɪənt]:
1. Riese III
2. riesig, Riesen- IV 4 (102)
giraffe [dʒə'rɑːf] Giraffe I
girl [gɜːl] Mädchen I
girlfriend ['gɜːlfrend] Freundin III
give [gɪv], **gave, given:**
1. geben I **give up** aufgeben III
2. give a talk (about) einen Vortrag / eine Rede halten (über) I
3. angeben IV 4 (106)
4. give sb. directions (to) jm. den Weg beschreiben (zu/nach) IV 3 (66)
given ['gɪvn] *siehe* **give**
°**giver** ['gɪvə] Geber/in, Spender/in
glad [glæd] froh, dankbar IV 1 (26)
glass [glɑːs] Glas II **a glass of milk** ein Glas Milch II
glasses *(pl)* ['glɑːsɪz] (eine) Brille II
°**global** ['gləʊbl] global
glove [glʌv] Handschuh II
glue [gluː] Klebstoff I
glue stick ['gluː stɪk] Klebestift I
glum [glʌm] niedergeschlagen IV 4 (103)
go [gəʊ], **went, gone:**
1. gehen; fahren I **How's it going?** Wie geht's? / Wie läuft's? IV 3 (74) **go by** vergehen, vorübergehen *(Zeit)* III **go by car/bus/...** mit dem Auto/Bus/... fahren I **go camping** zelten gehen II **go for a walk** spazieren gehen, einen Spaziergang machen I **go home** nach Hause gehen I **go in** hineingehen II **go on** weiterreden, fortfahren; weitermachen I **go on day trips** Tagesausflüge machen II **go on holiday** in Urlaub fahren II **My heart goes out to ...** Ich fühle mit ... / Mein Mitgefühl gilt ... IV 3 (79) **go sailing** segeln; segeln gehen I **go shopping** einkaufen gehen I **go together** zusammenpassen, zueinander passen III **go with sth.** zu etwas gehören, zu etwas passen I **Here we go.** Los geht's. / Jetzt geht's los. I
2. go red rot werden, erröten II
3. I'm going to sing a song. Ich werde ein Lied singen. / Ich habe vor ein Lied zu singen. II
4. Have a go. Versuch's mal. I
goal ['gəʊlkiːpə] Tor III
goalkeeper ['gəʊlkiːpə] Torwart, Torfrau III
goat [gəʊt] Ziege II
god, God [gɒd] Gott III
goddess ['gɒdes] Göttin III
go-kart ['gəʊ kɑːt] Gokart II
gold [gəʊld] Gold; golden, Gold- II
°**gold rush** ['gəʊldrʌʃ] Goldrausch
gone [gɒn] *siehe* **go**
good [gʊd]:
1. gut I **be good at kung fu** gut sein in Kung-Fu; gut Kung-Fu können I **Good luck!** Viel Glück! I **Good morning.** Guten Morgen. I
2. brav II
Goodbye. [,gʊd'baɪ] Auf Wiedersehen. I
good-looking [,gʊd'lʊkɪŋ] gutaussehend II
°**goods** *(pl)* [gʊdz] Waren, Güter
got [gɒt] *siehe* **get**
Have you got ...? Haben Sie ...? / Hast du ...? / Habt ihr ...? II
°**gourd** [gʊəd, gɔːd] Kalebasse, Kürbis
°**govern** ['gʌvən] regieren
government ['gʌvənmənt] Regierung III
grab [græb] schnappen, packen III
grade [greɪd]:
1. *(AE)* Jahrgangsstufe, Klasse IV 3 (73)
2. *(bes. AE)* (Schul-)Note, Zensur IV 4 (91)
°**gradually** ['grædʒuəli] allmählich
graffiti [grə'fiːti] Graffiti IV 4 (102)
gram [græm] Gramm II
grandfather ['grænfɑːðə] Großvater I
grandma ['grænmɑː] Oma I
grandmother ['grænmʌðə] Großmutter I
grandpa ['grænpɑː] Opa I
grandparents ['grænpeərənts] Großeltern II
granite ['grænɪt] Granit IV 4 (102)
graphics *(pl)* ['græfɪks] Grafiken IV 2 (53)
grass [grɑːs] Gras; Rasen II
grave [greɪv] Grab II
great [greɪt] großartig I
great-grandfather [,greɪt'grænfɑːðə] Urgroßvater IV 2 (46)
great-grandmother [,greɪt'grænmʌðə] Urgroßmutter IV 2 (46)
green [griːn] grün I
grew [gruː] *siehe* **grow**
grey [greɪ] grau I
groan [grəʊn]:
1. stöhnen II
2. Stöhnen II
ground [graʊnd]:
1. (Erd-)Boden II
2. ground sb. jm. Hausarrest/Ausgehverbot erteilen III
grounds *(pl)* [graʊndz] Gelände IV 4 (92)
group (of) [gruːp] Gruppe I
grow [grəʊ], **grew, grown:**
1. anbauen, anpflanzen I
2. wachsen II **grow up** erwachsen werden; aufwachsen III
grown [grəʊn] *siehe* **grow**
guard [gɑːd]:
1. bewachen III
2. Wachposten, Wache IV 3 (78)
guess [ges] raten, erraten I **And guess what!** Und stell dir/stellt euch vor! / Und weißt du/wisst ihr was? II **I guess ...** Ich nehme an, ... / Ich denke, ... IV 1 (17)
guest [gest] Gast III
guide [gaɪd] Fremdenführer/in; Reiseleiter/in II
guidebook ['gaɪdbʊk] Reiseführer III
guinea pig ['gɪni pɪg] Meerschweinchen I
guitar [gɪ'tɑː] Gitarre I **play the guitar** Gitarre spielen I
°**gumbo** ['gʌmbəʊ] Eintopfgericht
guy [gaɪz]:
1. Mann; Junge III
2. guys *(pl)* Leute III
gym [dʒɪm] Turnhalle I
gymnastics [dʒɪm'næstɪks] Gymnastik, Turnen I

H

habit ['hæbɪt] (An-)Gewohnheit IV 2 (41)
had [hæd] *siehe* **have**
hair [heə] Haar, Haare I
hairdresser ['heədresə] Friseur/in III
half [hɑːf]:
1. half past ten halb elf (10.30 / 22.30) I
°**2.** *(pl* **halves***)* [hɑːvz] Hälfte
°**3. half an hour** eine halbe Stunde
hamburger ['hæmbɜːgə] Hamburger II
hammer ['hæmə]:
1. Hammer III
2. hämmern III
hamster ['hæmstə] Hamster II
hand [hænd]:
1. Hand I
2. hand sth. in etwas abgeben; etwas einreichen II
hang [hæŋ], **hung, hung:**
1. hang sth. up etwas aufhängen II
2. hang out *(infml)* abhängen, rumhängen III

happen (to) ['hæpən] geschehen, passieren (mit) II
happiness ['hæpinəs] Glück IV 4 (104)
happy ['hæpi] glücklich, froh I
harbour ['hɑːbə] Hafen I
hard [hɑːd] schwer, schwierig; hart I
hardly ['hɑːdli] kaum IV 4 (102)
harmonica [hɑː'mɒnɪkə] Mundharmonika IV 2 (52)
has [hæz]: **he/she has** er/sie hat I
hat [hæt] Hut II
hate [heɪt] hassen III
have [hæv, həv], **had, had** haben I **have a cold** eine Erkältung haben, erkältet sein II **have a cough** Husten haben II **Have a go.** Versuch's mal. I **have a temperature** Fieber haben II **have a toothache/a headache/a sore throat** Zahnschmerzen/Kopfschmerzen/Halsschmerzen haben II **have breakfast** frühstücken I **have dinner** zu Abend essen I **have fun** Spaß haben, sich amüsieren I **have lunch** zu Mittag essen I **have to do** tun müssen I **Have you got ...?** Haben Sie ...?/Hast du ...?/Habt ihr ...? II **I'll have a tea/pizza/...** Ich nehme einen Tee/eine Pizza/... *(beim Essen, im Restaurant)* II
hay [heɪ] Heu II
he [hiː] er I
head [hed]:
1. Kopf II
2. **head for sth.** auf etwas zusteuern/zugehen/zufahren IV 2 (40)
headache ['hedeɪk]: **have a headache** Kopfschmerzen haben II
heading ['hedɪŋ] Überschrift III
head teacher [ˌhed 'tiːtʃə] Schulleiter/in III
headword ['hedwɜːd] Stichwort *(im Wörterbuch)* III
°**health** [helθ] Gesundheit
healthy ['helθi] gesund IV 2 (44)
hear [hɪə], **heard, heard** hören I
heard [hɜːd] *siehe* **hear**
heart [hɑːt] Herz II **My heart goes out to ...** Ich fühle mit .../Mein Mitgefühl gilt ... IV 3 (79)
heather ['heðə] Heide(kraut) III
heavy ['hevi]:
1. schwer *(von Gewicht)* II **heavy rain** starker Regen, heftiger Regen II
°2. *(infml)* ernst
°**hectare** ['hekteə] Hektar
held [held] *siehe* **hold**
helicopter ['helɪkɒptə] Hubschrauber, Helikopter IV 3 (79)
Hello. [hə'ləʊ] Hallo. / Guten Tag. I **Say hello to ... for me.** Grüß ... von mir. II
help [help]:
1. Hilfe I
2. helfen I **Help yourselves.** Greift zu! / Bedient euch! III
helpful ['helpfl] hilfreich IV 4 (98)
her [hɜː, hə]:
1. ihr, ihre I **her best friend** ihr bester Freund / ihre beste Freundin I
2. sie; ihr I
herb [hɜːb] (Gewürz-)Kraut IV 2 (41)
here [hɪə] hier; hierher I **Here we go.** Los geht's. / Jetzt geht's los. I **Here you are.** Bitte sehr. / Hier bitte. II **near here** (hier) in der Nähe I **over here** hier herüber II **up here** hier oben; nach hier oben II
hero ['hɪərəʊ], *pl* **heroes** Held/in III
hers [hɜːz] ihrer, ihre, ihrs II
herself [hɜː'self] sich III
hid [hɪd], **hidden** ['hɪdn] *siehe* **hide**
hide [haɪd]:
1. hid, hidden (sich) verstecken I:
°2. Haut, Fell
high [haɪ] hoch II
high school ['haɪ skuːl] *(USA)* Schule für 14-bis 18-Jährige IV 1 (17)
Highlands *(pl)* ['haɪləndz]: **the Highlands** das schottische Hochland III
highlight ['haɪlaɪt] hervorheben, markieren *(mit Textmarker)* II
hill [hɪl] Hügel I
him [hɪm] ihn; ihm I
himself [hɪm'self] sich III **he killed the alligator himself** er hat den Alligator selbst getötet IV 2 (46) **The director himself welcomed us.** Der Regisseur selbst hieß uns willkommen. IV 2 (46)
▶ S. 224 German "selbst"
hip [hɪp] Hüfte III
°**hippie** ['hɪpi] Hippie
his [hɪz]:
1. **his friend** sein Freund / seine Freundin I
2. seiner, seine, seins II
historic [hɪ'stɒrɪk] historisch *(geschichtlich bedeutsam)* IV 1 (16)
history ['hɪstri] Geschichte I
hit [hɪt], **hit, hit** schlagen; treffen (auf); *(Ball)* schlagen gegen II
hobby ['hɒbi] Hobby I
hold [həʊld], **held, held** halten I **Hold on a minute.** (*kurz auch:* **Hold on.)** Bleib / Bleiben Sie am Apparat. *(am Telefon)* II **hold onto sth.** sich an etwas festhalten III
hole [həʊl] Loch II
holiday ['hɒlədeɪ] Urlaub II **be on holiday/go on holiday** in Urlaub sein/in Urlaub fahren II **holidays** *(pl)* ['hɒlədeɪz] Ferien I
holidaymaker ['hɒlədeɪmeɪkə] Urlauber/in I
home [həʊm] Heim, Zuhause I **at home** daheim, zu Hause I **be home to sth.** Heimat sein für etwas; etwas beheimaten III **come/go home** nach Hause kommen/gehen I
°**homeland** ['həʊmlænd] Heimatland
°**homestead** ['həʊmsted] Heimstätte
hometown [ˌhəʊm'taʊn] Heimatstadt I
homework ['həʊmwɜːk] Hausaufgabe(n) I **Do your homework.** Mach deine Hausaufgaben. I **What's for homework?** Was haben wir als Hausaufgabe auf? I
honey ['hʌni] Honig; *(infml, als Anrede:)* Schatz, Schätzchen IV 2 (46)
honk [hɒŋk] hupen IV 4 (90)
honour ['ɒnə] Ehre II
hook [hʊk]:
1. Haken IV 2 (52)
2. an den Haken/an die Angel bekommen IV 2 (52)
hope [həʊp] hoffen I
horror ['hɒrə]: **in horror** entsetzt III
horse [hɔːs] Pferd I
hospital ['hɒspɪtl] Krankenhaus II
host family ['həʊst fæməli] Gastfamilie II
hostel ['hɒstl] Herberge, Wohnheim III
hostess ['həʊstəs] Gastgeberin *(in USA auch: Frau, die in einem Restaurant die Gäste in Empfang nimmt)* IV 3 (67)
hot [hɒt]:
1. heiß I
2. scharf (gewürzt) IV 2 (42)
hotel [həʊ'tel] Hotel II
hour ['aʊə] Stunde I **a one-hour concert** ein einstündiges Konzert III
▶ S. 219 a 9,740-foot swimming pool
house [haʊs] Haus I
how [haʊ] wie I **How are you?** Wie geht's? / Wie geht es dir/euch? I **How's it going?** Wie geht's? / Wie läuft's? IV 3 (74) **How do you know ...?** Woher weißt/kennst du ...? III **How do you like it?** Wie findest du es (sie/ihn)? / Wie gefällt es (sie/er) dir? I **How many?** Wie

viele? I **How much?** Wie viel? I **How much are ...?** Was kosten ...? I **How much is ?** Was kostet ...? I **How old are you?** Wie alt bist du? I **how to do** sth. wie man etwas macht / machen kann / machen soll III
however [haʊ'evə] aber; allerdings; jedoch IV 4 (102)
hug [hʌg]:
1. hug sb. jn. umarmen II
2. give sb. a hug jn. umarmen II
huge [hju:dʒ] riesig, sehr groß III
humour ['hju:mə] **sense of humour** (Sinn für) Humor III
hundred ['hʌndrəd]: **a hundred/one hundred** einhundert I
hung [hʌŋ] *siehe* **hang**
hungry ['hʌŋgri]: **be hungry** hungrig sein, Hunger haben II
hunt [hʌnt] jagen IV 2 (52)
°**hunter** ['hʌntə] Jäger/in
hurricane ['hʌrɪkən] Hurrikan, Orkan IV 2 (39)
hurry (up) ['hʌri] eilen; sich beeilen II
hurt [hɜ:t]:
1. (hurt, hurt) schmerzen, wehtun; verletzen II
2. verletzt II
hyphen ['haɪfən] Bindestrich II

I

I [aɪ] ich I **I'm ... (= I am ...)** Ich bin ... I **I'm from Plymouth.** Ich bin aus Plymouth. / Ich komme aus Plymouth. I
ice [aɪs] Eis II
ice cream [ˌaɪs 'kri:m] (Speise-)Eis I
ICT [ˌaɪ si: 'ti:] Informations- und Kommunikationstechnologie I
ID card [ˌaɪ 'di: kɑ:d] Personalausweis III
idea [aɪ'dɪə] Idee; Vorstellung I
°**identify sb./sth. (by sth.)** [aɪ'dentɪfaɪ] jn./etwas identifizieren (anhand von etwas)
°**identity** [aɪ'dentəti] Identität
if [ɪf]:
1. wenn, falls II **even if** selbst wenn II
2. ob IV 1 (29) **as if** als ob IV 1 (16)
ill [ɪl] krank II
illegal [ɪ'li:gl] illegal, ungesetzlich IV 3 (79)
image ['ɪmɪdʒ] Bild, Abbild; Vorstellung IV 1 (16)
imagine sth. [ɪ'mædʒɪn] sich etwas vorstellen I
immediately [ɪ'mi:diətli] sofort III
immigrant ['ɪmɪgrənt] Einwanderer/Einwanderin IV 1 (31)
°**immigration** [ˌɪmɪ'greɪʃn] Einwanderung
°**immunity** [ɪ'mju:nəti] Immunität
impatient [ɪm'peɪʃnt] ungeduldig IV 2 (52)
impolite [ˌɪmpə'laɪt] unhöflich III
important [ɪm'pɔ:tnt] wichtig I
impossible [ɪm'pɒsəbl] unmöglich II
impression [ɪm'preʃn] Eindruck III
impressive [ɪm'presɪv] beeindruckend IV 4 (88)
improve [ɪm'pru:v] verbessern; sich verbessern III
in [ɪn] in I **be in** zu Hause sein II **come in** hereinkommen I **in 1580** im Jahr 1580 I **in a loud/soft voice** mit lauter/sanfter Stimme II **in front of** vor *(räumlich)* I **in English** auf Englisch I **in the afternoon** nachmittags, am Nachmittag I **in the attic** auf dem Dachboden I **in the evening** abends, am Abend I **in the morning** morgens, vormittags, am Morgen/Vormittag I **in the photo/picture** auf dem Foto/Bild I
inch [ɪntʃ] Zoll (Längenmaß; 2,54 cm) IV 1 (17)
include [ɪn'klu:d] einschließen; beinhalten IV 1 (30)
including [ɪn'klu:dɪŋ] einschließlich; darunter (auch) III
°**increase** [ɪn'kri:s] (an)steigen, zunehmen
°**independent** [ˌɪndɪ'pendənt] unabhängig
Indian ['ɪndiən] Inder/in; indisch II
°**industry** ['ɪndəstri] Industrie
information (about/on) *(no pl)* [ˌɪnfə'meɪʃn] Information(en) (über) I **Information and Communications Technology** Informations und Kommunikationstechnologie I
ingredient [ɪn'gri:diənt] Zutat IV 2 (41)
°**inhabitant** [ɪn'hæbɪtənt] Bewohner/in
inside [ˌɪn'saɪd] (nach) drinnen I
instead [ɪn'sted] stattdessen II
instead of anstelle von, statt III
instrument ['ɪnstrəmənt] Instrument I
insult (to) ['ɪnsʌlt] Beleidigung (für) IV 4 (103)
insulted [ɪn'sʌltɪd] beleidigt IV 1 (24)
interaction [ˌɪntər'ækʃn] Interaktion, Umgang III
interest ['ɪntrəst]:
1. interest sb. jn. interessieren III
°**2.** Interesse **take interest in sth.** sich für etwas interessieren
interested ['ɪntrəstɪd]: **be interested (in)** interessiert sein (an), sich interessieren (für) II
interesting ['ɪntrəstɪŋ] interessant I
interrupt [ˌɪntə'rʌpt] unterbrechen II
interview sb. ['ɪntəvju:] jn. interviewen, jn. befragen I
into ['ɪntʊ]: **into the kitchen** in die Küche (hinein) I **be into sth.** *(infml)* etwas mögen, auf etwas stehen III
introduce [ˌɪntrə'dju:s]:
1. introduce sth./sb. (to sb.) etwas/jn. (jm.) vorstellen II
°**2.** einführen
introduction [ˌɪntrə'dʌkʃn] Einleitung, Einführung III
invade (a country) [ɪn'veɪd] (in ein Land) einmarschieren II
invent [ɪn'vent] erfinden III
investigate [ɪn'vestɪgeɪt] *(polizeilich)* untersuchen; ermitteln IV 3 (79)
invitation (to) [ˌɪnvɪ'teɪʃn] Einladung (zu, nach) II
invite sb. (to) [ɪn'vaɪt] jn. einladen (zu) II
°**inviting** [ɪn'vaɪtɪŋ] einladend, verlockend
irregular [ɪ'regjələ] unregelmäßig II
is [ɪz]: **Is it Monday?** Ist es Montag? I **Is that you?** Bist du's? / Bist du das? I **The book is ...** Das Buch kostet ... I
island ['aɪlənd] Insel II
isn't ['ɪznt]: **he/she/it isn't (= is not)** er/sie/es ist nicht ... I
°**issue** ['ɪʃu: 'ɪsju:] Thema, (Streit-)Frage, Angelegenheit
it [ɪt] er, sie, es I
it's ... (= it is) [ɪts] er/sie/es ist ... I
its name [ɪts] sein Name / ihr Name I
itself [ɪt'self] sich III **The room itself was OK, ...** Das Zimmer selbst war in Ordnung, ... IV 2 (46)
► S. 224 German "selbst"

J

jacket ['dʒækɪt] Jacke, Jackett II
jam [dʒæm] Marmelade I
January ['dʒænjuəri] Januar I
jealous (of) ['dʒeləs] neidisch (auf); eifersüchtig (auf) III
jeans *(pl)* [dʒi:nz] Jeans I
jelly ['dʒeli] *(AE)* Marmelade IV 1 (20)

jewellery *(BE)* **/ jewelry** *(AE) (no pl)* ['dʒuːəlri] Schmuck IV 2 (46)
jewels *(pl)* ['dʒuːəlz] Juwelen III
jigsaw ['dʒɪgsɔː] Puzzle II
job [dʒɒb]:
1. Job, (Arbeits-)Stelle I
2. Aufgabe II
join [dʒɔɪn]: **join a club** in einen Klub eintreten;sich einem Klub anschließen I **join in (sth.)** (bei etwas) mitmachen III
joke [dʒəʊk]:
1. Witz I
2. scherzen, Witze machen III
jolt [dʒəʊlt] Ruck, Stoß III
journey ['dʒɜːni] Reise, Fahrt II
judge [dʒʌdʒ]:
1. Richter/in III
°2. **judge sb. by ...** jn. nach ... beurteilen
judo ['dʒuːdəʊ] Judo I
juggle sth. ['dʒʌgl] mit etwas jonglieren II
juggler ['dʒʌglə] Jongleur/in II
juice [djuːs] Saft II
July [dʒu'laɪ] Juli I
jump [dʒʌmp]:
1. springen I **jump up** auf-, hochspringen II
2. Sprung I
June [dʒuːn] Juni I
just [dʒʌst]:
1. (einfach) nur, bloß I
2. gerade (eben), soeben II **just after ...** gleich nachdem ...; kurz nachdem ... II **just then** genau in dem Moment; gerade dann II
3. **just like ...** genau wie ... II **just as good/bad/...** genauso gut/schlecht/... III

K

kayak ['kaɪæk] Kajak III
keen [kiːn]: **be keen on doing sth.** wild darauf sein, etwas zu tun IV 1 (24) **be keen on sth.** wild auf etwas sein IV 1 (24)
keep [kiːp], **kept, kept:**
1. aufheben; behalten; aufbewahren III
2. **keep (on) doing sth.** etwas immer wieder / immer weiter tun; etwas ständig tun III
3. halten; erhalten III **keep to sth.** sich an etwas halten *(Plan, Zeitlimit)* IV 4 (90) **keep sth. up** etwas aufrechterhalten, etwas fortsetzen IV 4 (90) **keep sth. warm/alive** etwas warm halten; etwas am Leben (er)halten IV 4 (90)
▶ S. 232 (to) keep
ketchup ['ketʃəp] Ketchup III
key [kiː] Schlüssel II
keyword ['kiːwɜːd] Schlüsselwort I
kick [kɪk] treten III **free kick** Freistoß III **take a free kick** einen Freistoß ausführen III
kid [kɪd] *(infml)* Kind; Jugendliche(r) I
kill [kɪl] töten II
kilogram, kilo (kg) ['kiːləʊ,'kɪləgræm] Kilogramm, Kilo I **a 150-kilogram bear** ein 150 Kilogramm schwerer Bär IV 1 (29)
▶ S. 219 a 9,740-foot swimming pool
kilometre (km) ['kɪləmiːtə, kɪ'lɒmɪtə] Kilometer I **a ten-kilometre walk** eine Zehn-Kilometer-Wanderung IV 1 (29)
▶ S. 219 a 9,740-foot swimming pool
kind [kaɪnd] freundlich, nett II
kind [kaɪnd]: **a kind of ...** eine Art (von) ... I
kinda *(infml,* = **kind of**) ['kaɪndə] irgendwie IV 2 (40)
king [kɪŋ] König III
kit [kɪt] Ausrüstung I
kitchen ['kɪtʃɪn] Küche I
knee [niː] Knie II
°**kneel** [niːl] knien
knew [njuː] *siehe* **know**
knife [naɪf], *pl* **knives** [naɪvz] Messer II
knight [naɪt] Ritter II
knock [nɒk]: **knock (on sth.)** (an) klopfen (an etwas) III
know [nəʊ], **knew, known** wissen; kennen I **know about sth.** sich mit etwas auskennen; über etwas Bescheid wissen II **..., you know.** ..., weißt du. / ..., wissen Sie. I
known [nəʊn] *siehe* **know** **well-known** bekannt, wohlbekannt III
kung fu [ˌkʌŋ 'fuː] Kung Fu I

L

label ['leɪbl]:
1. beschriften; etikettieren II
2. Beschriftung; Schild, Etikett II
Ladies and gentlemen [ˌleɪdiz‿ən 'dʒentlmən] Meine Damen und Herren / Sehr geehrte Damen und Herren IV 1 (19)
lain [leɪn] *siehe* **lie**
lake [leɪk] (Binnen-)See II
lamb [læm] Lamm II
lamp [læmp] Lampe I
land [lænd]:
1. Land II
2. landen; an Land gehen II
°**landowner** ['lændəʊnə] Landbesitzer/in
°**landscape** ['lændskeɪp] Landschaft
language ['læŋgwɪdʒ] Sprache I
large [lɑːdʒ] groß II
last [lɑːst]:
1. **last night/Friday/weekend** letzte Nacht/letzten Freitag/letztes Wochenende I **the last exercise/biscuit** die letzte Übung/der letzte Keks I **last year's musical** das Musical vom letzten Jahr II
2. **at last** endlich, schließlich I
°3. dauern
late [leɪt] spät I **You're late.** Du bist spät dran. / Du bist zu spät. I **stay up late** lange aufbleiben II **the latest** das Neueste IV 3 (78)
°**lateness** ['leɪtnəs] Verspätung
later ['leɪtə] später I
laugh [lɑːf] lachen I
laughter ['lɑːftə] Gelächter III
law [lɔː] Gesetz III
lawn [lɔːn] Rasen IV 1 (29)
lay [leɪ] *siehe* **lie**
layout ['leɪaʊt] Layout, Gestaltung III
lead [liːd], **led, led** führen, leiten III
leader ['liːdə] Leiter/in III
leaf [liːf], *pl* **leaves** [liːvz] Blatt IV 1 (20)
lean [liːn] sich lehnen; sich beugen IV 1 (17)
learn [lɜːn] lernen I
least: at least [ət 'liːst] zumindest, wenigstens II
leather ['leðə] Leder IV 2 (52)
leave [liːv], **left, left:**
1. verlassen; zurücklassen I
2. (weg)gehen; abfahren II
3. lassen II **leave a message** eine Nachricht hinterlassen II **leave sth.** etwas übrig lassen II °**leave sth. out** etwas weglassen, auslassen
led [led] *siehe* **lead**
left [left]:
1. linke(r, s); (nach) links II **on the left** links; auf der linken Seite II **turn left** (nach) links abbiegen II
2. *siehe* **leave**
3. **be left** übrig sein III
leg [leg] Bein II
legal [liːgl] legal, gesetzlich IV 3 (79)
legend ['ledʒənd] Legende, Sage III
legendary ['ledʒəndri] legendär, berühmt IV 1 (25)

lemon [lemn] Zitrone IV 2 (42)
► S. 222 Food words
lend sb. sth., lent, lent [lend] jm. etwas leihen IV 4 (98)
lent [lent] *siehe* **lend**
lentil ['lentl] Linse (Gemüse) IV 2 (42)
► S. 222 Food words
less (than) [les] weniger (als) III
lesson ['lesn] (Unterrichts-)Stunde I **before lessons** vorm Unterricht I
let [let], **let, let** lassen I **Let me show you …** Lass mich dir … zeigen. I **Let's go.** Auf geht's. I **Let's go to Plymouth.** Lass(t) uns nach Plymouth gehen/fahren. I
letter ['letə]:
1. Brief I
2. Buchstabe I
letterbox ['letəbɒks] Briefkasten III
°**level** ['levl] Pegel
liberty ['lɪbəti] Freiheit IV 1 (12)
library ['laɪbrəri] Bibliothek, Bücherei I
licence ['laɪsəns]: **driver's license** *(AE)*, **driving licence** *(BE)* Führerschein, Fahrerlaubnis IV 4 (91)
lie [laɪ], **lay, lain** liegen II **lie down** sich hinlegen III
life [laɪf], *pl* **lives** [laɪvz] Leben I
°**lifestyle** ['laɪfstaɪl] Lebensstil
lift [lɪft]:
1. Mitfahrgelegenheit II **Can you give me a lift to the station?** Kannst du mich zum Bahnhof bringen/mitnehmen? II
2. Fahrstuhl, Aufzug III
light [laɪt]:
1. Licht I
2. **(lit, lit)** anzünden II **light sth. up** etwas erhellen *(aufleuchten lassen)* II
3. **light green/blue/…** hellgrün/blau/… IV 2 (43)
lightning *(no pl)* ['laɪtnɪŋ] Blitz(e) II **a flash of lightning** ein Blitz II
like [laɪk]:
1. mögen, gernhaben I **I like …** Ich mag … I **I don't like …** Ich mag … nicht. / Ich mag kein … I **I'd like …** Ich hätte gern … / Ich möchte … I **What would you like to eat?** Was möchtest du essen? I
2. **like boys** wie Jungen I **like that/like this** so *(auf diese Weise)* I **What's she like?** Wie ist sie? / Wie ist sie so? I
3. als ob III
°**likely** ['laɪkli]: **be likely to do** wahrscheinlich etwas tun (werden)
likes and dislikes *(pl)* [ˌlaɪks‿ən 'dɪslaɪks] Vorlieben und Abneigungen I
limit ['lɪmɪt]: **speed limit** Geschwindigkeitsbegrenzung, -beschränkung III
limited ['lɪmɪtɪd] beschränkt, begrenzt IV 2 (52)
limousine [ˌlɪmə'ziːn], ['lɪməziːn]] Luxuslimousine, Straßenkreuzer IV 3 (73)
line [laɪn]:
1. Zeile I
2. (U-Bahn-)Linie III
3. *(AE)* Schlange, Reihe *(wartender Menschen)* IV 1 (20) **stand/wait in line** *(AE)* Schlange stehen, sich anstellen IV 1 (20)
4. Leine, (Angel-)Schnur IV 2 (52)
link [lɪŋk]:
1. verbinden, verknüpfen III **be linked** verbunden sein III **linking word** Bindewort III
2. Link, Verknüpfung, Verbindung IV 3 (79)
lion ['laɪən] Löwe I
lip [lɪp] Lippe II
list [lɪst] Liste I
listen ['lɪsn] zuhören, horchen I **listen to sb.** jm. zuhören I **listen to sth.** sich etwas anhören I
lit [lɪt] *siehe* **light**
literature ['lɪtrətʃə] Literatur IV 4 (91)
litter bin ['lɪtə bɪn] Abfalleimer II
little ['lɪtl]:
1. klein I
2. **a little** ein bisschen, ein wenig, etwas IV 2 (52)
live [lɪv] leben; wohnen I
°**livelihood** ['laɪvlihʊd] Lebensunterhalt
lively ['laɪvli] lebendig, lebhaft IV 3 (69)
living room ['lɪvɪŋ ruːm] Wohnzimmer I
local ['ləʊkl] örtlich, Lokal-; am/vom Ort III
location [ləʊ'keɪʃn] Ort, Standort; Drehort IV 3 (80)
locker ['lɒkə] Schließfach, Spind IV 1 (17)
lonely ['ləʊnli] einsam II
long [lɒŋ] lang I **(the) longest …** der/die/das längste …; am längsten II **before long** schon bald III **not (…) any longer** nicht länger; nicht mehr IV 4 (103)
long shot ['lɒŋ ʃɒt] Totale, Totalaufnahme IV 4 (107)
look [lʊk]:
1. schauen I **look after sb.** auf jn. aufpassen; sich um jn. kümmern II **look around** sich umsehen, sich umdrehen; sich umschauen II **look at** anschauen, ansehen I **look closely** genau hinschauen II **look for sth.** etwas suchen I **look forward to sth.** sich auf etwas freuen II **look happy/angry** glücklich/wütend aussehen I **look into** sth. untersuchen, prüfen III **look out for sb./sth.** nach jm./etwas Ausschau halten IV 3 (67) **look sth. up** nachschlagen *(Wörter, Informationen)* III **look up** hochsehen, aufschauen II
2. **have a look (at sth.)** nachschauen; einen Blick auf etwas werfen III
lorry ['lɒri] Lastwagen, LKW III
lose [luːz], **lost, lost** verlieren II
lost [lɒst]:
1. *siehe* **lose**
2. **Get lost!** Verzieh dich! III
lot [lɒt]: **a lot of …/lots of …** viel …, viele … I **I like her a lot.** Ich mag sie sehr. II
loud [laʊd] laut I °**read sth. out loud** etwas vorlesen
loudspeaker [ˌlaʊd'spiːkə] Lautsprecher; Megaphon III
love [lʌv] lieben, sehr mögen I **I'd love to …** Ich würde sehr gern … II **Love, …** Alles Liebe, … / Liebe Grüße, … *(Briefschluss)* I
lovely ['lʌvli] schön, hübsch, herrlich II
°**low** [ləʊ] niedrig
luck [lʌk]: **Good luck!** Viel Glück! I
lucky ['lʌki]: **be lucky** Glück haben II
lunch [lʌntʃ] Mittagessen I **have lunch** zu Mittag essen I **What's for lunch?** Was gibt es zum Mittagessen? I
lunchtime ['lʌntʃtaɪm] Mittagszeit I **at lunchtime** mittags I

M

machine [mə'ʃiːn] Maschine, Gerät IV 3 (69)
mad [mæd] verrückt I
made [meɪd] *siehe* **make be made of sth.** aus etwas (gemacht) sein II
°**madhouse** ['mædhaʊs] Irrenhaus
magazine [ˌmægə'ziːn] Zeitschrift I
magic ['mædʒɪk] magisch, Zauber- II
magical ['mædʒɪkl] zauberhaft, wundervoll; magisch III
°**magnet** ['mægnət] Magnet
mail [meɪl] E-Mail II
main [meɪn] Haupt- II

°**major** ['meɪdʒə] bedeutende(r, s), wichtige(r, s)
make [meɪk], **made, made** machen; herstellen I **make friends** Freunde finden I **make sb. sth.** jn. zu etwas machen II **make sth. up** sich etwas ausdenken III **make sure that ...** sich vergewissern, dass ...; darauf achten, dass ...; dafür sorgen, dass ... II °**make the team** es ins Team schaffen **make tea/coffee/soup** Tee/Kaffee/ Suppe kochen IV 2 (42)
▶ S. 222 Food words
make-up ['meɪk_ʌp] Make-up II
malaria [mə'leəriə] Malaria III
mall [mɔ:l] (*kurz für:* **shopping mall**) (großes) Einkaufszentrum II
man [mæn], *pl* **men** [men] Mann I
manage sth. ['mænɪdʒ] etwas schaffen; etwas zustande bringen III
many ['meni] viele I **How many?** Wie viele? I
map [mæp] Landkarte; Stadtplan I **on the map** auf der Landkarte; auf dem Stadtplan I
March [mɑ:tʃ]:
1. März I
2. Marsch, Demonstration III
marcher [mɑ:tʃə] Demonstrant/in III
Mardi Gras [ˌmɑ:di 'grɑ:] Faschingsdienstag *(auch: die Karnevalsfeiern in New Orleans)* IV 2 (38)
marine [mə'ri:n] Meeres- IV 3 (66)
mark [mɑ:k]:
1. markieren II **mark sth. up** etwas markieren, kennzeichnen II
2. **stress mark** Betonungszeichen III
3. (Schul-)Note, Zensur IV 4 (91)
market ['mɑ:kɪt] Markt I
marry sb. ['mæri] jn. heiraten III **married (to)** verheiratet (mit) I
°**massacre** ['mæsəkə] Massaker
master ['mɑ:stə] Meister/in I
°**match sth. (to sth.)** [mætʃ] etwas (zu etwas) zuordnen
mate [meɪt] Kumpel, Freund III
material [mə'tɪəriəl] Material, Stoff III
maths [mæθs] Mathematik I
matter: What's the matter? ['mætə] Was ist denn? / Was ist los? I
may [meɪ] dürfen II **May I have a word with you?** Kann ich Sie kurz sprechen? II
May [meɪ] Mai I
maybe ['meɪbi] vielleicht I
mayor [meə] Bürgermeister/in II
me [mi:] mich; mir I **Me too.** Ich auch. I
meal [mi:l] Mahlzeit, Essen III **cook a meal** (ein) Essen kochen, eine Mahlzeit zubereiten IV 2 (42)
mean [mi:n], **meant, meant:**
1. bedeuten II
2. meinen, sagen wollen II
meaning ['mi:nɪŋ] Bedeutung II
meant [ment] *siehe* **mean**
meat [mi:t] Fleisch I
°**meatpacking** ['mi:tpækɪŋ] Fleischverarbeitung
media *(pl)* ['mi:diə] Medien III
°**mediate** ['mi:dieɪt] vermitteln *(auch sprachlich)*
mediation [ˌmi:di'eɪʃn] Sprachmittlung, Mediation I
medium shot ['mi:diəm ʃɒt] Halbtotale IV 4 (107)
meet [mi:t], **met, met:**
1. treffen; kennenlernen I **Meet your classmates.** Triff deine Mitschüler/innen. / Lerne deine Mitschüler/ innen kennen. I **Nice to meet you.** Freut mich, dich/euch/Sie kennenzulernen. I
2. sich treffen I
melt [melt] schmelzen II °**melting pot** Schmelztiegel
°**member** ['membə] Mitglied
memorial [mə'mɔ:riəl] Denkmal; Gedenk- III
memory ['meməri] Erinnerung II
men [men] *plural of* **man** I
mention ['menʃn] erwähnen IV 3 (83)
menu ['menju:] Speisekarte IV 2 (43)
message ['mesɪdʒ]:
1. Nachricht II
2. Botschaft, Aussage III
met [met] *siehe* **meet**
metal ['metl] Metall; Metall- IV 1 (12)
metre *(BE)* / **meter** *(AE)* ['mi:tə] Meter I
°**metropolis** [mə'trɒpəlɪs] Metropole
°**microprocessor** [ˌmaɪkrəʊ'prəʊsesə] Mikroprozessor
middle ['mɪdl] Mitte I
midnight ['mɪdnaɪt] Mitternacht I
might [maɪt]: **someone might like it** jemand könnte es mögen III
mile [maɪl] Meile II **for miles** meilenweit II **miles per hour** Meilen pro Stunde IV 3 (79)
milk [mɪlk] Milch I
million ['mɪljən] Million II
mind [maɪnd]:
1. Verstand, Sinn, Geist IV 1 (16) **read sb.'s mind** jemandes Gedanken lesen III **change your mind** es sich anders überlegen; seine Meinung ändern IV 4 (103)
2. **mind sth.** etwas dagegen haben III
°**mind map** ['maɪnd mæp] Mindmap
mine [maɪn]:
1. meiner, meine, meins II
2. Bergwerk III
3. Mine III
°**miner** ['maɪnə] Bergarbeiter/in
minute ['mɪnɪt] Minute I **Hold on a minute.** (*kurz auch:* **Hold on.**) Bleib / Bleiben Sie am Apparat. *(am Telefon)* II **wait a minute** Warte einen Moment. / Moment mal. I **a 30-minute ride** eine 30-minütige Fahrt IV 1 (29)
▶ S. 219 a 9,740-foot swimming pool
mirror ['mɪrə] Spiegel II
miss [mɪs]:
1. verpassen, verfehlen II
2. vermissen III
Miss [mɪs] Fräulein, junge Frau *(Anrede für eine Unbekannte)* IV 3 (72) **Miss Bell** Frau Bell *(übliche Anrede von Lehrerinnen)* I
missing ['mɪsɪŋ] verschollen, vermisst III **be missing** fehlen II
°**mission** ['mɪʃn] Mission
°**missionary** ['mɪʃənri] Missionar/in
mist [mɪst] (leichter) Nebel, Dunst(schleier) II
mistake [mɪ'steɪk] Fehler II
°**mix** [mɪks] Mischung
mobile (phone) [ˌməʊbaɪl 'fəʊn] Mobiltelefon, Handy I
model ['mɒdl]:
1. Model II
°2. Muster-
modern ['mɒdən] modern III
mom [mɑ:m] *(AE)* Mama, Mutti IV 1 (20)
moment ['məʊmənt] Moment I **at the moment** gerade, im Moment I
Monday ['mʌndeɪ, 'mʌndi] Montag I
money ['mʌni] Geld I
monkey ['mʌŋki] Affe I
monster ['mɒnstə] Monster I
month [mʌnθ] Monat I
monument (to) ['mɒnjumənt] Denkmal, Monument (für/zum Gedenken an) III
mood [mu:d] Laune, Stimmung IV 1 (24) **be in a good/bad mood** gute/ schlechte Laune haben IV 1 (24)
moon [mu:n] Mond I
moonlight ['mu:nlaɪt] Mondlicht III
moor [mɔ:], [mʊə] Hochmoor II
mop [mɒp]:
1. Wischmopp III
2. wischen *(Fußboden)* III

more [mɔː] mehr I **more beautiful (than)** schöner (als) II **more and more frequent / beautiful** immer häufiger / schöner IV 3 (79) **one more photo** noch ein Foto; ein weiteres Foto II **one more time** noch einmal, noch ein Mal II
morning ['mɔːnɪŋ] Morgen, Vormittag I **Good morning.** Guten Morgen. I **in the morning** morgens, vormittags, am Morgen/Vormittag I
most [məʊst]: **most people** die meisten Menschen II **most of them** die meisten von ihnen II **(the) most beautiful** der/die/das schönste ...; am schönsten II °**most every night** *(AE:* **= almost***)* fast jede Nacht
motel [məʊ'tel] Motel *(Hotel mit Zimmern und Garagen an einer Autostraße)* IV 3 (66)
mother ['mʌðə] Mutter I
motion ['məʊʃn]: **slow motion** Zeitlupe III
motor ['məʊtə] Motor III
°**motto** ['mɒtəʊ] Motto
mountain ['maʊntən] Berg II
mouth [maʊθ] Mund; Maul I
move [muːv]:
1. bewegen; sich bewegen I
2. **move (to)** umziehen (nach) II **move in** einziehen II **move into a house** in ein Haus einziehen II
2. Zug *(bei Brettspielen)* IV 1 (25)
movement ['muːvmənt] Bewegung III
movie ['muːvi] Film IV 2 (47)
movie theater ['muːvi θɪətə] *(AE)* Kino IV 2 (47)
mph (miles per hour) [ˌem piː‿'eɪtʃ] Meilen pro Stunde IV 3 (79)
MP3 player [ˌem piː 'θriː ˌpleɪə] MP3-Spieler I
Mr Brown ['mɪstə] Herr Brown I *(AE:* **Mr.***)* IV 3 (66)
Mrs Brown ['mɪsɪz] Frau Brown I *(AE:* **Mrs.***)* IV 3 (66)
Ms Brown [mɪz], [məz] Frau Brown *(AE:* **Ms.***)* IV 3 (78)
much [mʌtʃ] viel I **How much ...?** Wie viel ...? I **How much are / is ...?** Was kosten / kostet ...? I
mud [mʌd] Schlamm, Matsch II
muddy ['mʌdi] schlammig, matschig III
mug [mʌg] Becher II
mum [mʌm] Mama, Mutti I
murder ['mɜːdə] morden, ermorden IV 2 (47)
museum [mju'ziːəm] Museum I
mushroom ['mʌʃrʊm, 'mʌʃruːm] Pilz IV 2 (42)
► S. 222 Food words
music ['mjuːzɪk] Musik I
musical ['mjuːzɪkl]:
1. Musical II
2. **musical instrument** Musikinstrument III
musician [mju'zɪʃn] Musiker/in III
must [mʌst] müssen II **I mustn't do it** ['mʌsnt] ich darf es nicht tun II
my [maɪ] mein/e I **My birthday is in May.** Ich habe im Mai Geburtstag. I **My birthday is on 5th August.** Ich habe am 5. August Geburtstag. I **My name is ...** Ich heiße ... I
myself [maɪ'self] mich, mir III

N

name [neɪm]:
1. Name I **My name is ...** Ich heiße ... I **What's your name?** Wie heißt du? / Wie heißt ihr? I
2. (be)nennen III
narrator [nə'reɪtə] Erzähler/in; Sprecher/in IV 2 (55)
narrow ['nærəʊ]:
1. schmal, eng III
°2. **narrow sth. down** etwas eingrenzen
nation ['neɪʃn] Nation, Volk III
national ['næʃnəl] national, National- III
national anthem [ˌnæʃnəl‿'ænθəm] Nationalhymne IV 4 (102)
°**native** ['neɪtɪv] einheimisch
Native American [ˌneɪtɪv‿ə'merɪkən] amerikanischer Ureinwohner/amerikanische Ureinwohnerin IV 2 (41)
native speaker [ˌneɪtɪv 'spiːkə] Muttersprachler/in IV 2 (48)
natural ['natʃrəl] natürlich III
natural history Naturkunde III
nature *(no article)* ['neɪtʃə] Natur III
navy ['neɪvi] Marine I
near [nɪə] in der Nähe von, nahe (bei) I **near here** (hier) in der Nähe I
nearby ['nɪəbaɪ]: **a nearby town** eine nahegelegene Stadt II
nearly ['nɪəli] fast, beinahe III
necessary ['nesəsəri] notwendig, nötig IV 3 (69)
neck [nek] Hals II
need [niːd] brauchen, benötigen I **need to do sth.** etwas tun müssen II **we needn't do it** wir müssen es nicht tun, wir brauchen es nicht zu tun II
neighbour *(BE)* **/ neighbor** *(AE)* ['neɪbə] Nachbar/in II
neighbourhood *(BE)* **/ neighborhood** *(AE)* ['neɪbəhʊd] Viertel, Gegend, Umgebung; Nachbarschaft IV 1 (16)
neither ['naɪðə], ['niːðə]: **Me neither.** Ich auch nicht. III
nervous ['nɜːvəs] nervös, aufgeregt II
network ['netwɜːk] Netz, Netzwerk IV 1 (16)
neutral ['njuːtrəl] neutral IV 3 (79)
never ['nevə] nie, niemals I
new [njuː] neu I
news *(no pl)* [njuːz] Nachrichten; Neuigkeiten II
newspaper *(kurz auch:* **paper***)* ['njuːspeɪpə] Zeitung IV 1 (16)
New Year's Eve [ˌnjuː jɪəz‿'iːv] Silvester II
next [nekst]: **the next picture/question** das nächste Bild / die nächste Frage I **next year's musical** das Musical vom nächsten Jahr II
next to ['nekst tʊ] neben II
nice [naɪs] nett, schön I **Nice to meet you.** Freut mich, dich/euch/Sie kennenzulernen. I
night [naɪt] Nacht I **at night** nachts, in der Nacht I
nil [nɪl] null, Null III
nine [naɪn] neun I
no [nəʊ]:
1. nein I **No, that's wrong.** Nein, das ist falsch. / Nein, das stimmt nicht. I
2. kein, keine I **no sign of ...** keine Spur von ... II **it was no different** es war nicht anders III
°3. **no more** nicht (mehr) wieder
nobody ['nəʊbədi] niemand I
nod [nɒd] nicken II
noise [nɔɪz] Geräusch; Lärm III
noisy ['nɔɪzi] laut, lärmend, voller Lärm III
°**nomad** ['nəʊmæd] Nomade, Nomadin
°**non-** [nɒn] nicht-
noon [nuːn] Mittag IV 3 (72)
no one ['nəʊ wʌn] niemand I
normal ['nɔːməl] normal III
north [nɔːθ] Norden; nach Norden; nördlich III
northbound ['nɔːθbaʊnd] Richtung Norden III
north-east [ˌnɔːθ‿'iːs] Nordosten; nach Nordosten; nordöstlich III
northern ['nɔːðən] nördlich, Nord- III
north-west [ˌnɔːθ'west] Nordwesten; nach Nordwesten; nordwestlich III
nose [nəʊz] Nase II

not [nɒt] nicht I **not … any more** nicht mehr II **not … at all** überhaupt nicht(s), gar nicht(s); überhaupt kein/e, gar kein/e II **not … either** ['aɪðə], ['iːðə] auch nicht II **not even** (noch) nicht einmal II **not till three** erst um drei, nicht vor drei II **not … yet** noch nicht I
note [nəʊt]:
1. Notiz, Mitteilung II **make notes (on sth.)** (sich) Notizen machen (über/zu etwas) *(zur Vorbereitung)* II **take notes** (sich) Notizen machen *(beim Lesen oder Zuhören)* II
2. Note, Ton *(Musik)* III
°**3. note sth. down** etwas aufschreiben
nothing ['nʌθɪŋ] (gar) nichts I
notice ['nəʊtɪs] merken, bemerken IV 4 (91)
November [nəʊ'vembə] November I
now [naʊ] nun, jetzt I
nowhere ['nəʊweə] nirgendwo; nirgendwohin III **out of nowhere** (wie) aus dem Nichts III
number ['nʌmbə] Zahl, Nummer, Ziffer I
nurse [nɜːs] Krankenschwester, Krankenpfleger III
nut [nʌt] Nuss IV 2 (42)
▶ S. 222 Food words

O

o [əʊ] Null *(in Telefonnummern)* I
object ['ɒbdʒekt] Objekt II
ocean ['əʊʃn] Ozean I
o'clock: at 1 o'clock [ə'klɒk] um 1 Uhr / um 13 Uhr I
October [ɒk'təʊbə] Oktober I
octopus ['ɒktəpəs] Krake III
of [ɒv, əv] von I
of course [əv 'kɔːs] natürlich, selbstverständlich I
off [ɒf]: **be off** ausgeschaltet sein *(Radio, Licht usw.)* III **get/have a day off** einen Tag frei bekommen/haben III
°**offend sb.** [ə'fend] jn. verletzen, beleidigen
offensive [ə'fensɪv] beleidigend, Anstoß erregend IV 4 (102)
offer ['ɒfə] anbieten II
office ['ɒfɪs] Büro III
official [ə'fɪʃl]:
1. Beamte(r), Beamtin III
2. amtlich, Amts- III
often ['ɒfn, 'ɒftən] oft I
oh [əʊ]: **Oh, it's you.** Ach, du bist es. I **Oh dear!** Oje! II
oil [ɔɪl] Öl III
old [əʊld] alt I **How old are you?** Wie alt bist du? I
on [ɒn]:
1. auf I **on earth** auf der Erde II **on Monday** am Montag I **on Monday afternoon** am Montagnachmittag I **on the map** auf der Landkarte; auf dem Stadtplan I **on the phone** am Telefon II **on the plane** im Flugzeug II **on the radio** im Radio I **walk/run/sail/… on** weitergehen/-laufen/-segeln/… II
2. be on eingeschaltet sein, an sein *(Radio, Licht usw.)*; laufen, übertragen werden *(Programm, Sendung)* III
once [wʌns] einmal II **once a week/year** einmal pro Woche/Jahr II
one [wʌn] eins I **one by one** einer nach dem anderen II **one more photo** noch ein Foto; ein weiteres Foto II **one night/day** eines Nachts/Tages II **a white one** ein weißer/eine weiße/ein weißes II **this one** diese(r, s) II **two black ones** zwei schwarze II **Which one?** Welche(r, s)? II **the blue one** der/die/das blaue IV 2 (46) **the ones in Bourbon Street** die in Bourbon Street IV 2 (46) °**one-storey** *(BE)*, **one-story** *(AE)* [ˌwʌn'stɔːri] einstöckige(r, s)
▶ S. 223 one/ones
onion ['ʌnjən] Zwiebel IV 2 (42)
▶ S. 222 Food words
only ['əʊnli]:
1. nur, bloß I
2. erst II
3. the only … der/die/das einzige …; die einzigen… II
onto ['ɒntʊ] auf (… hinauf) I
open ['əʊpən]:
1. öffnen, aufmachen I; sich öffnen I
2. geöffnet, offen I
opinion [ə'pɪnjən] Meinung III **In my opinion …** Meiner Meinung nach … III
°**opportunity** [ˌɒpə'tjuːnəti] Gelegenheit, Möglichkeit, Chance
°**oppose sth.** [ə'pəʊz] etwas ablehnen, gegen etwas sein
opposite ['ɒpəzɪt]:
1. gegenüber (von) II
2. Gegenteil IV 3 (82)
or [ɔː] oder I
orange ['ɒrɪndʒ]:
1. orange I
2. Orange, Apfelsine I
order ['ɔːdə]:
1. bestellen II
2. Reihenfolge II
3. ordnen III
°**ordinary** ['ɔːdnri] gewöhnlich
organize ['ɔːgənaɪz] organisieren; ordnen III
originally [ə'rɪdʒənəli] ursprünglich III
other ['ʌðə] andere(r, s) I
otter ['ɒtə] Otter II
our ['aʊə] unser/e I
ours ['aʊəz] unserer, unsere, unseres II
ourselves [ɑː'selvz], [aʊə'selvz] uns III **We painted the room ourselves.** Wir haben das Zimmer selbst gestrichen. IV 2 (40)
▶ S. 224 German "selbst"
out ['aʊt]: **be out** nicht zu Hause sein, nicht da sein II **out and about** unterwegs II **out of …** aus … (heraus/hinaus) I °**out of work** arbeitslos
outdoor ['aʊtdɔː] Außen-, im Freien II
°**outlaw sth.** ['aʊtlɔː] etwas verbieten
outline ['aʊtlaɪn] Gliederung IV 3 (83)
outside [ˌaʊt'saɪd]:
1. draußen; nach draußen I
2. outside Rosie's Diner vor Rosie's Diner; außerhalb von Rosie's Diner II
°**outta** ['aʊtə] **(= out of)** aus (… heraus)
oval ['əʊvl] oval IV 2 (52)
oven ['ʌvn] Backofen IV 2 (42)
over ['əʊvə]:
1. über II **over here** hier herüber II **over there** da drüben, dort drüben II **over to …** hinüber zu/nach … II **run over (to)** hinüberrennen (zu/ nach) II
2. over 4 years über 4 Jahre; mehr als 4 Jahre I
3. be over vorbei sein, zu Ende sein I
own [əʊn]:
1. besitzen II
2. my own film/room/… mein eigener Film/mein eigenes Zimmer/… II **on my/your/their/… own** allein II
owner ['əʊnə] Besitzer/in III

P

p [piː] *Abkürzung für „pence", „penny"* I
packet ['pækɪt] Packung, Päckchen II
page [peɪdʒ] Seite I **What page are we on?** Auf welcher Seite sind wir? I

paid [peɪd] *siehe* **pay**
paint [peɪnt] (an)streichen; (an) malen II **painted** bemalt, angemalt II
painter ['peɪntə] Maler/in III
°**painting** ['peɪntɪŋ] Gemälde, Malerei
pair [peə]: **a pair (of)** ein Paar II
palace ['pæləs] Palast, Schloss III
palm tree ['pɑːm triː] Palme IV 2 (40)
pancake ['pænkeɪk] Pfannkuchen, Eierkuchen II
panic ['pænɪk] in Panik geraten III
pants *(pl)* [pænts] *(AE)* Hose IV 1 (20)
paper ['peɪpə]:
1. Zeitung I
2. Papier I **a piece of paper** ein Stück Papier III
parade [pə'reɪd] Parade, Umzug II
paragraph ['pærəgrɑːf] Absatz *(in einem Text)* II
paraphrase ['pærəfreɪz] umschreiben, anders ausdrücken IV 2 (43)
parents ['peərənts] Eltern II
park [pɑːk] Park I
parking lot ['pɑːkɪŋ lɒt] *(AE)* Parkplatz IV 3 (66)
parliament ['pɑːləmənt] Parlament III
parsley ['pɑːsli] Petersilie IV 2 (42)
► S. 222 Food words
part [pɑːt] Teil I **take part in sth.** an etwas teilnehmen II **part of speech** Wortart III
°**particularly** [pə'tɪkjələli] besonders; vor allem
partner ['pɑːtnə] Partner/in I
party ['pɑːti] Party I
pass [pɑːs]:
1. **pass sth./sb.** an etwas/jm. vorbeigehen/vorbeifahren II
2. **pass sth. (around)** etwas (herum) reichen II
3. bestehen *(Test, Prüfung)* IV 4 (91)
°4. **(late) pass** *etwa: ein Nachweis, dass der/die S sich bei der Schulverwaltung als verspätet gemeldet hat*
passport ['pɑːspɔːt] (Reise-)Pass III
password ['pɑːswɜːd] Passwort III
past [pɑːst]:
1. Vergangenheit II
2. vorbei (an), vorüber (an) II
half past ten halb elf (10:30 / 22:30) I **quarter past ten** Viertel nach zehn (10:15 / 22:15) I
°**pastor** ['pɑːstə] Pfarrer/in, Pastor/in
pat [pæt] tätscheln IV 3 (73)
path [pɑːθ] Pfad, Weg II
patriotism ['peɪtriətɪzəm] Patriotismus IV 4 (102)

°**patron saint** [ˌpeɪtrən'seɪnt] Schutzpatron/in
pattern ['pætn] Muster IV 2 (48)
pause [pɔːz] innehalten, pausieren; eine Pause einlegen II
pavement ['peɪvmənt] Gehweg, Bürgersteig III
paw [pɔː] Pfote, Tatze II
pay (for sth.) [peɪ], **paid, paid** (etwas) bezahlen II
PE [ˌpiː‿'iː] Sportunterricht, Turnen I
peace [piːs] Friede, Frieden III
°**keep the peace** die öffentliche Sicherheit wahren
pedestrian [pə'destrɪən] Fußgänger/in II
pedestrian zone [pə'destrɪən zəʊn] Fußgängerzone II
pen [pen] Kugelschreiber, Stift, Füller I
pence [pens] Pence *(plural of* **penny***)* I
pencil ['pensl] Bleistift I
pencil case ['pensl keɪs] Federmäppchen I
people ['piːpl] Leute, Menschen I
pepper ['pepə]:
1. Pfeffer I
2. Paprika(schote) IV 2 (42)
► S. 222 Food words
per [pə, pɜː] pro IV 3 (79) **miles per hour** Meilen pro Stunde IV 3 (79)
perfect ['pɜːfɪkt] perfekt, ideal I
perform [pə'fɔːm] auftreten *(Künstler/in)* III °**the performing arts** die darstellenden Künste
performance [pə'fɔːməns] Aufführung, Vorstellung, Auftritt IV 1 (29)
performer [pə'fɔːmə] Künstler/in, Performer/in III
period ['pɪəriəd] Unterrichtsstunde, Schulstunde IV 4 (91)
permission [pə'mɪʃn] Erlaubnis III **You need permission** Man benötigt eine Erlaubnis III
permit ['pɜːmɪt] Genehmigung, Erlaubnis(schein) IV 3 (79)
person ['pɜːsn] Person I
°**personality** [ˌpɜːsə'næləti] Persönlichkeit
pet [pet] Haustier I
phone [fəʊn]:
1. Telefon I
2. **phone sb.** jn. anrufen II **on the phone** am Telefon II **phone call** *(kurz auch:* **call**) Anruf; Telefongespräch II
photo ['fəʊtəʊ] Foto I **in the photo** auf dem Foto I **take photos** fotografieren, Fotos machen II

photograph ['fəʊtəgrɑːf] fotografieren III
phrase [freɪz]:
1. Ausdruck, (Rede-)Wendung I
°2. formulieren
Physical Education [ˌfɪzɪkl‿ˌedʒu'keɪʃn] Sportunterricht, Turnen I
piano [pi'ænəʊ] Klavier, Piano I
play the piano Klavier spielen I
pick [pɪk]:
1. **pick sb. up** jn. abholen II
2. **pick sth. up** etwas aufheben *(vom Boden)*, etwas hochheben II
picnic ['pɪknɪk] Picknick I
picture ['pɪktʃə] Bild I **in the picture** auf dem Bild I
pie [paɪ] Obstkuchen; Pastete IV 2 (52)
piece [piːs]: **a piece of paper** ein Stück Papier III
pig [pɪg] Schwein I
pigeon ['pɪdʒɪn] (Stadt-)Taube IV 1 (24)
pile [paɪl] Stapel, Haufen IV 2 (46)
pink [pɪŋk] pink, rosa I
pipe [paɪp] (Tabaks-, Dudelsack-) Pfeife III
°**pirate** ['paɪrət] Pirat/in
pitch [pɪtʃ] (Sport-)Platz, Spielfeld III
pity ['pɪti] **It was a pity that …** Es war schade, dass … III
pizza ['piːtsə] Pizza I
place [pleɪs] Ort, Platz, Stelle I **in second place** auf dem zweiten Platz; an zweiter Stelle III
°**plain** [pleɪn] Ebene
plan [plæn]:
1. Plan I
2. planen II
plane [pleɪn] Flugzeug II
planet ['plænɪt] Planet I
plant [plɑːnt]:
1. Pflanze II
2. pflanzen II
°**plantation** [plɑːn'teɪʃn] Plantage
plaster ['plɑːstə] (Heft-)Pflaster II
plastic ['plæstɪk] Plastik, Kunststoff II
plate [pleɪt] Teller I **a plate of …** ein Teller … I
platform ['plætfɔːm] Bahnsteig, Gleis III
play [pleɪ]:
1. spielen I **play the drums/ …** Schlagzeug/ … spielen I
2. abspielen *(CD, DVD)* I
3. Theaterstück I
player ['pleɪə] Spieler/in I
please [pliːz] bitte I
°**pledge of allegiance** [pledʒ], [ə'liːdʒəns] Treueschwur

pm: 4 pm [ˌpiː‿ˈem] 4 Uhr nachmittags / 16 Uhr I
pocket [ˈpɒkɪt] Tasche *(Mantel-, Hosentasche)* II
poem [ˈpəʊɪm] Gedicht II
point [pɔɪnt]:
1. Punkt I **point of view** Standpunkt III **from my point of view** von meinem Standpunkt aus gesehen; aus meiner Sicht III
2. **point to sth.** auf etwas zeigen, deuten I
3. **point sth. at sb.** etwas auf jn. richten I
4. **point sth. out (to sb.)** (jn.) auf etwas hinweisen III
5. **three point five** drei Komma fünf III
police *(pl)* [pəˈliːs] Polizei III
police officer [pəˈliːs‿ˌɒfɪsə] Polizist/in I
policeman [pəˈliːsmən] Polizist I
polite [pəˈlaɪt] höflich III
°**political** [pəˈlɪtɪkl] politisch
pony [ˈpəʊni] Pony II
pool [puːl] Schwimmbad, Schwimmbecken I
poor [pɔː, pʊə] arm I
popular (with) [ˈpɒpjələ] populär, beliebt (bei) III
°**populate** [ˈpɒpjuleɪt] besiedeln, bevölkern **thinly populated** dünn besiedelt
population [ˌpɒpjuˈleɪʃn] Bevölkerung, Einwohner(zahl) III
porch [pɔːtʃ] Veranda *(AE)*; Vorbau, Vordach *(BE)* IV 2 (46)
pork [pɔːk] Schweinefleisch IV 2 (42)
portion [ˈpɔːʃn] Portion III
position [pəˈzɪʃn] Platz, Position IV 4 (93)
possible [ˈpɒsəbl] möglich IV 3 (83)
post [pəʊst]:
1. posten, bekanntgeben III **Stay posted.** Bleib(t) auf dem Laufenden! IV 3 (78)
2. Posting (auf Blog), Blog-Eintrag III
postcard [ˈpəʊstkɑːd] Postkarte II
poster [ˈpəʊstə] Poster I
post office [ˈpəʊst‿ɒfɪs] Postamt II
pot [pɒt] Gefäß; Topf III **pot of tea** Kännchen Tee III
potato [pəˈteɪtəʊ], *pl* **potatoes** Kartoffel I **roast potatoes** *(pl) im Backofen in Fett gebackene Kartoffeln* I **sweet potato** Süßkartoffel IV 2 (52)
pound [paʊnd] Pfund *(Gewicht und britische Währung)* I **a three-pound ball** ein drei Pfund schwerer Ball IV 1 (29)
► S. 219 a 9,740-foot swimming pool
pour [pɔː] gießen II
°**poverty** [ˈpɒvəti] Armut
powder [ˈpaʊdə] Pulver IV 2 (42)
power [ˈpaʊə] Energie, Strom; Kraft, Stärke; Macht IV 3 (79)
°**powerful** [ˈpaʊəfl] mächtig
practical [ˈpræktɪkl] praktisch IV 1 (29)
practice [ˈpræktɪs] Übung I **it takes practice** [ˈpræktɪs] es erfordert Übung IV 4 (90)
practise *(AE:* **practice***)* [ˈpræktɪs] üben, trainieren I
prairie [ˈpreəri] Prärie, Grasland IV 4 (88)
prediction [prɪˈdɪkʃn] Vorhersage, Voraussage IV 3 (68)
prefer sth. (to sth.) [prɪˈfɜː] etwas (einer anderen Sache) vorziehen; etwas lieber tun (als etwas) III
prefix [ˈpriːfɪks] Präfix, Vorsilbe IV 3 (82)
prejudice (against) [ˈpredʒudɪs] Vorurteil (gegen), Voreingenommenheit (gegenüber) IV 2 (47)
prepare sth. [prɪˈpeə] etwas vorbereiten I; etwas zubereiten IV 2 (52)
present:
1. [ˈpreznt] Geschenk I
2. [ˈpreznt] Gegenwart II
3. **present sth. (to sb.)** [prɪˈzent] (jm.) etwas präsentieren, vorstellen II
presentation [ˌpreznˈteɪʃn] Präsentation, Vorstellung II
°**present-day** [ˌpreznt ˈdeɪ] heutige(r, s)
president [ˈprezɪdənt] Präsident/In III
press [pres] drücken III
pretend [prɪˈtend] so tun, als ob III
pretty [ˈprɪti] hübsch II
price [praɪs] (Kauf-)Preis I
pride (in sth.) [praɪd] Stolz (auf etwas) IV 4 (102)
principal [ˈprɪnsəpl] Schulleiter/in IV 4 (92)
°**print** [prɪnt]:
1. Druck; Print-
2. drucken
prison [ˈprɪzn] Gefängnis I
°**private** [ˈpraɪvət] privat
prize [praɪz] Preis, Gewinn II
probably [ˈprɒbəbli] wahrscheinlich II
problem [ˈprɒbləm] Problem II
process [ˈprəʊses] Prozess, Vorgang IV 3 (73)
°**produce** [prəˈdjuːs] produzieren, erzeugen, herstellen
profile [ˈprəʊfaɪl] Profil; Beschreibung, Porträt I
programme [ˈprəʊgræm] Programm *(auch im Theater usw.)*; (Radio-, Fernseh-)Sendung I **What programmes ...?** Welche (Art von) Sendungen ...? I
project [ˈprɒdʒekt] Projekt II
promise [ˈprɒmɪs]:
1. versprechen II
°2. Versprechen
pronounce [prəˈnaʊns] aussprechen III
pronunciation [prəˌnʌnsiˈeɪʃn] Aussprache I
property [ˈprɒpəti] Eigentum IV 4 (92)
protect sb./sth. (from sb./sth.) [prəˈtekt] jn./etwas (be)schützen (vor jm./etwas) III
protest [ˈprəʊtest] Protest IV 1 (29)
protest [prəˈtest] *(AE auch:* [ˈprəʊtest]*)* protestieren IV 1 (29)
protester [prəˈtestə], *(AE:* ˈprəʊtestə*)* Demonstrant/in IV 2 (47)
proud (of) [praʊd] stolz (auf) III
pub [pʌb] Kneipe, Lokal III
public [ˈpʌblɪk] öffentliche(r, s) III **the public** die Öffentlichkeit III **Don't do that in public.** Tu das nicht in der Öffentlichkeit. III
publish [ˈpʌblɪʃ] veröffentlichen III
pull [pʊl] ziehen II **pull sth. out** etwas herausziehen II
pullover [ˈpʊləʊvə] Pullover II
pumpkin [ˈpʌmpkɪn] Kürbis IV 2 (52)
punctuation [ˌpʌŋktʃuˈeɪʃn] Zeichensetzung II
punishment [ˈpʌnɪʃmənt] Bestrafung, Strafe III
puppet [ˈpʌpɪt] Marionette, Handpuppe II
purple [ˈpɜːpl] violett, lila I
°**purpose** [ˈpɜːpəs] Zweck
purse [pɜːs] Portemonnaie, Geldbörse III
push [pʊʃ] drücken, schieben, stoßen I
put [pʊt], **put, put** legen, stellen, *(etwas wohin)* tun I **put sth. on** etwas anziehen *(Kleidung)*; etwas aufsetzen *(Hut, Helm)* II °**Put up your hand.** Melde dich. / Heb deine Hand.

Q

qualify ['kwɒlɪfaɪ] sich qualifizieren IV 4 (90)
quarter ['kwɔːtə] Viertel (*auch:* Stadtviertel) IV 2 (38) **quarter past ten** Viertel nach zehn (10.15 / 22.15) I **quarter to eleven** Viertel vor elf (10.45 / 22.45) I
queen [kwiːn] Königin II
question ['kwestʃən] Frage I
question mark ['kwestʃən mɑːk] Fragezeichen II
queue [kjuː]:
1. Schlange stehen, sich anstellen II
2. Schlange, Reihe *(wartender Menschen)* III
quick [kwɪk] schnell II
quiet ['kwaɪət] ruhig, still, leise I
quite [kwaɪt] ziemlich; völlig, ganz III **quite a few** ziemlich viele IV 3 (82)
quiz [kwɪz] Quiz, Ratespiel I
quotation [kwəʊ'teɪʃn] Zitat IV 3 (78)
quote [kwəʊt] *(infml)* Zitat IV 3 (78)

R

rabbit ['ræbɪt] Kaninchen I
race [reɪs]:
1. Rennen II
2. rasen III
radio ['reɪdiəʊ] Radio I **on the radio** im Radio I
railroad *(AE)* ['reɪlrəʊd] Eisenbahn IV 1 (25)
railway *(BE)* ['reɪlweɪ] Eisenbahn IV 1 (28)
rain [reɪn]:
1. Regen II
2. regnen II
rainbow ['reɪnbəʊ] Regenbogen III
raincoat ['reɪnkəʊt] Regenmantel II
rainforest ['reɪnfɒrɪst] Regenwald II
rainy ['reɪni] regnerisch II
raise money (for sth.) [reɪz] Geld sammeln (für etwas) *(für wohltätige Zwecke)* II
rally ['ræli] Rallye II
ran [ræn] *siehe* **run**
rang [ræŋ] *siehe* **ring**
rat [ræt] Ratte I
raven ['reɪvn] Rabe III
reach [riːtʃ] erreichen III **reach over** die Hand ausstrecken III
react (to) [ri'ækt] reagieren (auf) III
reaction (to) [ri'ækʃn] Reaktion (auf) IV 3 (78)
read [riːd], **read, read** lesen I **read aloud** laut (vor)lesen II
ready ['redi] bereit, fertig I **get ready (for)** sich fertig machen (für); sich vorbereiten (auf) II
real ['riːəl] echt, wirklich III
really ['rɪəli] echt, wirklich I
reason ['riːzn] Grund, Begründung II **for this reason** aus diesem Grund IV 4 (92)
°**recently** ['riːsntli] vor Kurzem, neulich; in letzter Zeit
recipe ['resəpi] (Koch-)Rezept II
recognize ['rekəgnaɪz] erkennen III 4 (103)
recommend sth. (to sb.) [ˌrekə'mend] (jm.) etwas empfehlen IV 2 (41)
°**record** [rɪ'kɔːd] dokumentieren
recorder [rɪ'kɔːdə] Blockflöte II
red [red] rot I
°**reduce** [rɪ'djuːs] reduzieren, verringern
°**refer to sth.** [rɪ'fɜː] auf etwas verweisen, etwas erwähnen; sich auf etwas beziehen
referee [ˌrefə'riː] Schiedsrichter/in III
region ['riːdʒən] Region IV 4 (88)
regional ['riːdʒənl] regional III
register ['redʒɪstə] Klassenbuch; Register, Verzeichnis IV 4 (91)
regular ['regjələ] regelmäßig II
reins *(pl)* [reɪnz] Zügel III
°**relations** *(pl)* [rɪ'leɪʃnz] Beziehungen
relationship [rɪ'leɪʃnʃɪp] Beziehung, Verhältnis IV 4 (107)
relax [rɪ'læks] sich entspannen, sich ausruhen III
relaxed [rɪ'lækst] entspannt IV 3 (69)
relevant (to sth.) ['reləvənt] relevant, wichtig (für etwas) IV 2 (43)
religion [rɪ'lɪdʒən] Religion I
remember sth. [rɪ'membə]:
1. sich an etwas erinnern I
2. an etwas denken; sich etwas merken III
remind sb. [rɪ'maɪnd] jn. erinnern IV 2 (38)
°**remote** [rɪ'məʊt] abgelegen, abgeschieden
remote control [rɪˌməʊt kən'trəʊl], *(kurz auch:* **remote***)* Fernbedienung III
°**renewal** [rɪ'njuːəl] Erneuerung
repeat [rɪ'piːt] wiederholen II
reply (to) [rɪ'plaɪ] antworten (auf); erwidern, entgegnen III
report [rɪ'pɔːt]:
1. Bericht, Reportage II
2. berichten IV 1 (30)
republic [rɪ'pʌblɪk] Republik III
rescue ['reskjuː] retten II
research *(no pl)* ['riːsɜːtʃ] Recherche, Forschung(en) III
reservation *(kurz auch:* **rez***)* [ˌrezə'veɪʃn] Reservat, Reservation IV 4 (88)
reserve [rɪ'zɜːv]:
1. reservieren, buchen III
2. Schutzgebiet, Reservat IV 3 (66)
resident ['rezɪdənt] Bewohner/in, Anwohner/in IV 3 (79)
°**response** [rɪ'spɒns]: **in response to** als Antwort auf
responsible [rɪ'spɒnsəbl] verantwortlich II
rest [rest]:
1. Rest III
2. ruhen, sich ausruhen III
restaurant ['restrɒnt] Restaurant III
restroom *(AE)* ['restruːm] *(öffentliche)* Toilette, WC IV 1 (20)
result [rɪ'zʌlt] Ergebnis, Resultat III **as a result** folglich III
reveal [rɪ'viːl] offenbaren, preisgeben, verraten IV 3 (73)
revise [rɪ'vaɪz] überarbeiten; *(Lernstoff)* wiederholen III
revision [rɪ'vɪʒn] Wiederholung *(des Lernstoffs)* II
°**revolutionary** [ˌrevə'luːʃənəri] revolutionär
°**rewrite** [ˌriː'raɪt] neu schreiben, umarbeiten
rhyme [raɪm] Reim; Vers I
rhythm ['rɪðəm] Rhythmus III
rice [raɪs] Reis IV 2 (42)
► S. 222 Food words
rich [rɪtʃ] reich I
ridden ['rɪdn] *siehe* **ride**
ride [raɪd], **rode, ridden:**
1. reiten II
2. ride a bike Fahrrad fahren I
ride [raɪd] Fahrt *(auch Karussellfahrt u.Ä.)* II
riding ['raɪdɪŋ] Reiten I
right [raɪt]:
1. richtig I **sb. is right** jemand hat Recht I **Yes, that's right.** Ja, das ist richtig. / Ja, das stimmt. I **…, right?** …, nicht wahr? II
2. rechte(r, s); (nach) rechts II **on the right** rechts; auf der rechten Seite II **turn right** (nach) rechts abbiegen II
3. right after you gleich nach dir II **right behind you** direkt hinter dir, genau hinter dir II **right now** jetzt gerade II
°**rights** *(pl)* [raɪts] Rechte

ring [rɪŋ]:
1. **(rang, rung)** klingeln, läuten II
2. Ring II

rise up [ˌraɪz‿ˈʌp] aufragen, emporragen *(Berge, Säulen, Türme, …)* III
risen [ˈrɪzn] *siehe* **rise**
river [ˈrɪvə] Fluss I
road [rəʊd] Straße I **at 8 Beach Road** in der Beach Road (Nummer) 8 I **in Beach Road** in der Beach Road I
roar [rɔː]:
1. brüllen III
2. tosen, dröhnen IV 1 (17)

roast [rəʊst] braten *(im Backofen)* IV 2 (42) **roast beef** Rinderbraten I **roast potatoes** *(pl)* *im Backofen in Fett gebackene Kartoffeln* I
rock [rɒk]:
1. Fels, Felsen I
2. **rock (music)** Rock(musik) II

rocky [ˈrɒki] felsig, steinig II
rode [rəʊd] *siehe* **ride**
rodeo [ˈrəʊdiəʊ] Rodeo IV 4 (90)
role [rəʊl] Rolle *(in einem Theaterstück, Film)* II
roll [rəʊl] rollen II
°**roll-call** [ˈrəʊlkɔːl] Namensaufruf (zur Anwesenheitskontrolle)
roller coaster [ˈrəʊlə kəʊstə] Achterbahn IV 1 (29)
romantic [rəʊˈmæntɪk] romantisch; Liebes- III
roof [ruːf] Dach II
room [ruːm] Zimmer, Raum I
°**root** [ruːt] Wurzel
rope [rəʊp] Seil III
rose [rəʊz]:
1. Rose IV 1 (17)
2. *siehe* **rise**

round [raʊnd]:
1. **round the world** um die Welt II
2. **round sth. off (with sth.)** etwas (mit etwas) abschließen, vervollständigen IV 3 (83)

roundabout [ˈraʊndəbaʊt] Kreisverkehr II
route [ruːt] Strecke, Route III
routine [ruːˈtiːn] Routine II
°**row** [rəʊ] Reihe
royal [ˈrɔɪəl] königlich III
rubber [ˈrʌbə] Radiergummi I
rubbish [ˈrʌbɪʃ] Müll, Abfall II **rubbish bin** Mülltonne, Abfalleimer IV 3 (69)
rucksack [ˈrʌksæk] Rucksack I
rude [ruːd] unhöflich; unverschämt III
ruin [ˈruːɪn] Ruine II
rule [ruːl] Regel, Vorschrift II
ruler [ˈruːlə] Lineal I
run [rʌn]:
1. **(ran, run)** rennen, laufen I **run after sb.** hinter jm. herrennen I **run for your life** um sein Leben rennen IV 1 (16) °**run out** ausgehen
2. Punkt *(Kricket)*

rung [rʌŋ] *siehe* **ring**
°**rural** [ˈrʊərəl] ländlich, Land-

S

sacred [ˈseɪkrɪd] heilig IV 4 (102)
°**sacrifice** [ˈsækrɪfaɪs] Opfer(ung) ° **make a sacrifice** opfern
sad [sæd] traurig I
saddle [ˈsædl] Sattel III
sadness [ˈsædnəs] Traurigkeit IV 4 (104)
safe [seɪf] sicher, in Sicherheit III
said [sed] *siehe* **say**
sailing [ˈseɪlɪŋ]: **go sailing** segeln; segeln gehen I **sailing boat** Segelboot I
sailor [ˈseɪlə] Seemann, Matrose, Matrosin III
°**saint** [seɪnt] Heilige(r)
salad [ˈsæləd] Salat *(als Gericht oder Beilage)* I **fruit salad** Obstsalat I
salt [sɔːlt] Salz IV 2 (42)
► S. 222 Food words
samba [ˈsæmbə] Samba I
same [seɪm]: **the same as …** der-/die-/dasselbe wie … I
sand [sænd] Sand I
sandwich [ˈsænwɪtʃ, ˈsænwɪdʒ] Sandwich, (zusammengeklapptes) belegtes Brot I
sandy [ˈsændi] sandig, Sand- III
sang [sæŋ]
sank [sæŋk] *siehe* **sink**
sat [sæt] *siehe* **sit**
Saturday [ˈsætədeɪ, ˈsætədi] Samstag, Sonnabend I
sauce [sɔːs] Soße IV 2 (52)
saucepan [ˈsɔːspən] Kochtopf, Stieltopf IV 2 (42)
sausage [ˈsɒsɪdʒ] Wurst, Würstchen IV 2 (41)
save [ˈseɪv]:
1. **save sb. from sth.** jn. von/vor etwas retten III
2. **save a goal** ein Tor halten, abwehren III

saw [sɔː] *siehe* **see**
say [seɪ], **said, said** sagen I **Simon says …** [sez] Simon sagt … I
saying [ˈseɪɪŋ] Sprichwort, Redensart IV 3 (67)
scan sth. (for sth.) [skæn] etwas (nach etwas) absuchen III **scan a text** einen Text schnell nach bestimmten Wörtern/Informationen absuchen II
scare sb. [skeə] jn. erschrecken; jm. Angst machen III
scared [skeəd] verängstigt II
scarf [skɑːf], *pl* **scarves** [skɑːvz] Schal III
scary [ˈskeəri] unheimlich, gruselig I
scene [siːn] Szene I
schedule [ˈʃedjuːl] (Zeit-)Plan, Programm III
school [skuːl] Schule I **at school** in der Schule I **before school** vor der Schule *(vor Schulbeginn)* I **in front of the school** vor der Schule *(vor dem Schulgebäude)* I **school bag** Schultasche I
schoolyard [ˈskuːljɑːd] Schulhof I
science [ˈsaɪəns] Naturwissenschaft I
scientist [ˈsaɪəntɪst] Naturwissenschaftler/in III
scone [skɒn] *kleines rundes Milchbrötchen, leicht süß* I
score [skɔː]:
1. Treffer erzielen, Tor schießen III
2. Spielstand; Punktestand III

What's the score? Wie steht es?
scream [skriːm] schreien III
screen [skriːn] Bildschirm II **split screen** geteilter Bildschirm; Bildschirm(auf)teilung III
script [skrɪpt] Drehbuch; Manuskript IV 3 (73)
scroll [skrəʊl] scrollen III
sculpture [ˈskʌlptʃə] Skulptur IV 4 (88)
sea [siː] Meer I
seagull [ˈsiːgʌl] Möwe I
seal [siːl] Robbe I
search (for) [sɜːtʃ]:
1. Durchsuchung; Suche (nach) III
2. durchsuchen (nach); suchen (nach) III

season [ˈsiːzn] *(bes. AE)* Staffel *(einer Fernsehserie)* IV 3 (73)
seat [siːt] Sitz, Platz II
second [ˈsekənd]:
1. zweite(r, s) I **in second place** auf dem zweiten Platz; an zweiter Stelle III
2. Sekunde II

security [sɪˈkjʊərəti] Sicherheit, Sicherheits- IV 3 (78)
see [siː], **saw, seen** sehen; besuchen I **See you.** Bis gleich. / Bis bald. I **…, you see.** …, weißt du. II **see a doctor** einen Arzt/eine Ärztin

aufsuchen; zum Arzt gehen II
I see. Aha! / Verstehe. III
seed [si:d] Samen IV 1 (29)
seem (to be/do) [si:m] (zu sein/zu tun) scheinen III
seen [si:n] *siehe* **see**
segregation [ˌsegrɪˈgeɪʃn] Trennung *(nach Hautfarbe, Religion oder Geschlecht)* IV 2 (46)
selfie [ˈselfi] Selfie III
sell [sel], **sold, sold** verkaufen I
send sth. to sb. [send], **sent, sent** jm. etwas schicken, senden I
sense [sens]: **sense of humour** (Sinn für) Humor III °**make sense** plausibel klingen; Sinn haben
sent [sent] *siehe* **send**
sentence [ˈsentəns] Satz I **topic sentence** Satz, der in das Thema eines Absatzes einführt III
separate [ˈseprət] getrennt IV 3 (67)
separately [ˈseprətli] einzeln, separat IV 3 (67)
September [sepˈtembə] September I
serious [ˈsɪəriəs] ernst; ernsthaft III
service [ˈsɜːvɪs]:
1. Gottesdienst III
2. Dienst, Service IV 1 (16)
session [ˈseʃn] Sitzung, Einheit IV 4 (92)
set [set]:
1. Satz, Set II
2. set sth. up, set, set etwas errichten, aufbauen; etwas arrangieren IV 3 (73)
°**settler** [ˈsetlə] Siedler/in
seven [ˈsevn] sieben I
several [ˈsevrəl] mehrere, verschiedene III
°**sex** [seks] Sex
shadow [ˈʃædəʊ] Schatten *(den jemand/etwas wirft)* II
shake [ʃeɪk], **shook, shaken** schütteln II
shaken [ˈʃeɪkn] *siehe* **shake**
Shall I ...? [ʃæl] Soll ich ...? III
shallow [ˈʃæləʊ] flach, nicht tief III
°**shape** [ʃeɪp] gestalten, formen
share sth. [ʃeə] (sich) etwas teilen III
shark [ʃɑːk] Hai I
sharp [ʃɑːp] scharf IV 2 (52)
sharpener [ˈʃɑːpnə] Anspitzer I
she [ʃiː] sie I
sheep, *pl* **sheep** [ʃiːp] Schaf II
sheepdog [ˈʃiːpdɒg] Hütehund III
shelf [ʃelf], *pl* **shelves** [ʃelvz] Regal I
shell [ʃel] Muschel(schale) IV 3 (66)
shepherd [ˈʃepəd] Schäfer/in, Schafhirte/-hirtin III
shine [ʃaɪn], **shone, shone** [ʃɒn] scheinen (Sonne) III
shiny [ˈʃaɪni] glänzend IV 3 (78)
ship [ʃɪp] Schiff I
shirt [ʃɜːt] Hemd II
°**shock** [ʃɒk] schockieren
shocked [ʃɒkt] schockiert, entsetzt II
shoe [ʃuː] Schuh
shone [ʃɒn] *siehe* **shine**
shook [ʃʊk] *siehe* **shake**
shoot, shot, shot [ʃuːt] schießen; erschießen IV 2 (52) **shoot a film** einen Film drehen IV 3 (80)
shop [ʃɒp] Laden I **corner shop** Laden an der Ecke; Tante-Emma-Laden I
shop assistant [ˈʃɒp‿əˌsɪstənt] *(kurz auch:* **assistant**) Verkäufer/ in II
shopping [ˈʃɒpɪŋ]: **go shopping** einkaufen gehen I **do the/some shopping** einkaufen gehen; Einkäufe erledigen II **shopping centre** Einkaufszentrum II **shopping mall** *(großes)* Einkaufszentrum II
shore [ʃɔː] Ufer *(eines Sees)*, Strand II
short [ʃɔːt] kurz °**short form** Kurzform
shot [ʃɒt]:
1. Aufnahme, Foto; (Film) Einstellung, Szene IV 1 (17)
2. *siehe* **shoot** IV 2 (52)
should [ʃʊd], [ʃəd]: **You should ...** Du solltest ... / Ihr solltet ... II
shoulder [ˈʃəʊldə] Schulter II
shout [ʃaʊt] schreien, rufen I
show [ʃəʊ]:
1. zeigen I
2. Show, Vorstellung II
shower [ˈʃaʊə]: **have a shower** (sich) duschen III
shrimp [ʃrɪmp], *pl* **shrimp** *or* **shrimps** Garnele IV 2 (41)
shrub [ʃrʌb] Strauch, Busch IV 1 (29)
shy [ʃaɪ] schüchtern, scheu II
sick [sɪk] krank I **I feel sick.** Mir ist schlecht. II **be sick** sich übergeben II **I'm going to be sick.** Ich muss mich übergeben. II
side [saɪd] Seite II
sidewalk [ˈsaɪdwɔːk] *(AE)* Gehweg, Bürgersteig IV 1 (20)
sigh [saɪ] seufzen III
sights *(pl)* [saɪts] Sehenswürdigkeiten II
sign [saɪn] Schild; Zeichen I **no sign of ...** keine Spur von ... II
signal [ˈsɪgnəl] Signal, Zeichen III
silent [ˈsaɪlənt] still, leise III
silently [ˈsaɪləntli] lautlos; schweigend III
silliness [ˈsɪlinəs] Albernheit, Blödheit IV 4 (104)
silly [ˈsɪli]:
1. albern; blöd I
2. Dummerchen I
similar (to sth./sb.) [ˈsɪmələ] (etwas/jm.) ähnlich II
since 10 o'clock/... [sɪns] seit 10 Uhr/... III
sing [sɪŋ], **sang, sung** singen I **sing along** (with sb.) (mit jm.) mitsingen III
single [ˈsɪŋgl] ledig, alleinstehend I
sink [sɪŋk], **sank, sunk** sinken III
sister [ˈsɪstə] Schwester I
sit [sɪt], **sat, sat** sitzen; sich setzen I **sit down** sich hinsetzen I **sit up** sich aufsetzen III
°**sit-in** [ˈsɪt‿ɪn] Sit-in, Sitzstreik
situation [ˌsɪtʃuˈeɪʃn] Situation III
size [saɪz] Größe II
skates [skeɪts] Inlineskates I
skating [ˈskeɪtɪŋ] Inlineskaten, Rollschuhlaufen I
skill [skɪl] Fertigkeit II **study skills** Lern- und Arbeitstechniken I
skim a text [skɪm] einen Text überfliegen *(um den Inhalt grob zu erfassen)* IV 2 (53)
°**skin** [skɪn] Haut
skirt [skɜːt] Rock II
sky [skaɪ] Himmel II **in the sky** am Himmel II
skyline [ˈskaɪlaɪn] Skyline; Horizont III
skyscraper [ˈskaɪskreɪpə] Wolkenkratzer IV 1 (16)
slap [slæp] knallen, klatschen IV 4 (90)
slave [sleɪv] Sklave, Sklavin IV 2 (46)
slavery [ˈsleɪvəri] Sklaverei IV 2 (46)
sleep [sliːp], **slept, slept** schlafen I
sleepover [ˈsliːpəʊvə] Schlafparty I
slept [slept] *siehe* **sleep**
slide [slaɪd] Folie *(für Präsentationsprogramme)* III
slip [slɪp] (aus)rutschen III
slow [sləʊ] langsam I **slow motion** Zeitlupe III
small [smɔːl] klein I **small talk** Smalltalk *(spontan geführtes Gespräch in umgangssprachlichem Ton)* III
smell [smel] riechen I **smell sth.** an etwas riechen I
smile [smaɪl]:
1. lächeln I
2. Lächeln II
smiley [ˈsmaɪli] Smiley I
smoke [sməʊk] rauchen III

smoothie ['smu:ði] Smoothie, Fruchtshake III
smuggle ['smʌgl] schmuggeln I
smuggler ['smʌglə] Schmuggler/in I
smuggling ['smʌglɪŋ] der Schmuggel, das Schmuggeln I
snack [snæk] Snack, Imbiss I
snake [sneɪk] Schlange I
sneakers *(pl)* [sni:ks] Turnschuhe IV 1 (20)
sneeze [sni:z] niesen I
snow [snəʊ] Schnee II
so [səʊ]:
1. also; deshalb, daher I
2. **so cool/nice** so cool/nett I **so far** bis jetzt; bis hierher II
3. **so that ...** *(oft auch kurz:* **so ...***)* sodass, damit II
4. **So?/So what?** Und? / Na und? I
soccer ['sɒkə] *(AE)* Fußball IV 1 (20)
social ['səʊʃl] sozial, Sozial-, gesellschaftlich IV 3 (67) **social media** *(pl)* soziale Medien III **social studies** Sozialkunde IV 4 (91)
°**society** [sə'saɪəti] (die) Gesellschaft
sock [sɒk] Socke II
sofa ['səʊfə] Sofa I
soft [sɒft] weich II **in a soft voice** sanft; mit sanfter Stimme II **she sang softly** sie sang leise II
sold [səʊld] *siehe* **sell**
soldier ['səʊldʒə] Soldat/in III
solo ['səʊləʊ] Solo- II
solve [sɒlv] lösen III
some [sʌm] einige, ein paar; etwas I
somebody ['sʌmbədi] jemand I **somebody else** jemand anders III
someone ['sʌmwʌn] jemand I **someone else** jemand anders III
something ['sʌmθɪŋ] etwas I
sometimes ['sʌmtaɪmz] manchmal I
somewhere ['sʌmweə] irgendwo, irgendwohin IV 4 (90)
son [sʌn] Sohn II
song [sɒŋ] Lied, Song I
soon [su:n] bald I **as soon as** sobald, sowie III
sore [sɔ:]: **be sore** wund sein; wehtun II **have a sore throat** Halsschmerzen haben II
sorry ['sɒri]: **(I'm) sorry.** Tut mir leid. / Entschuldigung. I **I'm sorry about ...** Es tut mir leid wegen ... II **Sorry?** Wie bitte? IV 3 (66)
▶ S. 227 sorry
sound [saʊnd]:
1. klingen, sich anhören I
2. Geräusch; Klang I
°3. Laut **sound group** Lautgruppe
soup [su:p] Suppe I **make soup** Suppe kochen IV 2 (42)
▶ S. 222 Food words
sour ['saʊə] sauer, säuerlich IV 2 (42)
south [saʊθ] Süden; nach Süden; südlich III
southbound ['saʊθbaʊnd] Richtung Süden III
south-east [ˌsaʊθ‿'i:st] Südosten; nach Südosten; südöstlich III
south-west [ˌsaʊθ'west] Südwesten; nach Südwesten; südwestlich III
souvenir [ˌsu:və'nɪə] Andenken, Souvenir II
space [speɪs] Platz, Raum IV 1 (29)
spaghetti [spə'geti] Spagetti I
Spanish ['spænɪʃ] spanisch II
speak (to sb.) [spi:k]**, spoke, spoken** (mit jm.) sprechen I **speak out** den Mund aufmachen; sich (kritisch) äußern IV 2 (47)
speaker ['spi:kə] Sprecher/in
special ['speʃl] besondere(r, s) II
°**specialist** ['speʃəlɪst] Spezialist(in), Experte/Expertin
°**specific** [spə'sɪfɪk] spezifisch, genau
speech [spi:tʃ] (offizielle) Rede II **part of speech** Wortart III °**speech bubble** Sprechblase
speed [spi:d]:
1. Geschwindigkeit III **speed limit** Geschwindigkeitsbegrenzung, -beschränkung III
2. **speed up** beschleunigen, schneller werden IV 4 (90)
spell [spel] buchstabieren I
spelling ['spelɪŋ] Rechtschreibung; Schreibweise III
spend time/money (on) [spend]**, spent, spent** Zeit verbringen (mit); Geld ausgeben (für) III
spice [spaɪs] Gewürz IV 2 (41)
spicy ['spaɪsi] würzig, pikant IV 2 (42)
spinach ['spɪnɪtʃ] Spinat IV 2 (42)
▶ S. 222 Food words
°**spirit** ['spɪrɪt] Geist
splash sb. [splæʃ] jn. nass spritzen III
split screen [splɪt 'skri:n] geteilter Bildschirm; Bildschirm(auf)teilung III
spoke [spəʊk] *siehe* **speak**
spoken ['spəʊkn] *siehe* **speak**
°**spontaneous** [spɒn'teɪniəs] spontan
spoon [spu:n] Löffel II
sport [spɔ:t] Sport; Sportart I **do sport** Sport treiben I
spot [spɒt]:
1. Fleck, Punkt I
2. spot sb./sth. jn./etwas entdecken, erblicken IV 3 (66)
spray [spreɪ] (be)sprühen, sprayen IV 4 (102)
spread, spread, spread [spred] (sich) ausbreiten, verbreiten III
spring [sprɪŋ] Frühling II
square [skweə] Platz *(in der Stadt)* IV 1 (12)
square kilometre (sq km) [skweə] Quadratkilometer (km²) II
squash sth. [skwɒʃ] etwas zerdrücken, zerquetschen IV 3 (69)
stable ['steɪbl] (Pferde-, Kuh)Stall III
stadium ['steɪdiəm] Stadion III
stage [steɪdʒ] Bühne II
stairs *(pl)* [steəz] Treppe; Treppenstufen II
stall [stɔ:l] (Markt-)Stand II
stamp [stæmp] Stempel II
stand [stænd]**, stood, stood** stehen; sich (hin)stellen II **stand in line** *(AE)* Schlange stehen, sich anstellen IV 1 (20) **stand up (for/against sth./sb.)** aufstehen; eintreten/sich einsetzen (für/gegen etwas/jn.) IV 2 (47)
standard ['stændəd] Standard; Standard- III
star [stɑ:]:
1. (Film-, Pop-)Star I
2. Stern III
stare (at sb./sth.) [steə] (jn./etwas an)starren III
start [stɑ:t] anfangen, beginnen I
starving ['stɑ:vɪŋ]: **be starving** einen Riesenhunger haben III
state [steɪt]:
1. Staat III
2. Zustand IV 4 (95)
station ['steɪʃn] Bahnhof II
statue ['stætʃu:] Statue IV 1 (12)
stay [steɪ] bleiben II **stay up late** lange aufbleiben II **stay (at/with)** (vorübergehend) wohnen, übernachten (in/bei) III **Stay posted.** Bleib(t) auf dem Laufenden! IV 3 (78)
steal [sti:l]**, stole, stolen** stehlen IV 4 (92)
steep [sti:p] steil III
steering wheel ['stɪərɪŋ wi:l] Lenkrad IV 4 (90)
step [step]:
1. Schritt I
2. Stufe III
stew [stju:] Eintopf IV 2 (41)
stick [stɪk]:
1. Stock III
2. **stick sth. into sth., stuck, stuck** etwas in etwas stechen, stecken II

3. bleiben; kleben IV 1 (16)
still [stɪl]:
1. (immer) noch I
2. Standbild
stole [stəʊl] *siehe* **steal**
stolen ['stəʊlən] siehe **steal**
stomach ['stʌmək] Magen II
stone [stəʊn] Stein III
stood [stʊd] *siehe* **stand**
stop [stɒp]:
1. anhalten, stoppen I; aufhören II
2. Halt; Station, Haltestelle II
store [stɔː] *(AE)* Laden, Geschäft IV 1 (20)
storm [stɔːm] Sturm, Unwetter, Gewitter II
story ['stɔːri] Geschichte, Erzählung I
straight [streɪt] direkt, geradewegs III **straight on** geradeaus weiter II
strange [streɪndʒ] seltsam, komisch I
stranger ['streɪndʒə] Fremde(r), Unbekannte(r) IV 3 (67)
strawberry ['strɔːbəri] Erdbeere II
stream [striːm] Bach III
street [striːt] Straße I **at 14 Dean Street** in der Dean Street 14 I **in Dean Street** in der Dean Street I
street artist ['striːt‿ˌɑːtɪst] Straßenkünstler/in II
streetcar ['striːtkɑː] *(AE)* Straßenbahn IV 2 (47)
stress [stres]:
1. Betonung III **stress mark** Betonungszeichen III
2. betonen III
3. Stress IV 4 (98)
stretch [stretʃ] sich dehnen, sich strecken IV 3 (66) **stretch sth. out** etwas ausstrecken III
strict [strɪkt] streng IV 2 (52)
string [strɪŋ] Saite IV 2 (46)
strong [strɒŋ] stark, kräftig II
structure ['strʌktʃə]:
1. strukturieren, gliedern III
2. Struktur, Gliederung III
stuck [stʌk] *siehe* **stick**
student ['stjuːdənt] Schüler/in; Student/in I
studio ['stjuːdiəʊ] Studio I
study ['stʌdi] studieren; untersuchen, beobachten; lernen III
study poster ['stʌdi ˌpəʊstə] Lernposter II
study skills ['stʌdi ˌskɪlz] Lern- und Arbeitstechniken I
stuff [stʌf] *(infml)* Zeug, Kram III
stupid ['stjuːpɪd] dumm, blöd III
style [staɪl] Stil IV 2 (40)
sub-clause ['sʌbklɔːz] Nebensatz I
sub-heading ['sʌbˌhedɪŋ] Zwischenüberschrift; Kapitelüberschrift IV 2 (53)
subject ['sʌbdʒɪkt]:
1. Schulfach I
2. Subjekt II
submarine [ˌsʌbmə'riːn] U-Boot III
subtitle ['sʌbtaɪtl] Untertitel I
subway ['sʌbweɪ] *(AE)* U-Bahn IV 1 (12)
success [sək'ses] Erfolg III
°**successful** [sək'sesfl] erfolgreich
such [sʌtʃ]: **such a …** so ein/e …; solch ein/e … III °**such as …** wie zum Beispiel …
suddenly ['sʌdnli] plötzlich, auf einmal I
suffix ['sʌfɪks] Suffix, Nachsilbe IV 4 (104)
sugar ['ʃʊgə] Zucker IV 2 (42)
► S. 222 Food words
°**sugarcane** ['ʃʊgəkeɪn] Zuckerrohr
suggest sth. (to sb.) [sə'dʒest]:
1. (jm.) etwas vorschlagen III
suggestion [sə'dʒestʃən] Vorschlag IV 1 (25)
suit [suːt] Anzug III
sum sth. up [ˌsʌm‿'ʌp] etwas zusammenfassen III
summary ['sʌməri] Zusammenfassung III
summer ['sʌmə] Sommer II
summit ['sʌmɪt] Gipfel III
sun [sʌn] Sonne I
Sunday ['sʌndeɪ, 'sʌndɪ] Sonntag I
sung [sʌŋ] *siehe* **sing**
sunglasses *(pl)* ['sʌnglɑːsɪz] (eine) Sonnenbrille II
sunk [sʌŋk] *siehe* **sink**
sunny ['sʌni] sonnig II
sunset ['sʌnset] Sonnenuntergang III
°**šúŋkawakáŋ** [ˌʃʊŋkəwə'kɑːŋ] Pferd
supply [sə'plaɪ] Vorrat; Versorgung, Lieferung IV 3 (84)
support [sə'pɔːt]:
1. unterstützen III **support a team** eine Mannschaft unterstützen; Fan einer Mannschaft sein III
°**2.** **in support of sth./sb.** zur Unterstützung einer Sache/Person
suppose [sə'pəʊz] annehmen, vermuten III
°**Supreme Court** [suˌpriːm 'kɔːt] Oberster Gerichtshof
sure [ʃʊə], [ʃɔː] sicher II **make sure that …** sich vergewissern, dass …; darauf achten, dass …; dafür sorgen, dass … II **for sure** klar; ganz bestimmt IV 3 (73)
surface ['sɜːfɪs] Oberfläche III
surprise [sə'praɪz] Überraschung IV 4 (102)
surprised [sə'praɪzd] überrascht I
surprising [sə'praɪzɪŋ] überraschend IV 4 (102)
survive [sə'vaɪv] überleben III
swam [swæm] *siehe* **swim**
swamp [swɒmp] Sumpf IV 2 (39)
sweater ['swetə] *(bes. AE)* Pullover IV 1 (20)
sweet [swiːt]:
1. süß II **sweet potato** Süßkartoffel IV 2 (52)
2. Süßigkeit II
swim [swɪm], **swam, swum** schwimmen I
swimmer ['swɪmə] Schwimmer/in I
swimming pool ['swɪmɪŋ puːl] Schwimmbad, Schwimmbecken I
switch [swɪtʃ] wechseln IV 3 (73)
sword [sɔːd] Schwert I
swum [swʌm] *siehe* **swim**
syllable ['sɪləbl] Silbe II
symbol ['sɪmbl] Symbol II
°**synagogue** ['sɪnəgɒg] Synagoge
synonym ['sɪnənɪm] Synonym *(bedeutungsgleiches Wort)* IV 3 (82)
system ['sɪstəm] System IV 2 (47)

T

table ['teɪbl]:
1. Tisch I
2. Tabelle I
table tennis ['teɪbl tenɪs] Tischtennis II
tablet ['tæblət] Tablet III
take [teɪk], **took, taken:**
1. nehmen, mitnehmen; (weg-, hin) bringen I
2. *(Zeit)* brauchen; dauern II **take sth. off** etwas ausziehen *(Kleidung)*; etwas absetzen *(Hut, Helm)* II **take sth. out** etwas herausnehmen II **take control** Kontrolle übernehmen IV 1 (16) **take part in sth.** an etwas teilnehmen II **take photos** fotografieren, Fotos machen II **take place** stattfinden III **take care of sth.** sich (gut) um etwas kümmern; sorgfältig mit etwas umgehen IV 4 (92) °**take turns** sich abwechseln **take a walk** *(bes. AE)* spazieren gehen, einen Spaziergang machen IV 1 (28)
3. Einstellung, Take *(beim Film)* IV 3 (73)

takeaway ['teɪkəweɪ] *Restaurant/Imbissgeschäft, das Essen zum Mitnehmen verkauft; Essen zum Mitnehmen* II
taken ['teɪkən] *siehe* **take**
takeout ['teɪkaʊt] *(AE)* Essen zum Mitnehmen IV 1 (20)
talented ['tæləntɪd] begabt, talentiert II
talk [tɔːk]:
1. Vortrag, Referat, Rede I **give a talk (about)** einen Vortrag / eine Rede halten (über) I
2. talk (to) reden (mit), sich unterhalten (mit) I
tall [tɔːl] groß *(Person)*; hoch *(Gebäude, Baum)* II
tap [tæp] (an)tippen, (vorsichtig) klopfen II
target ['tɑːgɪt] Ziel, Zielscheibe IV 1 (16)
task [tɑːsk] Aufgabe I
taste [teɪst] schmecken I
tasty ['teɪsti] lecker II
taught [tɔːt] *siehe* **teach**
tax [tæks] (die) Steuer IV 4 (102)
taxpayer ['tækspeɪə] Steuerzahler/in IV 4 (102)
tea [tiː]:
1. Tee I
2. *leichte Nachmittags- oder Abendmahlzeit* II
teach [tiːtʃ], **taught, taught** unterrichten, lehren III
teacher ['tiːtʃə] Lehrer/in I **head teacher** Schulleiter/in III
team [tiːm] Team, Mannschaft I
tear [tɪə]:
1. Träne II
2. tear sth. down etwas abreißen IV 1 (28)
teaspoon ['tiːspuːn] Teelöffel II
technique [tek'niːk] Technik, Methode IV 4 (90)
°**technology** [tek'nɒlədʒi] Technik, Technologie
teen [tiːn] Teenager/in III
teeth [tiːθ] *plural of* **tooth**
telephone ['telɪfəʊn] Telefon I
tell sb. about sth. [tel], **told, told** jm. von etwas erzählen; jm. über etwas berichten I **tell sb. the way (to ...)** jm. den Weg (nach ...) beschreiben II **tell sb. (not) to do sth.** jn. auffordern, etwas (nicht) zu tun; jm. sagen, dass er/sie etwas (nicht) tun soll III

temperature ['temprətʃə] Temperatur II **have a temperature** Fieber haben II
ten [ten] zehn I
tennis ['tenɪs] Tennis I
tension ['tenʃn] Spannung, Anspannung III
tent [tent] Zelt II
term [tɜːm]:
1. Trimester II
2. Ausdruck, Begriff III
terrible ['terəbl] schrecklich, furchtbar II
°**territory** [territory] Territorium
terrorist ['terərɪst] terroristische(r, s); Terrorist/in IV 1 (16)
test ['test]:
1. Test, (Klassen-)Arbeit III
2. testen, prüfen III
text [tekst]:
1. text sb. jm. eine SMS schicken I
2. Text I; SMS II
text message ['tekst mesɪdʒ] *(kurz auch:* **text**) SMS II
than [ðæn], [ðən]: **bigger than** größer als II
Thank you. ['θæŋk juː] Danke. I **Thank you for listening.** Danke fürs Zuhören. II
Thanks. ['θæŋks] Danke. I **thanks to Maya** dank Maya II
Thanksgiving [θæŋks'gɪvɪŋ] Erntedankfest *(amerikanischer Feiertag am vierten Donnerstag im November)* IV 2 (41)
that [ðæt, ðət]:
1. der/die/das; die *(Relativpronomen)* II
2. dass *(Konjunktion)* I **it shows that ...** es zeigt, dass ... I
3. that group die Gruppe (dort), jene Gruppe I **that way** dort entlang; in die Richtung II
4. that's why deshalb, darum II
the [ðə] der, die, das; die I
theatre *(BE)* **/ theater** *(AE)* ['θɪətə] Theater II
their [ðeə] ihr I **their first day** ihr erster Tag I
theirs [ðeəz] ihrer, ihre, ihrs II
them [ðem, ðəm] sie; ihnen I
theme [θiːm] Thema II
themselves [ðəm'selvz] sich III
then [ðen] dann I
there [ðeə] da, dort; dahin, dorthin I **There are ...** Es sind ... / Es gibt ... I **There's ...** Es ist/gibt ... I **down there** dort unten; nach dort unten II **over there** da drüben, dort drüben II

thermometer [θə'mɒmɪtə] Thermometer II
these [ðiːz] diese, die (hier) I
they [ðeɪ] sie *(pl)* I **they're (= they are)** sie sind ... I
thick [θɪk] dick IV 1 (16)
thief [θiːf], *pl* **thieves** [θiːvz] Dieb/in I
°**thin** [θɪn] dünn
thing [θɪŋ] Sache, Ding, Gegenstand I
think [θɪŋk], **thought, thought** denken, glauben I **think of sth.** sich etwas ausdenken; an etwas denken II **think sth. of sth./sb.** etwas von etwas/jm. halten III
third [θɜːd]:
1. dritte(r, s) I
°**2.** Drittel
thirsty ['θɜːsti]: **be thirsty** durstig sein, Durst haben I
this [ðɪs]:
1. This is ... Dies ist ... / Das ist ... I
2. this place/break/subject dieser Ort / diese Pause / dieses Fach I **this afternoon/evening/...** heute Nachmittag/Abend/... II **this way** hier entlang; in diese Richtung II **this year's musical** das diesjährige Musical II
those [ðəʊz] die ... dort; jene ... I
though ['ðəʊ]: **even though** auch wenn; obwohl IV 4 (103)
thought [θɔːt]:
1. Gedanke III
2. *siehe* **think**
thousand ['θaʊznd] tausend; Tausend IV 1 (16)
three [θriː] drei I
threw [θruː] *siehe* **throw**
throat [θrəʊt] Hals, Kehle II **have a sore throat** Halsschmerzen haben II
through [θruː] durch I
throw [θrəʊ], **threw, thrown** werfen I
thrown [θrəʊn] *siehe* **throw**
thunder ['θʌndə] Donner II
Thursday ['θɜːzdeɪ, 'θɜːzdi] Donnerstag I
ticket ['tɪkɪt]:
1. Eintrittskarte I
2. Fahrkarte I
ticket office ['tɪkɪt‿ˌɒfɪs] Fahrkartenschalter; Kasse *(für den Verkauf von Eintrittskarten)* III
tide [taɪd] Gezeiten, Ebbe und Flut III
tighten ['taɪtn] spannen, festziehen, nachziehen IV 2 (46)

till [tɪl]: **till 1 o'clock** bis 1 Uhr I **not till three** erst um drei, nicht vor drei II
time [taɪm]:
1. Zeit; Uhrzeit I **at any time** jederzeit, zu jeder Zeit IV 4 (92) **at no time** nie IV 4 (92)
2. Mal II **at one time** zur selben Zeit, gleichzeitig III **feeding time** Fütterungszeit I **free time** Freizeit, freie Zeit I **What time is it?** Wie spät ist es? I
timeline ['taɪmlaɪn] Zeitstrahl, Zeitleiste IV 2 (41)
timer ['taɪmə] Zeitmesser IV 1 (25)
timetable ['taɪmteɪbl]:
1. Stundenplan I
2. Fahrplan III
tin [tɪn] Dose II
tinned [tɪnd] Dosen-; in Dosen IV 2 (42)
tip [tɪp] Tipp I
tired ['taɪəd] müde I
title ['taɪtl] Titel, Überschrift I
to [tu, tə]:
1. zu, nach I **count to ten** bis zehn zählen I **from … to …** von … bis … I
2. um zu II
3. Nice to meet you. Freut mich, dich/euch/Sie kennenzulernen. I
4. quarter to eleven Viertel vor elf (10.45 / 22.45)
toast [təʊst] Toast(brot) III
today [tə'deɪ] heute I
toe [təʊ] Zeh II
together [tə'geðə] zusammen I
toilet ['tɔɪlət] Toilette I
told [təʊld] *siehe* **tell**
tomato [tə'mɑːtəʊ], *pl* **tomatoes** Tomate II
tomorrow [tə'mɒrəʊ] morgen II
tongue [tʌŋ] Zunge II
tongue-twister ['tʌŋˌtwɪstə] Zungenbrecher II
tonight [tə'naɪt] heute Nacht, heute Abend III
too [tuː]:
1. auch I
2. too late/cold/big/… zu spät/kalt/groß/… I
took [tʊk] *siehe* **take**
tooth [tuːθ], *pl* **teeth** [tiːθ] Zahn II
toothache ['tuːθeɪk]: **have a toothache** Zahnschmerzen haben II
top [tɒp] Spitze; oberes Ende II; Spitzen- II **at the top (of)** oben, am oberen Ende (von) II
topic ['tɒpɪk] Thema, Themengebiet II **topic sentence** Satz, der in das Thema eines Absatzes einführt III
torch [tɔːtʃ]:
1. Taschenlampe II
2. Fackel II
tore [tɔː] *siehe* **tear** IV 1 (28)
torn [tɔːn] *siehe* **tear** IV 1 (28)
tortoise ['tɔːtəs] (Land-)Schildkröte III
total ['təʊtl]:
1. a total of … eine Gesamtsumme von …; insgesamt III
2. Gesamt- IV 2 (54)
totally ['təʊtəli] völlig, total IV 2 (54)
touch [tʌtʃ]:
1. berühren, anfassen I
2. get in touch (with sb.) (mit jm.) Kontakt aufnehmen; sich (mit jm.) in Verbindung setzen II **stay in touch (with sb.)** (mit jm.) Kontakt halten; (mit jm.) in Verbindung bleiben II
tough [tʌf] (knall)hart, schwierig IV 3 (69)
tour (of) ['tʊər‿əv] Rundgang, Rundfahrt, Reise (durch) I
°**tourism** ['tʊərɪzəm] Tourism
tourist ['tʊərɪst] Tourist/in I
towards the station/Mr Bell [tə'wɔːdz] auf den Bahnhof/Mr Bell zu, in Richtung Bahnhof/Mr Bell III
tower ['taʊə] Turm I
town [taʊn] Stadt I
town hall [ˌtaʊn 'hɔːl] Rathaus II
toy [tɔɪ] Spielzeug I
track [træk] (Bahn-)Gleis IV 1 (28)
tractor ['træktə] Traktor II
tradition [trə'dɪʃn] Tradition III
traditional [trə'dɪʃənl] traditionell II
trail [treɪl] Weg, Pfad III
train [treɪn]:
1. Zug II
2. trainieren II
trainer ['treɪnə] Turnschuh I
training ['treɪnɪŋ] Training(sstunde) I
tram [træm] Straßenbahn IV 2 (47)
translate [træns'leɪt] übersetzen II
translation [træns'leɪʃn] Übersetzung III
trash can ['træʃ kæn] *(AE)* Mülltonne, Abfalleimer IV 3 (69)
travel ['trævl] reisen I
traveller ['trævələ] Reisende(r) I
°**treaty** ['triːti] Vertrag
tree [triː] Baum I
trials *(pl)* ['traɪəlz] Turnier, Wettkampf III
trick [trɪk] Trick, Kunststück II
trip [trɪp] Ausflug; Reise I
trophy ['trəʊfi] Pokal; Trophäe I
tropical ['trɒpɪkl] tropisch, Tropen- IV 2 (40)
trouble ['trʌbl]: **be in trouble** in Schwierigkeiten sein; Ärger kriegen I
trousers *(pl)* ['traʊzəz] Hose II
truck [trʌk] Lastwagen, LKW III
true [truː] wahr I
trumpet ['trʌmpɪt] Trompete III
truth [truːθ] Wahrheit II
try [traɪ] (aus)probieren; versuchen I
T-shirt ['tiːʃɜːt] T-Shirt I
tube [tjuːb]: **the Tube** *(no pl)* die U-Bahn *(in London)* III
tuck [tʌk] stecken, klemmen IV 4 (90)
Tuesday ['tjuːzdeɪ, 'tjuːzdi] Dienstag I
tulip ['tjuːlɪp] Tulpe II
tune [tjuːn] stimmen *(Instrument)* IV 2 (46)
turkey ['tɜːki] Pute, Truthahn IV 1 (28)
turn [tɜːn]:
1. sich (um)drehen III **turn around** sich umdrehen I **turn left/right** (nach) links/rechts abbiegen II **turn sth. off/on** etwas aus-/einschalten II **turn to sb.** sich jm. zuwenden; sich an jn. wenden II **turn sth. up/down** etwas lauter/leiser stellen III
2. (It's) my turn. Ich bin dran / an der Reihe. I °**take turns** sich abwechseln *(etwas zu tun)*
tutor sb. ['tjuːtə] jn. unterrichten, jm. Stunden geben IV 3 (73)
TV [ˌtiː'viː] Fernsehen, Fernsehgerät I
twelve [twelv] zwölf I
twice [twaɪs] zweimal II **twice a week** zweimal pro Woche II
twins *(pl)* [twɪnz] Zwillinge I
two [tuː] zwei I
type (of) [taɪp] Art, Sorte, Typ IV 1 (30)
typical (of) ['tɪpɪkl] typisch (für) III

U

UK [ˌjuː 'keɪ]: **the UK (the United Kingdom)** das Vereinigte Königreich *(Großbritannien und Nordirland)* I
umbrella [ʌm'brelə] Schirm, Regenschirm I
°**unable** [ʌn'eɪbl]: **be unable to do sth.** etwas nicht tun dürfen/können
uncle ['ʌŋkl] Onkel I
under ['ʌndə] unter I
underground ['ʌndəgraʊnd]: **the underground** *(no pl)* die U-Bahn III 1 (14)

underline [ˌʌndəˈlaɪn] unterstreichen II
understand [ˌʌndəˈstænd], **understood, understood** verstehen I
understood [ˌʌndəˈstʊd] *siehe* **understand**
unfortunately [ʌnˈfɔːtʃənətli] leider, unglücklicherweise IV 1 (31)
unhappy [ʌnˈhæpi] unglücklich II
uniform [ˈjuːnɪfɔːm] Uniform I
unit [ˈjuːnɪt] Kapitel, Lektion I
united [juˈnaɪtɪd] vereinigt III **the United Kingdom** das Vereinigte Königreich III
unpack [ˌʌnˈpæk] auspacken III
unstoppable [ʌnˈstɒpəbl] unaufhaltsam, unaufhaltbar IV 3 (78)
until [ənˈtɪl] bis II **not until three** erst um drei, nicht vor drei III
unusual [ʌnˈjuːʒuəl] ungewöhnlich III
up [ʌp] hinauf, herauf; nach oben I **up and down** auf und ab; rauf und runter II **up here** hier oben; nach hier oben II **up to** bis (zu) II
°**upload sth.** [ˌʌpˈləʊd] etwas hochladen
upset [ˌʌpˈset] aufgebracht, gekränkt, mitgenommen III
upstairs [ˌʌpˈsteəz] oben; nach oben *(im Haus)* I
°**urban** [ˈɜːbən] städtisch, Stadt-
us [ʌs, əs] uns I
USA: the USA [ˌjuː‿es‿ˈeɪ] **(the United States of America)** die USA (die Vereinigten Staaten von Amerika) II
use [juːz] benutzen, verwenden I
usual [ˈjuːʒuəl] gewöhnlich, üblich III
usually [ˈjuːʒuəli] meistens, normalerweise, gewöhnlich I

V

vacation [vəˈkeɪʃn] *(AE)* Urlaub IV 1 (20)
valley [ˈvæli] Tal II
vast [vɑːst] riesig IV 4 (88)
vegetables *(pl)* [ˈvedʒtəblz] Gemüse I
vegetarian [ˌvedʒəˈteəriən] Vegetarier/in; vegetarisch IV 2 (42)
verse [vɜːs] Vers, Strophe II
°**version** [ˈvɜːʃn, ˈvɜːʒn] Version, Fassung
very [ˈveri] sehr I
°**victory** [ˈvɪktəri] Sieg **win a victory einen Sieg erringen**
video [ˈvɪdiəʊ] Video I **video camera** Videokamera I
view (of) [vjuː] Aussicht, Blick (auf) II **point of view** Standpunkt III **from my point of view** von meinem Standpunkt aus gesehen; aus meiner Sicht III
village [ˈvɪlɪdʒ] Dorf I
°**violence** [ˈvaɪələns] Gewalt
violin [ˌvaɪəˈlɪn] Violine, Geige III
VIP [ˌviː‿aɪ ˈpiː] Prominente(r) (very important person) IV 3 (72)
viral [ˈvaɪrəl]: **go viral** sich wie ein Virus ausbreiten / sich wie ein Lauffeuer verbreiten IV 3 (78)
visit [ˈvɪzɪt]:
1. besuchen I
2. Besuch II
visitor [ˈvɪzɪtə] Besucher/in, Gast II
vocabulary [vəˈkæbjələri] Vokabelverzeichnis, Wörterverzeichnis I
voice [vɔɪs] Stimme I **in a loud voice** mit lauter Stimme II
volcano [vɒlˈkeɪnəʊ] Vulkan III
volleyball [ˈvɒlibɔːl] Volleyball I
volunteer [ˌvɒlənˈtɪə] Freiwillige(r), Ehrenamtliche(r) III
°**vote** [vəʊt] wählen, abstimmen
vowel [ˈvaʊəl] Vokal, Selbstlaut II

W

°**waffle** [ˈwɒfl] Waffel
waist [weɪst] Taille II
wait (for) [weɪt] warten **(auf)** I **wait a minute** Warte einen Moment. / Moment mal. I **I can't wait to see ...** Ich kann es kaum erwarten, ... zu sehen. II **wait in line** *(AE)* Schlange stehen, sich anstellen IV 1 (20)
waiter [ˈweɪtə] Kellner IV 2 (43)
waitress [ˈweɪtrəs] Kellnerin IV 2 (43)
wake up [ˌweɪk‿ˈʌp], **woke up, woken up:**
1. aufwachen I
2. **wake sb. up** jn. wecken II
walk [wɔːk]:
1. Spaziergang I **go for a walk** spazieren gehen, einen Spaziergang machen I
2. (zu Fuß) gehen I
wall [wɔːl] Mauer; Wand II
wallet [ˈwɒlɪt] Portemonnaie, Geldbörse III
wander [ˈwɒndə] herumlaufen; herumirren II
want [wɒnt]: **want sth.** etwas (haben) wollen I **want to do sth.** etwas tun wollen I
war [wɔː] Krieg III
warm [wɔːm] warm II
warning [ˈwɔːnɪŋ] Warnung III
was [wɒz], [wəz]: **(I/he/she/it) was** *Vergangenheitsform von* **be** II
wash the dishes *(pl)* [ˌwɒʃ ðə ˈdɪʃɪz] das Geschirr abwaschen, spülen II
watch [wɒtʃ]:
1. Armbanduhr I
2. **watch sth.** sich etwas anschauen; etwas beobachten I **watch TV** fernsehen I **Watch out!** Pass auf! / Vorsicht! I
water [ˈwɔːtə] Wasser I **water fountain** *(bes. AE)* Trinkbrunnen IV 4 (90)
waterfall [ˈwɔːtəfɔːl] Wasserfall II
wave [weɪv]:
1. Welle II
2. **wave (at sb.)** (jm. zu)winken III **wave a flag** eine Fahne schwenken III
way [weɪ]:
1. Weg I **ask sb. the way** jn. nach dem Weg fragen II **by the way** übrigens III **No way!** Auf keinen Fall! / Kommt nicht in Frage! III **tell sb. the way** jm. den Weg beschreiben II **on the way to ...** auf dem Weg zu/nach ... I **that way** dort entlang; in die Richtung II **this way** hier entlang; in diese Richtung II
2. Art und Weise IV 1 (19)
► S. 217 way ("Art und Weise")
we [wiː] wir I
wear [weə], **wore, worn** tragen *(Kleidung)* I
weather [ˈweðə] Wetter II
website [ˈwebsaɪt] Website I
wedding [ˈwedɪŋ] Hochzeit, Trauung III
Wednesday [ˈwenzdeɪ, ˈwenzdi] Mittwoch I
wee *(besonders Scottish English, infml)* [wiː] klein III
week [wiːk] Woche I **a three-week holiday** ein dreiwöchiger Urlaub IV 1 (29)
► S. 219 a 9,740-foot swimming pool
weekend [ˌwiːkˈend] Wochenende I **at the weekend** am Wochenende I **on the weekend** *(bes. AE)* am Wochenende IV 4 (98)
weigh [weɪ] wiegen I
weird [wɪəd] seltsam, komisch III
weirdo [ˈwɪədəʊ] *(infml)* Spinner/in IV 1 (24)

welcome sb. (to) ['welkəm] jn. begrüßen (in), jn. willkommen heißen (in) III **Welcome to Plymouth.** Willkommen in Plymouth. I
well [wel]:
1. gut II **well-known** bekannt, wohlbekannt III **well-behaved** brav IV 1 (16)
2. gesund, gut II **I don't feel well.** Mir geht's nicht gut. / Ich fühle mich nicht gut. II
3. Well, ... Nun, ... / Also, ... / Na ja, ... I
Welsh [welʃ] Walisisch; walisisch III
went [went] *siehe* **got**
were [wɜː, wə]: **you were; we/you/ they were** *Vergangenheitsform von* **be** II
west [west] Westen; nach Westen; westlich III
westbound ['westbaʊnd] Richtung Westen III
western ['westən] westlich, West- III
°**westward** ['westwəd] in westlicher Richtung
wet [wet] nass I
whale [weɪl] Wal I
what? [wɒt] was? I **What about ...?** Wie wäre es mit ...? II **What about you?** Und du/ihr? **What colour is/are ...?** Welche Farbe hat/haben ...? I **What's up?** Was gibt's? / Was ist los? III **What's your poster about?** Wovon handelt dein Poster? / Worum geht es bei deinem Poster? I **What time is it?** Wie spät ist es? I **What's she like?** Wie ist sie (so)? **I don't know what to do** Ich weiß nicht, was ich tun soll.
whatever [wɒt'evə] was immer IV 4 (103)
► S. 235 whenever, wherever, whatever, whoever
wheat [wiːt] Weizen IV 4 (98)
wheel [wiːl]: *(kurz für:* **steering wheel***)* Lenkrad IV 4 (90) **big wheel** Riesenrad I
when [wen]:
1. wenn I
2. als II
3. when? wann? I
whenever [ˌwen'evə] wann (auch) immer; egal, wann IV 4 (103)
► S. 235 whenever, wherever, whatever, whoever
where? [weə] wo? / wohin? I **Where are you from?** Woher kommst du? I
wherever [weər'evə] wo immer IV 4 (103)
► S. 235 whenever, wherever, whatever, whoever
whether ['weðə] ob IV 4 (91)
which [wɪtʃ]:
1. der/die/das; die *(Relativpronomen)* II
2. welche(r, s) I **Which clubs/ jokes ...?** Welche Klubs/ Witze/...? I
while [waɪl]:
1. während III
2. eine Weile, einige Zeit III **for a while** eine Weile, eine Zeit lang III
whisper ['wɪspə] flüstern II
whistle ['wɪsl]:
1. pfeifen II
2. (Triller-)Pfeife III
3. Pfiff III
white [waɪt] weiß I
who [huː]:
1. wer I **Who danced with you?** Wer hat mit dir getanzt? I
2. wem/wen II **Who did you dance with?** Mit wem hast du getanzt? II
3. der/die/das; die *(Relativpronomen)* II
whoever [huː'evə] wer immer IV 4 (103)
► S. 235 whenever, wherever, whatever, whoever
whole [həʊl] ganze(r, s), gesamte(r, s) II
whose [huːz]:
1. whose? wessen? II
2. the men whose homes ... die Männer, deren Wohnungen ... IV 1 (29)
why [waɪ]: **why?** warum? I **that's why** deshalb, darum II
wide [waɪd] weit; breit III
wild [waɪld] wild II
wildfire ['waɪldfaɪə] Waldbrand, Buschbrand IV 3 (73)
wildlife ['waɪldlaɪf] Tierwelt, frei lebende Tiere IV 3 (66)
will [wɪl]: **we'll go (= we will go)** wir werden gehen II **I'll have a tea/ pizza/...** Ich nehme einen Tee/ eine Pizza/... *(beim Essen, im Restaurant)* II
win [wɪn], **won, won** gewinnen I
°**win a victory** einen Sieg erringen
wind [wɪnd] Wind II
window ['wɪndəʊ] Fenster I
windy ['wɪndi] windig II
wing [wɪŋ] Flügel III
winner ['wɪnə] Gewinner/in, Sieger/ in I
winter ['wɪntə] Winter II
wish [wɪʃ] wünschen II **I wish it was warmer.** Ich wünschte, es wäre wärmer. II
with [wɪð]:
1. mit I
2. bei I
within [wɪ'ðɪn] innerhalb (von) IV 1 (16)
without [wɪ'ðaʊt] ohne I
woke [wəʊk] *siehe* **wake**
woken ['wəʊkən] *siehe* **wake**
woman ['wʊmən], *pl* **women** ['wɪmɪn] Frau I
won [wʌn] *siehe* **win**
wonder ['wʌndə]:
1. sich fragen, gern wissen wollen III
2. Wunder III **No wonder ...** Kein Wunder ... IV 4 (90)
wonderful ['wʌndəfəl] wunderbar IV 4 (102)
wood [wʊd] Holz II
wooden ['wʊdn] hölzern; Holz- III
word [wɜːd] Wort I **word order** Wortstellung I
wordbank ['wɜːdˌbæŋk] „Wortspeicher" I
wore [wɔː] *siehe* **wear**
work [wɜːk]:
1. arbeiten I; funktionieren I
2. Arbeit I **work of art** Kunstwerk IV 1 (29) °**out of work** arbeitslos
workbook ['wɜːkbʊk] Arbeitsheft
°**worker** ['wɜːkə] Arbeiter/in
worksheet ['wɜːkʃiːt] Arbeitsblatt II
workshop ['wɜːkʃɒp]:
1. Workshop, Lehrgang II
2. Werkstatt III
worktop ['wɜːktɒp] (Küchen)Theke; Arbeitsplatte IV 2 (47)
world [wɜːld] Welt II **in the world** auf der Welt II
worm [wɜːm] Wurm I
worn [wɔːn] *siehe* **wear**
worried ['wʌrid] besorgt, beunruhigt I
worry (about) ['wʌri]:
1. worry (about) sich Sorgen machen (wegen, um) II
°**2.** Sorge
worse [wɜːs] schlechter, schlimmer II
worst [wɜːst] der/die/das schlechteste/schlimmste ...; am schlechtesten/ schlimmsten II
worth [wɜːθ] wert III
would [wʊd]: **What would you like to eat?** Was möchtest du essen? I **I'd like ... (= I would like ...)** Ich möchte ... I **I'd love to ...** Ich

würde sehr gern … II **I would have screamed too.** Ich hätte auch geschrien. IV 2 (46)
write [raɪt], **wrote, written** schreiben I **write sth. down** etwas aufschreiben II
written ['rɪtn] *siehe* **write**
wrong [rɒŋ]:
1. falsch, verkehrt I **No, that's wrong.** Nein, das ist falsch. / Nein, das stimmt nicht. I **What's wrong with you/Sam?** Was fehlt dir/Sam?; Was ist los mit dir/mit Sam? II
2. sb. is wrong jemand irrt sich; jemand hat Unrecht I
wrote [rəʊt] *siehe* **write**

Y

yard [jɑːd] *(AE)* Garten IV 1 (20)
year [jɪə]:
1. Jahr I **last/next year's musical** das Musical vom letzten/nächsten Jahr II **this year's musical** das diesjährige Musical II **a 70-year-old teacher** ein 70-jähriger Lehrer IV 1 (29)
▶ S. 219 a 9,740-foot swimming pool
2. Jahrgang(sstufe) I
yellow ['jeləʊ] gelb I
yes [jes] ja I **Yes, that's right.** Ja, das ist richtig. / Ja, das stimmt. I
yesterday ['jestədeɪ, 'jestədi] gestern I
yet [jet]: **Have you … yet?** Hast du schon …? II **not … yet** noch nicht I
yoga ['jəʊgə] Yoga I
yoghurt ['jɒgət] Joghurt I
you [juː]:
1. du; Sie; ihr; dir; dich; euch; Ihnen I
2. man III
young [jʌŋ] jung I
your [jɔː, jə] dein/e; euer/eure; Ihr/ Ihre I
yours [jɔːz] deiner, deine, deins; eurer, eure, eures II
yourself [jɔː'self]: **about yourself** über dich selbst I **Did you cook it yourself?** Hast du es selbst gekocht? IV 2 (46)
▶ S. 224 German "selbst"
yourselves [jɔː'selvz] euch; sich (bei „Sie") III
yummy *(infml)* ['jʌmi] lecker I

Z

zero ['zɪərəʊ] Null I
zoo [zuː] Zoo I
zoom in/out [zuːm] rein-/herauszoomen III

Das **German – English Dictionary** enthält den **Lernwortschatz** deines Englischbuchs.
Es kann dir eine erste Hilfe sein, wenn du vergessen hast, wie etwas auf Englisch heißt.

Wenn du wissen möchtest, wo das entsprechende englische Wort zum ersten Mal in deinem Englischbuch vorkommt, dann kannst du im **English – German Dictionary** (S. 237–266) nachschlagen.

Im **German – English Dictionary** werden folgende **Abkürzungen** verwendet:

sth. = something (etwas) sb. = somebody (jemand) jn. = jemanden jm. = jemandem
pl = *plural* (Mehrzahl) *infml* = *informal* (umgangssprachlich)

▶ Der Pfeil weist auf Kästen im **Vocabulary** (S. 214–236) hin, in denen du weitere Informationen zu diesem Wort findest.

1

in den 60er-Jahren (des 20. Jahrhunderts) in the 1960s [ˌnaɪntiːn'sɪkstiz]

A

ab: auf und ab up and down [ˌʌp‿ən 'daʊn]
abbiegen: (nach) links/rechts abbiegen turn left/right [tɜːn]
abdecken *(behandeln)* cover ['kʌvə]
Abend evening ['iːvnɪŋ] **am Abend** in the evening **zu Abend essen** have dinner ['dɪnə] **heute Nacht/Abend** this evening ['iːvnɪŋ] / tonight [tə'naɪt]
Abendbrot, -essen dinner ['dɪnə]
abends in the evening ['iːvnɪŋ]
Abenteuer adventure [əd'ventʃə]
aber but [bʌt], [bət], however [haʊ'evə]
Aber egal, … Anyway, … ['eniweɪ]
abfahren leave [liːv]
Abfall rubbish ['rʌbɪʃ]; *(AE)* garbage ['gɑːbɪdʒ]
Abfalleimer litter bin ['lɪtə bɪn]; rubbish bin ['rʌbɪʃ bɪn]; trash can *(AE)* ['træʃ kæn]
abgeben: etwas abgeben *(einreichen)* hand sth. in
abgeschnitten: von etwas abgeschnitten/abgetrennt sein be cut off from sth.
abhängen hang out [ˌhæŋ‿'aʊt] *(infml)*
abholen: jn. abholen pick sb. up [ˌpɪk‿'ʌp]
Abkürzung abbreviation [əˌbriːvi'eɪʃn]
Abneigungen: Vorlieben und Abneigungen likes and dislikes *(pl)* [ˌlaɪks‿ən 'dɪslaɪks]
abräumen *(Tisch)* clear [klɪə]
abreißen tear down [ˌteə 'daʊn]
Absatz *(Text)* paragraph ['pærəgrɑːf]
abschließen complete [kəm'pliːt]
etwas (mit etwas) abschließen round sth. off (with sth.)
abschreiben copy ['kɒpi]
absetzen: etwas absetzen *(Hut, Helm)* take sth. off [ˌteɪk‿ɒf]
absolut absolutely ['æbsəluːtli]
abspielen *(CD usw.)* play [pleɪ]
abstrakt abstract ['æbstrækt]
abstürzen crash [kræʃ]
▶ S. 215 (to) crash
absuchen: etwas (nach etwas) absuchen scan sth. (for sth.) [skæn]
abwaschen: das Geschirr abwaschen wash the dishes *(pl)* [ˌwɒʃ ðə 'dɪʃɪz]
Abwechslung: zur Abwechslung for a change [tʃeɪndʒ]
achten: darauf achten, dass … make sure that …
Achterbahn roller coaster ['rəʊlə kəʊstə]
Acker field [fiːld]
addieren (zu) add (to) [æd]
Adjektiv adjective ['ædʒɪktɪv]
Adresse address [ə'dres]
Adverb adverb ['ædvɜːb]
Affe monkey ['mʌŋki]
Aha! I see. [siː]
ähnlich: (etwas/jm.) ähnlich similar (to sth./sb.) ['sɪmələ]
Ahnung: Wir hatten keine Ahnung, wohin wir gehen sollten. We had no idea where to go.
Aktivität activity [æk'tɪvəti]
Akzent accent ['æksənt]
albern silly ['sɪli]
Albernheit silliness ['sɪlinəs]
alle all [ɔːl]; *(jeder)* everyone ['evriwʌn], everybody ['evribɒdi]
Allee avenue ['ævənjuː]
allein alone [ə'ləʊn]; on my/your/… own [əʊn] **ganz allein** all alone
alleinstehend *(ledig)* single ['sɪŋgl]
allerdings however [haʊ'evə]
allergisch (gegen etwas) allergic (to sth.) [ə'lɜːdʒɪk]
alles all [ɔːl]; everything ['evriθɪŋ]
Alles Liebe, … *(Briefschluss)* Love, … **alles in allem** altogether [ˌɔːltə'geðə]
Alligator alligator ['ælɪgeɪtə]
Alltags- everyday ['evrideɪ]
als **1.** *(zeitlich)* when [wen]; *(während)* as [æz], [əz]
2. als Kind as a child
3. als Erstes first [fɜːst]
4. größer/schöner als bigger/more beautiful than [ðæn], [ðən]
5. als ob like [laɪk] *(infml)*, as if [æz‿'ɪf]
also **1.** *(deshalb, daher)* so [səʊ]
2. Also, … Well, … [wel]
alt old [əʊld] **Ich bin zwölf Jahre alt.** I'm twelve years old. **Wie alt bist du?** How old are you?
Alter age [eɪdʒ] **… ist in deinem Alter** … is your age **ein Junge in deinem Alter** a boy of your age
am **1.** *(örtlich)* at [æ], [ət] **am Meer** by the sea [baɪ] **am Himmel** in the sky **Telefon** on the phone
2. *(zeitlich)* **am Abend** in the evening **am Montag/Dienstag/…** on Monday/Tuesday/… **am Morgen** in the morning **am Nachmittag** in the afternoon **am Samstagmorgen** on Saturday afternoon **am Wochenende** at the weekend
Ameise ant [ænt]
amtlich, Amts- official [ə'fɪʃl]
amüsieren: sich amüsieren have fun [fʌn] **Ich habe mich amüsiert.** I enjoyed myself.
an *(in Ortsangaben)* at [æ], [ət] **an britischen Schulen** at British schools **an sein** *(Radio, Licht usw.)* be on [ɒn]
anbauen *(anpflanzen)* grow [grəʊ]
anbieten offer ['ɒfə]

Andenken souvenir [ˌsuːvəˈnɪə]
andere(r, s) other [ˈʌðə] **ein(e) andere(r, s)** another [əˈnʌðə] **einer nach dem anderen** one by one **alle anderen** everybody else [els]
ändern; sich ändern change [tʃeɪndʒ]
anders *(verschieden)* different [ˈdɪfrənt] **es war nicht anders** it was no different **jemand anders** someone else [els]
Änderung change [tʃeɪndʒ]
Anfang beginning [bɪˈɡɪnɪŋ]
anfangen start [stɑːt]; begin [bɪˈɡɪn]
anfangs at first [ət ˈfɜːst]
anfassen touch [tʌtʃ]
Angel: an die Angel bekommen hook [hʊk]
Angelschnur line [laɪn]
angemalt painted [ˈpeɪntɪd]
angenehm comfortable [ˈkʌmftəbl]
Angewohnheit habit [ˈhæbɪt]
angreifen attack [əˈtæk]
Angriff attack [əˈtæk]
Angst: jm. Angst machen scare sb. [skeə] **Angst haben (vor etwas/jm.)** be afraid (of sth./sb.) [əˈfreɪd]
anhalten stop [stɒp]
Anhänger/in fan [fæn]
anhören 1. sich etwas anhören listen to sth. [ˈlɪsn] **Hör dir/Hört euch den Song an.** Listen to the song. **2. sich gut anhören** *(gut klingen)* sound good [saʊnd]
ankommen arrive [əˈraɪv]
anlächeln: jn. anlächeln smile at sb. [smaɪl]
anlocken attract [əˈtrækt]
anmalen paint [peɪnt]
annehmen *(vermuten)* suppose [səˈpəʊz] **Ich nehme an, …** I guess … [ɡes]
anordnen *(arrangieren)* arrange [əˈreɪndʒ]
anpflanzen grow [ɡrəʊ]
Anruf (phone) call [ˈfəʊn kɔːl]
anrufen: jn. anrufen phone sb. [fəʊn]; call sb. [kɔːl]
Ansage announcement [əˈnaʊnsmənt]
anschauen: sich etwas anschauen watch sth. [wɒtʃ]; look at sth. [lʊk]
anschließen: sich einem Klub anschließen join a club [dʒɔɪn]
Anschrift address [əˈdres]
ansehen: sich etwas ansehen watch sth. [wɒtʃ]; look at sth. [lʊk]
Anspitzer sharpener [ˈʃɑːpnə]
anstelle von instead of [ɪnˈsted‿əv]
anstellen: sich anstellen *(Schlange stehen)* queue [kjuː]; *(AE)* stand/wait in line [laɪn]
Anstieg climb [klaɪm]
Anstoß erregend offensive [əˈfensɪv]
anstreichen paint [peɪnt]
Antonym antonym [ˈæntənɪm]
Antwort answer [ˈɑːnsə]
antworten answer [ˈɑːnsə] **antworten (auf)** reply (to) [rɪˈplaɪ]
Anwohner/in resident [ˈrezɪdənt]
Anzeige *(Inserat)* advertisement [ədˈvɜːtɪsmənt]
anziehen attract [əˈtrækt] **etwas anziehen** *(Kleidung)* put sth. on [ˌpʊt‿ˈɒn] **sich schick anziehen** dress up [ˌdres‿ˈʌp]
Anziehungspunkt attraction [əˈtrækʃn]
Anzug suit [suːt]
anzünden light [laɪt]
Apfel apple [ˈæpl]
Apfelsine orange [ˈɒrɪndʒ]
April April [ˈeɪprəl]
Aquarienhaus aquarium [əˈkweəriəm]
Aquarium aquarium [əˈkweəriəm]
Arbeit work [wɜːk]; *(Job, Stelle)* job [dʒɒb]
arbeiten work [wɜːk]
Arbeitsauftrag assignment [əˈsaɪnmənt]
Arbeitsblatt worksheet [ˈwɜːkʃiːt]
Arbeitsheft workbook [ˈwɜːkbʊk]
Arbeitsplatte countertop [ˈkaʊntətɒp], counter [ˈkaʊntə], worktop [ˈwɜːktɒp]
Architekt/in architect [ˈɑːkɪtekt]
Ärger kriegen / haben be in trouble [ˈtrʌbl]
Argument argument [ˈɑːɡjumənt]
Arm arm [ɑːm]
arm poor [pɔː], [pʊə]
Armbanduhr watch [wɒtʃ]
Armee army [ˈɑːmi]
arrangieren: etwas arrangieren set sth. up
Art: eine Art (von) … a kind of … [kaɪnd], type (of) [taɪp] **Art und Weise** way
► S. 217 way ("Art und Weise")
Artikel article [ˈɑːtɪkl]
Arzt / Ärztin doctor [ˈdɒktə]
Asche *(Überreste)* ashes *(pl)* [ˈæʃɪz]
Astronaut/in astronaut [ˈæstrənɔːt]
Atem(zug) breath [breθ]
Atlantik: der Atlantik, der Atlantische Ozean the Atlantic (Ocean) [ətˈlæntɪk]
Atmosphäre atmosphere [ˈætməsfɪə]
Attraktion attraction [əˈtrækʃn]
auch: auch aus Berlin from Berlin too [tuː]; also from Berlin [ˈɔːlsəʊ] **Ich auch.** Me too. **auch nicht** not … either [ˈaɪðə], [ˈiːðə] **Ich auch nicht.** Me neither. [ˈnaɪðə, ˈniːðə]
auch wenn even though [ˌiːvn ˈðəʊ]
auf on [ɒn] **auf das Boot (hinauf)** onto the boat [ˈɒntʊ] **auf dem Bild / Foto** in the picture / photo **auf dem Dachboden** in the attic **auf der Welt** in the world **auf einmal** suddenly [ˈsʌdnli] **auf dem Weg zu / nach …** on the way to … **auf der Landkarte / dem Stadtplan** on the map **auf Deutsch / Englisch** in German / English **auf und ab** up and down [ˌʌp‿ən ˈdaʊn] **Auf welcher Seite sind wir?** What page are we on? **Auf Wiedersehen.** Goodbye.
aufbauen: etwas eufbauen set sth. up
aufbewahren keep [kiːp]
► S. 232 (to) keep
aufbleiben: lange aufbleiben stay up late
auffordern: jn. auffordern, etwas (nicht) zu tun tell sb. (not) to do sth. [tel]
Aufführung performance [pəˈfɔːməns]
Aufgabe task [tɑːsk]; exercise [ˈeksəsaɪz]; assignment [əˈsaɪnmənt]; job
Aufgabe, Arbeitsauftrag (in der Schule oder daheim zu erledigen)
aufgeben give up [ˌɡɪv‿ˈʌp]
aufgebracht upset [ˌʌpˈset]
aufgeregt *(gespannt)* excited [ɪkˈsaɪtɪd]; *(nervös)* nervous [ˈnɜːvəs]
aufhängen: etwas aufhängen hang sth. up [ˌhæŋ‿ˈʌp]
aufheben: etwas aufheben *(vom Boden)* pick sth. up [ˌpɪk‿ˈʌp] *(aufsparen)* keep [kiːp]
► S. 232 (to) keep
aufhören stop
aufmachen open [ˈəʊpən]
Aufnahme shot [ʃɒt]
aufnehmen: (mit jm.) Kontakt aufnehmen get in touch (with sb.) [tʌtʃ]
aufpassen: auf jn. aufpassen look after sb.
aufragen *(Berge, Säulen, Türme, …)* rise up [ˌraɪz‿ˈʌp]
aufrechterhalten: etwas aufrechterhalten keep sth. up [kiːp]
► S. 232 (to) keep

aufregend *(spannend)* exciting [ɪk'saɪtɪŋ]
aufrufen: die Namen aufrufen call out the names
aufschauen *(hochsehen)* look up [,lʊk_'ʌp]
aufschreiben: etwas aufschreiben write sth. down
aufsetzen: etwas aufsetzen *(Hut, Helm)* put sth. on [,pʊt_'ɒn] **sich aufsetzen** sit up
aufsparen keep [ki:p]
▶ S. 232 (to) keep
aufspringen jump up [,dʒʌmp_'ʌp]
aufstehen get up [,get_'ʌp]
Aufstieg climb [klaɪm]
aufsuchen: einen Arzt / eine Ärztin aufsuchen see a doctor
auftauchen *(erscheinen)* appear [ə'pɪə]
aufteilen: (sich) aufteilen (in), divide (into) [dɪ'vaɪd]
auftreten *(Künstler/in)* perform [pə'fɔ:m]
Auftritt performance [pə'fɔ:məns]
aufwachen wake up [,weɪk_'ʌp]
aufwachsen grow up [,grəʊ_'ʌp]
aufwecken: jn. aufwecken wake sb. up [,weɪk_'ʌp]
Aufzug lift [lɪft], elevator *(bes. AE)* ['elɪveɪtə]
Auge eye [aɪ]
Augenblick moment ['məʊmənt]
August August ['ɔ:gəst]
aus from [frɒm], [frəm] **aus … heraus / hinaus** out of … ['aʊt_əv] **aus etwas (gemacht) sein** be made of sth.
ausblasen: etwas ausblasen blow sth. out [,bləʊ_'aʊt]
ausdenken: sich etwas ausdenken think of sth.; make sth. up
Ausdruck term [tɜ:m]; *(Redewendung)* phrase [freɪz]
ausdrücken: anders ausdrücken paraphrase ['pærəfreɪz]
auseinander apart [ə'pɑ:t]
Auseinandersetzung argument ['ɑ:gjumənt]
Ausflug trip [trɪp]
ausgeben: Geld ausgeben (für) spend money (on) [spend]
Ausgehverbot: jm. Ausgehverbot erteilen ground sb. [graʊnd]
ausgezeichnet excellent ['eksələnt]
auskennen: sich mit etwas auskennen know about sth.
ausländisch foreign ['fɒrən]
Fremde(r), Unbekannte(r) stranger ['streɪndʒə]

ausmachen make sth. sth. [meɪk]
auspacken unpack [,ʌn'pæk]
ausprobieren try [traɪ]
auspusten: etwas auspusten blow sth. out [,bləʊ_'aʊt]
Ausrufezeichen exclamation mark [,ekskləˈmeɪʃn mɑ:k]
ausruhen: sich ausruhen rest [rest]; relax [rɪ'læks]
Ausrüstung kit [kɪt]; equipment *(no pl)* [ɪ'kwɪpmənt]
Aussage message ['mesɪdʒ]
ausschalten: etwas ausschalten turn sth. off [,tɜ:n_'ɒf]
Ausschau: nach jm./etwas Ausschau halten look out for sb./sth.
Ausschuss council ['kaʊnsl]
aussehen: glücklich / wütend / … aussehen look happy / angry / …
Außen- outdoor ['aʊtdɔ:]
außer except [ɪk'sept]
außerhalb von Rosie's Diner outside Rosie's Diner [,aʊt'saɪd]
äußern: sich (kritisch) äußern speak out
außerordentlich awfully ['ɔ:fli]
äußerst extremely [ɪk'stri:mli]
Aussicht view [vju:]
Aussprache pronunciation [prə,nʌnsi'eɪʃn]
aussprechen pronounce [prə'naʊns]
aussteigen get off [,get_'ɒf] **aus einem Bus / Flugzeug / Zug aussteigen** get off a bus / plane / train **aus einem Auto aussteigen** get out of a car
ausstrecken: etwas ausstrecken stretch sth. out [stretʃ] **die Hand ausstrecken** reach over [,ri:tʃ_'əʊvə]
aussuchen: (sich) etwas aussuchen choose sth. [tʃu:z]
Austausch exchange [ɪks'tʃeɪndʒ]
ausüben practise ['præktɪs]
Auswahl choice [tʃɔɪs]
auswählen choose [tʃu:z]
Auswirkung (auf) effect (on) [ɪ'fekt]
ausziehen: etwas ausziehen *(Kleidung)* take sth. off [,teɪk_ɒf]
Auszug (aus) excerpt (from) ['eksɜ:pt]
Auto car [kɑ:] **mit dem Auto fahren** go by car
Autogramm autograph ['ɔ:təgrɑ:f]
Autor/in author ['ɔ:θə]

B

Bach stream [stri:m]

backen bake [beɪk]
Backofen oven ['ʌvn]
Bad bath [bɑ:θ] **ein Bad nehmen** have / take a bath
baden *(in der Wanne)* have / take a bath [bɑ:θ]
Badezimmer bathroom ['bɑ:θru:m]
Bahnhof station ['steɪʃn]
Bahngleis track [træk]
Bahnsteig platform ['plætfɔ:m]
bald soon [su:n] **Bis bald.** See you. **schon bald** before long
Balkon balcony ['bælkəni]
Ball ball [bɔ:l]
Banane banana [bə'nɑ:nə]
Bar bar [bɑ:]
Bär bear [beə]
Barkeeper barman ['bɑ:mən]
Bart beard [bɪəd]
Basketball basketball ['bɑ:skɪtbɔ:l]
bauen build [bɪld]
Bauer / Bäuerin farmer ['fɑ:mə]
Bauernhaus farmhouse ['fɑ:mhaʊs]
Bauernhof farm [fɑ:m]
Baum tree [tri:]
Beamte(r), Beamtin official [ə'fɪʃl]
beantworten answer ['ɑ:nsə]
bearbeiten *(Texte, Videos)* edit ['edɪt]
Becher mug [mʌg]
bedeuten mean [mi:n]
Bedeutung meaning ['mi:nɪŋ]
Bedient euch! Help yourselves.
beeilen: sich beeilen hurry (up) [,hʌri_'ʌp]
beeindruckend impressive [ɪm'presɪv]
beenden: etwas beenden finish sth. ['fɪnɪʃ]; end sth.
beerdigen bury ['beri]
befragen: jn. befragen interview sb. ['ɪntəvju:]
begabt talented ['tæləntɪd]
Beginn beginning [bɪ'gɪnɪŋ]
beginnen start [stɑ:t]; begin [bɪ'gɪn]
begraben bury ['beri]
begrenzt limited ['lɪmɪtɪd]
Begriff term [tɜ:m] **im Begriff sein, etwas zu tun** be about to do sth. [ə'baʊt]
Begründung reason ['ri:zn]
begrüßen: jn. begrüßen (in) welcome sb. (to) ['welkəm]
behalten keep [ki:p]
▶ S. 232 (to) keep
behandeln *(abdecken)* cover ['kʌvə]
beheimaten: etwas beheimaten be home to sth. [həʊm]
beherrschen control [kən'trəʊl]
behutsam gently ['dʒentli]

bei *(in Ortsangaben)* at [æt], [ət] **bei den Blackwells zu Hause** at the Blackwells' house **bei Papa/Vati** at Dad's **bei jm. sein** be with sb. [wɪð]
beide both [bəʊθ]
Bein leg [leg]
beinahe almost ['ɔːlməʊst]; nearly ['nɪəli]
Beispiel example [ɪg'zɑːmpl] **zum Beispiel** for example
beißen bite [baɪt]
bekämpfen: jn. bekämpfen fight sb. [faɪt]
bekannt well-known [ˌwel'nəʊn]
bekanntgeben post [pəʊst]
beklagen: sich beklagen complain [kəm'pleɪn]
bekommen get [get]; *(Krankheit)* come down with
belebt busy ['bɪzi]
beleidigend offensive [ə'fensɪv]
beleidigt insulted [ɪn'sʌltɪd]
Beleidigung (für) insult (to) ['ɪnsʌlt]
beliebt (bei) popular (with) ['pɒpjələ]
bellen bark [bɑːk]
bemalt painted ['peɪntɪd]
bemerken notice ['nəʊtɪs]
Bemerkung comment ['kɒment]
benehmen: sich benehmen behave [bɪ'heɪv]
benötigen need [niːd]
benutzen use [juːz]
beobachten watch [wɒtʃ]; study ['stʌdi]
bequem comfortable ['kʌmftəbl]
Bereich area ['eəriə]
bereit ready ['redi]
bereits already [ɔːl'redi]
Berg mountain ['maʊntən]
bergab downhill [ˌdaʊn'hɪl]
Bergwerk mine [maɪn]
Bericht report [rɪ'pɔːt]
berichten report [rɪ'pɔːt] **jm. etwas berichten** tell sb. about sth. [tel]
berichtigen correct [kə'rekt]
berühmt (für, wegen) famous (for) ['feɪməs]
Berühmtheit *(berühmte Person)* celebrity [sə'lebrəti]
berühren touch [tʌtʃ] **peinlich berührt** embarrassed [ɪm'bærəst]
beschäftigen: sich mit etwas beschäftigen deal with sth. [diːl]
beschäftigt sein be busy ['bɪzi]
Bescheid: über etwas Bescheid wissen know about sth.
beschimpfen: jn. beschimpfen call sb. names
beschleunigen speed up [ˌspiːd‿'ʌp]
beschließen decide [dɪ'saɪd]
beschränkt limited ['lɪmɪtɪd]
beschreiben: (jm.) etwas beschreiben describe sth. (to sb.) [dɪ'skraɪb] **jm. den Weg (nach …) beschreiben** tell sb. the way (to …), give sb. directions (to …) [də'rekʃnz]
beschriften *(etikettieren)* label ['leɪbl]
Beschriftung *(Etikett)* label
beschweren: sich beschweren complain [kəm'pleɪn]
besiegen beat [biːt]
besitzen own [əʊn]
Besitzer/in owner ['əʊnə]
besondere(r, s) special ['speʃl]
besorgen: (sich) etwas besorgen get sth.
besorgt worried ['wʌrid]
besprühen spray [spreɪ]
besser better ['betə]
beste(r, s) best [best] **ihr bestes Buch** her best book **das Beste an …** the best thing about …
bestehen *(Test, Prüfung)* pass [pɑːs] **nicht bestehen** fail [feɪl]
bestellen order ['ɔːdə]
bestimmte(r, s) certain ['sɜːtn] **ganz bestimmt** for sure, definitely ['defɪnətli]
Bestrafung punishment ['pʌnɪʃmənt]
Besuch visit ['vɪzɪt]
besuchen: jn. besuchen visit sb. ['vɪzɪt]; see sb. [siː] **einen Kurs besuchen** attend a course [ə'tend]
Besucher/in visitor ['vɪzɪtə]
betonen stress [stres]
Betonung stress [stres]
Betonungszeichen stress mark
betreten enter ['entə]
Bett bed [bed]
beugen: sich beugen lean [liːn]
beunruhigt worried ['wʌrid]
Beutel bag [bæg]
Bevölkerung population [ˌpɒpju'leɪʃn]
bevor before [bɪ'fɔː]
bewachen guard [gɑːd]
bewegen; sich bewegen move [muːv]
Bewegung movement ['muːvmənt]
Bewohner/in resident ['rezɪdənt]
bewölkt cloudy ['klaʊdi]
bezahlen: (etwas) bezahlen pay (for sth.) [peɪ]
Beziehung relationship [rɪ'leɪʃnʃɪp]
Bibliothek library ['laɪbrəri]
Bild picture ['pɪktʃə], image ['ɪmɪdʒ] **auf dem Bild** in the picture
bilden form [fɔːm]
Bildschirm screen [skriːn] **geteilter Bildschirm** split screen [splɪt 'skriːn]
Bildunterschrift caption ['kæpʃn]
billig cheap [tʃiːp]
Bindestrich hyphen ['haɪfən]
Bindewort linking word ['lɪŋkɪŋ wɜːd]
bis **1.** till [tɪl]; until [ən'tɪl] **bis zwölf Uhr** till/until twelve o'clock **bis (spätestens) 20 Uhr** by 8 pm **bis jetzt** so far **Bis gleich. / Bis bald.** See you. **bis zehn zählen** count to ten **bis (zu)** up to **von … bis …** from … to …
2. bis auf *(außer)* except [ɪk'sept]
Bison (Amerikanischer) bison, *pl* bison ['baɪsn]
Biss, Bissen bite [baɪt]
bisschen: ein bisschen a bit [ə 'bɪt] a little ['lɪtl]
bitte please [pliːz] **Bitte sehr. / Hier bitte.** Here you are.
bitten: jemanden bitten, etwas zu tun ask sb. to do sth. [ɑːsk] **um etwas bitten** ask for sth.
bitter bitter ['bɪtə]
Bitterkeit bitterness ['bɪtənəs]
Blaskapelle brass band [ˌbrɑːs 'bænd]
Blatt leaf, *pl* leaves [liːf]
blau blue [bluː]
bleiben stay [steɪ], stick [stɪk] **(mit jm.) in Verbindung bleiben** stay in touch (with sb.) [tʌtʃ] **Bleiben Sie am Apparat.** Hold on a minute. [ˌhəʊld‿'ɒn], *(oft auch kurz:)* Hold on.
Bleistift pencil ['pensl]
Blick (auf) view (of) [vjuː] **einen Blick werfen (auf)** have a look (at)
blicken gaze [geɪz]
Blitz(e) lightning *(no pl)* ['laɪtnɪŋ] **ein Blitz** a flash of lightning
Block *(Häuser-, Wohnblock)* block [blɒk]
Blockflöte recorder [rɪ'kɔːdə]
blöd *(albern)* silly ['sɪli]; stupid ['stjuːpɪd]
Blödheit silliness ['sɪlinəs]
Blog-Eintrag post [pəʊst]
Blogschreiber/in blogger ['blɒgə]
blond blond *(bei Frauen oft:* blonde) [blɒnd]
bloß only ['əʊnli]; *(einfach nur)* just [dʒʌst]
blühen bloom [bluːm]
Blume flower ['flaʊə]
Blut blood [blʌd]
Blüte flower ['flaʊə]
Boden ground [graʊnd]
Bohne bean [biːn]
► S. 222 Food words
Boot boat [bəʊt]
Bootsfahrt cruise [kruːz]

Bord: an Bord (des Schiffes) on board (the ship) [ɒn 'bɔ:d]
Boss boss [bɒs]
Botschaft message ['mesɪdʒ]
Boulevard avenue ['ævənju:]
braten *(im Backofen)* roast [rəʊst], *(in der Pfanne)* fry [fraɪ]
Brathähnchen chicken ['tʃɪkɪn]
Bratpfanne frying pan ['fraɪɪŋ pæn]
brauchen need [ni:d]; *(Zeit)* take [teɪk] **du brauchst es nicht zu tun** you needn't do it ['ni:dnt]
braun brown [braʊn]
brav good [gʊd], **brav** well-behaved [ˌwelbɪ'heɪvd]
brechen *(kaputt gehen)* break [breɪk]
breit wide [waɪd]
brennen burn [bɜ:n]
Brief letter ['letə]
Briefkasten letterbox ['letəbɒks]
Brille glasses *(pl)* ['glɑ:sɪz]
bringen *(mit-, herbringen)* bring [brɪŋ]; *(weg-, hinbringen)* take [teɪk] **Kannst du mich zum Bahnhof bringen?** Can you give me a lift to the station? [lɪft]
Brise breeze [bri:z]
britisch British ['brɪtɪʃ]
Broschüre brochure ['brəʊʃə]
Brot bread [bred]
Brücke bridge [brɪdʒ]
Bruder brother ['brʌðə]
brüllen roar [rɔ:]
Brust(korb) chest [tʃest]
Buch book [bʊk]
buchen reserve [rɪ'zɜ:v]
Bücherei library ['laɪbrəri]
Buchstabe letter ['letə]
buchstabieren spell [spel]
bücken: sich bücken bend down
Bühne stage [steɪdʒ]
bunt colourful ['kʌləfl]
Burg castle ['kɑ:sl]
Bürgerrechte civil rights *(pl)* [ˌsɪvl 'raɪts]
Bürgersteig pavement ['peɪvmənt]; *(AE)* sidewalk ['saɪdwɔ:k]
Bürgermeister/in mayor [meə]
Büro office ['ɒfɪs]
Bus bus **mit dem Bus fahren** go by bus
Busch shrub [ʃrʌb]
Bushaltestelle bus stop
Butter butter ['bʌtə]
► S. 222 Food words

C

Café café ['kæfeɪ]
Cafeteria cafeteria [ˌkæfə'tɪəriə]
Cañon canyon ['kænjən]
Celsius Celsius (C) ['selsiəs]
► S. 220 Temperatures
Cent cent [sent]
Champion champion ['tʃæmpiən]
Chance chance [tʃɑ:ns]
Chaos chaos ['keɪɒs]
Chat chat [tʃæt]
chatten chat [tʃæt]
Chef/in boss [bɒs]
Chor choir ['kwaɪə]
Clown/in clown [klaʊn]
Comedyshow comedy ['kɒmədi]
Computer computer [kəm'pju:tə]
cool cool [ku:l]
Cornflakes cornflakes ['kɔ:nfleɪks]
Courage courage ['kʌrɪdʒ]
Cousin, Cousine cousin ['kʌzn]
Curry(gericht) curry ['kʌri]

D

da, dahin *(dort, dorthin)* there [ðeə] **da drüben** over there **nicht da sein** be out
Dach roof [ru:f]
Dachboden attic ['ætɪk] **auf dem Dachboden** in the attic
dagegen: etwas dagegen haben mind [maɪnd])
daheim at home [ət 'həʊm]
daher *(deshalb)* so [səʊ]
Dame: Meine Damen und Herren / Sehr geehrte Damen und Herren Ladies and gentlemen [ˌleɪdiz‿ən 'dʒentlmən]
damit ... so that ... *(oft auch kurz:* so ...)
danach after that ['ɑ:ftə], afterwards ['ɑ:ftəwədz]
dank Maya thanks to Maya
dankbar glad [glæd]
Danke. Thank you. ['θæŋk ju:]; Thanks. [θæŋks] **Danke fürs Zuhören.** Thank you for listening. **Danke, gut.** Fine, thanks.
dann then [ðen] **gerade dann** *(genau in dem Moment)* just then
darüber above [ə'bʌv]
darum that's why
darunter (von) below [bɪ'ləʊ] **darunter (auch)** *(einschließlich)* including [ɪn'klu:dɪŋ]
das *(Artikel)* the [ðə]
das *(Relativpronomen)* **1.** *(für Dinge)* which; that **2.** *(für Personen)* who; that
das (dort) *(Singular)* that [ðæt]; *(Plural)* those [ðəʊz] **das Auto dort** that car
dass that [ðæt], [ðət] **es zeigt, dass ...** it shows that ...
dasselbe wie ... the same as ... [seɪm]
Datum date [deɪt]
dauern *(Zeit brauchen)* take [teɪk]
davor: kurz davor sein, etwas zu tun be about to do sth.
Deck deck [dek]
dehnen: sich dehnen stretch [stretʃ]
dein(e) ... your ... [jɔ:], [jə]
deiner, deine, deins yours [jɔ:z]
Demonstrant/in marcher [mɑ:tʃə], protester [prə'testə]
Demonstration demonstration [ˌdemən'streɪʃn]; march [mɑ:tʃ]
denken think [θɪŋk] **an etwas denken** think of sth.; *(nicht vergessen)* remember sth. [rɪ'membə] **/ Ich denke, ...** I guess ... [ges]
Denkmal (für/zum Gedenken an) monument (to) ['mɒnjumənt]; memorial [mə'mɔ:riəl]
denn: Was ist denn? What's the matter? ['mætə]
deprimierend depressing [dɪ'presɪŋ]
der *(Artikel)* the [ðə]
der *(Relativpronomen)* **1.** *(für Personen)* who; that **2.** *(für Dinge)* which; that
der ... (dort) *(Singular)* that ... [ðæt]; *(Plural)* those ... [ðəʊz] **der ... (hier)** *(Singular)* this ... [ðɪs]; *(Plural)* these ... [ði:z]
deren: die Männer, deren Wohnungen ... the men whose homes ... [hu:z]
derselbe wie ... the same as ... [seɪm]
deshalb so [səʊ]; that's why
Design design [dɪ'zaɪn]
Designer/in designer [dɪ'zaɪnə]
Detail detail ['di:teɪl] **ins Detail gehen** go into detail
deuten: auf etwas deuten *(zeigen)* point to sth. [pɔɪnt]
deutlich clear(ly) [klɪə], ['klɪəli]
Deutsch; deutsch German ['dʒɜ:mən]
Dezember December [dɪ'sembə]
Dialog dialogue ['daɪəlɒg]
dich you [ju:]; *(Reflexivpronomen)* yourself [jɔ:'self]
dicht (bei, an) close (to) [kləʊs]
dick fat [fæt], thick [θɪk]
die *(Artikel)* the [ðə]

die *(Relativpronomen)* **1.** *(für Personen)* who; that **2.** *(für Dinge)* which; that
die … (dort) *(Singular)* that … [ðæt]; *(Plural)* those … [ðəʊz] **die … (hier)** *(Singular)* this … [ðɪs]; *(Plural)* these … [ði:z]
Dieb/in thief [θi:f] [θi:vz]
dieselbe(n) wie … the same as … [seɪm]
Dienst service ['sɜ:vɪs]
Dienstag Tuesday ['tju:zdeɪ, 'tju:zdi]
dies (hier) *(Singular)* this [ðɪs]; *(Plural)* these [ði:z] **dies (hier) ist …** this is … **dies (hier) sind …** these are …
diese(r, s): dieser Ort / diese Pause / dieses Fach this place/ break/subject **diese Leute** these people **Diese(r, s) hier.** This one.
▶ S. 223 one/ones
diesjährige(r, s): das diesjährige Musical this year's musical
digital digital ['dɪdʒɪtl]
Ding thing [θɪŋ]
dir you [ju:]; *(Reflexivpronomen)* yourself [jɔ:'self]
direkt straight [streɪt] **direkt hinter dir** right behind you [raɪt]
Dirigent/in director [də'rektə]
Disko disco ['dɪskəʊ]
Diskriminierung (von) discrimination (against) [dɪˌskrɪmɪ'neɪʃn]
Diskussion discussion [dɪ'skʌʃn]
Dollar dollar ($) ['dɒlə], buck *(infml)* [bʌk]
Dom cathedral [kə'θi:drəl]
Donner thunder ['θʌndə]
Donnerstag Thursday ['θɜ:zdeɪ, 'θɜ:zdi]
Doppel- double ['dʌbl]
Doppelpunkt colon ['kəʊlən]
Dorf village ['vɪlɪdʒ]
dort, dorthin there [ðeə] **dort drüben** over there **dort entlang** that way [weɪ] **dort unten** down there
Dose tin [tɪn] *(BE: für Essen)*, can *(AE; BE: für Getränke)* [kæn]
Dosen-; in Dosen tinned [tɪnd]
dramatisch dramatic [drə'mætɪk]
dran: Ich bin dran. (It's) my turn. [tɜ:n]
draußen outside [ˌaʊt'saɪd] **nach draußen** outside
Drehbuch script [skrɪpt]
drehen: sich drehen turn [tɜ:n] **einen Film drehen** shoot a film [ʃu:t]
Drehort location [ləʊ'keɪʃn]
drinnen inside [ˌɪn'saɪd] **nach drinnen** inside
dritte(r, s) third [θɜ:d]
dröhnen roar [rɔ:]
drüben: da drüben, dort drüben over there
drücken *(schieben, stoßen)* push; press [pres]
Dudelsack bagpipes *(pl)* ['bægpaɪps]
Dudelsackpfeifer/in, -spieler/in bagpiper ['bægpaɪpə]
dumm stupid ['stju:pɪd]
Dummerchen silly ['sɪli]
dunkel dark [dɑ:k]
Dunkelheit darkness ['dɑ:knəs]
durch through [θru:]
durchfallen *(Test, Prüfung)* fail [feɪl]
Durchsage announcement [ə'naʊnsmənt]
Durchsuchung search [sɜ:tʃ]
dürfen can [kæn], [kən]; may [meɪ]; be allowed to [ə'laʊd] **du darfst es nicht tun** you mustn't do it ['mʌsnt]
Dürre drought [draʊt]
Durst haben be thirsty ['θɜ:sti]
durstig sein be thirsty ['θɜ:sti]
DVD DVD [ˌdi:vi:'di:]

E

Ebbe: Es ist Ebbe. The tide is out. [taɪd]
eben *(soeben)* just [dʒʌst], *(flach)* flat [flæt]
echt real ['ri:əl]
Ecke corner ['kɔ:nə] **Church Road, Ecke London Road** on the corner of Church Road and London Road
egal: Aber egal, … *(Wie dem auch sei)* Anyway, … ['eniweɪ]
Ehre honour ['ɒnə]
Ehrenamtliche(r) volunteer [ˌvɒlən'tɪə]
Ei egg [eg]
Eierkuchen pancake ['pænkeɪk]
eifersüchtig (auf) jealous (of) ['dʒeləs]
eigene(r, s): mein eigener Film / mein eigenes Zimmer / … my own film/room/… [əʊn]
eigentlich in fact [ɪn 'fækt]; actually ['æktʃuəli]
Eigentum property ['prɒpəti]
eilen hurry ['hʌri]
Eimer bucket ['bʌkɪt]
ein(e) *(Artikel)* a, an [ə], [ən] **ein anderer … / eine andere … / ein anderes …** another … [ə'nʌðə] **einer nach dem anderen** one by one **eines Nachts/Tages** one night/day **ein paar** a few [ə 'fju:]; some [sʌm], [səm]
einbringen *(Heu)* bring in
eindrängen: sich in etwas eindrängen force your way into sth. [fɔ:s]
Eindruck impression [ɪm'preʃn]
einfach 1. *(nicht schwierig)* easy ['i:zi] **2. einfach nur** just [dʒʌst]
Einführung introduction [ˌɪntrə'dʌkʃn]
eingängig *(Melodie, Slogan)* catchy ['kætʃi]
eingeschaltet sein *(Radio, Licht usw.)* be on [ɒn]
einhundert a hundred, one hundred ['hʌndrəd]
einige a few [ə 'fju:]; some [sʌm], [səm]
einigen: sich auf etwas einigen agree on sth. [ə'gri:]
Einkäufe erledigen do the/some shopping ['ʃɒpɪŋ]
einkaufen shop [ʃɒp] **einkaufen gehen** go shopping ['ʃɒpɪŋ]; do the shopping / do some shopping
Einkaufszentrum shopping centre ['ʃɒpɪŋ sentə]; (shopping) mall [mɔ:l]
einladen: jn. einladen (zu) invite sb. (to) [ɪn'vaɪt]
Einladung (zu, nach) invitation (to) [ˌɪnvɪ'teɪʃn]
Einleitung introduction [ˌɪntrə'dʌkʃn]
einmal 1. once [wʌns] **noch einmal** again [ə'gen]; one more time **2. auf einmal** *(plötzlich)* suddenly ['sʌdnli] **3. (noch) nicht einmal** not even
einmarschieren (in ein Land) invade (a country) [ɪn'veɪd]
einpassen: etwas in etwas einpassen fit sth. into sth. [fɪt]
einreichen: etwas einreichen hand sth. in
eins one [wʌn]
einsam lonely ['ləʊnli]
einschalten: etwas einschalten turn sth. on [ˌtɜ:n_'ɒn]
einschlafen fall asleep [ˌfɔ:l_ə'sli:p]
einschließen include [ɪn'klu:d]
einschließlich including [ɪn'klu:dɪŋ]
einsetzen: sich einsetzen (für/gegen etwas/jn.) stand up (for/against sth./sb.) [ˌstænd_'ʌp]
einsteigen: in ein Auto/Taxi einsteigen get in(to) a car/taxi **in einen Bus / einen Zug / ein Flugzeug einsteigen** get on a bus/train/plane
Einstellung *(Film)* shot [ʃɒt]; take [teɪk]
einstürzen collapse [kə'læps]

Eintopf stew [stjuː]
Eintrag, Eintragung *(im Tagebuch, Wörterbuch)* entry ['entri]
eintreffen arrive [ə'raɪv]
eintreten enter ['entə] **in einen Klub eintreten** join a club [dʒɔɪn] **eintreten (für/gegen etwas/ jn.)** stand up (for/against sth./sb.) [ˌstænd‿'ʌp]
Eintritt entry ['entri]
Eintrittskarte ticket ['tɪkɪt]
Einwanderer/Einwanderin immigrant ['ɪmɪgrənt]
Einwohner(zahl) population [ˌpɒpju'leɪʃn]
Einzelheit detail ['diːteɪl] **auf Einzelheiten eingehen** go into detail
einzeln separately ['seprətli]
einziehen move in **in ein Haus einziehen** move into a house
einzige(r, s): **der/die/das einzige ...; die einzigen...** the only ... ['əʊnli]
Eis ice [aɪs]; *(Speiseeis)* ice cream [ˌaɪs 'kriːm]
Eisenbahn railroad *(AE)* ['reɪlrəʊd], railway *(BE)* ['reɪlweɪ]
ekelhaft disgusting [dɪs'gʌstɪŋ]
Elefant elephant ['elɪfənt]
elementar basic ['beɪsɪk]
Eltern parents ['peərənts]
E-Mail mail; email ['iːmeɪl]
empfehlen recommend [ˌrekə'mend]
Emotion emotion [ɪ'məʊʃn]
emotional emotional [ɪ'məʊʃənl]
emporragen *(Berge, Säulen, Türme, ...)* rise up [ˌraɪz‿'ʌp]
Ende end [end]; *(Abschluss)* ending **am oberen Ende (von)** at the top (of) **am unteren Ende (von)** at the bottom (of) ['bɒtəm] **zu Ende sein** be over ['əʊvə]
enden finish ['fɪnɪʃ]; end
endlich *(schließlich)* at last [ət 'lɑːst]; finally ['faɪnəli]
Endspiel final ['faɪnl]
Energie energy ['enədʒi], power ['paʊə]
eng narrow ['nærəʊ]
Englisch; englisch English ['ɪŋglɪʃ]
entdecken discover [dɪ'skʌvə] **jn./ etwas entdecken, erblicken** spot sb./sth. [spɒt]
Entdeckung discovery [dɪ'skʌvəri]
Entfernung distance ['dɪstəns]
entgegnen reply [rɪ'plaɪ]
entlang: die Straße / den Fluss / ... entlang along the street / the river / ... [ə'lɒŋ] **dort entlang** that way **hier entlang** this way [weɪ]
entscheiden: sich entscheiden decide [dɪ'saɪd]
Entscheidung decision [dɪ'sɪʒn]
Entschuldigung. **1.** *(Tut mir leid.)* (I'm) sorry. ['sɒri] **2. Entschuldigung, ... / Entschuldigen Sie, ...** *(Darf ich mal stören?)* Excuse me, ... [ɪk'skjuːz miː]
entsetzt shocked [ʃɒkt]; in horror ['hɒrə]
entspannen: sich entspannen relax [rɪ'læks]
entspannt relaxed [rɪ'lækst]
enttäuscht (von) disappointed (with) [ˌdɪsə'pɔɪntɪd]
Entwurf draft [drɑːft]
Episode episode ['epɪsəʊd]
er **1.** *(männliche Person)* he [hiː] **2.** *(Ding; Tier)* it [ɪt]
Erdbeere strawberry ['strɔːbəri]
Erde *(der Planet)* earth [ɜːθ] *(oft auch: Earth)* **auf der Erde** on earth
Ereignis event [ɪ'vent]
erfahren experience [ɪk'spɪəriəns]
Erfahrung(en) experience *(no pl)* [ɪk'spɪəriəns]
erfinden invent [ɪn'vent]
Erfolg success [sək'ses]
erforschen explore [ɪk'splɔː]
ergänzen (zu) add (to) [æd]
Ergebnis result [rɪ'zʌlt]
erhältlich available [ə'veɪləbl]
erhellen *(aufleuchten lassen)* light up [ˌlaɪt 'ʌp]
erinnern: sich an etwas erinnern remember sth. [rɪ'membə] **jn. erinnern** remind sb. [rɪ'maɪnd]
Erinnerung memory ['meməri]
erkältet sein have a cold [kəʊld]
Erkältung: eine Erkältung haben have a cold [kəʊld]
erkennen recognize ['rekəgnaɪz]
erklären: jm. etwas erklären explain sth. to sb. [ɪk'spleɪn]
erkranken an come down with
erkunden explore [ɪk'splɔː]
erlauben allow [ə'laʊ]
Erlaubnis permission [pə'mɪʃn], *(Erlaubnisschein)* permit ['pɜːmɪt]
erläutern: jm. etwas erläutern explain sth. to sb. [ɪk'spleɪn]
erleben experience [ɪk'spɪəriəns]
ermitteln investigate [ɪn'vestɪgeɪt]
ermorden murder ['mɜːdə]
ernst; ernsthaft serious ['sɪəriəs]
Erntedankfest *(amerikanischer Feiertag am vierten Donnerstag im November)* Thanksgiving [θæŋks'gɪvɪŋ]
erraten guess [ges]
erreichbar *(am Telefon)* available [ə'veɪləbl]
erreichen reach [riːtʃ]
errichten: etwas errichten set sth. up
erröten go red
erschaffen create [kri'eɪt]
erscheinen appear [ə'pɪə]
erschießen shoot [ʃuːt]
erschrecken: jn. erschrecken scare sb. [skeə]
erst only ['əʊnli] **erst um drei** *(nicht vor drei)* not till three
erstaunlich amazing [ə'meɪzɪŋ]
erste(r, s) first [fɜːst] **als Erstes** first **der erste Tag** the first day
ertrinken drown [draʊn]
erwachsen werden grow up [ˌgrəʊ‿'ʌp]
Erwachsene(r) adult ['ædʌlt]
erwähnen mention ['menʃn]
erwarten expect [ɪk'spekt] **Ich kann es kaum erwarten, ... zu sehen.** I can't wait to see ...
erwidern reply [rɪ'plaɪ]
erzählen (von) tell (about) [tel]
Erzähler/in narrator [nə'reɪtə]
Erzählung story ['stɔːri]
es it [ɪt] **es ist ... / es gibt ...** there's ... **es sind ... / es gibt ...** there are ... **Ach, du bist es.** Oh, it's you. **Bist du es?** Is that you?
essen eat [iːt] **zu Abend essen** have dinner **zu Mittag essen** have lunch
Essen *(Lebensmittel)* food [fuːd]
Esszimmer dining room ['daɪnɪŋ ruːm]
Etage floor [flɔː]
Etikett label
etikettieren label ['leɪbl]
etwas **1.** something ['sʌmθɪŋ]; *(in Fragen)* anything ['eniθɪŋ] **2.** *(ein bisschen)* some [sʌm], [səm]; a bit [ə 'bɪt]; a little ['lɪtl]
EU: die EU the EU [ˌiː 'juː] **die Europäische Union** the European Union [ˌjʊərəpiːən 'juːniən]
euch you [juː]; *(Reflexivpronomen)* yourselves [jɔː'selvz]
euer ... / eure ... your ... [jɔː], [jə]
eurer, eure, eures yours [jɔːz]
Euro euro (€) ['jʊərəʊ]
Europa Europe ['jʊərəp]
evakuieren evacuate [ɪ'vækjueɪt]
ewig *(für immer)* for ever [fər‿'evə] **Ich habe eine Ewigkeit kein Fleisch gegessen.** I haven't eaten meat for ages. [fər‿'eɪdʒɪz]
Ewigkeit: vor einer Ewigkeit ages ago ['eɪdʒɪz‿əˌgəʊ]

exotisch exotic [ɪɡ'zɒtɪk]
Experte/Expertin expert ['ekspɜːt]

F

Fabrik factory ['fæktri]
Fackel torch [tɔːtʃ]
Fahne *(Flagge)* flag [flæɡ]
fähig sein, etwas zu tun be able to do sth. ['eɪbl]
Fähre ferry ['feri]
fahren go [ɡəʊ]; *(ein Auto / mit dem Auto)* drive [draɪv] **in Urlaub fahren** go on holiday **mit dem Bus/Auto/Zug fahren** go by bus/car/train **Rad fahren** ride a bike **in/gegen etwas fahren** crash into sth. [kræʃ]
▶ S. 215 (to) crash
Fahrenheit Fahrenheit (F) ['færənhaɪt]
▶ S. 220 Temperatures
Fahrer/in driver [draɪvə]
Fahrerlaubnis *AE:* driver's license ['draɪvəz ˌlaɪsəns]; *BE:* driving licence ['draɪvɪŋ laɪsns]
Fahrkarte ticket ['tɪkɪt]
Fahrkartenschalter ticket office ['tɪkɪt‿ˌɒfɪs]
Fahrplan timetable ['taɪmteɪbl]
Fahrt drive [draɪv]
Fakt fact [fækt]
faktisch factual ['fæktʃʊəl]
Fahrrad bike [baɪk]
Fahrstuhl lift [lɪft], elevator *(bes. AE)* ['elɪveɪtə]
Fahrt journey ['dʒɜːni]; ride [raɪd]
fair fair ['feə]
Fall: Auf keinen Fall! No way! [ˌnəʊ 'weɪ]
fallen *(stürzen)* fall [fɔːl] **etwas fallen lassen** drop sth. [drɒp]
falls if [ɪf]
falsch wrong [rɒŋ] **Nein, das ist falsch.** No, that's wrong.
Familie family ['fæməli] **Familie Blackwell** the Blackwell family **eine vierköpfige Familie** a family of four
Fan fan [fæn]
fangen catch [kætʃ]
fantastisch fantastic [fæn'tæstɪk]
Farbe colour *(AE:* **color***)* ['kʌlə]
Farm farm [fɑːm]
Fasching carnival ['kɑːnɪvl]
fast almost ['ɔːlməʊst]; nearly ['nɪəli]
Februar February ['februəri]
Federmäppchen pencil case ['pensl keɪs]

fehlen be missing ['mɪsɪŋ] **die fehlenden Wörter** the missing words **Was fehlt Justin/dir?** *(Was ist los?)* What's wrong with Justin/you?
Fehler mistake [mɪ'steɪk]
Feier celebration [ˌselɪ'breɪʃn]
feiern celebrate ['selɪbreɪt]
fein fine [faɪn]
Feind/in enemy ['enəmi]
Feld field [fiːld]
Fels, Felsen rock [rɒk]
felsig rocky ['rɒki]
Fenster window ['wɪndəʊ]
Ferien holidays *(pl)* ['hɒlədeɪz]
Fernbedienung remote control *(kurz auch:* remote*)* [rɪˌməʊt kən'trəʊl]
Ferne distance ['dɪstəns]
fernsehen watch TV [ˌwɒtʃ tiː'viː]
Fernsehen, Fernsehgerät TV [ˌtiː'viː]
fertig **1. mit etwas fertig werden/sein** finish sth. ['fɪnɪʃ] **Wir sind fertig.** *(Wir haben es erledigt.)* We're finished. ['fɪnɪʃt]
2. *(bereit)* ready ['redi] **Wir sind fertig.** *(Wir sind bereit.)* We're ready. **sich fertig machen (für)** get ready (for)
Fertigkeit skill [skɪl]
Fest, Festival festival ['festɪvl]
festnehmen arrest [ə'rest]
festziehen tighten ['taɪtn]
fett fat [fæt]
Feuer fire ['faɪə]
Feuerwehrmann/-frau firefighter ['faɪəfaɪtə]
Feuerwerk fireworks *(pl)* ['faɪəwɜːks]
Feuerwerkskörper firework ['faɪəwɜːk]
Fieber haben have a temperature ['temprətʃə]
Figur figure ['fɪɡə]; *(in Roman, Film usw.)* character ['kærəktə]
Film film [fɪlm], movie ['muːvi]
filmen film [fɪlm]
Filzstift felt pen [ˌfelt 'pen]
Finale final ['faɪnl]
finden find [faɪnd] **Freunde finden** make friends **Wie findest du ...?** How do you like ...?
Finger finger ['fɪŋɡə]
Finsternis darkness ['dɑːknəs]
Fisch fish [fɪʃ]
flach *(Wasser)* shallow ['ʃæləʊ], *(Landschaft)* flat [flæt]
Flagge flag [flæɡ]
Flamme flame [fleɪm]
Flasche bottle ['bɒtl]
Fleck spot [spɒt]
Fleisch meat [miːt]
fliegen fly [flaɪ]

fliehen escape [ɪ'skeɪp]
fließen flow [fləʊ]
Flucht escape [ɪ'skeɪp]
Flügel wing [wɪŋ]
Flughafen airport ['eəpɔːt]
Flugzeug plane [pleɪn] **im Flugzeug** on the plane
Fluss river ['rɪvə]
flussabwärts downstream [ˌdaʊn'striːm]
flüstern whisper ['wɪspə] **..., sagte er flüsternd.** ..., he said under his breath. [breθ]
Flut flood [flʌd] **Es ist Flut.** The tide is in. [taɪd]
Flutlicht(lampe) floodlight ['flʌdlaɪt]
folgen follow ['fɒləʊ]
folglich as a result [rɪ'zʌlt]
Folie *(für Präsentationen mit Computerprogramm)* slide [slaɪd]
Form (von) form (of) [fɔːm]
formen form [fɔːm]
Forschung(en) research *(no pl)* ['riːsɜːtʃ]
fort away [ə'weɪ]
fortfahren *(weiterreden)* go on [ˌɡəʊ‿'ɒn]
fortsetzen: etwas fortsetzen continue sth. [kən'tɪnjuː], keep sth. up
▶ S. 232 (to) keep
Foto photo ['fəʊtəʊ], shot [ʃɒt] **auf dem Foto** in the photo **Fotos machen** take photos
Fotoapparat camera ['kæmərə]
fotografieren take photos; photograph ['fəʊtəɡrɑːf]
Frage question ['kwestʃn] **Fragen stellen** ask questions **Kommt nicht in Frage!** No way! [ˌnəʊ 'weɪ]
fragen ask [ɑːsk] **jn. nach dem Weg fragen** ask sb. the way **sich fragen** wonder ['wʌndə]
Fragezeichen question mark ['kwestʃən mɑːk]
Französisch; französisch French [frentʃ]
Frau **1.** woman ['wʊmən]
2. Frau Bell Mrs *(AE:* **Mrs.***)* Bell ['mɪsɪz]; Ms/Ms. Bell [mɪz], [məz]
Fräulein *(Anrede für eine Unbekannte)* Miss [mɪs]
frei free [friː] **einen Tag frei bekommen/haben** get/have a day off **frei haben** be free
Freiheit liberty ['lɪbəti]
Freistoß free kick [ˌfriː 'kɪk] **einen Freistoß ausführen** take a free kick
Freitag Friday ['fraɪdeɪ], ['fraɪdi]
Freiwillige(r) volunteer [ˌvɒlən'tɪə]

Freizeit free time [ˌfriː 'taɪm]
Freizeitaktivitäten free-time activities [ˌfriːtaɪm‿æk'tɪvətiz]
fremd foreign ['fɒrən]
Fremde(r), Unbekannte(r) stranger ['streɪndʒə]
Fremdenführer/in *(Reiseleiter/in)* guide [gaɪd]
freuen: sich auf etwas freuen look forward to sth. ['fɔːwəd] **Freut mich, dich/euch/Sie kennenzulernen.** Nice to meet you.
Freund/in friend [frend]; mate [meɪt]; boyfriend ['bɔɪfrend] **Freunde finden** make friends
Freundin girlfriend ['gɜːlfrend]
freundlich friendly ['frendli]; kind [kaɪnd]
Friede, Frieden peace [piːs]
Friedhof cemetery *BE:* ['semətri], *AE:* ['seməteri]
frieren be cold
frisch fresh [freʃ]
Friseur/in hairdresser ['heədresə]
froh *(glücklich)* happy ['hæpi]; *(dankbar)* glad [glæd]
Frosch frog [frɒg]
Frucht fruit [fruːt]
Fruchtshake smoothie ['smuːði]
früh early ['ɜːli]
Frühling spring [sprɪŋ]
Frühstück breakfast ['brekfəst]
frühstücken have breakfast
Frühstückspension bed and breakfast (B&B)
fühlen; sich fühlen feel [fiːl] **Ich fühle mich nicht gut.** I don't feel well. **Ich fühle mit ...** My heart goes out to ...
führen lead [liːd]
Führerschein *AE:* driver's license ['draɪvəz ˌlaɪsəns]; *BE:* driving licence ['draɪvɪŋ laɪsns]
füllen fill [fɪl]
Füller pen [pen]
funktionieren work [wɜːk]
für for [fɔː], [fə] **für immer** for ever [fər‿'evə]
furchtbar, fürchterlich terrible ['terəbl]; awful ['ɔːfl]
Fuß foot *(auch Längenmaß; ca. 30 cm)* [fʊt] **zu Fuß gehen** walk [wɔːk] **ein 9.740 Fuß langes Schwimmbad** a 9,740-foot swimming pool
▶ S. 219 a 9,740-foot swimming pool
Fußabdruck footprint ['fʊtprɪnt]
Fußball football ['fʊtbɔːl]; *(AE)* soccer ['sɒkə]
Fußboden floor [flɔː]
Fußgänger/in pedestrian [pə'destrɪən]
Fußgängerzone pedestrian zone [pə'destrɪən zəʊn]
Futter food [fuːd]
füttern feed [fiːd]
Fütterungszeit feeding time ['fiːdɪŋ taɪm]

G

Gabel fork [fɔːk]
Galerie gallery ['gæləri]
galoppieren gallop ['gæləp]
Gang corridor ['kɒrɪdɔː]
ganz quite [kwaɪt] **ganz allein** all alone
ganze(r, s) whole [həʊl] **das ganze Plymouth, ganz Plymouth** all of Plymouth **den ganzen Tag** all day **die ganze Zeit** all the time **ganzer Satz** full sentence **in der ganzen Stadt/auf der ganzen Welt** all over the city / the world
gar nichts nothing ['nʌθɪŋ]
Garnele shrimp, *pl* shrimp *oder* shrimps [ʃrɪmp]
Garten garden ['gɑːdn]; *(AE)* yard [jɑːd]
Gartenarbeit gardening ['gɑːdnɪŋ]
Gärtnern gardening ['gɑːdnɪŋ]
Gast guest [gest]
Gastfamilie host family ['həʊst fæməli]
Gastgeberin hostess ['həʊstəs]
Gatter gate [geɪt]
gebackene Kartoffeln *(im Backofen in Fett gebacken)* roast potatoes [rəʊst pə'teɪtəʊz]
Gebäude building ['bɪldɪŋ]
geben give [gɪv] **Es gibt ...** *(Singular)* There's ...; *(Plural)* There are ... **Gibt es (irgendwelche) ...?** Are there any ...? ['eni] **Was gibt es zum Mittagessen?** What's for lunch?
Gebiet area ['eəriə]
geboren sein/werden be born [bɔːn]
gebrochen broken ['brəʊkən]
Geburtstag birthday ['bɜːθdeɪ] **Ich habe am 5. Mai Geburtstag.** My birthday is on 5th May. **Ich habe im Mai Geburtstag.** My birthday is in May. **Wann hast du Geburtstag?** When's your birthday?
Gedanke thought [θɔːt] **jemandes Gedanken lesen** read sb.'s mind [maɪnd]
Gedenk- memorial [mə'mɔːriəl]
Gedicht poem ['pəʊɪm]
Gefahr danger ['deɪndʒə]
gefährlich dangerous ['deɪndʒərəs]
gefallen: Wie gefällt dir ...? How do you like ...?
Gefängnis prison ['prɪzn]
Gefühl feeling ['fiːlɪŋ]; emotion [ɪ'məʊʃn]
gefühlsbetont emotional [ɪ'məʊʃənl]
gegen against [ə'genst]
Gegend area ['eəriə]; *(Landschaft)* countryside ['kʌntrisaɪd] *(Stadt)* neighborhood *(AE)* / neighbourhood *(BE)* ['neɪbəhʊd]
Gegensatz contrast ['kɒntrɑːst]
Gegensatzwort antonym ['æntənɪm]
Gegenteil opposite ['ɒpəzɪt]
gegenüber (von) opposite ['ɒpəzɪt]
Gegenwart present ['preznt]
gehen go [gəʊ]; *(zu Fuß gehen)* walk [wɔːk] **ans Telefon gehen** answer the phone **einkaufen gehen** go shopping ['ʃɒpɪŋ]; do the/some shopping **kaputt gehen** break [breɪk] **Los geht's. / Jetzt geht's los.** Here we go. **nach Hause gehen** go home **segeln gehen** go sailing **spazieren gehen** go for a walk **zelten gehen** go camping **zum Arzt gehen** see a doctor **Mir geht's nicht gut.** I don't feel well. **Wie geht's? / Wie geht es dir/euch/Ihnen?** How are you? **Worum geht es in der Geschichte?** What is the story about? **Es geht um eine Möwe.** It's about a seagull.
gehören: (zu) jm. gehören belong to sb. [bɪ'lɒŋ] **zu etwas gehören** *(zu etwas passen)* go with sth.
Gehweg pavement ['peɪvmənt]; *(AE)* sidewalk ['saɪdwɔːk]
Geige violin [ˌvaɪə'lɪn]
Geist *(Gespenst)* ghost [gəʊst] *(Verstand)* mind [maɪnd]
gekränkt upset [ˌʌp'set]
Gel gel [dʒel]
Gelächter laughter ['lɑːftə]
Gelände grounds *(pl)* [graʊndz]
gelangen *(hinkommen)* get [get]
gelangweilt sein be/feel bored [bɔːd]
gelb yellow ['jeləʊ]
Geld money ['mʌni] **Geld sammeln (für etwas)** *(für wohltätige Zwecke)* raise money (for sth.) [reɪz] **Geld ausgeben (für)** spend money (on) [spend]
Geldbörse purse [pɜːs] *(bei Frauen)*; wallet ['wɒlɪt] *(bei Männern)*
Gelegenheit chance [tʃɑːns]

gemein: etwas miteinander gemein haben have sth. in common ['kɒmən]
Gemüse vegetables *(pl)* ['vedʒtəblz]
genannt werden *(heißen)* be called [kɔ:ld]
genau **1. genau in dem Moment** just then **genau wie …** just like … ['dʒʌst laɪk]; exact [ɪg'zækt] **2. genau hinschauen** look closely ['kləʊsli]
genauso gut/schlecht/… just as good/bad/… [dʒʌst]
Genehmigung permit ['pɜ:mɪt]
Generation generation [ˌdʒenə'reɪʃn]
genial *(großartig, glänzend)* brilliant ['brɪliənt]
genießen enjoy [ɪn'dʒɔɪ]
genug enough [ɪ'nʌf]
geöffnet open ['əʊpən]
Geografie geography [dʒi'ɒgrəfi]
Gerät machine [mə'ʃi:n]
gerade *(im Moment)* at the moment ['məʊmənt] **gerade dann** just then **gerade eben** just [dʒʌst] **jetzt gerade** *(in diesem Moment)* right now
geradeaus weiter straight on [streɪt_'ɒn]
geradewegs straight [streɪt]
Geräusch sound [saʊnd]; noise [nɔɪz]
gerecht fair ['feə]
Gericht *(Speise)* dish [dɪʃ]
gern: Ich tanze/singe/… gern. I like dancing/singing/… **Ich hätte gern …** I would like … **Ich würde gern gehen.** I would like to go. **Ich würde sehr gern gehen.** I'd love to go. **Was hättest du gern?** What would you like? [wʊd]
gernhaben like [laɪk]
gesamte(r, s) whole [həʊl] **Gesamt-** total ['təʊtəl]
Gesamtsumme: eine Gesamtsumme von … a total of … ['təʊtl]
Geschäft *(Laden)* shop [ʃɒp]; *(AE)* store [stɔ:]
geschäftig busy ['bɪzi]
geschehen (mit) happen (to) ['hæpən]
Geschenk present ['preznt]
Geschichte **1.** *(vergangene Zeiten)* history ['hɪstri] **2.** *(Erzählung)* story ['stɔ:ri]
geschieden divorced [dɪ'vɔ:st]
Geschirr: das Geschirr abwaschen / spülen wash the dishes *(pl)* ['dɪʃɪz]
Geschirrspüler dishwasher ['dɪʃwɒʃə]
Geschoss floor [flɔ:]
Geschwindigkeit speed [spi:d]
Geschwindigkeitsbegrenzung, -beschränkung speed limit ['spi:d ˌlɪmɪt]
Gesetz law [lɔ:]
gesetzlich legal [li:gl]
Gesicht face [feɪs]
Gesichtsausdruck facial expression [ˌfeɪʃl_ɪk'spreʃn]
gespannt *(aufgeregt)* excited [ɪk'saɪtɪd]
Gespenst ghost [gəʊst]
Gespräch conversation [ˌkɒnvə'seɪʃn]
Gestalt figure ['fɪgə]
Gestaltung layout ['leɪaʊt]
gestern yesterday ['jestədeɪ], ['jestədi]
gesund well [wel], healthy ['helθi] **Ich bin wieder gesund.** I'm well again.
Getränk drink [drɪŋk]
getrennt separate ['seprət]
gewidmet sein *(einer Sache/Person)* be dedicated to ['dedɪkeɪtɪd]
Gewinn *(Preis)* prize [praɪz]
gewinnen win [wɪn]
Gewinner/in winner ['wɪnə]
gewisse(r, s) certain ['sɜ:tn]
Gewitter storm [stɔ:m]
Gewohnheit habit ['hæbɪt]
gewöhnlich *(normalerweise)* usually ['ju:ʒuəli]; usual ['ju:ʒuəl]
Gewürz spice [spaɪs]
Gezeiten tide [taɪd]
gießen pour [pɔ:]
Gipfel summit ['sʌmɪt]
Giraffe giraffe [dʒə'rɑ:f]
Gitarre guitar [gɪ'tɑ:]
glänzend *(großartig)* brilliant ['brɪliənt], shiny ['ʃaɪni]
Glas glass [glɑ:s] **ein Glas Wasser** a glass of water
glauben believe [bɪ'li:v]; *(denken)* think [θɪŋk]
gleich nachdem … just after …
gleichzeitig at one time
Gleis platform ['plætfɔ:m]; track [træk]
Gliederung structure ['strʌktʃə]
gliedern structure ['strʌktʃə]
Gliederung outline ['aʊtlaɪn]
Glocke bell [bel]
Glück happiness ['hæpinəs] **Glück haben** be lucky **Viel Glück!** Good luck! [lʌk]
glücklich happy ['hæpi]
glücklicherweise fortunately ['fɔ:tʃənətli]
Gokart go-kart ['gəʊ kɑ:t]
Gold gold [gəʊld]
golden, Gold- gold ['gəʊld]
Gott god, God [gɒd]
Gottesdienst service ['sɜ:vɪs]
Göttin goddess ['gɒdes]
Grab grave [greɪv]
Graben ditch [dɪtʃ]
Grad degree [dɪ'gri:]
► S. 220 Temperatures
Graffiti graffiti [grə'fi:ti]
Grafiken graphics *(pl)* ['græfɪks]
Grafschaft *(in Großbritannien)* county ['kaʊnti]
Gramm gram [græm]
Granit granite ['grænɪt]
Gras grass [grɑ:s]
Grasland prairie ['preəri]
grau grey [greɪ]
grausam cruel ['kru:l]
Greift zu! Help yourselves.
Grenze border ['bɔ:də]
groß big [bɪg]; large [lɑ:dʒ]; *(Person)* tall [tɔ:l]
großartig great [greɪt]; brilliant ['brɪliənt]; awesome *(bes. AE, infml)* ['ɔ:səm]
Größe size [saɪz]
Großeltern grandparents ['grænpeərənts]
Großmutter grandmother ['grænmʌðə]
Großvater grandfather ['grænfɑ:ðə]
grün green [gri:n]
Grund reason ['ri:zn] **aus diesem Grund** for this reason ['ri:zn]
Grund- basic ['beɪsɪk]
Gruppe group (of) [gru:p]; *(Band)* band [bænd]
gruselig scary ['skeəri]
Gruß: Liebe Grüße, … *(Briefschluss)* Love, …
grüßen: Grüß … von mir. Say hello to … for me.
gucken look [lʊk]
gut good [gʊd]; *(gesundheitlich)* well; *(Adverb)* well [wel] **gut sein in Kung-Fu / gut Kung-Fu können** be good at kung fu **Danke, gut.** Fine, thanks. **Guten Morgen.** Good morning. [gʊd 'mɔ:nɪŋ] **Guten Tag.** Hello. [hə'ləʊ] **Mir geht's nicht gut. / Ich fühle mich nicht gut.** I don't feel well.
gutaussehend good-looking [ˌgʊd'lʊkɪŋ]
Gymnastik gymnastics [dʒɪm'næstɪks]

H

Haar, Haare hair [heə]
haben have [hæv], [həv]; have got **Durst haben** be thirsty ['θɜ:sti]

eine Erkältung haben have a cold [kəʊld] **Fieber haben** have a temperature ['temprətʃə] **Husten haben** have a cough [kɒf] **Zahnschmerzen/Kopfschmerzen/Halsschmerzen haben** have a toothache / a headache / a sore throat **Ich habe im Mai Geburtstag.** My birthday is in May. **jemand hat Recht** someone is right **jemand hat Unrecht** someone is wrong **Wann hast du Geburtstag?** When's your birthday?
Hafen harbour ['hɑːbə]; dock [dɒk]
Hähnchen chicken ['tʃɪkɪn]
Haken hook [hʊk] **an den Haken bekommen** hook
Hai shark [ʃɑːk]
halb elf (10.30 / 22.30) half past ten ['hɑːf pɑːst]
Halbtotale medium shot ['miːdiəm ʃɒt]
Hallo. Hello. [hə'ləʊ]
Hals neck [nek]; *(Kehle)* throat [θrəʊt]
Halsschmerzen haben have a sore throat [ˌsɔː 'θrəʊt]
Halt stop [stɒp]
halten hold [həʊld] **etwas von etwas/jm. halten** think sth. of sth./sb. **mit jm. Kontakt halten** stay in touch with sb. **einen Vortrag / eine Rede halten (über)** give a talk (about) **etwas warm halten** keep sth. warm [kiːp] **sich an etwas halten** keep to sth.
► S. 232 (to) keep
Haltestelle stop [stɒp]
Hamburger hamburger ['hæmbɜːɡə]; burger
Hammer hammer ['hæmə]
Hamster hamster ['hæmstə]
Hand hand [hænd]
handeln: Es handelt von einer Möwe. It's about a seagull. **Wovon handelt die Geschichte?** What is the story about?
Handschuh glove [ɡlʌv]
Handy mobile phone [ˌməʊbaɪl 'fəʊn], *(kurz auch:)* mobile; cell (phone) *(bes. AE)* [sel]
hängen hang out [ˌhæŋ_'aʊt]
hart hard [hɑːd], tough [tʌf]
hassen hate [heɪt]
Haufen pile [paɪl]
häufig frequent ['friːkwənt], common ['kɒmən]
Haupt- main [meɪn]
Hauptstadt capital ['kæpɪtl]
Hauptteil *(eines Textes)* body ['bɒdi]

Haus house [haʊs] **nach Hause gehen / kommen** go / come home **zu Hause** at home **zu Hause sein** be in **nicht zu Hause sein** be out
Hausarrest: jm. Hausarrest erteilen ground sb. [ɡraʊnd]
Hausaufgabe(n) homework ['həʊmwɜːk] **Hausaufgaben machen** do my/your/… homework **Was haben wir als Hausaufgabe auf?** What's for homework?
Häuschen *(Cottage)* cottage ['kɒtɪdʒ]
heftig: heftiger Regen heavy rain ['hevi]
Heide(kraut) heather ['heðə]
heilig sacred ['seɪkrɪd]
Heim *(Zuhause)* home [həʊm]
Heimat sein für etwas be home to sth. [həʊm]
Heimatstadt hometown [ˌhəʊm'taʊn]
heiraten: jn. heiraten marry sb. ['mæri]
heiß hot [hɒt]
heißen *(genannt werden)* be called [kɔːld] **Ich heiße …** My name is … **Wie heißt du?** What's your name?
hektisch busy ['bɪzi]
Held/in hero ['hɪərəʊ]
helfen help [help]
Helikopter helicopter ['helɪkɒptə]
hell bright [braɪt] **hellgrün/-blau/…** light green/blue/… [laɪt]
Hemd shirt [ʃɜːt]
heraus: aus … heraus out of … ['aʊt_əv]
heraus-: herausfinden find out; discover [dɪ'skʌvə] **herausnehmen** take out **herausziehen** pull out
herausfordern: jn. herausfordern (zu etwas) challenge sb. (to sth.) ['tʃælɪndʒ]
Herausforderung challenge ['tʃælɪndʒ]
Herausgeber/in editor ['edɪtə]
Herberge hostel ['hɒstl]
Herbst autumn ['ɔːtəm], fall *(AE)* [fɔːl]
hereinkommen come in [ˌkʌm_'ɪn]
Herr Schwarz Mr *(AE:* Mr.) Schwarz ['mɪstə] **Meine Damen und Herren / Sehr geehrte Damen und Herren** Ladies and gentlemen [ˌleɪdiz_ən 'dʒentlmən]
herrennen: hinter jm. herrennen run after sb. [ˌrʌn_'ɑːftə]
herrlich lovely ['lʌvli]
herüberkommen (zu/nach) come over (to)

herum: um … herum around … [ə'raʊnd]
herum-: herumirren wander ['wɒndə] **herumlaufen** walk around; wander **herumreichen** pass around **herumrennen** run around
herunter down [daʊn]
hervorheben *(mit Textmarker)* highlight ['haɪlaɪt]
hervorragend excellent ['eksələnt]
Herz heart [hɑːt]
Heu hay [heɪ]
heute today [tə'deɪ] **heute Nachmittag** this afternoon **heute Nacht/Abend** this evening / tonight [tə'naɪt]
hier here [hɪə] **Hier bitte.** *(Bitte sehr.)* Here you are. **hier entlang** this way **hier in der Nähe** near here **hier herüber** over here **hier oben** up here
hierher here [hɪə] **bis hierher** *(bis jetzt)* so far
Hilfe help [help]
hilfreich helpful ['helpfl]
Himmel sky [skaɪ]
hinauf: auf das Boot hinauf onto the boat ['ɒntʊ]
hinaufklettern (auf) climb [klaɪm]
hinaus: aus … hinaus out of … ['aʊt_əv]
hinbringen take [teɪk]
hinein: in die Küche hinein into the kitchen ['ɪntʊ]
hineingehen go in; enter ['entə]
hineinspringen dive in [ˌdaɪv_'ɪn]
hinfallen fall [fɔːl]
hinkommen *(gelangen)* get [ɡet]
hinlegen: sich hinlegen lie down [ˌlaɪ 'daʊn]
hinsetzen: sich hinsetzen sit down [ˌsɪt 'daʊn]
hinstellen: sich hinstellen stand [stænd]
hinten at the back [bæk] **nach hinten** to the back [bæk]
hinter behind [bɪ'haɪnd] **hinter jm. herrennen** run after sb. [ˌrʌn_'ɑːftə] **direkt / genau hinter dir** right behind you
Hintergrund background ['bækɡraʊnd]
hinüber zu/nach … over to … ['əʊvə]
hinüberrennen (zu/nach) run over (to)
hinunter down [daʊn]
hinunterbeugen: sich hinunterbeugen bend down [ˌbend_'daʊn]
hinzufügen (zu) add (to) [æd]

Hirsch deer [dɪə]
historisch *(geschichtlich bedeutsam)* historic [hɪ'stɒrɪk]
Hobby hobby ['hɒbi]
hoch high [haɪ]; *(Gebäude, Baum)* tall [tɔːl]
hochheben: etwas hochheben pick sth. up [ˌpɪk‿'ʌp]
Hochland: das schottische Hochland the Highlands (pl) ['haɪləndz]
Hochmoor moor [mɔː], [mʊə]
Hochschule college ['kɒlɪdʒ]
hochsehen *(aufschauen)* look up [ˌlʊk‿'ʌp]
hochspringen jump up
höchst extremely [ɪk'striːmli]
Hochzeit wedding ['wedɪŋ]
hoffen hope [həʊp]
höflich polite [pə'laɪt]
holen: (sich) etwas holen get sth.
Holz wood [wʊd]
hölzern; Holz- wooden ['wʊdn]
Honig honey ['hʌni]
horchen listen ['lɪsn]
hören hear [hɪə]
Horizont skyline ['skaɪlaɪn]
Hose trousers *(pl)* ['traʊzəz]; *(AE)* pants *(pl)* [pænts]
Hotel hotel [həʊ'tel]
hübsch pretty ['prɪti]; *(schön, herrlich)* lovely ['lʌvli]
Hubschrauber helicopter ['helɪkɒptə]
Hüfte hip [hɪp]
Hügel hill [hɪl]
Huhn chicken ['tʃɪkɪn]
Hund dog [dɒg]
Hunger haben be hungry ['hʌŋgri]
hungrig sein be hungry ['hʌŋgri]
hupen honk [hɒŋk]
Hurrikan hurricane ['hʌrɪkən]
Husten haben have a cough [kɒf]
Hut hat [hæt]
Hütehund sheepdog ['ʃiːpdɒg]

I

ich I [aɪ] **Ich auch.** Me too.
ideal *(perfekt)* perfect ['pɜːfɪkt]
Idee idea [aɪ'dɪə]
ihm him [hɪm]; *(bei Dingen, Tieren)* it
ihn him [hɪm]; *(bei Dingen, Tieren)* it
ihnen them [ðem], [ðəm]
Ihnen *(höfliche Anrede)* you [juː]
ihr(e) … *(vor Nomen; besitzanzeigend)*
1. *(zu „she")* her … [hɜː, hə]
2. *(zu „it")* its … [ɪts]
3. *(zu „they")* their … [ðeə]
Ihr(e) … *(vor Nomen; besitzanzeigend) (zur höflichen Anrede „you")* your … [jɔː, jə]
ihrer, ihre, ihrs *(zu „she")* hers [hɜːz]; *(zu „they")* theirs [ðeəz]
illegal illegal [ɪ'liːgl]
Imbiss snack [snæk]
immer always ['ɔːlweɪz] **immer noch** still [stɪl] **immer wieder** again and again **für immer** for ever [fər‿'evə] **etwas immer wieder / weiter tun** keep (on) doing sth. [kiːp]
► S. 232 (to) keep
immer häufiger / schöner more and more frequent / beautiful
in in [ɪn]; *(in Ortsangaben auch oft:)* at [æt], [ət] **in der Beach Road** in Beach Road **in der Beach Road 8** at 8 Beach Road **in der Nacht** at night **in der Nähe von** near **in der Schule** at school **in den Raum (hinein)** into the room **in Schwierigkeiten sein** be in trouble ['trʌbl]
Inder/in; indisch Indian ['ɪndiən]
Information(en) (über) information (about) *(no pl)* [ˌɪnfə'meɪʃn]
Informations-und Kommunikationstechnologie ICT [ˌaɪ siː 'tiː] (Information and Communication Technology)
Ingenieur/in engineer [ˌendʒɪnɪə]
Inhalt content ['kɒntent]
Inlineskaten skating ['skeɪtɪŋ]
Inlineskates skates [skeɪts]
innehalten *(eine Pause einlegen)* pause [pɔːz]
innerhalb (von) within [wɪ'ðɪn]
Insel island ['aɪlənd]
Inserat advertisement [əd'vɜːtɪsmənt]
insgesamt … a total of … ['təʊtl]; … altogether [ˌɔːltə'geðə]
Instrument instrument ['ɪnstrəmənt]
Interaktion interaction [ˌɪntər'ækʃn]
interessant interesting ['ɪntrəstɪŋ]
interessieren: sich interessieren (für) be interested (in) ['ɪntrəstɪd]
jn. interessieren interest sb.
interessiert sein (an) be interested (in) ['ɪntrəstɪd]
Internat boarding school ['bɔːdɪŋ skuːl]
interviewen: jn. interviewen interview sb. ['ɪntəvjuː]
irgendetwas? anything? ['eniθɪŋ]
irgendjemand? anybody? / anyone? ['enibɒdi, 'eniwʌn]
irgendwelche: Gibt es irgendwelche …? Are there any …? ['eni]
irgendwie kind of ['kaɪndəv], *(infml:)* kinda ['kaɪndə]
irgendwo, irgendwohin somewhere ['sʌmweə]
irren: jemand irrt sich *(jemand hat Unrecht)* someone is wrong [rɒŋ]

J

ja yes [jes] **Ja, das ist richtig. / Ja, das stimmt.** Yes, that's right.
Jacke, Jackett jacket ['dʒækɪt]
jagen hunt [hʌnt]
Jahr year [jɪə] **im Jahr 1580** in 1580 **ein 70-jähriger Lehrer** a 70-year-old teacher
► S. 219 a 9,740-foot swimming pool
Jahrestag anniversary [ˌænɪ'vɜːsəri]
Jahrgang, Jahrgangsstufe year [jɪə], *(AE)* grade [greɪd]
Jahrhundert century ['sentʃəri]
Januar January ['dʒænjuəri]
je: besser als je zuvor better than ever
Jeans jeans *(pl)* [dʒiːnz]
jede(r, s) … every … ['evri]; *(jede(r, s) einzelne)* each … [iːtʃ]
sonst jeder everybody else [els]
Jedenfalls, … *(Wie dem auch sei)* Anyway, … ['eniweɪ]
jeder *(alle)* everyone ['evriwʌn], everybody ['evribɒdi]
jederzeit, zu jeder Zeit at any time
jedoch however [haʊ'evə]
jemals ever ['evə] **Bist du jemals in … gewesen?** Have you ever been to …?
jemand somebody/someone ['sʌmbədi, 'sʌmwʌn]; *(in Fragen)* anybody? / anyone? ['enibɒdi, 'eniwʌn]
Finde jemanden, der … Find someone who …
jene(r, s): jener Ort / jene Fähre / jenes Kleid that place / ferry / dress
jene Leute those people
jenseits (von) beyond [bɪ'jɒnd]
jetzt now [naʊ] **jetzt gerade** right now **bis jetzt** so far
Job job [dʒɒb]
Joghurt yoghurt ['jɒgət]
Jongleur/in juggler ['dʒʌglə]
jonglieren: mit etwas jonglieren juggle sth. ['dʒʌgl]
jubeln cheer [tʃɪə]
Judo judo ['dʒuːdəʊ]
Jugendliche(r) kid [kɪd] *(infml)*

Juli July [dʒu'laɪ]
jung young [jʌŋ]
Junge boy [bɔɪ]; guy [gaɪ] *(infml)*
Juni June [dʒu:n]
Juwelen jewels *(pl)* ['dʒu:əlz]

K

Kaffee coffee ['kɒfi] **Kaffee kochen** make coffee
▶ S. 222 Food words
Kajak kayak ['kaɪæk]
Kakao cocoa ['kəʊkəʊ]
Kalender diary ['daɪəri]
kalt cold [kəʊld]
Kamera camera ['kæmərə]
Kamin fireplace ['faɪəpleɪs]
Kampf fight [faɪt]
kämpfen fight [faɪt] **gegen jn. kämpfen** fight sb.
Kanal canal [kə'næl] *(TV)* channel ['tʃænl]
Kaninchen rabbit ['ræbɪt]
Kännchen Tee pot of tea [pɒt]
Kante edge [edʒ]
Kantine canteen [kæn'ti:n]
kapieren: etwas kapieren get sth. [get] *(infml)*
Kapitän/in captain ['kæptɪn]
Kappe cap [kæp]
kaputt broken ['brəʊkən] **kaputt gehen** break [breɪk] **etwas kaputt machen** break sth.
Karneval carnival ['kɑ:nɪvl]
Karotte carrot ['kærət]
Karren cart [kɑ:t]
Karriere career [kə'rɪə]
Karte (an) card (to) [kɑ:d]
Kartoffel potato [pə'teɪtəʊ]
Käse cheese [tʃi:z]
Kasse *(in Geschäften)* cash desk ['kæʃ desk]; *(für den Verkauf von Eintrittskarten)* ticket office ['tɪkɪt‿ˌɒfɪs]
Kasten, Kästchen box [bɒks]
Kathedrale cathedral [kə'θi:drəl]
Katze cat [kæt]
kaufen buy [baɪ]
kaum hardly ['hɑ:dli]
Kehle throat [θrəʊt]
kein(e) no [nəʊ] **Es gibt/sind keine ...** There aren't any ... ['eni] **Ich bin kein Junge.** I'm not a boy. **Ich mag kein Rot.** I don't like red. **er hat keine Zeit** he doesn't have time **überhaupt kein(e) / gar kein(e) ...** not ... at all [ət‿'ɔ:l]
Keks biscuit ['bɪskɪt]; *(AE)* cookie ['kʊki]
Kellner waiter ['weɪtə]
Kellnerin waitress ['weɪtrəs]
kennen know [nəʊ]
kennenlernen meet [mi:t] **Freut mich, dich/euch/Sie kennenzulernen.** Nice to meet you.
kennzeichnen: etwas kennzeichnen mark sth. up [ˌmɑ:k‿'ʌp]
Kerze candle ['kændl]
Ketchup ketchup ['ketʃəp]
Kilogramm, Kilo (kg) kilogram ['kɪləgræm], kilo ['ki:ləʊ] (kg) **ein 150 Kilogramm schwerer Bär** a 150-kilogram bear
▶ S. 219 a 9,740-foot swimming pool
Kilometer (km) kilometre ['kɪləmi:tə], [kɪ'lɒmɪtə] (km) **eine Zehn-Kilometer-Wanderung** a ten-kilometre walk
▶ S. 219 a 9,740-foot swimming pool
Kind child [tʃaɪld]; *(infml)* kid [kɪd]
Kino cinema ['sɪnəmə], *(AE)* movie theater ['mu:vi θɪətə]
Kirche church [tʃɜ:tʃ]
Kiste box [bɒks]
Klang sound [saʊnd]
klar clear [klɪə], for sure
Klasse class [klɑ:s]
klasse awesome *(bes. AE, infml)* ['ɔ:səm]
Klassenbuch register ['redʒɪstə]
Klassenkamerad/in classmate ['klɑ:smeɪt]
Klassenzimmer classroom ['klɑ:sru:m]
klassisch classical ['klæsɪkl]
klatschen *(Beifall)* clap [klæp]; slap [slæp] **Klatscht in die Hände.** Clap your hands.
Klavier piano [pi'ænəʊ]
kleben stick [stɪk]
Klebestift glue stick ['glu: stɪk]
Klebstoff glue [glu:]
Kleid dress [dres]
Kleidung, Kleidungsstücke clothes *(pl)* [kləʊðz]
klein little ['lɪtl]; small [smɔ:l]
klemmen tuck [tʌk]
klettern climb [klaɪm] **auf einen Baum klettern** climb a tree
klicken click [klɪk]
Klima climate ['klaɪmət]
Klimawandel climate change
Klippe cliff [klɪf]
Klingel bell [bel]
klingeln ring [rɪŋ]
klingen sound [saʊnd]
klopfen (an etwas) knock (on sth.) [nɒk]; *(tippen)* tap [tæp]
Klub club [klʌb] **in einen Klub eintreten / sich einem Klub anschließen** join a club [dʒɔɪn]
klug clever ['klevə]
knallen slap [slæp] **in/gegen etwas knallen** crash into sth. [kræʃ]
▶ S. 215 (to) crash
Kneipe pub [pʌb]
Knie knee [ni:]
Knoblauch garlic ['gɑ:lɪk]
▶ S. 222 Food words
Koch, Köchin cook [kʊk]
kochen cook [kʊk] *(zum Kochen bringen)* boil [bɔɪl] **Tee/Kaffee/Suppe kochen** make tea/coffee/soup **Wer kocht heute Abend?** Who is going to cook / do the cooking this evening?
▶ S. 222 Food words
Kochtopf saucepan ['sɔ:spən]
Kohle coal [kəʊl]
kombinieren combine [kəm'baɪn]
komisch 1. *(lustig)* funny ['fʌni] 2. *(seltsam, merkwürdig)* funny; strange [streɪndʒ]; weird [wɪəd]
Komma comma ['kɒmə] **drei Komma fünf** three point five [pɔɪnt]
kommen come [kʌm]; *(gelangen, hinkommen)* get [get] **Ich komme aus Plymouth.** I'm from Plymouth. **Komm, Dad!** *(Na los, Dad!)* Come on, Dad. **Kommt nicht in Frage!** No way! **auf etwas kommen** *(Idee, Vorschlag)* come up with sth.
Kommentar comment ['kɒment]
Komödie comedy ['kɒmədi]
kompliziert complicated ['kɒmplɪkeɪtɪd]
König king [kɪŋ]
Königin queen [kwi:n]
königlich royal ['rɔɪəl]
Königreich: das Vereinigte Königreich the UK (the United Kingdom) [ˌju: 'keɪ, juˌnaɪtɪd 'kɪŋdəm]
konkret concrete ['kɒŋkri:t]
können can [kæn], [kən] **etwas tun können** be able to do sth. ['eɪbl] **ich kann nicht ... / du kannst nicht ...** *usw.* I can't ... / you can't ... *etc.* [kɑ:nt] **Kann ich Sie kurz sprechen?** May I have a word with you? **gut Kung-Fu können** be good at kung fu
konnte(n): ich konnte ... / du konntest ... *usw.* I could ... / you could ... *etc.* [kʊd]
könnte(n): Was könnte besser sein? What could be better? [kʊd],

[kəd] **jemand könnte es mögen** someone might like it [maɪt]
Konsonant consonant ['kɒnsənənt]
Kontakt: (mit jm.) Kontakt aufnehmen get in touch (with sb.) [tʌtʃ] **(mit jm.) Kontakt halten** stay in touch (with sb.)
Kontext *(Text-, Satzzusammenhang)* context ['kɒntekst]
Kontrast contrast ['kɒntrɑːst]
Kontrolle *(Überprüfung)* check [tʃek]; control [kən'trəʊl] **unter Kontrolle halten/bekommen** control [kən'trəʊl] **Kontrolle übernehmen** take control [kən'trəʊl]
kontrollieren *(überprüfen)* check [tʃek]; control [kən'trəʊl]
Konzert concert ['kɒnsət]
Koordinator/in coordinator [kəʊ'ɔːdɪneɪtə]
Kopf head [hed] **jm. durch den Kopf schießen** flash through sb.'s mind [flæʃ]
Kopfschmerzen haben a headache ['hedeɪk]
kopieren copy ['kɒpi]
Korb basket ['bɑːskɪt]
Körper body ['bɒdi]
korrekt correct [kə'rekt]
Korridor corridor ['kɒrɪdɔː]
korrigieren correct [kə'rekt]
kosten cost [kɒst] **Die Kamera kostet …** The camera is … **Die DVDs kosten …** The DVDs are … **Was / Wie viel kostet / kosten …?** How much is / are …?
kostenlos free
köstlich delicious [dɪ'lɪʃəs]
Kostüm costume ['kɒstjuːm]
krachen: in/gegen etwas krachen crash into sth. [kræʃ]
► S. 215 (to) crash
Kraft energy ['enədʒi], power ['paʊə]
kräftig strong [strɒŋ]
Krake octopus ['ɒktəpəs]
Kram stuff [stʌf] *(infml)*
krank sick [sɪk]; ill [ɪl]
Krankenhaus hospital ['hɒspɪtl]
Krankenschwester, -pfleger/in nurse [nɜːs]
Kraut herb [hɜːb]
Krebs *(Tier)* crab [kræb]
kreieren create [kri'eɪt]
Kreis circle ['sɜːkl]
Kreisverkehr roundabout ['raʊndəbaʊt]
Kricket cricket ['krɪkɪt]
kreuzen; sich kreuzen cross [krɒs]
Kreuzfahrt cruise [kruːz]
Kreuzotter adder ['ædə]
Kreuzworträtsel crossword ['krɒswɜːd]
Krone crown [kraʊn]
Küche kitchen ['kɪtʃɪn]
Küchentheke countertop ['kaʊntətɒp], counter ['kaʊntə], worktop ['wɜːktɒp]
Kuchen cake [keɪk]
Kugelschreiber pen [pen]
Kuh cow [kaʊ]
kühl cool [kuːl]
Kultur culture ['kʌltʃə]
kümmern: sich um jn. kümmern look after sb., take care of sth. [keə]
Kumpel mate [meɪt]
Kunst art [ɑːt] **Kunstwerk** work of art [ˌwɜːk‿əv‿'ɑːt]
Künstler/in artist ['ɑːtɪst]; performer [pə'fɔːmə]
Kunststoff plastic ['plæstɪk]
Kunststück trick [trɪk]
Kürbis pumpkin ['pʌmpkɪn]
Kurs: einen Kurs besuchen, an einem Kurs teilnehmen attend a course [ə'tend]
kurz short [ʃɔːt] **kurz nachdem …** just after …
Küste coast [kəʊst]

L

lachen laugh [lɑːf]
lächeln smile [smaɪl]
Lächeln smile [smaɪl]
Laden shop [ʃɒp]; *(AE)* store [stɔː] **Laden an der Ecke** *(„Tante-Emma-Laden")* corner shop ['kɔːnə ʃɒp]
Lage: In der Lage sein, etwas zu tun be able to do sth. ['eɪbl]
Lagerfeuer campfire ['kæmpfaɪə]
Lamm lamb [læm]
Lampe lamp [læmp]
Land *(auch als Gegensatz zur Stadt)* country ['kʌntri]; *(Grund und Boden)* land [lænd] **an Land gehen** land
landen land [lænd]
Landkarte map ['mæp] **auf der Landkarte** on the map
Landschaft *(ländliche Gegend)* countryside ['kʌntrisaɪd]
Landwirt/in farmer ['fɑːmə]
lang long [lɒŋ] **lange aufbleiben** stay up late **nicht länger** not (…) any longer ['lɒŋgə]
langsam slow [sləʊ]
langweilen: sich langweilen be/feel bored [bɔːd]
langweilig boring ['bɔːrɪŋ]
Lärm noise [nɔɪz] **voller Lärm** noisy ['nɔɪzi]
lärmend noisy ['nɔɪzi]
lassen **1.** let **Lass mich dir … zeigen.** Let me show you … **Lass(t) uns …** Let's … **2.** leave [liːv] **Lass bitte das Fenster offen.** Leave the window open, please. **etwas übrig lassen (für jn.)** leave sth. (for sb.) **etwas fallen lassen** drop sth. [drɒp] **3. Lass das!** *(Hör auf damit)* Stop it! *(infml)*
Lastwagen truck [trʌk]; lorry ['lɒri]
laufen run [rʌn] *(Programm, Sendung)* be on [ɒn] **Bleib(t) auf dem Laufenden!** Stay posted. ['pəʊstɪd]
Laune mood [muːd] **gute/schlechte Laune haben** be in a good/bad mood
laut loud [laʊd]; noisy ['nɔɪzi] **laut (vor)lesen** read aloud [ə'laʊd] **etwas lauter stellen** turn sth. up
läuten ring [rɪŋ]
lautlos silently ['saɪləntli]
Lautsprecher loudspeaker [ˌlaʊd'spiːkə]
Leben life [laɪf]
leben *(wohnen)* live [lɪv] *(am Leben sein)* be alive [ə'laɪv]
lebendig, lebhaft lively ['laɪvli]
lecker delicious [dɪ'lɪʃəs]; tasty ['teɪsti]; yummy ['jʌmi] *(infml)*
Leder leather ['leðə]
ledig *(alleinstehend)* single ['sɪŋgl]
leer empty ['empti]
legal legal [liːgl]
legen *(hinlegen, ablegen)* put [pʊt]
legendär legendary ['ledʒəndri]
Legende legend ['ledʒənd]
lehnen: sich lehnen lean [liːn]
lehren teach [tiːtʃ]
Lehrer/in teacher ['tiːtʃə]
Lehrgang workshop ['wɜːkʃɒp]
Leiche body ['bɒdi]
leicht *(einfach)* easy ['iːzi]
leid: Es tut mir leid wegen … I'm sorry about …
leider unfortunately [ʌn'fɔːtʃənətli]
leihen: jm. etwas leihen lend sb. sth., [lend] **sich etwas (aus)leihen (vom jm.), etwas entleihen** borrow sth. (from sb.) ['bɒrəʊ]
Leine line [laɪn]
leise quiet ['kwaɪət]; silent ['saɪlənt] **etwas leiser stellen** turn sth. down
leiten lead [liːd]
Leiter/in leader [liːdə]

Lenkrad (steering) wheel ['stɪərɪŋ wiːl]
lernen learn [lɜːn]; study ['stʌdi]
Lernposter study poster ['stʌdi pəʊstə]
lesen read [riːd] **jemandes Gedanken lesen** read sb.'s mind [maɪnd]
letzte(r, s) last [lɑːst]; final ['faɪnl] **letzte Nacht** last night **die letzte Übung** the last exercise **das Musical vom letzten Jahr** last year's musical
leuchtend bright [braɪt]
Leute people ['piːpl]; **guys** *(pl, infml)* [gaɪz]
Licht light [laɪt]
Lichtblitz flash [flæʃ]
Liebe: Alles Liebe, ... / Liebe Grüße, ... *(Briefschluss)* Love, ...
lieben love [lʌv]
lieber: etwas lieber tun (als etwas) prefer sth. (to sth.) [prɪ'fɜː] **Ich sollte lieber ...** I'd better ... (= I had better ...) ['betə]
Lieblings-: mein Lieblingsfoto my favourite *(AE:* favorite) photo ['feɪvərɪt]
Lied song [sɒŋ]
Lieferung supply [sə'plaɪ]
liegen lie [laɪ]
lila purple ['pɜːpl]
Lineal ruler ['ruːlə]
Linie line [laɪn]
Link link [lɪŋk]
linke(r, s) left [left] **auf der linken Seite** on the left **nach links** left **(nach) links abbiegen** turn left
Linse *(Gemüse)* lentil ['lentl]
▶ S. 222 Food words
Lippe lip [lɪp]
Liste list [lɪst]
Literatur literature ['lɪtrətʃə]
LKW truck [trʌk]; lorry ['lɒri]
Loch hole [həʊl]
Löffel spoon [spuːn]
Lokal pub [pʌb]
los: Los geht's. / Jetzt geht's los. Here we go. **Was ist los?** What's the matter? ['mætə] **Was ist los mit dir/Sam?** What's wrong with you/Sam?
löschen *(tilgen)* delete [dɪ'liːt]
lösen solve [sɒlv]
Löwe lion ['laɪən]
Luft air [eə]
Lust auf etwas/zu etwas haben fancy sth. ['fænsi]
lustig: sich über jn. / etwas lustig machen make fun of sb./sth. [fʌn]
Luxuslimousine limousine [ˌlɪmə'ziːn], ['lɪməziːn]

M

machen *(tun)* do [duː]; *(herstellen)* make [meɪk] **aus etwas gemacht sein** be made of sth. **einen Spaziergang machen** go for a walk [wɔːk] **Fotos machen** take photos **Hat es Spaß gemacht?** Was it fun? **jn. zu etwas machen** make sb. sth. **sich fertig machen (für)** get ready (for) ['redi] **sich Sorgen machen (wegen, um)** worry (about) ['wʌri] **wie man etwas macht / machen kann / machen soll** how to do sth.
Macht power ['paʊə]
Mädchen girl [gɜːl]
Magen stomach ['stʌmək]
magisch magic ['mædʒɪk]; magical ['mædʒɪkl]
Mahlzeit meal [miːl]
Mai May [meɪ]
Make-up make-up ['meɪk_ʌp]
Mal time [taɪm] **dieses Mal** this time **noch ein Mal** one more time
mal: (vorher) schon mal before [bɪ'fɔː] **Warst du schon mal hier?** Have you been here before?
Malaria malaria [mə'leəriə]
malen paint [peɪnt]
Maler/in painter ['peɪntə]
Mama mum [mʌm]; *(AE)* mom [mɑːm]
manchmal sometimes ['sʌmtaɪmz]
man you [juː]
Mann man [mæn]; guy *(infml)* [gaɪ]
Mannschaft team [tiːm]
Mantel coat [kəʊt]
Manuskript script [skrɪpt]
Marine navy ['neɪvi]
Marionette puppet ['pʌpɪt]
markieren mark (up) [mɑːk]; *(mit Textmarker)* highlight ['haɪlaɪt]
Markt market ['mɑːkɪt]
Marmelade jam [dʒæm]; *(AE)* jelly ['dʒeli]
Marsch march [mɑːtʃ]
März March [mɑːtʃ]
Maschine machine [mə'ʃiːn]
Material material [mə'tɪəriəl]
Mathematik maths [mæθs]
Matrose, Matrosin sailor ['seɪlə]
Matsch mud [mʌd]
matschig muddy ['mʌdi]
Mauer wall [wɔːl]
Maul mouth [maʊθ]
Medien: soziale Medien social media *(pl)* [ˌsəʊʃl 'miːdiə]
Meer sea [siː] **am Meer** by the sea
Meeres- marine [mə'riːn]
Meerschweinchen guinea pig ['gɪni pɪg]
Megaphon loudspeaker [ˌlaʊd'spiːkə]
Mehl flour ['flaʊə]
▶ S. 222 Food words
mehr more [mɔː] **nicht mehr** not ... any more; not ... any longer ['lɒŋgə]
Meile *(ca. 1,6 km)* mile [maɪl] **Meilen pro Stunde** mph [ˌem piː_'eɪtʃ] *(kurz für: miles per hour)*
meilenweit for miles [maɪlz]
mein(e) ... my ... [maɪ]
meinen *(sagen wollen)* mean [miːn]
meiner, meine, meins mine [maɪn]
meißeln carve [kɑːv]
meisten: die meisten Menschen most people [məʊst] **die meisten von ihnen** most of them
meistens usually ['juːʒuəli]
Meister/in master ['mɑːstə]
Meinung opinion [ə'pɪnjən] **Meiner Meinung nach ...** In my opinion ... **seine Meinung ändern** change your mind [maɪnd]
Menge *(Menschenmenge)* crowd [kraʊd]
Mensa *(Kantine)* canteen [kæn'tiːn]
Menschen people ['piːpl] **voller Menschen** crowded ['kraʊdɪd]
Menschenmenge crowd [kraʊd]
merken notice ['nəʊtɪs] **sich etwas merken** remember sth. [rɪ'membə]
Merkzettel crib sheet ['krɪb ʃiːt] *(infml)*
Messer knife [naɪf]
Metall; Metall- metal ['metl]
Meter metre *(AE:* meter) ['miːtə]
Methode technique [tek'niːk]
mich me [miː]; *(Reflexivpronomen)* myself [maɪ'self]
Milch milk [mɪlk]
Milchprodukte dairy products *(pl)* ['deəri prɒdʌkts]
Million million ['mɪljən]
Mimik facial expression [ˌfeɪʃl_ɪk'spreʃn]
Minute minute ['mɪnɪt] **eine 30-minütige Fahrt** a 30-minute ride
▶ S. 219 a 9,740-foot swimming pool
mir me [miː]; *(Reflexivpronomen)* myself [maɪ'self]

mit with [wɪð] **mit dem Bus fahren** go by bus **mit lauter Stimme** in a loud voice
Mitfahrgelegenheit lift [lɪft]
Mitgefühl: Mein Mitgefühl gilt ... My heart goes out to ...
mitgenommen upset [ˌʌp'set]
Mitlaut consonant ['kɒnsənənt]
mitnehmen: Kannst du mich zum Bahnhof mitnehmen? Can you give me a lift to the station? [lɪft] **Soll ich dich mitnehmen?** Do you want a lift?
Mitschüler/in classmate ['klɑːsmeɪt]
Mittag noon [nuːn] **zu Mittag essen** have lunch [lʌntʃ]
Mittagessen lunch [lʌntʃ]
mittags at lunchtime ['lʌntʃtaɪm]
Mittagszeit lunchtime ['lʌntʃtaɪm]
Mitte middle ['mɪdl]; *(Zentrum)* centre ['sentə]
Mitteilung note [nəʊt]
Mittelpunkt *(eines Bildes, Fotos)* focus ['fəʊkəs]
Mitternacht midnight ['mɪdnaɪt]
Mittwoch Wednesday ['wenzdeɪ, 'wenzdi]
Mobiltelefon mobile phone [ˌməʊbaɪl 'fəʊn], *(kurz auch:)* mobile; cell (phone) *(bes. AE)* [sel]
Möbel furniture *(no pl)* ['fɜːnɪtʃə]
möchte: Ich möchte ... (haben) I would like ... **Ich möchte gehen.** I'd like to go. **Was möchtest du (haben)?** What would you like? **Was möchtest du essen?** What would you like to eat?
Mode fashion ['fæʃn]
Model model ['mɒdl]
modern modern ['mɒdən]
mögen: etwas mögen like sth. [laɪk]; *(auf etwas stehen)* be into sth. *(infml)*
möglich possible ['pɒsəbl]
Möglichkeit chance [tʃɑːns]
Möhre carrot ['kærət]
Molkereiprodukte dairy products *(pl)* ['deəri prɒdʌkts]
Moment moment ['məʊmənt] **im Moment** at the moment **Warte einen Moment. / Moment mal.** Wait a minute.
Monat month [mʌnθ]
Mond moon [muːn]
Mondlicht moonlight ['muːnlaɪt]
Monster monster ['mɒnstə]
Montag Monday ['mʌndeɪ, 'mʌndi]
Monument (für/zum Gedenken an) monument (to) ['mɒnjumənt]
morden murder ['mɜːdə]
morgen tomorrow [tə'mɒrəʊ]
Morgen *(Vormittag)* morning ['mɔːnɪŋ] **am Morgen** in the morning
morgens in the morning ['mɔːnɪŋ]
Motor motor ['məʊtə]
Möwe seagull ['siːgʌl]
MP3-Player, MP3-Spieler MP3 player [ˌempiː'θriː ˌpleɪə]
müde tired ['taɪəd]
Müll rubbish ['rʌbɪʃ]; *(AE)* garbage ['gɑːbɪdʒ]
Mülltonne rubbish bin ['rʌbɪʃ bɪn]; trash can *(AE)* ['træʃ kæn]
Mund mouth [maʊθ]
Mundharmonika harmonica [hɑː'mɒnɪkə]
Münze coin [kɔɪn]
murmeln: ..., murmelte er. ..., he said under his breath. [breθ]
Muschel(schale) shell [ʃel]
Museum museum [mju'ziːəm]
Musical musical ['mjuːzɪkl]
Musik music ['mjuːzɪk]
Musiker/in musician [mju'zɪʃn]
Musikinstrument musical instrument
müssen have to ['hæv tə]; need to ['niːd tə]; must [mʌst] **du musst es nicht tun** you don't have to do it; you don't need to do it; you needn't do it ['niːdnt]
Muster pattern ['pætn]
Mut courage ['kʌrɪdʒ]
mutig brave [breɪv]
Mutter mother ['mʌðə]
Muttersprachler/in native speaker [ˌneɪtɪv 'spiːkə]
Mutti mum [mʌm]; *(AE)* mom [mɑːm]

N

Na: Na ja, ... Well, ... [wel] **Na los, Dad!** *(Komm, Dad!)* Come on, Dad. **Na und?** So? [səʊ]
nach 1. *(örtlich)* to [tu], [tə] **nach draußen** outside [ˌaʊt'saɪd] **nach drinnen** inside [ˌɪn'saɪd] **nach Hause gehen / kommen** go / come home **nach hinten / vorn** to the back [bæk] / front [frʌnt] **nach links / rechts** left / right **nach oben** *(im Haus)* upstairs [ˌʌp'steəz] **nach unten** down; *(im Haus)* downstairs [ˌdaʊn'steəz]
2. *(zeitlich)* after ['ɑːftə] **nach dem Frühstück** after breakfast **einer nach dem anderen** one by one **gleich nach dir** right after you
Viertel nach zehn (10.15 / 22.15) quarter past ten ['kwɔːtə pɑːst]
Nachbar/in neighbour *(AE:* neighbor) ['neɪbə]
Nachbarschaft neighborhood *(AE)* / neighbourhood *(BE)* ['neɪbəhʊd]
nachdem after ['ɑːftə] **gleich / kurz nachdem ...** just after ...
nachher afterwards ['ɑːftəwədz]
Nachmittag afternoon [ˌɑːftə'nuːn] **am Nachmittag** in the afternoon
nachmittags in the afternoon [ˌɑːftə'nuːn]
Nachricht message ['mesɪdʒ] **eine Nachricht hinterlassen** leave a message [ˌliːv‿ə 'mesɪdʒ]
Nachrichten news *(no pl)* [njuːz]
nachschauen have a look (at sth.)
nachschlagen *(Wörter, Informationen)* look sth. up
Nachsilbe suffix ['sʌfɪks]
Nachspeise dessert [dɪ'zɜːt]
nächste(r, s) next [nekst] **das Musical vom nächsten Jahr** next year's musical
Nacht night [naɪt] **in der Nacht** at night **heute Nacht** tonight [tə'naɪt]
Nachteil disadvantage [ˌdɪsəd'vɑːntɪdʒ]
Nachtisch dessert [dɪ'zɜːt]
nachts at night [ət 'naɪt]
Nähe: in der Nähe von near [nɪə] **hier in der Nähe** near here
Nahaufnahme close-up ['kləʊs‿ʌp]
nahe (bei) near [nɪə]; close (to) [kləʊs]
nahegelegen: eine nahegelegene Stadt a nearby town ['nɪəbaɪ]
Name name [neɪm] **Mein Name ist ...** My name is ...
Nase nose [nəʊz]
nass wet [wet] **jn. nass spritzen** splash sb. [splæʃ]
Nation nation ['neɪʃn]
national, National- national ['næʃnəl]
Nationalhymne national anthem [ˌnæʃnəl‿'ænθəm]
Natur nature *(no article)* ['neɪtʃə]
Naturkunde natural history [ˌnætʃrəl 'hɪstri]
natürlich natural ['nætʃrəl]; *(selbstverständlich)* of course [əv 'kɔːs]
Naturwissenschaft science ['saɪəns]
Naturwissenschaftler/in scientist ['saɪəntɪst]
neben next to ['nekst tʊ]
Nebensatz sub-clause ['sʌbklɔːz]

nehmen take [teɪk] **Ich nehme einen Tee / ...** *(beim Essen)* I'll have a tea/... **jn. am Arm nehmen** take sb. by the arm
neidisch (auf) jealous (of) ['dʒeləs]
nein no [nəʊ] **Nein, das ist falsch. / Nein, das stimmt nicht.** No, that's wrong.
nennen *(rufen, bezeichnen)* call [kɔːl]
nervös nervous ['nɜːvəs]
nett nice [naɪs]; kind [kaɪnd]
Netz, Netzwerk network ['netwɜːk]
neu new [njuː] **das Neueste** the latest ['leɪtɪst]
neugierig curious ['kjʊəriəs]
Neuigkeiten news [njuːz]
neutral neutral ['njuːtrəl]
nicht not [nɒt] **auch nicht** not ... either ['aɪðə], ['iːðə] **Geh nicht.** Don't go. [dəʊnt] **Ich auch nicht.** Me neither. ['naɪðə, 'niːðə] **Ich mag Grün nicht.** I don't like green. **Ich weiß (es) nicht.** I don't know. **nicht mehr** not ... any more **nicht vor drei** not till three **..., nicht wahr?** ..., right? **noch nicht** not ... yet [jet] **(noch) nicht einmal** not even
nichts not ... anything ['eniθɪŋ]
Nichts: (wie) aus dem Nichts out of nowhere ['nəʊweə]
nicken nod [nɒd]
nie never ['nevə]; at no time **(vorher) noch nie** never / not before
niedergeschlagen glum(ly) [glʌm, 'glʌmli]
niedlich, süß cute [kjuːt]
niemals never ['nevə]
niemand no one ['nəʊ wʌn], nobody ['nəʊbədi]; not anybody ['enibɒdi] / not anyone ['eniwʌn]
niesen sneeze [sniːz]
nirgendwo; nirgendwohin nowhere ['nəʊweə]
noch: noch ein Foto one more photo; another photo **noch einmal** again [ə'gen]; one more time **noch nicht** not ... yet [jet] **noch nicht einmal** not even **immer noch** still [stɪl] **(vorher) noch nie** never/ not before
Norden; nach Norden; nördlich north [nɔːθ] **Richtung Norden** northbound ['nɔːθbaʊnd]
nördlich, Nord- northern ['nɔːðən]
Nordosten; nach Nordosten; nordöstlich north-east [ˌnɔːθ‿'iːst]
Nordwesten; nach Nordwesten; nordwestlich north-west [ˌnɔːθ'west]
normal normal ['nɔːməl]
normalerweise usually ['juːʒuəli]
Note *(Musik)* note [nəʊt] *(Schulnote)* mark [mɑːk], grade *(bes. AE)* [greɪd]
Notfall, Not- emergency [ɪ'mɜːdʒənsi]
nötig necessary ['nesəsəri]
Notiz note [nəʊt] **(sich) Notizen machen** *(beim Lesen oder Zuhören)* take notes **(sich) Notizen machen (über/zu etwas)** *(zur Vorbereitung)* make notes (on sth.)
notwendig necessary ['nesəsəri]
November November [nəʊ'vembə]
Null zero ['zɪərəʊ]; *(in Telefonnummern)* o [əʊ]; *(Sport)* nil [nɪl]
Nummer number
nun now [naʊ] **Nun, ...** Well, ... [wel]
nur only ['əʊnli]; *(einfach nur)* just [dʒʌst]
Nuss nut [nʌt]
▶ S. 222 Food words

O

ob if [ɪf]; whether ['weðə]
oben *(an der Spitze, am oberen Ende)* at the top (of); *(im Haus)* upstairs [ˌʌp'steəz]; above [ə'bʌv] **hier oben** up here **nach oben** up; *(im Haus)* upstairs
Oberfläche surface ['sɜːfɪs]
oberhalb (von) above [ə'bʌv]
Objekt object ['ɒbdʒekt]
Obst fruit [fruːt]
Obstkuchen pie [paɪ]
Obstsalat fruit salad [ˌfruːt 'sæləd]
obwohl although [ɔːl'ðəʊ], even though [ˌiːvn 'ðəʊ]
oder or [ɔː]
offen open ['əʊpən]
offenbaren reveal [rɪ'viːl]
öffentliche(r, s) public ['pʌblɪk]
Öffentlichkeit (the) public ['pʌblɪk]
öffnen; sich öffnen open ['əʊpən]
oft often ['ɒfn], ['ɒftən]
ohne without [wɪ'ðaʊt]
Ohr ear [ɪə]
Ohrhörer earphones *(pl)* ['ɪəfəʊnz]
Ohrring earring ['ɪərɪŋ]
Oje! Oh dear! [dɪə]
okay OK [ˌəʊ'keɪ]; all right [ɔːl 'raɪt]
Oktober October [ɒk'təʊbə]
Öl oil [ɔɪl]
Oma grandma ['grænmɑː]
Onkel uncle ['ʌŋkl]
Opa grandpa ['grænpɑː]
Orange orange ['ɒrɪndʒ]
orange(farben) orange ['ɒrɪndʒ]
ordnen order ['ɔːdə]; organize ['ɔːgənaɪz]
Ordnung: in Ordnung *(okay)* all right [ɔːl 'raɪt]; OK [ˌəʊ'keɪ]
organisieren organize ['ɔːgənaɪz]; arrange [ə'reɪndʒ]
Orkan hurricane ['hʌrɪkən]
Ort place [pleɪs]; location [ləʊ'keɪʃn] **am/vom Ort** local ['ləʊkl]
örtlich local ['ləʊkl]
Osten; nach Osten; östlich east [iːst] **Richtung Osten** eastbound ['iːstbaʊnd]
Otter otter ['ɒtə]
oval oval ['əʊvl]
Ozean ocean ['əʊʃn]

P

paar: ein paar a few [ə 'fjuː]; some [sʌm]; [səm]; a couple ['kʌpl]
Paar: ein Paar a pair (of) [peə]; a couple ['kʌpl]
Päckchen packet ['pækɪt]
packen *(greifen, schnappen)* grab [græb]
Packung packet ['pækɪt]
Palast palace ['pæləs]
Palme palm tree ['pɑːm triː]
Panik: in Panik geraten panic ['pænɪk]
Papa dad [dæd]
Papier paper ['peɪpə]
Paprika(schote) pepper ['pepə]
▶ S. 222 Food words
Parade parade [pə'reɪd]
Park park [pɑːk]
Parkplatz car park ['kɑː pɑːk], parking lot *(AE)* ['pɑːkɪŋ lɒt]
Parlament parliament ['pɑːləmənt]
Partner/in partner ['pɑːtnə]
Party party ['pɑːti]
Pass auf! *(Vorsicht!)* Watch out! [ˌwɒtʃ‿'aʊt]
passen: zu etwas passen *(zu etwas gehören)* go with sth.
passieren (mit) happen (to) ['hæpən]
Passwort password ['pɑːswɜːd]
Pastete pie [paɪ]
Patriotismus patriotism ['peɪtriətɪzəm]
Pause break [breɪk] **eine Pause einlegen** pause [pɔːz]
pausieren pause [pɔːz]
peinlich berührt embarrassed [ɪm'bærəst]

Pence pence [pens]
perfekt perfect ['pɜːfɪkt]
Person person ['pɜːsn]; *(in Roman, Film, usw.)* character ['kærəktə]
Personalausweis ID card [ˌaɪ 'diː kɑːd]
Petersilie parsley ['pɑːsli]
▶ S. 222 Food words
Pfad path [pɑːθ]; trail [treɪl]
Pfannkuchen pancake ['pænkeɪk]
Pfeffer pepper ['pepə]
▶ S. 222 Food words
Pfeife *(Triller)* whistle ['wɪsl]
pfeifen whistle ['wɪsl]; pfeifen *(auf der Trillerpfeife)* blow the whistle [bləʊ]
Pferd horse [hɔːs]
Pflanze plant [plɑːnt]
pflanzen plant [plɑːnt]
Pflaster *(Heftpflaster)* plaster ['plɑːstə]
Pforte gate [geɪt]
Pfote paw [pɔː]
Pfund *(Gewicht und britische Währung)* pound (£) [paʊnd] **ein drei Pfund schwerer Ball** a three-pound ball
▶ S. 219 a 9,740-foot swimming pool
Piano piano [pi'ænəʊ]
Picknick picnic ['pɪknɪk]
piepen beep [biːp]
Pilz mushroom ['mʌʃrʊm, 'mʌʃruːm]
▶ S. 222 Food words
pink pink [pɪŋk]
Pizza pizza ['piːtsə]
Plan plan [plæn]; schedule ['ʃedjuːl]
planen plan [plæn]
Planet planet ['plænɪt]
Plastik plastic ['plæstɪk]
Platz place [pleɪs]; *(Sitz)* seat [siːt]; *(in der Stadt)* square [skweə]; *(Raum)* space [speɪs]; *(Position)* position [pə'zɪʃn]; **auf dem zweiten Platz** in second place
Plätzchen *(Keks)* biscuit ['bɪskɪt]
plötzlich suddenly ['sʌdnli]
Pokal *(Trophäe)* trophy ['trəʊfi]
Polizei police *(pl)* [pə'liːs]
Polizist/in police officer [pə'liːs‿ˌɒfɪsə]
Pommes frites chips *(pl)* [tʃɪps]; *(AE)* fries *(pl)* [fraɪz]
Pony pony ['pəʊni]
populär (bei) popular (with) ['pɒpjələ]
Portemonnaie purse [pɜːs] *(bei Frauen)*; wallet ['wɒlɪt] *(bei Männern)*
Portion portion ['pɔːʃn]
Porträt *(Personenbeschreibung)* profile ['prəʊfaɪl]
Position position [pə'zɪʃn]
Postamt post office ['pəʊst‿ɒfɪs]
posten post [pəʊst]
Poster poster ['pəʊstə]
Posting *(auf Blog)* post [pəʊst]
Postkarte postcard ['pəʊstkɑːd]
Präfix prefix ['priːfɪks]
praktisch practical ['præktɪkl]
Praline chocolate ['tʃɒklət]
Prärie prairie ['preəri]
Präsentation presentation [ˌprezn'teɪʃn]
präsentieren: (jm.) etwas präsentieren present sth. (to sb.) [prɪ'zent]
Präsident/in president ['prezɪdənt]
Preis **1.** *(Kaufpreis)* price [praɪs] **2.** *(Gewinn)* prize [praɪz]
Preiselbeere cranberry ['krænbəri]
preisgeben reveal [rɪ'viːl]
pro per [pə, pɜː]
probieren try [traɪ]
Problem problem ['prɒbləm]
Profil *(Personenbeschreibung, Porträt)* profile ['prəʊfaɪl]
Programm programme ['prəʊgræm] *(Zeitplan)* schedule ['ʃedjuːl]
Projekt project ['prɒdʒekt]
Prominente(r) VIP *(very important person)* [ˌviː‿aɪ 'piː]
Prospekt *(Broschüre)* brochure ['brəʊʃə]
Protest protest ['prəʊtest]
protestieren protest [prə'test] *(AE auch:* ['prəʊtest]*)*
Prozess process ['prəʊses]
prüfen *(überprüfen)* check [tʃek] **etwas prüfen** look into sth.
Prüfung exam [ɪg'zæm]
Publikum audience ['ɔːdiəns]
Pullover pullover ['pʊləʊvə], sweater *(bes. AE)* ['elɪveɪtə]
Pulver powder ['paʊdə]
Punkt point [pɔɪnt]; *(Satzzeichen)* full stop [ˌfʊl 'stɒp]; *(Fleck)* spot [spɒt]
Punktestand score [skɔː]
Pute turkey ['tɜːki]
putzen clean [kliːn]
Puzzle jigsaw ['dʒɪgsɔː]

Q

Quadratkilometer (km²) square kilometre (sq km) [skweə]
qualifizieren: sich qualifizieren qualify ['kwɒlɪfaɪ]
Querflöte flute [fluːt]
Quiz quiz [kwɪz]

R

Rabe raven ['reɪvn]
Rad *(Fahrrad)* bike [baɪk] **Rad fahren** ride a bike [ˌraɪd‿ə 'baɪk], cycle ['saɪkl]
Radiergummi rubber ['rʌbə]
Radio radio ['reɪdiəʊ] **im Radio** on the radio
Rallye rally ['ræli]
Rand edge [edʒ]
rasen race [reɪs]
Rasen lawn [lɔːn]
Rat **1.** *(Stadtrat, Gemeinderat u.Ä.)* council ['kaʊnsl] **2.** *(Ratschlag, Ratschläge)* advice *(no pl)* [əd'vaɪs]
raten **1.** guess [ges] **2. jm. raten, etwas zu tun** advise sb. to do sth. [əd'vaɪz]
Rathaus town hall [ˌtaʊn 'hɔːl]
Ratte rat [ræt]
rauchen smoke [sməʊk]
rauf und runter up and down [ˌʌp‿ən 'daʊn]
räumen clear [klɪə]
Reaktion (auf) reaction (to) [ri'ækʃn]
reagieren (auf) react (to) [ri'ækt]
Recherche research *(no pl)* ['riːsɜːtʃ]
Recht: jemand hat Recht someone is right
rechte(r, s) right [raɪt] **auf der rechten Seite** on the right **nach rechts** right **(nach) rechts abbiegen** turn right
Rechtschreibung spelling ['spelɪŋ]
Redakteur/in editor ['edɪtə]
Rede talk [tɔːk]; *(offiziell)* speech [spiːtʃ] **eine Rede halten (über)** give a talk (about)
reden (mit) talk (to) [tɔːk]
Redensart saying ['seɪɪŋ]
Referat talk [tɔːk] **ein Referat halten (über)** give a talk (about)
Refrain chorus ['kɔːrəs]
Regal shelf [ʃelf]
Regel rule [ruːl]
regelmäßig regular ['regjələ]
Regen rain [reɪn] **starker/heftiger Regen** heavy rain ['hevi]
Regenbogen rainbow ['reɪnbəʊ]
Regenmantel raincoat ['reɪnkəʊt]
Regenschirm umbrella [ʌm'brelə]
Regenwald rainforest ['reɪnfɒrɪst]
Regierung government ['gʌvənmənt]
Region region ['riːdʒən]
regional regional ['riːdʒənl]

Regisseur/in director [də'rektə]
regnen rain [reɪn]
regnerisch rainy ['reɪni]
Reh deer [dɪə]
reich rich [rɪtʃ]
reichen: etwas reichen pass sth. (around) [ˌpɑːs_ə'raʊnd]
Reihe *(wartender Menschen)* queue [kjuː] **Ich bin an der Reihe.** (It's) my turn. [tɜːn]
Reihenfolge order ['ɔːdə]
Reim rhyme [raɪm]
Reis rice [raɪs]
► S. 222 Food words
Reise trip [trɪp]; journey ['dʒɜːni]
Reiseführer guidebook ['gaɪdbʊk]
Reiseleiter/in guide [gaɪd]
reisen travel ['trævl]
Reisende(r) traveller ['trævələ]
reiten ride [raɪd]
Reiten riding ['raɪdɪŋ]
relevant (für etwas) relevant (to sth.) ['reləvənt]
Religion religion [rɪ'lɪdʒən]
rennen run [rʌn] **um sein Leben rennen** run for your life
Rennen race [reɪs]
Reportage report [rɪ'pɔːt]
Republik republic [rɪ'pʌblɪk]
Reservat, Reservation reservation *(kurz auch:* rez*)* [ˌrezə'veɪʃn]
reservieren reserve [rɪ'zɜːv]
Rest rest [rest]
Restaurant restaurant ['restrɒnt] *(kleines, preiswertes)* diner ['daɪnə]
Resultat result [rɪ'zʌlt]
retten rescue ['reskjuː] **jn. von/vor etwas retten** save sb. from sth. ['seɪv]
Rezept *(Kochrezept)* recipe ['resəpi]
Rhythmus rhythm ['rɪðəm]
richten: etwas auf jn. richten point sth. at sb. [pɔɪnt]
richtig right [raɪt]; correct [kə'rekt] **Ja, das ist richtig.** Yes, that's right.
Richter/in judge [dʒʌdʒ]
Richtung direction [də'rekʃn] **in die Richtung (dort)** that way **in diese Richtung** this way **in Richtung Bahnhof** towards the station [tə'wɔːdz] **Richtung Osten/...** eastbound ['iːstbaʊnd] / ...
riechen smell [smel] **an etwas riechen** smell sth.
Riegel *(Schokolade, Müsli)* bar [bɑː]
Riese giant ['dʒaɪənt]
riesig vast [vɑːst], giant ['dʒaɪənt]
Riesenhunger: einen Riesenhunger haben be starving ['stɑːvɪŋ]
riesig huge [hjuːdʒ]
Riesenrad big wheel [bɪg 'wiːl]
Rindfleisch beef [biːf]
Rinderbraten roast beef [ˌrəʊst 'biːf]
Ring ring [rɪŋ]
Ritter knight [naɪt]
Robbe seal [siːl]
Rock skirt [skɜːt]
Rock(musik) rock (music) [rɒk]
Rodeo rodeo ['rəʊdiəʊ]
Rolle *(Theaterstück, Film)* role [rəʊl]
rollen roll [rəʊl]
romantisch romantic [rəʊ'mæntɪk]
rosa pink [pɪŋk]
Rose rose [rəʊz]
rot red [red] **rot werden** go red
Route route [ruːt]
Routine routine [ruː'tiːn]
Ruck jolt [dʒəʊlt]
Rücken back [bæk]
Rückmeldung feedback ['fiːdbæk]
Rucksack rucksack ['rʌksæk], backpack ['bækpæk]
Rückseite back [bæk]
rufen call [kɔːl]; shout [ʃaʊt]
ruhen rest [rest]
ruhig *(leise)* quiet ['kwaɪət]; calm [kɑːm]
Ruhm fame [feɪm]
Ruine ruin ['ruːɪn]
rumhängen hang out [ˌhæŋ_'aʊt] *(infml)*
Rundgang, Rundfahrt (durch) tour (of) ['tʊər_əv]
runter: rauf und runter up and down [ˌʌp_ən 'daʊn]
runzeln: die Stirn runzeln frown [fraʊn]

S

Sache thing [θɪŋ]
sachlich, Sach- factual ['fæktʃuəl]
Sackpfeife bagpipes *(pl)* ['bægpaɪps]
Sackpfeifer/in bagpiper ['bægpaɪpə]
Saft juice [dʒuːs]
Sage legend ['ledʒənd]
sagen say [seɪ]
Sahne cream [kriːm]
Saite string [strɪŋ]
Salat *(Gericht, Beilage)* salad ['sæləd]
Salz salt [sɔːlt]
► S. 222 Food words
Samen seed [siːd]
sammeln collect [kə'lekt] **Geld sammeln (für etwas)** raise money (for sth.) [reɪz]
Samstag Saturday ['sætədeɪ, 'sætədi]
Sand sand [sænd]
Sandwich sandwich ['sænwɪtʃ], ['sænwɪdʒ]
sanft gently ['dʒentli] **mit sanfter Stimme** in a soft voice
Sattel saddle ['sædl]
Satz sentence ['sentəns] **Satz, der in das Thema eines Absatzes einführt** topic sentence [ˌtɒpɪk 'sentəns]
sauber clean [kliːn] **sauber machen** clean [kliːn]
sauer, säuerlich sour ['saʊə]
Säule column ['kɒləm]
Schach chess [tʃes]
schade: Es war schade, dass ... It was a pity that ... ['pɪti]
Schaf sheep [ʃiːp]
Schafenherde flock of sheep [flɒk]
Schäfer/in, Schafhirte/-hirtin shepherd ['ʃepəd]
schaffen create [kri'eɪt] **etwas schaffen** manage sth. ['mænɪdʒ]
Schal scarf [skɑːf]
scharf *(Messer)* sharp [ʃɑːp], *(gewürzt)* hot [hɒt]
Schatten *(einer Person, eines Gegenstandes)* shadow ['ʃædəʊ]
Schatz, Schätzchen honey *(infml, als Anrede)* ['hʌni]
schätzen: etwas schätzen, etwas zu schätzen wissen appreciate sb./sth. [ə'priːʃieɪt]
schauen look [lʊk]
Schauspiel drama ['drɑːmə]
Schauspieler/in actor ['æktə]
schauspielern act [ækt]
scheinen
1. *(Sonne)* shine [ʃaɪn]
2. **(zu sein / zu tun) scheinen** seem (to be/do) [siːm]
scherzen joke [dʒəʊk]
scheu shy [ʃaɪ]
Scheune barn [bɑːn]
schick: sich schick anziehen dress up [ˌdres_'ʌp]
schicken: jm. etwas schicken send sth. to sb. [send] **einem Freund / einer Freundin eine SMS schicken** text a friend [tekst]
schieben push [pʊʃ]
Schiedsrichter/in referee [ˌrefə'riː]
schießen shoot [ʃuːt] **jm. durch den Kopf schießen** flash through sb.'s mind [flæʃ]
Schiff ship [ʃɪp]
Schiffsreise cruise [kruːz]
Schild sign [saɪn]; *(Etikett)* label
Schimpfwort: jm. Schimpfwörter nachrufen call sb. names

Schinkenspeck bacon ['beɪkən]
Schirm umbrella [ʌm'brelə]
schlafen sleep [sli:p]; *(nicht wach sein)* be asleep [ə'sli:p]
Schlafparty sleepover ['sli:pəʊvə]
Schlafzimmer bedroom ['bedru:m]
schlagen hit [hɪt]; beat [bi:t]
Schlägerei fight [faɪt]
Schlagzeug drums *(pl)* [drʌmz]
Schlamm mud [mʌd]
schlammig muddy ['mʌdi]
Schlange
1. snake [sneɪk]
2. *(wartender Menschen)* queue [kju:]; *(AE)* line [laɪn] **Schlange stehen** queue; *(AE)* wait/stand in line
schlau clever ['klevə]
schlecht bad [bæd] **schlechter** worse [wɜ:s] **der/die/das schlechteste ...; am schlechtesten** worst [wɜ:st] **Mir ist schlecht.** I feel sick. **der/die/das schlechteste ...; am schlechtesten** worst [wɜ:st]
schließen close [kləʊz]
Schließfach locker ['lɒkə]
schließlich at last [ət 'lɑ:st]; finally ['faɪnəli]
schlimm bad [bæd] **schlimmer** worse [wɜ:s] **der/die/das schlimmste ...; am schlimmsten** worst [wɜ:st]
Schloss castle ['kɑ:sl]; palace ['pæləs]
Schluss end [end]; *(Abschluss)* ending ['endɪŋ]
Schlüssel key [ki:]
Schlüsselwort keyword ['ki:wɜ:d]
Schluss(folgerung) conclusion [kən'klu:ʒn]
schmal narrow ['nærəʊ]
schmecken taste [teɪst]
schmelzen melt [melt]
schmerzen hurt [hɜ:t]
Schmetterling butterfly ['bʌtəflaɪ]
Schmuck jewellery *(BE)* / jewelry *(AE)* *(no pl)* ['dʒu:əlri]
Schmuggel; das Schmuggeln smuggling ['smʌglɪŋ]
schmuggeln smuggle ['smʌgl]
Schmuggler/in smuggler ['smʌglə]
schmutzig dirty ['dɜ:ti]
schnappen grab [græb]
Schnee snow [snəʊ]
schneiden cut [kʌt]; *(Film, Video bearbeiten)* edit ['edɪt]
schnell fast [fɑ:st]; quick [kwɪk]
Schnitt! *(beim Filmen)* Cut! [kʌt]
schnitzen carve [kɑ:v]
schockiert shocked [ʃɒkt]
Schokolade chocolate ['tʃɒklət]
schön beautiful ['bju:tɪfl]; *(nett)* nice [naɪs]; *(herrlich)* lovely ['lʌvli]
schon already [ɔ:l'redi] **(vorher) schon mal** before **Hast du schon ...?** Have you ... yet? [jet]
Schrank cupboard ['kʌbəd]
schrecklich terrible ['terəbl]; awful ['ɔ:fl]
schreiben write [raɪt]
Schreibtisch desk [desk]
Schreibweise spelling ['spelɪŋ]
schreien shout [ʃaʊt]; cry [kraɪ]; scream [skri:m]
Schritt step [step], footstep ['fʊtstep]
schüchtern shy [ʃaɪ]
Schuh shoe [ʃu:]
Schule school [sku:l] **in der Schule** at school
Schüler/in student ['stju:dənt]
Schulfach (school) subject ['sʌbdʒɪkt]
Schulheft *(Übungsheft)* exercise book ['eksəsaɪz bʊk]
Schulhof schoolyard ['sku:ljɑ:d]
Schulleiter/in head teacher [,hed 'ti:tʃə], principal ['prɪnsəpl]
Schulstunde period ['pɪəriəd]
Schultasche school bag ['sku:l bæg]
Schulter shoulder ['ʃəʊldə]
Schüssel bowl [bəʊl]
schütteln shake [ʃeɪk]
schützen: jn./etwas (be)schützen (vor jm./etwas) protect sb./sth. (from sb./sth.) [prə'tekt]
Schutzgebiet reserve [rɪ'zɜ:v]
schwarz black [blæk]
schweigend silently ['saɪləntli]
Schwein pig [pɪg]
Schweinefleisch pork [pɔ:k]
schwer **1.** *(Gewicht)* heavy ['hevi]
2. *(schwierig)* difficult ['dɪfɪkəlt]; hard [hɑ:d]
Schwerpunkt focus ['fəʊkəs]
Schwert sword [sɔ:d]
Schwester sister ['sɪstə]
schwierig difficult ['dɪfɪkəlt]; hard [hɑ:d]
Schwimmbad, Schwimmbecken (swimming) pool [pu:l]
schwimmen swim [swɪm]
Schwimmer/in swimmer ['swɪmə]
schwindlig dizzy ['dɪzi] **ihr ist schwindelig** she feels faint [feɪnt]
scrollen scroll [skrəʊl]
See **1.** *(Binnensee)* lake [leɪk]
2. *(die See, das Meer)* sea [si:]
Seemann sailor ['seɪlə]
Segelboot sailing boat ['seɪlɪŋ bəʊt]
segeln sail [seɪl] **segeln gehen** go sailing ['seɪlɪŋ]
sehen see [si:]
Sehenswürdigkeiten sights *(pl)* [saɪts]
sehr very ['veri] **Bitte sehr.** Here you are. **Ich mag sie sehr.** I like her a lot. [ə 'lɒt] **Ich würde sehr gern ...** I'd love to ...
Seil rope [rəʊp]
sein *(Verb)* be [bi:]
sein(e) ... *(vor Nomen; besitzanzeigend)*
1. *(zu „he")* his ... [hɪz]
2. *(zu „it")* its ... [ɪts]
seiner, seine, seins his [hɪz]
seit: seit 10 Uhr since 10 o'clock [sɪns] **seit Wochen** for weeks
Seite **1.** side [saɪd] **auf der linken/rechten Seite** on the left/right
2. *(Buchseite)* page [peɪdʒ] **Auf welcher Seite sind wir?** What page are we on?
Sekunde second ['sekənd]
selbst: Hast du es selbst gekocht? Did you cook it yourself? [jɔ:'self] **..., wenn wir das Zimmer selbst streichen.** ... if we paint the room ourselves. [ɑ:'selvz], [aʊə'selvz] **Das Zimmer selbst war in Ordnung.** The room itself was OK. [ɪt'self] **er hat den Alligator selbst getötet** he killed the alligator himself [hɪm'self] **Der Regisseur selbst hieß uns willkommen.** The director himself welcomed us. [hɪm'self]
► S. 224 German "selbst"
selbst wenn even if ['i:vn‿ɪf]
Selbstlaut vowel ['vaʊəl]
selbstverständlich of course [əv 'kɔ:s]
Selfie selfie ['selfi]
seltsam strange [streɪndʒ]; weird [wɪəd]
senden: jm. etwas senden send sth. to sb. [send]
Sender channel ['tʃænl]
Sendung *(im Radio, Fernsehen)* programme ['prəʊgræm]
separat separately ['seprətli]
September September [sep'tembə]
Sessel armchair ['ɑ:mtʃeə]
setzen: sich setzen sit [sɪt] **sich (mit jm.) in Verbindung setzen** get in touch (with sb.) [tʌtʃ]
seufzen sigh [saɪ]
Show show [ʃəʊ]

sich 1. *(Reflexivpronomen)* herself [hɜːˈself]; himself [hɪmˈself]; itself [ɪtˈself]; themselves [ðəmˈselvz]; *(zur höflichen Anrede „Sie")* yourself [jɔːˈself]; yourselves [jɔːˈselvz] **2. sich (gegenseitig)** *(einander)* each other [iːtʃ_ˈʌðə]
sicher sure [ʃʊə], [ʃɔː] *(in Sicherheit)* safe [seɪf] *(bestimmt)* definitely [ˈdefɪnətli]
Sicherheit, Sicherheits- security [sɪˈkjʊərəti]
sie 1. *(Einzahl; weibliche Person)* she [ʃiː] **Frag sie.** Ask her. [hɜː] **2.** *(Einzahl; Ding, Tier)* it [ɪt] **3.** *(Mehrzahl)* they [ðeɪ] **Frag sie.** Ask them. [ðem, ðəm]
Sie *(höfliche Anrede)* you [juː, ju]
Sieger/in winner [ˈwɪnə]
Signal signal [ˈsɪgnəl]
Silbe syllable [ˈsɪləbl]
Silvester New Year's Eve [ˌnjuː jɪəz_ˈiːv]
singen sing [sɪŋ]
sinken sink [sɪŋk]
Sinn mind [maɪnd]
Situation situation [ˌsɪtʃuˈeɪʃn]
Sitz seat [siːt]
sitzen sit [sɪt]
Sitzung session [ˈseʃn]
Sklave, Sklavin slave [sleɪv]
Sklaverei slavery [ˈsleɪvəri]
Skulptur sculpture [ˈskʌlptʃə]
SMS text (message) [ˈtekst mesɪdʒ] **jm. eine SMS schicken** text sb.
Snack snack [snæk]
so 1. *(auf diese Weise)* like that / like this **so tun, als ob** pretend [prɪˈtend] **2. (nicht) so groß wie** (not) as big as [æz], [əz] **3. so nett/...** so nice/... [səʊ] **so ein/e ...** such a ... [sʌtʃ]
sobald as soon as [əz ˈsuːn_əz]
Socke sock [sɒk]
sodass ... so that ... *(oft auch kurz: so ...)*
soeben just [dʒʌst]
Sofa sofa [ˈsəʊfə]
sofort immediately [ɪˈmiːdiətli]
sogar even [ˈiːvn]
Sohn son [sʌn]
solch ein/e ... such a ... [sʌtʃ]
Soldat/in soldier [ˈsəʊldʒə]
sollen: Du solltest ... You should ... [ʃʊd], [ʃəd] **Soll ich ...?** Shall I ...? [ʃæl]
Solo- solo [ˈsəʊləʊ]
Sommer summer [ˈsʌmə]
Sonnabend Saturday [ˈsætədeɪ, ˈsætədi]
Sonne sun [sʌn]
Sonnenbrille sunglasses *(pl)* [ˈsʌnglɑːsɪz]
Sonnenuntergang sunset [ˈsʌnset]
sonnig sunny [ˈsʌni]
Sonntag Sunday [ˈsʌndeɪ, ˈsʌndi]
sonst: sonst jeder everybody else [els] **sonst etwas?** anything else?
Sorge: sich Sorgen machen (wegen, um) worry (about) [ˈwʌri]
Sorte type (of) [taɪp]
Soße sauce [sɔːs]
Souvenir souvenir [ˌsuːvəˈnɪə]
sowie *(sobald)* as soon as [əz ˈsuːn_əz]
sowohl ... als auch ... both ... and ... [bəʊθ]
sozial, Sozial- social [ˈsəʊʃl] **soziale Medien** social media *(pl)* [ˌsəʊʃl ˈmiːdiə] **Sozialkunde** social studies [ˌsəʊʃl ˈstʌdiz]
Spagetti spaghetti [spəˈgeti]
Spanisch; spanisch Spanish [ˈspænɪʃ]
spannen tighten [ˈtaɪtn]
spannend *(aufregend)* exciting [ɪkˈsaɪtɪŋ]
Spannung tension [ˈtenʃn]
Spaß fun [fʌn] **Spaß haben** have fun [fʌn] **Ich hatte Spaß.** I enjoyed myself.
spät late [leɪt] **Du bist spät dran. / Du bist zu spät.** You're late. **Wie spät ist es?** What time is it?
später later [ˈleɪtə]
spazieren gehen go for a walk [wɔːk], take a walk *(bes. AE)*
Spaziergang walk [wɔːk] **einen Spaziergang machen** go for a walk, take a walk *(bes. AE)*
Speisekarte menu [ˈmenjuː]
sperren block [blɒk]
Spickzettel crib sheet [ˈkrɪb ʃiːt] *(infml)*
Spiegel mirror [ˈmɪrə]
spielen play [pleɪ] **Gitarre/... spielen** play the guitar / the ...
Spieler/in player [ˈpleɪə]
Spielstand score [skɔː]
Spielzeug toy [tɔɪ]
Spinat spinach [ˈspɪnɪtʃ]
▶ S. 222 Food words
Spind locker [ˈlɒkə]
Spinner/in weirdo (infml) [ˈwɪədəʊ]
Spitze top [tɒp] **Spitzen-** top [tɒp]
Sport; Sportart sport [spɔːt] **Sport treiben** do sport
Sportunterricht PE [ˌpiː_ˈiː]
Sprache language [ˈlæŋgwɪdʒ]
sprayen spray [spreɪ]
sprechen speak [spiːk] **mit jm. sprechen** speak to sb. **Kann ich Sie kurz sprechen?** May I have a word with you?
Sprecher/in speaker [ˈspiːkə], narrator [nəˈreɪtə]
Sprichwort saying [ˈseɪɪŋ]
springen jump [dʒʌmp]
spritzen: jn. nass spritzen splash sb. [splæʃ]
sprühen spray [spreɪ]
Sprung jump [dʒʌmp]
spülen: das Geschirr spülen wash the dishes *(pl)* [ˌwɒʃ ðə ˈdɪʃɪz]
Spur: keine Spur von ... no sign of ... [saɪn]
Staat state [steɪt]
Stadion stadium [ˈsteɪdiəm]
Stadt town [taʊn]; *(Großstadt)* city [ˈsɪti]
Stadtplan map [mæp] **auf dem Stadtplan** on the map
Stadtviertel quarter [ˈkwɔːtə]
Staffel *(einer Fernsehserie)* season [ˈsiːzn]
Stammbaum family tree [ˈfæməli triː]
Stand *(Marktstand)* stall [stɔːl]
Standard; Standard- standard [ˈstændəd]
ständig: etwas ständig tun keep doing sth. [kiːp]
▶ S. 232 (to) keep
Standort location [ləʊˈkeɪʃn]
Standpunkt point of view [ˌpɔɪnt_əv ˈvjuː]
Stapel pile [paɪl]
Star star [stɑː]
stark strong [strɒŋ] **starker Regen** heavy rain [ˈhevi]
Stärke power [ˈpaʊə]
starren gaze [geɪz]
Station *(Haltestelle)* stop [stɒp]
statt instead of [ɪnˈsted_əv]
stattdessen instead [ɪnˈsted]
stattfinden take place [teɪk ˈpleɪs]
Statue statue [ˈstætʃuː]
Staub dust [dʌst]
stechen: etwas in etwas stechen stick sth. into sth. [stɪk]
stecken tuck [tʌk] **etwas in etwas stecken** stick sth. into sth. [stɪk]
stehen stand [stænd] **Schlange stehen** queue [kjuː]; *(AE)* wait/stand in line [laɪn] **auf etwas stehen** be into sth. *(infml)* **Wie steht es?** What's the score? [skɔː]
stehlen steal [stiːl]

steil steep [sti:p]
Stein stone [stəʊn]
steinig rocky ['rɒki]
Stelle place [pleɪs]; *(Job, Arbeitsstelle)* job [dʒɒb] **an zweiter Stelle** in second place
stellen *(hin-, abstellen)* put [pʊt] **eine Frage stellen** ask a question
Stempel stamp [stæmp]
sterben die [daɪ]
Stern star [stɑ:]
Steuer *(die)* tax [tæks]
Steuerzahler/in taxpayer ['tækspeɪə]
Stichwort *(im Wörterbuch)* headword ['hedwɜ:d]
Stiefel boot [bu:t]
Stift *(zum Schreiben)* pen [pen]
Stil style [staɪl]
still quiet ['kwaɪət]; silent ['saɪlənt]
Stimme voice [vɔɪs] **mit lauter Stimme** in a loud voice **mit sanfter Stimme** in a soft voice
stimmen *(Instrument)* tune [tju:n] **Ja, das stimmt.** Yes, that's right. [raɪt] **Nein, das stimmt nicht.** No, that's wrong. [rɒŋ]
Stimmung atmosphere ['ætməsfɪə], mood [mu:d]
Stirn: die Stirn runzeln frown [fraʊn]
Stock stick [stɪk]
Stockwerk floor [flɔ:]
Stoff material [mə'tɪəriəl]
stöhnen groan [grəʊn]
Stöhnen groan [grəʊn]
Stolz (auf etwas) pride (in sth.) [praɪd]
stolz (auf) proud (of) [praʊd]
stoppen stop [stɒp]
Stoß jolt [dʒəʊlt]
stoßen push [pʊʃ] **auf jn./etwas stoßen** *(zufällig)* come across sb./sth.
Strafe punishment ['pʌnɪʃmənt]
strahlend *(leuchtend hell)* bright [braɪt]
Strand beach [bi:tʃ]
Straße street [stri:t]; road [rəʊd]
Straßenbahn tram [træm], streetcar *(AE)* ['stri:tkɑ:]
Straßenkreuzer limousine [ˌlɪmə'zi:n], ['lɪməzi:n]
Straßenkünstler/in street artist
Strauch shrub [ʃrʌb]
Strecke route [ru:t]
strecken: sich strecken stretch [stretʃ]

streichen **1.** *(mit Farbe)* paint [peɪnt]
2. *(löschen)* delete [dɪ'li:t]
Streit argument ['ɑ:gjumənt]
streiten; sich streiten argue ['ɑ:gju:]
streng strict [strɪkt]
Stress stress [stres]
Strom power ['paʊə]
Strophe verse [vɜ:s]
Struktur structure ['strʌktʃə]
strukturieren structure ['strʌktʃə]
Stück piece [pi:s]
Student/in student ['stju:dənt]
studieren study ['stʌdi]
Studio studio ['stju:diəʊ]
Stufe step [step]
Stuhl chair [tʃeə]
Stunde hour ['aʊə]; *(Unterrichts-stunde)* lesson ['lesn], period ['pɪəriəd] **jm. Stunden geben** tutor sb. ['tju:tə] **ein einstündiges Konzert** a one-hour concert **ein Supermarkt, der 24 Stunden geöffnet ist** a 24-hour supermarket
► S. 219 a 9,740-foot swimming pool
Stundenplan timetable ['taɪmteɪbl]
Sturm storm [stɔ:m]
stürzen fall [fɔ:l] **in/gegen etwas stürzen** crash into sth. [kræʃ]
► S. 215 (to) crash
Subjekt subject ['sʌbdʒekt]
Suche (nach) search (for) [sɜ:tʃ]
suchen: etwas suchen look for sth. ['lʊk fɔ:]
Süden; nach Süden; südlich south [saʊθ]
Südosten; nach Südosten; südöstlich south-east [ˌsaʊθ_'i:st]
Südwesten; nach Südwesten; südwestlich south-west [ˌsaʊθ'west]
Suffix suffix ['sʌfɪks]
Sumpf swamp [swɒmp]
Suppe soup [su:p] **Suppe kochen** make soup
► S. 222 Food words
Süden: Richtung Süden southbound ['saʊθbaʊnd]
süß sweet [swi:t]
Süßigkeiten sweets [swi:ts]; *(AE)* candy ['kændi]
Süßkartoffel sweet potato [ˌswi:t pə'teɪtəʊ]
Symbol symbol ['sɪmbl]
Synonym *(bedeutungsgleiches Wort)* synonym ['sɪnənɪm]
System system ['sɪstəm]
Szene scene [si:n], *(Film)* shot [ʃɒt]

T

Tabelle table ['teɪbl]
Tablet tablet ['tæblət]
Tafel **1.** board [bɔ:d]
2. *(Schokolade)* bar [bɑ:]
Tag day [deɪ]
Tagebuch diary ['daɪəri]
Tagesausflüge machen go on day trips
Taille waist [weɪst]
Tal valley ['væli]
talentiert talented ['tæləntɪd]
Tante aunt [ɑ:nt]
Tante-Emma-Laden corner shop ['kɔ:nə ʃɒp]
Tanz dance [dɑ:ns]
tanzen dance [dɑ:ns]
Tanzfläche dance floor ['dɑ:ns flɔ:]
tapfer brave [breɪv]
Tasche bag [bæg]; *(Manteltasche, Hosentasche usw.)* pocket ['pɒkɪt]
Taschenlampe torch [tɔ:tʃ]; *(AE)* flashlight ['flæʃlaɪt]
Tasse cup [kʌp] **eine Tasse Tee** a cup of tea
Tatsache fact [fækt]
tatsächlich actually ['æktʃuəli]
tätscheln pat [pæt]
Tatze paw [pɔ:]
Taube pigeon ['pɪdʒɪn]
tausend; Tausend thousand ['θaʊznd]
Team team [ti:m]
Technik technique [tek'ni:k], technology [tek'nɒlədʒi]
Technologie technology [tek'nɒlədʒi]
Tee tea [ti:] **Tee kochen** make tea
► S. 222 Food words
Teelöffel teaspoon ['ti:spu:n]
Teil part [pɑ:t]
teilen: (sich) teilen (in), divide (into) [dɪ'vaɪd]
teilnehmen: an etwas teilnehmen take part in sth. [ˌteɪk 'pɑ:t] **an einem Kurs teilnehmen** attend a course [ə'tend]
Telefon telephone ['telɪfəʊn], *(kurz auch:)* phone **am Telefon** on the phone **ans Telefon gehen** answer the phone
Telefongespräch phone call ['fəʊn kɔ:l] (kurz auch: call)
Teller plate [pleɪt] **ein Teller ...** a plate of ... [pleɪt]
Temperatur temperature ['temprətʃə]
Tennis tennis ['tenɪs]
Termin appointment [ə'pɔɪntmənt]
terroristische(r, s); **Terrorist/in** terrorist ['terərɪst]

Test test [test]
testen test [test]
teuer expensive [ɪk'spensɪv]
Theater theatre, *(AE)* theater ['θɪətə]
Theaterstück play [pleɪ]
Theke countertop ['kaʊntətɒp] counter ['kaʊntə], worktop ['wɜːktɒp]
Thema theme [θiːm]; topic ['tɒpɪk]
Thermometer thermometer [θə'mɒmɪtə]
tief deep [diːp]
tiefgekühlt frozen ['frəʊzn]
▶ S. 222 Food words
Tier animal ['ænɪml] **frei lebende Tiere** wildlife ['waɪldlaɪf]
Tierwelt wildlife ['waɪldlaɪf]
Tipp tip [tɪp]
Tisch table ['teɪbl]
Tischler/in carpenter ['kɑːpəntə]
Tischtennis table tennis
Titel title ['taɪtl]
Toast(brot) toast [təʊst]
Tochter daughter ['dɔːtə]
Tod death [deθ]
Toilette toilet ['tɔɪlət] *(öffentliche, AE)* restroom ['restruːm]
Tomate tomato [tə'mɑːtəʊ]
Ton *(Musik)* note [nəʊt]
Topf pot [pɒt]
Tor *(Pforte, Gatter)* gate [geɪt]; *(Sport)* goal **ein Tor schießen** score (a goal) [skɔː]
Torwart, Torfrau goalkeeper ['gəʊlkiːpə]
tosen roar [rɔː]
tot dead [ded]
total totally ['təʊtəli]
Totale, Totalaufnahme long shot ['lɒŋ ʃɒt]
töten kill [kɪl]
Tourist/in tourist ['tʊərɪst]
Tradition tradition [trə'dɪʃn]
traditionell traditional [trə'dɪʃənl]
tragen carry ['kæri]; *(Kleidung)* wear [weə]
Trainer/in coach [kəʊtʃ]
trainieren practise ['præktɪs]; train [treɪn]
Training training ['treɪnɪŋ]
Traktor tractor ['træktə]
Träne tear [tɪə] **in Tränen ausbrechen** burst into tears [bɜːst]
Trauerfeier funeral ['fjuːnərəl]
Traum dream [driːm]
traurig sad [sæd]
Traurigkeit sadness ['sædnəs]
Trauung wedding ['wedɪŋ]
treffen; sich treffen meet [miːt] **etwas treffen** hit sth. **auf jn./etwas treffen** *(zufällig)* come across sb./sth.
Treffer: einen Treffer erzielen score [skɔː]
Trennung *(nach Hautfarbe, Religion oder Geschlecht)* segregation [ˌsegrɪ'geɪʃn]
Treppe; Treppenstufen stairs *(pl)* [steəz]
treten kick [kɪk]
Trick trick [trɪk]
Trillerpfeife whistle ['wɪsl]
Trimester term [tɜːm]
trinken drink [drɪŋk]
Trinkbrunnen drinking fountain *(bes. BE)* ['faʊntən], water fountain *(bes. AE)*
trocken dry [draɪ]
Trockenheit drought [draʊt]
Trommel drum [drʌm]
Trompete trumpet ['trʌmpɪt]
Tropen-, tropisch tropical ['trɒpɪkl]
Trophäe trophy ['trəʊfi]
Truthahn turkey ['tɜːki]
Tschüs. Bye. [baɪ]
T-Shirt T-shirt ['tiːʃɜːt]
Tulpe tulip ['tjuːlɪp]
tun do [duː] **so tun, als ob** pretend [prɪ'tend]
Tür door [dɔː]
Türklingel, -glocke doorbell ['dɔːbel]
Turm tower ['taʊə]
Turnen gymnastics [dʒɪm'næstɪks]; *(Sportunterricht)* PE [ˌpiː‿'iː] (Physical Education)
Turnhalle gym [dʒɪm]
Turnier trials *(pl)* ['traɪəlz]
Turnschuh trainer ['treɪnə], sneakers [sniːks]
Typ type (of) [taɪp]
typisch (für) typical (of) ['tɪpɪkl]

U

U-Bahn the underground *(no pl)* ['ʌndəgraʊnd]; *(AE)* subway ['sʌbweɪ]; *(in London)* the Tube [tjuːb] **U-Bahnlinie** line [laɪn]
üben practise ['præktɪs]
über **1.** *(räumlich)* over ['əʊvə]; above [ə'bʌv] **(quer) über die Straße** across the street [ə'krɒs] **2.** *(mehr als)* over ['əʊvə] **über 400 Jahre** over 400 years **3. über mich/dich/...** about me/you/... [ə'baʊt] **über dich selbst** about yourself [jɔː'self]
überall everywhere ['evriweə] **überall um sie herum** all around her
überarbeiten revise [rɪ'vaɪz]
überfliegen: einen Text überfliegen *(um den Inhalt grob zu erfassen)* skim a text [skɪm]
überfluten flood [flʌd]
überfüllt crowded ['kraʊdɪd]
übergeben: sich übergeben be sick **Ich muss mich übergeben.** I'm going to be sick.
überhaupt: überhaupt nicht(s) not ... at all [ət‿'ɔːl] **Und überhaupt, ...** And anyway, ... ['eniweɪ]
überleben survive [sə'vaɪv]
überlegen : es sich anders überlegen change your mind [maɪnd]
übernachten (in/bei) stay (at/with) [steɪ]
überprüfen check [tʃek]
Überprüfung check [tʃek]
überqueren cross [krɒs]
überraschend surprising [sə'praɪzɪŋ]
überrascht surprised [sə'praɪzd]
Überraschung surprise [sə'praɪz]
Überschrift title ['taɪtl]; heading ['hedɪŋ]
überschwemmen flood [flʌd]
Überschwemmung flood [flʌd]
übersetzen translate [træns'leɪt]
Übersetzung translation [træns'leɪʃn]
übertragen werden *(Programm, Sendung)* be on [ɒn]
üblich usual ['juːʒuəl]
U-Boot submarine [ˌsʌbmə'riːn]
übrig: übrig sein be left [left] **etwas übrig lassen** leave sth. [liːv]
übrigens actually ['æktʃuəli]; by the way [ˌbaɪ ðə 'weɪ]
Übung exercise ['eksəsaɪz] **es erfordert Übung** it takes practice ['præktɪs] **Übungsheft** exercise book
Ufer *(eines Sees)* shore [ʃɔː]
Uhr **1.** *(Armbanduhr)* watch [wɒtʃ]; *(Wand-, Turmuhr)* clock [klɒk] **2. 4 Uhr morgens** 4 am [ˌeɪ‿'em] **4 Uhr nachmittags / 16 Uhr** 4 pm [ˌpiː‿'em] **um 1 Uhr / 13 Uhr** at 1 o'clock [ə'klɒk]
Uhrzeit time [taɪm]
um **1.** *(örtlich)* **um ... (herum)** around ... [ə'raʊnd] **um die Welt** round the world [raʊnd] **2.** *(zeitlich)* **um 1 Uhr / 13 Uhr** at 1 o'clock [ə'klɒk] **3. um zu** to [tu], [tə]
umarmen: jn. umarmen give sb. a hug [hʌg]; hug sb. [hʌg]

umdrehen: sich umdrehen turn around [ə'raʊnd]

Umgang interaction [ˌɪntər'ækʃn]

Umgebung *(Stadt)* neighborhood *(AE)* / neighbourhood *(BE)* ['neɪbəhʊd]

umgehen: sorgfältig mit etwas umgehen take care of sth. [keə]

umher: in der Bücherei / auf dem Strand umher around the library/ beach [ə'raʊnd]

umher-: umherrennen run around [ˌrʌn‿ə'raʊnd] **umherspazieren** walk around

umschauen: sich umschauen look around [ˌlʊk‿ə'raʊnd]

umschreiben paraphrase ['pærəfreɪz]

umsehen: sich umsehen look around [ˌlʊk‿ə'raʊnd]

umsteigen change [tʃeɪndʒ]

umtauschen *(Geld)* change [tʃeɪndʒ]

Umwelt environment [ɪn'vaɪrənmənt]

Umweltschutz conservation [ˌkɒnsə'veɪʃn]

umziehen (nach) move (to) [muːv]

Umzug *(Parade)* parade [pə'reɪd]

unaufhaltsam, unaufhaltbar unstoppable [ʌn'stɒpəbl]

und and [ænd, ənd] **Und du? / Und was ist mit dir?** What about you? **Und? / Na und?** So? [səʊ]

ungeduldig impatient [ɪm'peɪʃnt]

Unfall accident [æksɪdənt]

ungefähr about [ə'baʊt]

ungesetzlich illegal [ɪ'liːgl]

ungewöhnlich unusual [ʌn'juːʒuəl]

unglaublich amazing [ə'meɪzɪŋ]

unglücklich unhappy [ʌn'hæpi]

unheimlich scary ['skeəri]

unhöflich impolite [ˌɪmpə'laɪt]; rude [ruːd]

Uniform uniform ['juːnɪfɔːm]

unmöglich impossible [ɪm'pɒsəbl]

Unrecht: jemand hat Unrecht someone is wrong [rɒŋ]

unregelmäßig irregular [ɪ'regjələ]

uns us [ʌs], [əs]; *(Reflexivpronomen)* ourselves [ɑː'selvz], [aʊə'selvz]

unser(e) ... our ... ['aʊə]

unsere(r, s) ours ['aʊəz]

unten *(am unteren Ende)* at the bottom (of) ['bɒtəm]; *(im Haus)* downstairs [ˌdaʊn'steəz]; **below** [bɪ'ləʊ] **dort unten** down there **nach unten** down; *(im Haus)* downstairs

unter under ['ʌndə]; below [bɪ'ləʊ]

unterbrechen interrupt [ˌɪntə'rʌpt]

unterhalb (von) below [bɪ'ləʊ]

unterhalten: sich unterhalten (mit) talk (to) [tɔːk]

Unterhaltung *(Gespräch)* conversation [ˌkɒnvə'seɪʃn]

unterrichten teach [tiːtʃ] **jn. unterrichten** tutor sb. ['tjuːtə]

Unterrichtsstunde period ['pɪəriəd]

Unterschied (zu) difference (to) ['dɪfrəns]

unterstreichen underline [ˌʌndə'laɪn]

unterstützen [sə'pɔːt]

untersuchen study ['stʌdi] **etwas untersuchen** look into sth. *(polizeilich)* investigate [ɪn'vestɪgeɪt]

Untertitel subtitle ['sʌbtaɪtl]

unterwegs out and about

unverschämt rude [ruːd]

Unwetter storm [stɔːm]

Ureinwohner: amerikanischer Ureinwohner/amerikanische Ureinwohnerin Native American [ˌneɪtɪv‿ə'merɪkən]

Urgroßvater great-grandfather

Urgroßmutter great-grandmother

Urlaub holiday ['hɒlədeɪ]; *(AE)* vacation [və'keɪʃn] **in Urlaub fahren/ sein** go/be on holiday/vacation

Urlauber/in holidaymaker ['hɒlədeɪmeɪkə]

Ursache cause [kɔːz]

ursprünglich originally [ə'rɪdʒənəli]

USA: die USA (die Vereinigten Staaten von Amerika) the USA [ˌjuː‿es‿'eɪ] (the United States of America)

usw. (und so weiter) etc. (et cetera) [et'setərə]

V

Vater father ['fɑːðə]

Vati dad [dæd]

Vegetarier/in; vegetarisch vegetarian [ˌvedʒə'teəriən]

Verabredung date [deɪt], appointment [ə'pɔɪntmənt]

Veranda porch *(AE)* [pɔːtʃ]

verändern; sich verändern change [tʃeɪndʒ]

Veränderung change [tʃeɪndʒ]

verängstigt scared [skeəd]

verantwortlich responsible [rɪ'spɒnsəbl]

verbessern; sich verbessern improve [ɪm'pruːv]

verbeugen: sich verbeugen bow [baʊ]

verbinden, verknüpfen link [lɪŋk]; combine [kəm'baɪn]

Verbindung link [lɪŋk] **sich (mit jm.) in Verbindung setzen** get in touch (with sb.) [tʌtʃ] **(mit jm.) in Verbindung bleiben** stay in touch (with sb.)

verbrannt burnt [bɜːnt]

verbreitet: weit verbreitet common ['kɒmən]

verbrennen burn [bɜːn]

verbringen: Zeit verbringen (mit) spend time (on) [spend]

verbunden sein be linked [kə'nektɪd]

verdienen *(Geld)* earn [ɜːn]

vereinbaren arrange [ə'reɪndʒ]

vereinigt united [ju'naɪtɪd] **das Vereinigte Königreich** the United Kingdom) [juˌnaɪtɪd 'kɪŋdəm]

verfehlen *(verpassen)* miss [mɪs]

verfügbar available [ə'veɪləbl]

Vergangenheit past [pɑːst]

vergehen *(Zeit)* go by

vergessen forget [fə'get]

vergewissern: sich vergewissern, dass ... make sure that ...

vergleichen compare [kəm'peə]

Vergnügungspark fun park

verhaften arrest [ə'rest]

verhalten: sich verhalten behave [bɪ'heɪv]

Verhältnis relationship [rɪ'leɪʃnʃɪp]

verheiratet (mit) married (to) ['mærɪd]

verkaufen sell [sel]

Verkäufer/in (shop) assistant ['ʃɒp‿əˌsɪstənt]

verkehrt wrong [rɒŋ]

verkleiden: sich verkleiden dress up [ˌdres‿'ʌp]

Verkleidung costume ['kɒstjuːm]

Verknüpfung link [lɪŋk]

verlassen leave [liːv]

verlegen embarrassed [ɪm'bærəst]

Verlegenheit: jn. in Verlegenheit bringen embarrass sb. [ɪm'bærəs]

verletzen hurt [hɜːt]

verletzt hurt [hɜːt]

verlieren lose [luːz]

vermissen miss [mɪs] **vermisst** missing ['mɪsɪŋ]

vermuten suppose [sə'pəʊz]

verneigen: sich verneigen bow [baʊ]

veröffentlichen publish ['pʌblɪʃ]

verpassen miss [mɪs]

verraten reveal [rɪ'viːl]

verrückt mad [mæd], crazy ['kreɪzi]

Vers *(Reim)* rhyme [raɪm]; *(Strophe)* verse [vɜːs]
verschieden different [ˈdɪfrənt]
Verschmutzung pollution [pəˈluːʃn]
verschollen missing [ˈmɪsɪŋ]
verschwinden disappear [ˌdɪsəˈpɪə]
Versorgung supply [səˈplaɪ]
versprechen promise [ˈprɒmɪs]
Verstand mind [maɪnd]
verstecken; sich verstecken hide [haɪd]
verstehen understand [ˌʌndəˈstænd] **Hast du es verstanden?** Did you get it? *(infml)* **Verstehe!** I see.
versuchen try [traɪ] **Versuch's mal.** Have a go.
verteidigen: jn./etwas verteidigen (gegen jn./etwas) defend sb./sth. (against sb./sth.) [dɪˈfend]
verursachen cause [kɔːz]
vervollständigen complete [kəmˈpliːt] **etwas (mit etwas) vervollständigen** round sth. off (with sth.)
verwenden use [juːz]
Verzieh dich! Get lost!
Video video [ˈvɪdiəʊ]
Videokamera video camera [ˈvɪdiəʊ kæmrə]
viel a lot (of); lots (of); much [mʌtʃ] **Viel Glück!** Good luck! [lʌk] **viel zu tun haben** be busy [ˈbɪzi] **Wie viel kosten/kosten …?** How much is/are …?
viele a lot (of); lots (of); many [ˈmeni]
vielleicht maybe [ˈmeɪbi]
Viertel quarter [ˈkwɔːtə], neighborhood *(AE)* / neighbourhood *(BE)* [ˈneɪbəhʊd] **Viertel nach zehn (10.15 / 22.15)** quarter past ten [ˈkwɔːtə pɑːst] **Viertel vor elf (10.45 / 22.45)** quarter to eleven [ˈkwɔːtə tʊ]
violett purple [ˈpɜːpl]
Violine violin [ˌvaɪəˈlɪn]
Virus: sich wie ein Virus ausbreiten go viral [ˈvaɪrəl]
Vogel bird [bɜːd]
Vogelschar flock of birds [flɒk]
Vokal vowel [ˈvaʊəl]
Volk nation [ˈneɪʃn]
Volksmusik folk music [ˈfəʊk ˌmjuːzɪk]
voll full (of) [fʊl]
vollenden complete [kəmˈpliːt]
Volleyball volleyball [ˈvɒlibɔːl]
völlig absolutely [ˈabsəluːtli]; quite [kwaɪt]; totally [ˈtəʊtəli]
Vollmond full moon [fʊl ˈmuːn]
vollständig complete [kəmˈpliːt]
von of [ɒv], [əv]; from [frɒm], [frəm] **ein Lied von …** a song by … [baɪ] **von … bis …** from … to …
voneinander entfernt apart [əˈpɑːt]
vor **1.** *(örtlich)* in front of [ɪnˈfrʌnt‿əv] **vor der Schule** *(vor dem Schulgebäude)* in front of the school; *(außerhalb der Schule)* outside the school [ˌaʊtˈsaɪd] **2.** *(zeitlich)* before [bɪˈfɔː] **vor der Schule** *(vor Schulbeginn)* before school **vor einer Woche** a week ago [əˈgəʊ] **Viertel vor elf (10.45 / 22.45)** quarter to eleven [ˈkwɔːtə tʊ] **nicht vor drei** *(erst um drei)* not till three
vorankommen *(zurechtkommen)* get on [ˌget‿ˈɒn]
Voraussage prediction [prɪˈdɪkʃn]
Vorbau porch *(BE)* [pɔːtʃ]
vorbei (an) past [pɑːst]
vorbei sein *(zu Ende sein)* be over [ˈəʊvə]
vorbei-: an etwas/jm. vorbeigehen pass sth./sb. [pɑːs] **vorbeikommen (bei)** come over (to)
vorbereiten: etwas vorbereiten prepare sth. [prɪˈpeə] **sich vorbereiten (auf)** get ready (for) [ˈredi]
Vordach porch *(BE)* [pɔːtʃ]
Vordergrund foreground [ˈfɔːgraʊnd]
Vorderseite front [frʌnt]
Voreingenommenheit (gegenüber) prejudice (against) [ˈpredʒudɪs]
Vorgang process [ˈprəʊses]
vorhaben: Ich habe vor, ein Lied zu singen. I'm going to sing a song.
vorher: vorher schon mal before **vorher noch nie** not … before, never … before
Vorhersage prediction [prɪˈdɪkʃn]
Vorlieben und Abneigungen likes and dislikes *(pl)* [ˌlaɪks‿ən ˈdɪslaɪks]
Vormittag morning [ˈmɔːnɪŋ]
vorn at the front [frʌnt] **nach vorn** to the front [frʌnt]
Vorrat supply [səˈplaɪ]
Vorschlag suggestion [səˈdʒestʃən]
Vorsicht! *(Pass auf!)* Watch out! [ˌwɒtʃ‿ˈaʊt]
vorsichtig careful [ˈkeəfl]
Vorsilbe prefix [ˈpriːfɪks]
vorspielen: etwas vorspielen act sth. out [ˌækt‿ˈaʊt]
Vorspielen, Vorsprechen *(Theater)* audition [ɔːˈdɪʃn]
vorstellen **1. (jm.) etwas vorstellen** *(präsentieren)* present sth. (to sb.) [prɪˈzent] **2. jn. (jm.) vorstellen** introduce sb. (to sb.) [ˌɪntrəˈdjuːs] **3. sich etwas vorstellen** imagine sth. [ɪˈmædʒɪn] **Stell dir vor, Dad …** Guess what, Dad …
Vorstellung **1.** *(Idee)* idea [aɪˈdɪə] **2.** *(Präsentation)* presentation [ˌprezn'teɪʃn] **3.** *(Show)* show [ʃəʊ], performance [pəˈfɔːməns]
Vorteil advantage [ədˈvɑːntɪdʒ]
Vortrag talk [tɔːk] **einen Vortrag halten (über)** give a talk (about)
vorüber (an) *(vorbei an)* past [pɑːst]
vorübergehen *(Zeit)* go by
vorübergehend wohnen (in/bei) stay (at/with) [steɪ]
Vorurteil (gegen) prejudice (against) [ˈpredʒudɪs]
vorziehen: etwas (einer anderen Sache) vorziehen prefer sth. (to sth.) [prɪˈfɜː]
Vulkan volcano [vɒlˈkeɪnəʊ]

W

wach awake [əˈweɪk]
Wache, Wachposten guard [gɑːd]
wachsen grow [grəʊ]
Wahl choice [tʃɔɪs]
wählen *(aussuchen)* choose [tʃuːz]; *(Telefonnummer)* dial [ˈdaɪəl]
wahr true [truː] **…, nicht wahr?** …, right?
während **1.** during [ˈdjʊərɪŋ] **2.** while [waɪl]
Wahrheit truth [truːθ]
wahrscheinlich probably [ˈprɒbəbli]
Währung currency [ˈkʌrənsi]
Wal whale [weɪl]
Walisisch; walisisch Welsh [welʃ]
Wald forest [ˈfɒrɪst]
Waldbrand wildfire [ˈwaɪldfaɪə]
Wand wall [wɔːl]
Wandschrank closet [ˈklɒzɪt]
wann? when? [wen]
wann (auch) immer whenever [ˌwenˈevə]
► S. 235 whenever, wherever, whatever, whoever
warm warm [wɔːm]
Warnung warning [ˈwɔːnɪŋ]
warten (auf) wait (for) [weɪt] **Warte einen Moment.** Wait a minute.
warum? why? [waɪ]
was? what? [wɒt]

was immer whatever [wɒt'evə]
▶ S. 235 whenever, wherever, whatever, whoever
Wasser water ['wɔːtə]
Wasserfall waterfall ['wɔːtəfɔːl]
Website website ['websaɪt]
Wechselgeld change [tʃeɪndʒ]
wechseln switch [swɪtʃ]
wechseln *(Geld)* change [tʃeɪndʒ]
wecken: jn. wecken wake sb. up [ˌweɪk_'ʌp]
weg away [ə'weɪ]
Weg way [weɪ]; *(Pfad)* path [pɑːθ]; trail [treɪl] **auf dem Weg zu/nach …** on the way to … **jm. den Weg (nach …) beschreiben** tell sb. the way (to …), give sb. directions (to …) [də'rekʃnz] **(jn.) nach dem Weg fragen** ask (sb.) the way; ask for directions [də'rekʃnz]
wegen: Es tut mir leid wegen … I'm sorry about …
weggehen leave [liːv]
wehtun 1. *(verletzen)* hurt [hɜːt] 2. *(wund sein)* be sore [sɔː]
weich soft [sɒft]
Weide field [fiːld]
Weihnachten Christmas ['krɪsməs]
weil because [bɪ'kɒz]
weinen cry [kraɪ]
weiß white [waɪt]
weit (entfernt) far [fɑː]; *(breit)* wide [waɪd] **weiter** further ['fɜːðə] **am weitesten** furthest ['fɜːðɪst]
weiter: geradeaus weiter straight on [streɪt_'ɒn]
weiter-: weitergehen/-laufen/-segeln/… walk / run / sail / … on **weitermachen/-reden** go on
Weizen wheat [wiːt]
welche(r, s) **1. Auf welcher Seite sind wir?** What page are we on? **Welche Farbe hat/haben …?** What colour is/are …? 2. *(aus einer begrenzten Anzahl)* which (one) [wɪtʃ] **Welche Klubs?** Which clubs ?
Welle wave [weɪv]
Welt world [wɜːld] **auf der Welt** in the world
wem? who? **Wem hast du es erzählt?** Who did you tell? **Mit wem hast du getanzt?** Who did you dance with?
wen? who? **Wen kennt Sam?** Who does Sam know?
wenden: sich an jn. wenden turn to sb. [tɜːn]
wenig: ein wenig a little ['lɪtl]
weniger (als) less (than) [les]
wenigstens at least [ət 'liːst]
wenn 1. *(zeitlich)* when [wen] 2. *(falls)* if [ɪf] **selbst wenn** even if ['iːvn_ɪf] **auch wenn** even though [ˌiːvn 'ðəʊ]
wer immer whoever [huː'evə]
▶ S. 235 whenever, wherever, whatever, whoever
wer? who? [huː] **Wer hat mit dir getanzt?** Who danced with you? **wer (sonst) noch?** who else? [els]
Werbespot, Werbung advertisement [əd'vɜːtɪsmənt]
werden become [bɪ'kʌm] **rot werden** go red **wütend/kalt werden** get angry/cold
werfen throw [θrəʊ]
Werkstatt workshop ['wɜːkʃɒp]
wessen? whose? [huːz]
Westen; nach Westen; westlich west [west] **Richtung Westen** westbound ['westbaʊnd]
westlich, West- western ['westən]
Wettbewerb competition [ˌkɒmpə'tɪʃn]; trials *(pl)* ['traɪəlz]
wetten bet [bet]
Wetter weather ['weðə]
wichtig important [ɪm'pɔːtnt], relevant ['reləvənt]
widerlich disgusting [dɪs'gʌstɪŋ]
wie 1. *(Fragewort)* how [haʊ] **Wie alt bist du?** How old are you? **Wie bitte?** Sorry? ['sɒri] **Wie findest du …? / Wie gefällt dir …?** How do you like …? **Wie geht's? / Wie geht es dir/euch?** How are you?; How's it going? **Wie heißt du?** What's your name? **Wie ist sie (so)?** What's she like? **Wie spät ist es?** What time is it? **Wie viel kostet/kosten …?** How much is/are …? **Wie war es?** What was it like? **Wie wäre es mit …?** What about …? **Wie dem auch sei, …** Anyway, … ['eniweɪ] **wie er (einmal) sagte …** as he said … **wie man etwas macht / machen kann / machen soll** how to do sth. 2. **wie Jungen** like boys [laɪk] **genau wie …** just like … 3. **der-/die-/dasselbe wie …** the same as … [æz], [əz] **(nicht) so groß wie** (not) as big as
wieder again [ə'gen] **immer wieder** again and again
wiederholen repeat [rɪ'piːt]; *(Lernstoff)* revise [rɪ'vaɪz]
Wiederholung *(des Lernstoffs)* revision [rɪ'vɪʒn]
wiegen weigh [weɪ]
wild wild [waɪld] **wild auf etwas sein** be keen on sth. [kiːn]
Willkommen in Plymouth. Welcome to Plymouth. ['welkəm] **jn. willkommen heißen (in)** welcome sb. (to) ['welkəm]
Wind wind [wɪnd]
windig windy ['wɪndi]
Winter winter ['wɪntə]
Wirbel: großen Wirbel um etwas machen make a fuss about sth. [fʌs]
wirklich real ['riːəl]; really ['rɪəli]
Wirklichkeit: in Wirklichkeit in fact [ɪn 'fækt]
Wirkung (auf) effect (on) [ɪ'fekt]
Wischmopp mop [mɒp]
wissbegierig curious ['kjʊəriəs]
wissen know [nəʊ] **…, weißt du. / …, wissen Sie.** …, you know.; …, you see. **Weißt du was** Guess what, Dad … **über etwas Bescheid wissen** know about sth.
Witz joke [dʒəʊk]
witzig funny ['fʌni]
wo immer wherever [weər'evə]
▶ S. 235 whenever, wherever, whatever, whoever
wo? where? [weə]
Woche week [wiːk] **ein dreiwöchiger Urlaub** a three-week holiday
▶ S. 219 a 9,740-foot swimming pool
Wochenende weekend [ˌwiːk'end] **am Wochenende** at the weekend, on the weekend *(AE)*
Wochentag day of the week
woher: Woher kommst du? Where are you from? **Woher weißt/kennst du …?** How do you know …?
wohin? where? [weə]
wohlbekannt well-known [ˌwel'nəʊn]
Wohlfahrtsorganisation, Wohltätigkeit, wohltätige Zwecke charity ['tʃærəti]
Wohnheim hostel ['hɒstl]
wohnen *(leben)* live [lɪv]; *(vorübergehend)* stay [steɪ]
Wohnung flat [flæt]; apartment [ə'pɑːtmənt]
Wohnwagen caravan ['kærəvæn]
Wohnzimmer living room ['lɪvɪŋ ruːm]
Wolke cloud [klaʊd]
Wolkenkratzer skyscraper ['skaɪskreɪpə]
wolkenlos cloudless ['klaʊdləs]
wollen: etwas haben wollen want sth. [wɒnt] **etwas tun wollen** want to do sth.
Workshop workshop ['wɜːkʃɒp]
Wort word [wɜːd]

Wortart part of speech [spiːtʃ]
Wortstellung word order ['ɔːdə]
Wovon handelt die Geschichte? What is the story about?
wund sein be sore [sɔː]
Wunder wonder ['wʌndə] **Kein Wunder …** No wonder … ['wʌndə]
wunderbar wonderful ['wʌndəfəl]
wundervoll magical ['mædʒɪkl]
wünschen wish [wɪʃ] **Ich wünschte, es wäre wärmer.** I wish it was warmer.
würde: Ich würde gern … I'd like to … **Ich würde sehr gern …** I'd love to …
Wurm worm [wɜːm]
Wurst, Würstchen sausage ['sɒsɪdʒ]
würzig, pikant spicy ['spaɪsi]
Wüste desert ['dezət]
wütend (auf jn.) angry (with sb.) ['æŋgri]

Z

Zahl number ['nʌmbə]; figure ['fɪgə]
zählen count [kaʊnt]
Zahn tooth [tuːθ]
Zahnarzt/-ärztin dentist ['dentɪst]
Zahnschmerzen haben have a toothache ['tuːθeɪk]
Zauber- magic ['mædʒɪk]
zauberhaft magical ['mædʒɪkl]
Zaun fence [fens]
z.B. (zum Beispiel) e.g. [ˌiː 'dʒiː]
Zeh toe [təʊ]
Zeichen sign [saɪn]; signal ['sɪgnəl]
Zeichensetzung punctuation [ˌpʌŋktʃu'eɪʃn]
zeichnen draw [drɔː]
Zeichnung drawing ['drɔːɪŋ]
zeigen show [ʃəʊ] **auf etwas zeigen** point to sth. [pɔɪnt]
Zeile line [laɪn]
Zeit time [taɪm] **eine unendlich lange Zeit** for ages ['eɪdʒɪz] **zur selben Zeit** at one time **Zeit verbringen (mit)** spend time (on) [spend]
Zeitleiste timeline ['taɪmlaɪn]
Zeitlupe slow motion [ˌsləʊ 'məʊʃn]
Zeitmesser timer ['taɪmə]
Zeitplan schedule ['ʃedjuːl]
Zeitschrift magazine [ˌmægə'ziːn]
Zeitstrahl timeline ['taɪmlaɪn]
Zeitung (news)paper ['njuːspeɪpə]
Zelt tent [tent]
zelten gehen go camping ['kæmpɪŋ]
Zeltplatz campsite ['kæmpsaɪt]
Zensur *(Schulnote)* mark [mɑːk], grade *(bes. AE)* [greɪd]
zentral, Zentral-, Mittel- central ['sentrəl]
Zentrum centre ['sentə], center *(AE)* **im Zentrum** downtown *(AE)* ['daʊntaʊn]
zerbrechen break [breɪk]
zerbrochen broken ['brəʊkən]
zerdrücken squash [skwɒʃ]
Zeremonie ceremony ['serəməni]
zerquetschen squash [skwɒʃ]
zerstören destroy [dɪ'strɔɪ]
Zeug stuff [stʌf] *(infml)*
Ziege goat [gəʊt] **Ziegenherde** flock of goats [flɒk]
ziehen pull [pʊl]
Ziel, Zielscheibe target ['tɑːgɪt]
ziemlich quite [kwaɪt], fairly ['feəli] **ziemlich viele** quite a few
Ziffer number ['nʌmbə]; figure ['fɪgə]
Zigarette cigarette [ˌsɪgə'ret]
Zimmerer/Zimmerin carpenter ['kɑːpəntə]
Zitat quotation [kwəʊ'teɪʃn], quote *(infml)* [kwəʊt]
Zitrone lemon [lemn]
► S. 222 Food words
Zoll *(Längenmaß; 2,54 cm)* inch [ɪntʃ]
zoomen: rein-/herauszoomen zoom in/out [zuːm]
zu **1.** *(örtlich)* to [tu], [tə] **2. zu spät/…** too late/… [tuː] **3. Es ist Zeit zu gehen.** It's time to go. **Nice to meet you.** Freut mich, dich/euch/Sie kennenzulernen.
zubereiten cook [kʊk], prepare [prɪ'peə]
Zucker sugar ['ʃʊgə]
► S. 222 Food words
zueinander passen go together [tə'geðə]
zuerst first [fɜːst]; *(anfangs)* at first [ət 'fɜːst]
zufahren: auf etwas zufahren head for sth. [hed]
Zug train [treɪn] *(bei Brettspielen)* move [muːv]
Zugabe encore ['ɒŋkɔː]
zugehen: auf etwas zugehen head for sth. [hed]
Zügel reins *(pl)* [reɪnz]
Zuhause home [həʊm]
zuhören listen ['lɪsn] **Hör mir zu.** Listen to me.
zukommen: auf jn. zukommen come up to sb.
Zukunft future ['fjuːtʃə]
zukünftige(r, s) future ['fjuːtʃə]
zulassen allow [ə'laʊ]
zum Beispiel for example [ɪg'zɑːmpl]
zumachen *(schließen)* close [kləʊz]
zumindest at least [ət 'liːst]
Zunge tongue [tʌŋ]
Zungenbrecher tongue-twister ['tʌŋˌtwɪstə]
zurechtkommen get on [ˌget‿'ɒn]
zurück back [bæk]
zurücklassen leave [liːv]
zusammen together [tə'geðə]
zusammenbrechen collapse [kə'læps]
zusammenfassen: etwas zusammenfassen sum sth. up [ˌsʌm‿'ʌp]
Zusammenfassung summary ['sʌməri]
Zusammenhang *(Text-, Satzzusammenhang)* context ['kɒntekst]
zusammenpassen go together [tə'geðə]
zusammenschlagen: jn. zusammenschlagen beat sb. up
zusätzlich extra ['ekstrə]
Zuschauer/innen *(Publikum)* audience ['ɔːdiəns]
Zustand state [steɪt]
zustande: etwas zustande bringen manage sth. ['mænɪdʒ]
zusteuern: auf etwas zusteuern head for sth. [hed]
zustimmen: jm. zustimmen agree with sb. [ə'griː]
Zutat ingredient [ɪn'griːdiənt]
Zutritt entry ['entri]
zuvor: besser als je zuvor better than ever **die Woche zuvor** the week before
zuwenden: sich jm. zuwenden turn to sb. [tɜːn]
zwei two [tuː] **zwei schwarze** two black ones
► S. 223 one/ones
zweimal twice [twaɪs]
zweisprachig bilingual [baɪ'lɪŋgwəl]
zweite(r, s) second ['sekənd] **auf dem zweiten Platz; an zweiter Stelle** in second place
Zwiebel onion ['ʌnjən]
► S. 222 Food words
Zwillinge twins *(pl)* [twɪnz]
zwischen between [bɪ'twiːn]
Zwischenüberschrift sub-heading ['sʌbˌhedɪŋ]

Unit 1

One day, two stories

1 g 2 j 3 b 4 i 5 h 6 a 7 f 8 e 9 c 10 d

Missing letters

1 I think **gray** is a really boring **color**. I never wear it. Blue, red and green are what I like. (AE)
2 I don't really have a **favourite** TV **programme**. I like everything! (BE)
3 I want to go to Paris to **practise** my French. And have a good time, of course! I love the fashions, too: their clothes are so **colourful**. (BE)
4 The **center** of town was crowded. There were thousands of people everywhere. It took me ten minutes to walk a hundred **meters**. (AE)
5 Airports are exciting places. They are full of **travelers** from all over the world. (AE)
6 Ladies and gentlemen, thanks for coming. It is an **honour** for me to speak to you today. (BE)

Ping pong prepositions

1 at/cooking 2 of/stores 3 for/theaters
4 to/cheese 5 about/planes 6 of/progress
7 from/cities

Two British tourists in Manhattan

1 see 2 neig**h**bourhood 3 ph**o**tos 4 breakfast
5 queue 6 delicious 7 bor**in**g 8 spe**n**d
9 memorial 10 vi**c**tims 11 pools 12 stood
13 museums 14 pizza 15 tickets 16 boa**t**
17 vie**w**s 18 h**a**rbour

The writer went for dinner in **Chinatown**.

What am I?

Central Park

Sentence building

1 Swimming in the sea is much nicer than in a pool, in my opinion.
2 He's so impatient that he hates waiting for longer than five minutes.
3 I enjoy playing sport more than watching it, and it keeps me healthy.
4 Nobody actually likes going to the dentist, but it's something we all have to do.
5 Travelling helps you to learn about how people in other countries live.
6 One of my favourite hobbies is playing video games and talking to my mates is another.
7 I don't mind reading stories, but I find writing really boring.

Remember, remember

a) 1 meeting
2 to take
3 to buy
4 going
5 seeing / thinking

b) 1 to bring
2 putting
3 seeing
4 to buy
5 to invite
6 telling

Two out of three

1 New York is a great city, but it's even **more** expensive **than** we had … thought it would be.
2 There weren't **as** many … people at the 9/11 Memorial **as** I had expected.
3 Central Park is **where** lots of people go to relax, **though** it's not the biggest … park in New York.
4 Even **though** we stayed **where** many of the famous sights are, we didn't see … everything in Manhattan.
5 Lots of … young people like the Bronx, but it doesn't attract **as** many tourists **as** Manhattan does.
6 Even **though** New York is an expensive place, a tasty meal … in Chinatown may cost less **than** you think.

Unit 2

Food words

1 Helen: lentil/garlic/mushrooms/spicy
2 Richard: baked/fried/boiled/bacon
3 Mark: dairy/cheese/butter/oil
4 Daisy: spaghetti/tinned/onions
5 Paul: pork/rice/mushrooms/spinach

Advice for teens

a) 1 a: serious
1 b: dentist
2 a: sports
2 b: tired
2 c: exercise
3 a: agreed
3 b: enjoys
4 a: instrument
4 b: hear

b) 1 Jay 2 Tilly
3 Aanan 4 Harriet

I wish …
1a) I wish we had left earlier.
1b) I wish we hadn't missed the first scene.
2a) I wish I hadn't forgotten my glasses.
2b) I wish I had remembered to take my glasses.
3a) My friend Jack wishes we had chosen a different film.
3b) He wishes it/the film hadn't been so frightening.
4a) I wish our/the seats had been closer to the screen
4b) I wish we hadn't sat so far back.
5a) I wish I/we had stayed at home.
5b) I wish I/we hadn't gone out.

Thanksgiving wordsearch
1 holiday 2 celebrated 3 fourth 4 traditional
5 save 6 eaten 7 president 8 families
9 miles 10 million 11 car 12 day

The right pair
1 am / will be 2 were / would find
3 don't leave / will miss 4 wasn't / weren't / would go
5 will ask / see 6 like / will give

Sentence halves
1 had gone / b. 2 went / g.
3 h. had forgotten 4 a. gave
5 f. weren't 6 c. had made
7 had seen / d. 8 was/were / e.

Rephrasing sentences
1 The beach was fairly empty.
2 The meal was absolutely delicious.
3 This room is a bit cold.
4 This street is very noisy.
5 Alex wasn't very polite.

Unit 3

Mixed up rubbish
a) Jutta:
1 apple 2 egg shells
3 banana 4 flowers
Markus:
1 brochure 2 newspapers
3 magazine 4 socks
Stefan:
1 Coffee filters 2 oranges 3 plastic bags
4 boxes 5 bottles
Simone:
1 pizza 2 box
3 posters 4 cinema tickets

b) 1 False – Jutta put everything in the brown bin.
2 True
3 False – Simone put things in two bins.
4 False – Stefan put the bottles, plastic bags and boxes in the yellow bin.

Who's the celebrity?
1 miles 2 blocks 3 feet
4 costs 5 cartoon 6 join
7 ceremony 8 honour 9 names

The celebrity is Elton John.

Join the words
1 shiny 2 celebrity 3 unstoppable 4 viral
5 security 6 common 7 discovery 8 channel

Unusual definitions
1-9-16: A cell phone is a device lots of teens can't live without.
2-11-17: A secret is something you tell everyone to tell nobody.
3-12-13: A teacher is a person who helps you solve problems you wouldn't have without them.
4-10-14: An argument is a discussion which goes on till the other person finally agrees with you.
5-8-15: A bed is a piece of furniture which becomes more comfortable when your alarm goes off.
6-7-18: Tomorrow is the best time to do the things people told you to do today.

Find the words
1 wrong 2 angry 3 loud
4 sweet 5 tall 6 weird

Vacation questions
1 Are you going to spend
2 How long are you going to stay
3 What are you going to do
4 Aren't you going to do / You're not going to do
5 Are you going to stay
6 are you going to travel
7 Where are you going to volunteer
8 Who are you going to volunteer
9 Are you going to write

Making a dialogue
2 going to give
8 I'm going to buy
5 I'll find; I'll go
4
6 that'll be
7 are you going to go
1
3 I'll meet

Mixed up sentences

1 The Walk of Fame, which is a major tourist attraction, celebrates stars of cinema, TV and theatre.
2 The Walk of Fame, which is an idea that many towns and cities have copied, began in L.A.
3 The Walk of Fame is a famous attraction in Los Angeles, which we visited last year.
4 Harry Potter, which is a series of books and films(,) and also a play, made J.K. Rowling famous.
5 Ian didn't enjoy the Harry Potter films, which he saw last year, as much as the books.
6 Daniel Radcliffe, who is one of thousands of celebrities on the Walk of Fame, was the star of the Harry Potter films.

Unit 4

School words

1 cafeteria 2 register 3 studies 4 assignment
5 grades 6 exam 7 science 8 periods

The fire alarm puzzle

a) 1 a. was studying b. wasn't listening c. heard d. arrived
2 a. was sitting b. didn't hear c. were listening
3 a. wasn't doing b. started c. put d. wasn't
4 a. was b. was having
5 a. wasn't doing b. was working c. went off

b)

Jack	Bryan	Sally
Cafeteria	Classroom	Library
Listening to music	Helping	Assignment
Third	Second	First

An invitation to a party

a) 1 – D – 5 – E – 2 – C – 4 – A – 6 – B – 3
b) 1 was having
2 hoped
3 wasn't
4 had
5 was
6 could
7 had arranged
8 opened
9 could
10 would need

Find the suffixes

A 1 colourful
2 darkness
3 sleepless
B 1 stressful
2 shyness
3 powerful
C 1 eventful
2 homeless
3 bitterness
D 1 heartless
2 powerless
3 sadness
E 1 cloudless
2 peaceful
3 happiness
F 1 loneliness
2 endless
3 helpful

Sentence halves

1 d – is tasting (activity)
2 g – tastes (state)
3 a – are having (activity)
4 f – have (state)
5 b – am thinking (activity)
6 h – think (state)
7 c – looks (state)
8 e – is looking (activity)

What did they say?

a) 1 d 2 e 3 f 4 b 5 c 6 a
b) 1 Jack said (that) the restaurant would be full and advised me to reserve a table.
2 Clara said (that) she hadn't eaten yet and asked me to make her a sandwich.
3 Tom said (that) there was nothing to do at home and suggested going to the cinema.
4 Lily said (that) it was Grandpa's birthday and reminded me to give him a call.
5 Harry said (that) he was sorry he couldn't join me at the beach and told me to have a nice time there.
6 Vera said (that) it was going to rain later and advised me to take an umbrella.

The or no *the*?

1 a. the b. the c. the d. (no *the*)
2 a. (no *the*) b. (no *the*) c. the d. (no *the*)
3 a. (no *the*) b. (no *the*) c. (no *the*) d. (no *the*)
4 a. the b. (no *the*) c. (no *the*) d. the

Arbeitsanweisungen

Wenn du eine Aufgabe bearbeitest, ist es wichtig, dass du die Arbeitsanweisungen richtig verstehst. Um genau zu wissen, was du zu tun hast, achte insbesondere auf das Hauptverb in der Arbeitsanweisung, z.B. Choose the right word / Join the two sentences.

Diese Arbeitsanweisungen findest du häufig im Schülerbuch.

Act out the dialogue.	Spielt den Dialog nach.
Add details/examples/ideas/words/...	Füge Details/Beispiele/Ideen/Wörter/... hinzu.
Agree on the best idea.	Einigt euch auf die beste Idee.
Check your answers/text/...	Überprüfe deine Anworten/deinen Text/...
Check with a partner.	Überprüfe (deine Antwort) mit einem Partner/einer Partnerin.
Choose the correct/right words.	Wähle die korrekten/richtigen Wörter.
Collect ideas/information/...	Sammle Ideen/Informationen/...
Comment on these ideas.	Kommentiere diese Ideen.
Compare with a partner.	Vergleiche mit einem Partner/einer Partnerin.
Complete the table/rule/sentence ...	Vervollständige die Tabelle/die Regel/den Satz ...
Correct the sentences.	Korrigiere die Sätze.
Decide if these statements are true.	Entscheide, ob diese Aussagen richtig sind.
Describe the picture/your hometown/...	Beschreibe das Bild/deine Heimatstadt/...
Discuss your ideas.	Diskutiert eure Ideen.
Explain your choice/ideas/opinion/...	Erkläre deine Wahl/Ideen/Meinung/...
Find examples/phrases/pictures/...	Finde Beispiele/Phrasen/Bilder/...
Give examples/reasons.	Nenne Beispiele/Gründe.
Join another pair.	Schließt euch einer anderen Zweiergruppe an.
Join the two sentences.	Verbinde die zwei Sätze.
Imagine you're ...	Stell dir vor, du bist ...
Listen to the dialogue.	Hör dir den Dialog an.
Look at the diagram/picture/stills/...	Schau dir das Diagramm/das Bild/die Standbilder an.
Make a list/table/....	Erstelle eine Liste/eine Tabelle/...
Make appointments with three partners.	Verabrede dich mit drei Partnern/Partnerinnen.
Make notes about/on your ideas.	Erstelle Notizen über deine Ideen.
Match the words to the pictures.	Ordne die Wörter den Bildern zu.
Note down the main information.	Notiere die wichtigsten Informationen.
Organize your information.	Ordne deine Informationen.
Practise the dialogue/phrases/...	Übe den Dialog/die Phrasen/...
Put the sentences/words in the right order.	Bring die Sätze in die richtige Reihenfolge.
Put the verbs in the correct form.	Bring die Verben in die richtige Form.
Rewrite the text.	Schreib den Text neu.
Swap texts.	Tauscht eure Texte.
Take notes about/on Kaya's feelings.	Mach dir Notizen über Kayas Gefühle.
Take turns.	Wechselt euch ab.
Think of a sentence.	Denk dir einen Satz aus.
Underline the syllable.	Unterstreiche die Silbe.
Use your notes/the simple past/ ...	Verwende deine Notzien/das simple past/ ...
Work in groups of three/four/...	Arbeitet in Dreier-/Vierergruppen.

Irregular verbs

infinitive	simple past	past participle	
(to) **be**	**was; were**	**been**	sein
(to) **beat**	**beat**	**beaten**	schlagen; besiegen
(to) **become**	**became**	**become**	werden
(to) **begin**	**began**	**begun**	beginnen, anfangen
(to) **bend**	**bent**	**bent**	sich bücken, sich beugen
(to) **bite** [aɪ]	**bit** [ɪ]	**bitten** [ɪ]	beißen
(to) **blow sth. out**	**blew**	**blown**	etwas auspusten, ausblasen
(to) **break** [eɪ]	**broke**	**broken**	brechen; zerbrechen
(to) **bring**	**brought**	**brought**	(mit-, her)bringen
(to) **build**	**built**	**built**	bauen
(to) **burst** into tears	**burst**	**burst**	in Tränen ausbrechen
(to) **buy**	**bought**	**bought**	kaufen
(to) **catch**	**caught**	**caught**	fangen
(to) **choose** [uː]	**chose** [əʊ]	**chosen** [əʊ]	aussuchen, (aus)wählen; sich aussuchen
(to) **come**	**came**	**come**	kommen
(to) **cost**	**cost**	**cost**	kosten
(to) **cut**	**cut**	**cut**	schneiden
(to) **do**	**did**	**done** [ʌ]	tun, machen
(to) **draw**	**drew**	**drawn**	zeichnen
(to) **drive** [aɪ]	**drove** [əʊ]	**driven** [ɪ]	(mit dem Auto) fahren
(to) **drink**	**drank**	**drunk**	trinken
(to) **eat**	**ate** [et, eɪt]	**eaten**	essen
(to) **fall**	**fell**	**fallen**	fallen, stürzen; hinfallen
(to) **feed**	**fed**	**fed**	füttern
(to) **feel**	**felt**	**felt**	fühlen; sich fühlen
(to) **fight**	**fought**	**fought**	(be)kämpfen
(to) **find**	**found**	**found**	finden
(to) **fly**	**flew**	**flown**	fliegen
(to) **forget**	**forgot**	**forgotten**	vergessen
(to) **freeze**	**froze**	**frozen**	(ge)frieren; zufrieren; einfrieren
(to) **get**	**got**	**got**	bekommen; holen; werden; gelangen
(to) **give**	**gave**	**given**	geben
(to) **go**	**went**	**gone** [ɒ]	gehen
(to) **grow**	**grew**	**grown**	wachsen; anbauen, anpflanzen
(to) **hang**	**hung**	**hung**	hängen
(to) **have**	**had**	**had**	haben
(to) **hear** [ɪə]	**heard** [ɜː]	**heard** [ɜː]	hören
(to) **hide** [aɪ]	**hid** [ɪ]	**hidden** [ɪ]	verstecken; sich verstecken
(to) **hit**	**hit**	**hit**	schlagen
(to) **hold**	**held**	**held**	halten
(to) **hurt**	**hurt**	**hurt**	schmerzen, wehtun; verletzen
(to) **keep**	**kept**	**kept**	behalten; aufheben, aufsparen; aufbewahren
(to) **kneel** [niːl]	**knelt** [nelt]	**knelt** [nelt]	knien
(to) **know** [nəʊ]	**knew** [njuː]	**known** [nəʊn]	wissen; kennen
(to) **lead** [iː]	**led**	**led**	führen, leiten
(to) **leave** [iː]	**left**	**left**	(weg)gehen; abfahren; (zurück)lassen; verlassen

infinitive	simple past	past participle	
(to) **lend sb. sth.**	**lent**	**lent**	jm. etwas leihen
(to) **let**	**let**	**let**	lassen
(to) **lie**	**lay**	**lain**	liegen
(to) **light** [aɪ]	**lit** [ɪ]	**lit** [ɪ]	anzünden
(to) **lose** [uː]	**lost** [ɒ]	**lost** [ɒ]	verlieren
(to) **make**	**made**	**made**	machen; herstellen
(to) **mean** [iː]	**meant** [e]	**meant** [e]	bedeuten; meinen
(to) **meet** [iː]	**met** [e]	**met**	treffen; sich treffen; kennenlernen
(to) **pay**	**paid**	**paid**	bezahlen
(to) **put**	**put**	**put**	(etwas wohin) tun, legen, stellen
(to) **read** [iː]	**read** [e]	**read** [e]	lesen
(to) **ride** [aɪ]	**rode**	**ridden** [ɪ]	reiten; (Rad) fahren
(to) **ring**	**rang**	**rung**	klingeln, läuten
(to) **rise up** [aɪ]	**rose**	**risen** [ɪ]	aufragen, emporragen
(to) **run**	**ran**	**run**	rennen, laufen
(to) **say** [eɪ]	**said** [e]	**said** [e]	sagen
(to) **see**	**saw**	**seen**	sehen
(to) **sell**	**sold**	**sold**	verkaufen
(to) **send**	**sent**	**sent**	schicken, senden
(to) **set sth. up**	**set**	**set**	etwas errichten, aufbauen; etwas arrangieren
(to) **shake**	**shook**	**shaken**	schütteln
(to) **shine**	**shone** [*BE:* ɒ, *AE:* əʊ]	**shone** [ɒ, əʊ]	scheinen (Sonne)
(to) **shoot** [uː]	**shot** [ɒ]	**shot** [ɒ]	schießen; erschießen
(to) **sing**	**sang**	**sung**	singen
(to) **sit**	**sat**	**sat**	sitzen; sich setzen
(to) **sleep**	**slept**	**slept**	schlafen
(to) **speak** [iː]	**spoke**	**spoken**	sprechen
(to) **spend**	**spent**	**spent**	(Zeit) verbringen; (Geld) ausgeben
(to) **spin around**	**spun**	**spun**	sich (im Kreis) drehen; herumwirbeln
(to) **spread** [e]	**spread** [e]	**spread** [e]	ausbreiten, verbreiten; sich ausbreiten, verbreiten
(to) **stand**	**stood**	**stood**	stehen; sich (hin)stellen
(to) **steal**	**stole**	**stolen**	stehlen
(to) **stick**	**stuck**	**stuck**	stechen, stecken
(to) **swear** [eə]	**swore**	**sworn**	schwören
(to) **swim**	**swam**	**swum**	schwimmen
(to) **take**	**took**	**taken**	(mit)nehmen; (weg-, hin)bringen; dauern
(to) **teach**	**taught**	**taught**	unterrichten, lehren
(to) **tear down** [teə]	**tore**	**torn**	abreißen
(to) **tell**	**told**	**told**	erzählen, berichten
(to) **think**	**thought**	**thought**	denken, glauben
(to) **throw**	**threw**	**thrown**	werfen
(to) **tread** [e]	**trod**	**trodden**	treten
(to) **understand**	**understood**	**understood**	verstehen
(to) **wake up**	**woke up**	**woken up**	aufwachen; (auf)wecken
(to) **wear** [eə]	**wore** [ɔː]	**worn** [ɔː]	tragen (Kleidung)
(to) **win**	**won** [ʌ]	**won** [ʌ]	gewinnen
(to) **write**	**wrote**	**written**	schreiben

Countries and continents

Country/Continent	**Adjective**	**Person**	**People**
Marco is from ***Italy****.*	*Pizza is* ***Italian****.*	*Marco is* ***an Italian****.*	***The Italians*** *invented pizza.*
Africa ['æfrɪkə] *Afrika*	African ['æfrɪkən]	an African	the Africans
Albania [æl'beɪniə] *Albanien*	Albanian [æl'beɪniən]	an Albanian	the Albanians
Asia ['eɪʒə, 'eɪʃə] *Asien*	Asian ['eɪʃn, 'eɪʒn]	an Asian	the Asians
Australia [ɒ'streɪliə] *Australien*	Australian [ɒ'streɪliən]	an Australian	the Australians
Austria ['ɒstriə] *Österreich*	Austrian ['ɒstriən]	an Austrian	the Austrians
Belarus [ˌbel'ruːs] *Weißrussland*	Belarusian [ˌbel'ruːsiən]	a Belarusian	the Belarusians
Belgium ['beldʒəm] *Belgien*	Belgian ['beldʒən]	a Belgian	the Belgians
Bosnia and Herzegovina ['bɒzniə ən ˌhɜːtsəgə'viːnə] *Bosnien und Herzegowina*	Bosnian ['bɒzniən]; Herzegovinian [ˌhɜːtsəgə'vɪniən]	a Bosnian; a Herzegovinian	the Bosnians; the Herzegovinians
Canada ['kænədə] *Kanada*	Canadian [kə'neɪdiən]	a Canadian	the Canadians
China ['tʃaɪnə] *China*	Chinese [ˌtʃaɪ'niːz]	a Chinese	the Chinese
Croatia [krəʊ'eɪʃə] *Kroatien*	Croatian [krəʊ'eɪʃn]	a Croatian	the Croatians
the **Czech Republic** [ˌtʃek rɪ'pʌblɪk] *Tschechien, die Tschechische Republik*	Czech [tʃek]	a Czech	the Czechs
Denmark ['denmɑːk] *Dänemark*	Danish ['deɪnɪʃ]	a Dane [deɪn]	the Danes
England ['ɪŋglənd] *England*	English ['ɪŋglɪʃ]	an Englishman / an Englishwoman	the English
Estonia [e'stəʊniə] *Estland*	Estonian [e'stəʊniən]	an Estonian	the Estonians
Europe ['jʊərəp] *Europa*	European [ˌjʊərə'piːən]	a European	the Europeans
Finland ['fɪnlənd] *Finnland*	Finnish ['fɪnɪʃ]	a Finn [fɪn]	the Finns
France [frɑːns] *Frankreich*	French [frentʃ]	a Frenchman / a Frenchwoman	the French
Germany ['dʒɜːməni] *Deutschland*	German ['dʒɜːmən]	a German	the Germans
(Great) Britain ['brɪtn] *Großbritannien*	British ['brɪtɪʃ]	a Briton ['brɪtn]	the British
Greece [griːs] *Griechenland*	Greek [griːk]	a Greek	the Greeks
Hungary ['hʌŋgəri] *Ungarn*	Hungarian [hʌŋ'geəriən]	a Hungarian	the Hungarians
Iceland ['aɪslənd] *Island*	Icelandic [aɪs'lændɪk]	an Icelander ['aɪsləndə]	the Icelanders
India ['ɪndiə] *Indien*	Indian ['ɪndiən]	an Indian	the Indians
Ireland ['aɪələnd] *Irland*	Irish ['aɪrɪʃ]	an Irishman / an Irishwoman	the Irish
Italy ['ɪtəli] *Italien*	Italian [ɪ'tæliən]	an Italian	the Italians
Jamaica [dʒəmeɪkə] *Jamaika*	Jamaika [dʒəmeɪkən]	a Jamaican	the Jamaicans
Kosovo ['kɒsəvəʊ] *Kosovo*	Kosovan ['kɒsəvən]	a Kosovan	the Kosovans
Latvia ['lætviə] *Lettland*	Latvian ['lætviən]	a Latvian	the Latvians
Lithuania [ˌlɪθju'eɪniə] *Litauen*	Lithuanian [ˌlɪθju'eɪniə]	a Lithuanian	the Lithuanians

Country/Continent	Adjective	Person	People
*Marco is from **Italy**.*	*Pizza is **Italian**.*	*Marco is **an Italian**.*	***The Italians** invented pizza.*
Luxembourg ['lʌksəmbɜːg] *Luxemburg*	Luxembourg	a Luxembourger ['lʌksəmbɜːgə]	the Luxembourgers
Macedonia [ˌmæsə'dəʊniə] *Mazedonien*	Macedonian [ˌmæsə'dəʊniən]	a Macedonian	the Macedonians
Malta ['mɔːltə] *Malta*	Maltese [mɔːl'tiːz]	a Maltese	the Maltese
Mexico ['meksɪkəʊ] *Mexiko*	Mexican ['meksɪkən]	a Mexican	the Mexicans
Moldova [mɒl'dəʊvə] *Moldawien*	Moldovan [mɒl'dəʊvən]	a Moldovan	the Moldovans
Montenegro [ˌmɒntɪ'niːgrəʊ] *Montenegro*	Montenegrin [ˌmɒntɪ'niːgrɪn]	a Montenegrin	the Montenegrins
the **Netherlands** ['neðələndz] *die Niederlande*	Dutch [dʌtʃ]	a Dutchman / a Dutchwoman	the Dutch
North America [ˌnɔːθ‿ə'merɪkə] *Nordamerika*	North American [ˌnɔːθ‿ə'merɪkən]	a North American	the North Americans
Northern Ireland [ˌnɔːðən‿'aɪələnd] *Nordirland*	Northern Irish [ˌnɔːðən‿'aɪrɪʃ]	a Northern Irishman / a Northern Irishwoman	the Northern Irish
Norway ['nɔːweɪ] *Norwegen*	Norwegian [nɔː'wiːdʒən]	a Norwegian	the Norwegians
Poland ['pəʊlənd] *Polen*	Polish ['pəʊlɪʃ]	a Pole [pəʊl]	the Poles
Polynesia [[ˌpɒlɪ'niːziə], [ˌpɒlɪ'niːʒə]] *Polynesien*	Polynesian [ˌpɒlɪ'niːziən], [ˌpɒlɪ'niːʒən]	a Polynesian	the Polynesians
Portugal ['pɔːtʃʊgl] *Portugal*	Portuguese [ˌpɔːtʃʊ'giːz]	a Portuguese	the Portuguese
Romania [ru'meɪniə] *Rumänien*	Romanian [ru'meɪniən]	a Romanian	the Romanians
Russia ['rʌʃə] *Russland*	Russian ['rʌʃn]	a Russian	the Russians
Scotland ['skɒtlənd] *Schottland*	Scottish ['skɒtɪʃ]	a Scot [skɒt]; a Scotsman / a Scotswoman	the Scots, the Scottish
Serbia ['sɜːbiə] *Serbien*	Serbian ['sɜːbiən]	a Serbian	the Serbians
Slovakia [sləʊ'vækiə] *die Slowakei*	Slovak ['sləʊvæk]	a Slovak	the Slovaks
Slovenia [sləʊ'viːniə] *Slowenien*	Slovenian [sləʊ'viːniən]	a Slovenian	the Slovenians
South America [ˌsaʊθ‿ə'merɪkə] *Südamerika*	South American [ˌsaʊθ‿ə'merɪkən]	a South American	the South Americans
Spain [speɪn] *Spanien*	Spanish ['spænɪʃ]	a Spaniard ['spænɪəd]	the Spanish
Sweden ['swiːdn] *Schweden*	Swedish ['swiːdɪʃ]	a Swede [swiːd]	the Swedes
Switzerland ['swɪtsələnd] *die Schweiz*	Swiss [swɪs]	a Swiss	the Swiss
Turkey ['tɜːki] *die Türkei*	Turkish ['tɜːkɪʃ]	a Turk [tɜːk]	the Turks
Ukraine [juː'kreɪn]	Ukrainian [juː'kreɪniən]	a Ukrainian	the Ukrainians
the **United Kingdom** [juˌnaɪtɪd 'kɪŋdəm] *das Vereinigte Königreich*	British ['brɪtɪʃ]	a Briton ['brɪtn]	the British
the **United States of America** [juˌnaɪtɪd ˌsteɪts‿əv‿ə'merɪkə] *die Vereinigten Staaten von Amerika*	American [ə'merɪkən]	an American	the Americans
Vietnam [ˌviːet'næm], [ˌviːet'nɑːm]	Vietnamese [viːˌetnə'miːz]	a Vietnamese	the Vietnamese
Wales [weɪlz] *Wales*	Welsh [welʃ]	a Welshman/-woman	the Welsh

Quellenverzeichnis

Titelbild
Shutterstock.com/IM_photo

Illustrationen
Stefan Bachmann (S. 42, 44, 128); **Roland Beier** (S. 227); **Carlos Borrell Eiköter** (Karten: U2, S. 4–5, 10–11); **Tobias Dahmen, Utrecht/www.tobidahmen.de** (S. 24, 25, 49, 67, 75, 129, 160, 164, 174, 188, 202); **Michael Fleischmann, Waldegg** (S. 216 skyline u. lockers, 217, 220, 224, 226, 232 alles zu *wheel*); **M. Burkhard Schulz** (S. 94, 132)

Abbildungen
Adobe (S. 4 un.: Rodrigo; S. 14 Bild B: Tupungato, Bild C: MarcelS. S. 39 Bild D: Rodrigo; S. 53: evgenyb; S. 60 Mütze: dianamower, Ei: lizascotty, Fingerhut: Constantinos, Teddy: teomakla, Spielzeugauto: robootb, Eintrittskarte: virtua73, Ball: Kletr, Foto: Gabriele Rohde, Flugticket: matthias21, Uhr: Scisetti Alfio; S. 65 Bild B: frank1crayon; S. 77 ob.: Peter; S. 79: toa555; S. 84: Mel Stoutsenberger; S. 93: Monkey Business; S. 111: pure-life-pictures; S. 120: f11photo; S. 123 Mi. li.: Natalia Bratslavsky; S. 201 un.: Miriam Dörr; S. 205: pressmaster; S. 221 li.: postsmth); **akg-images GmbH** (S. 16 ob.: Jason Hook; S. 121 un.: Jazz Archiv Hamburg); **Bonnie Glänzer** (S. 196 Wordcluster; S. 199); **Bridgeman Images** (S. 50 Mi.; S. 76 ob.: Granger, 2. v. un.: Photo © GraphicaArtis, un.: © Look and Learn; S. 96 2. v. un.: De Agostini Picture Library/F. Barbagallo; S. 97 2. v. ob.: Peter Newark American Pictures); **Cecile Niemitz-Rossant** (S. 40 ob. li. Hintergrund); **ClipDealer GmbH** (S. 60 Muschel: hadot); **Cornelsen/Inhouse** (S. 70); **Crooked Letter Films** (Filmstills S. 12 Bild C; S. 14 un.; S. 15 Bild D u. un.; S. 55; S. 204), **dpa Picture-Alliance** (S. 16 un.: AP Photo; S. 38 Bild A: AP Photo; S. 51 ob.: AP Photo, Mi.: X00044/Reuters; S. 96 un.: Photo12/Ann Ronan Picture Library; S. 121 ob.); **Imago Sportfotodienst GmbH** (S. 51 un.: ZUMA Press); **Imago Stock & People GmbH** (S. 23 un.: Bildbyran; S. 39 Bild C: Everett Collection; S. 47: United Archives International; S. 96 2. v. ob.: Danita Delimont; S. 98: Danita Delimont; S. 119: imago/ZUMA Press); **Interfilm Berlin Management GmbH** (Filmstills S. 107: Bloodlines/Christopher Nataanii Cegielski); **INTERFOTO** (S. 50 un.: Granger, NYC; S. 56 re.: Alinari; S. 88 Bild A: Danita Delimont/Angel Wynn; S. 96 ob.: SuperStock/Newberry Library; S. 108: Writer Pictures Ltd/Mathieu Bourgois; S. 123 un. re.: Danita Delimont/Angel Wynn; S. 125: Granger, NYC); **Julia Hintz** (Filmstills S. 36-37); **Laurence Harger** (S. S. 91 ob. re.); **Mauritius Images GmbH** (S. 4 Mi.: alamy stock photo/Nino Marcutti; S. 12 Bild A: alamy stock photo/Nino Marcutti; S. 13 Bild B: Westend61; S. 14 Bild A: alamy stock photo/Kevin Foy; S. 15 Bild E: alamy stock photo/Richard Ellis; S. 21: alamy stock photo/Richard Levine; S. 22 ob.: alamy stock photo/Olga Kolos, Mi.: alamy stock photo/Ryan Deberardinis, un.: alamy stock photo/dbimages; S. 23 ob.: alamy stock photo/M. Stan Reaves, Mi.: alamy stock photo/Edward Westmacott; S. 26: age fotostock; S. 28: alamy stock photo/Richard Levine; S. 29 re.: robertharding; S. 33: Onoky; S. 38 Bild B: alamy stock photo/peace portal photo; S. 40 ob. re.: alamy stock photo/Khairil Azhar Junos, un. li.: alamy stock photo/Edwin Remsberg, un. re.: alamy stock photo/Ian Dagnall; S. 41 ob. u. re.: alamy stock photo/Irene Abdou, un.: alamy stock photo/Reciprocity Images; S. 50 ob.: alamy stock photo/Montagu Images; S. 56 li.: Science Source; S. 77 2. v. un.: alamy stock photo/jvnimages; S. 81 un.: alamy stock photo/Jan Halaska; S. 87: alamy stock photo/hdh.n; S. 89 Bild F: alamy stock photo/Patti McConville; S. 102: alamy stock photo/Bill Bachmann; S. 112: alamy stock photo/Viacheslav Iakobchuk; S. 118 li.: alamy stock photo/The Picture Art Collection, re.: alamy stock photo/Pictorial Press Ltd; S. 123 ob. li.: alamy stock photo/Brad Mitchell, un. li.: alamy stock photo/Witold Skrypczak; S. 131: Jan Halaska; S. 148: Danita Delimont; S. 149: alamy stock photo/Barry Lewis; S. 201 ob.: alamy stock photo/Picture Partners); **Nigel Wilson Photography** (S. 40 ob. li. Tyler; S. 78); **Panther Media GmbH** (S. 81 ob.: Richard Šemík); **Rockfinch Ltd.** (Filmstills S. 91 ob. li.: Claire Cunningham, un. li. u. re.); **Sapna Richter** (S. 203; S. 208); **Shutterstock GmbH** (S. 4 ob.: TierneyMJ; S. 6 ob.: logoboom, un.: Trina Barnes; S. 8-9: TierneyMJ; S. 29 li.: Sabrina Tollenaers; S. 30: Richard Cavalleri; S. 39 Bild E: Elliott Cowand Jr; S. 40 Smileys: Ricardo Romero; S. 57: Nagel Photography; S. 60 Kette: Gavran333, Medaille: focal point, Lebkuchenherz: Andre Bonn, Kerze: Elena Schweitzer, Bauklötze: Nenov Brothers Images; S. 62: Monkey Business Images; S. 64 Bild A: Joakim Lloyd Raboff, Bild C: Min C. Chiu, Bild D: holbox; S. 65 Bild E: logoboom; S. 69: aleks333; S. 71: AridOcean; S. 76 2. v. ob.: Frank Bach; S. 77 2. v. ob.: yhelfman, un.: Machmarsky; S. 88 Bild C: Trina Barnes, Bild E: f11photo; S. 89 Bild B: Kaye Ray, Bild D: Martin Castrogiovanni; S. 97 un.: Joseph Sohm; S. 101: Perfect Wave; S. 114 ob.: Steve Heap; S. 115: NagyDodo; S. 123 ob. Mi.: Everett Historical, ob. re.: S. photo, un. Mi.: Doug Meek; S. 146: Masson; S. 147: Bonnie Taylor Barry; S. 150: SpeedKingz; S. 193: sarahdesign; S. 194: AVAVA; S. 207: Creaktiva; S. 213: Roman Babakin; S. 215: WarmWorld; S. 216 Rucksack li.: gresei, Rucksack re.: design56; S. 217: Gallinago_media; S. 218 ob.: DrMadra, Mi.: James Steidl, un. li.: veleknez, un. re.: Hurst Photo; S. 219 ob.: Marcio Jose Bastos Silva,

un. li.: 1000 Words, un. re.: Singkham; S. 221 Mi.: Lawkeeper, re.: Gayvoronskaya_Yana; S. 222 rice: mayakova, beans: Ekaterina Lin, lentils: baibaz, onions: andersphoto, peppers: topseller, mushrooms: Yasonya, spinach: Edvard Molnar, garlic: Maks Narodenko, parsley: Evgeny Karandaev, lemons: Volosina, nuts (Haselnüsse): Tim UR, nuts (Walnüsse): Dionisvera, butter: Multiart, salt + pepper: Elena Elisseeva, sugar: Garsya, flour: ddsign, frying pan: Petr Malyshev, saucepan: Levent Konuk, oven: photobank.ch; S. 223 ob. li.: tommaso lizzul, ob. re.: Jarp2, un. li.: Kunal Mehta, un. re.: mubus7; S. 224 ob.: ArtBitz, un.: Zack Frank; S. 225 cranberries: Dionisvera, sauce: sevenke, pumpkin: topseller, pumpkin pie: Foodio; S. 226: CoolKengzz; S. 227: Evlakhov Valeriy; S. 228 ob.: Sarawut Padungkwan, un.: yulia_lavrova; S. 229: Artisticco; S. 230: Dutourdumonde Photography; S. 232 ob. re.: Joseph Sohm, un.: tawatchai.m; S. 235 ob.: Gts, un.: albund); **Timothy Vogel** (S. 117)

Collagen

S. 17 (Cornelsen/M. Burkhard Schulz: Jasmine/Tyler: Cornelsen/Nigel Wilson Photography, Memorial: mauritius images/alamy stock photo/Melvyn Longhurst); **S. 46** (Cornelsen/M. Burkhard Schulz: Tyler/Betty: Cornelsen/ Nigel Wilson Photography, Sofa u. Teppich: shutterstock. com/Iriane Shiyan); **S. 52** (Cornelsen/M. Burkhard Schulz: Tyler/Betty/Eugene: Cornelsen/Nigel Wilson Photography, Truthahn: shutterstock.com/bikeriderlondon, Essen: shutterstock.com/Olga Nayashkova); **S. 66** (Cornelsen/M. Burkhard Schulz: Hailey/Eric: Cornelsen/Nigel Wilson Photography, Mailin/Ulrike: Cornelsen/Sapna Richter, Strand: shutterstock.com/Damian P. Gadal, Seeanemone: stock.adobe.com/Scott Bufkin); **S. 72 ob. li.** (Cornelsen/M. Burkhard Schulz: Hailey/Vater: Cornelsen/ Nigel Wilson Photography, Hotellobby: shutterstock.com/ August_0802), **ob. re.** (Cornelsen/M. Burkhard Schulz: Hailey: Cornelsen/Nigel Wilson Photography, Ralph (Bartender): Cornelsen/Sapna Richter, Bar: shutterstock. com/fiphoto), **un. li.** (Cornelsen/M. Burkhard Schulz: Hailey: Cornelsen/Nigel Wilson Photography, Bar: shutterstock.com/fiphoto, elegante Frau: shutterstock. com/katalinks), **un. re.** (Cornelsen/M. Burkhard Schulz: Hailey: Cornelsen/Nigel Wilson Photography, Mann: stock. adobe.com/flairimages, Hintergrund: shutterstock.com/ Gravicapa); **S. 73** (Cornelsen/Nigel Wilson Photography: Brandon/Dan: Cornelsen/Nigel Wilson Photography, Hintergrund: shutterstock.com/sunny_shine); **S. 90** (Cornelsen/M. Burkhard Schulz: Kaya/Drew: Cornelsen/ Nigel Wilson Photography, Mädchen li. u. Schüler im Hintergrund: shutterstock.com/Monkey Business Images, Hintergrund: stock-adobe.com/Imel900); **S. 99** (Cornelsen/M. Burkhard Schulz: Kaya/Jodi: Cornelsen/ Nigel Wilson Photography, Hintergrund: shutterstock.com/ Linda Z); **S. 103** (Cornelsen/M. Burkhard Schulz: Kaya/ Drew/Bobby: Cornelsen/Nigel Wilson Photography, Hintergrund: Laurence Harger)

Texte

S. 32–35 (VG WORT; Bill Wright: *Putting makeup on the fat boy*; Berlin: Cornelsen 2015); **S. 56–59** (VG WORT; Melba Pattillo Beals: *Warriors Don't Cry: A Searing Memoir of the Battle to Integrate Little Rock's Central High*; 2007); **S. 84–86** (VG WORT; Neal Shusterman und Jarrod Shusterman: *Dry*; Walker Books 2018); **S. 108–110** (VG WORT; Sherman Alexie: *The Absolutely True Diary of a Part-Time Indian*; Little, Brown and Company 2007); **S. 116–118** (VG WORT; Cecile Niemitz-Rossant: *Underground New York*; Berlin: Cornelsen 2009); **S. 120** (1000 Lights Music Limited/Webo Girl Publishing Inc; EMI Music Publishing Germany GmbH, Berlin/Neue Welt Musikverlag GmbH, Hamburg/Text: Miruais Ahmadzai, Madonna Ciccone); **S. 121** (EMI Music Publishing Ltd/ BMG Blue/Lenono Music/Unitunes; EMI Music Publishing Germany GmbH, Berlin/Budde Music Publishing GmbH/ BMG Rights Management GmbH, Berlin/Text: Carlos Alomar, David Bowie, John Lennon); **S. 125** (Blue Northern Publishing/Medicine Hat Music/W B Music Corp; Warner Bros Inc/Neue Welt Musikverlag GmbH, Hamburg/ Text: Robbie Robertson, William James Wilson)

Giving feedback to your classmates

✓ Choose criteria[1] for your feedback.

✎ Add other criteria you need, e.g. for feedback on a story.

TEXT — PRESENTATION

	CONTENT
✓	You covered the important points in the task.
✓	The information was interesting/new.
✓	You gave examples/details.
✓	You gave your opinion.
✓	You gave arguments for your opinion.
✎	Your story had a plot.[2]
	You described the characters.
	…

TEXT:

	STRUCTURE
✓	Your introduction said what the text is about.
✓	You used paragraphs.
✓	Each paragraph had a new idea.
✓	You had a conclusion.
✎	…

	LANGUAGE
✓	You used different adjectives and adverbs.
✓	You joined sentences with linking words.
✓	You used special vocabulary for the topic.
✓	Your spelling was correct.
✓	Your grammar was correct.
✎	…

PRESENTATION:

	STRUCTURE
✓	You introduced the topic.
✓	Your presentation had a clear structure.
✓	You showed your main points on a poster/…
✓	You summed up at the end.
✓	You invited us to ask questions.
✎	…

	COMMUNICATION
✓	You seemed relaxed.
✓	You made eye contact.
✓	You used notes.
✓	You spoke clearly.
✓	You explained your pictures.
✎	…

TIPS

1 Use the criteria you chose to assess[3] your classmate's work.

2 Give details when you say what a classmate did/didn't do well.
Always start with something positive.

Where	What
In the first paragraph you	wrote a good introduction ….
At the end of your presentation you	didn't ask if we had questions /…

3 Suggest how the classmate could do better.
You could try to use more linking words like **and** or **because** /use more pictures / …

[1] **criteria** *(pl)* [kraɪ'tɪəriə] Kriterien [2]**plot** [plɒt] Handlung [3](to) **assess** [ə'ses] einschätzen